METAPHOR
AND
THOUGHT

METAPHOR
AND
THOUGHT

Edited by
Andrew Ortony
University of Illinois

CAMBRIDGE UNIVERSITY PRESS

CAMBRIDGE

LONDON · NEW YORK · MELBOURNE

Essay Index

Published by the Syndics of the Cambridge University Press
The Pitt Building, Trumpington Street, Cambridge CB2 1RP
Bentley House, 200 Euston Road, London NW1 2DB
32 East 57th Street, New York, NY 10022, USA
296 Beaconsfield Parade, Middle Park, Melbourne 3206, Australia

First published 1979

Printed in the United States of America
Typeset by The Fuller Organization, Philadelphia, Pa.
Printed and bound by R. R. Donnelley & Sons Co., Crawfordsville, Ind.

Library of Congress Cataloging in Publication Data

Main entry under title:

Metaphor and thought.

1. Thought and thinking.   2. Metaphor.
I. Ortony, Andrew, 1942–
BF455.M47   169   78–32011
ISBN 0 521 22727 5 in hard covers
ISBN 0 521 29626 9 as a paperback

CONTENTS

PREFACE

In September 1977, a group of leading philosophers, psychologists, linguists, and educators gathered at the University of Illinois at Urbana-Champaign to participate in a multidisciplinary conference on metaphor and thought which was attended by nearly a thousand people. Most of the essays in this volume are substantially revised versions of papers presented at that conference. The conference was structured around a number of topics, and some of that structure has survived the transition to book form. Specifically, in both parts of the book there are three topics, each addressed by three papers. The second and third papers of these triplets are frequently devoted, at least in part, to a discussion of the first paper. The first part of the book contains two additional chapters; an opening one by Max Black that might be regarded as "scene setting," and a closing one by George Miller that might be regarded as a bridge between the two parts.

Because the conference constituted the genesis of this book, it is appropriate to acknowledge those groups and individuals whose help made it the success that it was. The principal source of funding for the conference was a contract from the National Institute of Education. Supplementary financial support was generously provided by a variety of sources within the University of Illinois. These included: the Advisory Committee to the Council of Academic Deans and Directors, the Center for Advanced Study, the College of Education, the College of Liberal Arts and Sciences, and the Office of the Chancellor. To all of these I should like to express my thanks. I should also like to express my appreciation to the National Academy of Education, whose award to me of a Spencer Fellowship helped in many concrete ways.

No large conference can function without a group of key people. In this case, Daniel Alpert, Jerry Morgan, and Hugh Petrie worked with me for nearly a year on the planning. Surprisingly, our frequent meetings often resulted in decisions, and the implementation of these decisions was largely effected through the dedicated efforts of Peggy Harris and Paula Sherman. To them, I owe a special word of thanks, for the doing is always so much more difficult than the talking.

The preparation of the final manuscript that resulted from all these efforts was no less onerous a task than the organization of the conference itself, partly because it was necessary to try to ensure that successive revisions of papers were not made totally in ignorance of revisions of related papers. (Readers should be cautioned that this undertaking may not have been in every case successful.) Apart from my gratitude to the authors for an unusually high level of cooperation in producing legible manuscripts within a reasonable time, my principal debt is to Michael Nivens, who was chiefly responsible for entering almost the entire manuscript onto computer files to facilitate editing, indexing, and general manuscript management. I also wish to thank Bonnie Anderson, who drew many of the illustrations.

With so diverse an array of topics there seemed little hope of achieving a coherent integration in an introductory chapter. It seemed more appropriate to attempt to identify the major questions, to highlight recurring themes, and to try to show how the individual chapters related to them. The constructive comments on various aspects of the introductory chapter made by William Alston, Janet Dougherty, Peter Haidu, Walter Kintsch, George Lakoff, and George Miller were very much appreciated. Thanks are also due to Eric Wanner. But, my greatest debt is due to my wife, Gillian. Her patience, understanding, and help at all stages of this project made it seem much easier than it really was.

Andrew Ortony

Urbana, Illinois
December 1978

CONTRIBUTORS

MAX BLACK
Department of Philosophy
Cornell University

RICHARD BOYD
Department of Philosophy
Cornell University

L. JONATHAN COHEN
The Queen's College
Oxford University

BRUCE FRASER
Department of Special Education
Boston University

THOMAS GREEN
Department of Foundations
  of Education
Syracuse University

THOMAS KUHN
Program in History and Philosophy
  of Science
Princeton University

SAMUEL LEVIN
Department of English
The Graduate School and
University Center
City University of New York

GEORGE MILLER
Laboratory of Experimental
  Psychology
The Rockefeller University

JERRY MORGAN
Department of Linguistics and
  Center for the Study of Reading
University of Illinois
  at Urbana-Champaign

ANDREW ORTONY
Department of Educational
  Psychology and Center for the
  Study of Reading
University of Illinois
  at Urbana-Champaign

ALLAN PAIVIO
Department of Psychology
University of Western Ontario

HUGH PETRIE
Department of Educational Policy
  Studies
University of Illinois
  at Urbana-Champaign

ZENON PYLYSHYN
Department of Computer Science
  and Department of
  Psychology
University of Western Ontario

MICHAEL REDDY
Department of Linguistics
Columbia University

DAVID RUMELHART
Department of Psychology
University of California
  at San Diego

JERROLD SADOCK
Department of Linguistics
The University of Chicago

DONALD SCHÖN
Department of Urban Studies
  and Planning
Massachusetts Institute of
  Technology

JOHN SEARLE
Department of Philosophy
University of California at Berkeley

ROBERT STERNBERG,
  ROBERT TOURANGEAU,
  AND GEORGIA NIGRO
Department of Psychology
Yale University

THOMAS G. STICHT
Teaching and Learning Group
National Institute of Education

Metaphor:
A Multidimensional Problem

ANDREW ORTONY

One of the dominant presuppositions of our culture is that the description and explanation of physical reality is a respectable and worthwhile enterprise – an enterprise that we call "science." Science is supposed to be characterized by precision and the absence of ambiguity, and the language of science is often thought to be correspondingly precise and unambiguous – in short, literal. Faith in literal language as the only adequate and appropriate tool for the objective characterization of reality has manifested itself in many ways. For example, in twentieth century philosophy it was an important underlying assumption of picture theories of meaning (e.g. Russell, 1956; Wittgenstein, 1921/1961). It reached one of its peaks in the doctrine of logical positivism, which was so pervasive amongst philosophers and scientists fifty years ago. A basic notion of positivism was that reality could be precisely described through the medium of language in a manner that was clear, unambiguous, and, in principle, testable – reality could, and should, be literally describable. Other uses of language were meaningless for they violated this empiricist criterion of meaning. One might say, therefore, that during the heyday of logical positivism, literal language reigned supreme.

However, a different approach is possible – an approach in which any truly veridical epistemological access to reality is denied. The central idea of this approach is that cognition is the result of mental *construction*. Knowledge of reality, whether it is occasioned by perception, language, memory, or anything else, is a result of going beyond the information given. It arises through the interaction of that information with the context in which it is presented, and with the knower's preexisting knowledge. This general orientation is the hallmark of the relativist view (E. Sapir, 1921; Whorf, 1956) that the objective world is not directly accessible, but is constructed on the basis of the constraining influences of human knowledge and language. In this kind of view – which provides no basis for a rigid differentiation between scientific language and other kinds – language, perception, and knowledge are inextricably interdependent.

Opposing beliefs along the lines of the two just described find their expression in a number of different areas. They can be found in anthropology, in sociology, in linguistics, in cognitive psychology, in epistemology and the philosophy of science, and even in literary theory (e.g. Bartlett, 1932; Berger & Luckmann, 1966; Blumer, 1969; Brooks & Warren, 1938; Chomsky, 1965; Greimas, 1970; Hanson, 1958; Hempel, 1965; Kant, 1787/1963; J. J. Katz, 1966; Lévi-Strauss, 1963; Neisser, 1967; Price, 1950; Sperber, 1975). Of course, different scholars subscribe to them to different degrees, and in different ways. Probably very few subscribe to them in the extreme forms which I have presented and few will agree with the labels I attach to them. Nevertheless, I shall refer to these opposing conceptions as "constructivism" and "nonconstructivism," fully recognizing that this terminology is far from ideal. It seems preferable, however, to attempt to relate two alternative approaches to metaphor – metaphor as an essential characteristic of the creativity of language; and metaphor as deviant and parasitic upon normal usage – to a more fundamental and pervasive difference of opinion about the relationship between language and the world.

The constructivist/nonconstructivist distinction provides an interesting perspective from which to view the essays in this collection. This is true even though the bulk of the contributions are at the constructivist end of the continuum. The constructivist approach seems to entail an important role for metaphors in both language and thought, but it also tends to break down the distinction between the metaphorical and the literal. Since, for the constructivist, meaning has to be constructed rather than merely "read off," the meaning of nonliteral uses of language does not constitute a special problem. The use of language is an essentially creative activity, as is its comprehension. To be sure, metaphors and other figures of speech may sometimes require a little more creativity than literal language, but the difference is quantitative, not qualitative. By contrast, the nonconstructivist position has metaphors as rather unimportant, deviant, and parasitic on "normal usage." If metaphors need explaining at all, their explanation will be in terms of violations of linguistic rules. Metaphors characterize rhetoric, not scientific discourse. They are fuzzy and vague, inessential frills, appropriate for the purposes of the politician and of the poet, but not for those of the scientist, who is attempting to furnish an objective description of physical reality.

As the various disciplines of human enquiry gained their independence over the centuries, adopting their own domains, techniques, and metalanguages, the study of metaphor survived as a curiosity in some, disappeared as irrelevant in others, and became the hallmark of only one, rhetoric. The area of literary theory called rhetoric was for centuries chiefly concerned with figurative language, especially tropes (see Preminger, 1974, for a detailed account of such troublesome terms as "literature," "rhetoric," "poetics," "figurative language," "trope," etc.). What for others was but an occasional means of communication, for the rhetorician became the principal object of study. Contemporary scholars of literature vary in their theoretical pursuasions almost along constructivist/nonconstructivist lines. There are those who challenge the literal/figurative distinction and the literary-text/nonliterary-text distinction, for example, the semioticians; and there are those who adhere to these distinctions, for example, the New Critics and some structuralists. Thus, literary scholars vary in the extent to which the study of metaphors and other tropes is central to their enterprise. Even so, until very recently, few would have denied that tropes (of which, metaphor is the archetype) are in some way special to literature. However, in many of the chapters that follow, it is implied that all language is tropological, the language of the scientist included. Again, the constructivist approach, with which this conclusion is principally associated, seems to threaten the distinction between the language of the poet and that of the scientist, by repudiating the distinction between the metaphorical and the literal upon which it is based.

Any serious study of metaphor is almost obliged to start with the works of Aristotle. Aristotle considered the general relationship of metaphor to language and its purpose in communication. His discussion of the issues, principally in the *Poetics* and in the *Rhetoric*, have remained influential to this day. He believed metaphors to be implicit comparisons, based on the principles of analogy, a view that translates into what, in modern terms, is generally called the *comparison* theory of metaphor. As to their use, he believed that it was primarily ornamental. Metaphors, in other words, are not necessary, they are just nice. Aristotle also considered the role of metaphors in definitions. In the *Topica* he urged that a distinction be made between genuine definitions and metaphors, arguing that it is necessary to be wary of the ambiguity and obscurity inherent in the latter.

A more contemporary influence on the theoretical study of metaphor was that of I. A. Richards. Not only did Richards (1936b) propose a set of useful terms for talking about metaphors (the "topic" or "tenor," the "vehicle," and the "ground"), he also proposed the "tensive" view – a view that emphasized the conceptual incompatibility between the terms in a metaphor (the topic and the vehicle), calling it the "tension."

More recently, there has been a growing interest in metaphor in a number of other disciplines. In linguistics, for example, an increasing concern with linguistic performance and pragmatics (in contrast to the emphasis on linguistic competence so characteristic of the Chomskian revolution), and an increasing interest in the nature of text, have resulted in more attention being given to nonliteral uses of language. In psychology, especially cognitive psychology, the processes involved in the comprehension of metaphors not only constitute an interesting challenge in themselves, but their specification also constitutes a good test for the power of theories of language comprehension in general. There are other disciplines in which metaphor is of some interest, for the topic is truly multidisciplinary. Some of them are represented in this book.

The chapters that follow deal with a variety of philosophical, linguistic, psychological, and educational issues pertinent to the study of metaphor. The emphasis on these disciplines is intended to maximize the prospects of revealing a concern for shared problems. Other disciplines are represented, but not so extensively. Thus, the focus of this book is mainly on the nature and role of metaphor from nonliterary perspectives, not because literary perspectives are unimportant, but because they have been so extensively dealt with elsewhere. It is to be hoped that the literary theorist will see some virtue in these new perspectives on old problems.

The questions that are dealt with in the first part of this book are the more microscopic ones. The examples used tend to be of metaphors at the word level, or at most, at the sentence level. By contrast, the second part takes a more macroscopic view. It concentrates not so much on individual metaphors, as on systems of metaphors, or metaphoric models (see, for example, Geertz, 1974). In such cases there often is a sentence level "root metaphor" (see, for example, V. W. Turner, 1974), but from it grow many shoots which, taken as a whole, constitute an entire system or way of looking at things. The questions addressed in Part I tend to concern the *nature* of metaphor, and of the theoretical machinery required to account for it. The larger questions in Part II, in which constructivist views predominate, relate to the *uses* of metaphors. How do they function in scientific language? How do they function in learning? And how do they function in decision making? These, essentially, are the two fundamental species of questions being addressed in this book – *What are metaphors?* and, *What are metaphors for?*

Max Black's chapter touches on both. One of his purposes is to further develop the *interaction* theory of metaphor, a theory whose germs can be found in the work of Richards (1936a), but which was first articulated in detail by Black (1962b). Black now seeks to specify the theory in terms that are not themselves metaphorical. He restricts his discussion to metaphors that he considers to be theoretically interesting, "vital" metaphors. In addressing the question of how to distinguish metaphors from nonmetaphors (the central "What are metaphors?" question), he suggests that the quest for an infallible criterion of "metaphorhood" is doomed to failure. Any criterion one cares to suggest, says Black, can be shown to break down under certain circumstances. The recognition that something is a metaphor depends, first, on our knowing what it is for something to be a metaphorical statement, and secondly, on our judgment that a metaphorical interpretation is preferable to a literal one. Black, then, seems to be saying that there are no necessary and sufficient conditions for something to be a metaphor, just as Wittgenstein (1953) had argued that there are no such conditions for something to be a game. Perhaps metaphors, too, are related by family resemblance, as Wittgenstein claimed games were. Black's conclusion that metaphors are recognized as such by users of the language in particular contexts, places metaphor in the domain, not of semantics – the study of the meaning – but of pragmatics – the study of speech acts and the contexts in which they occur (Stalnaker, 1972). So, for Black, the study of metaphor is broader in scope than would be the case were it to be just a problem in semantics.

Black's observations on the uses of metaphors foreshadow Boyd's on their role in scientific discourse. Black believes that some metaphors can function as "cognitive instruments." This notion is a more specific (less metaphorical) idea than his earlier claim that metaphors can "create" similarities that previously were not known to exist. Just as Boyd argues that some metaphors actually constitute scientific theories, so Black argues that some metaphors permit us to see aspects of reality that they themselves help to constitute. This general claim gives rise to two themes that surface repeatedly in the book. The first is the idea that something new is created when a metaphor is understood. As well as being explicit in Black's claims, and implicit in Boyd's, it appears to be of central importance to both Petrie and Schön. Meanwhile, it seems to be implicitly challenged by Searle, and somewhat incompatible with Miller's position. The resolution of an issue like this cannot be found in this book, or in any other. It is only partly an empirical question. Clearly, with respect to an individual, new knowledge can result from the comprehension of language in general, and to that extent, at least, it can result from the comprehension of metaphors in particular. But whether, for example, metaphors in some special way create new similarities by changes in word meanings, as Black (1962b) implied, depends, as Black now points out, on how one construes notions such as "creating similarities" and "changes in word meanings." Certainly one can come to see relationships that one did not see before, but whether exclusively by metaphor is doubtful. Certainly, in some sense, the interpretations of some of the words in metaphors are different from their interpretations in literal contexts, but whether that constitutes a change in word meanings is also doubtful. However, it is clear that the emergence of "something new" is a pivotal concept in Black's interaction theory of metaphor. If Black is right, then the idea needs to receive the kind of elaboration that he offers, at least as a first step.

Black's notion about the creation of similarities relates to a second theme; namely, that metaphors afford different ways of perceiving. This becomes of central importance in Part II, where it is particularly crucial to the papers of Schön, Reddy, and Petrie. Schön proposes that, in social contexts, "generative" metaphors may result in a sort of cognitive myopia, in which some aspects of a situation are unwittingly (?) emphasized at the expense of other, possibly equally important, ones. Reddy, applying Schön's notion to language itself, argues that the metaphors we use to talk about human communication encourage us to "see" that communication in the wrong way – they encourage us to see it from a nonconstructivist rather than from a constructivist perspective. Petrie redresses the balance somewhat; metaphor does not have to be the villain because the alternative ways of seeing that it affords are not only an advantage in educational contexts, but a necessary feature of them.

The arguments of both Sadock and Rumelhart raise serious questions about the distinction between literal and metaphorical meaning. Thus, in a sense, they share Black's doubts about the existence of a criterion for metaphors. Sadock believes that if linguistics is conceived of in a strict, traditional manner, then the study of metaphor does not constitute a proper part of it, because metaphors are features of language use rather than features of language per se. He argues that there seems to be no rational basis for distinguishing literal from metaphorical language at all. Where are we to draw the line? Why could it not be argued that the use of the word "lion" to refer to both the species in general, and the male members of that species in particular, is a kind of semantic, or metaphorical extension of the other? And, who is to say which is the "core" meaning, and which is the extended meaning? Thus, even at this simple level, there are questions about how to distinguish the metaphorical from the literal. Although those advocating more extreme positions, for example, Searle, are willing to agree that the notion of literal meaning is not without its problems, still that notion has to be presupposed in order for their accounts to get off the ground.

Rumelhart comes to a similar conclusion from a rather different starting point. His position is that the distinction between metaphorical and literal language does not have any psychological correlate in the underlying processes involved in their comprehension. The processes required to understand the one are the same as those required to understand the other. According to Rumelhart, metaphor plays a crucial role in language acquisition. In applying old words to new objects or situations, children engage in a kind of metaphorical extension. Sometimes these extensions are consistent with conventional uses of the word, and we preceive the child as having learned something more about that word's applications, and sometimes it is not consistent with conventional uses, and adults, in their wisdom, are quick to attribute an error to the child. Thus, when a child, having first learned to use the word "open" in the context of opening his mouth, uses the same word in the context of opening a door or a window, he is doing exactly the same thing as when he uses that word in the context of "opening" a light switch or a faucet. The only difference is that in the former cases the new uses are conventional (in English) while in the latter cases they are not (but, interestingly, they are in French, for example). Thus, from the point of view of an adult observer, in the former cases the child has learned something new that is appropriate, while in the latter case, what he says has all the ingredients of a novel metaphor. On this view, metaphor cannot be regarded as some kind of linguistic aberration that requires an extraordinary explanation. It has to be regarded as an essential ingredient of language acquisition, and consequently a natural and normal linguistic phenomenon. From Rumelhart's perspective, metaphor is still immensely important, but its role in language is now viewed quite differently. It is viewed from a radical constructivist position.

The pragmatic approach advocated by Black is probably not a typical pragmatic account. It is pragmatic in its reliance on context, but it does not follow the familiar Gricean tack (see, Grice, 1975; Searle, 1969.) However, both accounts are in sharp contrast to the semantic approach advocated by Cohen. Thus, whereas Black, Sadock, Rumelhart, and later, Searle and others, all take an essentially constructivist approach, Cohen provides an excellent example of the opposing viewpoint. For Cohen, metaphors can be accounted for solely within a theory of semantics – which is itself part of a general theory of language, rather than a theory of language use. Thus, Cohen attempts to characterize the kind of systematic violation of semantic rules that would be needed to explain the basis of metaphors. In particular, he examines rules that specify the cancellation of semantic features as a means of arriving at metaphorical meaning directly from literal meaning. His chapter is interesting and provocative, representing, as it does, a well-worked-out account based on a currently unfashionable approach to meaning. Cohen's position is that all that is required to account for metaphors is a set of essentially linguistic rules.

In marked contrast, Searle, in his chapter, sees the fundamentally important question as being much the same as for indirect speech acts; namely, What are the mechanisms whereby a sentence meaning can be related to the speaker's meaning? Searle discusses some candidate mechanisms, including the notion that the link between the two could be achieved by the hearer "calling to mind" appropriate relating elements. Searle distinguishes metaphors from indirect speech acts by suggesting that whereas in indirect speech acts the speaker intends to convey both the sentence meaning and the indirect meaning, in metaphors the intention can only be to convey the latter. Morgan's paper questions the power of Searle's notion of "calling to mind." Searle casts the net too wide, Morgan claims. Thus, while generally sympathetic to Searle's approach, Morgan is nevertheless unhappy with the details. Searle argues that if a literal interpretation is rejected, a metaphorical interpretation must be sought. Morgan argues that such an account is too vague, for it fails to distinguish between metaphors, mistakes, irony, and a host of other indirect speech acts.

Levin, too, is willing to accept the general thrust of Searle's approach, especially the separation of sentence meaning and speaker meaning – a separation that he sees as being of great theoretical value. However, Levin argues that the mechanism whereby metaphors are understood are more complex, and he advances two reasons for believing this. First, he suggests that the metaphorical transfer is artificially made unidirectional by the use of examples that introduce the predicate through the copula (X is a Y). Here, he says, it is difficult to conceive of a metaphorical transfer going from X to Y, rather than from Y to X. However, if we take something like "the brook smiled," we can see, he argues, that there is a choice as to whether to attribute to the brook properties characteristic of smilers, or whether to attribute to smiling characteristics of brooks. His second reservation is more radical. The kind of pragmatic approach advocated by Searle, he suggests, is well suited to metaphors that arise in everyday language. But another approach might be more appropriate for literary metaphors. In literary metaphors, linguistic construal – whereby the language is reinterpreted to fit the world – might be better replaced by phenomenal-istic construal, wherein a reader's model of the world is changed to accommodate a literal interpretation of the metaphor. This approach, suggests Levin, may provide a better basis for understanding what it is that poets are doing. What is defective, on this account, is not the use of language, but the model of the world that is being built up. The notion of phenomenalistic construal fits rather well with Miller's dis-cussion of the reading process – what it requires in literature is a sus-pension of disbelief, rather than a reinterpretation of the language.

The semantic and the pragmatic views of metaphor need not, per-haps, be quite as antithetical as their strongest proponents would have them. The radical pragmatics position accepts a notion of "literal meaning" (sentence meaning), that is alleged to deviate from the speaker's meaning. Therefore, it would be possible, at least in princi-ple, to conceive of the transformation mechanisms from the one to the other as involving precisely the kind of rules that the radical semantics position claims are required to account for metaphor. To be sure, the pragmatic approach is going to want more than that, but it is doubtful that it can get away with less than that. However, not all positions on this issue are amenable to such a rapprochement. Rumelhart, and to a lesser extent Miller, believe that there is no cognitive basis for a sharp distinction between the literal and the nonliteral. Rather, metaphoric-ity is a dimension along which statements can vary. Rumelhart clearly thinks that no special mechanisms need be postulated to account for the comprehension of metaphors – neither a pragmatically nor a semantically motivated reinterpretation is required. And, if no reinter-pretation is required, then the rules of the radical semanticists would appear to be left without any cognitive counterparts.

The controversy over whether or not metaphor can be dealt with purely within semantics reflects one of the broader questions that I identified at the outset: "What are metaphors?" The dispute concerns how metaphors should be broadly categorized – as a purely linguistic phenomenon, or as a more general, communication phenomenon. If metaphors can be handled by a purely linguistic theory, then there is no need to invoke extralinguistic knowledge to account for them. The alternatives seem to map quite directly onto the nonconstructivist and the constructivist approaches respectively. Black's paper urges us to consider genuine cases of nontrivial metaphors. But such "naturally occurring" metaphors are frequently incomprehensible if one does not consider the contexts in which they occur. (Indeed, in some cases they are incomprehensible even if one does!) So, if we have to refer to a context of use in order to know even if something is a metaphor, it would seem that a purely semantic account is too restrictive. Such an account cannot accommodate the observations of Black and Searle that in some contexts a speaker may intend to convey both the literal meaning of an utterance and a metaphorical meaning. Furthermore, it cannot even begin to explain that level of the comprehension of metaphors that Black calls "interaction." However, it is by no means clear that the kind of approach advocated by Searle would be any better suited to the explanation of interaction. Indeed, it could be argued that the three most widely held theories of metaphor, the *substitution view*, the *comparison view*, and the *interaction view*, are all equally compatible, or incompatible, with the semantics and the pragmatics approaches. Both approaches seem primarily concerned with the nature of the relationship between metaphorical meaning and surface meaning. Of course, Black is not really interested in what particular metaphors mean. As indicated above, he is concerned with giving an account of metaphor that satisfies an intuition that he and many others have, namely, that there is some special, emergent "new thing" that is created when a novel metaphor is understood – something new that is attributable to the metaphor rather than to its novelty.

The next chapters address the question of how metaphors are understood. The emergence of something new is considered by Paivio to be one of the central problems surrounding the comprehension of metaphors. He sees as a tool for its explanation the notion of integration, whereby disparate elements in the utterance are combined to yield something greater than the sum of their parts. He sees the concepts of similarity and relation as also being implicated, and his paper discusses these three central concepts and their relationship to metaphor. Paivio makes a number of suggestions about the way in which knowledge is represented in interacting visual and verbal modes – suggestions that relate to the role of imagery in metaphor. Coupled with these suggestions are some empirical predictions about the relative effectiveness of concrete versus abstract metaphorical vehicles. Paivio observes that very little research into the comprehension of metaphors has been undertaken by experimental psychologists, a situation that seems to be slowly rectifying itself.

Responding to Paivio's lament about the lack of empirical data, Fraser describes some systematically collected interpretative responses to a set of sentences. The sentences were constructed to be semantically anomalous, but Fraser's subjects were called upon to give them metaphorical interpretations, which they apparently did very willingly. Fraser found little consistency between the various interpretations offered, suggesting that in their interpretations, subjects were drawing heavily upon their own associations to, and knowledge about, the predicates requiring metaphorical interpretations. Fraser concludes that there is little agreement between people about the interpretation of metaphors. It ought, perhaps, to be noted that the subjects in Fraser's study might have been straining to make metaphorical interpretations of contextually unsupported sentences with no specific referents ("She is an octopus"). In more naturalistic cases, there might be more agreement. This is an outcome that seems to be demanded by the fact that people can and do communicate successfully using metaphors.

A question explicitly raised in Paivio's and in many of the other papers concerns the role of similarity in metaphors. This question is discussed in my own chapter. Although the emphasis is primarily on the role of similarity in similes, some attention is devoted to the relationship between similes and metaphors. One of the more controversial claims made is that similes cannot be construed as literal comparisons, a claim that seems to be made also by Searle, but which remains a point of widespread disagreement. Although no answer to the basic question "What are metaphors?" appears, one candidate solution – namely, that metaphors are implicit comparisons – is rejected. It is argued that the comparisons that underlie metaphors must themselves be regarded as nonliteral, or metaphorical. Consequently, there is no explanatory value in asserting that metaphors are comparisons unless one then goes on to explain the difference between literal comparisons and metaphorical ones.

The question of the role of comparisons in metaphors forms one of the major foci of Miller's chapter, with which Part I ends. Recognizing that one of the most persistent criticisms of the comparison theory of metaphor is its vagueness, Miller proposes a detailed and rigorous formal treatment of the various ways in which similarity statements can underlie metaphors. Miller also touches on a number of other issues that arise in the first part of the book. These include such notions as the recognition of metaphors, discussed by Black, the interpretation of metaphors, discussed principally by Searle, the construction of a world model to "fit" the metaphor, discussed by Levin, and the fundamental uniformity of the comprehension processes for literal and nonliteral language alike. All of these, and many other issues, are brought together in Miller's attempt to find a place for the comprehension of metaphors within a more general framework for the comprehension of text. While his discussion is, for the most part, restricted to sentence-level metaphors, his examples are analyzed with an unusual degree of penetration. Miller's paper can be viewed almost as easily as the opening chapter of Part II as the closing chapter of Part I.

One of the distinctions made in Black's chapter is that between appreciators and depreciators of metaphor. Part II starts with two powerful papers, by, if not depreciators, at least, skeptics. One of the principal themes running through Part II is that metaphors can provide a different way of seeing the world. If one believes that important social problems can be seen from "correct" and "incorrect" (or "healthy" and "unhealthy") perspectives (see, Geertz, 1974), then the question of whether metaphors may sometimes encourage an incorrect (and, consequently, a socially harmful or undesirable) view arises. Of course, this danger is present quite independently of metaphors – depreciators of metaphors, for example, might see problems that the appreciators neglect, as is apparent from Schön's paper. Schön's concern is social-policy planning, especially urban planning, and there he sees a situation in which society's ills receive conflicting descriptions, often couched as metaphors. These descriptions, these "stories people tell," these metaphors, carry with them implicitly, and often insidiously, natural "solutions." If slums are a cancer, then they are bad and have to be cured. So, depending on the social situation and what it is *seen as*, there is a constrained set of problem solutions which may well be wrong or inappropriate. Schön argues that this situation should be viewed as one of what he calls, "frame conflict"; the solution is "frame restructuring." Conflicts of frames, he claims, cannot be resolved by appeal to the facts, because all the "relevant" facts are already embedded in the metaphor. The solution, frame restructuring, involves the coordination and reconciliation of these conflicting descriptions. Thus, Schön's paper emphasizes the extent to which metaphors can constrain and sometimes dangerously control the way in which we construct the world in which we live. It is a warning to be wary of such "generative" metaphors, metaphors which generate their own solutions, because more often than not they will fail to present an objective characterization of the problem situation.

Reddy accepts Schön's arguments and conclusions, and develops a detailed example of a generative metaphor in a different domain, namely, language. In talking about English, the metalinguistic resources available and normally used are the result of what he calls the "conduit metaphor." This metaphor for communication in natural language is based on the notion that language is a carrier of ideas, thoughts, aspirations, and so on, so that all a hearer needs to do is to "unpack" the message and "take out" what was "in" it. Reddy argues that the conduit metaphor falsely presupposes a certain objectivity – an objectivity that ignores the contribution of the hearer's or reader's own knowledge and experience. He observes that it leads to erroneous attempts to solve various kinds of communications problems, and one might add, until quite recently it has also led to erroneous attempts to uncover the psychological processes involved in language comprehension. Reddy's paper contains an appendix of examples of the conduit metaphor in action. This appendix is in itself a major piece of work, providing linguists with an unusual corpus, as well as substantiating Reddy's claims about the pervasiveness of the root metaphor. The conduit metaphor that Reddy sees as being so misleading, turns out to be isomorphic with the nonconstructivist approach to language and cognition. The alternative analogy that he proposes (the "toolmakers paradigm") is Reddy's attempt to supplant that approach with the constructivist's. Reddy's main point, however, is fundamentally the same as Schön's, namely, that the way we talk about things (in Reddy's case, human communication, and in Schön's case, social problems) often depends on root metaphors that are essentially misleading and inaccurate.

The macroscopic views of Schön and Reddy (and of most of the other contributors to Part II) contrast, as I mentioned earlier, with the more microscopic views of the contributions in Part I. The chapter by Sternberg, Tourangeau, and Nigro provides a bridge between the two. These authors share most of Schön's conclusions, but they arrive at them from their own microscopic approach. They propose a theory of the processes involved in the generation and comprehension of metaphors, as well as a characterization of the representation of knowledge consistent with the operation of those processes. The basic notion that they employ in this regard is that of "semantic feature spaces." The idea is that a good metaphor utilizes regions in two remote conceptual spaces that occupy similar positions within each space. An important issue that they address is that of the "goodness" or "success" of a metaphor. This, they claim, depends on maximizing the distance between the different domains (feature spaces) involved, while minimizing the difference between the positions occupied by each term within each domain. This notion of the goodness or "aesthetic pleasingness" of a metaphor they contrast with a notion of the "comprehensibility" of a metaphor, which is enhanced by minimizing the distance between the domains themselves. From this it follows that the better the metaphor, the less comprehensible it is (up to some limit). The analysis that Sternberg et al. offer is consistent with the belief that metaphors are an important means of expressing ideas for which the language may not have any literal terms available. This is because, in their view, a function of metaphors can be to identify a point in the topic feature space such that the corresponding point in a different, vehicle, feature space, has no lexical items associated with it.

It might be argued that if the strongly constructivist views of people like Schön and Reddy (and Rumelhart and others) can be upheld, there would be important implications for theories of language, be they philosophical, linguistic, or psychological. For example, their views are quite inconsistent with a sharp distinction between semantics and pragmatics, or between language and knowledge. They are inconsistent with approaches based on formal logic, or with semantic systems like those of interpretative semantics (see Katz & Fodor, 1963) or generative semantics (see Lakoff, 1971). These latter approaches seem ill-equipped to deal with what many view as a central aspect of human thought and cognition, namely, the ability to understand the same thing from different points of view. The extreme nonconstructivist position is that cognition is understanding things in the way that they are, whereas the extreme constructivist position is that the notion of alternative ways of seeing is fundamental to cognition. So if metaphors are important because of their ability to provide alternative or new ways of "seeing," then so-called literal language may be too restricted because of its inability to provide those perspectives; and, consequently, approaches that attribute to literal language a privileged status vis-à-vis its access to reality will have to be regarded as essentially incorrect. This issue is central to Boyd's paper, a large part of which is concerned with the nature of our linguistic access to "objective reality." It also impinges on more general questions in the philosophy of science.

Metaphors seem to play an important role in scientific discovery, and in the formulation and transmission of new theories. This function, which has to do with the communication of new ideas, is the one on which Boyd concentrates in his paper. Boyd argues that sometimes metaphors are essential to the statement of novel scientific theories. Such metaphors he refers to as "theory-constitutive" metaphors. He is willing to concede that they may lack the linguistic precision that many have taken to be so important in scientific discourse. This imprecision, he argues, is a referential one. Imprecision is not a special feature of metaphors in scientific discourse, but of referring terms in general. Thus, Boyd sees the role of metaphors in the transmission of novel scientific conceptions as part of a more general theory of reference, albeit an essential part. A major contribution that Boyd makes is his proposal for a theory of reference that not only addresses many of the standard problems in epistemology associated with such theories, but that also offers a comfortable home for metaphors. His theory is cast in terms of the ability of general terms to provide "epistemic access" to important and interesting aspects of reality. Boyd's chapter offers, therefore, one answer to the question: "What are metaphors for?" They permit the articulation of new ideas, of which scientific theories are but a special case. It is a function that cannot always be fulfilled using literal language.

Kuhn for the most part accepts Boyd's position, but he sees the role of metaphors as being more extensive than Boyd does. Boyd limits his account to his theory-constitutive metaphors, while arguing that some uses of metaphors in science are purely exegetic (for example, the metaphor of atomic structure as a miniature solar system). Kuhn believes that even metaphors like this – where it is alleged that we know exactly what is the basis of similarity – require the employment of metaphor-like processes. He argues that we still need to distinguish between those aspects that are similar, and those that are not. Thus, Kuhn wants to extend an interactive account of metaphor to the use of models in general; they are not merely heuristic, pedagogical devices, they lie at the heart of theory change and transmission. For both Boyd and Kuhn, the necessity of metaphor lies in its role in establishing links between the language of science and the world that it purports to describe and explain. They agree in their unwillingness to restrict that function, as the nonconstructivist would, solely to literal language.

Pylyshyn, although finding the general thrust of Boyd's arguments attractive, poses a question raised earlier by Sadock about how one can decide whether something is a metaphorical or a literal description. He argues that, in fact, many of the examples that Boyd gives of metaphorical terms in cognitive psychology, are really examples of literal uses – particularly the concept of computation. Furthermore, Pylyshyn is concerned that it should be possible to distinguish between metaphors that are powerful, and those that are impotent, that is, between those that actually carry with them explanations as well as descriptions, and those that have no explanatory potential, although leaving their protagonists with an unwarranted and unhelpful "comfortable feeling" that something has been explained. Thus, two important points emerge from Pylyshyn's chapter. First, again, the point that distinguishing metaphors from literal uses of language is by no means an easy task, and, second, that the careless use of metaphors may do more harm than good.

I have suggested that the transmission of new scientific ideas and theories is but a special case of purveying ideas that are new (for the intended audience). We have a word for this general activity: "teaching." If one takes this line, then the role of metaphors in human thought and communication can be seen suddenly to blossom. Metaphor becomes ubiquitous, an everyday phenomenon in the lives of ordinary men, women, and perhaps especially, children. This is the position taken by Petrie, who argues that a principal function of metaphor is to permit the understanding of new concepts by an iterative process of successive approximations from the more familiar metaphorical vehicle. He sees this process as being analogous, in many important respects, to the account of the change of paradigms involved in scientific revolutions (Kuhn, 1970a). While Petrie argues that metaphors, or something like them, are necessary as the bridges between the known and the unknown, Green argues that they are not. Green maintains that reason and inference are normally quite sufficient to permit the learning of something radically new, if indeed, such learning ever takes place at all. Metaphors may sometimes help, but they cannot be always necessary. This seems to be the conclusion that Sticht reaches as well, although he goes on to discuss other uses of metaphors in education. He discusses the role of metaphors as indicators of comprehension, as frames of reference for producing text coherence, and as a tools for creative problem solving. Thus, in Sticht's chapter, the last, we find more proposals for answering the second major question which was raised at the outset: "What are metaphors for?"

The contribution of this book does not lie in the provision of definitive answers to the important questions; rather, it lies in the identification of these questions. Two central ones are: "What are metaphors?" (basically a theoretical issue), and "What are metaphors for?" (a more practical issue). These subsume a host of others raised at various places in the chapters that follow. How can metaphorical language be distinguished from literal language? How literal is literal language? Is the problem of metaphor one to be handled by a theory of language, a theory of language use, or both? Are the comprehension processes for metaphorical uses of language the same as those for literal uses? Can metaphors be reduced to comparisons? Is the reduction of metaphors to comparisons a fruitful approach to understanding the nature of metaphor? Are the comparisons to which one might attempt to reduce a metaphor themselves in need of explanation? Are metaphors necessary for the transmission of new scientific concepts? Are metaphors necessary for the transmission of new ideas in general? What dangers are there associated with the use of metaphors to describe new or problematical situations? These are but some of the questions discussed in the chapters that follow.

PART I

PART 1

More About Metaphor

MAX BLACK

This paper is intended to supplement the earlier study in which I introduced and defended an "interaction view of metaphor" (namely, Black, 1962b, referred to hereafter as *Metaphor*). A reader unfamiliar with that study will find a summary in the section entitled "The Interaction View Revisited."

I shall try here to amplify my original formulation by explicating the grounds of the metaphors of "interaction," "filtering," and "screening," which I used in trying to understand how metaphorical statements work. I shall add some suggestions about the relations of a metaphor to its grounding resemblances and analogies (somewhat neglected in *Metaphor*), with the hope of also shedding some further light on the connections between metaphors and models (for which, see Black, 1962c).

This occasion gives me an opportunity to take some notice of the numerous criticisms, mostly friendly, which *Metaphor* has received since its original publication. Pleased though I am at the widespread acceptance of the *interaction view*, I agree with Monroe Beardsley, Ted Cohen, Paul Ricœur, and others that more work will be needed before the power and limitations of this approach to the subject can be fully appreciated.

Reasons for current interest in metaphor

John Middleton Murry's essay, "Metaphor", (Murry, 1931), opens with the remark that, "Discussions of metaphor – there are not many of them – often strike us at first as superficial." Today both comments would be inappropriate. The extraordinary volume of papers and books on the subject produced during the past forty years might suggest that the subject is inexhaustible.[1]

Warren Shibles's useful bibliography (Shibles, 1971) has entries running to nearly three hundred pages and contains perhaps as many as four thousand titles. As for these discussions being superficial, one might rather complain today of ungrounded profundity, because so many writers, agreeing with Murry that "Metaphor is as ultimate as speech itself, and speech as ultimate as thought" (p. 1), rapidly draw ontological morals, while leaving the nature of metaphorical speech and thought tantalizingly obscure.

In the inconclusive debate between the appreciators and depreciators of metaphor, the former nowadays score most points. But they are characteristically prone to inflation. As Nowottny (1962, p. 89) puts it:

Current criticism often takes metaphor *au grand sérieux*, as a peephole on the nature of transcendental reality, a prime means by which the imagination can see into the life of things.

She adds:

[T]his attitude makes it difficult to see the workings of those metaphors which deliberately emphasize the frame, offering themselves as deliberate fabrications, as a prime means of seeing into the life not of things but of the creative human consciousness, framer of its own world.

Enthusiastic friends of metaphor are indeed prone to various kinds of inflation, ready to see metaphor everywhere, in the spirit of Carlyle, who said:

Examine language; what, if you except some primitive elements of natural sound, what is it all but metaphors, recognized as such or no longer recognized; still fluid and florid or now solid-grown and colourless? If these same primitive garments are the osseous fixtures in the Flesh-Garment Language then are metaphors its muscle and living integuments. (From S. J. Brown, 1927, p. 41)

This quotation illustrates a pervasive tendency for writers, including myself in *Metaphor*, to frame their basic insights in metaphorical terms.

A related inflationary thrust is shown in a persistent tendency, found in Aristotle's still influential treatment, and manifest in as recent a discussion as Nelson Goodman's *Languages of Art* (Goodman, 1968), to regard all figurative uses of language as metaphorical, and in this way to ignore the important distinctions between metaphor and such other figures of speech as simile, metonymy, and synecdoche.

To make a sufficiently intricate topic still harder to handle, the depreciators tend to focus upon relatively trivial examples ("Man is a wolf") that conform to the traditional "substitution view," and the special form of it that I called the "comparison view" (see Black, 1962b, especially pp. 30 – 37), whereas appreciators, in their zeal to establish "that metaphor is the omnipresent principle of language"

(Richards, 1936b, p. 92),[2] tend to dwell upon excitingly suggestive but obscure examples from Shakespeare, Donne, Hopkins, or Dylan Thomas, to the neglect of simpler instances that also require attention in a comprehensive theory.

Although I am on the side of the appreciators, who dwell upon what Empson and Ricœur call "vital" metaphors, I think their opponents (typically philosophers, scientists, mathematicians, and logicians) are right in asking for less "vital" or less "creative" metaphors to be considered. It may well be a mistaken strategy to treat profound metaphors as paradigms.

In what follows, I shall steer a middle course, taking as points of departure metaphors complex enough to invite analysis, yet sufficiently transparent for such analysis to be reasonably uncontroversial. My interest in this paper is particularly directed toward the "cognitive aspects" of certain metaphors, whether in science, philosophy, theology, or ordinary life, and their power to present in a distinctive and irreplaceable way, insight into "how things are" (for which, see the section entitled "Can a Metaphorical Statement Ever Reveal 'How Things Are'?". I shall leave the "poetic metaphors" invoked by Nowottny for another occasion.

What is the "mystery" of metaphor?

One writer, who might be speaking for many, says, "Among the mysteries of human speech, metaphor has remained one of the most baffling" (Boyle, 1954, p. 257). But what *is* this supposed mystery? Given the prevalence or, if we are to trust Richards and many other thinkers, the ubiquity of metaphor, metaphorical discourse might well seem no more mysterious than singing or dancing – and, one might add, no more improper or deviant.

In the sentence following the one I have quoted, Father Boyle refers to the "odd predilection for asserting a thing to be what it is not." So perhaps the "mystery" is simply that, *taken as literal,* a metaphorical statement appears to be perversely asserting something to be what it is plainly known not to be. (And that makes the metaphor user look like a liar or a deceiver.) When Juliet says to Romeo, "The light that shines comes from thine eyes," she surely cannot *really mean* that his eyeballs are lighting up the chamber; when Wallace Stevens says, "A poem is a pheasant," he cannot *really* mean that it flaps its wings and has a long tail – for such things are plainly false and absurd. But such "absurdity" and "falsity" are of the essence: in their absence, we should have no metaphor but merely a literal utterance. So a metaphor user, unless he is merely babbling, would seem, according to the ancient formula, to "say one thing and mean another." But why?

An intelligent child, hearing his scientist father refer to a "field of force," might ask – but with a twinkle in his eye, one hopes – "And who ploughs it?" In order to feel the supposed "mystery," one needs to recapture the naiveté of somebody who takes metaphorical utterances to be literal or the false naiveté of someone who pretends to do so. But to assume that a metaphorical utterance presents something as what it is plainly not – or to assume that its producer really does intend to say one thing while meaning something else – is to beg disastrously a prime question by accepting the misleading view of a metaphor as some kind of deviation or aberration from proper usage.

Somebody seriously making a metaphorical statement – say, "The Lord is my Shepherd" – might reasonably claim that he meant just what he said, having chosen the words most apt to express his thought, attitudes, and feelings, and was by no means guilty of uttering a crass absurdity. Such a position cannot be rejected out of hand.

The danger of an approach that treats literal utterance as an unproblematic standard, while regarding metaphorical utterance as problematic or mysterious by contrast, is that it tends to encourage reductionist theories: As the plain man might say, "If the metaphor producer didn't mean what he said, why didn't he say something else?" We are headed for the blind alley taken by those innumerable followers of Aristotle who have supposed metaphors to be replaceable by literal translations.

A sympathetic way of following Father Boyle's lead might be to start by asking what distinguishes a metaphorical statement from a literal one. That, of course, assumes that there is at least a prima facie and observable difference between metaphorical and literal statements – a donnée that seem to me initially less problematic than it does to some theorists. When a writer says, "Men are verbs, not nouns," a reader untrammeled by theoretical preconceptions about the ubiquity of metaphor will immediately recognize that "verbs" and "nouns" are not being used literally. Dictionaries do not include men as a special case of verbs, and a competent speaker will not list them as paradigm cases of the application of that word. And so in general, it would be relatively easy to devise tests, for those who want them, of the literal meaning of the word that is the metaphorical "focus" of a metaphorical utterance. Tacit knowledge of such literal meaning induces the characteristic feeling of dissonance or "tension" between the focus and its literal "frame."

Starting so, and acknowledging a clear prima facie difference between literal and metaphorical uses of expressions, need not, however, prejudge the validity of some "deeper" insight that might eventually reject the commonsensical distinction between the literal and the metaphorical as superficial and ultimately indefensible. But such a revisionist view needs the support of a thorough exploration of the implicit rationale of the common-sense distinction. An effort to do so will naturally concern itself with crucial supplementary questions about the point of using metaphors and, more generally, about the distinctive powers of metaphorical discourse.

Some writers, notably Coleridge, but not he alone, have imputed a peculiarly "creative" role to metaphor (for which, see the section entitled "Are Metaphors Ever 'Creative'?"). That a puzzle or mystery might be perceived in this connection can be supported by the following train of thought. A successful metaphor is *realized* in discourse, is embodied in the given "text," and need not be treated as a riddle. So the writer or speaker is employing conventional means to produce a nonstandard effect, while using only the standard syntactic and semantic resources of his speech community. Yet the meaning of an interesting metaphor is typically new or "creative," not inferable from the standard lexicon. A major task for theorists of metaphor, then, is to explain how such an outcome – striking for all its familiarity – is brought about.

We may usefully consider, for the sake of contrast, the situation of a participant in a rule-governed practice more tightly constrained than speech – say the game of chess. There, too, a creative aspect is readily discernible, because even if all the mistakes are waiting to be discovered (as a master once said) a player must still search for and ultimately *choose* his move: In most chess positions, there is no decision procedure and no demonstrably "correct" move. Yet the player's scope for creativity is sharply limited by the game's inflexible rules, which provide him always with a finite and well-defined set of options.

Imagine now a variation, say "epichess," in which a player would have the right to move any piece as if it were another of equal or inferior value (a bishop moving for once like a knight, say, or a pawn) – *provided the opponent accepted such a move.* There we have a primitive model of conversation and discourse, where almost any "move" is acceptable if one can get away with it; that is, if a competent receiver will accept it. But even here there are *some* constraints upon creativity: one cannot couple any two nouns at random and be sure to produce an effective metaphor. (If the reader doubts this, let him try to make sense of "a chair is a syllogism." In the absence of some specially constructed context, this must surely count as a failed metaphor.)

But what *is* a "creative," rule-violating metaphor producer really trying to do? And what is a competent hearer expected to do in response to such a move?

In *Metaphor,* I suggested that such questions, and most of the others posed by theorists of metaphor, might be regarded as concerned with "the 'logical grammar' of 'metaphor' and words having related meaning"; or as expressing "attempts to become clearer about some uses of the word 'metaphor'" (p. 25); or as the start of an effort "to analyze the notion of metaphor" (p. 26). Although this semantic emphasis has alienated some of my critics, I see no particular harm in it. There would be no substantial difference in an approach that was conceived, in a more ontological idiom, as an effort to "become clearer about the nature of metaphor." Indeed, I would regard the two formulas as equivalent.

Identifying the targets

The reader will have noticed my references to metaphorical statements. Indeed, my standing concern is with full metaphorical statements and, derivatively, with "statement-ingredients" (words or phrases used metaphorically) only as they occur in *specific* and relatively complete acts of expression and communication. (Hereafter, "metaphor" is usually short for "metaphorical statement.") A "statement," in my intended sense, will be identified by quoting a whole sentence, or a set of sentences, together with as much of the relevant verbal context, or the nonverbal setting, as may be needed for an adequate grasp of the actual or imputed speaker's meaning. I use "meaning" here for whatever a competent hearer may be said to have grasped when he succeeds in responding adequately to the actual or hypothetical verbal action consisting in the serious utterance of the sentence (s) in question.

As examples of such identifications of metaphorical statements, I offer:

(1) "L'homme n'est qu'un roseau, le plus faible de la nature, mais c'est un roseau pensant" (Pascal in the *Pensées*) – or, more briefly, Pascal's metaphor of man as a thinking reed.

(2) "You are a metaphor and they are lies/Or there true least where their knot chance unfurls." (William Empson, *Letter V*)

(3) Ezra Pound's metaphor of education as sheepherding (in his *ABC of Reading*, passim).

Of these metaphors, the last is relatively the most independent of its context and might be sufficiently identified, with supression of Pound's name, as "the metaphor of education as sheepherding." Yet, justice to

Pound's view might demand citation of relevant passages in his tract. Textual elaboration is more obviously needed to appreciate Pascal's deceptively simple metaphor or Empson's characteristically obscure one.

I propose to distinguish what is identified merely by a formula like "the metaphor of *A* as *B*," without further specification of its contextual use, as a metaphor-*theme*, regarded as an abstraction from the metaphorical statements in which it does or might occur, A metaphor-theme is available for repeated use, adaptation, and modification by a variety of speakers or thinkers on any number of specific occasions.[3]

One danger in attending mainly to what I have called metaphor-themes is that of postulating a standard response to a given metaphorical statement – a response determined by linguistic, conceptual, cultural, or other conventions. Such a view is untenable because a metaphorical statement involves a rule violation: There can be no rules for "creatively" violating rules.[4] And that is why there can be no *dictionary* (though there might be a thesaurus) of metaphors.

Any attempt to be more precise about the identifying and individuating criteria for metaphorical statements will be embarrassed by the following difficulty. The *very same* metaphorical statement, as I wish to use that expression, may appropriately receive a number of different and even partially conflicting readings. Thus Empson's metaphor, reproduced above, might be taken by one reader, but not another, as imputing falsity to the person addressed. We might choose to say that both were right about two different metaphors expressed in Empson's words; or, less plausibly, that one reader must have been mistaken. There is an inescapable indeterminacy in the notion of a *given* metaphorical-statement, so long as we count its import as part of its essence.

I hope these brief terminological remarks will serve for the present occasion. In what follows, I shall not insist pedantically upon using the qualifiers "-statement" or "-theme," usually leaving the context to resolve any possible ambiguity.

On classifying metaphors; and the importance of emphasis and resonance

Given the prevalence of metaphorical statements and their manifest versatility, a student of the subject would find some generally accepted classification helpful in making even the simplest distinctions: But at present, he is in an even worse situation than a biologist before Linnaeus. For the only entrenched classification is grounded in the trite opposition (itself expressed metaphorically) between "dead" and "live" metaphors. This is no more helpful than, say, treating a corpse as a special case of a person: A so-called dead metaphor is not a metaphor at all, but merely an expression that no longer has a pregnant metaphorical use.

A competent reader is not expected to recognize such a familiar expression as "falling in love" as a metaphor, to be taken *au grand sérieux*. Indeed, it is doubtful whether that expression was ever more than a case of catachresis (using an idiom to fill a gap in the lexicon).

If the "actuality" of a metaphor, its possessing the distinctive characteristics, whatever they may be, of genuine metaphorical efficacy, is important enough to be marked, one might consider replacing the dead and alive contrast by a set of finer discriminations: distinguishing perhaps between expressions whose etymologies, genuine or fancied, suggest a metaphor beyond resuscitation (a muscle as a little mouse, *musculus*); those where the original, now usually unnoticed, metaphor can be usefully restored (obligation as involving some kind of *bondage*); and those, the objects of my present interest, that are, and are perceived to be, actively metaphoric. Appropriate labels might be: "extinct," "dormant," and "active" metaphors. But not much is to be expected of this schema or any more finely tuned substitute. (I shall be concerned hereafter only with metaphors needing no artificial respiration, recognized by speaker and hearer as authentically "vital" or active.)

Given an active metaphorical statement, it would be useful to discriminate two aspects, which I shall call *emphasis* and *resonance*. A metaphorical utterance is *emphatic*, in my intended sense, to the degree that its producer will allow no variation upon or substitute for the words used – and especially not for what in *Metaphor* I called the "focus," the salient word or expression, whose occurrence in the literal frame invests the utterance with metaphorical force. Plausible opposites to "emphatic" might include: "expendable," "optional," "decorative," and "ornamental." (Relatively dispensable metaphors are often no more than literary or rhetorical flourishes that deserve no more serious attention than musical grace notes.) Emphatic metaphors are intended to be dwelt upon for the sake of their unstated implications: Their producers need the receiver's cooperation in perceiving what lies *behind* the words used.

How far such interpretative response can reach will depend upon the complexity and power of the metaphor-theme in question: Some metaphors, even famous ones, barely lend themselves to implicative elaboration, while others, perhaps less interesting, prove relatively rich in background implications. For want of a better label, I shall call metaphorical utterances that support a high degree of implicative elaboration *resonant*.

Resonance and emphasis are matters of degree. They are not independent: Highly emphatic metaphors tend to be highly resonant (though there are exceptions), while the unemphatic occurrence of a markedly resonant metaphor is apt to produce a dissonance, sustained by irony or some similarly distancing operation.

Finally, I propose to call a metaphor that is both markedly emphatic and resonant a *strong metaphor*. My purpose in the remainder of this paper is to analyze the raison d'être and the mode of operation of strong metaphors, treating those that are relatively "weak" on account of relatively low emphasis or resonance as etiolated specimens.

A weak metaphor might be compared to an unfunny joke, or an unilluminating philosophical epigram: One understands the unsuccessful or failed verbal actions in the light of what *would be* funny, illuminating, or what have you. Yet if all jokes are intended to be funny, and fail to the degree that they are not, not all metaphors aim at strength, and some may be none the worse for that.

Consider the following example from a letter of Virginia Woolf to Lytton Strachey:

"How you weave in every scrap – my god what scraps! – of interest to be had, like (you must pardon the metaphor) a snake insinuating himself through innumerable golden rings – (Do snakes? – I hope so)." (Nicolson & Trautmann, 1976, p. 205)

The snake metaphor used here should certainly count as weak in my terminology, because Strachey was intended to take the rich implicative background lightly.

The interaction view revisited

The interaction view which I presented in *Metaphor* was there characterized as an attempt "to become clearer about some uses of the word 'metaphor' – or, if one prefers the material model, to analyze the notion of metaphor" (pp. 25–6). In retrospect, I would prefer to think of my position as a help to understanding how strong metaphorical statements *work*. But this shift of formulation from conceptual analysis to a functional analysis, though potentially important, need not detain us.

The merits of the interaction view, a development and modification of I. A. Richards's valuable insights, should be weighed against those of its only available alternatives – the traditional "substitution view" and "comparison view" (a special case of the former). Briefly stated, the substitution view regards "the entire sentence that is the locus of the metaphor as replacing some set of literal sentences" (p. 31); while the comparison view takes the imputed literal paraphrase to be a statement of some similarity or analogy, and so takes every metaphor to be a condensed or elliptic simile (pp. 35–6).

The reader will notice that both of these views treat metaphors as *unemphatic*, in my terminology – in principle, expendable if one disregards the incidental pleasures of stating figuratively what might just as well have been said literally.

A brief summary of the preferred interaction view might consist of the following claims, based upon the concluding summary of *Metaphor* (pp. 44–5). I reproduce the original formulations, with minor improvements, appending afterthoughts in each case.

1. A metaphorical statement has two distinct subjects, to be identified as the "primary" subject and the "secondary" one.

In *Metaphor*, I spoke instead of the "principal" and "subsidiary" subjects. The duality of reference is marked by the contrast between the metaphorical statement's *focus* (the word or words used nonliterally) and the surrounding literal *frame*.

2. The secondary subject is to be regarded as a system rather than an individual thing.

Thus, I think of Wallace Stevens's remark that, "Society is a sea" as being not so much about the sea (considered as a thing) as about a system of relationships (the "implicative complex" discussed below) signaled by the presence of the word "sea" in the sentence in question. (In *Metaphor*, I proposed that the primary subject, also, be taken as a system. But it seems in retrospect needlessly paradoxical, though not plainly mistaken, to say that Stevens was viewing society, too, as a system of social relationships.) In retrospect, the intended emphasis upon "systems," rather than upon "things" or "ideas," (as in Richards) looks like one of the chief novelties in the earlier study.

3. The metaphorical utterance works by "projecting upon" the primary subject a set of "associated implications," comprised in the implicative complex, that are predicable of the secondary subject.

The label "implicative complex" is new. "Projection" is, of course, a metaphor, that will need further discussion. In the earlier study, I spoke of a "system of associated commonplaces" (which later provoked some pointed criticisms by Paul Ricœur). My notion was that the secondary subject, in a way partly depending upon the context of metaphorical use, determines a set of what Aristotle called *endoxa*, current opinions shared by members of a certain speech-community. But I also emphasized, as I should certainly wish to do now, that a metaphor producer may introduce a novel and nonplatitudinous "implication-complex."

4. The maker of a metaphorical statement selects, emphasizes, suppresses, and organizes features of the primary subject by applying to it statements isomorphic with the members of the secondary subject's implicative complex.

The mechanisms of such "projection" (a still serviceable metaphor) are discussed and illustrated in the next section.

5. In the context of a particular metaphorical statement, the two subjects "interact" in the following ways: (a) the presence of the primary subject incites the hearer to select some of the secondary subject's properties; and (b) invites him to construct a parallel implication-comlpex that can fit the primary subject; and (c) reciprocally induces parallel changes in the secondary subject.

This may be considered a crux for the interaction view (an attempted explication of Richards's striking image of the "interanimation of words"). Although I speak figuratively here of the *subjects* interacting, such an outcome is of course produced in the minds of the speaker and hearer: It is they who are led to engage in selecting, organizing, and projecting. I think of a metaphorical statement (even a weak one) as a verbal action essentially demanding *uptake*, a creative response from a competent reader. In *Metaphor*, I said – scandalizing some of my subsequent critics – that the imputed interaction involves "shifts in meaning of words belonging to the same family or system as the metaphorical expression" (p. 45). I meant, of course, a shift in the *speaker's* meaning – and the corresponding *hearers* meaning – what both of them understand by words, as used on the particular occasion.

How metaphorical statements work

Consider "Marriage is a zero-sum game." In this relatively "active" metaphor the implication-complex might be spelled out somewhat as follows:

(G1) A "game" is a *contest;*

(G2) between two opponents;

(G3) in which one player can win only at the expense of the other.

The corresponding system of imputed claims about marriage

depends crucially upon the interpretations given to "contest," "oppo
nents," and especially to "winning." One might try:

(M1) A marriage is a sustained struggle;

(M2) between two contestants;

(M3) in which the rewards (power? money? satisfaction?) of one con-
testant are gained only at the other's expense.

Here, the "projected" propositions can be taken literally – or
almost so, no matter what one thinks of their plausibility (the metaphor's aptness not being here in question).

Such a heavy-handed analysis of course neglects the ambience of the
secondary subject, the suggestions and valuations that necessarily
attach themselves to a game-theory view of marriage, and thereby suf-
fuse the receiver's perception of it: A marriage that can be seen as a
competitive "game" of skill and calculation is not the kind made in
heaven.

The relations between the three members of the implication complex (G1-3) in this relatively simple example and their correlated
statements about marriage (M1 – 3) are a mixed lot. M2 might be
said to predicate of marriage precisely what G2 does of a two-person
game (with some hesitation about the matching of "opponents" and
"contestants"); but in the shift from G1 to M1 it seems more plausible
to discern some similarity rather than strict identity; and in M3,
finally, "gain" must surely have an extended sense, by contrast with its
sense in G3, since marital struggles usually do not end in clear-cut conventional victories. The difficulty in making firm and decisive judgments on such points is, I think, present in *all* cases of metaphorical
statement. Since we must necessarily read "behind the words," we
cannot set firm bounds to the admissible interpretations: Ambiguity is
a necessary by-product of the metaphor's suggestiveness.

So far as I can see, after scrutinizing many examples, the relations
between the meanings of the corresponding key words of the two
implication complexes can be classified as (a) identity, (b) extension,
typically ad hoc, (c) similarity, (d) analogy, or (e) what might be
called "metaphorical coupling" (where, as often happens, the original
metaphor implicates subordinate metaphors).

Let us now idealize the connection between the two implication-complexes (G and M) in the following way: G consists of certain statements, say Pa, Qb, . . . , and aRb, cSd, . . . , while M comprises corresponding statements $P'a'$, $Q'b'$, . . . , and $a'R'b'$, $c'S'd'$, . . . , (where P
is uniquely correlated with P', a with a', R with R', and so on). Then
the two systems have, as mathematicians say, the same "structure";
they are isomorphic (see Eberle, 1970, for a lucid exposition of this

notion). One important deviation from the mathematical conception is that G is linked with M by a "mixed lot" of projective relations, as we saw in the game-marriage example, and not (as typically in mathematical contexts) by a single projective relation.

With such conceptions to hand, we need not speak metaphorically about "projecting" the secondary system. Viewed in this way (and neglecting the important suggestions and connotations – the ambience, tone, and attitudes that are also projected upon M) G is precisely what I have called in the past an "analog-model" (cf. Black, 1962c).[5] I am now impressed, as I was insufficiently so when composing *Metaphor*, by the tight connections between the notions of models and metaphors. Every implication-complex supported by a metaphor's secondary subject, I now think, is a *model* of the ascriptions imputed to the primary subject: Every metaphor is the tip of a submerged model.

Metaphors and similes

I have said that there is a similarity, analogy or, more generally, an identity of structure between the secondary implication-complex of a metaphor and the set of assertions – the primary implication-complex – that it maps. In "Poverty is a crime," "crime" and "poverty" are nodes of isomorphic networks, in which assertions about crime are correlated one-to-one with corresponding statements about poverty.

Hence, every metaphor may be said to mediate an analogy or structural correspondence. (That is the correct insight behind the classical comparison view of metaphor as elliptical or truncated simile.) Hence, also, every metaphorical statement may be said to implicate a likeness-statement and a comparison-statement, each weaker than the original metaphorical statement. ("I didn't say that he is *like* an echo; I said and meant that he *is* an echo!") But to perceive that a metaphor is grounded in similarity and analogy is not to agree with Whatley (1961) that "the simile or comparison may be considered as differing *in form only* from a metaphor" or with Bain (1888) that "the metaphor *is* a comparison implied in the use of a term" (cf. *Metaphor*, p. 36). Implication is not the same as covert identity: Looking at a scene through blue spectacles is different from *comparing* that scene with something else.

To call, "Poverty is a crime," a simile or comparison is either to say too little or too much. In a given context of utterance, "Poverty is like a crime" may still be figurative, and hardly more than a stylistic variant upon the original metaphorical statement. Burns might have said,

"My Love is a red, red rose," instead of "My Love is like a red, red rose," if the meter had permitted, with little semantic difference, if any. But to suppose that the metaphorical statement is an abstract or précis of a literal point-by-point comparison, in which the primary and secondary subjects are juxtaposed for the sake of noting dissimilarities as well as similarities, is to misconstrue the function of a metaphor. In discursively comparing one subject *with* another, we sacrifice the distinctive power and effectiveness of a good metaphor. The literal comparison lacks the ambience and suggestiveness, and the imposed "view" of the primary subject, upon which a metaphor's power to illuminate depends. In a metaphor as powerful as Pascal's, of man as a "thinking reed" (*un roseau pensant*), the supporting ground is disconcertingly simple, being intended chiefly to highlight human frailty and weakness (*faiblesse*). The figure's effect depends, in this instance, very much on the ambience.

It is helpful to remind oneself that "is like" has many uses, among them: to point to some obvious, striking, or salient resemblance as in, "Doesn't he look like Mussolini?" (where some such qualification as "*looks* like" or "*sounds* like" is needed); in an "open comparison," to mark the start of a detailed, literal point-by-point comparison; or as a mere stylistic variation upon the metaphorical form (which raises nearly all the questions I am here trying to answer).

Thinking in metaphors

The foregoing account, which treats a metaphor, roughly speaking, as an instrument for drawing implications grounded in perceived analogies of structure between two subjects belonging to different domains, has paid no attention to the state of mind of somebody who *affirms* a metaphorical statement. A good metaphor sometimes *impresses*, strikes, or seizes its producer: We want to say we had a "flash of insight," not merely that we were comparing *A* with *B*, or even that we were thinking of *A* as if it were *B*. But to say seriously, emphatically, that, "Life *is* the receipt and transmission of information," is at least to be thinking of life *as* the passage of information (but not that, merely). Similarly for all metaphorical utterances that are asserted and not merely entertained.

It might, therefore, be a large step forward in becoming clearer about what might be called *metaphorical thought* (a neglected topic of major importance) if we had a better grasp on what it is to think of something (*A*) *as* something else (*B*). What, then, is it to think of *A* as *B*?

Consider the relatively simple case of thinking of the geometrical figure sometimes called the "Star of David" in the following different ways:

(1) as an equilateral triangle set upon another of the same size (figure 1);

(2) as a regular hexagon, bearing an equilateral triangle upon each of its edges (figure 2);

(3) as three superimposed congruent parallelograms (figure 3);

(4) as the trace left by a point moving continuously around the perimeter of the Star and then around the interior hexagon;

(5) as in (4), but with the point tracing out the hexagon before moving to the outside.

One might ask a child to think of the figure in each of these ways in turn. In the difficult third case of the three parallelograms, he would probably need some help, so there is something that he can be taught to do. But what?

The images one forms in trying to obey instructions corresponding to these five aspects of the Star are heuristically essential. A slow learner might be helped by having the different geometrical forms outlined in contrasting colors or, in cases (4) and (5), by watching a moving pencil point actually produce the figure. But the comprehension could not consist merely in possessing such images, important as they may be: Any competent teacher would ask the learner such questions as whether the moving point could trace the whole figure continuously – or, in the simpler cases, whether the triangles in question had the same size and shape. A test of mastery is the ability to tease out the implications of the intended perceptual analysis.

So far, the case somewhat resembles what happens when we see some *A* as metaphorically *B*: The child sees the Star *as* superimposed parallelograms; a metaphor thinker sees life *as* a flow of information; both apply concepts that yield discovery; both manifest skills shown in ability to tease out suitable implications of their respective insights. But

Figure 1   Figure 2   Figure 3

this comparison is somewhat lame, because the child learner, unlike the metaphor thinker, has not yet been required to make *conceptual innovations*, the parallelograms he perceives being just those he had antecedently learned to draw and recognize.

So let us vary the illustration. One might ask a child to think of each of the following figures as a triangle: one composed of three *curved* segments; a straight line segment (viewed as a collapsed triangle, with its vertex on the base); two parallel lines issuing from a base segment (with the vertex "gone to infinity"); and so on. The imaginative effort demanded in such exercises (familiar to any student of mathematics) is not a bad model for what is needed in producing, handling, and understanding all but the most trivial of metaphors. That the use of the relevant concepts employed should *change* (so that "game" is *made* to apply to marriage; "information" to life; "reed" to man; and so on) seems essential to the operation.

Why stretch and twist, press and expand, concepts in this way – Why try to see *A* as metaphorically *B*, when it literally is not *B*? Well, because we *can* do so, conceptual boundaries not being rigid, but elastic and permeable; and because we often need to do so, the available literal resources of the language being insufficient to express our sense of the rich correspondences, interrelations, and analogies of domains conventionally separated; and because metaphorical thought and utterance sometimes embody insight expressible in no other fashion.

How do we recognize metaphors?

While praising the interaction theory, Monroe C. Beardsley has urged that it is:

... incomplete is not explaining what it is about the metaphorical attribution that *informs* us that the modifier is metaphorical rather than literal. (Beardsley, 1958, p. 161, italics added)

Elsewhere, Beardsley (1967) states the tasks of a theory of metaphor as follows:

The problem is to understand how that radical shift of intension [how the metaphorical modifer acquires a special sense in its particular context] comes about; *how we know that the modifier is to be taken metaphorically*; and how we construe or explicate its meaning correctly. (p. 285, italics added)

The supplement that Beardsley desires, therefore, seems to be some *diagnostic criterion*, as it might be called, for the occurrence of a metaphorical statement, some mark or indication that will allow its presence and metaphorical character to be detected. I use "diagnostic criterion" here to suggest a bodily symptom, such as a rash, that serves as a reliable sign of some abnormal state though not necessarily qualifying as a defining condition. But Beardsley may, after all, be seeking more ambitiously an observable and *necessary condition* for a statement to be metaphorical.

The need for some such identification criterion, essential or merely diagnostic, has been forcibly urged by other writers. Ina Loewenberg says:

Any satisfactory formulation of the principle of metaphor requires the identifiability of metaphors since they cannot be understood or produced unless recognized as such. (Loewenberg, 1973, p. 316)

Here *"the* principle of a metaphor" alludes to her contention that metaphors "exemplify a single principle of semantic change." If "identifiability" is taken in a broad sense, I could agree with Loewenberg's requirement, with a possible reservation about a "producer" being necessarily aware of using a metaphor. But the rest of her valuable essay shows that she, like Beardsley at least part of the time, is demanding what I have called a "diagnostic criterion" for a statement to be metaphorical.

Beardsley proceeds to offer such a diagnostic criterion as the cornerstone of his "controversion theory."[6] According to him, the recognizable mark of a metaphorical statement is that *taken literally* it would have to count as a logical contradiction or an absurdity, in either case something patently *false.*

An obvious objection is that this test, so far as it fits, will apply equally to such other tropes as oxymoron or hyperbole, so that it would at best certify the presence of some figurative statement, but not necessarily a metaphor. A more serious objection is that authentic metaphors need not manifest the invoked controversion, though many of them do. Suppose I counter the conversational remark, "As we know, man is a wolf – *homo homini lupus"* – by saying, "Oh, no, man is not a wolf but an ostrich."[7] In context, "Man is not a wolf" is as metaphorical as its opposite, yet it clearly fails the controversion test. The point is easy to generalize: The negation of any metaphorical statement can itself be a metaphorical statement and hence possibly true if taken literally. Nor need the examples be confined to such negatives. When we say, "He does indeed live in a glass house," of a man who actually lives in a house made of glass, nothing prevents us from using the sentence to make a metaphorical statement.

Our recognition of a metaphorical statement depends essentially upon two things: Our general knowledge of what it is *to be* a metaphor-

ical statement, and our specific judgment that a metaphorical reading
of a given statement is here preferable to a literal one. The decisive
reason for the choice of interpretation may be, as it often is, the patent
falsity or incoherence of the literal reading – but it might equally be
the banality of that reading's truth, its pointlessness, or its lack of congruence with the surrounding text and nonverbal setting. The situation in cases of doubt as to how a statement is best taken is basically
the same as that in other cases of ambiguity. And just as there is no
infallible test for resolving ambiguity, so there is none to be expected
in discriminating the metaphorical from the literal.

There is an important mistake of method in seeking an infallible
mark of the presence of metaphors. The problem seems to me analogous to that of distinguishing a joke from a nonjoke. If a philosopher,
whose children have trouble in deciding when he is joking, introduces
the convention that a raised thumb indicates seriousness, he might
sometimes be joking in raising his thumb! An explicit assertion that a
remark is being made metaphorically (perhaps the best candidate for a
reliable diagnostic sign) cannot guarantee that a metaphor is in question, for that does not depend simply upon its producer's intentions,
and the sign might itself be used metaphorically. Every criterion for a
metaphor's presence, however plausible, is defeasible in special circumstances.

If Beardsley and other critics of the interaction view are, after all,
not looking for a diagnostic criterion but rather something essential to
a metaphor's *being* a metaphor, my above rebuttals will miss their
mark. But then the tension of which Beardsley and others speak seems
to be only one feature of that peculiar mode of language use in which
a metaphor's focus induces a "projection" of a "secondary system," as
already explained in this paper. "Tension" seems to me somewhat less
suggestive than "interaction," but there is no point in quarrelling over
labels.

Are metaphors ever "creative"?

The production of a new metaphorical statement obviously introduces
some small change into a world that includes statements and the
thoughts they express, as well as clouds and rocks. Even the reaffirmation of an old metaphor can be viewed as a trivial insertion into the
world of a new token of a known statement-type. That metaphors
should be creative in this boring way is hardly worth mentioning
except for the sake of contrast.

Emphasis upon the alleged creativity of metaphors becomes more

interesting when they are viewed as miniature poems or poem fragments. But the production of a work of art would interest me here,
given the general thrust of this essay, only if such a work "tells us
something about the world." Indeed, I intend to defend the implausible contention that a metaphorical statement can sometimes generate
new knowledge and insight by *changing* relationships between the
things designated (the principal and subsidiary subjects). To agree
would be to assign a strong cognitive function to certain metaphors;
but to disagree is not necessarily to relegate them entirely to some realm
of fiction.[8] For it may be held that such metaphors reveal connections
without *making* them. (Would it not be unsettling to suppose that a
metaphor might be self-certifying, by generating the very reality to
which it seems to draw attention?)

In my earlier essay, I stated one form of what might be called the
"strong creativity thesis" in this way:

> It would be more illuminating in some of these cases [i.e., of metaphors
> imputing similarities difficult to discern otherwise] to say that the metaphor
> creates the similarity than to say that it formulates some similarity antece-
> dently existing (*Metaphor*, p. 37)

It will be noticed that the claim was explicitly hedged: to say, "it
would be more illuminating," to view some metaphors as ontologically
creative falls short of claiming that they *are* creative. Yet no remark in
Metaphor has provoked stronger dissent.

Khatchadourian (1968), in the course of a generally approving
account of the interaction view, thinks the thesis cannot be right. He
asks rhetorically, "How can one, anyway, literally create a feature or a
similarity by means of a metaphor?" (p. 235). Granting that a metaphor user "can bring into prominence *known* features . . . which he
thinks deserve special attention" (*ibid.*, my italics) and thereby "give
us a new vision or a new insight," Khatchadourian concludes that,
"The creation of some effect in the hearer or reader [does not involve]
the creation of a similarity between the principal and the subsidiary
subject" (p. 236).

Long ago, S. J. Brown (1927) summarily dismissed a related contention (on the part of Gustave Lanson) that, by means of metaphor,
"Our mind, perceiving a common quality in two different objects, or
*creating between them a relation which assimilates them to one
another,* names one of them by a term which suits, or belongs to, the
other" (p. 47; emphasis added). Brown says: "How the mind can create
a relation which does not previously exist, M. Lanson does not explain,
nor ought such explanation be expected of a writer on literary theory"

(*ibid.*). Such offhand rejection is clearly motivated by a picture of the "relation" in question as being "objective" or "out there" – existing quite as independently as the relation of "having-the-same-height-as": One rightly wants to deny that cubits can be added to stature by saying or thinking so. But this conception of some objective relation as antecedently existing is question-begging when applied to that variegated set of relations that we bundle together as "similarity."[9] When applied to the explication of metaphors, "is like" is not as sharply contrasted with "*looks* like" as "is taller than" is with "*looks* taller than." The imputed relations in a generative metaphor, one might say, must have a subjective as well as an objective aspect, but each may contribute to the other, as I hope to show. I shall try to make the strong creativity thesis at least plausible by considering a series of five answers to questions having the form, "Did X exist before it was perceived?"

(1) Did the other side of the moon exist before it was seen?

It would take a fanatical idealist to say no. We think, of course, of the rocks, plains, and mountains as having been there all the time, prior to observation. It is crucial to this conception – as contrasted with some of the following examples – that the existence of the physical objects and configurations in question is held to depend in no way upon the existence of human or other sentient beings, or upon their contingent possession and use of thought and language.

(2) Did genes exist before their existence was recognized by biologists?

The question might be rephrased as, "Did things properly *called* 'genes' exist before they were admitted into accepted biological theory?" An affirmative answer is no doubt used to contrast this case with those in which the "objects" in question were *synthesized* by human agency. *Qua* things found but not made, "natural" and not "artificial," genes – it must be agreed – were "there all the time," even before their existence was discovered. But it is less obvious that *genes* "were there all the time, waiting to be discovered." The term "gene" has its place within a man-made theory, in whose absence it would have no intelligible use: The relation between "gene" and what that term designates is more like that of a dot on a map and the city it represents than like that of a personal name and the person it designates. So the proper answer to this second question should be, "Yes and no."

(3) "Were there bankrupts before the financial institutions of the Western world were developed?"

If the question is taken in a literal sense, the only acceptable answer must be no. For here the allusion to man-made constructions (institutions rather than developed theory) is uncontroversial: "Bankrupt" (applied to someone judged insolvent on petition to a court of law) had no application before the requisite legal procedures had come into existence. A positive answer to the question would need to take the tortuously counterfactual form of: "*If* there had been the corresponding legal institutions (say in 1066), such-and-such a person would have been judged a bankrupt *if* the requisite petitions had been lodged."

(4) "Did the view of Mount Everest from a point one hundred feet above its summit exist before anybody had seen that view?"

An affirmative answer can be accepted only in the counterfactual sense proposed in the last paragraph: "If anybody had been in a position to view the mountain from the point specified, it *would* have looked as it does now from a plane flying overhead (i.e., the view has not changed)." But if we agree, we should reject the reifying mythology of the *unseen* view, "there all the time" and available for inspection like some ethereal emanation. The notion of a "view" implicates human beings as possible perceivers (though not as the creators and subjects of legal institutions, as in the last case): It is logically necessary that a view can be *seen* (viewed). Now, when a certain view is actually seen, that is a fact about the mountain as well as about the viewer – about a world that includes both. It is objectively true, not a matter of mere convention or whim, that the view of Everest from such-and-such a point has such-and-such features.

(5) Did the slow-motion appearance of a galloping horse exist before the invention of cinematography?

Here the "view" is necessarily mediated by a man-made instrument (though this might cease to be true if some mutant children were born with the power to see "slow motion" with one eye). And yet what is seen in a slow-motion film becomes a part of the world once it is seen.

The last example comes the closest to what I originally had in mind by the strong creativity thesis. If some metaphors are what might be called "cognitive instruments," indispensable for perceiving connections that, once perceived, are *then* truly present, the case for the thesis would be made out. Do metaphors ever function as such cognitive instruments? I believe so. When I first thought of Nixon as "an image surrounding a vacuum," the verbal formulation was necessary to my seeing him in this way. Subsequently, certain kinetic and visual images have come to serve as surrogates for the original verbal formulation, which still controls the sensory imagery and remains available for ready reaffirmation.

For such reasons as this, I still wish to contend that some metaphors enable us to see aspects of reality that the metaphor's production helps to constitute. But that is no longer surprising if one believes that the world is necessarily a world *under a certain description* – or a world

seen from a certain perspective. Some metaphors can create such a
perspective.

Can a metaphorical statement ever reveal "how things are"?

In the last section, my attention was fixed upon the creative or productive aspects of generative metaphors, in virtue of which they can sometimes function as cognitive instruments through which their users can
achieve novel views of a domain of reference. But a view, however
mediated, must be a view of *something*: My task here is to make some
suggestions about what that "something" is and how far its possession
can yield insight about "how things are."

I have chosen the unpretentious formula, "how things are," in order
to avoid the fixation of a number of writers who discuss the same topic
under the rubric, "Can metaphorical statements be *true*?"[10] Their strategy seems to me misguided and liable to induce distortion by focusing
exclusively upon that special connection between statement and reality
that we signal by the attribution of truth value. In ordinary language,
the epithet "true" has more restricted uses than philosophers usually
recognize.[11] It is most uncontroversially appropriate in situations
where the prime purpose is to state a "fact," that is, where the fact-stating statement in question is associated with some accepted procedure
for verification or confirmation: A witness who swears to "tell the truth
and nothing but the truth" is expected to "speak plainly," that is, to
eschew figurative language, and commits himself not only to refrain
from lying, but also to abstain from producing probability statements,
generalizations, explanations, and interpretations of actions (though
some of these excluded types of statements may in other contexts, for
example, those of scientific inquiry, be properly judged true or false).
In such fact-stating uses, the concepts of truth and falsity are closely
associated with such semantic paronyms as "lying," "believing," "knowing," "evidence," "contradiction," and others. The relevant linguistic
subpractice (or *Sprachspiel*, as Wittgenstein would call it) characteristically assumes agreement about ways of checking upon what is being
said, and about ways of contesting or qualifying such sayings.

Hence, one way to recognize that we are in *this* domain of language use is to consider whether supplementary questions such as, "Are
you perhaps lying?", "What's the evidence?", "How do you know?",
"Aren't you contradicting what you said a moment ago?", and the like
are in order. With such considerations in mind, we can readily dismiss
the question about whether metaphorical statements have truth values.
If somebody urges that, "Nixon is an image surrounding a vacuum," it

would be inept to ask soberly whether the speaker *knew* that to be so, or how he came to know it, or how we could check on the allegation, or whether he was saying something consistent with his previous assertion that Nixon was a shopkeeper. Such supplementary moves are never appropriate to any metaphorical statements except those degenerately "decorative" or expendable ones in which the metaphorical focus can be replaced by some literal equivalent. It is a violation of philosophical grammar to assign either truth or falsity to strong metaphors.

What lies behind the desire to stretch "true" to fit some such cases (as when somebody might quite intelligibly respond to the Nixon-metaphor by saying, "How true!") is a recognition that an emphatic, indispensable metaphor does not belong to the realm of fiction, and is not merely being used, as some writers allege, for some mysterious aesthetic effect, but really does say something (Nixon, if we are not mistaken, *is* indeed what he is metaphorically said to be).

Such recognition of what might be called the representational aspect of a strong metaphor can be accommodated by recalling other familiar devices for representing "how things are" that cannot be assimilated to "statements of fact." Charts and maps, graphs and pictorial diagrams, photographs and "realistic" paintings, and above all models, are familiar cognitive devices for *showing* "how things are," devices that need not be perceived as mere substitutes for bundles of statement of fact. In such cases we speak of correctness and incorrectness, without needing to rely upon those overworked epithets, "true" and "false."

This is the clue we need in order to do justice to the cognitive, informative, and ontologically illuminating aspects of strong metaphors. I have been presenting in this essay a conception of metaphors which postulates interactions between two systems, grounded in analogies of structure (partly created, partly discovered). The imputed isomorphisms can, as we have seen, be rendered explicit and are then proper subjects for the determination of appropriateness, faithfulness, partiality, superficiality, and the like. Metaphors that survive such critical examination can properly be held to convey, in indispensable fashion, insight into the systems to which they refer. In this way, they can, and sometimes do, generate insight about "how things are" in reality.

NOTES

The present paper is a slightly modified version of one appearing under the same title in *Dialectica*, Vol. 31, Fasc. 3–4, 1977, pp. 431–57. I wish to thank the publishers of *Dialectica* for granting permission to reprint it.

1 This reflection is sometimes attributed to Michel Bréal (1899). See his *Essai*, p. 115. But the subject he called "infini" was the special one of the influence of metaphors upon the extension and renewal of a standard lexicon, of which he provides numerous illustrations.

2 Richards says that this "can be shown by mere observation."

3 It might be thought puzzling that while the act of producing a metaphorical statement is a datable event, its semantic content can be described, referred to, and discussed at any time: consequently, what by definition seems to be subjective, as produced by a particular speaker or thinker, has an *import*, as one might say, that is sufficiently stable or objective – in spite of violating the background linguistic conventions – to be available for subsequent analysis, interpretation, and criticism. But is this really more puzzling than the fact that what a tennis player did in his last serve can be talked about (more or less) at any subsequent time?

4 For this reason, my analogy of "epichess" may be somewhat misleading. For in that game, there was a "super-rule" of sorts that determined *how* and *when* the rules of ordinary chess might be violated. In view of what looks like the essential lawlessness of metaphorical transgression, I am less sanguine than other writers about the prospects of treating the production of a metaphorical statement as a speech act in Austin's sense. I, too, wish to attend particularly to what a metaphor user is doing and what he expects his auditor to do. But I see little profit in modeling this primal situation on that of a promise giver (Austin's paradigm case), where the consequences of the performative statement are determined by a speech community's *conventions*.

5 To these might be added the following optional implications, that would readily occur to somebody familiar with game theory, though not to a layman:

(G4) There is no rational procedure for winning in a single play.

(G5) A "maximin" strategy (playing to minimize possible losses) may, though controversially, be considered rational.

(G6) Playing a long-run "mixed strategy" (alternating available moves randomly but in a predetermined frequency) is (again, controversially) a "solution."

These further implications would, of course, strengthen the metaphor and heighten its interest.

6 This conception might, accordingly, be regarded as a generalization of S. J. Brown's view of metaphor as an "analogy between . . . two relations" (p. 71). I differ from him in admitting any number of predicates and relations in isomorphic correlation – and in laying less stress than he does upon analogy, that tantalizingly suggestive but obscure notion.

7 In later writing, he called his view the "Revised Verbal Opposition Theory" (Beardsley, 1962, passim). The preferred later title indicates his interest in explaining the supposed "tension between the subject and the modifier by which we are alerted to something special, odd and startling in the combination" (p. 285). Here, he has in mind what would be an essential and not merely a diagnostic feature of metaphor.

8 This is an adaptation of an example used by Binkley (1974). See also Ted Cohen (1976) which also contains many counterexamples to Beardsley's thesis.

9 According to Oakeshott (1959), all "poetic imagining" (as in the use of indispensable metaphors) is concerned with "fictions," which would be radically misconstrued as "contributions to an enquiry into the nature of the real world." He adds: "When it is said that poetic imagining is 'seeing things as they really are' . . . we seem to have been inveigled back into a world composed, not of images but of cows and cornfields" (pp. 45–6). Contrast with this Wallace Stevens's (1957) dictum: "Metaphor creates a new reality from which the original appears to be unreal" (p. 169).

10 For which, see John Whatley's (1961) illuminating essay. I agree with him that, "To say, as philosophers sometimes at least imply, that 'A is like B' designates a 'similarity relation' tends to group like-statements to statements of physical, temporal and other purely objective relationships" (p. 112). On the whole, Whatley tends to stress nonobjective uses of "like"; but he also says of some uses that, "There is, in all but peculiar circumstances, some very definite sense in which these resemblances must correspond to fact" (p. 113).

11 Unsurprisingly, a notable exception is Austin (1961), who says: "We become obsessed with 'truth' when discussing statements, just as we become obsessed with 'freedom' when discussing conduct . . . Not merely is it jejune to suppose that all a statement aims to be is 'true', but it may further be questioned whether every 'statement' does aim to be true at all. The principle of Logic, that 'Every proposition must be true or false', has too long operated as the simplest, most persuasive and most pervasive form of the descriptive fallacy" (p. 98–9).

METAPHOR
AND
LINGUISTIC THEORY

Figurative Speech and Linguistics

JERROLD M. SADOCK

Introduction

I take synchronic linguistics to be the study of those aspects of human communication that are unique to natural language, no matter whether they are principled and inhere specifically in the nature of human language or are arbitrary features of particular languages. All nonliteral speech, then, including metaphor, falls outside the domain of synchronic linguistics, for nonliteral acts having nothing to do with natural language occur and parallel those that we perform by using language.

The study of metaphor, specifically, would not be a proper subject for synchronic linguistics for the reason that the basis of metaphor is a kind of indirection that is shared with nonlanguage behavior. Whatever might be unclear about the way metaphor is used and understood, I take it for granted that the underlying principles governing metaphor are of a general psychological sort and are thus not specifically linguistic. While the intellectual faculties that are involved might be *prerequisites* to speech, they are independent of it. The fact that a certain group of stars in the night sky reminded someone of a bull and the fact that a lion on a warrior's shield suggests that its bearer is brave are, I think, nonlinguistic instances of the same analogical urge that functions in the issuance and apprehension of metaphor.

Other figures of speech, from anacoluthon to zeugma, have counterparts in realms of behavior other than speaking, but here I am interested particularly in the nonliteral figures of speech, of which metaphor is one. Metonymy, synecdoche, hyperbole, understatement, irony, and euphemism (especially the sort that have been labeled "indirect speech acts") are the most important nonliteral figures of speech, besides, of course, metaphor. They all rest their success upon an apparent clash between what is done (i.e., what is *said*) and what is intended. They therefore comprise an important natural class of speech acts.

Nonliteral figures differ from one another in the way in which what is said is connected with what is intended. In irony, what is said is (roughly) the opposite of what is intended. Overstatement and understatement are either more or less (in senses along the lines of Horn, 1976 or Gazdar, 1976) than what is intended. Euphemism is the saying of something innocuous that either hints at, or establishes a precondition of, some possibly offensive intended act.

In metaphor, the locus of the indirection is one part of an utterance, namely a predication. The predication may be buried inside a noun phrase, as in Aristotle's example "the sunset of life," or it may be overt, as in the sentence, "Life has a sunrise and a sunset." But all of these types of figures are alike in that they communicate in an indirect way what might have been communicated directly in terms of the conventions of a language. For this reason, they have an effect over and above what would accompany the direct accomplishment of the intended effect. As I shall argue, the fact of nonliteralness is crucially important to our understanding of the way that language functions as an integrated communicative system. Therefore in what follows, I will not restrict my attention to metaphor, but will freely examine other sorts of linguistic indirection in an effort to explicate what I consider to be the most important property of metaphor as far as linguistic pursuits go, namely its nonliteralness.

Now, linguistic figuration does differ from the general psychological tendencies to analogize and generalize, in that it is an aspect of social behavior. For this reason it is governed by whatever natural or arbitrary principles govern other aspects of social interaction. Paramount among these are the sorts of rules that Grice (1975) has called cooperative maxims, rules that govern our interactions for our mutual benefit, which are, ceteris paribus, always assumed to be in force. Because linguistic figuration is ordinarily voluntary social action, it has been assumed by Grice to be subject to all general conditions on such activities. Grice would trace the recognition of figurative, or nonliteral language use, to apparent violations of one or another of these principles. I am convinced that he is right and that his treatment is superior in all respects to others, such as that of Reddy (1969). When the literal sense of an uttered monologue, sentence, phrase, or word is in apparent conflict with the cooperative principle – by seeming to be irrelevant, false, or lacking in justification – the hearer is forced to seek a figurative, but cooperative, intent behind the utterance. The production of figurative speech is then reflexively governed by the speaker's awareness of the hearer's expectation of cooperative behavior on his (the speaker's) part.

Thus, the abilities that allow and control the nonliteral use of natural language expressions are not specifically linguistic faculties and hence figuration does not fall within the domain of linguistics, at least under the narrow definition that I suggested above. But that is not to say that the phenomenon of figurative speech is of no interest to the linguist. On the contrary, there are at least two ways in which a proper understanding of metaphor and other tropes is critical to the linguist.

Figuration and semantic change

First, there is the indisputable fact that figurative language is one of the most productive sources of linguistic change. In particular, reanalysis of figures of speech as literal signs is clearly the most important source of semantic change. It is a commonplace that most lexical items prove to be dead metaphors that were alive and kicking at some time in the past. (In a similar fashion, essentially nonlinguistic articulatory and perceptual facts are the source for first phonetic, and then phonological, changes in language.)

Therefore, if the mechanism of metaphor were better understood, we would have a better grasp of the principles of semantic change and this, in turn, would yield a better understanding of synchronic grammar and grammars. Languages are the way they are in part because of historical accident, because of common psychology and experience, but also in part because of constraints peculiar to language. Not knowing a great deal about the way languages change, one may mistake basically diachronic facts for synchronic facts, and basically psychological or sociological facts for linguistic facts.

To make matters worse, the essentially nonliguistic forces behind language change are mostly constant across time, culture, and language. We find that the same sorts of semantic shifts crop up over and over. (Similarly, the same sorts of phonological changes are attested in language after language.) Lacking detailed knowledge of what produces these changes, the error of labeling such cross-language facts "language universals" is easy to commit.

It is probably the case that, in any language, vowels will be nasalized before nasal consonants at a sufficiently rapid rate of speech. It happens, of course, that this phonetic phenomenon gets incorporated into the grammars of individual languages, but the tendency toward nasalization is universal. But is it a *linguistic* universal? I think not. An accurate ballistic description of the organs of speech, and particularly of the tongue and velum, would predict allegro nasalization *whether there was speech or not*. It seems, therefore, to be a grave error to write a specifically linguistic universal nasalization rule or rule schema, as

Chomsky and Halle (1968) do. There is, to be sure, a universal tendency toward vowel nasalization, but it is no more a reflection of our
specifically linguistic makeup than the fact that people will stumble if
they dance the polka too fast is a fact about our specifically terpsicho-
rean abilities. True, this universal phonetic tendency has insinuated
itself into the grammars of numerous languages (usually due to other
changes in the linguistic system that have nothing to do with nasalization) but this is mere historical accident. Now I am *not* saying that
all phonological universals are nonlinguistic in origin, nor am I saying
that all phonological change has its roots in phonetics. But some universals are surely to be explained by reference to principles that
impinge on language, rather than to principles that constitute language.

Analogously, much semantic change has its origin in metaphor, or
some other figure of speech, and in some cases the metaphor is so
obvious that it shows up in numerous languages and therefore might
be misdescribed as a universal tendency of language rather than a natural tendency of thought. One case in point is the widespread occurrence of spatial metaphors for temporal relations. In English we say "at
3:00," just as we say "at the corner of Fourth and Green," we say
"within an hour," "throughout the year," "before Monday," "toward
the end of the month," and so on. Even the otherwise locative deic-
tics "here" and "there" pop up in temporal usages in the forms "here-
tofore" and "thereafter." Facts like these are by no means unique to
English. Eskimo has four suffixes that represent the spatial relations "X
is located at Y," "X (moves) toward Y," "X (moves) away from Y,"
and "X (moves) from one end of Y to the other." Some of these same
suffixes are used in the temporal mode as well and very little needs to
be said about their meaning, since the metaphor of space for time is so
readily understood. Compare, for example, Greenlandic "ukiume" (in
the winter) with "igdlume" (in the house); and "ukiukut" (throughout the winter) with "nunakut" (across the land).

Facts like these could prompt linguists to suggest a language universal to the effect that the same morphemes express both spatial and temporal relations. But it seems to me that this is rather a fact that owes
its existence to universal human psychology, perception, and experience and is quite independent of language. Accidents of history do
often elevate this metaphor to the status of a grammatical fact. The
metaphor in English (and Eskimo) is imperfect in that, for example,
words like "during" and "previously" refer only to time, while "in
front of" and "in back of" refer only to space. Closely related languages
can differ in the use of relational elements in the spatial and temporal

modes. For example, German "um" translates English "around" when it refers to space but "um 8 Uhr" means "at 8:oo," and not "around 8:oo." Thus it is clear that the underlying metaphor has been conventionalized, to a certain extent, in English and German, and I suspect that this is true in most other other languages as well. Nevertheless, there is no need to postulate a *linguistic* universal to explain this cross-linguistic syncretism: It is due to the inevitable freezing of a metaphor so natural that it has occurred to people of nearly all cultures.

Figuration and synchronic grammar

As I stated earlier, and as many before me have pointed out, frequent figurative phrases can come to be directly associated with the senses that they previously conveyed only indirectly. That is, metaphors and other figures of speech can become idioms.

Pure idioms convey what they do entirely conventionally, whereas figures of speech achieve their effect for principled reasons having to do in part with some conventional meaning – the so-called literal meaning. Individual lexical items with their ordinary senses are thus idioms of a kind since there is no principled basis for their meaning what they do. Now the problem that the existence of figurative speech poses for the synchronic description of language is this: Which effects of the use of chunks of the language are purely conventional (arbitrary, idiomatic) and which effects follow from extralinguistic principles? What, in other words, do the morphemes of a language mean and what can these meanings be used to convey?

One manifestation of this problem is in the difficulty that a careful linguist encounters in trying to decide whether a lexical item, construction, or sentence is gramatically ambiguous or whether it is univocal but allows, besides the literal interpretation, a figurative understanding. That true ambiguities exist in natural languages seems undeniable. There is no conceivable reason why the word "swallow" should designate a particular sort of bird and an action of the throat – but it does. Similarly the fact that a sentence like, "He found her home" can be taken in two very different ways, one parallel to "He found me home" and the other parallel to "He found my home," seems inexplicable on natural grounds and must be relegated to the grammar of English – the repository of arbitrary, conventional facts of the language.

At the same time, it is indisputable that certain univocal words, phrases, and so on, have two or more effects for natural reasons. In such cases, one use is literal and the rest are figuratively based upon it.

One clear set of examples is discussed by L. J. Cohen (1971). Should we treat the noun "flower" as lexically ambiguous because it can be used to refer to the sexual organs of plants as well as likenesses of them in paint or plastic? Such a treatment is quite inplausible because it would require us to treat every concrete noun in the language as similarly ambiguous. The theory that "flower," "rabbit," and "cyclotron," for example, are all homonyms would also not explain why it is that any new noun that comes into the language would admit of both understandings. If I announce that I have just invented an electric dinner fork and if I dub it a "flibbus," no one needs to consult a lexicographer to find out whether it would be acceptable to refer to the likeness of this technological miracle as a "flibbus" as well.

By far the more pleasing account of these facts would be just the one suggested by Cohen, namely that "flower," "flibbus," and so on, have only one sense each, a literal sense, but that we may metonymically speak of any semblance of a thing by using the name of the thing itself. Thus a sentence such as, "This is a flower," said while pointing to a conglomeration of pigment on canvas would be, strictly speaking, false. But its metonymical intent is plain enough. The utterance is perfectly acceptable under the circumstances, although it is literally false.

Indirect speech acts provide examples of syntactic configurations that might be analyzed as ambiguous or as having one true sense and a parasitic figurative use. In some cases, the double understanding should be branded as an arbitrary, grammatically specified fact of the language (which might well have had a principled historical origin), but in other cases, the proper analysis would treat the indirect effect as a sort of figuration.

A more subtle version of the same problem has to do with the proper specification of the synchronic meaning of morphemes, or concatenations of them, regardless of whether they are ambiguous. The problem involves linguistic material which is semantically complex in the sense that its meaning seems to involve a conjunction of terms. Thus the meaning of "bachelor" somehow involves the notions male and unmarried. Most often, of course, there does not seem to be any necessary connection between the various components of the meaning of such items. But it sometimes happens that one aspect of the meaning of a lexical item is figuratively dependent on the rest of the meaning. Uncontroversial examples are hard to find, but the following cases strike me as having some plausibility.

The infinitive-taking verb "fail" appears to have two components to its meaning. "Alfred failed to finish the exam" indicates not only that Alfred did not finish the exam, but moreover that he tried. Now the standard analysis of this lexical item (as represented, for example, in the work of Karttunen and Peters, 1975); treats both aspects of the import of "fail" as completely conventional. But it can also be suggested that the only conventional import of "fail" is that of the negative. The implication that some effort was made would be merely a suggestion or, in Grice's terms, a conversational "implicature" that rests on the literal sense per se. The implicature would be triggered in part because of the additional syntactic baggage that sentences with "fail" require as compared to simple negative sentences. I shall not attempt a lengthy account of the nonconventional treatment of certain parts of the effect of lexical items like "fail" here, because I am only trying to illustrate a sort of analysis and not (necessarily) trying to produce a correct one.

A slightly different example is provided by sets of lexical items for approximately the same thing. Most if not all members of such sets will differ from one another in connotation if not denotation. Thus, a light current of air through a house is called "a breeze" if we like it and "a draft" if we don't. The former term might be claimed to encompass (among other things) the specification "pleasant," and the latter the specification "unpleasant." But it seems more plausible to say that one of these terms is neutral (or unmarked) with respect to the speaker's attitude and only figuratively acquires an additional force in virtue of the fact that it stands in contrast to some connotatively nonneutral (or marked) lexical item.

The importance of the problem

The stated goal of one major brand of modern linguistics is to make explicit the relationship between form and meaning. One group of modern philosophers sees as its goal the construction of a truth definition for the sentences of a natural language. Neither of these objectives is achievable unless we first understand, at least intuitively, what the sentences of a language mean – as opposed to what they can be used to convey. Stated differently, we must know which aspects of the communication achieved by an utterance are achieved solely through the agency of meaning conventions of the linguistic system, and which are achieved indirectly through figuration of one sort or another.

We cannot hope to provide a semantic representation for sentences of English unless we are able to determine whether a sentence such as, "John is the Rock of Gibraltar," is ambiguous and should be grammatically associated with separate meanings, or not. Put in terms of formal logic, we must have grounds for saying whether this sort of sentence is true or false in the state of affairs where John is, in fact, an unfailing friend, but not a geological formation at the entrance to the Mediterranean, if a complete truth definition for the sentences of English is to be constructed.

There are innumerable examples, both in syntax and lexicography, where the choice between ascribing what an utterance conveys to conventional meaning or to figurative import is not at all easy to make. I shall list here a few such cases. While we might be prejudiced toward one or the other treatment, I must stress that both possibilities are open.

Consider the words "lion," "goose," and "newt." The first two of these allow two interpretations each. "Lion" can be used to refer to any member of the species *Leo leonis*, or more specifically, to a male of that species. "Goose" can indicate a particular sort of fowl, or particularly the females of that kind. "Newt," by contrast to the previous two words, cannot be used in a sex-specific way. Now these facts seem accidental enough to warrant separating the more inclusive and more specific uses of "lion" and "goose" into two separate, but related lexical entries, one a semantic extension of the other. On the other hand, this lexical complication could be avoided by claiming that the words "lion" and "goose" are univocal, but allow a *figurative* extension. And here there are two further choices. Either we could say that "lion," for example, properly refers only to the male of the species and that through a kind of synecdoche it can be used to refer to the whole species, or we could say that "lion" has only a generic sense but through metonymy can be used in an apparently more specific way.

This second type of figurative account resembles Grice's mode of explanation in that it postulates a weak sense that takes on greater specificity when it is invoked in a particular context. The argument may be supported by claiming that it is the existence of a word "lioness" (which does specifically indicate the female) that bolsters the more specific suggestion of maleness that surrounds the use of "lion." The first kind of explanation, while also tantamount to the claim that figurative, or nonliteral, use is involved, is like L. J. Cohen's in that the basic sense is claimed to be rather strong, but that it may, under appropriate circumstances, be used loosely. At any rate, it is not clear whether *any* use of "lion" involves figuration. The word might still be lexically ambiguous.

There is only one way to understand the expression, "a likely story." It signifies something on the order of "an unlikely story." Now are we to take this as an idiom in English or should we rather treat this as an instance of irony? There is evidence on both sides.

First, on the side of irony, is the fact that the expression indicates just what an ironical interpretation of the apparent literal sense would be expected to be. "A plausible story" suggests just the same thing, when used ironically. Also on the side of a figurative treatment is the fact that it is difficult to disagree with a statement like, "That's a likely story." Neither "No, it's not" nor "Yes, it is" seems like the appropriate way to indicate that one thinks that the story in question *is* plausible. The same holds for clear cases of irony and, in fact, most examples of nonliteral speech. Since they are not intended to be taken literally, they are not as open to rebuttal as literal utterances. This immunity to contradiction may, in fact, be one of the purposes of figuration. Indubitable idioms, on the other hand, can readily be denied. The response, "No, he didn't," to the statement, "Bill kicked the bucket," straightforwardly means, "Bill didn't die."

On the side of "idiomaticity" is, principally, the fact that the import of the expression is quite rigidly fixed. It never conveys what its component words would suggest that it should.

There is a discrepancy between the most natural effects of the following sentences and the meanings they ought to have in virtue of the meanings of their parts: "Uncle Scrooge has money"; "A fraction of the people voted Libertarian"; "Tiny Tim was a man of stature"; "Be a man"; "A number of my friends are literate." The ordinary understanding involves what appears to be a variety of understatement: "to have money" ("nerve," "muscles," "brains," etc.) indicates having a great deal of that commodity. "A number of X" usually indicates "a large number." (Conversely, "a fraction" indicates "a small fraction.") Now in these cases, the figurative source of the use of these locutions is obvious and fairly plausible.

But if the assumption of univocality plus figuration is the correct account in these cases, why not in the following case as well? The words "tall," "big," "heavy," "intelligent," "wide," and so on, indicate something on the order of "more (adj.) than average," when used in the formula "X is (adj.)." Further, as has often been pointed out, a different use is found in expressions like, "X is as (adj.) as Y," "X is N units (adj.)," "X is more (adj.) than Y." Here the adjective simply means that the entity of which it is predicated has the property to some degree, namely the degree specified in the sentence. Thus arises the famous fact that sentence (1) does not seem to entail (2).

(1) Bolivar is five feet tall.
(2) Bolivar is tall.

The parallel with the case of expressions like "to have money," "a number," and so on, should be obvious. It is also the case that (3) does not entail (the ordinary understanding of) (4).

(3) The number of my friends that are literate is two.

(4) A number of my friends are literate.

Thus, by parity of reasoning, it should be possible, perhaps desirable, to treat "tall" and other basic graded adjectives as having only one sense wherever they occur, but as allowing a use as a kind of understatement. "John is tall" would be taken as meaning (strictly) that John has height to some extent. But – because of its obviously trivial sense – it will ordinarily be used figuratively to indicate much more. While this treatment is possible, it is disturbing. But, if it is wrong, how do we know it is?

"Some X" almost always indicates, among other things, "not all X." Horn (1976) very convincingly argued that it does not *mean* this, but only suggests it. He proposed a mechanism along the following lines as giving rise to the conversational implicature (that is, to the additional figurative understanding): "all" is a "stronger" quantifier than "some." Speakers are constrained to say as much as is required. Therefore in using any quantifier, a speaker implicates that no stronger quantifier could have been used.

Now consider the way we understand a sentence such as (5):

(5) Bill has written almost twenty articles.

We will usually (maybe always) take an utterance of this sentence as indicating that the number of articles Bill has written is not much less than twenty. "Almost" in this use seems to have a compound significance: "almost N" indicates "not much less than N but not N." The question thus arises as to whether both parts of the understanding of "almost" are independent, conventional aspects of its meaning. It is possible, at least in principle, to treat one of these as figuratively dependent on the other. Note that the expression "not much less than N" usually indicates "not N," without apparently meaning it. Therefore it is not implausible to treat "almost" as meaning *only* something like "not much less than N," and figuratively, albeit invariably, suggesting in addition "not N." But is this the right analysis? Is (5) true, false, or neither, if Bill happens to have written exactly twenty articles?

Thus there appear to be many cases where it is difficult to determine where meaning leaves off and figuration begins. Each such case is a stumbling block in the path of the linguist whose goal is the formalization of the principles linking meaning and form. Likewise, these are examples that will prevent the construction of formal truth definitions for natural languages until the issue of conventionality versus figurative effect is resolved.

Testing for convention and figuration

If the distinction between figurative, nonconventional effect and literal conventional meaning is real, it ought to correlate with properties that could serve as touchstones for distinguishing them in the difficult cases. Indeed, several such tests have been suggested, principally by Grice (1975). I have criticized these tests at length elsewhere (Sadock, 1976, 1978) and shown, to my satisfaction at least, that in the truly intractable cases, the tests do not give reliable results. I would like to give a brief indication here of what I found wrong with these tests: I shall leave out a few which are quite patently circular: tests that require that we know beforehand what an expression means in order to gain results as to what that expression conveys figuratively, that is, as to what it does not mean.

1. *Calculability:* If C is figuratively conveyed by an utterance of an expression *E*, then there should be some rational scheme for figuring out that the speaker intended to convey *C* based on whatever else *E* *conventionally* means.

Criticisms:
  a. Almost any effect is calculable, starting from almost any utterance.
  b. If *E* in fact *means C*, *C* might still be calculable.
  c. One needs to know (at least part of) the conventional meaning beforehand. How is this knowledge gained?

2. *Context dependence:* Whether an uttered expression is taken figuratively will depend on context. Further, the speaker's knowledge will play a role in deciding whether a particular utterance will be interpreted as having been intended to have a particular figurative intent.

Criticism:
  a. This cannot serve to distinguish figuration from genuine ambiguity. Context plays a role in determining which of two senses of an uttered expression must have been intended, and the utterer is aware of this and uses his knowledge to help insure that his intentions are properly grasped. Worse, the mechanisms of disambiguation and the apprehension of figurative intent are similar. The principal logical tool, I believe, is elimination of alternatives. Given the choice between intention *A* and *B*, *B* is favored if *A* is false, irrelevant, unjustified, and so on. The only difference is that in the case of disambiguation, both *A* and *B* are literal senses, but

in the cases of apprehension of figuration, *A* is a literal sense and *B* a figurative intent.

3. *Translatability:* Figures of speech translate well into other languages. Idioms (i.e., noncompositional, but literal, collocations) do not.

Criticisms:

a. Some idioms, namely those that have arisen from "natural" figures of speech will also translate well (see discussion of the space-for-time metaphor.)

b. Some figures of speech may differ in popularity from one culture to another. It is said that irony is rarely used in the Southern United States. Such a difference could make translation of a genuine figure of speech difficult.

4. *Paraphrasability:* Figures of speech are paraphrasable *salva sensu*. Idioms generally are not. (This is Grice's nondetachability criterion.)

Criticisms:

a. This begs the question to a certain extent. Paraphrase involves substitution of one expression for another *with the same meaning*. But this test is supposed to tell us what the literal meaning of an expression is. It could be claimed (rather implausibly) that "boot the pail" does not replace "kick the bucket" without important changes in significance, because "boot" does not mean quite the same thing as "kick" and because "pail" does not mean quite the same thing as "bucket." It *has* been claimed (somewhat more plausibly) that "Are you able to close the door?" does not have the same effect as, "Can you close the door?" because "be able" is not identical in meaning to "can."

b. Certain figures depend for their effect not just on what is said, but *how* it is said. Litotes, or double negation, ought to be logically equivalent to a simple positive, but it has a different effect because of its form. In such cases (i.e., where Grice would say that the maxim of manner has been flouted) paraphrase does not work.

5. *Commitment:* A speaker is held responsible for the literal content of his utterance, but he may without oddity, deny – or otherwise behave as if he did not intend – any figurative significance that might be attached to his utterance. (This is Grice's cancellability test).

Criticism:

a. This holds just as much for cases of genuine ambiguity. A speaker can always deny one proper sense of a strictly ambiguous utterance, or behave as if he does not hold to that sense, without giving the appearance of holding contradictory beliefs.

6. *Reiterability:* Since figurative effect is not literal content, a pos-

sibly figurative expression, E, may be conjoined with an expression M whose literal content is similar to the potential figurative effect of E and no redundancy should result.

Criticisms:

a. As above.

b. Some redundancy is tolerated in natural language, for example, "He entered into an agreement," or, in some varieties of English, "He repeated the process again" (i.e., "He did it a second time").

7. *Incontrovertibility:* Figurative effects are nonpolemical. They have a rather personal, emotive character, and thus are difficult to contest. Literal senses, including those that are idiomatic, are, on the other hand, easy to deny. When I respond, "No, he didn't," to the statement, "Bill kicked the bucket," I obviously mean that Bill did not die.

Criticisms:

a. The test applies only to declarative sentences, but the phenomenon of nonliteral speech is not limited to these.

b. No theory backs up this test. It seems to work in the clearer cases, but it is not clear why.

8. *Interaction with grammar:* Conventional content often suffers grammatical idiosyncrasies; figurative effects do not.

Criticisms:

a. It is often difficult to say what is a grammatical fact and what is not.

b. Some parts of the grammar will be regular enough that nothing will be grammatically peculiar.

9. *Normality:* Figurative language is superficially odd; literal language it not. (A version of a test suggested by Abraham, 1975).

Criticisms:

a. The criterion is vague, at best.

b. Idioms are also odd, at least from a very superficial point of view.

10. *Appropriate responses:* One responds to the literal content of a figurative utterance rather than to its intended significance. (A version of a test used by Searle, 1975).

Criticisms:

a. Almost any response is, on occasion, appropriate to almost any utterance. Thus sequences such as, "Is today Monday?" "Well, this is Paris." are perfectly fine dialogues. Much research indicates that this criterion is simply false.

b. The criterion conflicts with criterion 6.

I consider the criticisms offered here to be serious enough that these tests, singly or in combination, can at most be taken as suggestive. None of them provides a sufficient criterion for convention or its absence nor, as far as I can see, does any conjunction of them. There-fore, the important question of defining the boundary between literally and nonliterally conveyed communication is not answered. The prob-lem that verbal figuration poses for the linguist (and the logician) thus remains unsolved.

Variability of the results

When it comes to applying these tests, it appears clearly that they have to do not with properties that utterance/understanding pairs either have or do not have, but rather with properties that such pairs possess in varying degrees. If, indeed, these are criteria that distinguish between conventional meaning and figurative effect, then we are faced with a situation that mainstream formal linguistics is not equipped to deal with. American linguistic theory, at least, pretty much without regard to whether it is practiced in Massachusetts, Illinois, or Califor-nia, assumes that each sentence of a natural language is mapped onto a finite number of distinct meanings (semantic representations, readings, etc.). That is, a sentence either does or does not have any particular meaning, a sentence either is or is not ambiguous, two sentences either are or are not paraphrases, and so on. But the tests appear to indicate that a particular aspect of the understanding of a given utterance may be more-or-less conventional, and more-or-less figurative.

Calculability not only turns out to be a variable property – it would seem it would have to be. Given enough steps, just about any effect could be worked out on the basis of the utterance of nearly any sen-tence. Put differently, there is no limit to the possible figurative signifi-cances of any given utterance.

Let us say that E is some expression in a natural language and that $U_c(E)$ is the utterance of E on some occasion c. Further, let us say that $U_c(E)$ conveys P (where P is a proposition, or something like that). Now either $U_c(E)$ conveys P in virtue of the fast that E *means* P, or the intent to convey P is calculated on the basis of the fact that E (with its meaning, whatever it is) has been uttered on occasion c. If the calculation is short and obvious, then it is quite plausible that $U_c(E)$ only figuratively con-veys P, whereas if the required calculations are cumbersome and far-fetched, then it is easier to believe that $U_c(E)$ conveys P because E conventionally means P. Thus the calculability criterion gives us hier-archical results ranking examples in terms of the likelihood of their being instances of figuration.

It should be apparent that context dependence is also a matter of degree. Whether $U_c(E)$ conveys P will always depend to a certain extent

on the nature of c, *even when E means P*. Namely, $U_c(E)$ will *not* convey
P, even if E means P, in just those contexts where E is taken as figurative.
When I say, "John is a genius," and intend it ironically – and am taken
as having intended it ironically – I convey my feeling that John is not
very clever, but I do not simultaneously convey my feeling that he is
extremely smart. So it is not just a matter of whether the conveying of P
depends on context or not that indicates that an effect is figurative
or literal. Rather, it is a matter of *how much* the success of the effect
depends on context. The more reference to context is required in the
account of how P is conveyed, the more it seems that E does not mean
P and conversely, the weaker the role of context in the success of
$U_c(E)$ conveying P, the more it seems that E must have P as part of its
conventional meaning.

Translatability is also a matter of degree. We cannot expect that all
idioms are such that they have no counterparts in any other language.
Particularly in the case of idioms based historically upon very natural
metaphors, or other figures of speech, translatability might well be
rather good. Such idioms will appear to be closer to figuration than
those that are grounded in more implausible or unique images. On the
other hand, figures of speech that require reference to some very specific unusual cultural fact for their interpretation will translate more
poorly than figures that rest only on common human experience. Such
figures have some of the character of idioms – at least according to the
translatability test.

The other tests also give variable results, as the reader may determine for himself. It appears, then, that $U_c(E)$ can in principle convey P not just figuratively or conventionally, but often to some extent
in both ways.

Variable conventionality and linguistic theory

One way of allowing for degrees of conventionality in communication would simply be to rewrite the theory. Consider the case of a puta-
tively ambiguous expression that could also be considered to be univocal but to allow, on occasion, a figurative interpretation.

Indirect speech acts are a much-discussed case in point. Disputed
examples have been analyzed as ambiguous between a straightforward
compositional sense and an idiomatic (noncompositional) sense by
some researchers, and, by others, as unambiguous but capable of producing a figurative effect when they are put to use in conversation.
The figure of speech that would seem to play a role in the production
and comprehension of the most popular varieties of indirect speech

acts is euphemism; indirect means are chosen because the intended action is too offensive, prying, pushy, or embarrassing, to approach directly. An act that in and of itself is less of an affront, but which hints at the true intent of the utterance, is therefore resorted to.

Let us say that it has been decided, according to the criteria above, that the sentence, "Can you close the door?" is exactly fifty percent conventionalized as a request to close the door. Now instead of the grammar just spewing out meaning/form pairs, as in the older conception, let us say that the grammar produces ordered triples, where the first element is a meaning, the second a syntactic form, and the third a number n, $0 > n > 1$, which is an index of conventionality. In the case at hand, the index would be $\emptyset.5$. But what do we gain from such a description? What interpretation are we to give it? What shall we say about the truth value of declarative sentences with indexes of conventionality less than 1? It seems to me that this brute-force description is almost totally unenlightening. At best it is a means of acknowledging the fact that conventionality is not an off-on switch, but in no sense can it be looked upon as an account, let alone an explanation, of the phenomenon.

One novel and promising suggestion has recently been made by Morgan (1978). He distinguishes between conventions of usage and conventions of language. An ordinary meaning convention (e.g., that the word "dog" in English designates members of the set of dogs) is a convention of language. Conventions of usage concern appropriate linguistic means for accomplishing specified purposes (possibly on specified occasions).

Morgan's idea is that the more specific the conventional means, the more the convention comes to resemble a convention of language, that is, a meaning. He also notes that there is a qualitative difference between conventional means that make no reference to expressions in a natural language and those that do. The former kind might more appropriately be called conventional "methods" (my term), while the word "means" might better be reserved for conventionally specified expressions.

It can be seen that these distinctions provide four qualitatively different degrees of conventionalization:

1. The totally nonconventional. The purpose is accomplished by whatever linguistic methods and means the speaker feels will be effective. True figures of speech belong in this category, because the methods of accomplishing the purpose are presumably not culture, or language, specific.
2. Conventional methods, but no conventional means. Morgan cites

several examples in indirect speech acts. Irony might be an example from among the more traditional varieties of figures of speech since (as I mentioned earlier) irony barely exists in some cultures, such as that of the Southern Unites States, whereas its use is endemic in others, – for instance, the Yiddish-speaking cultures of Eastern Europe. The kennings of old Germanic poetry are also examples. While these are generally just metaphors (albeit rather obscure ones), there is an element of the conventional in their use, because (a) they are restricted to a certain kind of poetry, and (b) certain notions (ships, swords, the sea, death) are almost obligatorily communicated in this indirect fashion.

3. Conventional methods and conventional means. Most of the sticky examples come under this heading. Most proverbs, I would think, are like this, too. Here one idea is expressed figuratively by reference to another conventionally specified idea. In addition, the very words to be used in expressing this second idea are conventionally established. We say, "Too many cooks spoil the broth," not "A superabundance of chefs ruins the consommé," to get across the notion that someone's help is not desired.

4. No conventional methods but conventional means. These are Morgan's conventions of language. The difference between this class of examples and the previous two classes is that there is no rationale for the fact that particular forms in the language can be used to accomplish certain ends. True idioms, as well as lexical items (mini-idioms) and arbitrary, but functional, syntactic patterns belong here.

By providing two intermediate levels of conventionality, Morgan's ideas hold out the hope of resolving the dilemma that figurative speech creates for linguistic theory. I find this prospect exciting.

Conclusions

In summary, I see the importance of metaphor to linguistics as two-fold. First, metaphor and other varieties of nonliteral figures of speech are the locus of semantic change in natural language. The facts of semantic change and their implications for universal grammar can only be grasped if we have a thorough understanding of the principles of linguistic figuration.

Second, I have argued that a large part of English (and presumably of other natural languages as well) is in flux; the pragmatic effect of numerous figures of speech are on the way to becoming part of the conventional content of the expressions that are used to convey them. But this process occurs by stages so that in most cases the communicative value of an expression that began life as a metaphor or as some other trope is partially conventional and partially not. This fact makes untenable one of the most cherished assumptions of modern formal linguistics, namely the assumption that conventional content and linguistic form are connected by a discrete function. Thus, while figuration in general, and metaphor in particular, are not specifically linguistic phenomena, their study is of the utmost importance to an understanding of the part that grammar itself plays in natural language communication.

The Semantics of Metaphor

L. JONATHAN COHEN

Metaphor as a feature of sentence-readings

Professor Sadock's position is that metaphor is not a linguistic problem at all, because the mechanisms underlying metaphor exist independently of language. The use of "a lion on a warrior's shield," he says, manifests "the same analogical urge that functions in the issuance and apprehension of verbal metaphors." But it is vital here to distinguish metaphor, on the one hand, from similes and other nonmetaphorical analogies, on the other. There is certainly no special linguistic problem about such explicitly figurative sentences as (1) or (2):

(1) He is as brave as a lion.
(2) He is like a father to her.

The linguistic problem arises instead because of implicit figuration, as in (3) or (4):

(3) He is a lion in battle.
(4) The child is father to the man.

The problem is to explain how such sentences can have the meaning they do, when they are false or nonsensical if taken literally. In other words, the analogical urge operates sometimes in literal speech, sometimes in metaphorical. It can produce both and so cannot explain the difference between the two.

My own position, as against Sadock's, is that the fundamental problem about metaphor is a problem for our theory of *langue*, not for our theory of *parole*. But I speak here only about metaphor, and not about other figures such as irony, litotes, allegory, or simile.

Various considerations operate in favor of this position, although they neither severally nor jointly entail it.

First, if the synchronic description of a language takes no account of metaphor, it provides an inadequate basis for diachronic explanations of semantic innovation. Language is full of dead metaphors like "inflamed passion," "feeble argument", or "rain of blows": How have they got there?

Again, it is clearly characteristic of certain categories of artificial languages that they must lack any possibility of metaphor. Programming-languages for computers, like Fortran, or interpreted formal systems, like Carnap's, would be very seriously flawed in the performance of the tasks for which they are severally designed if they allowed their component words or symbols to be attributed new and unstipulated meanings in certain contexts. It is arguable, therefore, that we radically blur the difference between these kinds of artificial languages on the one side, and ordinary natural languages, like English (or artificial languages for everyday use, like Esperanto), on the other, if we do not allow essentially for the possibility of metaphor in our analysis of the latter. For example, it is characteristic of a natural language sentence like (5)

(5) He is a lion

that it is indefinitely rich in possible meaning. Alongside one or more literal readings it admits also an indefinite variety of metaphorical ones. A theory that does not allow this will never satisfy the intuitions of people who are expert in the use of language, like the best creative writers. (The French classical tradition was an exception, but a self-conscious and theoretically motivated one.)

Thirdly, metaphor cannot be explained within a theory of speech acts, because a supposed speech act of metaphorizing would differ from standard types of speech act in an important respect. If Tom utters the sentence

(6) I am sorry,

he may well be apologizing. But, if I utter the sentence

(7) Tom said that he was sorry,

I am not apologizing myself; I am just reporting Tom's apology. The original speech act is overridden by the passage from oratio recta to oratio obliqua. Now metaphor behaves quite differently. When Tom describes his friend by saying

(8) The boy next door is a ball of fire,

Tom's description can be fully understood only by someone who understands the metaphor. But equally, if I myself report later

(9) Tom said that the boy next door is a ball of fire,

my report of Tom's utterance can also be fully understood only by someone who understands the metaphor. The metaphor is not overridden by the passage from oratio recta to oratio obliqua: the oratio obliqua sentence contains the same element of metaphorical meaning that the oratio recta contained. Arguably, therefore, metaphorical meaning inheres in sentences, not just in speech acts. We should be perfectly happy to say here, "What Tom said is true," not just, "What Tom meant is true."

This point is a very serious difficulty for anyone, like Searle (cf. his paper in the present volume) who wants to construe metaphor solely in terms of speaker's meaning – the meaning of the utterance rather than of the sentence uttered. The metaphoricalness, or special character, of (8) is preserved under transformation into indirect discourse: The apology-making character of (6) is not. Why is this? The simplest explanation seems to be that metaphoricalness is a property of sentences. Those, like Searle, who wish to reject such an explanation bear the onus of presenting a convincing alternative one. Otherwise their theory limps.

No doubt the linguistic context of utterance often fails to provide sufficient cues for us to disambiguate a metaphorical sentence. We must turn then to whatever features of the nonlinguistic setting are relevant. But just the same is true of nonmetaphorical sentences, as with the meaning of "unsatisfactory," say, in

(10) He's unsatisfactory.

It would be a mistake to suppose that this familiar component of communicational situations provides any special support for a speech-act theory of metaphor.

Fourthly, if our linguistic theory gives no account of metaphor, it may well make so much the poorer a contribution to the framework within which psycholinguistic investigations are carried on. Language-learning infants often speak in metaphors without knowing the literal meanings of the sentences they utter (Cohen & Margalit, 1972, p. 470).

But there is another reason why the stock attitude of linguistic theorists to metaphor is incorrect; and this reason is an intrinsically stronger one, because it looks inwardly to the structure of synchronic semantics, rather than outwardly to the use of semantic analyses in etymological explanations, in comparisons between natural and artificial languages, in speech-act theory, or in psychological inquiry. I have in mind a certain choice that exists in the methodology of natural language semantics, which I shall refer to as the choice between the method of cancellation and the method of multiplication. This choice arises in relation to quite a range of other problems besides that of metaphor; and my argument will be that whatever choice of method is made to deal with metaphor both reinforces, and is reinforced by, the choice of the same method in the other cases. In particular, if we need to introduce the method of cancellation into our semantics in order to deal with certain kinds of nonmetaphorical sentences, we might just as well exploit its potential for the analysis of metaphor.

Let us turn briefly from metaphor to examine these other, nonmetaphorical cases. Consider the differences between

(11) It wasn't an insult because it was not intended as such

and

(12) It was an unintentional insult.

Clearly the word "insult" might be described by a compositional semantics as occurring in a sense that is +INTENTIONAL in (11), but not in (12). But such a description chooses what I have called the method of cancellation. It supposes that the occurrence of the adjective "unintentional" in (12) has cancelled the +INTENTIONAL feature in this occurrence of the word "insult," (because the retention of that feature would render the sentence self-contradictory). We need then, for the description of (11) and (12), just one lexical entry for "insult," alongside some general set of rules for semantic feature-cancellation in the process of composing sentential meaning. Correspondingly both (11) and (12) are unambiguous.

Alternatively, however, we could employ the method of multiplication. We could have two lexical entries: "insult₁" which is +INTENTIONAL, and "insult₂" which is $+/-$INTENTIONAL. We would then dispense here with the use of any rules for semantic cancellation, and both (11) and (12) would now be ambiguous. One of the two underlying sentences for (11) would have the same meaning as on our previous interpretation of (11), the other would be rather a non sequitur. Similarly, one of the two underlying sentences for (12) would be self-contradictory, the other would have the same meaning as our previous interpretation. But what is crucial here is that the alternative to the method of cancellation is a method that doubles the number of relevant lexical entries.

Perhaps I should add here that there is not a third – quasi-Gricean – possibility. It will not do to say that "insult" never has the feature +INTENTIONAL but carries with it, in normal contexts, a conversational implicature of intentionality, which happens to be cancelled in (12). The reason why this possibility is not available is because it cannot explain the force of the "because . . ." clause in (11). (In regard to the logical particles of natural language, Grice's theory of implicatures does afford an alternative approach to the method of cancellation, but arguably an inferior one. See L. J. Cohen, 1971; L. J. Cohen, 1977a[1].)

It would be easy to give many more examples of the issue about +INTENTIONAL, which is a particularly familiar hazard in the register of jurisprudence. But other kinds of example are also frequent. Consider

(13) I tried to warn him but he didn't hear me

and

(14) I warned him, but he didn't hear me.

The method of cancellation would describe the word "warn" as occurring in a sense that is +UPTAKE in (13) but not in (14). But the method of multiplication would generate two correspondingly different lexical entries for the word "warn."

Another familiar feature in relation to which we are faced with a choice between the method of cancellation and the method of multiplication is the feature +ANIMATE. Consider the difference between

(15) A lion eats ten pounds of meat a day

and

(16) A stone lion needs no feeding.

According to the method of cancellation, the feature +ANIMATE is present in the occurrence of "lion" in (15), but is cancelled in (16): according to the method of multiplication the lexeme "lion₁" occurs in (15) and a different lexeme, "lion₂" occurs in (16). A vast number of analogous examples can be given, like "china dog," "plastic flower," and so one. The method of cancellation avoids the need to multiply lexical entries in order to deal with such phrases. But the method of multiplication promotes a second lexical entry, with the sense "replica of a lion," "replica of a dog," "replica of a flower." Of course, one could hope to avoid cancelling or multiplying anything in relation to "lion" if one supposed that "stone" in (16) meant "stone replica of a." But the focus of methodological choice – choice between the method of cancellation and the method of multiplication – has now just shifted to "stone." The contrast is now between the occurrence of "stone" in (16) and its occurrence in

(17) A stone wall surrounds the garden.

Again the feature for mode of functioning, or mode of operation, would be at issue for a word like "car" in such sentence pairs as

(18) We will pack the luggage into the car

and

(19) We will pack the car into the luggage.

The method of cancellation allows us to suppose the same lexeme occurs in the composition of both (18) and (19). The method of multiplication requires us to suppose two lexical entries in relation to every inanimate object as well as in relation to every plant or animal: one for the name of the original, and a second for the name of its replica.

If we are always to prefer the method of multiplication wherever possible, our linguistic theory can hardly have anything of interest to say about metaphor. Consider, for example

(20) Their legislative program is a rocket to the moon.

The method of multiplication can either treat (20) as involving some neologism that could, if it becomes established in the language, figure as "rocket₂" in a listing of English lexemes. Metaphor is then reduced to polysemy. Or alternatively the method of multiplication could reduce metaphor to simile by adding to the ordinary copula a second lexeme "is$_2$," in the sense of "is like," and making similar additions for other predicative morphemes. In neither case will metaphor appear as anything other than a rather peripheral or superficial item in the immense motley of lexical variety. Its existence will have no particularly close dependence on certain special modes of sentential composition, and those linguists who have postponed its treatment until they have an adequate semantics for nonmetaphorical sentences will be immune to any charge of methodological hysteron proteron.

But is it right to adopt the method of multiplication in cases like (12), (14), (16), and (19)? Scientific inquiry tends to make more progress if it avoids unnecessary multiplications of entities, and it is this Ockhamian policy that the method of cancellation pursues. If we could formulate principles controlling feature-cancellation in the composition of sentence meanings we should gain a powerful, general insight into the semantics of natural language, which will be forever denied us if we are content to follow the method of multiplication and merely list or catalogue its proliferation of lexical entries. No doubt there are some points at which the method of cancellation ceases to pay dividends. Where the meanings of a polyseme have grown apart and taken on different positive features, like "funny" meaning "comic" and "funny" meaning "strange," the best procedure may well be to follow the method of multiplication and treat the word semantically just as if it were a homonym. Where a particular combination of words, like "kick the bucket," has lost all touch with the component words' meanings in other combinations, the phrase may need to be listed as an idiom alongside single words and have its own lexical entry. But the fact that in such circumstances we are forced into falling back on the method of multiplication constitutes no argument against pursuing, wherever possible, the economies and insights that are afforded by the method of cancellation. The method of multiplication merely records what meanings exist, without explaining how they are generated. It lists elements but does not explore relations.

The problem of feature-cancellation

What then should be said about metaphor in a componential semantics if our policy in analysing the composition of sentence meanings is to be the Ockhamian one of preferring, wherever possible, the method of cancellation to the method of multiplication? Clearly we have to regard metaphorical meaning as being put together by a different kind of cancellation from that which appears in nonmetaphorical cases like (12), (14), (16), and (19). But what is the nature of the difference?

Let us distinguish broadly between those semantical features that represent attributes which are empirical, immediately evident, or relatively obvious, and those which are inferential, intellectually appreciated, or relatively latent. It will be convenient to refer to these groups of features as "empirical" and "inferential," respectively, though determinate classification will often be difficult and there are bound to be many borderline issues. Then a tempting hypothesis is that in the normal, literal cases it tends to be inferential features (though not necessarily all of them) that are cancelled, whereas in metaphorical sentences it is empirical features (though again not necessarily all of them) that tend to be cancelled. Thus in the examples considered earlier the cancelled features +INTENTIONAL, +ANIMATE and +UPTAKE are all inferential ones. But in the metaphorical sentence (20), the legislative program is presumably said to be a rocket only in a sense that has shed such empirical features as +MATERIAL, +AIR-CLEAVING, +CYLINDRICAL, and so on, which are incompatible with the features of "legislative program," while retaining such features as +FAST-MOVING, +FAR-AIMING.

Such a hypothesis seems to jibe well with the common use of metaphor to enliven discussion of an abstract subject with concrete imagery. And it would be no objection to this hypothesis that even the uncancelled features in a word's metaphorical occurrence may also sometimes be empirical ones, as in

(21) Jane has the face of a wild rose

or

(22) The clouds are made of pure gold.

For, though a woman's face may share the color of a wild rose blossom, or even have a similar shape, it certainly lacks other empirical properties associated with wild roses, such as their spiky stems; and though sunset clouds share the color of pure gold, they certainly lack its tangibility.

Nevertheless, there are at least two reasons why this hypothesis is unsatisfactory.

First, even nonmetaphorical cancellation sometimes removes empirical features, as in

(23) They have produced a new breed of animal — a hornless cow. The feature +HORNED is certainly an empirical one, but it is cancelled from the sense of "cow" in (23) without any intuitable semblance of metaphor. We need a hypothesis that will explain why an empirical description in which one or more of a lexeme's empirical features have been cancelled is metaphorical in (21) and (22) but not in (23).

Secondly, in some cases of metaphorical cancellation there seem to be no empirical features available for removal. Consider, for example,

(24) The troop movements ordered by Wellington were logarithmic in their strategy: By adding complementary · units to one another in a particular location, he obtained the same effect as if he had multiplied the number of mutually ill-assorted units in that location.

Here we have an image taken from the highly abstract subject matter of mathematics and applied to the somewhat less abstract topic of military strategy.

It would appear that a more satisfactory hypothesis might be one which exploited the concept of a semantic category. On this view, cancellation would be metaphorical, if and only if, the features cancelled were intrinsic to the lexeme's superordinate semantic category. Thus in (12), (14), (16), and (19), it might be argued, the category remains essentially unaltered. We are still dealing with a name for a type of speech act in (12) as in (11), and in (14) as in (12): we are still dealing with a name for a type of physical object in (16) as in (15), and in (19) as in (18). On the other hand in (20) we are dealing with a name for something – a legislative program – that does not belong in the same semantic category as "rocket," and in (24) we have a shift from the name of a mathematical operation to the description of a military one. So far so good.

But the trouble here is that what we should need to count as a semantic category for dealing with some sentences cuts across what we should need to count as a semantic category for dealing with others. Thus to maintain the nonmetaphoricalness of (16) we need to think of both lion and stone lion as belonging in a single category, that of PHYSICAL OBJECT. Yet "face" and "rose" also seem to belong in this category, though we should need to think of them as belonging in different categories in order to explain the metaphoricalness of (21) by the proposed hypothesis. If criteria for sameness and difference of semantic category in a natural language have to be systematically adapted to native-speakers' intuitions of metaphoricalness, we can no longer appeal to categorical structure for an explanation of the differences between metaphorical and nonmetaphorical cancellation. The description of categorical structure would be just a restatement of this difference.

I was once inclined therefore (Cohen & Margalit, 1972) to favor a third hypothesis, which relies neither on the "empirical – inferential" distinction nor on the concept of a semantic category. The assumption that lies behind this third hypothesis is that, for theoretical purposes, semantic features should not be classified dichotomously, whether as empirical or inferential, or as categorical or noncategorical, or in any other way, but should rather be arranged in an order of decreasing semantic importance. Then a cancellation would be metaphorical if and only if it removes the most important feature or features. For example, *gold* would be said to have a metaphorical occurrence in (22) because its most important feature +METALLIC would be cancelled.

Now there are several good reasons, quite apart from this issue of metaphorical and nonmetaphorical cancellation, why a semantic theory for natural language should assume the semantic features appropriate in this or that area of a language's vocabulary to be at least partially ordered in importance, rather than merely coordinate with one another. One reason is that we need such an assumption in diachronic semantics. It explains why in borderline cases, where there is a choice between either modifying one word to fit a novel or unusual situation or modifying another, we may be inclined to choose the modification that makes less of an inroad into the core of a word's meaning. For example, the verb naming the action of a hang-glider is "to glide," not "to parachute." A second reason is that to suppose an ordering of this kind provides a certain room for maneuver in the philosophical analysis of a concept. The claim to be concerned only with the nuclear sense of a concept may provide a valid excuse for not pursuing the analysis of the concept into those thickets of refinement where the argument gets bogged down in dealing with ingenious but farfetched counterexamples. Thirdly, it can be shown (L.J. Cohen, 1970, p. 35ff.; 1977b, p. 129ff.) that any inductive processing mechanism, like a vocabulary-learning infant, which seeks to learn from the variety of its experiences rather than from the mere multiplicity of experiences of one particular kind, must impose some importance-ordering on the relevant patterns of variation.

However, I do not want to digress here into issues that belong more properly to other inquiries than to linguistic theory. Suffice it to say that the most serious mistake in the Wittgensteinian family-resemblance theory about the meanings of certain descriptive terms is its incompatibility with the assumption of some kind of importance-ordering for semantic features. And any theory of metaphor must operate within the framework of this assumption. Nevertheless, it will not do at all to say, as I once said (Cohen & Margalit, 1972, p. 484), that metaphorical cancellation is distinguished by its always being the cancellation of semantically important features. After all +ANIMATE hardly seems much less important a feature than +METALLIC. Yet its cancellation in (16) does not render the sentence's meaning metaphorical. Moreover, importance is a matter of degree, but though metaphors may be better or worse, a phrase's or sentence's meaning seems to be *either* literal *or* metaphorical.

How in any case is semantical importance to be graded? We must certainly distinguish carefully here between semantical and practical importance – between what is relevant for the applicability of a generic name, and what is relevant for attitudes towards things of the kind named. It may be highly relevant to your mobility whether you have a drivable car or only a toy one, and highly relevant to your safety whether a cow has horns or not. But what counts for semantical importance is the capacity to falsify propositions about the applicability of terms, not the capacity to falsify propositions about what practical course of action is possible or desirable. Hence the features that are relatively more important from a semantical point of view are those that are relatively more distinctive and specific. Because they are less probable (that is, have greater prior improbability in the universe of feature-instantiations), they carry more information. And if that is how semantic importance is to be graded, I suspect that most metaphorical cancellation, like all nonmetaphorical cancellation, begins at the lower end of the scale. Rather general features like +ANIMATE or +METALLIC are highly eligible for cancellation because they are semantically unimportant; whereas features representing specific peculiarities of appearance or behavior are considerably less eligible for cancellation because they are semantically much more important.

The relevance of the topic–comment distinction

So, though it is quite clear that some metaphorical cancellation occurs at the upper end of the scale, as in, for example,

(25) The poor used to be the blacks of Europe,

the difference between metaphorical and nonmetaphorical cancellation cannot depend on either the nature or the semantic importance of the feature cancelled. But if this difference does not depend on which kinds of elements are connected by the cancellation-relation, and if feature-cancellation itself is a uniform operation, then perhaps we shall get a clue to what the difference does depend on from the direction of the cancellation-relation, as determined by the grammatical functions of the expressions related. If we can distinguish within any phrase or sentence in which cancellation occurs, between the topic-expression – the expression that would normally be isolated by the particle "wa" in Japanese – and the comment-expression, or between the head and the modifier, then metaphorical cancellation seems normally (exceptions are considered below) to be imposed by the topic-expression on the comment-expression, or part of it, or by the head on the modifier, whereas nonmetaphorical cancellation is imposed by the comment-expression on the topic-expression, or part of it, or by the modifier on the

head. Thus cancellation runs from "legislative program" to "rocket" in
(20), from "clouds" to "gold" in (22), from the second sentence in
(24) to "logarithmic," and from "Europe" to "blacks" in (25). But it
runs from "unintentional" to "insult" in (12), from "but he didn't
hear me" to "warned" in (14), from "stone" to "lion" in (16), from
"into the luggage" to "car" in (19), and from "hornless" to "cow" in
(23).

We have still to explain, however, just why it is that the direction of
feature-cancellation normally varies thus from sentence to sentence or
sentence-sequence to sentence-sequence. One might perhaps have
expected, prior to examining instances, that an operation of this kind
would always run in the same direction. Why does that not happen? I
suggest that the explanation lies in the overriding linguistic need to
make the topic of a sentence or sentence-sequence easily identifiable.
Ease of topic-identification must be conserved under variations in the
amount of feature-cancellation. If the extent of cancellation (considered as a function of the number and importance of features cancelled) is relatively small, as in (12), (14), (16), (19) or (23), cancellation runs naturally from comment-expression to topic-expression–
parallel to the normal direction of modification. But when cancellation
is relatively extensive, as in (20), (21), (24), (26), and (27), easy
identification of the topic is preserved by the cancellation's running
from the topic-expression to the comment-expression; and it is thus,
in the grammatically well-formed sentences of a language, that what
we commonly call metaphors arise. Of course, a good or apt metaphor
will not involve too much cancellation, because then it will have too
few points of similarity with that for which it is a metaphor. But if
there is too little cancellation in a word or phrase it will not be a
metaphor at all. An expression has a metaphorical occurrence in a sentence-sequence if and only if the extent of cancellation (from the
expression's semantic features) is so great as to exclude it from identifying a topic independently of some special circumstance (such as an
ad hoc convention, a relevant previous sentence in the sequence, a
familiar linguistic practice, and so on).

If we consider apparent exceptions to this principle, they will all be
found, I suspect, to rely on certain special circumstances for their plausibility. For example,

(26) The brightest star in my sky has just run off with the milkman
is obviously a sentence in which the topic is identified by a metaphorical expression. But this is possible just because the metaphor is a trite
one.[2] An original or unfamiliar metaphor, unaided by context, would
not identify a topic with any clarity. For example, the sentence "The

sparkle on summer dew has just run off with the milkman" is a kind of nonsense if considered as an isolated unit. But its topic would become quite apparent if it occurred in some suitable sequence of sentences that contained

(27) My wife is the sparkle on summer dew

as an earlier element. Somehow or other, whether by being more readily intelligible, or by being present at least in the first occurrence of metaphor, the comment-making use of a metaphor is primary and any topic-identifying use is secondary and derivative.

A number of amplificatory points need to be made in conclusion.

First, I take it that lexical entries for a natural language can draw no clear distinction between features that are supposed to be "purely linguistic" and features that are supposed to represent common knowledge or commonly accepted beliefs. The *Concise Oxford Dictionary* (6th ed., 1976) tells us quite appropriately that lions are found in Africa and South Asia and that privet is much used for hedging. There is no confusion here between the function of a dictionary and the function of an encyclopedia. We need encyclopedias to tell us things that are not common knowledge, not things that are. Of course, all a word's semantic features have to be ordered for importance, and the type of feature that we are inclined to call "common knowledge" is normally a relatively unimportant one. Because it is less important it is less insisted upon, and sentences articulating it are more easily treated as synthetic propositions. However, such features frequently provide a vital part of the residual analogy that a metaphorical sentence seeks to convey.

Secondly, I am not claiming that the same order of importance for semantic features extends throughout a language's vocabulary. For example, while the features determining visible appearance are highly relevant for animal names, they are clearly not so relevant for the lexemes that name social roles, such as "policeman," "president," or "banker." The main differences between such lexemes are revealed by inferential rather than empirical features. A plain-clothes policeman is still a policeman, and a water-skiing banker is still a banker.

Thirdly, each of the sentences that I have discussed so far is either obviously literal or obviously metaphorical. Many others are ambiguous between these two possibilities. For example, the sentence

(28) It will never get off its launching pad

has not only a (familiar) literal meaning but also a metaphorical one – in which it might be uttered as a reply to the utterance of (20). The sentences that are normally called metaphorical ones, like (20), (21), (22), (24), (25), (26), or (27), are sentences that appear absurd or flagrantly false if we try to give them a literal reading. But to know how we should understand an utterance of (20) we need to know its topic. Or we could say, in general, that though there is normally a presumption in favor of a literal interpretation, this presumption can be rebutted by suitable contextual cues. Correspondingly in *langue*, if we always consider not just isolated sentences but sufficiently long sentence-sequences, we can take any such sequence to be a literal one throughout, unless this involves an absurdity that would disappear on a metaphorical interpretation.

Fourthly, I have assumed throughout that we cannot dispense with some kind of compositional approach to the semantics of natural language if we are to achieve any determinate progress – anything more than pious generalities – in this area of inquiry. An analytic – resolutive methodology, as so many other sciences can testify, leads us naturally into a deeper understanding of richly structured wholes, and the meaning of a natural language sentence, whether literal or metaphorical, is certainly such a whole. But once a compositional approach is accepted we can scarcely avoid being led, for the reasons already canvassed, to prefer what I have called the method of cancellation to the method of multiplication, to recognize the significance of the direction in which feature-cancellation operates, and to explain the choice of this direction by reference to the extent of the cancellation and the need to conserve ease of topic-identification. I do not underestimate the immense difficulty and complexity of the task that anyone would undertake who sought to construct a rigorously adequate theory of cancellation. But in the present paper I have been concerned rather to argue the more general issue: How intrinsic to linguistic theory is the problem of metaphor and what, in general, is the best solution for it? I have also not been concerned at all with the corresponding psychological problem: How are metaphors invented and comprehended? But it is reasonable to suppose that until the linguistic problem has a definitive solution, the psychological one cannot be adequately articulated.

NOTES

I am grateful to Dr. Gillian Cohen for some very helpful comments on an earlier draft of the present paper.

1 The discussion of proposition-compounding particles, like "or" and "if," in these papers could be extended to quantifiers like "some." For example, either "some" has a cancelable semantic feature that implies "not all" or its use normally carries a conversational implicature "not all." A Gricean treatment would begin to run into difficulties with sentences like

If some of the money has already been found, the rest will be found quite soon.

Note that it would be unreasonable to expect that semantic cancelability
will be preserved when such a word is disambiguated by compound phrases
like "a part but only a part" and "a part or even the whole,'" respectively.
2 It is tempting to think that some proverbs claim a certain kind of metaphorical truth alongside their literal truth, as in

A stitch in time saves nine.

If this is the correct way to regard such proverbs, the metaphor will be as
trite as the proverb is familiar.

Some Problems with the Notion of Literal Meanings

DAVID E. RUMELHART

In his paper, Professor Sadock brings to the fore a fundamental
dilemma of semantic analysis as practiced by many linguists and
modern philosophers. The approach adopted by these workers is committed to the existence of a sharp distinction between what an utterance might *mean* (that is, its literal meaning) and what that utterance
is, or can be, used to *convey*. (See, for example, Searle's chapter [this
volume] which emphasizes the distinction between "sentence meaning"
and "utterance meaning.") To a linguist interested in form–meaning
pairs, or to a philosopher interested in truth conditions on expressions,
this distinction might be crucial. In these cases, the concern is to build
a theory of literal meaning and to assign conveyed meanings to the
application of unspecified psychological processes not specific to language. As a psychologist, I find myself primarily interested in the
mechanisms whereby meanings are conveyed. Whatever role "literal
meanings" (as defined by these linguists and philosophers) might play
in the comprehension of language (that is, in the determination of
what some utterance conveys), psychological theory must concern itself
with conveyed meanings.

Sadock, arguing from a linguistic perspective, makes an interesting
comparison between what he calls *figurative* and what he calls *conventional* language use. His analysis leads him to conclude that "conventional" and "figurative" do not form two well-defined categories of
utterances as implied by most theories of language. Rather a particular
utterance may be more-or-less figurative and more-or-less conventional.
Conventionality and figurativeness are at two ends of a scale. Purely
figurative and purely conventional utterances are, at best, rare. Moreover, he points out that the classic approaches to semantics require
such a distinction; yet they are incapable of providing a rational basis
for it. Hence, a new approach is clearly required.

Interestingly, looking at language from a psychological point of
view, one can be led to a somewhat similar conclusion. I shall argue
that the distinction between literal and metaphorical language is

rarely, if ever, reflected in a qualitative change in the psychological processes involved in the processing of that language.[1] I argue that the classification of an utterance as to whether it involves literal or metaphorical meanings is analogous to our judgment as to whether a bit of language is formal or informal. It is a judgment that can be reliably made, but not one which signals fundamentally different comprehension processes.

I have been led to these conclusions through two sorts of considerations. First, in attempting to develop psychologically plausible models of *literal* language comprehension, I have been forced to consider comprehension mechanisms with enough power to interpret literal and metaphorical language alike. Second, both theoretical considerations of the language-acquisition process and empirical observations of the language of children suggest that far from being a special aspect of language, which perhaps develops only after children have full control of literal language, figurative language appears in children's speech from the very beginning.

Language comprehension and metaphor

First, I want to discuss a fairly typical observation on the child's use of language. Consider the following observation of one of my children making a perfectly ordinary remark. One day I was driving down a freeway with my wife and two children when one of my sons, age eight, remarked: "Hey, Mom, my sock has a hangnail." My wife, quietly, and without special note, responded: "Don't worry about it, I'll fix it when we get home," and the topic was dropped. I was the only one of the four who even noticed anything unusual in this interchange. Here, a new metaphor was created, produced, and comprehended without the slightest awareness by either of the primary participants.

This free and easy use of words in a "nonliteral" fashion is, I believe, not at all unusual. It does not require special note because it is not special. Children and adults alike produce and understand metaphorical utterances constantly. A logical consideration of some of the problems of language acquisition and the production of so-called semantic errors by children offers, I believe, some insight into the naturalness of this process. To begin, of course, children are unaware of the "correct" domain of application for a particular lexical item. Presumably, a child learns a lexical item with respect to some particular domain of reference that in no way exhausts the set of situations to which the word can be correctly applied. In this domain of original use, some of the features of the use situation presumably are relevant, and others presumably are not. Normally speaking, the process of language comprehension and production for a young child not fully familiar with the conventional range of application of a term must proceed through a process of fitting the aspects of the current situation into the closest lexical concept already available. Often this will conform with the conventional application of the term and it will therefore appear that the child is using the bit of language "literally." Just as often, the child will apply the concepts in a nonstandard way and appear to generate "nonliteral" or "metaphorical" speech. Thus, for example, if the term "open" is learned in the context of (say) a child's mouth being open, and then it is applied to a door or a window, the child will appear merely to be demonstrating an understanding of the term. On the other hand, if the child uses the term "open" to mean "turn on" (as with a television set or a light) the child will be perceived as having produced a metaphor. Yet the process of applying words to situations is much the same in the two cases – namely that of finding the best word or concept to communicate the idea in mind. For the child the production of literal and nonliteral speech may involve *exactly* the same processes.

The same arguments just made for production apply equally well for comprehension. When trying to understand an utterance, the child must make use of the situations associated with the various lexical items at hand and try, as well as possible, to construct a cogent interpretation of the utterance (in light of the current context). As a rule, this will involve the extension of concepts from one domain to another. Those extensions may or may not correspond to the intentions of the speaker and the utterance may or may not contain words used in a nonliteral way, but the child's process is the same in either case. If a child has difficulty understanding metaphorical language (as judged by an adult), this is presumably due to the child's difficulty in making the connection between his or her conception of the situation underlying the lexical items used and the situation at hand, not because of any inherent inability to apply terms learned in one context to another. This process must be the only way a child can learn to comprehend language at all.

Thus, the child's language-acquisition process should not be construed, as it often seems to be, as a process of first learning literal language and then, after that is thoroughly mastered, moving on into nonliteral language. Rather, it would appear that the child's early comprehension and production processes involve the production and comprehension of what is for the child *nonconventional* (and probably) nonliteral language. Thus, I believe that the processes involved in the comprehension of nonliteral speech are part of our language production and comprehension equipment from the very start, and that far from being a special aspect of linguistic or pragmatic competence, it is the very basis for this competence.

At first blush, this fact – that metaphor is natural and widespread in our speech, not having any apparent special status – is remarkable. How is it that falsehoods such as my son's comment can pass for normal speech? The answer I think, arises not so much through a careful analysis of metaphor as through a careful analysis of so-called literal language. Before pressing this issue, however, let me turn to the traditional view of meaning and metaphor to see why this fact should be so remarkable.

The traditional program of semantic analysis (cf. Katz & Fodor, 1963) provides a set of *meanings* for the individual lexemes of the language and then provides a set of *rules of composition* whereby the individual meanings of the lexemes are *combined* to form the *meaning of the sentence*. Likewise, for any discourse, the meanings of the individual sentences of the discourse can be combined to form the meaning of the discourse. Meanings built up in this way are the *literal meanings* of the sentence or discourse. Arguably, this program of semantic analysis can provide a reasonable account of the *conveyed meanings* (that is, what the listener understands upon hearing the sentence uttered in some context) of many sentences in English. However, as Sadock has pointed out, this is not always the case. Sometimes, as in the case of my son's comment, such an analysis simply does not work. We cannot suppose that there was an *actual* hangnail on my son's sock. Yet, unless we assume that the lexical entry for "hangnail" includes provision for a thread hanging from something (an after-the-fact interview held later the same day indicated that my son knew that the thread hanging from his sock was not a *real* hangnail), we are forced to the conclusion that the literal meaning of such an utterance offers no account of its conveyed meaning. At this point, there are four possible moves that can be made.

1. We could reject the traditional program of semantics and try to formulate a new account of both literal and conveyed meanings.
2. We could retain the traditional program, but assume that metaphor and other cases of figurative language represent mere curiosities to be accounted for by some other theory entirely.
3. We could assume that the traditional theory works correctly for most cases and that some additional processing is required when the literal meaning is nonsensical or violates some rule of conversation.
4. We could modify the traditional theory to make it work for metaphor as well as literal language.

Sadock has opted for alternative (3) and Cohen for option (4). I believe that neither of these alternatives will work, and that (1) will be necessary. For the most part, options (2) and (3) have been the most popular and, in fact, accounts along these lines have been mildly successful. This success has had a number of unfortunate (in my view) effects on the development of theories of language comprehension.

First, for example, it has led to the view that language is *actually understood* by the individual's looking up the meanings of the lexemes in some "internal lexicon" and then putting them together to form the meaning of the entire sentence. Second, it has led to the supposition, for literal sentences, that the literal meaning (as derived from the appropriate rules of concatenation) and the conveyed meaning are often identical. Third, it has led to the view that the conveyed meaning of a discourse consists of a simple concatenation of the meanings of the individual sentences of the discourse. Finally, it has tended to put metaphor and other similar cases of nonliteral speech into a special category. Related to this is the idea that we use special mechanisms to deal with nonliteral language, mechanisms that are different from those employed in processing literal speech.

In my view, each of these positions is suspect. But they have so dominated thought about semantics and meaning that psychologists interested in meaning have often accepted them without adequate analysis. They therefore warrant serious scrutiny, and I shall devote the remainder of this paper to a more detailed discussion of their defects and their repair.

Is literal meaning necessary to get the conveyed meaning?

The first supposition, namely, that language is comprehended by first computing the literal meaning and then, if it violates some rule of conversation (e.g., Grice's, 1975, maxim of relevance), somehow calculating the conveyed meaning, has already developed a strong hold in psychology. Clark and Lucy (1975), for example, have proposed the following three-stage model for the comprehension of indirect requests. They argue that in order to comprehend such a request (e.g., "Must you do *x*," meaning "Do not do *x*"), a person must : (a) determine the literal meaning of the utterance (presumably by a simple composition of lexeme meanings); (b) compare the literal meaning so determined with various contextual and conversational rules to decide if the literal meaning could also be the intended meaning; (c) if the literal meaning is determined inappropriate, apply additional rules to determine the indirect, or conveyed, meaning.

Here we have a model which takes very seriously the distinction between literal and conveyed meaning, and which assumes that the determination of literal meaning is a necessary step on the way toward finding the conveyed meaning – at least of an indirect request. In a recent study, a student of mine, Ray Gibbs, set out to test this model. The critical sentences of his study were sentences like, "Must you open the window," which can function either as indirect requests meaning something like, "Don't open the window!" or literally with an interpretation of the form, "Is it necessary that you open the window?" In his experiment, these sentences could either appear out of context with the subject judging whether one or the other of these paraphrases was the correct one, or they appeared in the context of one of two stories, in which one or the other of these two interpretations was clearly demanded. In both cases, the sentence was immediately followed by one or the other of the two paraphrases and the subjects had to judge whether or not the paraphrase was correct. The results showed that whereas out of context it took longer to determine that the indirect-request paraphrase could be true of the statement – thereby confirming the sequential model for out-of-context sentences – it took no longer to verify the correct indirect request paraphrase when the sentence occurred in context. Thus, when indirect requests occur in an appropriate context, they can be understood as quickly as when the literal interpretation of the same statement is required. However, with no supporting context, the indirect-request reading of the statements takes longer to verify. So, whereas the sequential model may be correct for sentences occurring out of context, we cannot be determining the literal readings first *in* context, since in context the two sentence-types are processed and verified equally quickly.

Are conveyed meanings ever literal meanings?

It is often claimed that although figurative language is problematic for the sort of semantic theories under discussion, *normally* the conveyed meaning and the literal meanings are the same. The problems only arise for these special cases. I suspect that, on the contrary, the same problems arise for literal language as for figurative language. In both cases, what is conveyed is not easily determined from the meanings of the individual lexical items of the utterance; and in both cases, the interpretation seems to depend on knowledge well beyond definitions of the terms involved. There are no rules whereby lexical meanings can be combined to generate conveyed meanings. I believe that the processes involved in the comprehension of nonfigurative language are no less dependent on knowledge of the world than those involved in figurative language. Any theory rich enough to generate the meanings people actually assign to nonfigurative language is rich enough to deal with figurative language as well. In this section I look at a few cases of nonfigurative language in order to illustrate some of the problems a theory of "literal" speech must face and then suggest a mechanism that I believe is rich enough to deal with nonfigurative speech. In the following sections I indicate how this same mechanism can be employed for figurative language.

Linguistic utterances are always interpreted in some context. The context of utterance, along with any knowledge available to the listener, may potentially be employed in the process of constructing an interpretation of the utterance. Moreover, I suspect that this knowledge is not employed in any ad hoc way, say simply as a filter in choosing among the various possible readings a sentence might have. Rather, these elements play a central role in determining what interpretations are possible for a given utterance. Consider the following two examples:

(1) If you mow the lawn, I'll pay you $5;
(2) If you are a senator, you are over thirty-five.

People seem to interpret the "if" in these two sentences in rather different ways. In the first case, the "if" is normally interpreted to mean "if and only if," whereas, in the second, a simple implication reading is obtained. If we were to take the concatenation view of meaning construction, we would be led to suggest one of three possible explanations for this phenomenon: First, perhaps "if" is ambiguous between the simple implication and bi-conditional readings. The bi-conditional is selected in (1) and the simple implication in (2). Second, perhaps "if" is univocal, and people simply misunderstand (1). Third, perhaps the true meaning of "if" is the conditional reading, but through some conversational implicature or another, in (1) it is interpreted to mean "if an only if."

I find none of these explanations very convincing. It seems unlikely that the first is the case since both sentences should exhibit the same ambiguity and they seem not to do so. The second merely denies the claim that (1) *conveys* the bi-conditional. The third, while the most plausible of the three, offers no clue as to what maxims are violated or how the respective readings are settled upon.

There is, however, an explanation rather more obvious than these. Namely, the claim that the difference in interpretation has nothing at all to do with the word "if," nor with the meaning of any of the individual lexemes. Rather it depends on our *real world knowledge,* of business contracts, of senators, of payments, and so on. In the case of

(1), we know that we get paid only if we do the work we contract to do. No work, no pay. Hence the conveyed meaning is a product of our social knowledge. In (2), we know that senators are rather few and far between and that they tend to need quite a lot of political experience. Knowing that someone is over thirty-five provides very little evidence that a person is a senator. This and numerous other similar examples lead me to posit the following very general account of the comprehension process – which, as I hope to show, is applicable to literal and figurative language alike. The process of comprehension is identical to the process of selecting and verifying conceptual schemata to account for the situation (including its linguistic components) to be understood. Having selected and verified that some configuration of schemata offers a sufficient account for the situation, it is said to be understood. As I use the term, a "schema" is taken to be an abstract representation of a generalized concept or situation, and a schema is said to "account for a situation" whenever that situation can be taken as an instance of the general class of concepts represented by the schema. Thus, in the case of (1), a listener presumably brings to mind schemata involving the formation of business contracts in which one works in exchange for pay. The sentence is then presumably understood *as a case of this general schema,* and the biconditional interpretation is a natural consequence of this interpretation. This approach is, I believe, quite different from the "standard" approach. The standard view emphasizes the "bottom up" processes of constructing meaning from smaller component meanings. Nonlinguistic knowledge comes into play only *after* the set of possible meanings have been selected. My approach suggests that comprehension, like perception, should be likened to Hebb's paleontologist (Hebb 1949) who uses his beliefs and knowledge about dinosaurs in conjunction with the clues provided by the bone fragments available to construct a full-fledged model of the original. In this case, the words spoken and the actions taken by the speaker are likened to the clues of the paleontologist, and the dinosaur, to the meaning conveyed through those clues. On this view, the processing is much more "top down" in that internal hypotheses are actively imposed on the observed utterances.

Now consider how this general framework would deal with the following:

(3) The policeman raised his hand and stopped the car.

The comprehension of this utterance through the mechanisims I envision would involve searching memory for a schema to account for the described event. There are probably many possible accounts of this event, but perhaps the most likely is one involving a traffic cop who is signalling to a driver to stop his car. Note that this brings under consideration a number of concepts that are not mentioned in the sentence itself. For example, this interpretation requires that the car has a *driver* and that the policement stopped the car by signaling with his hand to the driver, who then most likely puts his *foot* on the *brake* of the car causing it finally to halt. It is difficult to imagine how the meanings of the individual lexemes could be put together in such a way as to generate such an interpretation. Moreover, it seems unlikely that the example is in any way an instance of figurative language. Here we have the literal interpretation of an utterance clearly dependent on our knowledge of policemen, cars, how policemen are known to signal to drivers, and so forth. It would seem that no model can account for the interpretation of this sentence without itself incorporating all of this rather general knowledge. The situation is even more complicated than this. Suppose that we had been given the knowledge that there was no driver in the car and that the policeman in question was really Superman in disguise. We would then get a very different interpretation. We would probably understand that Superman had *physically* stopped the car by bracing his legs and putting his hand on the car thus preventing further forward motion. Clearly, our knowledge of the nature of cars, people, and Superman, and of the conventions whereby policemen signal drivers, are all essential in making these interpretations.

In summary then, the supposition that conveyed meanings are *ever* identical to *literal meanings* (where literal meanings are assumed to be those given by a compositional semantic theory) is surely suspect. The problems of determining conveyed meanings of literal sentences are no less difficult (I believe) than finding those of figurative ones.

The meaning of discourses

I have, over the past several years, been involved in a study of the processes whereby people interpret stories. It was here that it became clearest to me that literal meanings – in the sense implied by the advocates of compositional theories – and conveyed meanings deviated in even the most mundane cases. It also became clear to me that a schema-based notion of the comprehension process is the most viable alternative account. A careful look at almost any story and the interpretations given to it makes this abundantly clear. Consider the following brief passage:

Business had been slow since the oil crisis. Nobody seemed to want anything really elegant anymore. Suddenly the door opened and a well-dressed man entered the showroom. John put on his friendliest and most sincere expression and walked toward the man.

Although the example is merely a fragment, most people generate a rather clear interpretation of this story. Apparently, John is a car salesman fallen on hard times. He probably sells rather large elegant cars – most likely Cadillacs. Suddenly a good prospect enters the showroom where John works. John wants to make a sale. To do that, he must make a good impression on the man. Therefore he tries to appear friendly and sincere. He also wants to talk to the man to deliver his sales pitch. Thus, he makes his way over to the man. Presumably, had the story continued, John would have made the sales pitch and, if all went well, sold the man a car.

How do people arrive at such an interpretation? Clearly, people do not arrive at it all at once. As the sentences are read, schemata are activated, evaluated, and refined or discarded. When people are asked to describe their various hypotheses as they read the story, a remarkably consistent pattern of hypothesis generation and evaluation emerges. The first sentence is usually interpreted to mean that business is slow *because* of the oil crisis. Thus, people are led to see the story as about a business which is somehow dependent on oil and, consequently, suffering. Frequent hypotheses involve either the selling of cars, or of gasoline. A few interpret the sentence as being about the economy in general. The second sentence, about people not wanting elegant things anymore, leads readers with the gas-station hypothesis into a quandary. Elegance just does not fit with gas stations. The gas station hypothesis is weakened, but not always rejected. On the other hand, people with hypotheses about the general economy or about cars have no trouble incorporating this sentence into their emerging interpretation. In the former case, they conclude that it means that people do not buy luxury items, and in the latter, they assume it means that people tend not to buy large elegant cars – Cadillacs – anymore. The third sentence clinches the car interpretation for nearly all readers. They are already looking for a business interpretation – that most probably means a selling interpretation – and when a *well-dressed man* enters the door he is immediately labeled as someone with money — a prospective buyer. The word *showroom* clearly invalidates the gas-station interpretation and strongly implicates automobiles, which are often sold from a showroom. Moreover, the reference to a specific event does not fit at all well with the view that the passage is a general discussion of the state of the economy. Finally, with the introduction of *John,* we have an ideal candidate for the seller. John's actions are clearly those stereotypic of a salesman. John wants to make a sale and his *putting on* is

clearly an attempt on his part to "make a good impression." His movement toward the man fits nicely into this interpretation. If he is a salesman, he must make contact with the man and deliver the stereotypic
pitch.

The process outlined here is, I believe, typical of the processes
involved in understanding language. There is no sense in which the
meanings of sentences are simply compounded to derive the meanings
of discourses. Again, although this story fragment contained no metaphorical statements, the processes of active hypothesis testing and evaluation employed in deriving an interpretation of such a passage is
also required for deriving an interpretation of metaphorical material. There is no reason to suppose that metaphorical understanding is
in any way an extension beyond normal understanding. As I will discuss, I believe that it is an aspect of the quality of the account, rather
than the processes whereby an account is reached, that distinguishes
metaphorical from literal language.

Are metaphorical uses of language special?

As I have indicated previously, it is perhaps an unfortunate consequence of accepting the strong distinction between literal language
and metaphorical language that we tend to miss the strong similarities
between the comprehension processes employed in the two cases. There
is a tendency to miss the lessons that I believe metaphorical language
has for models of literal-language comprehension and thought. A large
portion of the language that we ordinarily use is based on metaphor.
Perhaps one of the best examples of this is in the so-called dual-func-
tion adjective.

Although we often have strong intuitions about what is *literally true*
and what is only *metaphorically true*, the judgments are not always
easy and, more importantly, they often have substantial implications
about the nature of metaphor. Consider, as an example, the sentence
   (4) John is a cold person,
when uttered in a context in which it is interpreted to mean that John
is unemotional. Is this sentence *literally* true? There are three possible
answers to this question.
   1. No, it is not literally true, John is not actually *cold*, the sense in
      which he is cold is metaphorical, not literal.
   2. Yes, cold is a word with several senses: one of these senses involves
      being unemotional, and in that sense of cold it is literally the case
      that John is cold.
   3. Well, yes and no. The use of cold to mean unemotional was
      originally metaphorical, but is now conventional. It is now merely

an idiom. There is a sense in which idioms are *never* literally true, but it is not a figurative use either. Perhaps it is better to say that in our idiom John is literally a cold person, but were the words used according to their normal meanings, we would not say that he was cold, but that he was unemotional.

I think it is important to get clear in our minds which one of these three answers we believe to be best. I suspect that, depending on which it is, we get a substantially different notion about how language-comprehension processes operate. If we choose the first alternative, metaphor in language is absolutely ubiquitous and the existence of nonmetaphorical language is questionable. Nearly always, when we talk about abstract concepts, we choose language drawn from one or another concrete domain. A good example of this is our talk about the mind. Here we use a spatial model to talk about things that are clearly nonspatial in character. We have things "in" our minds, "on" our minds, "in the back corners of" our minds. We "put things out" of our minds, things "pass through" our minds, we "call things to mind," and so on. It is quite possible that our primary method of understanding nonsensory concepts is through analogy with concrete experiential situations.

I believe that alternative (2) will never work. It is clearly not the word "cold" that has two meanings. We could also have said: John is a cool person, or John is a warm person, or even John is a block of ice. In all of these cases, it would seem much more economical to say, not that the word has two meanings, but rather that temperature and emotional states are analogous to one another in a certain way. The meanings of the terms "cold" and "warm" presumably do not have to be learned independently; rather, the learning of one clearly reinforces and modifies the use of the other. Surely, the learner of the language just learns the general model and can *productively* derive these and other cases of applying temperature words to emotional states.

In many ways, (3) is the most pleasing of the three answers. It would be nice if we could discount these troublesome cases and concentrate on cases of "real" metaphor. However, I suspect that to include these as cases of idioms is to strain the concept of idiom beyond its breaking point. Clearly, unlike idioms such as "kick the bucket" or "pull my leg," these idioms are very productive. We can always generate new cases based on the "conventional" analogy. It, therefore, seems to me that we are left with (1). Moreover, I believe that most metaphor works in just the same way, by reference to analogies that are known to relate the two domains. Consider, as an example, the metaphor discussed in Ortony's chapter in this volume.

(5) Encyclopedias are gold mines.

How are we to understand it? According to the schema theory of comprehension suggested above, the task for the comprehender is to find a schema within which this utterance is coherent. Here we have a case of predication, the process of interpretation presumably involves applying the schemata suggested by the predicate term to the subject term. Thus, the interpretation that the speaker is asserting that we should view an encyclopedia as a gold mine is entertained. In general, predication suggests that the characteristic properties of the predicate concept are to be applied to the subject concept. In this case, we find that the "gold mine" schema fits only partially, although certain of the primary characteristics of gold mines can be shown to be true of encyclopedias (such as the characteristic of containing something of value – if only you look for it), other characteristics (such as being underground) do not hold. I suspect that it is the unevenness of account – certain primary features of the gold mine schema fit very well, others not at all – that leads to the metaphorical flavor of statements such as this. The interpretation process, I believe, is no different here than for a literal predication, the outcome is simply different. We say that a statement is literally true when we find an existing schema that accounts fully for the data in question. We say that a statement is metaphorically true when we find that although certain primary aspects of the schema hold, others equally primary do not hold. When no schema can be found which allows for a good fit between any important aspects of the schema and the object for which it is said to account, we are simply unable to interpret the input at all.

NOTE

1 I except here particularly obscure cases in which the interpretation of a piece of language is not immediately given in our awareness, but instead requires a lengthy reasoning process – extending from several seconds to several years. Still, this process, which is sometimes required for particularly obscure figurative uses, has its counterpart in nonfigurative uses such as mathematics and scientific discourse. The full understanding of such discourse can often require rather lengthy reasoning processes and thus may well employ qualitatively different comprehension strategies.

METAPHOR
AND
PRAGMATICS

Metaphor

JOHN R. SEARLE

Formulating the problem

If you hear somebody say, "Sally is a block of ice," or "Sam is a pig," you are likely to assume that the speaker does not mean what he says literally but that he is speaking metaphorically. Furthermore, you are not likely to have very much trouble figuring out what he means. If he says, "Sally is a prime number between 17 and 23," or "Bill is a barn door," you might still assume he is speaking metaphorically, but it is much harder to figure out what he means. The existence of such utterances – utterances in which the speaker means metaphorically something different from what the sentence means literally – poses a series of questions for any theory of language and communication: What is metaphor, and how does it differ from both literal and other forms of figurative utterances? Why do we use expressions metaphori-cally instead of saying exactly and literally what we mean? How do metaphorical utterances work, that is, how is it possible for speakers to communicate to hearers when speaking metaphorically inasmuch as they do not say what they mean? And why do some metaphors work and others not?

In my discussion, I propose to tackle this latter set of questions – those centering around the problem of how metaphors work – both because of its intrinsic interest, and because it does not seem to me that we shall get an answer to the others until this fundamental question has been answered. Before we can begin to understand it, however, we need to formulate the question more precisely.

The problem of explaining how metaphors work is a special case of the general problem of explaining how speaker meaning and sentence or word meaning come apart. It is a special case, that is, of the prob-lem of how it is possible to say one thing and mean something else, where one succeeds in communicating what one means even though both the speaker and the hearer know that the meanings of the words uttered by the speaker do not exactly and literally express what the speaker meant. Some other instances of the break between speaker's utterance meaning and literal sentence meaning are irony and indirct speech acts. In each of these cases, what the speaker means is not identical with what the sentence means, and yet what he means is in various ways dependent on what the sentence means.

It is essential to emphasize at the very beginning that the problem of metaphor concerns the relations between word and sentence meaning, on the one hand, and speaker's meaning or utterance meaning, on the other. Many writers on the subject try to locate the metaphorical element of a metaphorical utterance in the sentence or expressions uttered. They think there are two kinds of sentence meaning, literal and metaphorical. However, sentences and words have only the meanings that they have. Strictly speaking, whenever we talk about the metaphorical meaning of a word, expression, or sentence, we are talking about what a speaker might utter it to mean, in a way that departs from what the word, expression, or sentence actually means. We are, therefore, talking about possible speaker's intentions. Even when we discuss how a nonsense sentence, such as Chomsky's example, "Colorless green ideas sleep furiously," could be given a metaphorical interpretation, what we are talking about is how a speaker could utter the sentence and mean something by it metaphorically, even though it is literally nonsensical. To have a brief way of distinguishing what a speaker means by uttering words, sentences, and expressions, on the one hand, and what the words, sentences, and expressions mean, on the other, I shall call the former *speaker's utterance meaning*, and the latter, *word*, or *sentence meaning*. Metaphorical meaning is always speaker's utterance meaning.

In order that the speaker can communicate using metaphorical utterances, ironical utterances, and indirect speech acts, there must be some principles according to which he is able to mean more than, or something different from, what he says, whereby the hearer, using his knowledge of them, can understand what the speaker means. The relation between the sentence meaning and the metaphorical utterance meaning is systematic rather than random or ad hoc. Our task in constructing a theory of metaphor is to try to state the principles which relate literal sentence meaning to metaphorical utterance meaning. Because the knowledge that enables people to use and understand metaphorical utterances goes beyond their knowledge of the literal meanings of words and sentences, the principles we seek are not included, or at least not entirely included, within a theory of semantic competence as traditionally conceived. From the point of view of the hearer, the

problem of a theory of metaphor is to explain how he can understand
the speaker's utterance meaning given that all he hears is a sentence
with its word and sentence meaning. From the point of view of the
speaker, the problem is to explain how he can mean something different from the word and sentence meaning of the sentence he utters. In
light of these reflections, our original question, How do metaphors
work? can be recast as follows: What are the principles that enable
speakers to formulate, and hearers to understand, metaphorical utterances? and How can we state these principles in a way that makes it
clear how metaphorical utterances differ from other sorts of utterances
in which speaker meaning does not coincide with literal meaning?

Because part of our task is to explain how metaphorical utterances
differ from literal utterances, to start with we must arrive at a characterization of literal utterances. Most – indeed all – of the authors I have
read on the subject of metaphor assume that we know how literal
utterances work; they do not think that the problem of literal utterances is worth discussing in their account of metaphor. The price they
pay for this is that their accounts often describe metaphorical utterances in ways that fail to distinguish them from literal ones.

In fact, to give an accurate account of literal predication is an
extremely difficult, complex, and subtle problem. I shall not attempt
anything like a thorough summary of the principles of literal utterance
but shall remark on only those features which are essential for a comparison of literal utterance with metaphorical utterance. Also, for the
sake of simplicity, I shall confine most of my discussion of both literal
and metaphorical utterance to very simple cases, and to sentences used
for the speech act of assertion.

Imagine that a speaker makes a literal utterance of a sentence such
as

(1) Sally is tall
(2) The cat is on the mat
(3) It's getting hot in here.

Now notice that in each of these cases, the literal meaning of the sentence determines, at least in part, a set of truth conditions; and because
the only illocutionary force indicating devices (see Searle, 1969) in the
sentences are assertive, the literal and serious utterance of one of these
sentences will commit the speaker to the existence of the set of truth
conditions determined by the meaning of that sentence, together with the
other determinants of truth conditions. Notice, furthermore, that in each
case the sentence only determines a definite set of truth conditions relative to a particular context. That is because each of these examples has
some indexical element, such as the present tense, or the demonstrative

"here," or the occurrence of contextually dependent definite descriptions, such as "the cat" and "the mat."

In these examples, the contextually dependent elements of the sentence are explicitly realized in the semantic structure of the sentence: One can see and hear the indexical expressions. But these sentences, like most sentences, only determine a set of truth conditions against a background of assumptions that are not explicitly realized in the semantic structure of the sentence. This is most obvious for (1) and (3), because they contain the relative terms "tall" and "hot." These are what old-fashioned grammarians called "attributive" terms, and they only determine a definite set of truth conditions against a background of factual assumptions about the sort of things referred to by the speaker in the rest of the sentence. Moreover, these assumptions are not explicitly realized in the semantic structure of the sentence. Thus, a woman can be correctly described as "tall" even though she is shorter than a giraffe that could correctly be described as "short."

Though this dependence of the application of the literal meaning of the sentence on certain factual background assumptions that are not part of the literal meaning is most obvious for sentences containing attributive terms, the phenomenon is quite general. Sentence (2) only determines a definite set of truth conditions given certain assumptions about cats, mats, and the relation of being on. However, these assumptions are not part of the semantic content of the sentence. Suppose, for example, that the cat and mat are in the usual cat-on-mat spatial configuration, only both cat and mat are in outer space, outside any gravitational field relative to which one could be said to be "above" or "over" the other. Is the cat still *on* the mat? Without some further assumptions, the sentence does not determine a definite set of truth conditions in this context. Or suppose all cats suddenly became lighter than air, and the cat went flying about with the mat stuck to its belly. Is the cat still on the mat?

We know without hesitation what are the truth conditions of, "The fly is on the ceiling," but not of, "The cat is on the ceiling," and this difference is not a matter of meaning, but a matter of how our factual background information enables us to apply the meanings of sentences. In general, one can say that in most cases a sentence only determines a set of truth conditions relative to a set of assumptions that are not realized in the semantic content of the sentence. Thus, even in literal utterances, where speaker's meaning coincides with sentence meaning, the speaker must contribute more to the literal utterance than just the semantic content of the sentence, because that semantic content only determines a set of truth conditions relative to a set of assumptions made by the speaker, and if communication is to be successful, his assumptions must be shared by the hearer (for further discussion of this point, see Searle, 1978).

Notice finally that the notion of similarity plays a crucial role in any account of literal utterance. This is because the literal meaning of any general term, by determining a set of truth conditions, also determines a criterion of similarity between objects. To know that a general term is true of a set of objects is to know that they are similar with respect to the property specified by that term. All tall women are similar with respect to being tall, all hot rooms similar with respect to being hot, all square objects similar with respect to being square, and so on.

To summarize this brief discussion of some aspects of literal utterance, there are three features we shall need to keep in mind in our account of metaphorical utterance. First, in literal utterance the speaker means what he says; that is, literal sentence meaning and speaker's utterance meaning are the same; second, in general the literal meaning of a sentence only determines a set of truth conditions relative to a set of background assumptions which are not part of the semantic content of the sentence; and third, the notion of similarity plays an essential role in any account of literal predication.

When we turn to cases where utterance meaning and sentence meaning are different, we find them quite various. Thus, for example, (3) could be uttered not only to tell somebody that it is getting hot in the place of utterance (literal utterance), but it could also be used to request somebody to open a window (indirect speech act), to complain about how cold it is (ironical utterance), or to remark on the increasing vituperation of an argument that is in progress (metaphorical utterance). In our account of metaphorical utterance, we shall need to distinguish it not only from literal utterance, but also from these other forms in which literal utterance is departed from, or exceeded, in some way.

Because in metaphorical utterances what the speaker means differs from what he says (in one sense of "say"), in general we shall need two sentences for our examples of metaphor – first the sentence uttered metaphorically, and second a sentence that expresses literally what the speaker means when he utters the first sentence and means it metaphorically. Thus (3), the metaphor (MET):

(3) (MET) It's getting hot in here.

corresponds to (3), the paraphrase (PAR):

(3) (PAR) The argument that is going on is becoming more vituperative

and similarly with the pairs:

(4) (MET) Sally is a block of ice

(4) (PAR) Sally is an extremely unemotional and unresponsive person

(5) (MET) I have climbed to the top of the greasy pole (Disraeli)

(5) (PAR) I have after great difficulty become prime minister

(6) (MET) Richard is a gorilla

(6) (PAR) Richard is fierce, nasty, and prone to violence.

Notice that in each case we feel that the paraphrase is somehow inadequate, that something is lost. One of our tasks will be to explain this sense of dissatisfaction that we have with paraphrases of even feeble metaphors. Still, in some sense, the paraphrases must approximate what the speaker meant, because in each case the speaker's metaphorical assertion will be true if, and only if, the corresponding assertion using the PAR sentence is true. When we get to more elaborate examples, our sense of the inadequacy of the paraphrase becomes more acute. How would we paraphrase

(7) (MET) My Life had stood – a Loaded Gun –
　　　　In Corners – till a Day
　　　　The Owner passes – identified
　　　　And carried Me away – (Emily Dickinson)?

Clearly a good deal is lost by

(7) (PAR) My life was one of unrealized but readily realizable potential (a loaded gun) in mediocre surroundings (corners) until such time (a day) when my destined lover (the owner) came (passed), recognized my potential (identified), and took (carried) me away.

Yet, even in this case, the paraphrase or something like it must express a large part of speaker's utterance meaning, because the truth conditions are the same.

Sometimes we feel that we know exactly what the metaphor means and yet would not be able to formulate a literal PAR sentence because there are no literal expressions that convey what it means. Thus even for such a simple case as

(8) (MET) The ship ploughed the sea,

we may not be able to construct a simple paraphrase sentence even though there is no obscurity in the metaphorical utterance. And indeed metaphors often serve to plug such semantic gaps as this. In other cases, there may be an indefinite range of paraphrases. For example, when Romeo says:

(9) (MET) Juliet is the sun,

there may be a range of things he might mean. But while lamenting the inadequacy of paraphrases, let us also recall that paraphrase is symmetrical relation. To say that the paraphrase is a poor paraphrase of the metaphor is also to say that the metaphor is a poor paraphrase of its paraphrase. Furthermore, we should not feel apologetic about the fact that some of our examples are trite or dead metaphors. Dead metaphors are especially interesting for our study, because, to speak oxymoronically, dead metaphors have lived on. They have become dead through continual use, but their continual use is a clue that they satisfy some semantic need.

Confining ourselves to the simplest subject–predicate cases, we can say that the general form of the metaphorical utterance is that a speaker utters a sentence of the form "S is P" and means metaphorically that S is R. In analyzing metaphorical predication, we need to distinguish, therefore, between three sets of elements. Firstly, there is the subject expression "S" and the object or objects it is used to refer to. Secondly, there is the predicate expression "P" that is uttered and the literal meaning of that expression with its corresponding truth conditions, plus the denotation if there is any. And thirdly, there is the speaker's utterance meaning "S is R" and the truth conditions determined by that meaning. In its simplest form, the problem of metaphor is to try to get a characterization of the relations between the three sets, S, P, and R^1, together with a specification of other information and principles used by speakers and hearers, so as to explain how it is possible to utter "S is P" and mean "S is R," and how it is possible to communicate that meaning from speaker to hearer. Now, obviously, that is not all there is to understand about metaphorical utterances; the speaker does more than just assert that S is R, and the peculiar effectiveness of metaphor will have to be explained in terms of how he does more than just assert that S is R and why he should choose this roundabout way of asserting that S is R in the first place. But at this stage we are starting at the beginning. At the very minimum, a theory of metaphor must explain how it is possible to utter "S is P" and both mean and communicate that S is R.

We can now state one of the differences between literal and metaphorical utterances as applied to these simple examples: In the case of literal utterance, speaker's meaning and sentence meaning are the same; therefore the assertion made about the object referred to will be true if and only if it satisfies the truth conditions determined by the meaning of the general term as applied against a set of shared background assumptions. In order to understand the utterance, the hearer does not require any extra knowledge beyond his knowledge of the rules of language, his awareness of the conditions of utterance, and a set of shared background assumptions. But, in the case of the metaphorical utterance, the truth conditions of the assertion are not determined by the truth conditions of the sentence and its general term. In order to understand the metaphorical utterance, the hearer requires something more than his knowledge of the language, his awareness of the conditions of the utterance, and background assumptions that he shares with the speaker. He must have some other principles, or some other factual information, or some combination of principles and information that enables him to figure out that when the speaker says, "*S* is *P*," he means "*S* is *R*." What is this extra element?

I believe that at the most general level, the question has a fairly simple answer, but it will take me much of the rest of this discussion to work it out in any detail. The basic principle on which all metaphor works is that the utterance of an expression with its literal meaning and corresponding truth conditions can, in various ways that are specific to metaphor, call to mind another meaning and corresponding set of truth conditions. The hard problem of the theory of metaphor is to explain what exactly are the principles according to which the utterance of an expression can metaphorically call to mind a different set of truth conditions from the one determined by its literal meaning, and to state those principles precisely and without using metaphorical expressions like "call to mind."

Some common mistakes about metaphor

Before attempting to sketch a theory of metaphor, I want in this section and the next to backtrack a bit and examine some existing theories. Roughly speaking, theories of metaphor from Aristotle to the present can be divided into two types.[2] Comparison theories assert that metaphorical utterances involve a *comparison* or *similarity* between two or more *objects* (e.g., Aristotle, 1952a, 1952b; Henle, 1965), and semantic interaction theories claim that metaphor involves a *verbal opposition* (Beardsley, 1962) or *interaction* (Black, 1962b) between two *semantic contents,* that of the expression used metaphorically, and that of the surrounding literal context. I think that both of these theories, if one tries to take them quite literally, are in various ways inadequate; nonetheless, they are both trying to say something true, and we ought to try to extract what is true in them. But first I want to show some of the common mistakes they contain and some further common mistakes made in discussions of metaphor. My aim here is not polemical; rather, I am trying to clear the ground for the development of a theory of metaphor. One might say the endemic vice of the comparison theories is that they fail to distinguish between the claim that the statement of the comparison is part of the *meaning,* and hence the *truth*

conditions, of the metaphorical statement, and the claim that the statement of the similarity is the *principle of inference,* or a step in the
process of *comprehending,* on the basis of which speakers produce and
hearers understand metaphor. (More about this distinction later.) The
semantic interaction theories were developed in response to the weaknesses of the comparison theories, and they have little independent
argument to recommend them other than the weakness of their rivals:
Their endemic vice is the failure to appreciate the distinction between
sentence or word meaning, which is never metaphorical, and speaker or
utterance meaning, which can be metaphorical. They usually try to
locate metaphorical meaning in the sentence or some set of associations
with the sentence. In any event, here are half a dozen mistakes, which I
believe should be noted:

It is often said that in metaphorical utterances there is a change in
meaning of at least one expression. I wish to say that on the contrary,
strictly speaking, in metaphor there is never a change of meaning;
diachronically speaking, metaphors do indeed initiate semantic
changes, but to the extent that there has been a genuine change in
meaning, so that a word or expression no longer means what it previously did, to precisely that extent the locution is no longer metaphorical. We are all familiar with the processes whereby an expression
becomes a dead metaphor, and then finally becomes an idiom or
acquires a new meaning different from the original meaning. But in a
genuine metaphorical utterance, it is only because the expressions have
not changed their meaning that there is a metaphorical utterance at
all. The people who make this claim seem to be confusing *sentence*
meaning with *speaker's* meaning. The metaphorical utterance does
indeed mean something different from the meaning of the words and
sentences, but that is not because there has been any change in the
meanings of the lexical elements, but because the speaker means something different by them; speaker meaning does not coincide with sentence or word meaning. It is essential to see this point, because the
main problem of metaphor is to explain how speaker meaning and sentence meaning are different and how they are, nevertheless, related.
Such an explanation is impossible if we suppose that sentence or word
meaning has changed in the metaphorical utterance.

The simplest way to show that the crude versions of the comparison
view are false is to show that, in the production and understanding of
metaphorical utterances, there need not be any two objects for comparison. When I say metaphorically

(4) (MET) Sally is a block of ice,

I am not necessarily quantifying over blocks of ice at all. My utterance
does not entail literally that

(10) $(\exists x)$ (x is a block of ice),

and such that I am comparing Sally to x. This point is even more obvious if we take expressions used as metaphors which have a null extension. If I say

(11) Sally is a dragon

that does not entail literally

(12) $(\exists x)$ (x is a dragon).

Or, another way to see the same thing is to note that the negative sentence is just as metaphorical as the affirmative. If I say

(13) Sally is not a block of ice,

that, I take it, does not invite the absurd question: Which block of ice is it that you are comparing Sally with, in order to say that she is not like it? At its *crudest*, the comparison theory is just muddled about the referential character of expressions used metaphorically.

Now, this might seem a somewhat minor objection to the comparison theorists, but it paves the way for a much more radical objection. Comparison theories which are explicit on the point at all, generally treat the statement of the comparison as part of the meaning and hence as part of the truth conditions of the metaphorical statement. For example, Miller (this volume) is quite explicit in regarding metaphorical statements as statements of similarity, and indeed for such theorists the meaning of a *metaphorical* statement is always given by an explicit *statement* of similarity. Thus, in their view, I have not even formulated the problem correctly. According to me, the problem of explaining (simple subject–predicate) metaphors is to explain how the speaker and hearer go from the literal sentence meaning "S is P" to the metaphorical utterance meaning "S is R." But, according to them, that is not the utterance meaning; rather the utterance meaning must be expressible by an explicit statement of similarity, such as "S is like P with respect to R," or in Miller's case, the metaphorical statement "S is P" is to be analyzed as, "There is some property F and some property G such that S's being F is similar to P's being G." I will have more to say about this thesis and its exact formulation later, but at present I want to claim that though similarity often plays a role in the *comprehension* of metaphor, the metaphorical assertion is not necessarily an *assertion* of similarity. The simplest argument that metaphorical assertions are not always assertions of similarity is that there are true metaphorical assertions for which there are no objects to be designated by the P term, hence the true metaphorical statement cannot possibly presuppose the existence of an object of comparison. But even where there are objects of comparison, the metaphorical assertion is not necessarily an assertion of similarity. Similarity, I shall argue, has to do with the production and understanding of metaphor, not with its meaning.

A second simple argument to show that metaphorical assertions are not necessarily assertions of similarity is that often the metaphorical assertion can remain true even though it turns out that the statement of similarity on which the inference to the metaphorical meaning is based is false. Thus, suppose I say,

(6) (MET) Richard is a gorilla

meaning

(6) (PAR) Richard is fierce, nasty, prone to violence, and so forth.

And suppose the hearer's inference to (6 PAR) is based on the belief that

(14) Gorillas are fierce, nasty, prone to violence, and so forth,

and hence (6 MET) and (14), on the comparison view, would justify the inference to

(15) Richard and gorillas are similar in several respects; *viz*, they are fierce, nasty, prone to violence, and so forth,

and this in turn would be part of the inference pattern that enabled the hearer to conclude that when I uttered (6 MET) I meant (6 PAR). But suppose ethological investigation shows, as I am told it has, that gorillas are not at all fierce and nasty, but are in fact shy, sensitive creatures, given to bouts of sentimentality. This would definitely show that (15) is false, for (15) is as much an assertion about gorillas as about Richard. But would it show that when I uttered (6 MET), what I said was false? Clearly not, for what I meant was (6 PAR), and (6 PAR) is an assertion about Richard. It can remain true regardless of the actual facts about gorillas; though, of course, what expressions we use to convey metaphorically certain semantic contents will normally depend on what we take the facts to be.

To put it crudely, "Richard is a gorilla," is just about Richard; it is not literally about gorillas at all. The word "gorilla" here serves to convey a certain semantic content other than its own meaning by a set of principles I have yet to state. But (15) is literally about both Richard and gorillas, and it is true if and only if they both share the properties it claims they do. Now, it may well be true that the hearer employs something like (15) as a step in the procedures that get him from (6 MET) to (6 PAR), but it does not follow from this fact about his *procedures of comprehension* that this is part of the *speaker's utterance meaning* of (6 MET); and, indeed, that it is not part of the utterance meaning is shown by the fact that the metaphorical statement can be *true* even if it turns out that gorillas do not have the traits that the metaphorical occurrence of "gorilla" served to convey. I am not saying that a metaphorical assertion can *never* be equivalent in meaning to a statement of similarity – whether or not it is would depend on the intentions of the speaker; but I am saying that it is not a necessary feature of metaphor – and is certainly not the point of having metaphor – that metaphorical assertions are equivalent in meaning to statements of similarity. My argument is starkly simple: In many cases the metaphorical statement and the corresponding similarity statement cannot be equivalent in meaning because they have different truth conditions. The difference between the view I am attacking and the one I shall espouse is this. According to the view I am attacking, (6 MET) *means* Richard and gorillas are similar in certain respects. According to the view I shall espouse, similarity functions as a comprehension strategy, not as a component of meaning: (6 MET) says that Richard has certain traits (and to figure out what they are, look for features associated with gorillas). On my account the P term need not figure literally in the statement of the truth conditions of the metaphorical statement at all.

Similar remarks apply incidentally to similes. If I say,

(16) Sam acts like a gorilla

that need not commit me to the truth of

(17) Gorillas are such that their behavior resembles Sam's.

For (16) need not be about gorillas at all, and we might say that "gorilla" in (16) has a metaphorical occurrence. Perhaps this is one way we might distinguish between figurative similes and literal statements of similarity. Figurative similes need not necessarily commit the speaker to a literal statement of similarity.

The semantic interaction view, it seems to me, is equally defective. One of the assumptions behind the view that metaphorical meaning is a result of an interaction between an expression used metaphorically and other expressions used literally, is that all metaphorical uses of expressions must occur in sentences containing literal uses of expressions, and that assumption seems to me plainly false. It is, incidentally, the assumption behind the terminology of many of the contemporary discussions of metaphor. We are told, for example, that every metaphorical sentence contains a "tenor" and a "vehicle" (Richards, 1936a) or a "frame" and a "focus" (Black, 1962b). But it is not the case that every metaphorical use of an expression is surrounded by literal uses of other expressions. Consider again our example (4): In uttering, "Sally is a block of ice," we referred to Sally using her proper name literally, but we need not have. Suppose, to use a mixed metaphor, we refer to Sally as "the bad news." We would then say, using a mixed metaphor

(18) The bad news is a block of ice.

If you insist that the "is" is still literal, it is easy enough to construct examples of a dramatic change on Sally's part where we would be inclined, in another mixed metaphor, to say

(19) The bad news congealed into a block of ice.

Mixed metaphors may be stylistically objectionable, but I cannot see that they are necessarily logically incoherent. Of course, most metaphors do occur in contexts of expressions used literally. It would be very hard to understand them if they did not. But it is not a logical necessity that every metaphorical use of an expression occurs surrounded by literal occurrences of other expressions and, indeed, many famous examples of metaphor are not. Thus Russell's example of a completely nonsensical sentence, "Quadrilaterality drinks procrastination," is often given a metaphorical interpretation as a description of any postwar four-power disarmament conference, but none of the words, so interpreted, has a literal occurrence; that is, for every word the speaker's utterance meaning differs from the literal word meaning.

However, the most serious objection to the semantic interaction view is not that it falsely presupposes that all metaphorical occurrences of words must be surrounded by literal occurrence of other words, but rather, that even where the metaphorical occurrence is within the context of literal occurrences, it is not in general the case that the metaphorical speaker's meaning is a result of any interaction among the elements of the sentence in any literal sense of "interaction." Consider again our example (4). In its metaphorical utterances, there is no question of any interaction between the meaning of the "principal subject" ("Sally") and the "subsidiary subject" ("block of ice"). "Sally" is a proper name; it does not have a meaning in quite the way in which "block of ice" has a meaning. Indeed, other expressions could have been used to produce the same metaphorical predication. Thus,

(20) Miss Jones is a block of ice

or

(21) That girl over there in the corner is a block of ice

could have been uttered with the same metaphorical utterance meaning.

I conclude that, as general theories, both the object comparison view and the semantic interaction view are inadequate. If we were to diagnose their failure in Fregean terms, we might say that the comparison view tries to explain metaphor as a relation between references, and the interaction view tries to explain it as a relation between senses and beliefs associated with references. The proponents of the interaction view see correctly that the mental processes and the semantic processes involved in producing and understanding metaphorical utterances cannot involve references themselves, but must be at the level of intentionality, that is, they must involve relations at the level of beliefs, meanings, associations, and so on. However, they then say incorrectly that the relations in question must be some unexplained, but metaphorically described, relations of "interaction"[3] between a literal frame and a metaphorical focus.

Two final mistakes I wish to note are not cases of saying something false about metaphors but of saying something true which fails to distinguish metaphor from literal utterance. Thus it is sometimes said that the notion of similarity plays a crucial role in the analysis of metaphor, or that metaphorical utterances are dependent on the context for their interpretation. But, as we saw earlier, both of these features are true of literal utterances as well. An analysis of metaphor must show how similarity and context play a role in metaphor different from their role in literal utterance.

A further examination of the comparison theory

One way to work up to a theory of metaphor would be to examine the strengths and weaknesses of one of the existing theories. The obvious candidate for this role of stalking horse is a version of the comparison theory that goes back to Aristotle and can, indeed, probably be considered the common-sense view – the theory that says all metaphor is really literal simile with the "like" or "as" deleted and the respect of the similarity left unspecified. Thus, according to this view, the metaphorical utterance, "Man is a wolf," means "Man is like a wolf in certain unspecified ways"; the utterance, "You are my sunshine," means "You are like sunshine to me in certain respects," and "Sally is a block of ice," means "Sally is like a block of ice in certain but so far unspecified ways."

The principles on which metaphors function, then, according to this theory are the same as those for literal statements of similarity together with the principle of ellipsis. We understand the metaphor as a shortened version of the literal simile.[4] Since literal simile requires no special extralinguistic knowledge for its comprehension, most of the knowledge necessary for the comprehension of metaphor is already contained in the speaker's and hearer's semantic competence, together with the general background knowledge of the world that makes literal meaning comprehensible.

We have already seen certain defects of this view, most notably that metaphorical statements cannot be equivalent in meaning to literal statements of similarity because the truth conditions of the two sorts of statements are frequently different. Furthermore, we must emphasize that even as a theory of metaphorical comprehension – as opposed to a theory of metaphorical meaning – it is important for the simile theory that the alleged underlying similes be literal statements of similarity. If the simile statements which are supposed to explain metaphor are themselves metaphorical or otherwise figurative, our explanation will be circular.

Still, treated as theory of comprehension, there does seem to be a large number of cases where for the metaphorical utterance we can construct a simile sentence that does seem in some way to explain how its metaphorical meaning is comprehended. And, indeed, the fact that the specification of the values of R is left vague by the simile statement may, in fact, be an advantage of the theory, inasmuch as metaphorical utterances are often vague in precisely that way: it is not made *exactly* clear what the R is supposed to be when we say that S is P, meaning metaphorically that S is R. Thus, for example, in analyzing Romeo's metaphorical statement, "Juliet is the sun," Cavell (1976, pp. 78 – 9) gives as part of its explanation that Romeo means that his day begins with Juliet. Now, apart from the special context of the play, that reading would never occur to me. I would look for other properties of the sun to fill in the values of R in the formula. In saying this I am not objecting to either Shakespeare or Cavell, because the metaphor in question, like most metaphors, is open-ended in precisely that way.

Nonetheless, the simile theory, in spite of its attractiveness, has serious difficulties. First, the theory does more – or rather, less – than fail to tell us how to compute the value of R exactly: So far it fails to tell us how to compute it at all. That is, the theory still has almost no explanatory power, because the task of a theory of metaphor is to explain how the speaker and hearer are able to go from "S is P" to "S is R," and it does not explain that process to tell us that they go from "S is P" to "S is R" by first going through the stage "S is like P with respect to R" because we are not told how we are supposed to figure out which values to assign to R. Similarity is a vacuous predicate: any two things are similar in some respect or other. Saying that the metaphorical "S is P" implies the literal "S is like P" does not solve our problem. It only pushes it back a step. The problem of understanding literal similes with the respect of the similarity left unspecified is only a part of the problem of understanding metaphor. How are we supposed to know, for example, that the utterance, "Juliet is the sun," does not mean "Juliet is for the most part gaseous," or "Juliet is 90 million miles from the earth," both of which properties are salient and well-known features of the sun.

Yet another objection is this: It is crucial to the simile thesis that the

simile be taken literally; yet there seem to be a great many metaphorical utterances where there is no relevant literal corresponding similarity between S and P. If we insist that there are always such similes, it
looks as if we would have to interpret them metaphorically, and thus
our account would be circular. Consider our example (4), "Sally is a
block of ice." If we were to enumerate quite literally the various distinctive qualities of blocks of ice, none of them would be true of Sally.
Even if we were to throw in the various beliefs that people have about
blocks of ice, they still would not be literally true of Sally. There
simply is no class of predicates, R, such that Sally is literally like a
block of ice with respect to R where R is what we intended to predicate metaphorically of Sally when we said she was a block of ice. Being
unemotional is not a feature of blocks of ice because blocks of ice are
not in that line of business at all, and if one wants to insist that blocks
of ice are literally unresponsive, then we need only point out that that
feature is still insufficient to explain the metaphorical utterance meaning of (4), because in that sense bonfires are "unresponsive" as well,
but

(22) Sally is a bonfire

has a quite different metaphorical utterance meaning from (4). Furthermore, there are many similes that are not intended literally. For
example, an utterance of "My love is like a red, red rose" does not
mean that there is a class of literal predicates that are true both of my
love and red, red roses and that express what the speaker was driving
at when he said his love was like a red, red rose.

The defender of the simile thesis, however, need not give up so
easily. He might say that many metaphors are also examples of other
figures as well. Thus, "Sally is a block of ice" is not only an example
of metaphor, but of hyperbole as well.[5] The metaphorical utterance
meaning is indeed derived from the simile, "Sally is like a block of
ice," but then both the metaphor and the simile are cases of *hyperbole*;
they are exaggerations, and indeed, many metaphors are exaggerations.
According to this reply, if we interpret both the metaphor and the
simile hyperbolically, they are equivalent.

Furthermore, the defender of the simile thesis might add that it is
not an objection to the simile account to say that some of the respects
in which Sally is like a block of ice will be specified metaphorically,
because for each of these metaphorical similes we can specify another
underlying simile until eventually we reach the rock bottom of literal
similes on which the whole edifice rests. Thus "Sally is a block of ice"
means "Sally is like a block of ice," which means "She shares certain
traits with a block of ice, in particular she is very cold." But since

"cold" in "Sally is very cold" is also metaphorical, there must be an underlying similarity in which Sally's emotional state is like coldness, and when we finally specify these respects, the metaphor will be completely analyzed.

There are really two stages to this reply: First, it points out that other figures such as hyperbole sometimes combine with metaphor, and, secondly, it concedes that some of the similes that we can offer as translations of the metaphor are still metaphorical, but insists that some recursive procedure of analyzing metaphorical similes will eventually lead us to literal similes.

Is this reply really adequate? I think not. The trouble is that there do not seem to be any literal similarities between objects which are cold and people who are unemotional that would justify the view that when we say metaphorically that someone is cold what we mean is that he or she is unemotional. In what respects exactly are unemotional people like cold objects? Well, there are some things that one can say in answer to this, but they all leave us feeling somewhat dissatisfied.

We can say, for example, that when someone is physically cold it places severe restrictions on their emotions. But even if that is true, it is not what we meant by the metaphorical utterance. I think the only answer to the question, "What is the relation between cold things and unemotional people?" that would justify the use of "cold" as a metaphor for lack of emotion is simply that as a matter of perceptions, sensibilities, and linguistic practices, people find the notion of coldness associated in their minds with lack of emotion. The notion of being cold just is associated with being unemotional.

There is some evidence, incidentally, that this metaphor works across several different cultures: It is not confined to English speakers (cf. Asch, 1958). Moreover, it is even becoming, or has become, a dead metaphor. Some dictionaries (for example, the *O.E.D.*) list lack of emotion as one of the meanings of "cold." Temperature metaphors for emotional and personal traits are in fact quite common and they are not derived from any literal underlying similarities. Thus we speak of a "heated argument," "a warm welcome," "a lukewarm friendship," and "sexual frigidity." Such metaphors are fatal for the simile thesis, unless the defenders can produce a literal R which S and P have in common, and which is sufficient to explain the precise metaphorical meaning which is conveyed.

Because this point is bound to be contested, it is well to emphasize exactly what is at stake. In claiming that there are no sufficient similarities to explain utterance meaning, I am making a negative existential claim, and thus not one which is demonstrable from an examination of a finite number of instances. The onus is rather on the similarity theorist to state the similarities and show how they exhaust utterance meaning. But it is not at all easy to see how he could do that in a way that would satisfy the constraints of his own theory.

Of course, one can think of lots of ways in which any S is like any P, e.g., ways in which Sally is like a block of ice, and one can think of lots of F's and G's such that Sally's being F is like a block of ice's being G. But that is not enough. Such similarities as one can name do not exhaust utterance meaning and if there are others that do, they are certainly not obvious.

But suppose with some ingenuity one could think up a similarity that would exhaust utterance meaning. The very fact that it takes so much ingenuity to think it up makes it unlikely that it is the underlying principle of the metaphorical interpretation, inasmuch as the metaphor is obvious: There is no difficulty for any native speaker to explain what it means. In "Sam is a pig," both utterance meaning and similarities are obvious, but in "Sally is a block of ice," only the utterance meaning is obvious. The simpler hypothesis, then, is that this metaphor, like several others I shall now discuss, functions on principles other than similarity.

Once we start looking for them, this class of metaphors turns out to be quite large. For example, the numerous spatial metaphors for temporal duration are not based on literal similarities. In "time flies," or "the hours crawled by," what is it that time does and the hours did which is literally like flying or crawling? We are tempted to say they went rapidly or slowly respectively, but of course "went rapidly" and "went slowly" are further spatial metaphors. Similarly, taste metaphors for personal traits are not based on properties in common. We speak of a "sweet disposition" or a "bitter person," without implying that the sweet disposition and the bitter person have literal traits in common with sweet and bitter tastes which exhaust the utterance meaning of the metaphorical utterance. Of course, sweet dispositions and sweet things are both pleasant, but much more is conveyed by the metaphor than mere pleasantness.

So deeply embedded in our whole mode of sensibility are certain metaphorical associations that we tend to think there *must* be a similarity, or even that the association itself is a form of similarity. Thus, we feel inclined to say that the passage of time *just is like* spatial movement, but when we say this we forget that "passage" is only yet another spatial metaphor for time and that the bald assertion of similarity, with no specification of the respect of similarity, is without content.

The most sophisticated version of the simile thesis I have seen is by

George Miller (this volume), and I shall digress briefly to consider some of its special features. Miller, like other simile theorists, believes that the meanings of metaphorical statements can be expressed as statements of similarity, but he offers a special kind of similarity statement (rather like one of Aristotle's formulations, by the way) as the form of "reconstruction" of metaphorical statements. According to Miller, metaphors of the form "*S* is *P*", where both *S* and *P* are noun phrases, are equivalent to sentences of the form

(23) $(\exists F)(\exists G)\,\{\text{SIM}\,[F\,(S),\,G\,(P)]\}$.

Thus, for example, "Man is a wolf," according to Miller would be analyzed as

(24) There is some property *F* and some property *G* such that man's being *F* is similar to a wolf's being *G*.

And when we have metaphors where a verb or predicate adjective *F* is used metaphorically in a sentence of the form "*x* is *F*" or "*xF*'s", the analysis is of the form

(25) $(\exists G)(\exists y)\,\{\text{SIM}\,[G\,(x),F\,(y)]\}$.

Thus, for example, "The problem is thorny" would be analyzed as

(26) There is some property *G* and some object *y* such that the problem's being *G* is similar to *y*'s being thorny.

I believe this account has all the difficulties of the other simile theories – namely, it mistakenly supposes that the use of a metaphorical predicate commits the speaker to the existence of objects of which that predicate is literally true; it confuses the truth conditions of the metaphorical statement with the principles under which it is comprehended; it fails to tell us how to compute the values of the variables (Miller is aware of this problem, he calls it the problem of "interpretation" and sees it as different from the problem of "reconstruction"); and it is refuted by the fact that not all metaphors have literal statements of similarity underlying them. But it has some additional problems of its own. In my view, the most serious weakness of Miller's account is that according to it the semantic contents of most metaphorical utterances have too many predicates, and, in fact, rather few metaphors really satisfy the formal structure he provides us with. Consider, for example, "Man is a wolf." On what I believe is the most plausible version of the simile thesis, it means something of the form

(27) Man is like a wolf in certain respects *R*.

We could represent this as

(28) $\text{SIM}_R\,(\text{man, wolf})$.

The hearer is required to compute only one set of predicates, the values for *R*. But according to Miller's account, the hearer is required to compute no less than three sets of predicates. Inasmuch as similarity is a vacuous predicate, we need to be told in which respect two things are similar for the statement that they are similar to have any informative content. His formalization of the above metaphorical utterance is

(29) $(\exists F)\,(\exists G)\,\{\text{SIM}\,[F\,(\text{man},\,G\,(\text{wolf})]\}.$

In order to complete this formula in a way that would specify the respect of the similarity we would have to rewrite it as

(30) $(\exists F)\,(\exists G)\,(\exists H)\,\{\text{SIM}_H\,[F\,(\text{man}),\,G\,(\text{wolf})]\}.$

But both the reformulation (30), and Miller's original (29), contain too many predicate variables: When I say, "Man is a wolf," I am not saying that there are some *different* sets of properties that men have from those that wolves have, I am saying they have the *same* set of properties (at least on a sympathetic construal of the simile thesis, that is what I am saying). But according to Miller's account, I am saying that man has one set of properties F, wolves have a different set of properties G, and man's having F is similar to wolves having G with respect to some other properties H. I argue that this "reconstruction" is (a) counterintuitive, (b) unmotivated, and (c) assigns an impossible computing task to the speaker and hearer. What are these F's, G's and H's supposed to be? and, How is the hearer supposed to figure them out? It is not surprising that his treatment of the interpretation problem is very sketchy. Similar objections apply to his accounts of other syntactical forms of metaphorical utterances.

There is a class of metaphors, that I shall call "relational metaphors," for which something like his analysis might be more appropriate. Thus, if I say

(8) The ship ploughed the sea

or

(31) Washington is the father of his country,

these might be interpreted using something like his forms. We might treat (8) as equivalent to

(32) There is some relation R which the ship has to the sea and which is similar to the relation that ploughs have to fields when they plough fields;

and (31) as

(33) There is some relation R which Washington has to his country and which is like the relation that fathers have to their offspring.

And (32) and (33) are fairly easily formalized *à la* Miller. However, even these analyses seem to me to concede too much to his approach: (8) makes no reference either implicitly or explicitly to fields and

(31) makes no reference to offspring. On the simplest and most plausible version of the simile thesis (8) and (31) are equivalent to:

(34) The ship does something to the sea which is like ploughing

and

(35) Washington stands in a relation to his country which is like the relation of being a father.

And the hearer's task is simply to compute the intended relations in the two cases. By my account, which I shall develop in the next section, similarity does not, in general, function as part of the truth conditions either in Miller's manner or in the simpler version; rather, when it functions, it functions as a strategy for interpretation. Thus, very crudely, the way that similarity figures in the interpretation of (8) and (31) is given by

(36) The ship does something to the sea (to figure out what it is, find a relationship like ploughing)

and

(37) Washington stands in a certain relationship to his country (to figure out what it is, find a relationship like that of being a father).

But the hearer does not have to compute any respects in which these relations are similar, inasmuch as that is not what is being asserted. Rather, what is being asserted is that the ship is doing something to the sea and that Washington stands in a certain set of relations to his country, and the hearer is to figure out what it is that the ship does and what the relations are that Washington stands in by looking for relations similar to ploughing and being a father of.

To conclude this section: The problem of metaphor is either very difficult or very easy. If the simile theory were true, it would be very easy, because there would be no separate semantic category of *metaphors* – only a category of *elliptical utterances* where "like" or "as" had been deleted from the uttered sentence. But alas, the simile theory is not right, and the problem of metaphor remains very difficult. I hope our rather lengthy discussion of the simile theory has been illuminating in at least these respects. First, there are many metaphors in which there is no underlying literal similarity adequate to explain the metaphorical utterance meaning. Second, even where there is a correlated literal statement of similarity, the truth conditions, and hence the meaning of the metaphorical statement and the similarity statement, are not, in general, the same. Third, what we should salvage from the simile theory is a set of strategies for producing and understanding metaphorical utterances, using similarity. And fourth, even so construed, that is, construed as a theory of interpretation rather than of meaning, the simile theory does not tell us how to compute the respects of similarity or which similarities are metaphorically intended by the speaker.

The principles of metaphorical interpretation

The time has now come to try to state the principles according to which metaphors are produced and understood. To reiterate, in its simplest form, the question we are trying to answer is, How is it possible for the speaker to say metaphorically "*S* is *P*" and mean "*S* is *R*," when *P* plainly does not mean *R*; furthermore, How is it possible for the hearer who hears the utterance "*S* is *P*" to know that the speaker means "*S* is *R*"? The short and uninformative answer is that the utterance of *P* calls to mind the meaning and, hence, truth conditions associated with *R*, in the special ways that metaphorical utterances have of calling other things to mind. But that answer remains uninformative until we know what are the principles according to which the utterance calls the metaphorical meaning to mind, and until we can state these principles in a way which does not rely on metaphorical expressions like "calls to mind." I believe that there is no single principle on which metaphor works.

The question, "How do metaphors work?" is a bit like the question, "How does one thing remind us of another thing?" There is no single answer to either question, though similarity obviously plays a major role in answering both. Two important differences between them are that metaphors are both restricted and systematic; restricted in the sense that not every way that one thing can remind us of something else will provide a basis for metaphor, and systematic in the sense that metaphors must be communicable from speaker to hearer in virtue of a shared system of principles.

Let us approach the problem from the hearer's point of view. If we can figure out the principles according to which hearers understand metaphorical utterances, we shall be a long way toward understanding how it is possible for speakers to make metaphorical utterances, because for communication to be possible, speaker and hearer must share a common set of principles. Suppose a hearer hears an utterance such as, "Sally is a block of ice," or "Richard is a gorilla," or "Bill is a barn door." What are the steps he must go through in order to comprehend the metaphorical meaning of such utterances? Obviously an answer to that question need not specify a set of steps that he goes through consciously; instead it must provide a rational reconstruction of the inference patterns that underlie our ability to understand such metaphors. Furthermore, not all metaphors will be as simple as the cases we shall be discussing; nonetheless, a model designed to account for the simple cases should prove to be of more general application.

I believe that for the simple sorts of cases we have been discussing, the hearer must go through at least three sets of steps. First, he must have some strategy for determining whether or not he has to seek a metaphorical interpretation of the utterance in the first place. Secondly, when he has decided to look for a metaphorical interpretation, he must have some set of strategies, or principles, for computing possible values of R, and third, he must have a set of strategies, or principles, for restricting the range of R's – for deciding which R's are likely to be the ones the speaker is asserting of S.

Suppose he hears the utterance, "Sam is a pig." He knows that that cannot be literally true, that the utterance, if he tries to take it literally, is radically defective. And, indeed, such defectiveness is a feature of nearly all of the examples that .we have considered so far. The defects which cue the hearer may be obvious falsehood, semantic nonsense, violations of the rules of speech acts, or violations of conversational principles of communication. This suggests a strategy that underlies the first step: *Where the utterance is defective if taken literally, look for an utterance meaning that differs from sentence meaning.*

This is not the only strategy on which a hearer can tell that an utterance probably has a metaphorical meaning, but it is by far the most common. (It is also common to the interpretation of poetry. If I hear a figure on a Grecian Urn being addressed as a "still unravish'd bride of quietness," I know I had better look for alternative meanings.) But it is certainly not a necessary condition of a metaphorical utterance that it be in any way defective if construed literally. Disraeli might have said metaphorically

(5) (MET) I have climbed to the top of the greasy pole,
though he had in fact climbed to the top of a greasy pole. There are various other cues that we employ to spot metaphorical utterances. For example, when reading Romantic poets, we are on the lookout for metaphors, and some people we know are simply more prone to metaphorical utterances than others.

Once our hearer has established that he is to look for an alternative meaning, he has a number of principles by which he can compute possible values of R. I will give a list of these shortly, but one of them is this: *When you hear "S is P," to find possible values of R look for ways in which* S *might be like* P, *and to fill in the respect in which* S *might be like* P, *look for salient, well known, and distinctive feature of* P *things.*

In this case, the hearer might invoke his factual knowledge to come up with such features as that pigs are fat, gluttonous, slovenly, filthy, and so on. This indefinite range of features provides possible values of R. However, lots of other features of pigs are equally distinctive and well known, for example, pigs have a distinctive shape and distinctive bristles. So, in order to understand the utterance, the hearer needs to go through the third step where he restricts the range of possible R's. Here again the hearer may employ various strategies for doing that but the one that is most commonly used is this: *Go back to the* S *term and see which of the many candidates for the values of* R *are likely or even possible properties of* S.

Thus, if the hearer is told, "Sam's car is a pig," he will interpret that metaphor differently from the utterance, "Sam is a pig." The former, he might take to mean that Sam's car consumes gas the way pigs consume food, or that Sam's car is shaped like a pig. Though, in one sense, the metaphor is the same in the two cases, in each case it is restricted by the S term in a different way. The hearer has to use his knowledge of S things and P things to know which of the possible values of R are plausible candidates for metaphorical predication.

Now, much of the dispute between the interaction theories and the object comparison theories derives from the fact that they can be construed as answers to different questions. The object comparison theories are best construed as attempts to answer the question of stage two: "How do we compute the possible values of R?" The interaction theories are best construed as answers to the question of stage three: "Given a range of possible values of R, how does the relationship between the S term and the P term restrict that range?" I think it is misleading to describe these relations as "interactions," but it seems correct to suppose that the S term must play a role in metaphors of the sort we have been considering. In order to show that the interaction theory was also an answer to the question of stage two, we would have to show that there are values of R that are specifiable, given S and P together, that are not specifiable given P alone; one would have to show that S does not *restrict* the range of R's but in fact, creates new R's. I do not believe that can be shown, but I shall mention some possibilities later.

I said that there was a variety of principles for computing R, given P – that is, a variety of principles according to which the utterance of

P can call to mind the meaning *R* in ways that are peculiar to meta-phor. I am sure I do not know all of the principles that do this, but here are several (not necessary independent) for a start.

Principle 1

Things which are *P* are by definition *R*. Usually, if the metaphor works, *R* will be one of the salient defining characteristics of *P*. Thus, for example,

(38) (MET) Sam is a giant
will be taken to mean
(38) (PAR) Sam is big,
because giants are by definition big. That is what is special about them.

Principle 2

Things which are *P* are contingently *R*. Again, if the metaphor works, the property *R* should be a salient or well known property of *P* things.

(39) (MET) Sam is a pig
will be taken to mean
(39) (PAR) Sam is filthy, gluttonous, sloppy, and so on.
Both principles 1 and 2 correlate metaphorical utterances with literal similes, "Sam is like a giant," "Sam is like a pig," etc. Notice in connec-tion with this principle and the next that small variations in the *P* term can create big differences in the *R* terms. Consider the differences between "Sam is a pig," "Sam is a hog," and "Sam is a swine."

Principle 3

Things which are *P* are often said or believed to be *R*, even though both speaker and hearer may know that *R* is false of *P*. Thus,

(7) (MET) Richard is a gorilla
can be uttered to mean
(7) (PAR) Richard is mean, nasty, prone to violence, and so on,
even though both speaker and hearer know that in fact gorillas are shy, timid, and sensitive creatures, but generations of gorilla mythology have set up associations that will enable the metaphor to work even though both speaker and hearer know these beliefs to be false.

Principle 4

Things which are *P* are not *R*, nor are they like *R* things, nor are they believed to be *R*, nonetheless it is a fact about our sensibility, whether culturally or naturally determined, that we just do perceive a connection, so that utterance of P is associated in our minds with R properties.

Thus,

(4) (MET) Sally is a block of ice

(40) (MET) I am in a black mood

(41) (MET) Mary is sweet

(42) (MET) John is bitter

(43) (MET) The hours
$\left\{ \begin{array}{l} \text{crept} \\ \text{crawled} \\ \text{dragged} \\ \text{sped} \\ \text{whizzed} \end{array} \right\}$
by as we waited for the plane

are sentences that could be uttered to mean metaphorically that: Sally is unemotional; I am angry and depressed; Mary is gentle, kind, pleasant, and so on; John is resentful; and the hours seemed (of varying degrees of duration) as we waited for the plane; even though there are no literal similarities on which these metaphors are based. Notice that the associations tend to be scalar: degrees of temperature with ranges of emotion, degrees of speed with temporal duration, and so forth.

Principle 5

P things are not like R things, and are not believed to be like R things, nonetheless the condition of being P is like the condition of being R. Thus, I might say to someone who has just received a huge promotion

(44) You have become an aristocrat,

meaning not that he has personally become *like* an aristocrat, but that his new status or condition is like that of being an aristocrat.

Principle 6

There are cases where P and R are the same or similar in meaning, but where one, usually P, is restricted in its application, and does not literally apply to S. Thus, "addled" is only said literally of eggs, but we can metaphorically say

(45) This soufflé is addled

(46) That parliament was addled

and

(47) His brain is addled.

Principle 7

This is not a separate principle but a way of applying principles 1 through 6 to simple cases which are not of the form "*S* is *P*" but relational metaphors, and metaphors of other syntactical forms such as those involving verbs and predicate adjectives. Consider such relational metaphors as

(48) Sam devours books

(8) The ship ploughs the sea

(31) Washington was the father of his country.

In each case, we have a literal utterance of two noun phrases surrounding a metaphorical utterance of a relational term (it can be a transitive verb, as in (48) and (8) but it need not be, as in (31)). The hearer's task is not to go from "*S* is *P*" to "*S* is *R*" but to go from "*S P*-relation *S'* " to "*S R*-relation *S'* " and the latter task is formally rather different from the former because, for example, our similarity principles in the former case will enable him to find a property that *S* and *P* things have in common, namely, *R*. But in the latter, he cannot find a· relation in common, instead he has to find a relation *R* which is different from relation *P* but similar to it in some respect. So, as applied to these cases, principle 1, for example, would read

P-relations are by definition *R*-relations.

For example, *ploughing* is by definition partly a matter of moving a substance to either side of a pointed object while the object moves forward; and though this definitional similarity between the *P*-relation and the *R*-relation would provide the principle that enables the hearer to infer the *R*-relation, the respect of similarity does not exhaust the context of the *R*-relation, as the similarity exhausts the content of the *R* term in the simplest of the "*S* is *P*" cases. In these cases, the hearer's job is to find a relation (or property) that is similar to, or otherwise associated with, the relation or property literally expressed by the metaphorical expression *P*; and the principles function to enable him to select that relation or property by giving him a respect in which the *P*-relation and the *R*-relation might be similar or otherwise associated.

Principle 8

According to my account of metaphor, it becomes a matter of terminology whether we want to construe metonymy and synecdoche as special cases of metaphor or as independent tropes. When one says, "*S* is *P*," and means that "*S* is *R*," *P* and *R* may be associated by such relations as the part – whole relation, the container – contained relation, or even the clothing and wearer relation. In each case, as in metaphor proper, the semantic content of the P term conveys the semantic content of the R term by some principle of association. Since the principles of metaphor are rather various anyway, I am inclined to treat metonymy and synecdoche as special cases of metaphor and add their principles to my list of metaphorical principles. I can, for example, refer to the British monarch as "the Crown," and the executive branch of the U.S. government as "the White House" by exploiting systematic principles of association. However, as I said, the claim that these are special cases of metaphor seems to me purely a matter of terminology, and if purists insist that the principles of metaphor be kept separate from those of metonymy and synecdoche, I can have no nontaxonomical objections.

In addition to these eight principles, one might wonder if there is a ninth. Are there cases where an association between P and R that did not previously exist can be created by the juxtaposition of S and P in the original sentence? This, I take it, is the thesis of the interaction theorists. However, I have never seen any convincing examples, nor any even halfway clear account, of what "interaction" is supposed to mean. Let us try to construct some examples. Consider the differences between

(49) Sam's voice is $\left\{ \begin{array}{l} \text{mud} \\ \text{gravel} \\ \text{sandpaper} \end{array} \right\}$

and

(50) Kant's second argument for the transcendental deduction is so much $\left\{ \begin{array}{l} \text{mud} \\ \text{gravel} \\ \text{sandpaper} \end{array} \right\}$

The second set clearly gives us different metaphorical meanings – different values for R – than the first trio, and one might argue that this is due not to the fact that the different S terms restrict the range of possible R's generated by the P terms, but to the fact that the different combinations of S and P create new R's. But that explanation seems implausible. The more plausible explanation is this. One has a set of associations with the P terms, "mud," "gravel," and "sandpaper." The principles of these associations are those of principles 1 through 7. The different S terms restrict the values of R differently, because different R's can be true of voices than can be true of arguments for transcendental deductions. Where is the interaction?

Because this section contains my account of metaphorical predication, it may be well to summarize its main points. Given that a speaker and a hearer have shared linguistic and factual knowledge sufficient to enable them to communicate literal utterance, the following principles are individually necessary and collectively sufficient to enable speaker and hearer to form and comprehend utterances of the form "S is P," where the speaker means metaphorically that S is R (where $P \neq R$).

First, there must be some shared strategies on the basis of which the hearer can recognize that the utterance is not intended literally. The most common, but not the only strategy, is based on the fact that the utterance is obviously defective if taken literally.

Second, there must be some shared principles that associate the P term (whether the meaning, the truth conditions, or the denotation if there is any) with a set of possible values of R. The heart of the problem of metaphor is to state these principles. I have tried to state several of them, but I feel confident that there must be more.

Third, there must be some shared strategies that enable the speaker and the hearer, given their knowledge of the S term (whether the meaning of the expression, or the nature of the referent, or both), to restrict the range of possible values of R to the actual value of R. The basic principle of this step is that only those possible values of R which determine possible properties of S can be actual values of R.

Metaphor, irony, and indirect speech acts

To conclude, I wish to compare briefly the principles on which metaphor works with those on which irony and indirect speech acts work. Consider first a case of irony. Suppose you have just broken a priceless K'ang Hsi vase and I say ironically, "That was a brilliant thing to do." Here, as in metaphor, the speaker's meaning and sentence meaning are different. What are the principles by which the hearer is able to infer that the speaker meant, "That was a stupid thing to do," when what he heard was the sentence, "That was a brilliant thing to do"? Stated very crudely, the mechanism by which irony works is that the utterance, if taken literally, is obviously inappropriate to the situation. Since it is grossly inappropriate, the hearer is compelled to reinterpret it in such a way as to render it appropriate, and the most natural way to interpret it is as meaning the *opposite* of its literal form.

I am not suggesting that this is by any means the whole story about irony. Cultures and subcultures vary enormously in the extent and degree of the linguistic and extralinguistic cues provided for ironical utterances. In English, in fact, there are certain characteristic intonational contours that go with ironical utterances. However, it is important to see that irony, like metaphor, does not require any conventions, extralinguistic or otherwise. The principles of conversation and the general rules for performing speech acts are sufficient to provide the basic principles of irony.

Now consider a case of an indirect speech act. Suppose that in the usual dinner-table situation, I say to you, "Can you pass the salt?" In this situation you will normally take that as meaning, "Please pass the salt." That is, you will take the question about your ability as a request to perform an action. What are the principles on which this inference works? There is a radical difference between indirect speech acts, on the one hand, and irony and metaphor, on the other. In the indirect speech act, the speaker means what he says. However, in addition, he means something more. Sentence meaning is part of utterance meaning, but it does not exhaust utterance meaning. In a very simplified form (for a more detailed account, see Searle, 1975), the principles on which the inference works in this case are: First, the hearer must have some device for recognizing that the utterance might be an indirect speech act. This requirement is satisfied by the fact that in the context, a question about the hearer's ability lacks any conversational point. The hearer, therefore, is led to seek an alternative meaning. Second, since the hearer knows the rules of speech acts, he knows that the ability to pass the salt is a preparatory condition on the speech act of requesting him to do so. Therefore, he is able to infer that the question about his ability is likely to be a polite request to perform the act. The differences and similarities between literal utterances, metaphorical utterances, ironical utterances, and indirect speech acts are illustrated in Figure 4.

The question of whether all metaphorical utterances can be given a literal paraphrase is one that must have a trivial answer. Interpreted one way, the answer is trivially yes; interpreted another way, it is trivially no. If we interpret the question as, "Is it possible to find or to invent an expression that will exactly express the intended metaphorical meaning R, in the sense of the truth conditions of R, for any metaphorical utterance of 'S is P,' where what is meant is that S is R?" the answer to that question must surely be yes. It follows trivially from the Principle of Expressibility (see Searle, 1969) that any meaning whatever can be given an exact expression in the language.

If the question is interpreted as meaning, "Does every existing language provide us exact devices for expressing literally whatever we wish to express in any given metaphor?" then the answer is obviously no. It is often the case that we use metaphor precisely because there is

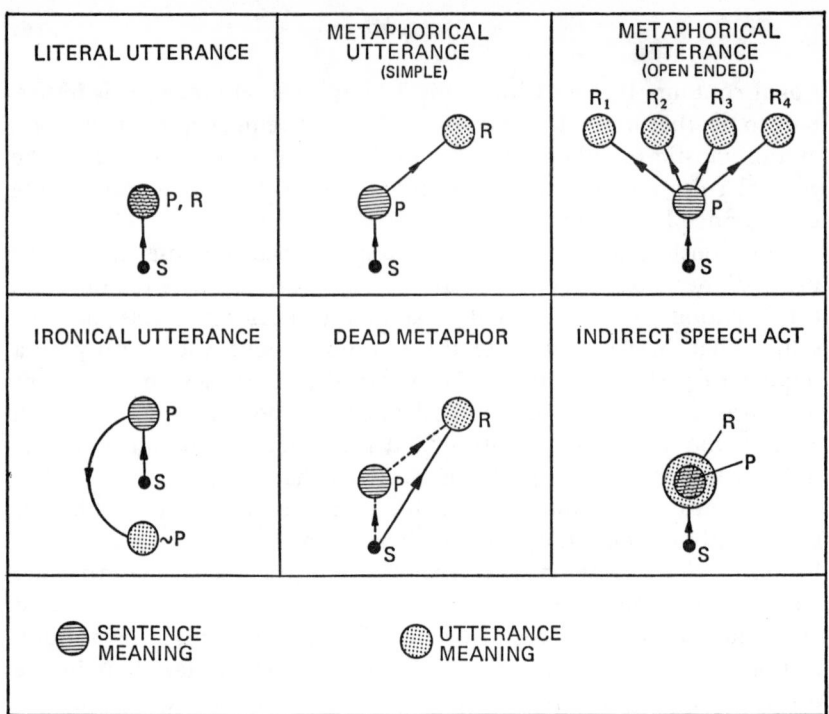

Figure 4. A graphical comparison of the relations between sentence meaning and utterance meaning where the sentence meaning is S is P and the utterance meaning is S is R, that is, where the speaker utters a sentence that means literally that the object S falls under the concept P, but where the speaker means by his utterance that the object S falls under the concept R.

   a. *Literal Utterance.* A speaker says S is P and he means S is P. Thus the speaker places object S under the concept P, where P = R. Sentence meaning and utterance meaning coincide.

   b. *Metaphorical Utterance (simple).* A speaker says S is P but means metaphorically that S is R. Utterance meaning is arrived at by going through literal sentence meaning.

   c. *Metaphorical Utterance (open ended).* A speaker says S is P, but means metaphorically an indefinite range of meanings, S is R_1, S is R_2, etc. As in the simple case, utterance meaning is arrived at by going through literal meaning.

   d. *Ironical Utterance.* A speaker means the opposite of what he says. Utterance meaning is arrived at by going through sentence meaning and then doubling back to the opposite of sentence meaning.

   e. *Dead Metaphor.* The original sentence meaning is bypassed and the sentence acquires a new literal meaning identical with the former metaphorical utterance meaning. This is a shift from the metaphorical utterance (simple), *b* above, to the literal utterance, diagram *a*.

   f. *Indirect Speech Act.* A speaker means what he says, but he means something more as well. Thus utterance meaning includes sentence meaning but extends beyond it.

no literal expression that expresses exactly what we mean. Furthermore, in metaphorical utterances, we do more than just state that S is R; as figure 4 shows, we state that S is R by way of going through the meaning of "S is P." It is in this sense that we feel that metaphors somehow are intrinsically not paraphrasable. They are not paraphrasable, because without using the metaphorical expression, we will not reproduce the semantic content which occurred in the hearer's comprehension of the utterance.

The best we can do in the paraphrase is reproduce the truth conditions of the metaphorical utterance, but the metaphorical utterance does more than just convey its truth conditions. It conveys its truth conditions by way of another semantic content, whose truth conditions are not part of the truth conditions of the utterance. The expressive power that we feel is part of good metaphors is largely a matter of two features. The hearer has to figure out what the speaker means – he has to contribute more to the communication than just passive uptake – and he has to do that by going through another and related semantic content from the one which is communicated. And that, I take it, is what Dr. Johnson meant when he said metaphor gives us two ideas for one.

NOTES

I am indebted to several people for helpful comments on earlier drafts of this article, and I especially want to thank Jerry Morgan, Andrew Ortony, Paul Rauber, and Dagmar Searle.

1 It is essential to avoid any use – mention confusions when talking about these sets. Sometimes we will be talking about the words, other times about meanings, other times about references and denotations, and still other times about truth conditions.

2 I follow Beardsley (1962) in this classification.

3 Even in Black's clarification (this volume) of interaction in terms of "implication-complexes" there still does not seem to be any precise statement of the principles on which interaction works. And the actual example he gives, "Marriage is a zero-sum game," looks distressingly like a comparison metaphor: "Metaphor is *like* a zero-sum game in that it is an adversary relationship between two parties in which one side can benefit only at the expense of the other." It is hard to see what the talk about interaction is supposed to add to this analysis.

4 By "literal simile," I mean literal statement of similarity. It is arguable that one should confine "simile" to nonliteral comparisons, but that is not the usage I follow here.

5 Furthermore, it is at least arguable that "block of ice" functions metonymously in this example.

Standard Approaches to Metaphor and a Proposal for Literary Metaphor

SAMUEL R. LEVIN

The stimulating and valuable part of Searle's paper stems from his adaptation of speech-act theory to the problem of metaphor. In particular, the prizing apart of "sentence meaning" and "utterance meaning" makes possible a motivated allocation of that portion of a metaphor's meaning that cannot be read off from the sentence in which it is expressed. In this respect, his treatment marks an advance over other accounts, which like his own, recognize that metaphor comprises meaning in excess of, or differing from, what can be deduced from its sentence vehicle, but which do not provide, as his does, a theoretical framework in which that excess or difference is given an appropriate rendering.

Despite this and other merits of his paper, however, I do not think that his account of metaphor is as superior to those that were previously available as Searle attempts to show. That he can propose his account as markedly superior results, I believe, from his adopting towards the received theories very strict standards of argument, while allowing for his own a much more liberal application of those standards. A good part of the difference that Searle sees between his account of metaphor and those in the received theories results simply from this inconsistency.

The comparison theory and the interaction theory

Two of the received theories of metaphor that Searle discusses are the *comparison* theory and the *interaction* theory. He introduces his discussion of these theories by the following observations:

Comparison theories assert that metaphorical utterances involve a *comparison* or *similarity* between two or more *objects,* and semantic interaction theories claim that metaphor involves a *verbal opposition* or *interaction* between two *semantic contents,* that of the expression used metaphorically, and that of the surrounding literal context. I think that both of these theories, if one tries to take them quite literally, are in various ways inadequate.

Searle argues against the comparison theory that it claims existence for the objects being compared and, inasmuch as existence is not a necessary requirement for successful metaphor, the claim is false. This strikes me as an arbitrary criticism. We should remember that for the implementation of Searle's theory a whole panoply of information – intentional, factual, and pragmatic – is required. Although these types of information are not as precisely defined and allocated in the theories that Searle criticizes as they are in his own, they are just as clearly operative. None of the theories that Searle criticizes would limit itself to objects per se or semantics proper. Thus the comparison theory does not require that it be objects pure and simple which enter into the comparison; the comparison may very well – and, in the event, probably will – involve properties. To understand "Bill is a gazelle" it is immaterial whether one has ever seen a gazelle. Of course, we know they exist. What is important, however, and what provides the basis for our understanding the utterance, is that we are aware that certain properties (including speed of foot) are commonly attributed to gazelles. In the same way, we understand "Sally is a dragon" because of certain properties commonly associated with dragons. If one wishes, one can argue that we cannot know anything about dragons, since there are none; we can only know the meaning of "dragon." That meaning, though, would have to include a heavy load of intentional and factual information if it were to explain how we interpret the utterance, at which point it becomes unclear what is gained in faulting the comparison theory for implying the existence of objects. The entailment of objects, we should notice, follows from the use in comparison theories of properties commonly associated with those objects. In most cases this entailment holds. But if we can dispose of properties – which are the operative factors – in the absence of objects, it does not seem to me that an unsatisfied entailment need be reckoned fatal to the theory.

   Alternatively, if it should be insisted that the entertainment of properties presupposes objects, and that therefore the comparison theory indeed is about objects, then just about any theory of metaphor would require as a necessary condition that one be able to quantify over its objects. In this case, however, Searle's criticism would lose all point, since it would then also apply to his own theory as well as to the interaction theory.[1]

   Concerning the semantic interaction theory, Searle objects first that "one of the assumptions behind the view that metaphorical meaning is a result of an interaction between an expression used metaphorically and other expressions used literally, is that all metaphorical uses of expressions must occur in sentences containing literal uses of expressions, and that assumption seems to me plainly false." He reasons that in place of "Sally is a block of ice," where "Sally" would be the literal context, one could "refer to Sally" as "the bad news." Thus the utterance, "The bad news is a block of ice" (in which neither noun phrase is used literally) would still be a metaphor (albeit mixed). Unless, however, "the bad news" had previously been predicated of "Sally," so that we *knew* that it referred to Sally, the utterance would strike us as nonsense, not even as a mixed metaphor. Similarly, that "quadruplicity drinks procrastination" can be given a metaphoric interpretation merely reflects the inventiveness of readers. On Searle's own account, it fails as a metaphor, inasmuch as it was no part of Russell's intention in writing it to have it understood metaphorically.

Searle's other objection to the semantic interaction theory is that "it is not in general the case that the metaphorical speaker's meaning is a result of any interaction among the elements of the sentence in any literal sense of 'interaction'." His argument here is not explicit, but it appears to be based on the Millean view that proper names have no meaning – they merely designate their referents. That would seem to be the point of claiming that "the same metaphorical predication" could be produced by "Sally," "Miss Jones," and "that girl over there in the corner" in the context of "is a block of ice," where, presumably, the three noun phrases refer to the same person. Now when Searle comes to set out his own account, he allows himself a much wider latitude where "semantics" is concerned; thus he includes factual knowledge, speakers' beliefs, associations, perceptions, attitudes, and so forth. Obviously, if this range of capabilities were to be applied in determining the signification of a proper name, the upshot would be more than simple reference to an individual. Thus, if provision is made for employment of all these capabilities in the interaction theory, Searle could not cite proper names as invalidating that theory. Conversely, if one were to disallow these capabilities to Searle's own account of metaphor, it would suffer the same handicap where proper names are concerned that he alleges against the interaction theory.

The semantic inadequacy that Searle attributes to the interaction theory in the preceding connection is curious in light of the description that he gives elsewhere of that theory. He says:

The proponents of the interaction view see correctly that the mental processes and the semantic processes involved in producing and understanding metaphorical utterances cannot involve references themselves, but must be at the level of intentionality, that is, they must involve relations at the level of beliefs, meanings, associations, and so on. However, they then say incorrectly that the relations in question must be some unexplained, but metaphorically described relations of "interaction" between a literal frame and a metaphorical focus.

If the proponents of the interaction view see correctly that the mental and semantic processes involved in producing and understanding metaphorical utterances must be at the level of intentionality, as Searle defines that notion, then those processes should not be thought to be suspended where proper names are concerned. As to Searle's claim that the relevant relations are relegated to some "unexplained, but metaphorically described, relations of 'interaction' between a literal frame and a metaphorical focus", I would propose as one quite literal and serviceable description of those relations the account given in Black (1962b).

To work up to his own account of metaphor, Searle goes on to examine a view "that goes back to Aristotle: . . . the theory that says all metaphor is really literal simile with the 'like' or 'as' deleted and the respect of the similarity left unspecified." For all practical purposes, this view and the comparison theory are one and the same (see Beardsley, 1967, p. 285). In any case, Searle goes on to say,

We understand the metaphor as a shortened version of the literal simile. Since literal simile requires no special extralinguistic knowledge for its comprehension, most of the knowledge necessary for the comprehension of metaphor is already contained in the speaker's and hearer's semantic competence. . . .

Concerning this approach, Searle argues that despite its attractiveness, it is ultimately inadequate, in that although it indicates that a similarity is supposed to obtain between the two terms of the simile, it provides no means that would enable us to ascertain what the similarity consists in. This is true. When Aristotle in the *Rhetoric* (III.4) writes:

When the poet says of Achilles: 'he rushed on like a lion', it is a simile; if he says, 'a lion, he rushed on', it is a metaphor: for because both are courageous, he transfers the sense and calls Achilles a lion,

he does not tell us by what means the attribute of courage is selected as the respect in which Achilles and a lion are similar.

Here one is reminded of the comparison which Chomsky has drawn between traditional and generative grammarians (Chomsky, 1964, p. 918). He points out that the goal of a traditional grammar is "(at least) as far-reaching as that of a generative grammar. . . ." He goes on to say, "However, it is important to bear in mind that even the most careful and complete traditional grammar relies in an essential way on the intuition and intelligence of the user, who is expected to draw the correct inferences from the many examples and hints . . . presented by the grammar." Aristotle's account of metaphor is in the spirit of the traditional grammàrians. What, however, about Searle's? Certainly, the enumeration of some half-dozen informally expressed principles on the basis of which the attributes ("the possible values of R") are selected does not approach the rigor and explicitness of a generative grammar. In drawing this analogy, I do not wish to be thought as downgrading Searle's accomplishment. I wish, rather, to suggest that the difference between Searle's theory and those he criticizes is essentially one of degree.

I would sum up my criticism of Searle's paper by saying that the theoretical framework that he provides, in which an explicit distinction is drawn between sentence meaning and utterance meaning, represents an advance in our understanding of how metaphor works. I would add, however, that the insights of the received theories are a good deal more consistent with those in his own account than Searle allows.

Directionality and construal mechanisms

A limitation of the comparison approach – one that applies as well to Searle's development of it – is that it treats metaphor in a one-sided fashion. According to this view, something is compared to some other thing in respect of that other thing's properties or characteristics. However, when the example used to illustrate the process is one in which the copula *be* introduces the predicate – and such are the examples one customarily uses on this view – the predilection is to assume that the object referred to by the subject term is being compared to the denotation of the predicate term. Even though implicit in these comparisons is the word "like," which we might expect to be symmetrical, the word order, and the topic – comment relationship imposed by it, more or less dictate that the subject be compared to the predicate and not the reverse. Especially is this true if the subject term is a proper noun. Thus, in "Bill is a wolf" or "Sally is a block of ice," one tends to think of the objects Bill and Sally as being modified through a comparison with the concepts of wolf and block of ice, respectively.[2] When our examples take this form, it is not likely that in our metaphoric interpretation we should modify our conception of wolves or blocks of ice in consequence of comparing these concepts with those of the individual Bill or Sally. As far as metaphor in general is concerned, however, it is just as possible for one term of the comparison to modify the other as it is for the reverse procedure to take place. The fact becomes clear when we introduce different grammatical forms of metaphor. Consider, for example,

(1a) The $\overleftarrow{\text{brook}}$ smiled

(1b) The $\overrightarrow{\text{brook}}$ smiled.

A priori (1) may be construed either with the concept of brook being modified or with the concept of smiling modified. In the former case (1a) we get an interpretation in which the brook, provided with certain human characteristics, smiled; in the latter case (1b) we get an interpretation in which the brook glistened or sparkled. In terms of comparison, we might say that in (1a) the brook is compared to the concept of smiling in the respect that smiling is an activity normally engaged in by humans. In (1b) we might say that the activity of smiling is compared to the concept of a brook in respect of the latter's being a liquid object. In (1a) the result is a personification of the brook; in (1b) it is a dispersonification of smiling.

From the preceding considerations, it appears that comparison suggests itself as a rationale for metaphor primarily on the basis of examples with copulative *be*. And with this type of example, it is almost compulsory to construe in one direction only. As examples like (1) show, however, many utterances allow for metaphoric construal in either direction. In such examples, moreover, it does not seem to be comparison that is the process actually at work in the construal. Comparison may figure as the basis on which the process of construal is carried out, but it itself cannot be that process. The process actually involved is one of transfer and amalgamation, where from the total range of elements associated with one term of the comparison, a subset is selected that is compatible or viable with elements of the other term. The process as described here is on a par theoretically with the interaction theory and with the second and third steps of Searle's own formulation. I believe, however, that it more accurately defines the actual mechanism of construal than does either of those ideas.

The amalgamation of elements may take a variety of forms. We see two of those forms in the construals that we have made of our example (1). In the construal according to (1a), the property of humanness, on being transferred from the concept of smiling, has been combined with our conception of a brook – with the result that we have a personification. The amalgamation here has taken the form, we might say, of fusion. In the construal according to (1b), liquidness – a property or attribute of brooks – on being transferred, has taken the place of the property corresponding to it in the concept of smiling, which would be that of humanness. Whatever "smiling" means, that meaning is modified to mean what "smiling" would mean if predicated of a liquid object. With this amalgamation as a basis, the interpretation of glistening or sparkling is arrived at. The amalgamation here has taken the form, we might say, of displacement.[3]

These amalgamation processes are not ad hoc; they are part of a store of such processes that are available a priori and from which selection is made in the construal of particular cases. Particular cases will, by their form and their context of utterance, more or less determine which amalgamative process should be applied for their proper construal; theoretically, however, any and all of those processes can be applied in an individual case. Thus, if in (1a) we had used displacement instead of fusion as the amalgamative process, the construal would have yielded an interpretation in which the brook would have had its liquidness displaced by humanness; the result would be not a personified brook, but a human being with certain characteristics of a brook, say a person who is cool, or clean, or active. In the same way, if in (1b) we had used fusion instead of displacement as the amalgamative process, the construal would have yielded not a "glistening brook" but a brook characterized by an appearance that was a cross between glistening and smiling.

The two latter interpretations offered above may seem strained and so call into question the claim that the amalgamative processes described earlier really are viable in the construal of metaphors. There is, however, empirical evidence for the a priori availability of these amalgamative processes; it takes the form of numerous dead metaphors, which at the time of their original construal must have implemented these very types of amalgamation. Thus, in the appropriate context, the word "wolf" in "Bill is a wolf" is interpreted as a human being with wolflike characteristics. To arrive at this interpretation the amalgamative process employed is that of displacement. If an utterance like "The wolf finally got married," should be produced in appropriate circumstances, the interpretation and amalgamative process would be the same – displacement. If fusion had been used instead of displacement, we should now have in such expressions personification of the wolf. If the utterance, "The wolf finally got married," should occur in a beast fable or children's story, on the other hand, we, in fact, would interpret the utterance in terms of personification, thus we would have amalgamated in terms of fusion.[4]

Among the dead metaphors in which the amalgamative process of displacement can be reconstructed are expressions in which "pig" means a person who is dirty or gluttonous, "ox" means a person who is strong or stubborn, and "rock" means a person who is firm or reliable.

Dead metaphors in which the process of fusion can be reconstructed may be observed in, "Justice is blind," "Time waits for no man," and similar expressions.

Other dead metaphors which similarly provide evidence for the viability of these and other amalgamative processes could be cited. It is in fact the case that inspection of dead metaphors will show that a fairly wide variety of amalgamative processes have been at work in the interpretation of metaphoric utterances. There is no reason to think that these processes do not continue to be productive.

A proposal for literary metaphor

Implicit in Searle's account of metaphor (and in other accounts as well) is the assumption that, given an incompatibility between the utterance and conditions in the world, the conditions are to be taken as fixed, and it is the utterance that must be construed. Now this is not a logically necessary position. We may, if we like, assume that, in the face of an incompatibility between what is asserted in an utterance and conditions as they obtain in the world, we regard the utterance as fixed and construe the world. Instead, that is, of construing the utterance so that it makes sense in the world, we construe the world so as to make sense of the utterance. On this account, "defectiveness" is located in the world (i.e., the actual world), not in the utterance. "Deviant" utterances are taken literally; they mean what they say – what gives is the world.

Employing this conception of metaphor, the states of affairs depicted by the linguistic expressions (taken at face value) have somehow to be rationalized. The depicted states of affairs will be incongruous, outlandish, or preternatural compared to the conditions that obtain in the actual world. They will than be "terrestrialized," i.e., construed against one's knowledge of the physical and empirical aspects of the actual world. This terrestrialization proceeds by way of phenomenalistic construal.[5] If in a poem a star is said to smile, we interpret that as a phenomenalistic metaphor for gleaming or sparkling; if the wind is said to whistle, we interpret that as a phenomenalistic metaphor for producing a high-pitched sound. Everything is reversed, as the following diagram (in which deviance is presupposed) shows: In the standard approaches to metaphor, the construal is linguistic; it involves the process represented in Figure 5 by the move around the northeast corner of the parallelogram. L_1 is taken as deviant, it is construed as L_2, and the latter is mapped onto the actual world, W_1. In my proposal, the construal is phenomenalistic; it involves the process represented in Figure 5 by the move around the southwest corner of the par-

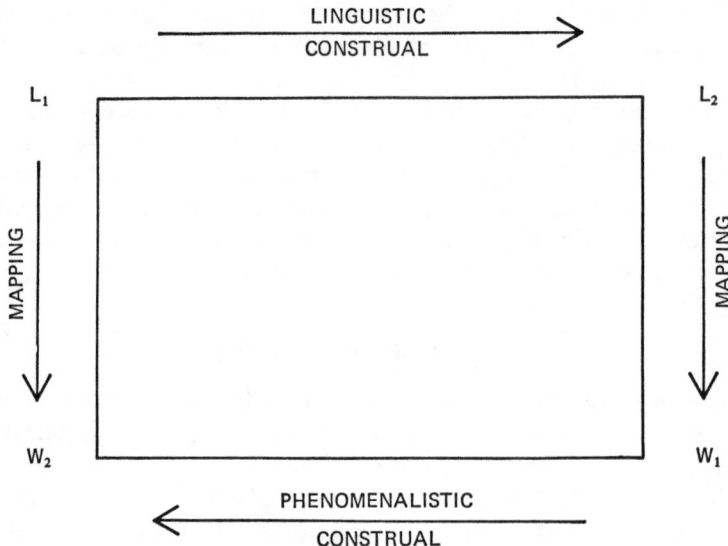

Figure 5. The two logics of metaphoric construal.

allelogram. L_1 is taken literally, it is mapped onto a possible world, W_2, then the conditions described in that world by L_1 are construed via an importation of facts as they are known to obtain in the actual world, W_1. The result of the construal process, in both cases, is an interpretation – of the language in the first case, of a world in the second.

For an account of metaphor in ordinary language, the foregoing proposal has little, if anything, to recommend it. If, however, our concern is with metaphor as it occurs in literary language, particualrly in lyric poetry, then the proposal, it seems to me, has certain merits. Before moving to a consideration of those merits, however, let us see what effect the proposal has when applied in an actual case. Consider the following poem by Emily Dickinson:

> The mountain sat upon the plain
> In his eternal chair,
> His observation omnifold,
> His inquest everywhere.
> The seasons prayed around his knees,
> Like children round a sire:
> Grandfather of the days is he,
> Of dawn the ancestor.

A standard type of interpretation might include observations like the following: In the first two lines the mountain's being located or situated in a certain place is expressed metaphorically by "sat . . . in his eternal chair"; that it rises higher than its surroundings is expressed metaphorically in lines 3 and 4; line 5, "the seasons prayed around his knees," is a metaphor for the mountain's steadfastness throughout the years; lines 7 and 8 contain metaphors for its extreme age. Assuming that the preceding observations adequately reflect a standard approach to metaphoric analysis, we would draw the inference that Emily Dickinson experienced a rather ordinary vision, or conception – that of a mountain's being high and old – and proceeded to make an interesting if unspectacular poem out of that conception by contriving to express it in an extraordinary arrangement of language.

If we invert the approach, we countenance a world in which the mountain has the properties attributed to him: he actually sits on an eternal chair; he looks everywhere; he has knees, around which the seasons pray; and so on. On this view it is not the language that is remarkable, it is the conception; given the conception, the linguistic description of it follows straightforwardly. On reading this description, however, we need to modulate the images described in the poem into such as make sense given our knowledge of facts in the actual world. We thus, by phenomenalistically construing the descriptions in the poem, return to a conception of the mountain as being situated in a certain place, as rising higher than its surroundings, as being very old, and so on.

I shall not attempt here to give any logical or formal arguments in support of my proposal for the way metaphor works in poetry. It seems to me, however, that a number of long-established critical canons concerning the role and function of poets and the nature of the poetic act are provided with some theoretical foundation by this proposal. Thus, poets have been characterized as "seers," poems as "worlds." Without some such conception of metaphor as that proposed in this paper, these characterizations – if they are not indeed mere rhetoric – are no more than metaphors themselves. If, however, we think of the images in a poem in terms of what the language literally represents, then it is consistent to regard the poet as a seer, a *vates*, a prophet, inspired, even somehow mad – all of which are functions or conditions that have traditionally been attributed to the poet. Moreover, the claim that the poet is a creator and the poem a world is also lent credence by the view of metaphor espoused here. If the language of the poem is taken literally, then the world depicted by it is indeed a creation. For that world is achieved not by some simple and uninteresting modification of the actually obtaining state of affairs, but rather by a radical and fundamental departure from that state. The result, we might say, is an "impossible" possible world. Such a world is not simply experienced; it is created.

I assume at the beginning of each lyric poem the following utterance, (I), to be implicit on the part of the poet: "I imagine (myself in) and invite you to conceive a world in which . . ." What has been said earlier in this section about the function of the poet and the nature of the poetic act is thus to be understood as following from the poet's being in a certain psychological state, that expressed by the verb "imagine." The reflexive pronoun in (I) reflects the fact that it is not the poet proper who describes the world represented in the poem, but a projection of himself or herself, a "persona."

The invitation addressed to the reader in (I) must be accepted for the poetic transaction to take place. Acceptance implies the "willing suspension of disbelief" asserted by Coleridge to be the condition of poetic faith. It presumes the literal interpretation of the language of the poem, which in turn entails phenomenalistic construal.

NOTES

1 I include the interaction theory here because, although in the first analysis it disposes of semantic and pragmatic elements, ultimately it associates those elements with properties (see e.g., Beardsley, 1962, p. 294).

2 In this section, there may appear to be an uncritical mingling of reference to objects and their properties with reference to concepts and conceptions. I do not think that any serious problem should be caused by this. In any event, the attempt to systematize the usage, to speak consistently in either ontological or epistemological terms — and to separate these from talk of meanings — would result in a needlessly pedantic exposition.

3 In the preceding discussion, I have referred to properties like "humanness" and "liquidness," properties which in a formal account would be expressed in terms of semantic markers. I wish to make it clear, however, that the features "humanness" and "liquidness," ranking high as they do on a scale of semantic "markerese," are used in this context chiefly for illustrative purposes. The fact is that in the process of amalgamation, the elements that may be called into play may include elements that are analytic of the objects and activities designated in the metaphor, that are synthetic with respect to those objects and activities, or that represent factual beliefs concerning those objects and activities; in short, a wide range of pragmatic, as well as semantic, factors may figure in the construal process.

4 The two interpretations above involving displacement, it should be noted, result from transfer in opposite directions — from the subject to the predicate in "Bill is a wolf," and from the predicate to the subject in "The wolf finally got married."

5 For some discussion of phenomenalistic construal, as well as for a fuller account of the view of metaphor proposed here, see Levin (1977), particularly Chapters 6 and 7.

An interesting passage that seems to imply phenomenalistic construal occurs in *Paradise Lost* (V. 563 – 76). After the angel Raphael has mentioned the fall of angels from heaven and the Adam has asked to be told more about it,
Raphael replies:

> High matter thou injoinst me, O prime of men,
> Sad task and hard, for how shall I relate
> To human sense th' invisible exploits
> Of warring Spirits; how without remorse
> The ruin of so many glorious once
> And perfet while they stood; how last unfould
> The secrets of another world, perhaps
> Not lawful to reveal? yet for thy good
> This is dispenc't, and what surmounts the reach
> Of human sense, I shall delineate so,
> By lik'ning spiritual to corporal forms,
> As may express them best, though what if Earth
> Be but the shaddow of Heav'n, and things therein
> Each to other like, more then on earth is thought?

When Raphael says that he will delineate what surmounts the reach of human sense by likening spiritual to corporal forms, he is undertaking to construe phenomena of a preternatural sort into a guise that will be familiar to Adam and then to describe the phenomena as they appear in the latter guise. The first part of this process is phenomenalistic construal.

The Milton passage was brought to my attention by Samuel Mintz in conversation.

Observations on the Pragmatics of Metaphor

JERRY L. MORGAN

Introduction

I am persuaded that the main points in Professor Searle's paper are correct, but there are a few arguments which leave me unsatisfied. I agree with his point that metaphor can only be understood by close attention to the distinction between "sentence meaning" and "utterance meaning," and that metaphor must be considered a case of the latter, not the former. But I find some aspects of his proposal for a proper treatment of metaphor tantalizingly vague or incomplete. In particular, it seems to me that his discussion of "call to mind" casts the net too wide, capturing some things that are not in the same boat as clear cases of metaphor. Moreover, there are some difficult leaps in his three-step analysis of metaphor, and I think that his proposal avoids dealing with an important question about its nature. I have a few other quibbles that I shall mention along the way, though I do not think they are a serious threat to Searle's analysis, with which, as I have said, I generally agree.

The proper domain of the analysis of metaphor

The distinction Searle makes between sentence meaning and utterance meaning is a crucial one, not only for metaphor, but for the study of meaning in general. The mistake of overlooking this distinction has constantly plagued work on meaning by linguists, and I think recognition of the importance of the distinction is a real advance.

Searle argues that metaphor is a matter of utterance meaning, hence a pragmatic problem, rather than a semantic one. This is a point worth dwelling on, because there have been proposals made for accounts of metaphor that could be construed as semantic treatments. For example, one well-known position on metaphor (Matthews, 1971) is that it always involves violation of "selection restrictions," rendering metaphor a kind of semantic deviance. At its simplest, this approach is no more than a putative method for detecting metaphors. It says nothing about how language users are able to make sense of supposedly deviant sentences. But a more serious objection is that this characterization of metaphor is just plain wrong, a point made forcefully by Reddy (1969), and Ortony, Schallert, Reynolds, and Antos (1978). Reddy points out that perfectly sensible sentences can be used metaphorically. He makes this point with some thoroughly convincing examples, including the following:

(1) He suspected that most of his listeners were sympathetic to the position that selection restrictions were totally inadequate. But he attacked the sputtering tyrant once again, if only to place his little penknife alongside the daggers of his companions. (p. 242)

And he observes that

(2) The rock is becoming brittle with age

could be used either literally or metaphorically; it could be used literally in the context of a group of people on a geology expedition, metaphorically in the context of a group of students walking out of the office of some staunch old professor emeritus (p. 242). So the theory that all metaphors are semantically anomalous in some way cannot stand.

Another approach to metaphor that could be construed as semantic is one involving a meaning change of some sort, wherein a "semantic feature" of some element in the sentence is changed, or some kind of operation results in a change in the meaning of the sentence. Searle rejects this approach out of hand, but I think it is worth a closer look, in part because it is a sidelight on the need for more precise language in discussion of metaphor.

There are a number of senses in which we might take the term "change in meaning" as a description of the interpretation of metaphor. I shall try to show that on close examination the only sense that makes sense is one that is indistinguishable from Searle's position.

First, I must sort out what one might mean by "meaning" in the phrase, "change of meaning." As far as I can see, there are only two possibilities. One might mean the meaning that is assigned to the sentence by the compositional rules of the language being used. But on this interpretation, metaphor as change of meaning is clearly incoherent. Taken literally, a claim that an instance of metaphor involves a change in meaning in this sense can only mean that the meaning is not what it used to be; either the original meaning has been replaced by a new meaning – the metaphorical one – or the new meaning has been added beside the old (literal) one. Any other construal of "change" would be metaphorical. Thus the claim that interpretation of metaphor involves a change in meaning would imply that by using a sentence metaphorically, one somehow changes the compositional rules of the language so that that sentence henceforth has a different, or an additional, literal meaning. Clearly this is not what is meant by the phrase "change of meaning" as applied to metaphor. While it is logically possible, I suppose, for there to be a language community so insane that the rules of the language are changed every time some speaker produces a metaphor, it seems to me that this is not in general the case. If I say, "John is a wall." meaning thereby to convey that he is immovable, the rules of English remain intact, including those that assign conventional meaning to the word "wall."

Then we might take "meaning" in another sense, that is, in the sense of Searle's speaker meaning – whatever it is that the speaker has in mind to convey by his utterance. But obviously this kind of meaning is not subject to change in the comprehension process. The speaker means whatever he means, something it makes no sense to speak of changing.

But there is a way to make sense of "changing" the sentence meaning. Namely, that starting with the literal meaning, one constructs a modified version that differs in some way from the original literal meaning. But this is not in any literal sense a "change" in sentence-meaning. It is no more accurate to call this process "change in meaning" than it is to say that constructing a slightly modified version of the Louvre in Peoria constitutes a "change" in the Louvre. The case of metaphor is parallel. There is no sense in which meaning is, strictly speaking, changed. Rather, one starts with a meaning, then performs some operation that produces a second thing that could be called a meaning, which is related in some way to the first meaning. We have as a result two different meanings, one in some way derivative of the other, but it is not accurate to say that anything has been changed.

The next question is, What sort of operation is it that is involved in this so-called change? Searle proposes that it is a matter of utterance meaning, of figuring out by inference in context what the speaker intends to convey by saying what he says. But an advocate of a semantic treatment of metaphor might reply that the involvement of inference and context is not sufficient grounds for concluding that the matter is pragmatic. For inference and context are also involved in matters of literal meaning – in resolving ambiguity, for example. If I say to somebody, "The chicken is ready to eat," one could plausibly argue that the hearer must use knowledge of context, rules of conversation, and so forth, to infer which of the two literal meanings of the sentence I intended to convey. Just so with metaphor: there are two meanings, a literal one and a metaphoric one, and the hearer is required to infer which one was intended. Then metaphor is no different from any other kind of duality of meaning.

But, in fact, there is an important difference. In the case of ambiguity, the relation between the two meanings is a coincidence of the language, so that the same two meanings might well be translated into separate sentences in another language. But in the case of metaphor one of the meanings is derivative in some way from the other. If I say, "John is a wall," the metaphorical reading is not a coincidental second meaning, but *derivative* of the literal meaning. Moreover, the number of metaphorical readings a sentence can have is not some small number (as in the case of multiple literal meanings), but an open set. "John is a wall" can have any number of metaphorical interpretations, depending on context – whether it is said, for example, by a teacher about a student, by a football coach about an offensive lineman, by anybody about a fat person, and so on. Furthermore, the process by which the metaphorical interpretation is derived from the literal meaning, whatever that process is, cannot be just some kind of formal linguistic operation on literal meaning, because as Searle points out, metaphor can be based not only on properties involved in literal meaning, but on associations, myths, and things we happen to know about the things referred to in the literal meaning. It is not really from the literal meaning that the metaphor is calculated, but from a complete understanding, an enriched sort of meaning with all the pragmatic gaps filled in. This is most clearly demonstrated by the fact that one can make metaphors indirectly, by using a nonmetaphorical sentence to conversationally implicate something that can only be understood as metaphor, as in something like

(3) A: How can I make John feel at home?
    B: Buy him some Purina Hog Chow,

an example of an indirect conveyance of a frozen metaphor. Or, if asked about John's level of enthusiasm, I might say the following literally impeccable sentence:

(4) Somebody should set a match to him on the Fourth of July,

meaning thereby to convey indirectly that John is a firecracker, itself a metaphor.

My claim is, then, that when the phrase "change of meaning" is closely examined, it turns out to make no sense if taken literally; and if one seeks for the spirit of the phrase by taking it metaphorically, then it leads to the same conclusions Searle reaches in his paper – that metaphor is a matter of utterance meaning, and that the proper domain for an account of metaphor is pragmatics, not semantics. Moreover, I think talking of metaphor as a kind of meaning is a mistake itself, in that it naturally leads to thinking of metaphor as a property

of sentences. But I think it is not a property of the sentence, but a
matter of what one *does* in saying the sentence. To make clearer what
I mean, let me compare metaphors with indirect speech acts. Although
I do not mean to say that metaphor is just another kind of indirect
speech act, there is an important similarity.

   If I say to someone who is sitting on my hat,

   (5) You're sitting on my hat,

as an indirect way of getting him off it, it is not my *sentence* that
informs him that I wish he would get off my hat, but what I have *done*
by saying the sentence. I have informed my interlocutor that he is sitting on my hat. If I could inform him in some nonlinguistic manner,
the effect would be the same. It is clear to him that I want him to
know he is sitting on my hat, for why else would I say it? Then for
what purpose would I want him to know it? My purpose is obvious,
given the right context. My interlocutor will infer that my reason for
informing him was that if he were aware of his position, he would
change it. Moreover, he would rightfully infer that it was my intention
that he make this inference from my informing him. Now, clearly it is
a grave mistake to try to attach this hint to the meaning of the sentence. It is an inference one might reasonably make about what I
intend in *doing* what I do, informing being just one of those things
one can do by linguistic means. So a proper treatment of this kind of
indirect meaning belongs not in a theory of sentence meanings, but in
a theory of acts, in particular in that subpart of a theory of acts that
deals with the special case of communicative acts. Just so with metaphor. I think Black (this volume) puts his finger on an important
point in saying that when Stevens writes, "A poem is a pheasant," he
means not that a poem is *like* a pheasant, but that it *is* a pheasant.
One might draw the same conclusion from the fact that (6) could be
used metaphorically:

   (6) John's not just *like* a tree, he *is* a tree.

If I am right that it can be used metaphorically, then it would appear
that no simple simile theory can deal with this case, since it asserts the
metaphor but denies the simile. Metaphors are *not* just grammatical
variants of similes. When one says

   (7) John's mind is a meadow in winter,

one takes a position on the truth of this very sentence, just as one
always does in asserting. And it is by so *doing* that metaphor is conveyed, not by the sentence as a semantic object. The hearer does not
just carry out some operation on the semantics of the sentence; he
must picture what the world would be like if the sentence were true, or
he could never know that I do not mean to be taken literally. Then he
must figure out what the world could be like to lead me to make such

an outrageously false assertion. He constructs a picture of the world that is as close as relevantly and sensibly possible to the world that corresponds to the literal meaning of the sentence.

I suppose that the interpretation of metaphor I am arguing for is one of overstatement. But clearly there is more to it than that. The interpretation of metaphor is not, as one might conclude, just a matter of getting rid of it, by turning it back into literal meaning; it is not just literal meaning in disguise.

Some criticisms of Searle

First, some minor criticisms concerning Searle's arguments against simile theory. To begin with, I think it is necessary to make a distinction between clear cases of metaphor and cases that have become conventional in one way or another, yet are not idioms. A clear case of metaphor is one not previously encountered, which one must really figure out. The second kind, which I shall call a "stored metaphor," just to have a way of talking about it, is a metaphor with which everybody is familiar, on its way to becoming an idiom, but still, in fact, understood figuratively. Several of Searle's examples are clearly of this kind. On being told, for example, that one is a pig, one does not greet it as a new metaphoric problem, to be figured out afresh via Searle's rules. One already has the knowledge that the phrase is used metaphorically to say something about personal habits, and recalls this information immediately. Recognizing the phrase, one knows immediately what is intended. It is an institutionalized metaphor, and knowledge that the phrase "a pig" is used this way short circuits the process of figuring out the metaphor from literal meaning (for a discussion of "short-circuited" indirect speech acts, see Morgan, 1978). Surely, it is obvious that one does not process, "John is a pig," in the same way that one processes, "John is a kangaroo." One knows immediately what is meant in the former case; the latter takes a little figuring. These stored metaphors are different from fresh metaphors in that they are *not* processed by first trying to make sense of the literal meaning, then, failing, trying to construe it as a figure of speech. This can be seen in that in a context where both the literal and the figurative senses are appropriate, the effect is of a pun. For example, if a lamp fetishist had a special passion for a certain lamp and kept it lit constantly, he could say,

(8) This lamp is the light of my life,

and have it work as a pun (albeit a feeble one). Or one could say of the comic-book character, the Flame, that he is a "ball of fire," and achieve the same punlike effect. Now, if the figurative sense were calculated only as a default reading when the literal reading was rejected, we should expect such puns to be impossible. The figurative reading would never be reached, since the literal one is sensible and relevant. This is, in fact, the case with genuine metaphor: Trying to make such puns with a fresh metaphor does not work. If one said

(9) The King Tut exhibit is a pharaoh's burial treasure,

intending to convey that the exhibit was worth a lot of money, there is little chance that the metaphor would be conveyed, since the literal meaning makes sense and is in fact true. On the other hand,

(10) John's bank account is a pharaoh's burial treasure,

is more likely to work as metaphor, because the literal reading is likely to be rejected.

The upshot of this is that some apparent metaphors are fresh and must be calculated or figured out, others are stored, labeled as figures of speech, a kind of instant metaphor – just add water and stir – and are recognized as such and understood immediately, probably because of some look-up strategy like, "Try the largest chunk first." This class of institutionalized metaphors, which I call "stored metaphors," is quite different from the class of fresh metaphors – and therefore dubious as a test case for an understanding of metaphor – if I am right in assuming that it is fresh metaphor that is the central problem for a theory of metaphor, with stored metaphor to be treated derivatively. And I think at least some of Searle's examples are of this kind. If so, they are not useful ammunition in an attack on a simile theory of metaphor.

In fact, as Searle himself acknowledges, some of them might not even be metaphors at all, but idioms, such that the expression is now truly ambiguous, assigned two *literal* meanings by the rules of English. And an odd kind of nonliteral use (I hesitate to call it metaphor) can be built on idioms. For example, it is clear that the phrase, "kick the bucket," is an idiom, having as a second literal meaning the meaning of "die," so that

(11) John kicked the bucket

is truly ambiguous. Speakers can exploit this special kind of ambiguity in a creative way, as in,

(12) When John kicked the bucket, he knocked it into the next county

used to describe a particularly spectacular death; likewise,

(13) John put his foot in his mouth and most of his leg as well,

used to convey that John really said the wrong thing, or similar word-play on ambiguity like

(14) I'm so low I have to look up to tie my shoelaces.

One might propose, then, that the word "cold" is a kind of idiom for having "unresponsive," and similar attributes, as a second literal meaning, and that, "Sally is a block of ice," is an exploitation of this ambiguity, in a way similar to the examples above.

Finally, another way to save simile theory from Searle's claim that "Sally is a block of ice" has no meaning as a literal simile is to deny his premise that there is no similarity between cold things and unresponsive people. In fact, some of his later examples indirectly raise this possibility for escape. It is clear that metaphor can be built on *mythical* similarities that everybody knows are not really true. Searle cites the case of gorillas and their image; concerning owls there is a shared myth that they are wise. Foxes are clever, snakes sneaky, and so on. Metaphors, or at least stored metaphors, can be built on such myths, inasmuch as everybody knows that everybody knows the myths, even though everybody knows, further, that nobody *believes* the myths. One might propose, then, the "cold" is such a myth – that there is a shared myth that unresponsive people are cold, and that metaphor or figures of speech can exploit that myth, even though nobody really believes the myth is literally true.

It seems to me that these various possibilities for reinterpreting Searle's examples weaken his case against simile theory, insofar as his case depends on those examples.

As an aside, I should say that I do not share Searle's confidence about the cross-cultural validity of his examples. Figurative usage differs cross-culturally according to differences in shared beliefs, including the sort of myth that I have discussed. In fact, it seems to me to follow from Searle's point that metaphor can be constructed on myths, that we should find cross-cultural differences in metaphor corresponding to differences in such connotations and myths. Out of curiosity, I checked with some friends from abroad on the figurative uses of Searle's examples and a few others. The consultants were Nepali, Arab, and Chinese. I checked for figurative use of "blue," "yellow," "green," "cold," "warm," "square," "bad news," "sunset," "dawn," "moon," "sun," "wolf," "pig," "fox," and "dirt." I found as many differences as similarities. None accepted "warm" as a figurative counterpart of "cold." I was told that in Arabic, there are two words for "cold," only one of which has Searle's figurative use. One could conclude from this that one has to *learn* that "warm" is used figuratively to mean friendly, responsive, and so on.

Regarding Searle's proposal, my most serious complaint is not that it is wrong, but that it leaves some important questions unanswered. The first of these has to do with the nature of metaphor. In Searle's schema, if literal meaning is found to violate rules of conversation – by being nonsensical, obviously false, or merely irrelevant – the next step is to infer that a metaphor (or one of a few other things) is intended.

One can see how to get part way to this inference. If the sentence meaning is deviant, and the speaker is rational, then the speaker cannot intend (just) the sentence meaning. Then, assuming that the speaker means to convey anything at all, it must be different from sentence meaning. But if the speaker is rational, then there was some purpose in uttering the sentence he did. Therefore, there must be some connection between the meaning of the sentence and the meaning the speaker intends to convey.

This far one can get. But it is not clear how to get to the inferred conclusion that the connection of sentence meaning to speaker meaning is a metaphoric one. Is this a natural inference that could be made by any reasoning being? Or does it depend on prior knowledge that there is such a thing as metaphor that people use occasionally for certain purposes? If some rational being from another galaxy could be imbued with a grammar of English and enough knowledge of the world to get along, but no exposure to either the concept of metaphor or any example of metaphor, would he instantly recognize a metaphor for what it was the first time he encountered one? Or would he have to be told, or learn by example, what a metaphor is and its rules and purpose? Is metaphor a natural function of the mind, or a concept that must be learned? This is an empirical question, but I speculate that metaphor is a natural function of the mind.

The second step, the method of determining the possible (set of) properties that are being metaphorically predicated, Searle characterizes with the phrase, "call to mind," and gives a taxonomy of subcases, remarking that there are surely more subtypes. The question here is, Is it possible to replace this list with one or two generalizations from which the list can be derived as a consequence, or are we stuck with an arbitrary list of unknown length? The phrase, "call to mind," is surely too general. First of all, and obviously, there must be some condition to the effect that the thing "called to mind" was intended by the speaker. This avoids labeling as metaphor all sorts of random, private associations in the hearer's mind that the speaker does not intend to provoke, and may not even know about. I think this kind of condition is implicit in Searle's schema.

Second, there are things that are intuitively different from metaphor, though perhaps a subtype of figurative speech, that could be characterized as calling to mind a second meaning, due to rejection of the literal meaning. But before I give an example of this kind, I must establish that there are cases where an entire sentence is used metaphorically, without any particular part of the sentence corresponding to any particular part of what is metaphorically described. For example, if somebody is asked about the status of his tenure case and replies with (15) or (16),

(15) The sky is darkening

(16) It's clouding up,

there is no particular thing "the sky" or "it" refers to; the whole sentence serves as a metaphor, and somehow calls to mind an unpleasant state of affairs that can be applied to his tenure case. Now to the troublesome case. What is there that sets cases like (15) and (16) apart from cases like (17):

(17) Q: How do you like the soufflé?

A: On the whole, I'd rather be in Philadelphia.

Given the right set of beliefs, one can convey by saying the latter sentence that the soufflé is as bad as death. The inference that this is the intended meaning rests on knowledge that it is said (and it does not matter whether it is true or not) that this sentence is the epitaph on W. C. Fields' headstone. The intended meaning there, of course, is, "better in Philadelphia than dead." If the hearer knows this story, the response will call to mind what Fields supposedly meant by it, and by inferential steps I will not go into, the hearer will infer that a parallelism is intended wherein the soufflé is like death. Perhaps this kind of thing ought to be included in the general category of metaphor. I am not sure how to decide whether it should or not, save by arbitrary definition. At any rate, it is clearly different from, "Juliet is the sun."

Some further indications that "call to mind" is too general: My wife's most vivid memory of a certain village in the Balkans (I shall call it Pazari, though that is not its name) is of a certain official who was an obnoxious sexist. Any mention of Pazari immediately calls to mind this unpleasant man. Knowing this, why can I not, when speaking to my wife, use (18)

(18) John is Pazari,

to convey metaphorically that John is an obnoxious sexist? Or again, everybody who knows my father knows that he is a machinist; it is an important part of his life, and a salient property for people who know him. But I cannot imagine any circumstances under which (19)

(19) John is my father,

could be used to convey metaphorically to anybody that John is a machinist.

In the same way, Searle's inclusion of metonymy and synecdoche lets in some things that seem intuitively to deserve separate status. If "call to mind" includes the part – whole, container – contained, clothing – wearer, and similar associational relationships, then the following, consistency dictates, all qualify as metaphors:

(20) The kettle is boiling (i.e., its contents)

(21) IBM dropped 30 points (i.e., its stock)

(22) Read Chapter 3 of Chomsky for tomorrow (i.e., the book he wrote)

(23) Turn on the fish (i.e., the burner of the stove on which the pan containing the fish is located, in order to cook the fish).

It is not clear to me what senses of the word "Washington" are literal, but I suspect at least two of the following four sentences would probably count as metaphor in Searle's system:

(24) Washington covers a lot of land (that is, the physical structure, or the abstract plot of land)

(25) Washington elected a new mayor (that is, the people who live there)

(26) Washington rejected the Albanian proposal (that is, the executives of the government whose capitol is there)

(27) Washington was founded in 1942 (that is, the abstract legal entity).

These strike me as unlike central cases of metaphor in being prosaic and unexciting, lacking the quasi-magical properties one usually thinks of metaphor as having. The difference is not merely the difference between predicating and referring expressions; one can get the central kind of metaphor in referring expressions as well, as in (28) and (29).

(28) My tender rosebud has left me

(29) The brightest star in my sky has run off with the milkman.

The difference between these and (20),

(20) The kettle is boiling,

resides in the *purpose* of choosing an expression that refers only indirectly to the object in question. The reason for choosing "the kettle" to refer to the contents of the kettle is mere convenience, as far as I can see. It serves to call to mind for the hearer the intended referent, and that is all there is to it. But in the other example, there is a purpose beyond this – to inform or remind the hearer, by choice of referring expression, of the emotional role and importance of the referent.

This relates to my final point of the "call to mind" relation: It seems to me that the most common type of "call to mind" connection in metaphors of the street, that is, in ordinary conversation, have a common property: The salient properties involved in the metaphor tend to be those with "affective" value (in the sense of Osgood et al., 1957); that is, some emotional or evaluative aspect. This relates, no doubt, to an important question that goes unanswered in Searle's system: What is the purpose of metaphor? Why does a speaker choose to use metaphor at all, instead of literal language? Searle apparently assumes that the fundamental questions of metaphor can be dealt with and understood without worrying about its purpose. I am suspicious of this assumption. In the case of indirect speech acts, the usual purpose of indirectness is just that: indirectness. The hearer's observation that the speaker is choosing to do things indirectly has important consequences for matters of politeness and other aspects of social interaction. To overlook this fact is to miss a potential source of explanation of difficult facts. For example, taking into account the purpose of indirectness provides a potential explanation for the fact that the oddness of preverbal "please" increases with indirectness: Preverbal "please" is a fairly direct indication of a request; thus to put it in a sentence intended to convey a request very indirectly is self-defeating, hence strange, as in

(30) *I wonder if anybody's going to please bring me a drink.

The answer to the question of the purpose of metaphor is surely not a simple one. It is not indirectness in the same sense as in indirect speech acts. And it is not mere convenience, a lazy inclination to use metaphor because an equally effective literal utterance would be too much work. Surely its purpose is more than the enjoyment of puzzle solving. There is something special about metaphor and its purpose that goes beyond the purpose of other kinds of indirect speech. The picture of metaphor one often gets, as I mentioned earlier, is of something to be eliminated as quickly as possible, to get down to the literal meaning that the metaphor covers up. If this were all there were to it, then the real question about metaphor would be, "Why bother?" Until we get at the question of why metaphor is used, I doubt that we will ever understand what it is.

METAPHOR
AND
PSYCHOLOGY

Psychological Processes in the Comprehension of Metaphor

ALLAN PAIVIO

For the student of language and thought, metaphor is a solar eclipse. It hides the object of study and at the same time reveals some of its most salient and interesting characteristics when viewed through the right telescope. The object is linguistic meaning. Metaphor obscures its literal and commonplace aspects while permitting a new and subtle understanding to emerge. Thus, metaphor highlights the phenomenon of semantic creativity, the capacity of language users to create and understand novel linguistic combinations that may be literal nonsense. An advertisement that urges you to, "Put a tiger in your tank," is anomalous semantically but not in what it symbolizes for the driver who likes to take off with a roar. Of course, everyone knows that most metaphors are not newly created by their users, but all were once novel and new ones arise constantly even in the most commonplace of conversations. Thus, semantic productivity must be regarded as a salient design feature of metaphorical language, just as syntactic productivity is of language in general, despite the repetitiousness of specific grammatical constructions in everyday speech. However, we know even less about the psychology of semantic creativity than we do about syntactic creativity, and the former must be counted among the most challenging theoretical problems that confront those who are interested in a scientific understanding of language behavior.

The degree of semantic creativity in metaphorical language, and the problem it poses for language theory, have been emphasized recently by a number of psychologists (e.g., Anderson & Ortony, 1975; Bransford & McCarrell, 1975; Honeck, Riechmann, & Hoffman, 1975; Olson, 1970). Honeck et al. (1975), using proverbs to study the problem, found that conceptually related interpretations and stories were judged to be highly relevant to target proverbs and also served as effective prompts for the recall of the latter in a memory task. For example, "Your actions are bound to be accounted for eventually," was the relevant prompt for the proverb, "In due time, the fox is brought to the furrier." The authors emphasized that the interpretations did not share any major vocabulary, phrase structure, or propositional structure with the corresponding proverbs. Thus, they concluded that no existing theory adequately describes the semantic relationship between a proverb and its interpretations. Similar arguments have been made by Anderson and Ortony (1975) in regard to the general problem of polysemy in language comprehension which, they argue, requires a theory that provides for the construction of a novel particularized representation that integrates the disparate elements of linguistic expressions and does so in an infinitely productive way. Most contemporary and traditional approaches to linguistic semantics, and to semantic memory, lack the necessary flexibility and integrative power, or so it is claimed by those who adopt the constructivist approach. Be that as it may, most theorists would at least agree that the apparent creativity involved in the use of metaphor poses a major conceptual challenge for students of language, regardless of their theoretical preferences.

While not pretending to solve the problem to the complete satisfaction of anyone, I hope to show that some of the theoretical ideas and research findings arising from recent studies of memory and cognition have direct relevance for the student of metaphor, providing both clarification and testable hypotheses concerning the comprehension of metaphor.

I discuss, first, the psychological issues associated with metaphorical behavior. Second, I review some traditional and recent psychological approaches to those issues, including an analysis based on relevant aspects of a general theoretical approach to language and thought, which I have previously discussed briefly in relation to the problem of metaphor (Paivio, 1971, Chap. 13). In what follows, I shall sometimes use the term "metaphor" to refer to metaphorical or figurative expressions in general, but the paradigm case will be the similarity metaphor in which *topic* and *vehicle* are the key terms. Thus, in my introductory expression, "Metaphor is a solar eclipse," the topic is "metaphor" and the vehicle is "solar eclipse." Whatever it is that they have in common that permits a figurative interpretation is the *ground*.

Psychological problems related to metaphor

Metaphorical behavior includes both motivational and cognitive aspects. One motivational issue concerns the reasons for the creation of metaphorical expressions: Why do they arise at all in communication? Ortony (1975) has discussed the problem in terms of a general assumption and three hypotheses related to it. The general assumption is that metaphor fulfills the necessary communication function of conveying continuous experiential information, using a discrete symbol system. The three hypotheses pertain to the way in which metaphor fulfills this general function. One hypothesis is that a metaphor provides a compact way of representing the subset of cognitive and perceptual features that are salient to it. A metaphor allows large "chunks" of information to be converted or transferred from the vehicle to the topic. The second is the "inexpressibility" hypothesis, which states that a metaphor enables us to talk about experiences which cannot be literally described. The third is the hypothesis that, perhaps through imagery, metaphor provides a vivid and, therefore, memorable and emotion-arousing representation of perceived experience. These functions obviously implicate cognitive processes, but they are intended to explain what motivates the use of metaphor in communication.

The other side of the motivational issue has to do with the effect of incongruity and novelty on the hearer. C. Anderson (1964) discussed the effects of metaphorical novelty in terms of Berlyne's (1960) theory of arousal induction and reduction: The incongruity of metaphor induces arousal, which the person seeks to reduce by means of a "conceptual resolution" of the disparate elements. The motivational basis of metaphorical expression has been of particular interest to psychoanalysts as well as students of poetry (see Billow, 1977). Such views have received almost no direct research attention by psychologists interested in metaphor. Moreover, they have not clarified the cognitive problem of the comprehension of metaphor, and I shall not pursue them further in this paper.

The comprehension of metaphor is basically a cognitive problem which centers around the following question: How does a novel conceptual entity arise from apparently disparate parts? It is central in regard to production, as well as comprehension, of metaphor; for the creator of the metaphor must first grasp the significance of a metaphorical relation before it is uttered. The problem as stated entails the concepts of *similarity, relation*, and *integration*, as well as the idea of novelty. Similarity and relation are implied in definitions of metaphor. According to one definition, linguistic metaphor involves "the application of a word or expression that properly belongs to one context to express meaning in a different context because of some real or implied similarity in the reference involved (C. Anderson, 1964, p. 53)." The basis of similarity may lie in shared attributes of some kind, as in referring to a submissive person as a "sheep." Or it may involve relational similarity, as in the proportional metaphor in which four or more elements of a sentence are related proportionately (Billow, 1977, p. 82). So, the injunction to, "Put a tiger in your tank," which a well-known gasoline company used a few years ago, could be analyzed as a proportionate metaphor which implies that a certain gasoline is to a car as power is to a tiger.

The centrality of the concepts of similarity and relation is particularly interesting because both are old and thorny conceptual problems in psychology. Similarity has always played a key role in the analysis of generalization, transfer of training, and forgetting in tasks ranging from motor performance to paired associate learning of nonsense syllables (see, for example, Osgood, 1953). The basis of similarity, however, continues to be a theoretical puzzle. An operational definition seems straightforward in the case of formal similarity, which can be defined in terms of the number of identical elements shared by two stimuli, although the concept of identical elements itself was highly controversial in the early debates concerning transfer of training. The analysis of meaning similarity is even more difficult, particularly in regard to the nature of the common elements. It became necessary to invoke such concepts as "functional equivalence," "response similarity," and "mediated similarity," all of which also led to conceptual problems in their own right. These problems are further accentuated in the case of metaphor, which involves a particularly subtle form (or forms) of semantic similarity. They have rarely been raised, let alone solved, in that context. Osgood (1953) represents a notable exception to this generalization, for he was an early contributor to the theoretical interpretation of mediated similarity as well as metaphor. More recently, Tversky (1977) has proposed a weighted feature-matching approach to similarity, which appears to solve some of the classical problems, generates novel predictions, and has testable implications for metaphor (e.g., see Ortony's discussion of the present paper in this volume).

The concept of relation has been historically prominent in perceptual psychology, particularly in the context of the "transposition problem" (Reese, 1968), where the debate turned on the degree to which an organism will respond to relations as compared to absolute stimulus quantities. Gestalt psychologists championed the view that relational responding usually predominates. The gestalt view is particularly relevant to the assumption that the comprehension of metaphor involves a special kind of relational perception or response (cf. Verbrugge & McCarrell, 1977).

The concept of relation is also implicated in another key term, integration, because relational perception is often interpreted as involving the perception of a new entity, which is distinct from the related elements considered separately. This conceptualization extends directly to metaphor, where, according to one writer, "The two (or more) ideas of the metaphor work together to produce a new concept for which there may be no other expression (Billow, 1977, p. 82)."

All of these concepts – similarity, relation, and novel integration – are implicated in the various psychological approaches to metaphor, to which I now turn.

Psychological approaches to metaphor

All psychological studies of metaphor involve *mediational approaches*, in the sense that they are concerned with processes that mediate the similarity, relational, and integrative reactions involved in the comprehension of metaphor. Contemporary cognitive psychologists would interpret such processes primarily in terms of structural and functional characteristics of long-term or *semantic memory*. Skinner's (1957) analysis is an apparent exception, since he rejects mediational and cognitive terminology. Nonetheless, close examination suggests that he, too, must assume mediational responses to explain metaphorical extension.

The Skinnerian interpretation is based on the idea of generalization of verbal responses to properties of stimuli that happen to be present along with the salient discriminative stimuli when the responses were originally reinforced. The following examples can be used to illustrate how some common figurative expressions may have arisen by such a mechanism (Winokur, 1976, pp. 57ff.). The verbal response "eye" would be reinforced in the presence of a stimulus cluster which includes, in addition to an eye, a "person," together with such properties as "recessed," "oval," "near the top," "part," "surrounded by flesh," and "contains fluid." Later, some of the parts occur as part of another whole, and the verbal response will also tend to occur. A needle, for example, would include the parts "recessed," "oval," "near top," and "part," hence the metaphorical verbal response, "eye of needle." This approach implies quite a different interpretation of the novelty of metaphorical behavior than is the case in more traditional analyses. The response is not *created* by the speaker, it is simply *controlled* by stimuli through the mechanism of generalization.

The analysis apparently does not depend on any elaborate mediating process, unless one seeks explanations for generalization itself and inquires into the nature of the identity of the "parts" in two very dissimilar wholes. Other examples more obviously call for mediational constructs. For example, Skinner's analysis of, "Juliet is the sun," is explicitly couched in terms of a common mediating reaction. Thus, "The metaphorical extension might have been mediated by, say, an emotional response which both the sun and Juliet evoked in [Romeo] (1957, p. 97)."

Contemporary memory theorists would analyze comprehension of metaphor primarily as a problem of long-term, or semantic, memory (for example, Kintsch, 1972). This is implicit in the idea that metaphor is a problem of meaning, which is based on long-term memory information associated with the terms of the metaphor. Comprehension accordingly involves the retrieval of such information from long-term memory. The nature and organizational structure of the information is crucial to the analysis of metaphor, because that structure will determine what attributes of the topic and vehicle will be likely to enter into, or mediate, the metaphorical relationship, given that there is access to those attributes by appropriate retrieval cues.

Different theories assume different mediating structures. Traditional verbal associative theory assumes that the relation is mediated by the structure of verbal associations. Imagery-based theories might stress the structural similarities in perceptual memories. Other theories stress overlap in abstract semantic representations, which may be organized into networks or hierarchies. Each class of theory asserts or implies that the click of comprehension of a metaphor depends on some kind of structural match in regard to the information activated by the linguistic metaphor, or the construction of some new, relational entity from such information.

But comprehension also involves "episodic memory," a term introduced by Tulving (1972) to refer to memories of specific, dated events, such as a particular list of words that one is required to memorize in a laboratory experiment. In the case of metaphor comprehension, one's episodic memory for the metaphorical expression, and the linguistic context in which it was uttered, must be taken into account along with extralinguistic factors. The linguistic context includes the ongoing topic of conversation. The extralinguistic context includes the general communicational setting and the persons involved in the exchange. All of these situational stimuli will determine precisely what semantic memory information is relevant to the interpretation of the metaphor. In brief, the metaphorical expression and the situation provide the *retrieval context* that guides the "search" through long-term memory. Since the linguistic aspects of the retrieval context are episodic events that fade rapidly, their influence will depend on their memorability, which in turn depends on such long-term memory characteristics as their concreteness or meaningfulness.

The preceding account provides a general framework for the analysis of metaphor in terms of mediation processes, long-term memory infor-

mation, retrieval cues, and the like. I turn now to a more specific analysis of such processes in relation to metaphorical behavior, particularly
comprehension. Four approaches are considered, one based on imagery,
another on verbal associations, a third on abstract representations, and
a fourth on a dual-coding approach that combines imagery and verbal
processes in a systematic analysis.

Perceptual experience and imagery

Traditionally, metaphor has been analyzed in terms of perceptual
imagery of a rather abstract nature. Susanne Langer, for example,
wrote that "Metaphor is our most striking evidence of *abstractive
seeing*, of the power of the human mind to use presentational symbols"
(1948 reprint, p. 14). Conversely, the symbolic function of images is
revealed in "their tendency to become metaphorical . . . [they are] our
readiest instruments for abstracting concepts from the tumbling stream
of impressions" (p. 117). These symbolic images are not only comprised of visual ingredients but are complex elements more appropriately described as "fantasies." They derive from experience, but the
original perception of experience is "promptly and spontaneously
abstracted, and used symbolically to represent a whole kind of actual
happening" (p. 118). Further abstraction of this literal generality
under appropriate circumstances results in a metaphorical fantasy, a
figurative meaning.

Langer finds the origin of metaphorical thinking, not in language
but in the nature of perception itself, in abstractive seeing. Her
account is in striking agreement with Arnheim's (1969) analysis of
visual perception as an abstractive process. Particularly relevant is an
experiment by one of Arnheim's students, in which observers were
asked to describe their impressions of two paintings of quite different
style, shown side by side. One painting was then replaced by another
and the effects of this new combination on the perception of the
remaining picture were noted. These changes had strong effects, often
leading to distortions in the perception of a picture. The experiments
were actually "designed to illustrate the psychological mechanism on
which metaphors are based in literature. There, the pairing of two
images throws into relief a common quality and thereby accomplishes a
perceptual abstraction without relinquishing the context from which
the singled out quality draws its life" (p. 62). The confrontation of
the two images "presses for relation," which produces changes in the
related items – changes in keeping with the structure of the context.
Even single pictures can be vehicles for such perceptual abstractions, as

Kennedy (1976) has demonstrated, particularly in regard to movement indicators in static pictures. Postural cues, lines of motion, and the like, are essentially pictorial metaphors that elicit sensations, or images, of movement.

A number of other psychologists have also emphasized the perceptual basis of the metaphor without necessarily referring explicitly to imagery. Roger W. Brown (1958) suggested that metaphorical extensions involving the vocabulary of sensations, as when words like "warm," "cold," "heavy," and "dull" are applied to personality and social manners, may be based on "correlations of sense data in the non-linguistic world" (p. 154). Asch (1958) referred to functional similarities between the referents of metaphors and corresponding literal terms. Osgood (1953) related metaphor to the intersensory experience of "synesthesia," a form of imagery. Werner and Kaplan (1963) reported that subjects who were required to express relational statements in terms of lines or images often did so in an abstract, metaphorical way. Such interpretations do not in themselves *explain* how the perceptual processes and images achieve their abstract functions, nor how they become linked to language, but they do emphasize the primacy of such processes in the origins of metaphor.

Despite the traditional emphasis on the relation of metaphor to perception and imagery, only a few studies have directly investigated the effects of relevant variables on the comprehension of metaphor. Billow (1975) studied, among other things, the effect of pictorial accompaniment on the comprehension of similarity metaphors in children. For example, "The branch of the tree was her pony," was accompanied by a picture of a girl riding on the branch of a tree. Billow's results suggested that pictures facilitated comprehension significantly, although the effect was not large (about 10 percent above a prior presentation of the metaphors without any pictures). Moreover, the pictures also produced interference; 26.3 percent of the changes in interpretation when pictures were presented were from an initially correct to an incorrect interpretation. Billow concluded that "the results emphasized the linguistic nature of the metaphor task and the relatively minor input supplied by pictorial accompaniment" (p. 421). It is important to note, however, that the results do not justify the conclusion that *imagery* played only a minor role in the task. The metaphors were originally "chosen for their relative concreteness. The compared objects were tangible and shared an attribute referring to tangible qualities or familiar actions for functions" (p. 416). Thus, the metaphorical sentences themselves were high in image-evoking value and the pictures presumably added little relevant imagery – and sometimes contributed irrelevant detail that led to erroneous interpretations.

The effectiveness of the imagery value of metaphorical expressions was demonstrated in an experiment by Honeck, Riechmann, and Hoffman (1975). Subjects were presented high- or low-imagery proverbs (as determined by subjects' ratings on imagery), accompanied by interpretations that were either conceptually related to the proverbs in varying degree, or were unrelated to them. The interpretations subsequently served as prompts for the recall of the proverbs in a memory task. The results showed that related interpretations were more effective recall-prompts than were unrelated ones, but only for high-imagery proverbs. Story-prompts similarly interacted with proverb imagery level in a second experiment. The results suggest that imagery is somehow involved in the comprehension and recall of some metaphors, but its role is not clear from the research, and the authors, in fact, proposed an interpretation in terms of an abstract, possibly imagery-free, conceptual base (this class of hypothesis is discussed below in more detail). Their preference was partly motivated by an unpublished experiment, which showed that subjects recognized interpretations of proverbs better after instructions to encode them for their literal meanings. Such a finding does not necessarily rule out imagery as an effective process, however, since metaphorical imagery may be quite different from literal imagery. As suggested earlier, it appears to be of a symbolic, or abstract, nature. I shall return to these points later.

Verbal associative processes

Verbal interpretations of metaphor attribute the similarity relation between the key terms to common verbal associations. The common associations may vary in their remoteness, that is, their position in the hierarchy of associations to the key terms. Presumably, the more remote the common associates, the longer it would take to "find" them and the more difficult the metaphor would seem. The influence of contextual factors can be similarly analysed in terms of the concept of "associative priming," which refers to the modifying effect of contextual stimuli on the associations that are most likely to occur to individual words.

The associative model has often been applied to anecdotal data or literary examples, but direct research studies of metaphor from this viewpoint are relatively scarce. Koen (1965) obtained experimental evidence for the model in a situation in which subjects selected either a *metaphor* or a *literal* word to complete a sentence, such as, "The sandpiper ran along the beach leaving a row of tiny STITCHES/MARKS in the sand." They were instructed to choose the word ("stitches" or "marks") most closely related to the group of ideas suggested by four cue words, which, according to associative data obtained from a separate group of subjects, were more often associated with either the metaphorical word, or the literal word, or equally often with each. The results showed that the metaphor was greatly preferred over the literal word when cued by its frequent associates, but not otherwise. The finding is consistent with the verbal associative interpretation, but it does not necessarily rule out imagery as an effective variable. It could be argued, for example, that the cue words simply aroused images that were more "compatible" with the image aroused by the sentence when completed by one rather than the other critical word. Nonetheless, verbal mediation is a plausible mechanism, and I shall accept it as a partial explanation, together with other processes, when I turn later to my own account.

Abstract representations

The third approach differs from the imagery and verbal associative interpretations in the assumption that the mediating process in metaphor comprehension is abstract, rather than modality specific. Osgood (1953, 1963) was probably the first psychologist to apply such a theory systematically to the analysis of language phenomena, including metaphor. His theoretical work, in fact, began with the analysis of synesthesia. For Osgood, the basis of similarity, or transfer, in synesthesia and metaphor is in the common affective reactions that are aroused by different sensory stimuli and by words. "Evaluation," "potency," and "activity" are the primary components of these affective reactions, according to factor-analytic studies. Osgood proposed that,

the highly generalized nature of the affective reaction system – the fact that it is independent of any particular sensory modality and yet participates with all of them – is at once the reason why Evaluation, Potency, and Activity appear as dominant factors *and* the psychological basis for metaphor and synesthesia. It is because such diverse sensory experiences as a *white* circle (rather than black), a *straight* line (rather than crooked), a *rising* melody (rather than a falling one), a *sweet* taste (rather than a sour one), a *caressing* touch (rather than an irritating scratch . . . [it is because all these diverse experiences] can share a common affective meaning that one easily and lawfully translates from one sensory modality into another in synesthesia and metaphor (1963, pp. 246–7).

The common affective reactions are abstract in the sense that they are independent of "particular sensory modality," as well as in the sense that the representational affective reactions themselves are assumed to be abstractions of reactions originally made to things. Specifically, Osgood views the representational process as a simultaneous bundle of response-like components which differentiate among classes of meaning.

I do not know of any studies of metaphor comprehension that are explicitly based on Osgood's theory, but the research on the semantic differential itself provides extensive indirect support for the relevance of the model. When individuals use scales such as "fast – slow," "hard – soft," and "weak – strong" to rate such diverse concepts as "mother" and "democracy," they obviously must do so in a metaphorical way. Moreover, the emergence of stable factors indicates that individuals within a culture largely agree in their metaphorical interpretations of the relationship between the specific concepts that are rated and the bipolar terms in the rating scales. Such agreement is necessary if the model is to be relevant to the comprehension of metaphorical expressions, which must be amenable to common interpretations if they are to be used for communicative purposes within a linguistic community. Indeed, there is considerable cross-cultural generality in the metaphorical application of a nonverbal visual form of the semantic differential to translation-equivalent words (Osgood, 1963, p. 247-248). These observations suggest that it would be profitable to study metaphor comprehension more directly, using the semantic differential approach.

Others have recently suggested a variety of different abstract representational approaches to the analysis of metaphor. Malgady and Johnson (1976) proposed a model in which metaphor processing is described in terms of elementary units of meaning called "cognitive features." Features are inferred from association data, most particularly adjectival, descriptive associations to nouns (cf. Johnson, 1970). This aspect renders it operationally similar to the verbal associative approach, but features are theoretically viewed as units that are more elementary and abstract than words. In this general respect, although not in its details, the conceptual approach is similar to that of Osgood. Malgady and Johnson's experiment involved measures of similarity of constituents, as well as goodness and interpretability of metaphors involving noun pairs that were initially chosen to be high or low in rated similarity. The pair members were modified by adjectives that were associatively related to (a) both nouns together (e.g., "soft hair is shiny silk"), (b) each noun separately ("long hair is elegant silk"), (c) the opposite (nonadjacent) noun in the pair ("elegant hair is long silk"), or (d) neither noun ("distant hair is fatal silk"). A fifth condi-tion involved two unmodified nouns ("hair is silk"). It was found that constituent similarity, goodness, and interpretability were all related to the pattern of modification. Metaphors in which the adjectives were associated with both nouns were generally highest in constituent simi-larity, goodness, and interpretability. The three variables were moder-ately intercorrelated when the individual nouns were initially high in similarity, but interpretability was essentially uncorrelated with con-stituent similarity and metaphorical goodness when the nouns were low in similarity.

Malgady and Johnson interpreted their results in terms of the idea that, in metaphor interpretation, the constituents are encoded into a single feature representation. The degree of similarity of the constitu-ent nouns, together with adjectival modifiers, will influence the integ-rity of the whole. Similar but "deviant" constituents, such as the noun pairs in this experiment, will be synthesized into a well-organized whole that is readily interpreted and viewed as a good metaphor. Dis-similar noun constituents usually result in a disintegrated representa-tion that is difficult to interpret, and goodness will be judged only on the basis of phase similarity.

The idea that the separate, feature-defined meanings of the constitu-ents are assumed to form a single representation with a qualitatively distinct meaning is intriguing. The problem remains, however, of fur-ther specifying the psychological nature of the elementary features and, more particularly, of the novel integrated representation that presum-ably results from their combination. Given their definition in terms of controlled associations, the features could be interpreted in verbal asso-ciative terms unless independent evidence suggests otherwise. In fact, there is reason to believe that descriptive associations are related to sev-eral different processes. A. N. Katz (1976) factor-analysed a variety of measures obtained on concept instances, including descriptive associa-tive norms available in Underwood and Richardson (1956). The asso-ciations consisted of sense-impression words, the frequency of which defined the relative dominance level of the instance with respect to a given sensory attribute. Thus "globe" has a higher dominance level than "pearl" with respect to the attribute "round," because "round" was a more frequent response to the former. It can be seen that associa-tions define a subset of features in the Malgady and Johnson sense. Katz found that the dominance level correlated substantially with sev-eral different measures, including "image salience" (the degree to which the attribute is a salient aspect of the image aroused by the instance), the rank of the attribute in the verbal associative hierarchy, and the judged goodness of the instance as an example of a sense-impression category. In fact, dominance level had loadings from three different factors and was unrelated to a fourth. Subsequent experiments showed that each of these factors independently predicted the ease of concept discovery. These results suggest that the elementary cognitive features and integrated representations involved in the metaphor research might be similarly decomposable into different components, including verbal associative and imagistic mechanisms, and each might play a role in metaphor comprehension. In regard to imagery, it is interesting that Johnson (1977) himself has recently stressed the perceptual basis of metaphor processing, without necessarily implying that the perceptual process "spills over" into conscious imagery.

The ultimate nature of the abstract representational process is similarly indefinite in other current theories of metaphor processing. I have already referred to the conceptual base hypothesis proposed by Honeck and his co-workers. They left the characteristics of the conceptual base relatively undefined except for the assertion that it is abstract and perhaps imagery-free. A number of psychologists have proposed similar views recently (for example, Brewer, 1975; Anderson & Ortony, 1975) in regard to the semantic processing of sentences. Verbrugge and McCarrell (1977) stressed the perceptual origins and relational nature of the common abstract representations that emerge in metaphor processing. The support for such representations emerged from a series of experiments in which the recall of metaphors was prompted by the topic, vehicle, or ground of the metaphor. Thus, for the metaphor, "Billboards are warts on the landscape," the prompts were "billboards," "warts," or the (implicit) ground, "are ugly protrusions on the surface." The grounds from a different list served as irrelevant prompts. The results of one experiment showed that topic, vehicle, and relevant ground were all effective prompts, in that they produced recall levels that far exceeded levels obtained with the irrelevant prompts. The interesting result, of course, is the high recall with grounds as prompts, since they contained no words that appeared in the related sentences. Other experiments showed that the ground was a more effective prompt for the entire metaphor than for either topic or vehicle alone, and that the prompting effects could not be explained in terms of pre-experimental verbal associations between grounds and metaphoric components.

Verbrugge and McCarrell concluded that metaphor processing involves the recognition of an abstract resemblance, or abstract relation, between the vehicle and topic domains, which is more than the sum of the attributes of each constituent. However, the precise nature of this abstract perceptual relation and how it arises from the separate parts remain unspecified, as do the abstract representational mechanisms postulated by Malgady and Johnson (1976) and Honeck et al. (1975). In this respect, the situation is comparable to the one that prevails in a variety of recent approaches to sentence memory (see Marschark & Paivio, 1977, for a discussion).

A dual-coding approach

The preceding views all have merit, but each suggested process is incomplete and insufficient in itself. Here, I discuss a dual-coding approach, which in principle combines the imagery and verbal associative views, in the sense that both processes are assumed to be cooperatively involved in language and thought, including metaphor processing. The two processes represent the activity of independent but interconnected systems that are specialized for picking up, storing, organizing, retrieving, and manipulating stimulus information. The imagery system deals with information concerning concrete objects and events, the verbal system with linguistic information. Independence implies that the systems can be active separately or in parallel. Interconnections between the systems permits information to be transferred from one to the other or, more accurately, for one system to initiate activity in the other. Thus, words can evoke imagery, and concrete events can evoke verbal descriptions. The systems are assumed to differ qualitatively in the nature of the information they handle and generate. The imagery system presumably constructs synchronously organized, integrated informational structures, analogous to the continuous, structural layout of the perceptual world. Thus, imaginal representations (not necessarily experienced in the form of conscious imagery) are assumed to have just those properties that would account for the integrated representation that appears to emerge when a metaphor is understood. The verbal system organizes discrete linguistic units into higher-order sequential structures. Taken together, these assumptions imply that the two systems can contribute independently, yet cooperatively, to tasks such as metaphor comprehension. They provide the cognitive mechanisms for conveying continuous experiential information, using a discrete symbol system – the communication function that Ortony (1975) considers so essential to metaphor. I shall now consider more specifically how these processes might contribute to metaphor comprehension, supporting my suggestions with relevant experimental studies where available.

Dual coding enhances the probability of finding a common ground in long-term memory. The first point is that two independent, but interconnected, sources of information in long-term memory increase the probability of finding a connection between topic and vehicle. The mechanism is simply additivity of independent systems. A relevant verbal-associative connection might be found in verbal memory, or some similarity might be found in the imagistic referents of the topic and vehicle, or both processes might contribute somehow to the construction of an integrated symbolic image, or a reasonable verbal interpretation, that could constitute the ground of the metaphor.

The additivity hypothesis has been supported in memory experiments and other tasks. Memory studies have shown that the availability of nonverbal images increases verbal recall. For example, pictures are recalled better than words, and concrete words that readily evoke images are recalled better than abstract, low-imagery words. A number of findings suggest that these differences can be explained partly in terms of dual coding (Paivio, 1975a). The reasoning is that pictures of familiar objects are highly likely to be named implicitly during input, concrete words are quite likely to evoke images, and abstract words are most likely simply to be named and rehearsed. Dual coding similarly provides a partial explanation of the facilitating effect of instructions to use imagery mnemonics on verbal recall: Such techniques ensure that an imaginal representation will be added to the verbal base. It is particularly relevant here that such techniques are most effective when they are used in associative learning tasks, which require the mental construction of a link connecting two unrelated terms, much as one is required to do in understanding a new metaphor.

There is evidence that subject-generated imaginal mediators are sometimes related metaphorically to the memorized items. Some of our experiments have required subjects to learn pairs of abstract nouns, using images. Such image-mediated learning is understandable only in terms of concretization, or instantiation, of the abstract information. Occasionally, this seemed to occur in the form of an image that symbolized both members of a pair. For example, one subject reported "boy scout" as the imaginal mediator for the pair "chance – deed." The image in this case is clearly metaphoric, symbolizing in a single representation a complex idea that incorporates the meaning of both terms: a boy scout is someone who takes the "chance" (or opportunity) to do a good "deed." The example is relevant here, because the metaphorical connection was constructed by the subject himself, in a manner analogous to the discovery of a common ground between the vehicle and topic of a novel metaphor. The discovery presumably involved dual coding in that the image had to be generated from verbal cues.

Another study illustrates more directly the discovery of a common mediator. It involved a concept learning task (Katz & Paivio, 1975). We asked subjects to learn pairs in which nonsense words were associated with instances of several concepts. The subject's task was to learn the concepts that were represented by the nonsense words. Although the specific instances did not differ in imagery value, the to-be-learned concepts themselves were either high or low in imagery value. Thus, "a four-footed animal" is relatively high in imagery, whereas "an optical instrument" is relatively low in imagery value. In addition, some individuals were instructed to use visual imagery to learn the pairs, whereas others were not. The results showed that the imagery value of the conceptual categories, as well as imagery instructions, facilitated concept acquisition. We interpreted this to mean that the addition of high-imagery conditions increased the probability that concept learning would be mediated by either imaginal or verbal representations, or both. The study is relevant to metaphor interpretation, because such interpretation is analogous to concept discovery. The subject must discover what the vehicle and topic have in common in a semantic, conceptual sense. Our experiment demonstrated that verbal conditions that encourage image arousal also facilitate concept discovery.

Finally, there is considerable evidence that imagery contributes to the comprehensibility of sentences (Klee & Eysenck, 1973; O'Neill & Paivio, 1978; Paivio & Begg, 1971). The general assumption is that imagery provides an additional (subjective) referential context for the interpretation of a sentence. It is reasonable to suppose that imagery contributes similarly to the comprehension of metaphorical expressions. Note, however, that the context could be inappropriate if it draws attention to its literal aspects. This point was mentioned earlier in connection with Honeck's research on proverb recall. Suggestive evidence emerged from a study in which subjects rated normal and anomalous sentences for comprehensibility (O'Neill & Paivio, 1978). In the anomalous case, selection restrictions were violated by interchanging nouns from different sentences. The pertinent result was that anomalous sentences were rated as less sensible than normal ones, but the manipulation had little effect on imagery ratings. Something similar might occur in the case of novel metaphorical expressions that initially seem somewhat anomalous – if they contain highly concrete terms, one might easily image those terms without arriving at an appropriate metaphorical understanding. On the other hand, if the situation draws attention to nonliteral possibilities, concrete terms might prompt figurative interpretations of anomalous sentences as well as of metaphors.

Pollio and Burns (1977), for example, found that subjects could interpret anomalous sentences under instructions to do so, and that many of
the interpretations were metaphorical in nature. The study did not
indicate whether imagery played any special role in such figurative
interpretations, but it does suggest ways of investigating the problem.

The discussion now turns to the qualitative differences that might
result in different contributions by the two systems.

Integrated images make for efficient information storage. The organizational characteristics of the imagery system provide for a large storehouse of potentially relevant information. The assumption is that imagistic information in long-term memory is organized synchronously
into large, integrated chunks. This idea goes back to the British asso-
ciationists, who distinguished between simultaneous and successive
associations. The former are especially characteristic of visual perception and imagery, although they can be multimodal as well. Think of
the sun and you simultaneously think of the sky. Imagine your home
and you have available, more or less at once, its components and
contents — windows, doors, rooms, furniture, colors, and so on. Integration also implies redintegration, so that access to part of the structure tends to redintegrate the whole. This means that a large amount
of information becomes quickly available when it is stored in the form
of integrated images.

Relevant evidence again comes from laboratory studies of associative
memory. Begg (1972) showed that high imagery phrases, such as
"white horse," tended to be remembered as holistic units, as though
each phrase took up no more memory space than either word alone.
Abstract phrases, such as "basic theory," on the other hand, seemed to
take up twice as much memory space as the individual words, as
though the words were concatenated onto each other. Begg's theoretical explanation was that the concrete phrases activate holistic long-
term memory images, in which the components are unitized in a single
representation, for example, an animal that is at once a horse and
white.

To appreciate the implications of this analysis for metaphor, consider the vehicle in the expression, "A metaphor is a solar eclipse."
The term "solar eclipse" will tend to arouse a compound image that
includes the blackened center, together with the glowing ring that surrounds it. Both components, obscurity and light, will then be simultaneously available to arouse further associations relevant to the metaphorical context. These may involve further imagery, or the component
information may be described verbally, and the descriptions, in turn,

evoke further verbal associations or imagery; and so on, in a continuous exchange until a reasonable interpretation is achieved.

Imagery ensures processing flexibility. The synchronous nature of imaginal representations also promotes efficient memory search, because such information can be processed in a way that is flexible and relatively free from sequential constraints. If I ask you how many windows there are in your house, you will probably arrive at the answer by imagining your house from different positions and counting the windows from the image. You could do so by working around the house in either direction, inside or out. By contrast, the processing of organized verbal information in long-term memory is sequentially constrained to a high degree. We can recite the alphabet forward more quickly than backward, and backward recitation of a poem would be painfully slow.

The idea of flexible processing applies also to the generation of novel, integrated images from unrelated words. Segal (1976; described in Paivio, 1975b) presented his subjects with sets of two, three, or four nouns and required them to generate either meaningful images, which they drew, or sentences, which they wrote. Segal measured reaction time from the point of exposure of the words to the moment when the subject pressed a key to indicate completion of the task. The interesting result was that image generation time increased only slightly as the number of items increased, whereas sentence generation time increased sharply with set size. This was predicted from the idea of differences in sequential constraints: Things can be put together in various ways in a meaningful image, but words do not enjoy the same freedom in sentences.

The flexibility of image processing implies a special advantage in creative discovery and invention; specifically, it makes for speed and efficiency in the search for relevant information, as well as in the construction of novel combinations from component information. The implication for metaphor comprehension is that imagery can increase the efficiency of the search for relevant information, as well as the generation of a novel, integrated representation that would constitute the common ground for vehicle and topic. However, the term "relevant" is crucial in this context. A completely unconstrained search, or constructive process, could not guarantee metaphorical relevance. I assume that relevance is ensured by the retrieval cues provided by the terms of the metaphor and the constraints associated with verbal processes.

Topic and vehicle as retrieval cues for relevant information. Relevance requires a guided search through long-term memory, which is initiated

by appropriate retrieval cues. This function is served by the metaphorical expression itself, together with contextual information. I propose
that the vehicle and topic are the key terms, and that the former is
usually prepotent because, by definition, its properties are to be "conveyed" to the topic. Moreover, the concreteness of the vehicle should
be crucial, because a concrete term provides rapid access to information-rich images.

The idea originates with paired-associate learning tasks, in which the
concreteness of image-evoking value of stimuli and responses have been
systematically varied. Individuals are presented with pairs of nouns
varying in concreteness or nouns paired with pictures. They are then
presented with one member of each pair and are required to recall its
associate. It turns out that recall accuracy depends particularly on the
concreteness of the item that is presented as the retrieval cue: Pictures
or concrete nouns are good reminders for their associates, abstract
nouns are not. This effect was metaphorically expressed as the "conceptual peg" hypothesis: Concrete nouns and pictures are effective pegs
for storage and retrieval of associated information (Paivio, 1963;
Paivio & Yarmey, 1966).

In the case of metaphor comprehension, I extend the idea to the
retrieval of relevant information from long-term memory. The vehicle
serves as an efficient conceptual peg for metaphor comprehension to
the extent that it promotes retrieval of images and verbal information
that intersects with information aroused by the topic. Retrieval of integrated images will be particularly useful for reasons already discussed:
they are information-rich and in addition they permit flexible processing.

Direct experimental evidence is lacking on the hypothesis as a whole,
although aspects of it are supported by recent experimental findings
and some informal observations. The experimental findings bear on
the asymmetry of the topic and vehicle. Verbrugge and McCarrell
(1977) found that the vehicle was generally superior to the topic as a
retrieval cue for the entire metaphor. This supports the special salience
of the vehicle in episodic memory for the metaphorical expression, but
it does not necessarily follow that the vehicle is also prepotent in
retrieval of information from semantic memory or other aspects of the
comprehension process. Moreover, Verbrugge and McCarrell's study
did not provide any evidence on the role of imagery in their task nor
was it intended to do so.

Tversky's (1977) demonstration that similarity relations are not
symmetrical is also relevant to the present hypothesis. Specifically, he
found systematic asymmetries in comparative tasks (*A* is like *B*) as well

as production tasks (producing the most similar response to a given stimulus). The direction of the asymmetry was determined by the relative salience (that is, judged prominence, figural goodness, prototypicality) of the two stimuli, so that similarity was greater when the less salient stimulus was compared to the more salient one than vice versa. Thus, if B is more salient than A, A is more likely to be compared with and viewed as similar to B than B to A (see also Rosch, 1975a). The application to metaphor and simile is obvious: such expressions should be more acceptable when the more salient noun serves as the vehicle than when it serves as the response. Moreover, Tversky suggested that the interpretation of similes and metaphors involves "scanning the feature space and selecting the features of the referent that are applicable to the subject" (1977, p. 349). The relevant point in the present context is not the feature model per se, but Tversky's emphasis on the priority of the vehicle (i.e., the referent) in the interpretation process. That aspect seems consonant with the present hypothesis, but Tversky's analysis is open to alternative interpretations (e.g., Harwood & Verbrugge, 1977; Ortony, this volume).

I have made some informal observations that bear more directly on these features of the hypothesis. I asked a number of my colleagues and graduate students to interpret the "meta-metaphor" that introduced this talk, namely, the statement that "for the student of language and thought, metaphor is a solar eclipse." I then asked them to describe how they arrived at their interpretation. Most agreed at least partly with the interpretation that I had in mind when I constructed the expression. This part was the idea that in a metaphor, as in an eclipse, something is obscured. In addition, several respondents gave interpretations completely in agreement with my own, saying, for example, that both metaphor and eclipse enlighten while they obscure, that they cover up the real thing so that you can see it better, or that they block out the central stuff so that you can see the subtle stuff around it better.

What would be expected in regard to their introspective reports concerning the manner of arriving at an interpretation? The hypothesis that the vehicle functions as a conceptual peg suggests that it should have been processed before the topic, and as an image. This seemed to be generally the case. One person spontaneously reported that the statement made no sense until he imaged an eclipsed sun. Another said that he first imaged a partial eclipse and then a full one. A third said that he certainly imaged "that thing with all the fuzzy stuff around it." And so on. There was one exception, who said that he first thought of what metaphor might be for the student of language, then what an eclipse means for the student of astronomy, and then what the two have in common. He *may* have imaged, he said; but it did not seem salient. It is interesting that this respondent is also the only one whose interpretation did not include the idea of something being covered up or obscured. He referred instead to "exotic events from which one can learn something." This certainly is an appropriate interpretation, although not the most common one for this group of respondents. His interpretation and his introspections are consistent with the conclusion that he used the topic rather than the vehicle as his conceptual peg, whereas the others apparently were drawn to use the vehicle in that role. Both strategies are logically possible, but one was generally preferred.

The theoretical analysis has some obvious testable implications. For example, metaphors could be constructed so that the concreteness of the topic and the vehicle are independently varied. Concreteness of either term should facilitate interpretation (as measured, for example, by its speed and appropriateness) but concreteness of the vehicle should have the greater effect. Moreover, the interpretation should more often be initiated by the vehicle than by the topic, although this may be modified by the relative concreteness level of the two terms. Such implications come to mind easily and I mentioned these only to indicate that the hypothesis has heuristic as well as explanatory value.

Verbal processes keep search and retrieval on track. I have suggested that imagery contributes specifically to the speed of accessing long-term memory, and to the speed and flexibility of search for information that would provide the basis of a relevant interpretation of a metaphor. I propose, finally, that relevance itself is largely determined by the verbal system. The sequential nature of verbal processes contributes to an orderly, logical sequence in the flow of ideas (cf. Paivio, 1975b). In brief, the verbal system keeps the search process "on track" in regard to the goal of discovering a relevant relational idea. Thus, in my thematic metaphor, the image of a solar eclipse could lead to flights of fantasy bearing no relevance to the meaning of metaphor for a student of language. It is one's episodic memory for the verbal concepts themselves that keeps one from being blinded by the glare of the solar image and thereby stumbling aimlessly through one's memory storehouse.

Conclusion

I have reviewed some psychological research findings and theories relevant to the comprehension of metaphor. The theoretical ideas are for the most part highly speculative, because relevant research is still scarce. Moreover, the basic problem of comprehension itself is only poorly understood. I have expressed the hope that the study of metaphor might lead to a better conceptualization of comprehension in general. This implies that "ordinary language" and metaphor are continuous phenomena, involving common cognitive and linguistic processes. Research might prove otherwise but, in any case, without it we shall never know. Much of the psychological research on metaphor to date has not been directed at really fundamental problems in the area. Such work might require the systematic development of a large pool of novel metaphors that vary in type, difficulty, concreteness, and whatever other dimensions may seem relevant. It may demand systematic extensions of some of the traditional paradigms that have been developed in verbal memory and language research. It would require detailed factual information on precisely how people respond to a novel metaphorical expression. I suggested a few possibilities in connection with the role of the vehicle and topic as retrieval cues, but such informal approaches need to be translated into systematic observational studies and experiments before real progress can be made in this area.

NOTE

The author's research cited in this chapter was supported by grants from the National Research Council of Canada.

The Interpretation
of Novel Metaphors

BRUCE FRASER

Paivio concludes his chapter with the lament that much of the psychological research on metaphor to date has not been directed at really fundamental problems in the area. In the last paragraph, he writes:

Such work might require the systematic development of a large pool of novel metaphors that vary in type, difficulty, concreteness, and whatever other dimensions may seem relevant. It may demand systematic extensions of some of the traditional paradigms that have been developed in verbal memory and language research. It would require detailed factual information about precisely how people respond to a novel metaphorical expression.

The present chapter describes a first step towards redressing this lack of relevant research.

The particular issues I am addressing involve the last point raised by Paivio, namely, the nature of the speaker's response to a novel metaphor. However, I want to go further than just determining the facts of what interpretation is provided by the native speaker to a novel metaphorical utterance and suggest that in order to evaluate such facts, we must examine the following general question: To what extent is the interpretation of a metaphorical expression (or at least the most probable interpretation) predictable on the basis of the linguistic properties of the utterance alone? There are several subquestions: If the metaphorical utterance is given out of context, do speakers agree on the most likely interpretation? Where speakers differ, are the differences explainable in terms of speaker characteristics, such as age, education, sex, cultural background, and the like? Where there is agreement, can we specify the properties which give rise to this agreement, and if so, are these properties part of the linguistic characterization of the sentence used, or more a component of the belief system of the language users?

Since the questions I am raising cannot be adequately answered through introspection, a portion of this chapter will deal with the details of an empirical attempt to arrive at some of the answers. First, however, I shall establish a framework by providing a partial account of metaphor: what it is, and how it is signaled.

What is a metaphor?

Although I shall talk as though all metaphors were the same, there is, in fact, a continuum. At one end there is what might be called the *live metaphor*, at the other end the *dead metaphor*. The latter is simply an idiom, which was once a live metaphor, but which is now to be treated as a conventionalized form in the language. The phrase "to kick the bucket," once used literally and then metaphorically to refer to the final struggles of animals lashed by their feet to a beam called a "bucket," has now lost any sense of its original source. On the other hand, there are expressions such as "John is married to his tennis game" or "Irrigate your mind a little" that require both a context and a certain creativity to interpret adequately. It is only these last that I shall be concerned with here.

Now, it may seem redundant and unnecessary to try to provide a definition of metaphor. After all, the topic has been discussed by many eminent writers (for example, Aristotle; Black, 1962b; Dubois et al., 1970; Koestler, 1964; Richards, 1936a), and one might expect to find an acceptable definition amongst such writings. Perhaps one can, but at the risk of replowing old ground, I want to address the question anew, looking at metaphor within the context of a more general theory of pragmatics. The main point that underlies this orientation is an obvious fact about metaphor, but one that is often overlooked in the linguistic literature, namely, that a metaphor involves the *use* of language. As such, metaphor is not to be accounted for within the grammar of a language – at least not in the sense of grammar proposed by Chomsky, which, although having undergone various modifications in the last fifteen years, is still intended to be a characterization of the language user's knowledge about the relationship between strings of sounds and their meanings, and not the knowledge about how such sentences might be used in context to communicate intentions. Black (1962b) presents this view when he writes:

The rules of our language determine that some expressions must count as metaphors; . . . but we must also recognize that the established rules of language leave wide latitude for individual variation, initiative, and creation. There are indefinitely many contexts (including nearly all the interesting ones) where the meaning of a metaphorical expression has to be reconstructed from the speaker's intentions (and other clues) because the broad rules of standard usage are too general to supply the information needed . . .

to know what the user of a metaphor means, we need to know how seriously he treats the metaphorical focus . . . We must not expect the "rules of language" to be of much help in such inquiries. (There is accordingly a sense of "metaphor" that belongs to "pragmatics" rather than to "semantics" – and this sense may be the one most deserving of attention.) (pp. 29–30)

Black does not provide an account of what he means by "pragmatics," but since he contrasts it with "semantics" in the passage cited, I think we can take it as being consistent with the recent work that is aimed at developing a theory of pragmatics – a theory which attempts to explain how it is that a speaker can consistently exploit factors of the context of speaking, as well as the manner in which something is said, to convey to the hearer an utterance meaning that differs from the literal meaning of the linguistic expression he has used. The literal interpretation of the sentence, "Where are your shoes?" for example, is a request for information about the location of the hearer's shoes. Spoken by a mother to a child late for school, the utterance takes on (or we may assert that on many such occasions it takes on) the meaning of "Get going"; spoken by a nurse to an elderly patient, it may be intended to mean "I offer to get your shoes for you if you tell me where they are," and so forth.

The precise domain of such a theory, as well as its relationship to a theory of grammar, is a subject of current disagreement. This need not concern us here, though there are several concepts we shall need for the subsequent discussion.[1]

The first of these involves the choices a speaker may make in determining how to convey his intended meaning. There is one major distinction, that of speaking literally versus speaking nonliterally. To speak literally is to intend to convey the literal meaning of the sentence uttered; that is, to mean what you say. On the other hand, to speak nonliterally (figuratively) is to intend to convey *not* the literal meaning of the sentence uttered but, rather, some different meaning – one that is related in some conventional way to the literal meaning. A good example of the nonliteral use of language is found in irony. For example, I might be driving you in my car when someone from the right-hand lane cuts in front of us to make a left-hand turn, thereby causing me to slam on the brakes. My response might be to say, "I just love people who don't signal." (I might also say several other things, but they are not relevant here.) Clearly, the native speaker of English who has heard my utterance would recognize that I did not mean what I said, that I was speaking ironically, and that my intended meaning was something like, "I really hate people who don't signal."

Note, however, that the sentence I used in being ironic is, in fact, a well-formed English sentence which has a clear literal interpretation. It just happens that I do not want to be taken as intending to convey this meaning at this particular moment. I shall argue later that metaphors involve only language used nonliterally.

It is, however, important to recognize that metaphor is not the only use of nonliteral language. I have already mentioned how irony ("I just love people who don't signal") requires that the speaker intend the expression nonliterally. Hyperbole, another rhetorical device, involves the conveying of a proposition that so distorts the obvious truth that the hearer recognizes the nonliteral intention on the speaker's part; for example, when one says, "Thousands showed up," when in fact hundreds were there. Synecdoche involves the substitution of one term for another within a predetermined hierarchy. Jakobson and Halle (1956) suggested that this replacement is of a syntagmatic sort, as opposed to metaphor, in which the replacement is paradigmatic. For synecdoche, one referring term replaces another that is either more general or more particular than the actual term itself. What binds the two terms together may be based on anatomical classification (for example, "all hands on deck"), or a perceptual relationship (for example, "Get that smell out of here," where "smell" is referring to the bag of garbage). Metonymy, on the other hand, involves a replacement of a term where the relationship of the first to the second is felt to be more functional: cause/effect, actor/action, container/contained, and the like. We find examples like the "lands belonging to the Crown," "The White House announced that. . . ," and "The Fords won all the prizes at le Mans this year." None of the expressions above can be taken literally, and each reflects a substitution of one term for another because of some preexisting relationship. An interesting analysis can be found in J.D. Sapir (1977).

A second distinction involves what it is that we convey to a hearer when we say something. Without going into any detail, I think we can adopt the position of Searle (1969) who argues that every sentence carries two sorts of information. It carries information that signals the intended propositional content, and it carries information that signals the intended speech act force. In a sentence such as, "I promise that I will be there," the propositional content is clear and unambiguous: "I will be there." And the intended force of promising is also clear and unambiguous. In other sentences, the information signaling the force and propositional content may be collapsed, and in some cases, incomplete. For the purposes of this discussion, I shall be concerned only with the propositional content of the example sentences, and I shall usually treat them as simple propositions, rather than as compound propositions.

Let us return to the question posed at the beginning of this section: What is a metaphor? As a working definition, I define a metaphor as: "an instance of the non-literal use of language in which the intended propositional content must be determined by the construction of an analogy."[2] I shall now elaborate on this definition.

First, that a metaphor does not exist without someone saying something seems clear. I think there would be general agreement that in seriously uttering, "My brother is a spinster," or "The chairman plowed through the discussion," one is using a metaphor. However, to claim that the sentence "My brother is a spinster" *is* a metaphor seems just wrong. To say that the sentence "contains" a metaphor also seems unacceptable, because, at least in our view, a metaphor results from the speaker intending to use an expression nonliterally, and sentences surely do not have intentions. Of course, it might be fair to conclude that the use of the sentence would ordinarily involve the intention to speak metaphorically.

The requirement that a metaphor involve only the nonliteral use of language is perhaps more controversial. Sentences such as, "John is a pig," "The chairman plowed through the discussion," and "Sheathe your impatience" are often suggested as incontestable examples of metaphor. Moreover, it is pointed out that they are all semantically anomalous and thus *cannot* be interpreted literally – they are literally meaningless. But just as there are many semantically anomalous expressions used metaphorically, so there are many which are semantically unexceptional; that is, there is an acceptable literal interpretation. Suppose, for example, that we are discussing my neighbors and I remark that "John is our priest," referring to John, who is, in fact, a plumber, but who provides us counsel. I have used a perfectly acceptable sentence, but one which I intend to be taken nonliterally in that context. Clearly I do not believe what I say, nor do I expect you to take me to believe it. The point here is not whether or not there are more metaphors which rest on semantically acceptable or unacceptable expressions; rather, the point is that, acceptable or not, the speaker *intends* the expression to be taken nonliterally. We return to this point in the following section, which deals with the signaling of a metaphor.

If the above claim restricting metaphors to the intended nonliteral use of language is correct, it should be clear that the truth or falsity of a sentence intended metaphorically is irrelevant. For semantically anomalous declarative sentences which cannot be interpreted literally, the issue of their being true or false cannot arise. In such cases, if the speaker is serious about the conversation and trying to communicate something, the hearer *must* take the expression as being nonliterally intended in order to understand it. For imperative sentences such as, "Root out your faults, one by one," which are intended as orders of some sort, the issue of truth also cannot arise. The same is true for sentences which have an interrogative form but which are used metaphorically. Sentences such as, "John is our priest," which are semantically well formed may or may not reflect a true or false claim. But this is beside the point if the speaker intends the expression to be taken nonliterally, thereby intending the hearer to infer some different interpretation of the utterance.

The final point in the definition which bears clarification is the requirement that the interpretation of a metaphor requires that the hearer establish an analogy. Indeed, a metaphor is often defined as a type of analogy, as an implicit comparison, whereas a simile is called an explicit comparison. Aristotle, for example, called a simile "a metaphor with a preface." I must point out, however, that whereas I am arguing that a metaphor is a proposition used nonliterally which requires the establishing of an analogy for its interpretation, a metaphor is *not* an analogy. An analogy must play a crucial role in the interpretation of a metaphor, but this is analogous to saying that some sort of polarity reversal must play a role in the interpretation of irony. From the latter, it does not follow that irony is a type of polarity reversal. The form of this analogy is discussed by Miller (this volume), and in Fraser (1977), where I discuss in some detail the nature of the required analogy and the process of metaphorical interpretation. There, I not only argue that all metaphors should be treated in a similar way, but I also propose some pragmatic rules of metaphor interpretation, sensitive to the grammatical form of the metaphorical utterance.

How is a metaphor signaled?

I have suggested in the preceding section that a metaphor involves a nonliteral use of language. At issue now is how a speaker signals this intention. There appear to be three basic approaches.

The most obvious, though seldom mentioned, way to signal a metaphor is to announce it. To say, for example, "Speaking metaphorically, Harry is married to his work," is to make explicit that you intend the utterance to be taken nonliterally and to receive metaphorical processing.[3] In addition, the use of terms such as "practically," "actually," or "virtually," as in "He virtually purred at the news," often serve to announce the intention to use a metaphor.

The second, and probably the most noted way to signal a metaphorical intent is to use a semantically anomalous sentence.[4] Examples such as, "Harry is a wastebasket," when talking about Harry, or "The crowd floated through the market," when discussing the crowd, represent such cases. As will be discussed later, not all semantically anomalous propositions are intended to be metaphorically interpreted.

The third device to signal metaphorical intention is to use a sentence which is pragmatically anomalous. In such cases, the sentence is literally meaningful (in contrast to the case above), but the propositional content represents a possible state of affairs that is clearly false or irrelevant under the conditions of utterance.

Let us consider the following examples, not all intended metaphorically. First, "John is our priest," under the circumstance of talking about John, our unreligious next-door neighbor; second, "That remark reflects an outstanding sensitivity," said to someone who had just made a remark in front of the hostess about the tasteless dinner, and third, "He swallowed gallons of water," said of someone who nearly drowned. All of these sentences are clearly meaningful, but all are, in the stipulated context, clearly untrue, and all signal the need for a nonliteral interpretation. However, while the former seems to be a clear case of metaphor, the second is an example of irony, the third of hyperbole.

Unfortunately, I have no adequate analysis that will successfully identify which figurative use of language has been intended. Various linguists have informally suggested that irony is always accompanied by a characteristic nasal intonation, but there is no empirical evidence. Such an intonation may well sometimes accompany intended irony, but it is by no means a necessary condition for it. Rather, there appears to be but one clear method to differentiate ironic from metaphorical or hyperbolic intention: if the meaning of the proposition is, roughly speaking, directly opposite to the meaning one might expect from the speaker under the circumstances, then irony is intended; if the meaning does not fall into this category, then metaphor or hyperbole is a possibility. One can, of course, ask how the hearer is to know "what is expected" in a given utterance context. I have no adequate answer to this at present. That the example, "He swallowed gallons of water," is a case of hyperbole, rather than irony or metaphor, seems clear. But here again, we have no definite way of "proving" it.

To summarize, I have suggested that there are three ways of signaling a metaphorical intent. First, the speaker can simply announce his intention to have the utterance interpreted as a metaphor. Second, the speaker can use a semantically anomalous sentence; such cases appear unequivocally to be instances of the speaker signaling a metaphorical intent. Third, the speaker can use a meaningful sentence, but one whose content, given the context of utterance, is either obviously false or simply irrelevant. Here there are three possibilities: The speaker can be intending to signal irony, hyperbole, or metaphor. The first of these would seem to be signaled if the expected propositional content is directly opposed to that expressed. Hyperbole would seem to be signaled if the predication overstates or understates the abilities or actions of the propositional subject referent. And finally, as a default case, metaphor would seem to be signaled if neither of the first two is indicated.

All the examples considered so far have involved cases in which the propositional subject directly referred to the focus of the conversation. There are, however, at least two other rhetorical devices which rely on the nonliteral use of the proposition expressed, but for both of these, the propositional subject does not directly refer to the conversational focus. As we have indicated earlier, synecdoche involves a syntagmatic replacement of what would be the appropriate directly referring term by an indirectly referring one, where the two are related by some predetermined hierarchy; for example, "The sail appeared on the horizon," where "sail" is used to refer to the entire object, the ship. Metonymy, on the other hand, involves a replacement of the focus term by another term related in some functional way to the first. For example, "The White House announced . . ." uses the term "the White House" for the direct term, "the president." Although I have not discussed the rules that guide the interpretation of either metonymy or synecdoche, they would seem to bear close resemblance to those involved in metaphorical interpretation.

There may, of course, be problems with the account of how a metaphor is signaled that has been presented in this section. I may have overlooked a nonliteral use of language that will confound the recognition problem, or I may be oversimplifying the task of recognition by choosing examples too obvious. However, I think the basic outline of the program is sound, and I now wish to turn to the question initially posed concerning the interpretation of novel metaphors.

A pilot study

To pursue my response to Paivio's challenge to provide some real data on the interpretation of novel metaphorical expressions, I developed a set of test items which were clearly semantically anomalous, thereby signaling the need for a metaphorical interpretation. The principal questions I wished to investigate were those posed initially in this paper:

First, if a metaphorical utterance is given out of context, do speakers agree on the most likely interpretation? My hypothesis was that they would not, since context plays such a crucial role.

Second, where speakers do differ, are their differences explainable in terms of speaker characteristics, such as age, education, sex, cultural background, and the like? My hypothesis was that they would be, particularly with respect to cultural orientation.

Third, where there is agreement, can the properties which give rise to this agreement be inferred, and to what extent are such properties part of the linguistic description of the utterance? My hypothesis was that we can specify the properties, but that they relate to connotative aspects (salient features) of the lexical items involved rather than any denotative lexical information.

There was, however, a second agenda; namely, to determine the extent to which metaphors and the similes which appear to be related structurally to them (for example, "John is a pig" and "John is like a pig") receive the same zero-context interpretation. Although various linguists have speculated informally on the translatability of metaphors to similes, and vice versa, no one, to my knowledge, has enquired empirically into the similarity of hearer interpretation.

To investigate some of these questions, at least at a preliminary level, we constructed four sets of twenty-eight sentences, each sentence having been judged clearly semantically anomalous by two or more native speakers. The groups consisted of declarative sentences having the following form:

Group A: "He's an X"
Group B: "She's an X"
Group C: "He's like an X"
Group D: "She's like an X."

Thus, groups A and B contained metaphorical expressions, differing only in the gender of the subject; groups C and D contained similes, again differing only in the subject gender. By using only pronominal subjects, I hoped to avoid specific images associated with a more specific noun phrase. The values of the X in the test were nouns chosen in as completely an unsystematic fashion as possible: A list of objects observed or mentioned during a day was compiled, and from it twenty-eight objects were selected which seemed "interesting," and which clearly would not receive a semantically acceptable interpretation in the test frame. No attempt was made to control the conceptual categories from which values for the X were chosen.

The subjects for this first set of judgments consisted of ten men and thirty women, all native English-speaking college students in the greater Boston area. The age range was from nineteen to thirty-eight; the mean was twenty-six. No attempt was made to control for ethnic or cultural background.

Each subject was given a set of pages stapled together, consisting of a set of instructions followed by 30 separate examples: These included two practice examples ($X=$"dog," $X=$"snail") followed by seven from each of the four groups. The sheets of items were arranged in several random orders within each group of 28. Four different test sets of 28 items were compiled, thereby exhausting the (4×28) 112 test items.

Results

The basic question – whether a metaphor in zero-context receives a consistent interpretation – was answered clearly in the negative, except for the two practice items ("He is a dog" and "She is like a snail" – dogs are nearly always ugly; snails are almost always slow). Several examples will illustrate this. Combining the metaphor and simile responses, for the $X=$"termite" cases, the following (edited) responses were obtained:

He: is a pest, is destructive, eats a lot, eats a little, is little, tears at your sense of self, bores into any conversation, is deceptive, picks things apart, is a parasite, is always worrying about you, is always in the way, is petty, is undermining, is insidious, is devious;

She: is nosey, is always eating, is tiny, eats you out of everything, is a pain in the ass, spends money quickly, is small, is bothersome, is a leech, is relentless, hides, is unwanted, keeps nagging, digs into others' business, is destructive, has a small brain, is dumb, is afraid of herself.

For $X=$"a peanut butter and jelly sandwich":

He: is always falling on his face, is delicious, is mediocre, is difficult to get rid of, is mushy minded, is sweet, has no backbone, is nice but dull, is easy going, is All American, is an acceptable substitute when no one else is around, is well put together, kids like him, is sometimes boring but basically good for you, is ubiquitous, is plain, is uninteresting;

She: is a good standby, is a slob, is mushy, is hard to get rid of, has got it, has no backbone, is a "common type," is plain, has mush for brains, is nice to have around, is not refreshing, is familiar.

For $X=$"a compass":

He/She: is stylish, is well-oriented, is rigid and set in direction, always does the right thing, is scientific, always knows where and how to go, follows you if he likes you, is very aware, has a good sense of direction, is indecisive, is decisive, has a girl in every place, is disorganized, is well organized.

For $X=$"a ripe banana":

He: is soft, is an OK person, is malleable, is mushyheaded, "too dirty to write down," is old and worn, is outmoded, is overripe, is soft, is all yellow, is nice, is friendly, is always ready, is harmless, is eccentric, is good now but rotten soon, is well hung, is phallic;

She: is oversexed, is raring to go, is crazy, stands out to be picked on, has appeal, is mushy, is too soft, is fully developed, is hot to trot, is voluptuous, is provocative, is soggy, is sensitive, is easy to hurt, is slender, takes care of herself, is waiting to be peeled, is too fat, is available.

Finally, for $X=$"an octopus":

He: is all arms, climbs, does a lot, is clumsy, is aggressive, is motor-oriented, is into everything, can't keep his hands off girls, is grabby (these last three a number of times);

She: does lots at once, is always hugging and touching, has fingers in many pies, is domineering, is manipulative, is great on first dates, is all over the place, touches everything, is grabby.

I think that without much fear of argument, I can conclude that for the zero-context interpretation of the similes and metaphors with pronominal subjects, but separated in terms of the sex of the referent of whom the expression is predicated, there is no one "most-probable" interpretation. Whether this would be true for nonpronominal subjects is an open question.

Four things, however, do stand out from the examples above, which I have taken to be representative. First, there is often a clear interpretation in terms of a positive or negative evaluation of the expression. Predicating "termite" of someone nearly always produced a negative interpretation. This might, of course, follow from the shared belief that termites are generally undesirable. For the case of $X=$"a caterpillar," however, where we might expect caterpillars to be pretty generally disliked, there were many more positive responses; for example, "He has potential," "She is very smooth," and "He is slow and cautious." Perhaps some general criteria of disdain can explain these differences.

Second, there is often (though not always) a significant distinction between the predication of the expression for "he" as opposed to "she" for both male and female judges. If a male is an octopus, he is nearly always aggressive, all hands, after a woman, oversexed, and only occasionally a busy person. A female who is an octopus, however, is much less aggressive, and grabby, and is more often seen as busy, liberated, ambitious, and the like.

Third, although none of the examples was (consciously) picked for any sexual connotation, nearly every test item evoked two or more interpretations which were sexually oriented. It is easy to see how this might arise with "a ripe banana," "an octopus," and "a geometric figure"; but one is far less likely to predict such a response with "a peanut butter and jelly sandwich" ("She's a good standby"), "a compass" ("He has a girl everyplace"), "a caterpillar" ("She's a good date, crawls all over you"), "a pack of chewing gum" ("She's cheap"). These sexual interpretations were by no means located solely with one or two individuals (though one person did seem to get carried away), nor were they made predominantly by the male as opposed to the female judges. One subject suggested that the reason for this might be that metaphors are so often used as a device to mask sexual information; I know of no empirical evidence which bears on this.

Fourth, and finally, though there is wide variation in the interpretations provided by the judges, they do not vary totally indiscriminately. Leaving aside those more idiomatic expressions (for example, "He's a dog," "She's a pig"), we can analyze the aspect of the X being evoked by the expression as relating what is believed to be (a) a physical characteristic; (b) a behavioral characteristic; or, (c) a functional characteristic of the object. Many of the interpretations fit into one of these three categories. Take, for example, the case $X=$"a woodchuck," where, in terms of the above framework, we find:

1. *Physical*: has buckteeth, is ugly, is fat, is hairy;
2. *Behavioral*: is industrious, is an introvert, is shy, eats continually, waddles, is always digging, is a careful eater, is plodding, is persistent;
3. *Functional*: (None, but a possibility would be "predicts spring").

However, we also have:

He: is timely, wears glasses, is always in your business, is a workhorse, needs braces, . . .

which do not appear to fit well into this classification, although there are associations which can be suggested. For nearly each of the test X's, the same sort of analysis resulted: Many of the interpretations could be easily related to one of the three aspects of the referent as was done above for "a woodchuck"; in all cases, however, there was a substantial residue which did not seem amenable to this classification. Whether this residue would increase with more subjects, or whether it was an artifact of the present research remains to be clarified.

To summarize, though there is often a definite orientation to the interpretation (positive/negative), often an obvious differentiation between the interpretation when predicated of a male versus a female, sometimes a definite sexual connotation, and sometimes some properties of the X that can be related to the interpretation, there is little evidence of the kind of consistency that would be needed to predict a zero-context interpretation.[5] This, of course, is exactly what one would hope, if the interpretation of a metaphor is to be based within the rules of language *use*, rather than within the rules of grammar. That is, to the extent to which a metaphorical interpretation is determined by the context in which it is uttered, the least consistent interpretations should be the zero-context ones.

I have much less to say on the other questions I raised. There was no evidence that the sex of the judge played any role in the resulting interpretation, though with a larger sample some effect might have become apparent. Since the other possibly important variables, such as education, and cultural and ethnic background were not controlled, I cannot comment on their roles.

The purpose of providing both metaphor and simile test items was, as indicated, to determine if there was any difference in their interpretation. Since the range of responses was so large, it was not possible to find any clear-cut trends. One, however, that did appear to be tenable is the following: The simile was more likely than the metaphor to evoke an interpretation involving the behavior of the X. For example, for "She's like a caterpillar," there were several responses of the sort, "She's in the process of development," whereas there were none for "She's a caterpillar." For "He's like a frog," there were several "He jumps around a lot;" but there was only one such response for "He's a frog." Whether such a trend would show significance on conventional statistical tests remains to be seen.

In conclusion, I began this chapter by indicating that I wanted to respond to Paivio's challenge by investigating the interpretation of novel metaphors. I think that I have done so in a small but significant way. I have presented some precise, factual information about how native speakers interpret novel metaphors, and I have indicated that these interpretations suggest strongly that there is little consistency across speakers, thereby supporting the position that the interpretation of metaphor is based within a theory of language use, not a theory of grammar. Paivio says that "A metaphor is a solar eclipse." I suggest, rather that "Metaphors are black holes in the universe of language": We know that they are there; many prominent people have examined them; they have had enormous amounts of energy poured into them; and, sadly, no one yet knows very much about them.

NOTES

I have benefited greatly from discussions with Jean Fraser, John Ross, and George Miller on the ideas presented here. All, however, have expressed reservations about them!

1 In Fraser (forthcoming), I argue that a theory of pragmatics and a theory of illocutionary acts are equivalent. This appears to be the position of J. J. Katz (1976), as well as that of Bach and Harnish (forthcoming). Searle (1969, 1975) does not mention the term "pragmatics" but does make it clear that in his view, illocutionary acts cannot be separated from a theory of semantics. R. Lakoff (personal communication) sees pragmatics to encompass a much larger domain, perhaps that suggested by Hymes (1973) under the term "communicative competence."

2 In Fraser (1977) I argue that it is only the predicating expression of the propositional content that must be determined by use of an analogy, and that the referring expression (the propositional subject) is unequivocal. Miller (this volume) takes this position as well.

3 Interestingly, we do not find the expressions, "Speaking similely," or "Speaking in a simile," to be acceptable ways to indicate that a simile is intended, perhaps because the presence of "like," "as," or other predicates of similitude serves the purpose. Nor do we find "Speaking ironically," which cannot be for that reason, since there are no syntactic or semantic indicators of irony which can be indicated only by certain performance features, most notably intonation.

4 As various linguists have pointed out, there is a fine line to be drawn between where syntactic generalizations end, and semantic ones begin. Some, in fact, argue that such a distinction is both irrelevant and impossible. It is not necessary for me to take sides in this argument here, inasmuch as all I require is an agreement that certain propositions cannot be interpreted literally because of the propositional structure and the meanings of the individual lexical items.

5 One obvious way to investigate predictabililty would be to ask the judges to provide salient characteristics for each of the X's and then determine if these correspond to their responses.

The Role of Similarity in Similes and Metaphors

ANDREW ORTONY

Professor Paivio's chapter is like a tool kit; it provides the wherewithal for undertaking a serious examination of our problem. The question that now has to be asked is: Does the kit contain the right tools? I suspect that the answer is the same as for most kits. For the problem at hand, some of the tools are useful and some are not. I am going to concentrate on the tool that I believe to be most important of all, namely *similarity*. I shall also discuss briefly two other issues that are raised by Paivio, namely, integration and relation.

Paivio argues that the central question surrounding the comprehension (and the production) of metaphors concerns the way in which a novel conception arises from apparently disparate parts. This question, he claims, involves three important concepts, namely those of integration, relation, and similarity. Similarity is involved because the two terms in a metaphor share attributes. Relation is implicated, because a metaphor may take advantage of common relations, and also because of its involvement in integration. Integration is significant because of the emergence of something new, presumably a result of integrating certain aspects of the parts. As I have said, I think that the most important of these three concepts is that of similarity. For that reason, I shall devote most of my attention to the role of similarity in metaphors, and especially in similes. I think that integration deserves a more thorough treatment than I am able to give it, while relation probably gets more than it deserves.

Accepting the importance of the question Paivio takes to be the central one, I shall start by making a few observations about integration and relation. Paivio does not have much to say about integration beyond the fact that it gives rise to a gestaltlike representation. He presumably believes that this representation finds its home primarily in the imagery system, rather than in the linguistic system. But he cannot claim that it lies exclusively there, because he believes that abstract concepts having little or no image-evoking value are primarily handled by the linguistic system. If this is true, then it follows that metaphors involving very abstract ideas will be processed primarily in the linguistic system, such ideas having few if any connections to the imagery system. However, it does not seem likely that the linguistic system, as Paivio describes it, is able to achieve the integration of disparate elements into a coherent whole. The kinds of representational systems that seem most suited to this task are the abstract representational systems that have been proposed by various psychologists, often of substantially different persuasions in other respects (for example, Anderson & Bower, 1973; Bransford & McCarrell, 1974; Kintsch, 1974; Norman & Rumelhart, 1975; Rumelhart & Ortony, 1977; Pylyshyn, 1973). Paivio does not appear to be very enthusiastic about such proposals.

The second concept that Paivio considers to be important in metaphors is that of relation. Relation, without doubt, plays a role there, as it does in language in general, but I am not at all convinced that the distinction between similarity metaphors and proportional metaphors, which Paivio raises, is a very fruitful one, in spite of its illustrious origins. When metaphors involve common relations, as they do in proportional metaphors, their essential structure seems to me to be the same as that of similarity metaphors. Typically, similarity metaphors have two terms – the first term, often called the *topic*; and the second term, often called the *vehicle*. A similarity metaphor such as, "The man is a sheep," gains its currency from the fact that there is something in common between the topic (man) and the vehicle (sheep). In a proportional metaphor the only difference is that the topic and the vehicle refer to relations rather than to objects.[1] Thus, relations are no more nor less important to the nature of metaphors than are objects. Both are important in that they constitute the kinds of things that tie language to reality, but neither of them are powerful tools for explaining specific linguistic phenomena. To rely on them as basic explanatory devices would be like relying on grass to explain the operation of a lawn mower. When the lawn mower breaks, one calls in a mechanically minded repairman, not a horticulturalist who specializes in grass!

As Paivio observes, the underlying notion of a proportional metaphor is that of analogy. What the metaphor does is to express the analogy in an indirect fashion by leaving out certain of its components. George Miller's chapter in this volume is most relevant in this connection. At the same time, as with similes, the proportional metaphor expresses a similarity between relations that are not really alike. An example of a proportional metaphor, that is, a metaphorical expression of an analogy, may clarify this point. A recent paper by Billow (1975) provides one with: "My head is an apple without any core." This has to be interpreted as asserting that the relationship between my head (or at least, someone's) and something or other, is the same as the relationship between an apple and its nonexistent core. Clearly, part of what is involved in understanding this is the solution of an analogy of the form, "X is to ? as Y is to Z." What makes it a metaphor is not the fact that common relations are involved, but rather the fact that, literally interpreted, the assertion is false. It is false because the relations that are allegedly similar, are not in fact similar at all. I shall have more to say on this question in due course. Actually, such a proportional metaphor can easily be reduced to a "similarity" metaphor by creating a predicate out of the relation, to give: "My head is (like) a coreless apple." The purpose of this apparently fruitless (sic) manipulation is to suggest that the role played by relations in the comprehension and production of metaphors does not have any special significance. Whatever the processes are that enable people to understand metaphors, these processes result in a coherent interpretation of something that if taken literally is either false or meaningless with respect to the context in which it occurs. Whether the implicit comparison involves relations or objects seems to be a relatively unimportant question; some analogies are literal analogies and some are not. In either case, they involve alleged similarities – similarities between relations between objects, rather than between objects themselves. So, as Paivio implies, the question of relations has to be subsumed partly under that of integration, and partly under that of similarity, which I take to be the guts of the problem, and which I shall now discuss.

It is often claimed that metaphors are merely implicit comparisons, to be contrasted with similes, which are explicit ones. I have very little faith in this view: first, because I do not think that it is true of all metaphors; and second, because even if it were, it would be totally unilluminating. The fact that metaphors are frequently used to make comparisons, if it is a fact, does not mean that metaphors *are* comparisons. A metaphor is a kind of *use* of language, whereas a comparison is a kind of psychological process, which while quite possibly an essential component of certain kinds of language use, is not the same thing as such a use.

In any event, it is probably not possible to map all metaphors into similes; and if it is not, then it becomes necessary to explain why some implicit comparisons are incapable of being made explicit. But a more serious problem with the claim is that even if it were true, or even if it is interpreted in a way that makes it plausible, it has no explanatory power unless it is assumed that the comparison, implicit in a metaphor and explicit in its corresponding simile, is a *literal* comparison, i.e., a literal use of language. If this assumption were true, then the claim would suggest a reductionist program whereby metaphors could be reduced to literal language. But, if the assumption is false, as I shall argue it is, then the comparisons involved in both metaphors ("John is an ox") and in similes ("John is like an ox") still require explanations, because they cannot be construed as literal uses of language. In other words, the problems posed by the existence of metaphors are also posed by the existence of similes, so that the reduction of metaphors to similes will contribute nothing to their solution.

The fact that metaphors are not to be identified with comparisons, however, does not mean that the process of making comparisons is not of the utmost importance in the comprehension of metaphors. I shall argue that the process of making comparisons is of fundamental importance in the comprehension of similes, and that the process can be construed in such a way as to make it perfectly appropriate for metaphors, even though, unlike similes, they lack the surface structural linguistic signals (e.g., the presence of the word "like") which invite an attempt to make a comparison. Given my unwillingness to equate metaphors with "literal" similes (which I take to be a contradiction in terms), I feel well justified in concentrating my efforts on similes, hoping thereby to distill the more general notion of "nonliteral" as a prelude to understanding what is involved in the comprehension of metaphors. For convenience, I shall sometimes refer to the terms in a simile in the same way as to the terms in a metaphor, using "topic" for the first term and "vehicle" for the second.

Comparisons are more or less successful or appropriate to the degree to which the things being compared are, or can be found to be, similar. So, if understanding similes and metaphors involves making comparisons, and if making comparisons involves making similarity judgments, then we need to focus on the nature of these judgments. That is why I think Paivio is right to treat similarity as a central concept. But the current situation in psychology concerning the analysis of similarity, particularly of meaning similarity, is not quite as gloomy as Paivio suggests. A recent paper by Tversky (1977) attests to this fact. Tversky describes how, in most approaches to similarity, the degree of similarity between two terms is represented by an inverse function of the distance between their representations in a multidimensional space (e.g., Carroll & Wish, 1974; Henley, 1969; Rumelhart & Abrahamson, 1973; and Shepard, 1974). As Paivio suggests, these approaches have their shortcomings. One is that they are only appropriate for certain kinds of stimuli; namely those for which a small number of dimensions can be found (for example, colors and tones). But for our purposes, there is a particularly serious problem. Since the distance between two points

(say, *A* and *B*) in an *n*-dimensional Euclidian space is the same whether
measured from *A* to *B* or from *B* to *A*, it follows that such models of
similarity entail something that is empirically false; namely, that people's
similarity judgments are symmetrical.[2] As Tversky notes in passing,
similes and metaphors are very good counterexamples, for if the terms in
them are reversed they may become meaningless, or their meaning may
change substantially. This tends to be less true for literal comparisons.
So, for example, blackberries are probably like raspberries to the same
degree that raspberries are like blackberries, and for the same reasons.
By contrast, billboards are probably more like warts than warts are like
billboards; and even if they are not, asserting that billboards are like
warts would mean something quite different from asserting that warts
are like billboards. If the similarity relation were independent of the
relative position of the terms in it, then those positions should make
only a stylistic, not a semantic, difference.

Finding geometric models of similarity unsatisfactory, Tversky offers
an alternative account – an account based on feature matching. In
this context, a feature is to be thought of as an attribute or predicate
in a rather general sense, so that a feature of *X* is "something that is
known about *X*." The basis of Tversky's model, put in words, is that
the degree of similarity between two objects is a weighted function of
their intersecting features minus a weighted function of the features
distinctive to one and of the features distinctive to the other. Tversky
presents a good deal of evidence for the goodness of fit between similarity ratings predicted by his model and those reported by subjects, both
for visual and verbal materials. Toward the end of his paper he says:

> It appears that people interpret metaphors by scanning the feature space and
> selecting the features of the referent [vehicle] that are applicable to the sub-
> ject [topic] . . . The nature of this process is left to be explained.
>   There is a close tie between the assessment of similarity and the interpreta-
> tion of metaphors. In judgments of similarity one assumes a particular feature
> space, or a frame of reference, and assesses the quality of the match between
> the subject and the referent. In the interpretation of similes, one assumes a
> resemblance between the subject and the referent, and searches for an inter-
> pretation of the space that would maximize the quality of the match. (p. 349)

I think that, for the most part, Tversky is right, and that his account
goes a long way toward civilizing what Paivio sees as an underdevel-
oped area. However, in my discussion I shall not use the term "feature." I am anxious to avoid giving the impression that I am referring
to semantic features in the traditional sense, for I am not. I am really
referring to "subschemata," that is, to knowledge representations that
are constituent structures of the representations of the entities being

compared. A more detailed discussion of subschemata, and schema theory in general, can be found in Rumelhart and Ortony (1977). Now, although I am referring to subschemata, it is very awkward to talk about "subschema matching," so I shall use the term "predicate" which, I think, does pretty much the same job. A predicate can be attributed to, or predicated of something. It can represent knowledge, a belief, or an attitude about or toward something, and that is just what I want.

In returning to the topic of similarity, I should like to start by comparing an ordinary statement of comparison with a simile. Certainly, both have the surface structure of explicit comparisons, as can be seen from (1) and (2).

(1) Encyclopedias are like dictionaries

(2) Encyclopedias are like gold mines.

But I am going to argue that whereas (1) is a literal comparison (encyclopedias really are like dictionaries), (2) is a nonliteral comparison (encyclopedias are not really like gold mines). I have two principal arguments in support of this conclusion, and because I think that it is an important conclusion to establish, and because many people find it counterintuitive and simply assert that it is false, I shall spell out the arguments in detail.

The first argument pertains to the intuitions of ordinary people, as opposed to those of the theoreticians, who are so prone to ignore them. If one asks someone whether encyclopedias are really like gold mines one never gets a straightforward positive answer. Very often one gets a straightforward negative answer, particularly if the question is posed in contrast to the question: "Are encyclopedias really like dictionaries?" This must mean that people do not believe that (2) is true; they are more likely to say that it is false. By contrast, they normally believe that (1) is true. So, there is a prima facie case for saying that (2) is false. Related to this fact, is a linguistic fact, namely, that similes such as (2) are much more likely to be found in conjunction with hedges such as "sort of," "kind of," "in a way," and so on. Indeed, when people do not straightforwardly deny the truth of assertions like (2) their acceptance of them is invariably accompanied by some kind of hedge. So, I think that there is evidence that people generally will assent to the truth of an ordinary comparison without hesitation, whereas they are very willing to deny the truth of a simile if they are encouraged to evaluate its truth in the same literal way they use for ordinary comparisons. Consequently, I am inclined to believe that typically ordinary comparisons are literally true (if they are appropriately intended as such), while similes are literally false.

My second argument is a kind of *reductio ad absurdum.* Suppose one argues the other side of the issue. Suppose, that is, that one vigorously maintains that similes are literally true. On what basis is that argument advanced? The answer is that it is based on the belief that to some degree, and in some respect or respects, everything is like everything else. So, if everything is like everything else, then certainly encyclopedias are like gold mines, and they are also like ice cream, infinity, and anything else you care to think of. But this argument has some curious consequences, the most serious of which seems to be this. If all similarity statements are true by virtue of the fact that everything is like everything else, then there is no possibility of a similarity statement ever being false. This means that similarity statements are necessarily true, which means that they are tautologies. Since tautologies convey no new information, similarity statements can convey no new information. Apart from this conclusion being absurd, it is plainly false, for to say that the structure of an atom is similar to the structure of the solar system, can indeed be to say something that conveys new information. In fact, it is a fairly standard way of teaching the rudiments of atomic physics. Furthermore, if similarity statements have the characteristic (one that is not shared by any other class of widely used statements) of being always true, another problem arises. One of the reasons that assertions are meaningful is that there always exists the possibility that they are false, just as with orders there exists the possibility that they will not be obeyed, and with promises, that they will not be kept. There is nothing contradictory about asserting that encyclopedias are not like gold mines, yet there would have to be if one were to accept the position described above. Thus, again, I find myself forced to conclude that to deny that some similarity statements can be false is an untenable position, and if they can be false, there seems to be no objection to saying that similes, if interpreted like ordinary comparisons, constitute good examples of false similarity statements.

I have several times used the phrase "similes, interpreted like ordinary comparisons," or phrases like it. The time has now come to explain what that is supposed to mean. When we are faced with a similarity statement that is literally true, it is always the case that some of the predicates that are important to one of the terms are also important to the other term. The interpretation of ordinary similarity statements can therefore be regarded as involving the determination of shared high-salient predicates in much the way that Tversky envisions it. The point about similes is that this procedure will produce *no* such shared predicates at all, unless those predicates are themselves interpreted metaphorically.[3] In his chapter in this volume, Searle makes much the same point. Now, if the ordinary procedure for interpreting similarity statements involves finding shared high-salient predicates, and if, as both Tversky's theory and my intuitions tell me, one of the features determining the degree of similarity is the quality of the match, or the number of shared high-salient predicates, then, since the terms in a simile have no such shared predicates, the procedure will fail to find anything important in common between the two terms. Thus, to say that they are alike, is either false, or metaphorical. So, from now on I am going to refer to ordinary similarity statements as being "literal comparisons" and I am going to refer to similes as being "nonliteral" comparisons. The question that now has to be answered is: "What are the processes involved in arriving at a coherent interpretation of a nonliteral comparison?"

According to Tversky, one "assumes a resemblance . . . and searches for an interpretation of the space that would maximize the quality of the match." But how does one know to do that, rather than to do what he says has to be done for literal comparisons, namely to assume the feature space and find the match? Tversky seems to be proposing two related but different operations, but the surface structures of the comparisons provide no clues as to which one is applicable. Perhaps the default process is that for literal comparisons; then, if no match is found, the space is reinterpreted to produce one. But suppose the process for interpreting literal comparisons were just the one that Tversky says applies in the case of metaphors, namely, finding predicates of the second term that are applicable to the first. Then, the same process might work for both literal comparisons and for nonliteral comparisons (similes). Of course, this process ought not to succeed if just any old predicates can be applied, since the predicate "is a thing" can be trivially applied to both gold mines and encyclopedias. We will have to restrict the predicates to be applied, at least initially, to salient ones. Paivio's interesting suggestion that concrete vehicles are better than abstract ones, may thus relate to the fact – if it is a fact – that concrete terms have more salient predicates associated with them than do abstract terms, as well as to the fact that they are more accessible. Before proceeding, it is important to point out that the distinction between salient and nonsalient predicates is not a sharp one. In extreme cases, however, it is obvious. There are doubtless large individual differences resulting from the different conceptions and experiences that different people have of things. My use of the notion of salience here is based on an operational definition, a solution that may satisfy psychologists, but that probably leaves philosophers cold.

The concepts of gold mines and encyclopedias, like all concepts, have predicates associated with them, which vary in their salience according to the context in which they are used (see Anderson & Ortony, 1975). Suppose that the comparison process takes the predicates of "gold mines" and tries to apply them to "encyclopedias," starting with the most salient. We get back to Tversky's notion of matching by having the criterion for a predicate applying to a concept as being the appearance of that predicate somewhere in the topic concept's internal structure. Now, there are either very few – or more likely, no – high-salient predicates of "gold mines" that are also high-salient predicates of "encyclopedias"; and for that reason I have suggested that (2) is not a literal comparison; but there are high-salient predicates of "gold mines" that are lower-salient predicates of "encylopedias," and for that reason (2) is an interpretable comparison. This leads to the following account: in a comparison, "A is like B," if high-salient predicates of B are also high-salient predicates of A, then the comparison is a literal one and the two referents will be judged as being "really" similar. If a high-salient predicate of B is a less-salient predicate of A while there are high-salient predicates of B that cannot be applied to A at all, then we have a simile. If no high-salient predicate of B can be applied to A then the comparison is either uninterpretable, or nonsense (if there is a difference).

It should be noted that similes can easily be modified so as to come very close to being literal comparisons. If a modifier is introduced that is in fact an attribute with respect to which both terms are comparable, then by temporarily increasing the salience of that attribute for the A term, the comparison may result in a match of high-salient predicates. So we can think of modifiers as emphasizing (that is, increasing the salience of) predicates that correspond to them, and consequently they serve to identify the matching salient predicates, by specifying them and accentuating them. Thus, while (3) is a simile, (4) is much more like a literal comparison.

(3) His face was like a beet.

(4) His face was red like a beet.

The difference between the two is that in (4) the salience of a predicate of the unfortunate referent's face has been increased, thus rendering a match of high-salient predicates, whereas in (3) the match is of high- to low-salient predicates. It seems, therefore, that whether a particular use of language on a particular occasion is literal or nonliteral, is a question of degree rather than a question of kind.

I shall now review some preliminary data that I have collected which relate to the role of shared salient predicates in literal and nonliteral comparisons. In a predicate elicitation task, subjects were asked to list the predicates of 40 terms; 10 terms were given to each of four groups of subjects. The 40 items were derived from 10 triplets of comparisons. Each triplet contained a simile such as (2) and two literal comparisons, one for each of the terms in the simile. Thus, if (2) was the simile, (1) would be one of the literal comparisons (for encyclopedias), and (5) would be the other (for gold mines).

(1) Encyclopedias are like dictionaries.
(2) Encyclopedias are like gold mines.
(5) Gold mines are like oil wells.

Subjects listed an average of just over six predicates for each of their ten items. Having listed the predicates for a particular item, each subject ranked the predicates for importance and then indicated how many of them, in order of importance, were felt to be necessary to identify the item to someone who did not know what it was. This was taken as the operational definition of salience. Subjects rated an average of about three predicates per term as being salient. The predicated similarities were computed in accordance with Tversky's formula; the resulting values were always much lower for the similes than for the literal controls.

The point of interest for the moment, however, is the relative likelihood of shared predicates appearing for the literal and nonliteral comparisons. Referring now only to salient predicates, about twenty-five percent of those listed for terms in literal comparisons were listed for both the terms, compared with only about one percent for similes. If these values are weighted according to the frequency of mention, the difference becomes even more dramatic. These data show that the terms from the similes had virtually no common salient predicates, whereas those in the literal comparisons had many. The conclusion to be drawn is that if, in saying that two things are similar, one means that they have important things in common, then the data strongly suggest that similes, or at least the terms in them, are not in fact similar, whereas the terms in literal comparisons are. This, of course, is not to say that a similarity between the terms in a simile cannot be found, but in finding such resemblances, the interpretation of the simile would cease to be a literal interpretation.

It is instructive to look at a particular example to see the relationships between high- and low-salient predicates. Consider the simile expressed in (6), which was alluded to earlier.

(6) Billboards are like warts.

Table 1 lists the predicates that were most frequently mentioned as being salient for each term. These predicates are listed in order of likelihood of mention. The most frequent one was listed by over ninety

TABLE 1

Billboards	Warts
are used for advertising	are found on the skin
are found by the roadside	are usually removed
are large	are ugly
etc.	are growths
	etc.

percent of the subjects, and the less frequent ones, by about forty per-cent. It would not be unreasonable to use the probability of inclusion as a salient predicate as a first-order approximation to the degree of sa-lience. On this basis, one would have to say that .40 was a high value. That happens to be the value for "ugly" with respect to warts. Now "ugly" did not occur at all as a high-salient predicate of "billboards," but it was listed as a predicate with a probability of about .07. Thus it seems justifiable to say that being ugly is a high-salient predicate of warts, though a low-salient predicate of "billboards." Notice that there is no high-salient predicate shared by each of the terms, so that the comparison expressed by (6) is a nonliteral comparison, or simile, rather than a literal comparison. Billboards are not really like warts, they are only like warts metaphorically speaking.

I argued earlier that there was a big difference between asserting (6) and asserting (7).

(7) Warts are like billboards.

An interpretation of (7) would involve finding high-salient predicates of "billboards" that are low-salient predicates of warts. So, one might suppose that the point of uttering (7) would be to emphasize the fact that warts can be large and conspicuous, and so on, rather than that they are ugly, for these are high-salient predicates of billboards that are applicable to warts. The lack of symmetry in nonliteral comparisons is thus due to the fact that the terms have nonoverlapping sets of salient predicates. Literal comparisons may also be asymmetrical due to the fact that some applicable predicates of one of the terms are not high-salient predicates of the other. But, since there are always shared salient predicates of both, the lack of symmetry is less obvious and less radical. The difference between the meanings of (6) and (7), seems to me to be far greater than that between (8) and (9).

(8) Warts are like sores.

(9) Sores are like warts.

In this pair, the primary difference is due to the change in what is being talked about; the basis of the comparison is substantially the same in each case, even though it might not be identical. The same is true for the raspberries and blackberries case discussed earlier. In any event, one thing is certain; any treatment of similes and metaphors must account for the fact that they are radically asymmetrical. The account I have offered seems capable of doing that if nothing else.

My discussion of the role of similarity has so far been primarily concerned with establishing an empirical criterion to distinguish literal from nonliteral comparisons. This criterion has been cast in terms of the degree to which high-salient predicates of the second term are high- or low-salient predicates of the first. I have suggested a way in which the same process could underlie the comprehension of both literal and nonliteral comparisons. The process would be a "predicate application" process whereby known salient predicates of the vehicle would be applied – as it were, experimentally – to the topic. But if we unpack the notion of "application," what do we get? If the process involves trying to apply a predicate to the topic, what criteria are there for determining whether the application was successful or possible? As we saw earlier, one way is to see if the predicate being applied is already known to be a predicate of the topic. So, it may be that predicate matching has to be construed as an integral part of the predicate application process, a part that is sometimes successful and sometimes not. This then raises the question of what happens if the to-be-applied predicate is not already a predicate of the topic (for the reader or hearer). If a great deal is known about the topic, matching could play a major role. But if little is known, insufficient to give a coherent match, it will be to no avail. Furthermore, in such cases, the process of predicate *selection*, in which predicates that *can* be applied *are* applied, may be much less efficient than a process of predicate *rejection* in which all predicates of the vehicle are assumed to apply unless there is some fundamental incompatibility. What is here being suggested is this: When very little is known about the topic, predicates from the vehicle which are clearly incompatible with it are rejected; the manner in which, and extent to which, the other predicates do apply is hardly determined at all. On the other hand, if a great deal is known about the topic, the predicates that apply are selected and the resulting interpretation is more specific and more restricted. This distinction has, I think, some important consequences with respect to the creation of the "novel conceptual entity" that Paivio talks about, and I shall return to it shortly.

The position that I have adopted is still basically one that denies any fundamentally important difference in the processing of literal and nonliteral comparisons. I am inclined to believe that this is true for literal and metaphorical uses of language in general. Of course, there are cases in which a hearer or reader may fail to come up with a coherent interpretation using the processes we have described. There are often occasions upon which one says to oneself: "I wonder what on earth that was supposed to mean." In such cases, I think that some relatively more deliberate problem-solving strategies are brought to bear, initiated by a kind of Gricean pragmatic analysis (see Grice, 1975), as described in the chapter by Searle. Such an analysis would require a person to relate the utterance meaning to the speaker meaning by resolving apparent violations of the implicit conventions governing linguistic interactions. Specifically, I assume that when the reader or hearer fails to (sensibly) interpret something which he or she has reason to believe was intended to be meaningful, there follows an attempt to render the violation of the conventions (probably those of being relevant and of being sincere) only apparent. The hearer would then assume that there is a detectable basis for comparison and would engage in processes that might help find it. But, of course this general account applies equally well to obscure literal uses of language. There may be a difference in the particular linguistic conventions that are violated, but a deliberate "figuring out of the intended meaning" is certainly not something that is necessarily restricted to nonliteral uses of language (Ortony, Schallert, Reynolds, & Antos, 1978).

A reasonable complaint that could be made at this juncture is that my discussion has centered around similes and has left their relevance for the topic of metaphor to the imagination. So I shall now devote a few moments to talking about that relationship. Insofar as the comprehension of metaphor involves making comparisons, one might suppose that the processes required to comprehend metaphors would overlap with those required to comprehend similes. It has been argued, for example by Kintsch (1974), that the comprehension of metaphor in fact proceeds by the conversion of the metaphor into a simile. But even if one were to accept this suggestion (assuming that the conversion is always possible, which I doubt), the manner in which, and the reason for which, the conversion takes place still has to be explained. Consider (10) which is a metaphorical statement of the simile, (2).

(10) Encyclopedias are gold mines.

When a hearer (or reader) encounters (10) in a particular context, there might come a point at which he realizes that if it is interpreted literally it is either false or nonsensical. And, unlike a simile, it does not have the surface characteristics of a comparison; so even though the processes for interpreting similes may be the same as those for interpreting literal comparisons, there is initially no reason to suppose that those processes are engaged. It first has to be thought of as though it were a comparison, a comparison which cannot be literally true since (10) is not. It may be that the comprehension processes for comparisons then comes into play. One possibility is that in such "attributive" metaphors predicates are attributed to the topic in just the same way as in similes, inapplicable predicates of the vehicle getting left behind. In some cases this may well happen, but I doubt that it does in all. In other cases an additional mechanism is required, namely a mechanism that relates sentence meanings to speaker meanings, as described above. This is the approach taken by Searle in his chapter.

Finally, I want to introduce a distinction between "predicate promotion" metaphors and "predicate introduction" metaphors – a distinction that relates to the one between predicate selection and predicate rejection that I mentioned a little while ago. In a predicate promotion metaphor it is assumed that the hearer (and presumably the speaker) knows enough about the topic to recognize that what is implicitly being said of it is true. Such metaphors often involve generic terms. Consider (10) again: Most people know that encyclopedias are a source of knowledge, and that sources of knowledge are useful and desirable, and so forth. It is predicates such as these that one might expect to be applicable to "gold mines." When somebody understands the metaphor in this way, I want to argue that he already knows that the predicates in question are true of the A term, so that the information extractable from the metaphor is old information and it is recognized as such by the speaker and hearer. Consequently, all that the hearer does in comprehension is to promote the salience of the relevant predicates for the A term. But there is another possibility, namely, cases where the hearer knows very little about the topic, and in comprehending the metaphor, discovers something new about it; or at least makes inferences about something previously unknown. In these cases I want to say that from the hearer's point of view, the metaphor is a predicate introduction metaphor, namely, one in which the salience of an existing predicate (or set of predicates) cannot be increased, because they are not yet predicates of the A term at all; they are introduced as new predicates as a result of the comprehension process.

I have been arguing that in similes, high-salient predicates of the vehicle are low-salient predicates of the topic, and this distinguishes similes from literal comparisons, where the match is of high to high-salient predicates. But now we can see that something more is happening. Consider (11), for example:

(11) Attila the Hun had manners like a cesspool.

Suppose someone utters (11) and the hearer knows nothing more specific about Attila the Hun than that he was a renowned barbarian. Then, although no high-salient predicates of cesspools are low-salient predicates of Attila, or of his manners, (11) is interpretable, and most people will interpret it correctly. Less salient predicates that the speaker has for Attila may include things like "being extremely unpleasant," "having repulsive manners" and so on. These are not attributes of Attila the Hun at all from the hearer's point of view. Indeed, the purpose of the simile may be to introduce these ideas. So, perhaps we should say the following: A simile, by using high-salient predicates of the vehicle that are lower-salient predicates of the topic, if they are predicates at all, has the effect of emphasizing or promoting the salience of those predicates if they were low-salient, and of introducing them if they were not there at all. In predicate promotion metaphors, the predicates are already there, and they get promoted or emphasized. In predicate introduction metaphors, they are not already there and they get introduced. I think that it might be the case that predicate introduction metaphors are one of the cornerstones of insight. Their comprehension results in richer representations – representations that may be to some extent inappropriate because they exclude only what is flagrantly incompatible. Their richness is partially a consequence of this. The predicates that are transferred from the vehicle to the topic are more holistic, less discrete, and can include perceptual and emotive aspects. As I have argued elsewhere (see, Ortony, 1975; 1976), this may bring them closer to perceptual representations than most language-initiated representations. I think that this may be why imagery is so important in metaphors, as I am sure Paivio and others believe. This more coherent, holistic representation helps us to see things in different ways. And, as has often been argued, seeing things in different ways is a necessary prerequisite for scientific discovery. As Whitehead put it: "Fundamental progress has to do with the reinterpretation of basic ideas."

Although I have argued that similes and metaphors are usually processed in much the same way as is literal language, there remain important differences between the two, differences which concern their uses and functions in communication. And there is another difference too. All uses of language tend to stretch it; but in literal uses, language bounces back. Metaphors stretch language beyond its elastic limit.

NOTES

I am particularly indebted to David Rumelhart. Some of the ideas in this paper are at least partially a result of hours of discussion with him. I also wish to acknowledge the help afforded me by a Spencer Fellowship awarded

by the National Academy of Education. The work described herein was also
supported by a contract from the National Institute of Education.

1 By "objects" I do not wish to imply "physical objects," but rather those entities, real or imaginary, which can enter into relations. For the dangers of
treating "objects" as "physical objects," see the chapter by Searle.

2 It should be noted, however, that there have been proposals to modify geometric models so as to avoid this difficulty (see, for example, Krumhansl,
1978).

3 This is a complicated question that is beyond the scope of this paper. However, it is important to realize that it does not have to lead to infinite
regress. One can argue for a recursive comprehension process. The stop rule
would either be a detection of a match prior to reaching some processing
threshold, or the failure to do so. In this case, the result might be an awareness of failure to comprehend.

Images and Models, Similes and Metaphors

GEORGE A. MILLER

I shall try to defend a version of the traditional view that a metaphor is an abbreviated simile, and that the thought provoked is the kind required to appreciate similarities and analogies. In the nineteenth century that kind of thought was called "apperception."

"Apperception" is one mentalistic term that has not been rehabilitated by cognitive psychologists in recent years; perhaps it is time we got around to it. For Herbart (1898) "apperception" was a general term for those mental processes whereby an attended experience is brought into relation with an already acquired and familiar conceptual system. Today our psychological journals are full of terms like "encoding," "mapping," "categorizing," "inference," "assimilation and accommodation," "attribution," and so on; perhaps "apperception" would be a useful superordinate for all of them.

If I understand Herbart correctly, his general claim was that new things are learned by being related to things already known; he built his educational psychology on the belief that if teachers know what their pupils know, they can relate ideas they want to teach to ideas the pupil has already mastered. Although Herbart's term has passed from fashion, the educational philosophy of maximizing transfer of training seems as sensible now as it did a century ago. In my view, much of the scientific interest of an analysis of metaphor derives from what it might contribute to a theory of apperception appropriate to the psychological and educational concepts of the twentieth century.

In order to stay within manageable limits, I shall ignore the sort of root metaphors whose detailed development can motivate elaborate literary or scientific constructions; I shall concentrate on what might be called local metaphors, which can enrich a single phrase or sentence. And, since any metaphor can be written, I shall refer to the recipient of the metaphor as "the reader."[1]

Textual concepts

The need to understand how people relate new ideas to old is particularly acute in the psychology of reading. As a person reads and understands a passage, the new information he encounters has to be related both to his store of general knowledge – to his "apperceptive mass," as it used to be called – and to his internal representation of the passage itself. As new information is added, of course, it becomes part of the old information to which further new information can be added, and so a "textual concept" grows as reading proceeds. Reading with comprehension is a test-tube example of apperception in action. I shall first sketch my view of the apperceptive processes involved in reading comprehension, then discuss the comprehension of expressions of similitude, and finally consider metaphor as posing a particular kind of apperceptive difficulty.

Remembering

What happens as we read a descriptive prose passage? If we attend closely and try to understand, we do more than move our eyes along the lines and mumble words to our inner ear. It changes us. When we finish reading, we have something that we did not have before we began. The psychological problem is how to characterize the change that occurs in a reader when he has carefully read a passage of straight, expository, descriptive prose.

Images. One approach is introspective. Indulge me, therefore, by participating in an experiment in self-observation. Below is a descriptive passage taken from Henry Thoreau's (1937) *Walden*. Read it attentively, but at the same time try to keep track of what is going on as you read:

Near the end of March, 1845, I borrowed an axe and went down to the woods by Walden Pond, nearest to where I intended to build my house, and began to cut down some tall, arrowy white pines, still in their youth, for timber . . . It was a pleasant hillside where I worked, covered with pine woods, through which I looked out on the pond, and a small open field in the woods where pines and hickories were springing up. The ice in the pond was not yet dissolved, though there were some open spaces, and it was all dark-colored and saturated with water.

My introspections on reading this passage persuade me that I built something in my imagination – a sort of mental picture to which I added details as I encountered successive phrases and sentences. Let me call what I was building an "image." Since I am well aware that what took shape in my mind was different from a photographic image, or a perceptual image, of the episode and landscape that Thoreau was describing, I need to qualify this label in order to mark the difference:

I shall call it a "memory image" whenever I feel there is danger of confusing it with something more substantial or detailed.

My memory image grew piecemeal in roughly the following way. First I read that the time was late March; I formed no image at this point, but filed it away for possible use later. (This is not a satisfactory account: I shall return to "March, 1845" below.) Next, I saw an indistinct Thoreau borrow an axe from an even less distinct somebody and walk, axe in hand, to some woods near a pond. The following phrase turned the trees into white pines, and I saw Thoreau, his back toward me, swinging his axe on them. The next sentence introduced a hillside; suddenly the ground in my image tilted and the scene became firm. Then it was a simple matter to add the pond, the open field, the melting ice.

I make no substantive claims about my personal imagery, which I know to be predominantly visual; you may have smelled the piney woods or heard the axe biting into the trees. My point is that I felt I was doing something constructive as I read the passage; the result of this constructive mental activity was a memory image that summarized the information I had extracted from the passage. Although the memory image remained vague in many respects, it was nonetheless a particular image, just as the prose passage by Thoreau is a particular passage. Indeed, part of my memory image was an image of the passage itself, as well as the scene it described.

One way to characterize the change that occurs in reading, therefore, is to say that you construct an image as part of the process of understanding the passage, and that the image helps you to remember what you have read. It helps you to remember in the following sense. If, after putting down the book, you were asked to repeat what you have read, you would probably not be able to repeat it verbatim. Nevertheless, you could reactivate your memory image and describe it, thus generating a different prose passage, but one that (if your memory is good) would be roughly equivalent to the original passage that inspired the memory image. Many psychological experiments have shown that people forget some details and embellish others, so the process is not perfect. But the memory image provides some record of the passage and of information extracted from it – a record that is constructed as the passage is read, phrase by phrase.

The iconic character of memory images should not be exaggerated. The passage from Thoreau was deliberately selected; many others would have been far more difficult to visualize. Moreover, some people claim not to have such imagery; they search their mental furniture in vain for anything resembling a picture of the description they are reading. If we are to believe these people (and I do), there must be other ways to remember what is read. Let me generalize what I mean by "memory image," therefore, to include all mental processes that can construct a particular record of a particular passage and of the information extracted from it. For some people, it is convenient to exploit the apparently enormous storage capacity of the perceptual system in order to construct this record, but that is not the only way, and, for some passages, it is not even an easy way to construct and preserve that record in all its individual particularity. For highly abstract passages, the memory image may be predominantly an image, visual or auditory, of the text itself.

All of this is surely familiar to anyone who has thought about it, but I have gone over it in order to make clear what I mean by a memory image, and what the intuitive basis is for claims that understanding a passage like this one is a constructive mental process.

I shall add only one point that is sometimes overlooked when memory images are discussed: the vagueness of the image is critical to its utility. If memory images had to be completely detailed, like photographs, they could not preserve the incomplete information given by written descriptions. Thoreau did not describe every detail of the hillside above Walden Pond; a reader who wants to remember accurately what Thoreau *did* describe had better not clutter the memory image with details that were not provided. It may be impossible to construct an image that does not contain *some* extraneous information that is merely suggested, not entailed, by the text (Anderson & Ortony, 1975); a reader lacking any knowledge of the New England countryside, for example, would not construct the same image as a reader who knew it well. My point is simply that such additions from general knowledge are potential sources of error, even when they appear highly probable in the given context.

Models. This account of imagery formation will be persuasive to many people, but let me now describe another way to characterize what went on as I read the sample passage.

First, I cleared my mind of other matters. This initial attitude was one in which, potentially, any state of affairs at all could be represented. When I read the first sentence and encountered Thoreau borrowing an axe, I used that information to narrow down the variety of possible states of affairs to just those that included Thoreau borrowing an axe. When I read next that he went down to the woods by Walden Pond, I narrowed the potential set even further, now to those that included Thoreau with his axe walking to the woods by Walden Pond. As I continued to pick up information from the passage, I used it phrase by phrase to restrict the set of possible states of affairs that I was considering. By the time I finished, I had narrowed down this set considerably, but there were still indefinitely many alternatives left— alternatives I had not gathered sufficient information to distinguish among.

When I described my imagery, I described the process as *constructive*. The second account I have given is not constructive, but *selective*. As each item of information is understood and added to the image, it is used to select a smaller subset of possible states of affairs compatible with the image. Constructing something is not the same as selecting it. Moreover, the end product is different. The constructive process results in a memory image, a single representation of a scene whose particularities correspond closely to the particularities of the passage. The selective process, on the other hand, results in a collection of possible states of affairs that correspond to the written passage only with respect to their shared features, but which differ from one another in all other respects.

On first hearing the selective account, many people feel it violates common experience. It is hard enough to hold one memory image before the mind's eye. How could anyone deal with an indefinitely large collection of images simultaneously? I agree completely with this complaint. Indeed, I would insist on it, because it shows so clearly that whatever the mental representations are that the reader is selecting among, they cannot be images. If we are to take the selective hypothesis seriously, we must be clear that the sets of possible states of affairs among which the reader is choosing are not images. The simplest way to remember that is to give these sets a different name. I shall call them "models" of the passage. Since there are many different kinds of models (Black, 1962a), however, I shall call them *semantic models* when there is any possibility of confusion.

A semantic model for a given text, then, is the set of all possible states of affairs in which all of the information in the memory image for that text is true. In order to be a member of this set, any particular state of affairs must be consistent with all of the information the reader has been given. All of the facts stated in the description are necessarily true in the model – they are true of every element in the set. Any facts that would contradict the facts stated in the description are necessarily false. And any facts that have neither been given nor contradicted are possibly true – they are true of some state of affairs contained in the model, but need not be true of all.

Semantic models are more abstract than memory images. A model is a set of things, but I have not yet characterized those things – all I have said is that they are not images. We could, without violating the spirit of the selective hypothesis, think of them as potential, but as yet unimagined, images. Or, in keeping with a more linguistic interpretation, we could think of the model as the passage plus the set of all possible continuations of the passage. As we read the passage, we construct a memory image that enables us to narrow the set of possible continuations.

Consider models from the author's point of view. Thoreau had something in mind when he wrote the passage we read. If he wrote it as a description of an actual scene – if his model contained just one representation of a unique state of affairs it is not difficult to understand how he could have used the model to determine that every sentence he wrote was true of that scene. On the other hand, if he was writing from memory, he had probably forgotten many specific details, in which case the model selected by his image contained more than one representation compatible with what he remembered, but he could still use his model to insure that every sentence he wrote was true in the model.

That is how semantic models are usually thought of. It is assumed that the model is given in advance, and sentences expressing various facts can then be judged as necessarily or possibly true or false in that model. In short, *an author uses a semantic model to select true descriptive sentences.*

Now consider models from the reader's point of view. Initially, the reader has a very general model if he has any at all. The reader is given, not a model, but a text, a string of descriptive sentences. He must discover a model that is compatible with those sentences – a model that includes the author's model as a subset. The reader's basic assumption must be that the sentences he is given are true. Then his task becomes just the reverse of the author's: *a reader uses the true descriptive sentence to select a model* (Cushing, 1977).

Textual concepts. I have now presented two ways to characterize what goes on when a person reads a passage of descriptive prose. Since they seem different, you might be tempted to ask which is correct. I claim that both are correct.

A reader has both a memory image and a model. They serve related but different purposes. The memory image serves as a mental surrogate for the descriptive passage itself. It is a historical record, accurate just to the extent that it contains all, and only, the information in the passage. The model, on the other hand, keeps the mind open to future possibilities. Its importance might be illustrated as follows:[2] reinstate your image of Thoreau's scene and use it to decide whether there was any snow. The passage did not mention snow; if your memory image is accurate, it will not have any snow either. If all that you had were this image, you would have to answer no, because there is no snow in your memory image. Yet you know that the fact that Thoreau did not mention snow in what you read does not mean that there was none. If you answer yes, however, you may be going too far beyond the information given. For all you know, the next sentence may say, "There was no snow that winter." All you can say is, "It is possible that there was snow, but I don't know yet."

What does your ignorance imply? If you were looking at a real scene and someone asked whether there was any snow, you would have little difficulty answering. In order to know that you do not know, there must be some mental machinery that supplements your memory image. That additional machinery is the semantic model, which differs from a real scene in being a whole set of representations of alternative states of affairs, some with snow and some without. Bishop Berkeley once argued that there can be no abstract ideas, because ideas are images and images are particular; you cannot have an image that simultaneously contains snow and does not contain snow. In order to answer Berkeley's objection, we must supplement images with models. Models, by definition, contain alternative representations that are incompatible with one another.

Images, insofar as they preserve information provided by the preceding discourse, are creatures of the pragmatic theory of language. That is to say, different sentences can lead to the construction of the same image, and the same sentence in different contexts can lead to the construction of different images. How a person constructs an image that a given passage is intended to describe on some particular occasion of its use is a central problem for any pragmatic theory of language. Models, on the other hand, provide a mechanism for assigning truth-values, and to that extent they are creatures of the semantic theory of language. There is no conflict here. The image, like the text it enables us to remember, is a particular image, corresponding to a particular list of criteria for selecting an abstract model compatible with that list.[3]

In short, remembering a descriptive prose passage depends on two complementary and mutually supporting processes, one constructive and particular, the other selective and abstract. The constructive process preserves the particular criteria given by the passage for the selection of an abstract model consisting of all the potential states of affairs that could satisfy those criteria.

I shall call the combined image/model that emerges during the process of reading the reader's "concept" of the passage; and I shall call the constructive/selective processes that are involved his "synthesis" of that concept. If the extension of a concept is understood to be the set of things that are instances of that concept, then the reader's model corresponds to the extension of his concept of the passage; if the intension of a concept is what a person must know in order to determine its extension, then the reader's image corresponds to the intension of his concept of the passage. In this respect, a reader's concept of a particular text is similar to the sentential and lexical concepts that are used to synthesize it. Since not all concepts are equivalent, however, I shall refer to the reader's concept of a text he is reading as a "textual concept" whenever there may be danger of misunderstanding.

At this point, I could begin to talk about metaphor. I could claim that a metaphor poses an apperceptive problem. I shall get around to such a claim eventually, but my account is still deficient in a very important respect.

Understanding

The study of reading comprehension is more than a study of how a reader extracts information by decoding, parsing, and interpreting a text, or how he uses that information to construct an image of the passage that will enable him to select a model of its possible continuations. It must also be a study of problem solving (Thorndike, 1924), in which anything the reader knows about the world, or about the uses to which texts are put, can be exploited to help him solve the problem: What concept did the author have in mind when he selected these particular sentences? In order to understand a passage, readers must relate the textual concept they are synthesizing to their general store of knowledge and belief.

Grounds. A notion that has received much attention is that one understands a sentence if one knows the conditions under which it could be true. There are good reasons to think this notion is too narrow, but let us take it seriously for a moment. It presumes that you already know a great deal about whatever it is that the sentence is about; you are expected to search what you know for the truth conditions of the sentence. Psychologically, this means that in order to understand a sentence you must establish a particular kind of relation (a verifiability relation) between the concept that the sentence expresses and your general knowledge of the world. If you cannot establish that relation, you do not understand the sentence; if nobody can establish the relation, the sentence is (presumably) meaningless.

A broader relation than verifiability must be established between the text and general knowledge. What that relation is and how it is established are central problems for the psychology of apperception. I have no solution to offer, but, in order to hold a place for whatever solution the future may bring, let us say that you understand a sentence if you know the conditions under which a person would use it. Use conditions are sufficiently broader than truth conditions to cover most apperceptive relations. I shall speak of use conditions as the author's "grounds" for what he says, and shall assume that the appreciation of the grounds for a sentence is drawn largely from general knowledge and belief about situations or events similar to those described or imagined in the textual concept.

Under this formulation, you can understand sentences that defy verification if you can appreciate the author's grounds for using them. We cannot completely abandon the notion of truth, however, because readers cannot begin to search for the author's grounds unless they are willing to accept what is said as true of the concept the author has in mind. In passages intended to convey literal truth, of course, use conditions are not very different from truth conditions, but not all writing is intended to convey literal truth. We must, therefore, reconsider the reader's truth assumption.

The truth assumption. I have said that the semantic model selected for a text contains all possible developments of the text that do not contradict anything in the memory image. The apperceptive problem concealed in this formulation is "contradict." I can illustrate it by supposing that the first sentence of Thoreau's passage had read as follows:

Near the end of March, 1845, I borrowed an axe and drove my automobile to the woods by Walden Pond, nearest to where I intended to build my house. . . .

You would immediately see a contradiction, since there were no automobiles in 1845.

Where does the knowledge required to recognize this contradiction come from? Not from the memory image. I, at least, have no more trouble imagining automobiles in 1845 than I had revising Thoreau's passage. And not from the model selected for the passage, since (as described so far) the model is constrained only by the image. The source of the contradiction is elsewhere. Somewhere in my store of general knowledge, I have the information required to infer that automobiles did not exist in 1845. General knowledge must play a role in the process of understanding. It must provide some grounds for what the author has written.

What happens when we encounter a contradiction? Obviously, the comprehension system does not blow a fuse and quit. In this example, we recognize that Thoreau could not have written the passage. Someone who lived since the invention of the automobile must have written it. Either the genre is not what it seemed to be – it is parody, perhaps, or science fiction – or perhaps there has been a misprint – "1945" being accidentally printed as "1845." That is to say, we revise our concept of the passage in such a way as to preserve our assumption that our textual concept is true.

It is banal to insist that reading comprehension depends in some way on general knowledge not given in the text. But how general knowledge makes its contribution is often misunderstood. We might, for example, think of the model for a passage as being selected, not solely on the basis of information extracted from the text, but from all the information the individual has gained from his experience throughout life, up to and including however much of the text he has just read. In a sense, this view is correct, as is indicated in recall by the intrusion of other knowledge that was not explicitly stated or entailed in the original text. On the other hand, it cannot be completely true, since if the textual concept of the present passage is not kept distinct from other knowledge in some degree, the memory image cannot serve its purpose – when asked to recall a text, any fragment of previous experience might be described. We must assume, therefore, that the memory image for a text is isolated from general knowledge as a record of the current episode. A reader will normally assume that what he knows about the real world can apply to the world he is reading about (unless the text says otherwise), but if he confuses those two worlds, he will not be able to recall the text accurately.

Another reason the memory image cannot be assimilated directly into general knowledge is that truth in the model must be kept distinct from truth in the so-called real world, or in our general knowledge of that world. Literary critics have long argued about the sense in which fiction in general, and poetry in particular, can be said to be true or false. Some claim that truth and falsity are irrelevant to the acceptance of such works, but I believe that Empson (1967) is on the right track when he says, "The point is not that their truth or falsity is irrelevant, but that you are asked to imagine a state of mind in which they would appear true" (p. 12). In my terms, by accepting them as true, a reader can hope to converge on the model that the author had in mind, which may or may not coincide with what the reader knows or believes about the real world. If, as in the example just given, we find an assertion that contradicts what we know or believe about the world, we cannot abandon our working assumption that what we have read is true in the model we are selecting. We must hold on to the truth assumption at all costs. If we are not to abandon our effort to understand, we must select a model that makes the passage true – even though that selection may tax our ingenuity.

Fortunately, people can be enormously ingenious in such matters. The extreme test of a reader's truth assumption is provided by the form of humor that deliberately compounds absurdities. An example (source unknown) that amuses children:

> One bright day in the middle of the night
> Two dead boys got up to fight.
> Back to back they faced each other,
> Drew their swords and shot each other.
> A deaf policeman heard the noise
> And came and killed those two dead boys.

Accepting such nonsense goes beyond the willing suspension of disbelief – belief is not even involved. Yet it is possible to construct an image for this jingle (spectral boys, swords that shoot bullets), and the general scenario (trouble between boys attracts police) is sufficiently familiar to hold it together in spite of the flat contradictions in every line. The lengths to which a reader will go in order to maintain the assumption that what he reads is true – true in his model of the text, at least – should not be underestimated. So strongly does this assumption constrain the reader that an author can exploit it to create a wide variety of special effects, of which humor is but one.

The reader's assumption of truth is not limited to the special case of texts that are intended to communicate objective truth. Thinking ahead to metaphor, it should be obvious why a distinction between "true in fact" and "true in the model" is required. Metaphors are, on literal interpretation, incongruous, if not actually false – a robust sense of what is germane to the context and what is "true in fact" is necessary for the recognition of a metaphor, and hence general knowledge must be available to the reader. Not every statement that is literally incongruous or false is a metaphor, of course, but it must be true in the model. Whether to invent a fictitious state of affairs or to search for an alternative interpretation that could be true in the real world represents an important decision that a reader must make: Whether, for example, "rusty joints" is taken as a figurative description of an old man or conjures up a rusty machine can have important consequences for a reader's comprehension of the text. But whatever trick a reader uses to preserve the truth assumption, a distinction between "true in fact" and "true in the model" must be included in any general theory of textual comprehension.

Metaphor presents an apperceptive problem. A metaphor that is literally false of the real world can still be added to our image and used to constrain our model, but it creates a tension between our conception of the real world and our conception of the world that the author had in mind. In order to be able to make as much use as possible of what we know about similar situations in the real world, we try to synthesize a textual concept as near to our concept of reality as possible – we try to add the metaphorical information in such a way that its truth conflicts as little as possible with our conception of the real world. That is to say, we try to make the world that the author is asking us to imagine resemble the real world (as we know it) in as many respects as possible.

If an author says that x is y when we know in fact that x is not y, we must try to imagine a world in which x is y. This act of imagination is facilitated if, in the real world, x is like y in some respects, for then we can take their similarities as the author's grounds for saying that x is y. If he says, for example, "Man is a wolf," we can honor the truth assumption by attributing properties of wolves to men (in much the way we would deal with "Man is an animal"). If however, the author says, "Typhoons are wheat," we shall have difficulty simultaneously selecting a model in which this statement is true and preserving resemblances between that model and the real world. Resemblances between x and y enable us to minimize the tension between our textual concept and our concept of reality, thus maximizing our ability to use what we already know.

It is tempting to make a stronger claim, namely, that resemblances enable a reader to understand what the author meant and that this understood information, rather than the literal statement, is added to the textual concept. For example, if an author says, "Man is a wolf," a reader might understand this sentence to have meant "Man is like a wolf," and add this information to the textual concept. It is indeed true that an attempt to understand "Man is a wolf" causes a reader to explore those respects in which men and wolves are similar, but to add "Man is like a wolf" to the textual concept violates the truth assumption that is a reader's only basis for determining the author's state of mind. "Man is a wolf" is a much stronger claim, and if that is what the author said, readers must assume that that is what the author meant.

"Man is a wolf" is false in fact. If it must be regarded as true, it can only be regarded as true in the textual concept the reader is synthesizing. In order to understand it, however, the reader must associate it with "Man is like a wolf" or, even weaker, "Man seems like a wolf (to the author)." The simile cannot be added to the textual concept, because that is not what the author said, but it does provide a basis on which a reader can understand why the author might have said, "Man is a wolf." Thus, the reader synthesizes a concept of the author, as well as a concept of what the author wrote.

The important point, however, is that when an author says something literally false or contradictory, readers do not translate it into something true and then assume that that was what the author meant to say. Rather, they assume that what the author said is true in the state of affairs he is describing, then search their general knowledge for plausible grounds for saying that in the given context. Their search for those grounds, however, is guided by whatever resemblances and analogies they can find between the world of the text and the world of reality.

Comparison statements

Since Aristotle, students of metaphor have said that it is used to express resemblances or analogies. Although it has long been recognized that there are figures of speech that look like metaphors and do not express resemblances or analogies, so great is Aristotle's authority that many followers have either ignored them or argued that they are not really metaphors. But whether or not similitude is a defining property of metaphor, no one could disagree with the claim that many metaphors are apperceived in terms of resemblances. I must, therefore, say a few general words about expressions of similitude before turning to their role in metaphor.

Directionality

In the abstract, most people assume that similarity is symmetric – that if A is similar to B, then B must be similar to A, and that either way of saying it is equivalent to saying that A and B are similar. This assumption is not above question, even at an abstract level, but at the level of the linguistic expression of similarities it is surely false (Tversky, 1977).

To begin with as pure a case as possible, let me take mathematical equality as my starting point. Everyone knows that "$=$" denotes a symmetric relation, that if $x = y$, then $y = x$. From a psychological point of view, however, even this symbol of total similarity is used asymmetrically. For example, you will not have to search through many algebra texts to find expressions like the following:

(1) $y = ax + b$

where "a" and "b" are constants and "x" and "y" are unknowns. As every student knows, this equation can be used to derive other equations:

(2) $y - b = ax$

(3) $x = (y - b) / a$

All three equations, and indefinitely many others that could be invented, convey the same information and, in all three cases, the term on the left of the equals sign could be interchanged with the term on the right without changing the truth conditions for the equation. Nevertheless, (1) and (3) are special, for psychological reasons: (1) says that if you know what x is, you can multiply it by a and add b in order to find out what y is; (3) says that if you know what y is, you can subtract b and divide the remainder by a in order to find out what x is. The convenience of (1) and (3) comes from the fact that we usually know or assume the value of one variable and want to find the corresponding value of the other variable. The equations are perfectly symmetric, but the way we use them is not: (1) and (3) respect the way we use them.

A similar observation holds for analogies. Verbal analogies of the form, "Day is to light as night is to darkness," characteristically allow many permutations of terms: "Day is to night as light is to darkness," "Darkness is to light as night is to day," and so on. In the abstract, therefore, verbal analogies, like equations, seem to have no intrinsic directionality. As soon as we consider how authors use analogies, however, we find that the context imposes a direction, that it is no longer possible to rearrange freely the order of the terms. An author who says, "Money is to a university as fuel is to an engine," is telling the reader something about money in a university, namely, that it is like fuel in an engine. If you know what fuel does for an engine, you can transfer that knowledge to the relation between money and universities. "Fuel is to money as an engine is to a university" would tell the reader something very different.

In order to stay close to equality, consider definitions of words. Suppose you do not know what a pickle is and decide to look the word up in a dictionary. You will find a definition along the following lines:

    (4) *pickle*: any article of food, especially cucumbers, that has been preserved in brine or vinegar.

Here again the asymmetry is respected: "pickle" is defined as a function of food, especially cucumbers. If you know what cucumbers are, you can find out what pickles are by soaking cucumbers in brine or vinegar. Something new is defined in terms of something it is assumed you already know. Of course, if you do not know what cucumbers are, you will have to pursue your research further until, if you are lucky, you encounter some defining terms that are familiar.

Moving one step further away from equality, consider lay definitions. Suppose a child asks you what a zebra is. You might respond:

    (5) A zebra is like a horse, except that it has stripes.

You would assume that the child knows what a horse is and you would explain the unknown word in terms of the known word.

The word "like" in (5) marks it as a simile; if you delete it, as in:

    (6) A zebra is a horse with stripes,

some scholars might say that you had used a metaphor. However, others would deny it was a metaphor on the grounds that "horse" is commonly used (by synecdoche?) to denote the genus *Equus*, in which case (6) is a perfectly satisfactory definition. My purpose, however, is not to quibble about the bounds of metaphor, but to point to a pervasive directionality in our expression of similarities, a directionality that is not restircted to metaphorical expressions (Rosch, 1975a). If we revise the phrasing of (6) to obtain:

    (7) A horse is a zebra without any stripes,

the direction is reversed; knowledge of zebras is taken for granted and used to explain what a horse is.

If we find asymmetry in the expression of equalities, analogies, and definitions, we should not be surprised to find it also in the expression of weaker degrees of similarity. Consider an example:

    (8) John's wife resembles his mother
    (9) John's mother resembles his wife
    (10) John's wife and mother resemble each other.

Leaving aside questions of John's oedipal problems, (8) is what you would say to someone who knew John's mother and was asking about his wife, (9) is what you would say to someone who knew John's wife and was asking about his mother, and (10) is what you would say to someone who knew John's wife and mother equally well.

Another example can be patterned on Thoreau's passage:

(11) I went to a place near to where I intended to build my house
(12) I intended to build my house near to a place where I went
(13) The place where I went and the place where I intended to build my house were near to each other.

It was natural for Thoreau to use the pattern in (11), because the preceding text had already established that he intended to build a house – it answers the question, "Where did you go?" by relating it to something already known. On the other hand, (12) seems to assume that the reader already knows of some place where Thoreau habitually went, and is being given new information about the intended location of his house. And (13) is neutral; the reader is assumed to be equally knowledgeable about both. Note especially that the directionality of (8) and (9), and of (11) and (12), are different – sufficiently different to imply different intentions on the part of the author.

The reason for this directionality is transparent, but let me make it explicit. New knowledge is assimilated apperceptively by being related to old knowledge (see Haviland & Clark, 1974). One of the easiest ways to impart new knowledge is to state its relation to something already known. The old knowledge may be either general information that the author can assume everyone knows, or it can be knowledge imparted earlier in the same text.

I will borrow a pair of terms from medieval logic to characterize this directionality. I will call the concept that is being talked about the "referent," and the concept to which the referent is being related the "relatum."[4] In sentences of the form, A is similar to B, for example, A is the referent and B the relatum. The reader is expected to transfer features of the relatum B to the referent A.

The distinction between referent and relatum enables a reader to determine what should be added to the memory image he is constructing. It is always the referent, enriched by the relatum, that should be added to the image; the relatum is either already part of the image or is part of general knowledge. Consider, for example:

"I didn't know he'd been married before."
"John's first wife looked like his mother. She came from Chicago."

In these sentences, it is clear that the antecedent of the anaphoric pronoun "she" is John's first wife, not his mother. This follows because the wife is the referent and the referent is added to the memory image; the relatum indicates how, where, or why the referent is to be qualified.

In terms of the distinction between old and new information, it should be noted that there is a sense in which both the referent and the relatum of a simile are old information. The referent is what the sentence is about; if a reader is to connect the sentence to the concept, its referent must already have been introduced. The relatum is something the reader is assumed to know already, either from the passage or from general knowledge. The new information in a simile is the statement of a similarity between the referent and the relatum. A more precise terminology, therefore, might distinguish between old, current, and new information: the relatum is old information, the referent is the current topic, and the relation of similarity between them is new information.

Classification of comparison statements

Comparison statements are easily recognizable by their use of one or another copula of similitude: "like," "is like," "acts like," "looks like," "as," "is as *Adj* as," "resembles," "reminds me of," "is the same as," "is similar to," "the same way," and so on. Different copulas of similitude are not interchangeable; they impose different syntactic requirements on the constituents being compared, and often have different meanings, but those differences will not concern us here.

I shall distinguish three types of comparison statements: literal comparisons, similes, and analogies. In literal comparisons, the grounds are obvious. For example, "John's wife is like his mother" can be understood to mean that a description of John's wife would include many of the same features as would a description of John's mother. In similes, the grounds for the comparison are not obvious. For example, "John's wife is like his umbrella" might be understood to mean that she is very thin or that she protects him, or in some other way. Analogies generally involve four terms, since they are patterned after the arithmetic analogies of proportionality: for example, 3:4::9:12, or, more generally, $x:y::nx:ny$. "The toes are to the foot as the fingers are to the hand" is a comparison statement using the copula of similitude "as," but the grounds for the comparison are not stated explicitly.

In all three types, however, it is possible for a reader to assume that the statement is true, and all three can be taken as the basis for metaphors.

Declarative sentences of the form, "*A* is like *B*," can be understood as expressing true statements to the effect that the author has observed a resemblance between *A* and *B*. That the grounds for the resemblance may be obscure does not imply that such sentences are not true descriptions of the author's state of mind. If "statement" seems too strong for the expression of subjective and possibly idiosyncratic impressions, one could still say that the author was using the comparison statement to make a proposal (Loewenberg, 1975b) or a claim (Fraser, this volume) to which another person could reasonably assent or dissent. The reader, who is under the requirement to regard whatever an author writes as true in the semantic model he is selecting, should face no special problem with comparison statements if the referent, which is already part of the reader's textual concept, is simply qualified by the new information that (in the author's view) it resembles the relatum.

The qualification will not be understood, however, unless the reader can discover the grounds for the claimed resemblance, and that is the central problem of interpretation. In the nonobvious comparison, "John's wife is like his umbrella," it makes a difference whether the grounds of similarity are that John's wife is very thin or that John uses his wife to protect himself from unpleasant situations. In "A woman without a man is like a fish without a bicycle," it helps to know that the author is a proponent of women's liberation and to recognize the rejected allusion to a fish out of water. Once an interpretation is assigned, however, a simile poses no further apperceptive difficulties.

One type of comparison statement that might seem to contradict this claim includes such similes as, "My love is like a red, red rose." It is not a real rose that the author had in mind, but a symbolic rose – a flower that, in our culture, has become symbolic of love. Or, to take a more extreme example, "John eats like a pig" is not an expression of an observed similarity between John's eating and a pig's eating. A person who had never seen a pig could use it if he had learned that, in our culture, the pig is a symbol of uncouth gluttony. In some cases, symbolism can be tested by translation. To the extent that the relatum is a symbol rather than a sign (Sperber, 1975), there could be languages into which the simile could not be translated directly, but would have to be translated indirectly by using the expression for the corresponding symbol, rather than the corresponding referent.[5] The reader of a symbolic simile must respect the symbolism; but once the simile is interpreted symbolically, it can be accepted as true in the model that the reader is selecting.

The importance of this point becomes clearer if it is also accepted that all the varieties of comparison statements are related to metaphors. Metaphors characteristically pose apperceptive problems: either they assert something that strains the reader's truth assumption, or they seem to bear no apparent relation to the reader's textual concept. This apperceptive problem is reduced if there is a resemblance between the reader's concept of reality and what the author has written. Finding that resemblance can be viewed as a process of paraphrasing the metaphor as a comparison statement. The reconstructed comparison is not then added to the reader's textual concept – the reader must honor what the author wrote – but it does enable the reader to construct an image for the text (in which the metaphor must be true) that resembles his conception of reality (in which the corresponding comparison could be true) as closely as possible. Whereas a comparison statement expresses a resemblance, a metaphor merely calls attention to it.

The outline of the argument should now be clear. In order to find a compromise between the requirements of the truth assumption and the need to relate the textual concept as closely as possible to general knowledge and belief, the reader must search for resemblances between the textual concept and general knowledge. These resemblances, which are the grounds for the metaphor, can be formulated as comparison statements. Once found and interpreted, the comparison is not added directly to the textual concept, but is used as a basis for imagining a minimally divergent state of affairs in which the metaphorical claim is true.

Similes

A simile is a comparison statement involving two unlike things. Precisely how unlike they must be before the comparison qualifies as a simile is not well defined, but the indistinctness of the boundary will not pose any problems for the present discussion.

I assume that there are two aspects to understanding a simile: (1) recognizing that a simile has occurred, and (2) interpreting the grounds for the simile and the author's reasons for using it in the given context.

Recognition. Similes contain a copula of similitude. Presumably, they are processed in the same way any other comparison statement is processed, so the initial step of simile recognition is the recognition that a comparison statement has occurred. It is probably only after some processing has occurred and the grounds for the comparison are found to be nonobvious (Ortony, this volume) that a reader is able to say with assurance that the comparison is a simile.

Interpretation. Interpretation of a simile may require an inference as to the grounds the author had for the claim of similitude. The inference may be based on the antecedent text, on general knowledge, or both. Let me give a simile and context and try to characterize the comprehension of literal prose:

I told him that everything would be all right. Telling John not to worry is like telling the wind not to blow. It made things worse, because he started arguing with me.

As I read the passage, I construct a memory image of the author and a worried friend. I hear the author tell his friend John that everything will be all right, but John continues to worry. John is so worried that he starts arguing with the author.

Although the passage mentions the wind blowing, the wind is not added to my memory image for the content of the passage. (If it were, the wind would have been a possible antecedent for the anaphoric pronoun "it" that begins the third sentence.) The referent of the simile, "Telling John not to worry is like telling the wind not to blow," is "Telling John not to worry"; I add this referent to my image, which is used to select a model in which the referent, not the relatum, is the antecedent of "it." The fact that the wind was mentioned, however, may be added verbatim to my memory image of the passage itself.

More interesting, however, is how I know (1) that telling John everything would be all right is the same as telling John not to worry, and (2) that John continued to worry. On the face of it, the sentence, "Telling John not to worry is like telling the wind not to blow," is an interruption of the literal narrative (it could be called a simile that is used as a sentential metaphor: see rule M3 below). The reader is thereby warned that special processing is required to integrate this sentence into the narrative. In this case, however, the additional processing is relatively simple: (1) is explained by general knowledge that people worry because they think everything is not all right; (2) is explained by the transfer of features from the relatum to the referent. Before the referent of a simile is added to the image, certain features are transferred to it from its relatum. What is the most obviously transferable feature of the relatum, "telling the wind not to blow"? Futility. When futility is transferred to the referent, it is implicated that the admonition failed, that John continued to worry. (Note, incidentally, that the futility of talking to the wind is also drawn from general knowledge, not from lexical knowledge.)

My account of this simile is still not complete, however. Comparing John with the wind does more than indicate that he continued to worry on this occasion. It attributes to John the trait of being an inveterate worrier. If the wind did not blow, it would not be the wind; if John did not worry, he would not be John. This feature, too, can be transferred, in this case from the argument of the relatum to the argument of the referent.

It is an understatement to say that the mechanism of this transference is not well understood. I have spoken here as if all the conceptual features required to characterize the referent literally were preserved and some features of the relatum were simply added on, as if an old friend were dressed in new clothes. This way of speaking is surely too simple, even for this example, and other examples seem to work differently. Black (1962b) speaks of the interaction of the two terms as a "filtering" process – the relatum provides a filter through which the referent is viewed – which suggests that some of the literal features of the referent are subtracted, rather than that new features are added. "Honest work is like prayer," for example, would be subtractive, since all features of honest work other than those associable with prayer – respect, devotion, dedication, perhaps – seem to be filtered out. The complexity of this transfer process poses a central problem for psychological research, a problem that becomes even more pressing when we turn to the analysis of metaphors (Ortony, 1975).

What makes a simile striking, of course, is an author's sensitivity to previously unnoticed resemblances; it can link together two spheres of knowledge or experience in novel and revealing ways. In such cases, finding grounds for the comparison may be a nontrivial task. When Eliot writes, for example, "the evening is spread out against the sky like a patient etherised upon a table," it challenges us to search for the similarity in our own experience of evenings and etherized patients – and may affect the way we see an evening sky thereafter. Similes are less interesting than metaphors only in that the terms of the similitude are explicit and require less work from a reader. As far as interpretation is concerned, it is important to recognize that similes can pose all the apperceptive problems that metaphors can.

With these examples of similes in mind, I should like to formulate some generalizations about them. This task will be much easier, however, if I interrupt the argument at this point in order to introduce some notations for the concepts that are involved in comparison statements and metaphors.

Some conceptual notation

A simple notation for conceptual functions and arguments will serve our present purposes (Miller & Johnson-Laird, 1976; Miller, 1978). For example, the sentence, "The patient slept," has an intransitive verb, and the sentential concept it expresses can be represented as a function with a single argument: SLEEP (the patient), where small capitals indicate the *function* and lower case letters indicate the *argument*. In a fully developed semantic theory it would be necessary to indicate how this function is computed. I would claim that SLEEP is a function that maps animate arguments into truth values, but since in the situation we are considering, the reader is constrained to assume that the value of all such functions is "true," I shall not pursue these matters, important as they are.

The general form that such sentential concepts take can be represented as F (x). It is conventional to say that functions taking a single argument express properties of the argument – in this case, sleeping is a property attributed to or predicated of the patient. The sentence, "He writes poetry," has a transitive verb and can be said to express a sentential concept with two arguments: WRITE (he, poetry), where the general form is F (x, y). It is conventional to say that functions taking two or more arguments express relations between those arguments – in this case, "he" and "poetry" are related by "writing."

This notation for concepts should be reasonably transparent, but two complications will be needed later. First, it is possible (by a formal operation known as abstraction; see note 6) to treat relations as properties. For example, it is sometimes convenient to represent the concept expressed by sentences like, "He writes poetry," as WRITE POETRY (he), where writing poetry is a property attributed to "he."

Second, arguments are sometimes omitted. For example, the verb "eat" can be used either transitively or intransitively. For reasons having nothing to do with metaphorical language, it is convenient to assume that the mental lexicon contains a single entry for "eat" as a transitive verb; conceptually, "eat" expresses a relation between an eater and the eaten. It is also recorded in this lexical entry, however, that the second argument of "eat" need not be specified. One way to do this is to use the existential quantifier "∃" to bind the argument without assigning it a value (Bresnan, 1978). Thus, "John is eating" expresses the sentential concept (∃y)EAT (john, y), which can be paraphrased as "John is eating something." In this way, we can explain the fact that it is sensible to ask, "What is John eating?" whereas it would not be sensible to ask, "What is the patient sleeping?" The point, however, is that omitting arguments from a conceptual representation is required for other reasons than the reason to be proposed later, when comparison statements will be related to metaphors by omitting arguments.

If all features of a sentential concept G (y) are also features of a sentential concept F (x), then F (x) entails G (y); if G (y) also entails F (x), then the two concepts are identical. I will use SIM to represent the relation of similitude between concepts:

S1. SIM[F (x), G (y)]

will be the general form from comparison statements, and will be used to mean that the two concepts have some features in common, but that neither entails the other. SIM can be expressed by a variety of copulas of similitude, as already indicated. I shall always use F (x) or F (x, x') to indicate the referent of the simile and G (y) or G (y, y') to indicate the relatum. Although S1 is given for a comparison between properties of x and y, I shall take it as standing in for comparisons between relational concepts as well. The features that two concepts may share must be understood broadly; they are not constrained to semantic markers, truth conditions, or logical entailments of the sort that result from semantic decomposition of the particular words used to express the simile. The shared features constitute the grounds for the expressed similitude, and identifying them is the first step in interpreting the comparison.

In this notation, "The brain works the way a machine computes" would be taken as expressing the sentential concept:

(14) SIM [WORK (the brain), COMPUTE (a machine)]

where "the way" expresses SIM, which links two constituent sentential concepts, "the brain works" and "a machine computes," having some (but not all) features in common.

Parts of S1 can be omitted in a comparison statement (as long as an expression for SIM is preserved): "The brain is like a machine," for example, expresses the sentential concept:

(15) SIM (the brain, a machine)

where SIM relates two nominal concepts, not two sentential concepts. I claim, however, that the missing functions are understood conceptually, and, therefore, "The brain is like a machine" can be taken as expressing the underlying concept:

(16) $(\exists F \ (\exists G) \{SIM[F$ (the brain), G (a machine)]$\}$

which can be paraphrased as "Some properties of the brain are like some properties of a machine," just as "John is eating" can be paraphrased as "John is eating something." This claim is summarized in a general rule for transforming a comparison of nominal concepts into a comparison of sentential concepts:

S2. SIM $(x, y) \longrightarrow (\exists F) (\exists G) \{SIM [F (x), G (y)]\}$

Note that the functions F and G, which are missing from the left side of rule S2, are introduced in the right side as variables bound by existential quantifiers. S2 is a reconstructive rule for comparison statements, but it illustrates the kind of rule that will be proposed below for reconstructing comparisons that underlie metaphors.

Both S1 and S2 are intended as psychological, not linguistic, structures. In particular, when F and G are implicit, the reader is not constrained to some particular linguistic expression that must replace them but is free to explore a range of conceptual possibilities. For example, in the symbolic simile "My love is like a rose," rule S2 entitles us only to the paraphrase "Some properties of my love are like some properties of a rose." The reader is then free to consider such alternative properties as "beautiful," "thorny," or (closer to what the author probably had in mind) "affects me."[6] To paraphrase "My love is like a rose" as "My love affects me as a rose affects me" is to go far beyond the kind of recoverable deletions sanctioned by syntactic theories.

Analogies

In its broadest definition, any expression of similarity or resemblance can be called an analogy; in that general sense, we say that similes express analogies. In a narrower sense, however, analogies are stated between four terms: $x:x'::y:y'$. This is the sense familiar to psychologists from verbal analogy tests, where a person is required to judge an analogy true or false, or to determine an appropriate value for the fourth term. Let us consider the relation of such analogies, narrowly defined, to the conceptual form of comparison statements characterized in S1.

Take a simple example: "Toe is to foot as finger is to hand." SIM is expressed by "as," and on that basis it is recognized as a comparison statement. The arguments linked by SIM, however, are neither sentential nor nominal concepts, but idioms peculiar to analogies. Let us represent them in the general form "$x:x'$." Then the example can be said to express the concept SIM [(toe:foot), (finger:hand)], where the missing constituents of S1 are the functions F and G. The missing function is symbolized by ":" and is the same for both arguments, so we can assume that F = G. In order to reconstruct the comparison statement, therefore, we need a variant of rule S2:

S3. SIM $[(x:x'), (y:y')] \longrightarrow (\exists F)\{SIM [F(x,x'), (y,y')]\}$.

When we apply S3 to the example, the result can be paraphrased as "There is some relation between toe and foot that is similar to the relation between finger and hand." F is left for the reader to choose: it could be, say, "is part of" or "there are five per" (or both). Then the paraphrase could be either "The toe is part of the foot as the finger is part of the hand" or "There are five toes per foot as there are five fingers per hand." Note that the same function must be used for both arguments of the simile: "The toe is part of the foot as there are five fingers per hand" is nonsense.

Reasoning by analogy usually proceeds as follows. It is noticed that SIM $[F(x, x'), F(y, y')]$ and, assuming H (y, y') is already known, it is conjectured that H (x, x'). In the example just considered, a child might notice that the toe is a part of the foot in the same way a finger is a part of the hand, and assuming it is already known that there are five fingers per hand, the child might reason by analogy that there are five toes per foot. In less trivial examples, the analogy might lead to a tentative hypothesis to be tested empirically.

The productivity of reasoning by analogy is not limited to four-term analogies. A more literary example is "His thoughts flow like a river, deep and clear," where the root simile that his thoughts follow one another as a river flows is elaborated: his thoughts are profound as a river is deep; his thoughts are intelligible as a river is clear. The same arguments – "his thoughts" and "a river" – are compared in several respects.

Such parallels suggest that we should search for deeper relations between analogy and simile. We might follow J. D. Sapir's (1977) suggestion that analogy be regarded as a kind of thought process, and simile as one product of such thought. Given an analogy between four terms, $x:x'::y:y'$, eight valid analogies can be stated:[7]

$$(17) \quad x:x'::y:y' \quad x:y::x':y' \quad x':x::y':y \quad y:x::y':x'$$
$$y:y'::x:x' \quad x':y'::x:y \quad y':y::x':x \quad y':x'::y:x$$

Thus, analogies allow combinatorial play that might well be part of an author's thinking as he decides how to express some similitude in a particular context. Moreover, when x' and y' are superordinate terms for x and y, respectively, the analogy can take the form $x:\text{F}::y:\text{G}$. For example "Washington was an American" and "Napoleon was a French-man" can be represented as AMERICAN (washington) and FRENCHMAN (napoleon); the uninteresting comparison "Washington was an American as Napoleon was a Frenchman" expresses the concept SIM [AMERICAN (washington), FRENCHMAN (napoleon)]. If we play combinatorially with the underlying analogy, however, we will come across $\text{F}:\text{G}::x:y$, or "Americans are to Frenchmen as Washington was to Napoleon," which might be an idea that a chauvinistic American author would want to express.

Metaphors

Perhaps the simplest way to characterize a metaphor is as a comparison statement with parts left out. This is, of course, the traditional view of metaphor, as indicated in *Webster's New International Dictionary* (2nd ed.), where we are told, "A metaphor may be regarded as a compressed simile," the comparison implied in the former being explicit in the latter." Making the comparison explicit is the first riddle that a reader must solve.

This characterization is a version of what is generally called the comparison view of metaphor, to which Black (1962b) has objected on the grounds that "it suffers from a vagueness that borders on vacuity" (p. 37). Black is not alone in his criticism of the traditional dogma,[8] but if vagueness is a fault of this view, we should not abandon it before attempting to clarify it. I shall argue that the comparison view of metaphor can be made considerably less vague, and that the result of doing so leaves the process of interaction, which Black takes to be the crux of the problem, in much clearer relief.

Relation to comparison statements

In principle, three steps, recognition, reconstruction, and interpretation, must be taken in understanding metaphors, although in the simplest instances the processing may occur so rapidly that all three blend into a single mental act. I shall discuss recognition and reconstruction here, and postpone interpretation until later (p. 240).

I have claimed that metaphors produce a problem of apperception because the reader's textual concept departs from known facts about the real world. It would be natural to claim, therefore, that the recognition of this discrepancy is the recognition that a metaphor has occurred. On this view, a reader recognizes that something is false or unrelated to the preceding context, examines it, and decides to activate a mental subroutine for the interpretation of metaphors.

This characterization may be correct, but it is not the only possibility. One alternative is that readers process metaphors in the same way that they would process any literal expression. That is to say, perhaps no special attention is paid to the falsity or irrelevance of the metaphor, because readers are bound by the nature of their task to take whatever they read as true in the replica of the author's concept that they are synthesizing, and to assume that there is an internal coherence to the text. Readers do not balk when nonexistent people are described performing fictional acts; perhaps they accept metaphors the same way, as true in the textual concept. But just as readers understand what they read by relating it to what they know about the real world, so readers try to understand metaphors by relating them to something that could be true in the real world.

According to this alternative view, recognition that an expression is a metaphor would be post hoc, based on a review of the mental processes it initiated. If the text says, "He is a pain in the neck," perhaps it is processed mentally in much the same way as "He is a lawyer" might be: "he" is assigned to the class of things labeled "pain in the neck."

In order to understand this assignment, however, the reader must relate it to what he knows of the real world, where "people" and "pain" label disjunct categories. This relation can be established with the minimal discrepancy between the text and reality by searching for resemblances. If it were the case that in the real world the person in question affected people as a pain in the neck affects them, then the author's sentence, "He is a pain in the neck," could be understood in terms of the related comparison statement. But the reader must remember that the author did not say, "He affects me like a pain in the neck"; the author said, "He is a pain in the neck," and the reader must try to imagine a state of mind in which this assignment would be true.

If the author had said, "He is a lawyer," "he" would be assigned to the class of things labeled "lawyer" and this assignment would also be understood in terms of the reader's knowledge of the real world. In this case, however, understanding does not lead to disjunct categories that must be reconciled in terms of assumed similarities. The post hoc realization that the processing required to understand the metaphor was different from what would be required to understand a literal expression would provide a basis for recognizing that the expression was a metaphor and that, outside the textual context, it acould not be literally true.

Since the recognition of metaphors may not be an antecedent psychological process, prior to the search for similarities to general knowledge, I shall turn instead to the reconstructive step. Once reconstruction is clear, I shall reconsider recognition (p. 239), and shall claim that recognizing a metaphor must be a more complex process than recognizing a comparison statement.

Reconstruction of the implied comparison is a critical step in understanding a metaphor (Kimtsch, 1974). I assume that reconstruction is a psychological process equivalent to the formation of a concept having the structure of S1. The comparison statement cannot be taken as the meaning of the metaphor, because it will have different truth conditions, but it represents a possible situation in the real world that could provide a basis for the author's use of the metaphor.

All metaphors omit any expression of the relation of similarity, SIM. For example, comparisons of the form "x is like y" can be converted into metaphors by simply replacing "is like" with "is." Thus, even such literal comparisons as "His wife is like his mother" can be transformed into the much stronger claim, "His wife is his mother." In this case, understanding the metaphor requires the reinsertion of "is like," and the comparison so reconstructed provides a basis for understanding the sentence as a metaphor. Probably this reconstruction goes on in parallel with processing "His wife is his mother" as a literal expression, because the sentence must be regarded as true in the textual concept, but then context and general plausibility are used to decide which of the two interpretations probably provided the author's grounds for using the sentence on the given occasion.

When the terms of a comparison statement are clauses or sentences, however, the simple substitution of "is" for "is like" is not always possible. For example, "The crowd rushed through the door like a river bursting through a dam" will not admit the simple omission of "like." We can obtain a metaphor, however, by nominalizing the initial sentence: "The crowd rushing through the door was a river bursting through a dam." But sometimes nominalization does not suffice: "The rich must enjoy their leisure as the poor must perform their duties" is different from "The rich who must enjoy their leisure are the poor who must perform their duties," for example; more drastic steps are required to eliminate "like": "The rich must perform leisure" was Thorstein Veblen's solution. There may be comparisons that cannot be expressed as metaphors, but the point is not crucial to my argument. I should like to relate all metaphors to comparison statements, not promote all comparisons into metaphors.

Classification of metaphors

I shall begin with the simplest cases. Take "Man is like a wolf." If "is like" is replaced by "is," we obtain Plautus's metaphor, "Man is a wolf." This pattern is found when a nominal concept is used metaphorically. Conceptually, SIM [F (man), G (wolf)] becomes BE (man, wolf) or WOLF (man).[9] (In English, a form of *be* is usually required to express concepts like WOLF (man), but this is not always the case. Sometimes $y(x)$ can be expressed simply as "y of x": "coat of paint," "family of mankind," "filing cabinet of memory," "river of time," "ship of state," "stream of consciousness," "tree of life" are all metaphors that can be understood in terms of comparison statements of the form "x is like a y.")

"Man is a wolf" is a clear violation of categories – men are not wolves – but readers, who are committed to the assumption that all sentences have to be true in the model they are selecting, must figure out what to do with it. They can understand the author's grounds for using the sentence by reconstructing the conceptual basis of the comparison, "Man is like a wolf," and they can then proceed to interpret that comparison statement. Note that, as in the case of comparison statements, it is the referent, man, that will appear in the image; no wolf will be added to the cast of characters in the reader's concept of the text. Note also that assigning man to the category of wolves endows him with wolflike properties drawn from either lexical knowledge of *wolf* or general knowledge, factual or symbolic, of wolves. And note finally that a careful reader will remember that the author said, "Man is a wolf," which cannot be synonymous with "Man is like a wolf," because the two have different truth-values.

If the riddle of a metaphor is to be solvable, the conceptual elements of the comparison that are left out cannot be chosen haphazardly. What the metaphor is about can be inferred if the argument x of the referent of S1 is preserved; if the implied comparison is to be recoverable, something from the relatum must also be preserved. In some metaphors, SIM, F, and G are omitted, but the argument x of the referent is retained and the relatum is represented by its argument y. The constraints can also be satisfied if the relatum is represented by its function G, instead of its argument y. This pattern is found when a predicative concept is used metaphorically: SIM, F, and y are omitted, but the function G is predicated of the argument x.

For example, "Root out your faults one by one" might be based on a concept that could be expressed by a comparison statement like "Eliminate your faults as you would root out weeds, one by one." Conceptually, the metaphor is ROOT OUT (your faults); when it is reconstructed as a comparison, it becomes SIM [ELIMINATE (your faults), ROOT OUT (weeds)]. As Empson (1967, p. 339) points out, the same idea can lead to a different metaphor: "Rid your soul of weeds," in which case the formula for the metaphor would be RID OF WEEDS (your soul), and the corresponding comparison would be SIM [RID OF FAULTS (your soul), RID OF WEEDS (your garden)]. In either case, however, the metaphor applies the function of the relatum to the argument of the referent of the corresponding comparison statement.

We have seen two patterns of omissions, both of which can be summarized in general rules.

Nominal metaphors. When a nominal concept y is expressed by a noun phrase that is used metaphorically, we have:

M1. BE $(x,y) \longrightarrow (\exists F)(\exists G) \{SIM [F (x), G (y)]\}$

where "BE" is some form of the verb "to be." Sinces a noun phrase is used metaphorically in M1, I shall call these *nominal metaphors.*

A common metaphoric figure follows the format, x is the y of x': "This is the leg of a table," "The lion is the king of beasts," "Britain was the ruler of the waves," "George Washington was the father of his country," "André Weil is the Bobby Fischer of mathematics," and so on. Such proportional metaphors are most easily understood as incomplete analogies (J.D. Sapir, 1977): for example, lion : beasts : : king :y'. An analogy that we have already considered can be used to illustrate how such metaphors are formed: toes · foot : : fingers : hand becomes "The toes are the fingers of the foot," where the fourth term is omitted. Note, however, that the freedom of rearrangement indicated in (17) is not available here. If we take the derived analogy, toes : fingers : : foot : hand, we obtain "The toes are the foot of the fingers," which is nonsense.

In order to see that "The toes are the fingers of the foot" can be formulated as an instance of M1, take the metaphor as "the toes are the fingers," or BE (toes, fingers). Then, by M1:

(18) BE (toes, fingers) $\longrightarrow$ ($\exists$F) ($\exists$G) {SIM [F (toes), G (fingers]}

which can be paraphrased as "Some property of the toes is like some property of the fingers." If we assume that the relation of the finger to the hand is H, we can define the function G by abstraction from H (y, hand):

(19) G $= \lambda y.$ H (y, hand)

Since H is also the relation of the toe to the foot, we can also use it by abstraction to define F:

(20) F $= \lambda x.$H (x, foot)

Then the relation of (18) to the underlying analogy can be seen as follows:

(21) BE (toes, fingers) $\longrightarrow$

($\exists$H) ($\exists x$) ($\exists y$) [SIM {[λx . H (x, foot)] (toes),

[λy . H (y, hand)] (fingers)}]

$=$ ($\exists$H) {SIM [H (toe, foot), H (finger, hand)]},

which is the analogy toe:foot::finger:hand expressed according to rule S3.

Since proportional metaphors are based on analogic comparisons, they provide particularly clear examples of the relation between metaphor and the thought processes involved in analogic thinking. The point to be noted here, however, is that they conform to rule M1.

Predicative metaphors When a predicative concept G is expressed by a predicate phrase (verb, verb phrase, or predicate adjective) that is used metaphorically, we have:

M2. G (x) $\longrightarrow$ ($\exists$F) ($\exists y$) {SIM [F (x), G (y)]}

Since a predicate phrase is used metaphorically in M2, I shall call these "predicative metaphors."[10]

Rules M1 and M2, like S1, stand in for relational metaphors as well as for those involving properties (having a single argument). For example, an author's grounds for saying, "The rich perform leisure," can be reconstructed by substituting relations for properties in M2:

(22) PERFORM (the rich, leisure) $\longrightarrow$

($\exists$F) ($\exists y, y'$) {SIM [F (the rich, leisure), PERFORM (y, y')]}.

The first step in interpreting this comparison is to find appropriate values for the missing terms. As already suggested, "the poor" and "duties" can serve as y and y', and "enjoy" can serve as F. With these substitutions, the right side of (22) can be interpreted as:

(23) PERFORM (the rich, leisure) $\longrightarrow$ SIM (ENJOY (the rich, leisure),

PERFORM (the poor, duties)].

There is a pun here (as there often is in metaphors: Reddy, 1973) between the performance of a duty and the performance of a play. The dramatic sense of "perform" would suggest "actors" and "their parts" as values for y and y'. It is left to the reader to decide which interpretation (if not both) provided the author's grounds for the metaphor in the particular context of use.

A possible objection to this approach is that it seems to demand that F and G in M1 or F and y in M2 be particular words already present in the English lexicon, and that the reconstruction is not correct unless we are able to infer the exact words that the author had in mind. Since metaphor is often used to repair a gap in the lexicon, any demand for particular words is highly questionable. Moreover, the author may or may not have had some particular words in mind; as he did not use them, we can never know. In that respect, there can be no uniquely correct comparison statement.

This is a forceful objection and should be respected whenever these reconstructive rules are used. All that these rules entitle us to is the claim that some properties or arguments will complete the conceptual structure of an underlying comparison: we can rewrite a metaphorical concept in the format of a concept expressible by a comparison statement as in (18) or (22). The search for suitable values to convert (18) to (21) or (22) to (23) is, strictly speaking, a matter of interpretation, not reconstruction. A variety of words may be appropriate, or there may be none at all. The claim is not that the author had particular words in mind, but that he had a general concept – resemblance, comparison, analogy – that we are trying to appreciate and make explicit. Such concepts have a structure, and S1 makes that structure explicit. Rules M1 and M2 merely indicate what conceptual elements are missing in the metaphoric expression of the concept. Thus, M1 and M2, like S1, should be viewed as psychological, not linguistic, rules.

Another possible objection is that these rules are too simple and mechanical to characterize adequately the complexity of the mental processes involved in the comprehension of metaphor. When metaphors are complex, however, most of the complexity occurs in the process of interpretation. If we are to respect the speed with which an intelligent reader is able to grasp a simple metaphor, the reconstruction had better be as simple and mechanical as possible. With complex metaphors, of course, much longer times will be required to explore alternative interpretations, which may require alternative reconstructions, with uncertain results even for literary experts. But it is interpretation, not reconstruction, that can be complicated.

Sentential metaphors. Still another objection would be that M1 and M2 do not apply to metaphors that use an otherwise unobjectionable sentence in an incongruous context, as when, for example, "John has lost his marbles" appears in a text that otherwise has nothing to do with marbles. However, these, too, can be encompassed in this framework if we introduce a third general rule:

$$\text{M3. } G(y) \longrightarrow (\exists F)(\exists x)\{\text{SIM}[F(x), G'(y)]\}$$

In such cases, which I shall call "sentential metaphors," nothing of the referent is preserved in the metaphor; the entire sentential concept $F(x)$ must be inferred from the text or context. Grice's (1975) notion of "implicature" may be particularly relevant here.

We have, therefore, classified metaphors into three types according to the constituents of the underlying comparison statement that are omitted:

Nominal metaphors: BE (x, y) when an x is not a y.
Predicative metaphors: G (x) when an x is not G.
Sentential metaphors: G (y) when y is not a discourse referent.

If S1 is accepted as a correct conceptual representation of the underlying comparison, then it is possible to claim that this classification is complete.

Of the five terms in S1 – SIM, F, x, G and y – two, SIM and F, are always omitted in a metaphor. The omission of SIM is necessary because the words expressing it are the characteristic marker of a simile; the omission of F is necessary because the purpose of a metaphor is to create a substitute for a literal F. We are left, therefore, with three terms, x, G, and y, of which two are always retained; if only one were retained, there would be no incongruity to mark the expression as a metaphor. When G is omitted and x and y retained, we obtain a nominal metaphor; when y is omitted and G and x retained, we obtain a predicative metaphor; when x is omitted and G and y retained, we obtain a sentential metaphor. Since there are only three possible pairs of three things taken two at a time, rules M1, M2, and M3 together exhaust the possibilities, and the resulting classification can be said to be complete.

Test Cases

It would be a simple matter to show that a wide variety of metaphors have the conceptual structure given in these rules. No number of such demonstrations, however, would really test their completness. For that, we must search for potential exceptions to the rules.

One type of exception poses a problem for any theory that assumes metaphors are always expressions of resemblance or analogy. "Giddy brink," for example, is not based on a simile of the form "A dangerous brink is like a giddy feeling," as rule M2 might suggest. It is possible to claim that the copula is not similitude, but causality:

(24) GIDDY (brink) $\longrightarrow$ CAUSE [DANGEROUS (brink), GIDDY (feeling)].

The structure of rule M2 would thus remain intact, although CAUSE rather than SIM would be the copulative relation in the source expression.[11]

Richards (1936a, p. 108) offers a more imaginative interpretation of "giddy brink," however, in which the observer's own giddiness is projected onto the brink that causes it. This analysis is roughly equivalent to saying that "I stood on the giddy brink" should be understood as "I stood giddily on the brink" plus projection. Richards's analysis has the advantage of fitting other examples, like "He drank a mournful cup of coffee," where CAUSE is as inappropriate as SIM, but where "He mournfully drank a cup of coffee" plus projection provides a reasonable interpretation. This projective conversion of adverbs into misplaced adjectives results in a trope that poses many of the same apperceptive problems as do metaphors, but that cannot be resolved by the reconstruction of an underlying simile. If the brink or the cup of coffee could be construed as part of a larger situation, it might be possible to classify such tropes as instances of synecdoche or metonymy.

Another type of expression that looks like a metaphor but does not seem to express a resemblance or analogy can occur when two arguments of a relation are reversed, as in "John bores poetry" or "Golf plays John." If rule M2 is imposed willy-nilly, the resulting similes do not capture the natural interpretations. Most people I have asked have said that these figures of speech (if they mean anything at all) mean that something about John (his dullness, his compulsiveness) is expressed by reversing the conventional agent – patient roles: John is not prepared to appreciate poetry, or John plays golf obsessively. The rules I have given, however, make no provision for reversing the order of arguments within a function, so if these expressions are metaphors, they are counterexamples to the present analysis. My own preference is to classify them as instances of personification and irony.

One possible difficulty is that it may not always be clear whether a metaphor is nominal or predicative, and thus a reader will not know whether to reconstruct it by rule M1 or M2. "A watchdog committee," for example, seems at first glance to be a predicative metaphor, and M2 leads to the not implausible paraphrase, "Some property of the committee is like a watchdog of something." But "watchdog" is a noun that is being pressed into service here as an adjective; if we treat it as a noun in a nominal metaphor, M1 leads to "Some property of the committee is like some property of a watchdog," which is a clear improvement. But the choice is not always obvious. Consider the following pair of metaphors:

(25) a. John is married to his work.

b. John is married to a gem.

The attempt here is to find a case, like (25b), where the formula must apply to an argument inside the analysis required for (25a), i.e., to a noun phrase inside a predicate phrase. Consider (25a) first. If we apply rule M2, we obtain:

(26) MARRIED TO (john, his work) $\longrightarrow$ SIM [RELATED TO (john, his work), MARRIED TO (a person, a spouse)].

This reconstruction is based on the assumption that the underlying comparison is something like, "John is related to his work the same way a person is married to a spouse." If we follow the same analysis with (25b), however, the result is:

(27) MARRIED TO (john, a gem) $\longrightarrow$ SIM [RELATED TO (john, a gem), MARRIED TO (a person, a spouse)].

The comparison reconstructed in this manner is "John is related to a gem the same way a person is married to their spouse." Since this is not how we would normally understand (25b), we seem to have found a counterexample.

In order to defend my analysis, therefore, I must argue that (25b) is not a counterexample. The first step is to argue that, to someone unfamiliar with this weary "gem" metaphor, the comparison constructed in (27) might be a perfectly plausible paraphrase. Indeed, (25b) seems more interesting when I see it in this fresh manner. In short, (27) is a possible, though not the conventional, reconstruction of (25b). The second step is to argue for an alternative way to obtain the more conventional result: as a nominal metaphor rather than a predicate metaphor. In order to make this point, it is convenient to paraphrase (25b) so that the conventional interpretation is unavoidable:

(28) [The person] John is married to [is] a gem.

This expansion emphasizes the conventional sense of (25b), and the result is a nominal metaphor that can be reconstructed according to M1:

(29) BE (the person john is married to, a gem) $\longrightarrow$

　　　SIM [F (the person john is married to), G (a gem)],

which says that some property F of the person John is married to is similar to some property G of gems. The final step in the defense is to argue that this second reconstruction is also available for (25a). As before, we rephrase (25a),

(30) [The person] John is married to [is] his work,

which can be reconstructed to give the comparison, "The person John is married to is like his work." It is not clear how this simile should be interpreted, but it suggests to me that the person John is married to makes him work like an employee.

We see, therefore, that (25a) and (25b) both permit (at least) two reconstructions, which accords well with the notorious subtlety of metaphoric analysis. The difference between the two derivations is a difference in the scope of the metaphor; the apparent counterexample arises from the fact that the conventional scope of one is different from the conventional scope of the other. It might be proposed that some further rule should be formulated to govern the correct scope, but that would be unwise. Much better, in my opinion, to take (25) as a demonstration of the possibility of different reconstructions, and leave to context the task of selecting the more appropriate one on any given occasion.

Still another test is provided by mixed metaphors. Ortony, Reynolds, and Arter (1978) quote Ronald Reagan as saying, "The ship of state is sailing the wrong way down a one-way street." The underlying comparison is presumably:

(31) SIM [SAIL (ship of state), DRIVE WRONG WAY (someone)].

If rule M2 were respected, the result would be "The ship of state is driving the wrong way down a one-way street," but this is hardly an improvement. Either metaphor alone would be unexceptionable: "The country is driving the wrong way down a one-way street," or "The ship of state is sailing in the wrong direction." But these, too, are no better. As Ortony, Reynolds, and Arter remark, Reagan said exactly what he meant. Pedants should keep their hands off such effective communication. I must admit, therefore, that mixed metaphors can violate M2 and get away with it. But I cannot resist adding that the general validity of the rules is evidenced by the fact that we are aware they have been violated.

Not all compound metaphors are incongruous; some poets have excelled at nesting one inside another. Unraveling such constructions may require an algebra of metaphor that goes well beyond the rules offered here. We can catch a glimpse of the latent complexities by analyzing an example.

Consider these lines from Dryden: "A fiery soul, which, working out its way,/ Fretted the pygmy body to decay,/ And o'er informed the tenement of clay." An old sense of "inform" is "give form to" (the communicative sense presumably derives from the need to give form to your ideas before expressing them) and a closely related sense is "to be the formative principle of" or "animate." If we consider only the fragment, "A fiery soul . . . informed the tenement of clay," the comparison underlying it is something like "His passionate soul was related to his body as fire informs the clay," or, conceptually:

(32) SIM [RELATED TO (passionate soul, body), INFORM (fire, clay)].

A straightforward application of M2, however, would yield, "A passionate soul informed his body," which, given the close relation of "inform" and "animate," is hardly a metaphor at all. In order to force the relatum of (32) to the surface, Dryden elaborated the metaphor. First, he used another metaphor to link "fiery" and "soul":

(33) FIERY (soul) $\longrightarrow$ SIM [PASSIONATE (soul), FIERY (furnace)].

Next, he draws on two more figures: "The body is (like) the tenement of the soul" and "The body is (like) clay." When the second is nominalized (following a general rule that relates, for example, "The boat is aluminum" to "the boat of aluminum"), and substituted into the first figure, the result is, "The body of clay is like the tenement of the soul," which is the simile corresponding to "tenement of clay":

(34) TENEMENT OF (clay) $\longrightarrow$ SIM [BODY OF (clay),
       TENEMENT OF (soul)]

Now, when (33) and (34) are substituted for the arguments of the referent in (32), we can finally represent Dryden's line:

(35) INFORM (fiery soul, tenement of clay) $\longrightarrow$
      SIM [RELATED TO (fiery soul, tenement of clay),
      INFORM (fire, clay)].

A full paraphrase in terms of all the comparisons we have reconstructed might go something like this: "As fire informs the clay, so a soul as passionate as a fiery furnace was related to his body, which is like the tenement of his soul." Not only is this paraphrase stylistically awkward, it is harder to understand than Dryden's metaphors. As an interpretation, it would be a mockery.

Since "fiery soul" and "tenement of clay" were probably familiar metaphors even in Dryden's time, we can surmise that he did little more than juxtapose them in an interesting way. The conceptual analysis in (35) is no flow chart of the author's mental operations, nor does it exhaust all we would like to know about such constructions. It is intended simply to illustrate the intricate conceptual structure that can be hidden in a line of only moderate metaphorical complexity. I would speculate that, although we have no algebra for nested metaphors, we can pick them off one by one – compounding does not discredit the reconstructive rules in principle.

Adverbial metaphors provide still other test cases. As described, the rules hold for only noun and verb or adjective phrases. What are we to make of expressions like "Rapidly is wastefully," or "He shouted silently"?

Conceptually, a predicate adverb is an operator that maps a function into another function. "He ran" expresses the concept RUN (he); the concept expressed by "He ran rapidly" can be represented as [RAPIDLY (RUN)] (he), where [RAPIDLY (RUN)] is the new function. Using this notation, expressions like "He shouted silently" can be seen as special cases of rule M2,

(36) [SILENTLY (SHOUT)] (he) $\longrightarrow$

$\qquad$ ($\exists$F) ($\exists$y) [SIM {[SILENTLY (F)] (he), SHOUT (y)}],

which would be paraphrased as "He did something silently like someone shouting." Such examples can, therefore, be accommodated in the present account.

Examples like "Rapidly is wastefully," however, have the conceptual structure

(37) ($\exists$F) ($\exists$x) [BE {[RAPIDLY (F)] (x), [WASTEFULLY (F)] (x)}]

which would be paraphrased as "To do something rapidly is to do it wastefully"; the general idea is that "wastefully" can be substituted for "rapidly" in any F (x) . As in "Haste makes waste," it is not clear that any resemblance or analogy is being expressed; the relation seems to be one of causation or identity. If these expressions are considered to be metaphors, they are counterexamples to the present theory. Like metaphors, they involve ellipsis, but, unlike metaphors, they do not involve comparison.

The merits of the reconstructive rules should not be overstated. Cases not involving similitude can possibly be counted as exceptions; so, perhaps, can cases that do not involve the metaphorical use of a noun phrase, predicate phrase, or sentence (in Dylan Thomas's "a grief ago," "ago" is not a predicate adjective). Although most of the metaphors that have been discussed in the extensive literature on this topic can be reconstructed as comparisons by a relatively mechanical application of the rules, no doubt a determined critic could find still other exceptions.

Recognition reconsidered

These various test cases provide a basis for reconsidering what cognitive processes might be involved in the recognition that some expression is a metaphor. According to the view presented here, recognition is equivalent to the reconstruction of SIM in the underlying conceptual representation. In this view, therefore, it would be plausible to argue that the appropriateness of SIM cannot be determined until a reader has understood the components well enough to evaluate possible relations between them.

Take BE (x, y) as an example. If a sentence expresses an entailment, as in "Trees are plants," we might assume that there is a reconstructive process of the form:

E1. BE (tree, plant) $\longrightarrow$ ($\exists$F) ($\exists$G) {ENTAIL [F (tree), G (plant)]},

where the entailment is verified by determining that all properties of plants are also properties of trees. That is to say, if all properties of y must also be properties of x, the appropriate reconstruction is as an entailment. If the sentence expresses a contingent relation, as in "This tree is a landmark," we might imagine that there is a reconstructive process of the form:

A1. BE (tree, landmark) $\longrightarrow$ ($\exists$F) ($\exists$G) {ATTRIBUTE [F (tree),
      G (landmark)]},

where the contingency is understood as adding all the properties of landmarks to the properties of this tree. That is to say, if all properties of y could be properties of x, yet are not entailed, the appropriate reconstruction is as an attribution. These formulations of E1 and A1 are designed to show their similarity to M1, and thus to suggest that part of the cognitive activity required to understand a sentence expressing a concept of the form BE (x, y) is the determination of which relation is appropriate. A general statement of the reconstructive process, therefore, would be:

G1. BE $(x, y) \longrightarrow$ ($\exists$R) ($\exists$F) ($\exists$G) {R [F (x), G (y)]}.

In order to determine an appropriate value for R, a reader must first understand F (x) and G (y). If the sentence is a metaphor, like "A

tree is an umbrella," neither E1 nor A1 will be judged appropriate, but
the reader may decide that $R = SIM$. Only at this point would it be
possible to judge that the expression was a nominal metaphor.

A similar generalization of M2 is possible. For example, "Trees are
woody" would follow:

E2. WOODY (tree) $\longrightarrow$ ($\exists$F) ($\exists y$) {ENTAIL [F (tree), WOODY (y)]},

and "Trees are beautiful" would follow:

A2. BEAUTIFUL (tree) $\longrightarrow$ ($\exists$F) ($\exists y$) {ATTRIBUTE [F (tree),
   BEAUTIFUL (y)]},

leading to the general rule:

G2. G (x) $\longrightarrow$ ($\exists$R) ($\exists y$) {R [F (x), G (y)]},

where once again the selection of $R = SIM$ must await the processing
of the related constituent expressions, and the recognition that the
expression was a predicative metaphor would be post hoc.

Recognition of a sentential metaphor would also be post hoc, since
the sentence itself would not require SIM, but after it had been understood, it would be recognized as unrelated to the antecedent text.

According to this view, therefore, a special recognition process is
unnecessary. It would not be necessary first to recognize that an expression is metaphorical and then to resort to some special subroutine for
processing it. Metaphorical expressions would be processed just as literal expressions are, up to the point where SIM must be introduced.

Interpretation

In sentences like "John is eating," where one conceptual argument of
the verb is omitted, a reader understands that John is eating something. It is not necessary to know precisely what John is eating in order
to understand what has been claimed. Similarly, in sentences like
"John is a wolf," where the properties of the two arguments are omitted, a reader understands that some properties of wolves are to be
attributed to John. It is not necessary to know precisely what property
of wolves is to be attributed to John in order to understand what has
been claimed. Just as "John is eating" cannot lead to a unique determination of what John is eating, so "John is a wolf" cannot lead to a
unique determination of John's lupine properties.

It would be futile, therefore, to view the interpretive process as a
search for the uniquely correct interpretation of a simile or metaphor.
Nevertheless, there is a set of alternative interpretations that are plausible. In the case of "John is eating," the missing argument is understood to be something edible: lunch, enchiladas, strawberry shortcake,

or whatever. What is given places constraints on what can be understood, but without determining it uniquely. Similarly, in the case of "John is a wolf," the missing properties are understood to be something attributable to both wolves and men: properties descriptive of appearance, disposition, behavior, or whatever. For "John is eating," the constraints are conventional, whereas for "John is a wolf" they are not. In the case of similes and metaphors, therefore, it is necessary to search the text and context for the author's grounds. This search process is one of interpretation. Interpretation is not a search for a unique paraphrase of the implicit comparison, but rather a search for grounds that will constrain the basis of the comparison to a plausible set of alternatives.

Sometimes the grounds for a comparison statement are relatively obvious, but when they are obscure, interpretation becomes especially important. Examples of nonobvious comparisons are provided by oxymora – figures like "a mournful optimist" or "a laborious idleness" – where grounds for conjoining antonymous words must be found.

Are oxymora metaphors? If so, they provide a special challenge for comparison views of metaphor (Beardsley, 1962). Since oxymora combine opposites, they seem to express contrasts, not comparisons, and it can be argued that, on the comparison view, they should not be analyzed in the same way as metaphors.

Let us treat "a cruel kindness" by rule M2, as if it were a predicative metaphor. Conceptually:

(38) CRUEL (kindness) $\longrightarrow$ $(\exists F)(\exists y)$ {SIM [F (kindness), CRUEL (y))]}.

As a comparison, "Some property of kindness is like something cruel." This paraphrase does not seem absurd to me, especially if I think of it as referring to some particular act of kindness, rather than to kindness generically. From the comparison, moreover, we can explain the direction of transfer: "a cruel kindness" is not the same as "a kind cruelty"; an oxymoron does more than merely contrast two opposing ideas.

The puzzle that remains, however, is to understand the circumstances under which a kindness could be cruel, and that puzzle is much the same for the comparison statement as for the oxymoron. Was the kindness so overwhelming that it created a cruel obligation for the beneficiary? The problem posed by oxymora is not that they cannot be recast as comparisons, but that reconstructing the comparison does so little to help us understand what the author had in mind.

Although the need for interpretation in addition to reconstruction is obvious in the case of oxymora, interpretation is also necessary in the case of more conventional metaphors. In every case, given a reconstructed comparison, a reader must try to appreciate how and why the author felt the referent was similar to the relatum, and what the similarity contributes to the larger concept of the text in which it occurs. A reconstruction that may seem acceptable out of context can prove unacceptable when seen in a broader perspective, in which case it may be necessary to seek alternative reconstructions. Thus, reconstruction and interpretation are mutually interacting processes. Their separation in theory is no sharp dichotomy, but more a difference in emphasis.

Finding appropriate classes of referents and relata is, strictly speaking, part of the task of interpretation. In order to make the discussion definite, let us assume that the author has given us some predicative metaphor having the conceptual structure $G(x)$, where x is something that G is not normally predicated of. $G(x)$ will, of course, be added to the image, but it will be understood (related to other knowledge) by finding a plausible basis for the use of such an expression, that is, by reconstruction a concept of the form $(\exists F)(\exists y) \{\text{SIM}[F(x), G(y)]\}$ and interpreting it. In this case, our initial degrees of freedom in interpretation will be the freedom to choose values for F and y. Two readers who choose different values for F and y will, of course, arrive at different interpretations of the metaphor, but even the same choices of F and y can lead to different interpretations. Choosing these values is only part of the interpretive task.

Consider first the selection of y, since this often seems the less critical choice. Usually it is sufficient to take as y whatever is the most generic argument G is conventionally predicated of. If, for example, the metaphoric concept is $\text{COMMIT}(x)$, then we search for something y such that $\text{COMMIT}(y)$ is highly predictable: "faux pas," "adultery," "suicide," "murder," or, more generally, a "crime." We will choose a generic argument, since the author is telling us that x is one of the generic class of things that COMMIT can be predicated of. In Auden's lines, "Thou shalt not sit/With statisticians nor commit/A social science," for example, the concept expressed by the metaphor is COMMIT (a social science) and thus social science is assigned to the class of things, namely crimes, that are most commonly committed; precisely which crime Auden had in mind (if any) we can never know.

If you were to ask what features to transfer from y to x, I would answer, "Whatever features are necessary in order to include x in the class of things that G is commonly predicated of." What effect this may have on the concept of x is a question that must be considered separately in every instance – in some cases it will be much more obvious than in others – but the reinterpretation of *x* as a kind of *y* is part, and sometimes the most important part, of interpreting the metaphor.

A more difficult step, however, is the choice of an F that stands in an appropriate relation to both *x* and G. We could, of course, proceed as before: ask what function is most commonly predicated of *x*. In the case of "commit a social science," this procedure is not much help, since there is nothing that stands out as the chief predicate applied to this argument: "study," "practice," "like," "subsidize," are all acceptable, but so are "forget," "ignore," "dislike," "criticize." The mystery: how do we know (and we do know) that the basis for Auden's metaphor is a comparison of the form, "Practicing a social science is like committing a crime," and not a comparison of the form, "Criticizing a social science is like committing a crime"?

Let us turn to G for help in finding an appropriate F. Reinhart (1976) suggests that the effect of F should be to delete certain semantic features of G – that G should be allowed to stand as the function applied to *x*, but that only those semantic features of G that are compatible with F are to be effective. "Commit" means to perform, or even more generically, to do, but with unpleasant connotations. If we delete all semantic features that serve to differentiate "commit" from "do," the comparison becomes "Doing a social science is like committing a crime," and the poet's message is "Thou shalt not do a social science." If, on the other hand, we delete all semantic features that differentiate "commit" from "criticize," the unpleasant connotations of "commit" will not be deleted, since "criticize" shares them, so the comparison would become "Doing something unpleasant to a social science is like committing a crime," and the poet's message would be "Thou shalt not do anything unpleasant to a social science," e.g., criticize it or, if Auden were punning, commit it to prison.

This version of filtering theory works well enough, but still does not explain why we prefer a positive over a negative version of F. The answer to that question, I believe, must come from the context. The whole poem points to Auden's opinion of social science. Given that opinion, "do," "perform," "practice," and the like, yield the only consistent interpretation; with F = "criticize," the poem self-destroys. A person who understood "Thou shalt not commit a social science" to mean "Thou shalt not commit a social science to memory" would not recognize that a metaphor had occurred, and a person who understood it to mean "Thou shalt not commit a social science to prison" would presumably regard it as an instance of metonymy. A person who understands the poem can only understand the metaphor to mean "Thou shalt not practice a social science."

The moral is not merely that interpretation is complicated, but that it requires an internally coherent configuration of all four terms. The interpretation of the referent cannot be independent of the interpretation of the relatum. When Richards (1936a) speaks of the "interaction" of two ideas to produce a new, resultant idea, different from either in isolation, at least part of what he means is that the reconstruction must produce a result that is internally coherent and interpretable, and that such a result cannot be obtained without taking full account of both ideas, their interrelations, and their relation to the context.

Another example may illustrate more dramatically that interpretation must be consistent with the context in which the metaphor is used. In most contexts, "Sheathe thine impatience" would probably be reconstructed by M2 as follows:

(39) SHEATHE (impatience) $\longrightarrow$ SIM [RESTRAIN (impatience),
     SHEATHE (SWORD)],

where y is taken to be "sword" because swords are the chief objects that we think of putting into sheaths. The choice of F is again somewhat moot; "conceal," "contain," or "hold back" would probably serve as well as "restrain." This reconstruction would be appropriate if the metaphor were spoken in a conventional social situation. In the context of a woman speaking to her lover, however, a second level of interpretation can be added on the basis of the simile that a penis is like a sword, in which case a variety of interpretations of F compatible with "sheathe" are possible. We can imagine contexts, therefore, that require totally different arguments for y and functions for F.

The importance of interpretation is clearest when repair is most dubious, when rule M2 produces an obviously inadequate simile. Consider, for example, Beckett's phrase, "waiting till my corpse is up to scratch." Leaving aside the pun on Old Scratch (an old jocular term for the devil), I take this to mean "waiting to die," but the inadequacy of that paraphrase is obvious. When I force "my corpse is up to scratch" into a comparison statement, the best I can do is: "A corpse that is ready for burial is like a body that is up to scratch." But what an odd relatum! The question, "Is Samuel's body up to scratch?" would not normally be understood as asking whether Samuel is dead – just the opposite.

Part of the power of Beckett's phrase comes from irony; if the irony is removed by rephrasing it as "waiting till my body is ready for burial," the impact is lost along with the metaphor. It is obvious that this attempt to provide a literal paraphrase of the metaphor falls far short of a translation; as Black says, "it fails to be a translation because it fails to give the insight that the metaphor did" (1962a, p. 46). The steps involved in reconstructing a comparison will often leave us far short of a satisfactory interpretation. Although we can tease out a pun, a simile, and an irony by relatively routine analysis, interpretation must go beyond that.

I am no expert at squeezing out everything a phrase will yield, but I can offer a candidate interpretation. Beckett does not say "waiting to die" because everyone is dying all the time. Death is merely the final stage in the progressive corpsification of the body. But this idea is carried one step further by irony: we are asked to see death as an achievement. If these notions are on the right track, it is obvious that interpretation must include more than the characterization of a transfer, either subtractive or additive, of conceptual features from the relatum to the referent.

The search for a theory of interpretation usually presupposes that it must begin with lexical concepts assignable to x, y, F, and G, including, perhaps, any general knowledge associated with these concepts and any affect that words expressing them may arouse. A discussion of the interpretation of metaphors leads very naturally, therefore, into a discussion of lexical knowledge. Since this is a vast topic on which I have written elsewhere at considerable length (Miller & Johnson-Laird, 1976), I shall try to discuss it here suggestively, not exhaustively.

Lexicalization

The organization of a person's memory for the meanings of words in his language has become a topic for much psychological speculation and research in recent years. One attraction of metaphor for cognitive psychologists is that it might contribute to a better understanding of lexical memory. The judgment that a word can literally denote some novel instances involves an appreciation of the similarity of that instance to instances previously encountered; SIM represents a basic psychological function. And, as Paivio (this volume) points out, the meanings that are combined in a metaphor must be retrieved from the reader's memory for what the words conventionally mean and how they are normally used.

The interpretation of the comparison underlying a novel metaphor sometimes requires merely that a subsidiary meaning of a word be favored over its core meaning. For example, Reinhart (1976) comments that the interpretation of "green ideas" depends on selecting a subsidiary meaning of "green," unripe. (Should we take this to mean that "green ideas" is not a metaphor?) Note, however, that "green ideas" can be reconstructed by rule M2:

(40) GREEN (idea) $\longrightarrow$ SIM [UNDEVELOPED (idea), GREEN (fruit)].

Reinhart makes the point that when we hear the literal warning, "Don't eat that apple; it's green," as we are about to eat an apple that is not green in color, we must do precisely the same thing we do for "green ideas": pass over the color sense of "green" in favor of the unripe sense. On the assumption that "green" has several alternative meanings, the problem of finding an appropriate sense in an apparently metaphorical use is not basically different from the problem of finding an appropriate sense in a literal use. The rapid disambiguation of polysemous words on the basis of context is one of the standard enigmas facing any theory of language comprehension.

These considerations add further plausibility to the suggestion that "green apple" is processed in the same manner as "green idea":

(41) GREEN (apple) $\longrightarrow$ ENTAIL [UNDEVELOPED (apple), GREEN (fruit)],

which follows rule E2; ENTAIL is appropriate because all properties of green fruit are also properties of undeveloped apples. This proposal levels any sharp boundary between the literal and figurative uses of words, which is consistent with easy passage of overused metaphors into subsidiary senses – of "green," in this example, from a metaphor based on the color of unripe fruit to a subsidiary sense, unripe, applicable to many other nouns.

Metaphor is frequently cited as a source of polysemy. For example, there was presumably a time in the history of English when "leg" was not used to refer to a part of a table. At that time, therefore, "leg of a table" might have been a metaphor based on a comparison of the form:

(42) LEG (table) $\longrightarrow$ SIM [SUPPORT (table), LEG (animal)].

With repeated use, however, "leg" acquired another meaning as the name for a part of a table. (Stern, 1965, calls this type of meaning change "adequation.") We are still able to recognize the similarity that led to the original metaphor, but we understand "leg of a table" literally by rejecting the animal-part sense in favor of the furniture-part sense in appropriate contexts.

The adequation of a metaphor is only one way subsidiary senses can creep into the lexicon. I have discussed elsewhere (Miller, 1978) semantic extensions that are common to many different words, and have proposed that such lexical regularities should be called construal rules. I shall not review this claim that people appreciate regular relations between a core sense and various extended senses of many words, since the status of such rules is still a matter for investigation. But, however the regularities are formulated, some extensions are easily understood on first hearing. Since a metaphoric interpretation of a word can be viewed as a semantic extension of that word's core meaning – a radical extension, in some cases – it would obviously be worthwhile to look for correspondences between construal rules and metaphorical interpretations. If metaphor often involves favoring an extended meaning over the core meaning of a word, students of metaphor should be interested in how such extended meanings arise.

The danger I see in regarding the metaphorical use of a word as merely an extension of that word's meaning is that it tempts us to over-simplify our view of metaphor. In novel metaphors, it is not the meanings of the words that change, but rather our beliefs and feelings about the things that the words refer to. I have claimed that the reader must imagine a world in which the metaphor, however incongruous it may seem, is true. Readers try to be conservative in imagining such different worlds, but the exercise cannot help but broaden their conception of what a world can be. If we think of metaphor as nothing more than pouring new meanings into old words, we shall be hard pressed to understand how metaphor can enrich the way we see the world, or why word meanings change so slowly.

Conclusion

A psychological theory of metaphor should be guided by two objectives. On the one hand, it should attempt to account for the comprehension of metaphorical language in the same terms used to account for the comprehension of nonmetaphorical language. On the other hand, it should attempt to discover what literal comprehension must be if metaphoric comprehension is to be explained in terms of it. Taken together, these objectives imply that we must extend our theories of literal comprehension until they are sufficiently powerful to account for metaphorical comprehension.

I have taken apperception as the central process in textual comprehension – the process of assimilating new information by relating it to things already known. A concept of the text is synthesized on the assumption that whatever the author has written is true in the conceptual world that he is describing, and that the reader is trying to replicate. What is true in the text, however, may be very different from what is true in the real world; the textual concept and the concept of reality must be kept distinct.

Metaphor poses an apperceptive problem, because metaphors are either false in the real world or apparently unrelated to the textual concept. Although readers must take what the metaphor says as true in the world that they are trying to synthesize from the text, they can only understand that world if they can find a basis in the real world that might have led the author to think of the metaphor. This search begins by attending to those features of the textual world that are similar to what is known of the real world, since those features can provide a basis for relating the textual world to what the reader already knows.

The grounds for a metaphor, therefore, can be formulated as relations of similitude that can be expressed as comparison statements. A set of rules for reconstructing those comparisons has been proposed, and an argument has been presented that the resulting classification of metaphors is complete. How the reconstructed comparisons are interpreted has been discussed, but many important problems of interpretation are left unsettled.

In this way, I have attempted to account for the comprehension of metaphorical language in terms of the comprehension of comparison statements. And I have tried to argue that the comprehension of literal language requires all of the apperceptive psychological machinery needed to account for the comprehension of comparison statements.

NOTES

Preparation of this manuscript was supported in part by a grant from the National Institute of Education to the Rockefeller University. The title is intended to acknowledge my intellectual debt to the work of Max Black. More personal acknowledgements are due to Bruce Fraser and Morris Halle for conversations that helped me to understand better what the problem of metaphor is, and to Andrew Ortony and John Ross for helpful comments on an earlier draft.

1 Metaphors occur in conversation as well as in written prose and poetry; these different settings undoubtedly impose different demands on both the source and addressee of a metaphoric expression. Inasmuch as I do not intend to explore such differences, however, I have chosen to focus on readers (to the exclusion of speakers and hearers, and the near exclusion of authors). I hope that this decision will not seriously compromise what I shall say about those aspects of metaphor I do intend to explore.

2 I am indebted to Steven Cushing for this way to illustrate the point.

3 The image has the logical status of a list of presuppositions, containing constants or bound variables, which restrict (or relativize) the domain of interpretation over which variables in the model can be quantified (Cushing, 1977).

4 Tversky (1977) calls the referent the "subject" and the relatum the "referent." If I understand Chomsky (1971) correctly, the referent is a conceptual instance of what he calls the (linguistic) "focus," and the relatum is a conceptual instance of what he calls the (linguistic) "presupposition" of a sentence.

5 If I understand Black (1962b) correctly, what I call a "symbol" is what he calls the "system of associated commonplaces." Bruce Fraser has suggested to me that the distinction between literal and symbolic should not be viewed as a dichotomy, but as a continuum, comparable to the continuum between creative and idiomatic expressions. The criterion of nontranslatability, if it can be used at all, would have to be used with caution. Asch (1958) has pointed out that the use of certain adjectives (e.g., "warm," "hard," "straight") to describe both properties of objects and properties of persons is sufficiently universal to justify challenging the common assumption that their application to persons is a metaphorical extension of their meaning in objective contexts. If some symbol proved to be similarly universal, its translatability could not be used to argue that it was not a symbol.

6 Strictly speaking, the verb "affect" is a relation, not a property: "My love affects me" expresses the sentential concept AFFECT (my love, me). It is possible to treat a relation as a property, however, by exploiting the logical abstraction operator λ. Thus, the relation F (x, x') can be used to define a new function, λx.F (x, x'), which is a property that takes x as its argument. In the example: λx.AFFECT $(x,$ me) defines a new function (that can be represented as AFFECT ME) which is a property that can take "my love" or "a rose" as its argument x. By using that abstraction operator it is possible to deal with comparisons in which the functions F and G have different numbers of arguments. For example, "Fog swirls like a cat rubs its back" compares a function of one argument, SWIRL (fog), with a function of two arguments, RUB (cat, its back). We can define a new function RUB ITS BACK $= \lambda x$.RUB $(x,$ its back), in which case the conceptual structure of the simile can be written SIM[SWIRL (fog), RUB ITS BACK (cat)], which conforms to S1.

7 There are also degenerate analogies: $x:x::x:x$, or $x:x::y:y$, or $x:y::x:y$, which are valid regardless of the values of x and y (Sternberg, 1977a).

8 The history of the comparison view is reviewed by Mooij (1976), who concludes that the case against it is not convincing. Most objections, he says, are to "a careless application of the comparison view rather than the comparison view itself" (p. 60).

9 More precisely, 7 (y) is attributed to F (x). Applying the abstraction operator to SIM[F (x), G (y)] enables us to define a new function λF (x).SIM[F (x), G (y)], which is a property that can take F (x) as its argument. If we represent this new function as SIM G (y), as in note 6, we obtain [SIM G (y)] [F (x)] as an alternative formulation of S1 for comparisons: SIMILAR TO G (y) is attributed to F (x). When SIM is omitted, we obtain [G (y)] [F (x)]. Since, in the example, both F and G are implicit, the paraphrase of

[G (a wolf)] [F (man)] will be "Some properties of a wolf are attributed to be properties of man." Note that in literal statements of categorization, like "Man is a primate," this same paraphrase is possible, but the simile would be odd because all properties of a primate are properties of man, and we do not use "some" when we know that "all" is appropriate.

10 If I understand Richards (1936b) correctly, the referent $F(x)$ of the underlying comparison is what he calls the "tenor" and the relatum $G(y)$ is what he calls the "vehicle" of the metaphor. And if I understand Black (1962b) correctly, the argument y (in M_1) or the function G (in M_2) is what he calls the "focus," and the argument x of the referent is what he calls the "frame" of the metaphor. J. D. Sapir (1977), calls the referent the "continuous term" (since it is commensurate or continuous with the topic of discourse) and calls the relatum the "discontinuous term" of the metaphor.

11 A similar and probably related situation exists in the morphology of compound words, where an even greater variety of relational predicates must be inferred. Thus, a bulldog is a dog that "resembles" a bull, but a honeybee is a bee that "makes" honey, an armchair is a chair that "has" arms, a garden party is a party that is "in" a garden, and so on. Levi (1974) has proposed a list of six "recoverably deletable predicates" (CAUSE, HAVE, MAKE, USE, BE, IN, but no predicate of similitude) that will account for many such constructions.

PART II

METAPHOR
AND
SOCIETY

Generative Metaphor: A Perspective on Problem-Setting in Social Policy

DONALD A. SCHÖN

Introduction

Much of the interest in metaphor on the part of linguists and philosophers of language has had to do with metaphor as a species of figurative language which needs explaining, or explaining away. (See, for a notable example, Searle, this volume. Two classic articles, Black, 1962b, and Beardsley, 1967, are also in this vein.) Metaphor, in this tradition, is a kind of anomaly of language, one which must be dispelled in order to clear the path for a general theory of reference or meaning. There is a very different tradition associated with the notion of metaphor, however – one which treats metaphor as central to the task of accounting for our perspectives on the world: how we think about things, make sense of reality, and set the problems we later try to solve.[1] In this second sense, "metaphor" refers both to a certain kind of product – a perspective or frame, a way of looking at things – and to a certain kind of process – a process by which new perspectives on the world come into existence. In this tradition, metaphorical utterances – "Man is a wolf" along with the rest of the rather dreary repertoire of hallowed examples – are significant only as symptoms of a particular kind of SEEING-AS, the "meta-pherein" or "carrying over" of frames or perspectives from one domain of experience to another. This is the process which, in the remainder of this paper I shall call generative metaphor.[2]

In the second tradition, there are two central puzzles. The first has to do with interpretation. From what people say and do, especially in problematic situations, how ought we to infer how they are *thinking* about those situations, whether their thinking involves a generative metaphor and, if so, what it is. This is the hermeneutic problem,[3] the problem of the interpretation of texts in a very broad sense, the problem of literary criticism. The concern here is to understand the kinds of inferences by which such interpretations are made, the sorts of evidence pertinent to them, and the criteria by which they should be judged and tested.

The second puzzle has to do with generativity. It is nothing less than the question of how we come to see things in new ways. Conceiving of generative metaphor as a special case – a special version of SEEING-AS by which we gain new perspectives on the world – we ask how the process of generative metaphor works. What is the anatomy of the making of generative metaphor?

In this paper, I shall be considering aspects of both of these puzzles as they crop up in a particular domain, that of social policy.

For some twenty years, it has been a powerful, indeed a dominant, view that the development of social policy ought to be considered as a problem-solving enterprise. In opposition to this view, I have become persuaded that the essential difficulties in social policy have more to do with *problem setting* than with problem solving, more to do with ways in which we frame the purposes to be achieved than with the selection of optimal means for achieving them. It becomes critically important, then, to learn how social policy problems are actually set and to discover what it means to set them well or badly.[4]

Problem settings are mediated, I believe, by the "stories" people tell about troublesome situations – stories in which they describe what is wrong and what needs fixing. When we examine the problem-setting stories told by the analysts and practitioners of social policy, it becomes apparent that the framing of problems often depends upon metaphors inderlying the stories which generate problem setting and set the directions of problem solving. One of the most pervasive stories about social services, for example, diagnoses the problem as "fragmentation" and prescribes "coordination" as the remedy. But services seen as fragmented might be seen, alternatively, as autonomous. Fragmented services become problematic when they are seen as the shattering of a prior integration. The services are seen something like a vase that was once whole and now is broken.

Under the spell of metaphor, it appears obvious that fragmentation is bad and coordination, good. But this sense of obviousness depends very much on the metaphor remaining tacit. Once we have constructed the metaphor which generates the problem-setting story, we can ask, for example, whether the services appropriate to the present situation are just those which used to be integrated, and whether there may not be benefits as well as costs associated with the lack of integration. In short, we can spell out the metaphor, elaborate the assumptions which flow from it, and examine their appropriateness in the present situation.

The notion of generative metaphor then becomes an interpretive tool for the critical analysis of social policy. My point here is not that we *ought* to think metaphorically about social policy problems, but that we *do* already think about them in terms of certain pervasive, tacit generative metaphors; and that we ought to become critically aware of these generative metaphors, to increase the rigor and precision of our analysis of social policy problems by examining the analogies and "disanalogies" between the familiar descriptions – embodied in metaphors like "fragmented services" – and the actual problematic situations that confront us.

The train of thought which leads me to argue for greater awareness of the metaphors which generate our setting of social policy problems also leads me to propose an argument about the making of generative metaphor.

When we become attentive to the framing of social problems, we thereby become aware of conflicting frames. Our debates over social policy turn often not on problems but on dilemmas. The participants in the debate bring different and conflicting frames, generated by different and conflicting metaphors. Such conflicts are often not resolvable by recourse to the facts – by technological fixes, by tradeoff analyses, or by reliance on institutionalized forms of social choice. Indeed, these stubborn conflicts of perspective, full of potential for violent contention, have become in their own right issues of social policy. The question then arises as to whether it is possible by *inquiry* to achieve the restructuring, coordination, reconciliation, or integration of conflicting frames for the construction of social problems. If so, what is the nature of this inquiry?

I shall argue that we are sometimes intuitively able to engage in reciprocal inquiry by which conflicting frames are reconstructed and coordinated. And I shall propose that "frame restructuring" is in several crucial respects similar to the making of generative metaphor. These two kinds of processes seem to me to have a family resemblance, and our efforts to account for them can be mutually illuminating.

I shall pursue this line of thought by considering two examples – the first drawn from the domain of technology, and the second, from the field of housing policy. I shall consider in the first example the making of a generative metaphor, and in the second, a conflict of two ways of setting a social policy problem (each generated by a metaphor of its own) – a conflict which is resolved in a particular context through a process of frame restructuring and coordination, which resembles in several important respects the cognitive work involved in the making of generative metaphor.

The making of generative metaphor: a technological example

Some years ago, a group of product-development researchers was considering how to improve the performance of a new paintbrush made with synthetic bristles.[5] Compared to the old natural-bristle brush, the new one delivered paint to a surface in a discontinuous, "gloppy" way. The researchers had tried a number of different improvements. They had noticed, for example, that natural bristles had split ends, whereas the synthetic bristles did not, and they tried (without significant improvement resulting) to split the ends of the synthetic bristles. They experimented with bristles of different diameters. Nothing seemed to help.

Then someone observed, *"You know, a paintbrush is a kind of pump!"* He pointed out that when a paintbrush is pressed against a surface, paint is forced through the *spaces between bristles* onto the surface. The paint is made to flow through the "channels" formed by the bristles when the channels are deformed by the bending of the brush. He noted that painters will sometimes *vibrate* a brush when applying it to a surface, so as to facilitate the flow of paint.

The researchers tried out the natural and synthetic bristle brushes, thinking of them as pumps. They noticed that the natural brush formed a *gradual curve* when it was pressed against a surface whereas the synthetic brush formed a shape more nearly an angle. They speculated that this difference might account for the "gloppy" performance of the bristle brush. How then might they make the bending shape of the synthetic brush into a gentle curve?

This line of thought led them to a variety of inventions. Perhaps fibers could be varied so as to create greater density in that zone. Perhaps fibers could be bonded together in that zone. Some of these inventions were reduced to practice and did, indeed, produce a smoother· flow of paint.

Paintbrush-as-pump is an example of what I mean by a generative metaphor.

In ordinary discourse, we call a paintbrush "paintbrush" and we call a pump, "pump." Paintbrushes and pumps are two quite different things and it is not appropriate to call one thing by the other's name. It is true that we can subsume both paintbrushes and pumps under a more general category; for example, they are both examples of tools. But when we think of the two things as tools, we also recognize that they are designed and used for different purposes, and that they operate according to different mechanisms. Hence, we would describe them differently. We might say, for example, that paintbrushes serve to "spread paint on a surface" whereas pumps serve to "move a quantity of liquid from one place to another." We might say that a pump works by "pushing or sucking liquid through a channel" whereas one makes a paintbrush work by "dipping it in paint and then transferring the paint to a surface by wiping the brush across that surface."

When one of the researchers said, "You know, a paintbrush is a kind of pump!" he was himself thinking of the paintbrush as a pump, seeing it as a pump, and he was inviting the other researchers to do likewise. In the language of description, we might say that he was taking the ordinary description of "pump" – something on the order of "an instrument that moves liquid from one place to another by pushing or sucking it through a channel" – as a putative description of "paintbrush." It is as though he were posing a kind of riddle ("How is a paintbrush a pump?") which, once entertained, led him and the other researchers to notice new features of the brush and of the painting process. The constellation of notions familiarly associated with pumping (what Black [1962b] calls the "associated commonplaces") the researchers project onto the painting situation, transforming their perception of pumping. They notice the spaces *between* the bristles, for example, rather than just the bristles; and they think of these spaces as channels through which paint can flow. One might say that the spaces which had been background become foreground elements, objects of attention in their own right, as in a pump the contained space called a "channel" is a foreground element with a special name of its own. Rather than perceiving the paint as adhering to the surface of the bristles (later scraped off onto a surface), they now see the paint as flowing through the channels formed by the bristles. They can then pay attention to the different bending angles of the natural and synthetic brushes, noting how these different angles make for different ways of compressing channels and thereby affecting the pumping of liquid through the channels; and they can incorporate this observation into a new explanation of the differences in the brushes' performance. They invent ways to smooth out the bending angle of the synthetic brush in order to make it pump (not wipe) paint more evenly onto the surface.

Paintbrush-as-pump became a *metaphor* for the researchers.[6] One can characterize the metaphor-making process by saying that the researchers, who had begun by describing painting in a familiar way, entertained the description of a different, already-named process (pumping) as an alternative description of painting; and that in their redescription of painting, both their perception of the phenomenon and the previous description of pumping were transformed. What makes the process one of metaphor making, rather than simply of redescribing, is that the new putative description already belongs to what is initially perceived as a different, albeit familiar thing; hence, everything one knows about pumping has the potential of being brought into play in this redescription of painting. There is, in this sense, great economy and high leverage in this particular kind of redescription.[7] To use the language of "seeing" rather than "describing,"[8] we can also say that the researchers were engaged in seeing *A* as *B*, where *A* and *B* had previously seemed to them to be different things. Every instance of metaphor making is an instance of SEEING-AS, though not every instance of SEEING-AS involves metaphor making. (For example, someone might see □ as a box). In metaphor making, *A* and *B* are initially perceived, named, and understood as very different things – so different that it would ordinarily pass as a mistake to describe one as the other. It is the restructuring of the perception of the phenomena named by *"A"* and *"B"* which enables us to call "metaphor" what we might otherwise have called "mistake."

Not all metaphors are generative. In the researchers' talk about the paintbrush problem, for example, they also spoke of painting as "masking a surface." But this metaphor did not generate perceptions of new features of the paintbrush nor did it give rise to a new view of the problem. Paintbrush-as-pump was a *generative* metaphor for the researchers in the sense that it generated new perceptions, explanations, and inventions.

It is possible in this account to notice several important features of the process of making a generative metaphor. The researchers had, to begin with, certain ways of describing the brush and the painting process, but these descriptions were unsatisfactory. They did not lead to a setting of the technological problem that enabled it to be solved; they did not provoke invention. The triggering of the generative metaphor ("A paintbrush is a kind of pump!") occurred while the researchers were involved in the concrete, sensory experience of using the brushes and feeling how the brushes worked with the paint. The researchers used words like "gloppy" and "smooth" to convey some of the qualities of the phenomena they were experiencing. It seems to me very likely that the triggering of the metaphor occurred because the researchers were immersed in experience of the phenomena.

Once the metaphor had been triggered, one might say that the researchers *mapped* their descriptions of "pump" and "pumping" onto their initial descriptions of "paintbrush" and "painting." But this would be at least partly incorrect. For in the first instance, the two descriptions resisted mapping. It was only after elements and relations of the brush and the painting had been regrouped and renamed (spaces between bristles made into foreground elements and called "channels," for example) that the paintbrush could be seen as a pump.

It is important to note that the researchers were able to see painting as similar to pumping before they were able to say "similar with respect to what."[9] At first, they had only an unarticulated perception of similarity which they could express by doing the painting and inviting others to see it as they did, or by using terms like "squeezing" or "forcing" to convey the pumplike quality of the action. Only later, and in an effort to account for their earlier perception of similarity, did they develop an explicit account of the similarity, an account which later still became part of a general theory of "pumpoids," according to which they could regard paintbrushes and pumps, along with washcloths and mops, as instances of a single technological category.

It would be seriously misleading, then, to say that, in making their generative metaphor, the researchers first "noticed certain similarities between paintbrushes and pumps." For the making of generative metaphor involves a developmental process. It has a life cycle. In the earlier stages of the life cycle, one notices or feels that A and B are similar, without being able to say similar with respect to what. Later on, one may come to be able to describe relations of elements present in a restructured perception of both A and B which account for the pre-analytic detection of similarity between A and B, that is, one can formulate an *analogy* between A and B. Later still, one may construct a general model for which a redescribed A and a redescribed B can be identified as instances. To read the later model back onto the beginning of the process would be to engage in a kind of historical revisionism.

Problem setting in social policy

My second example of generative metaphor will be drawn from a very different field, that of social policy; and here I shall pay particular attention to the issue of housing.

In introducing this field, I should like first to observe that it has come to be dominated, at least in the United States over the last twenty or thirty years, by a particular perspective – a perspective under which inquiry into social policy is regarded as a form of problem solving.

The problem-solving perspective contains three central components. It directs our attention, first of all, to the search for solutions. The problems themselves are generally assumed to be given. Thus, it is assumed that we know, or can easily voice, the problems of cities, the problems of the economy, the problems of population control, but that we cannot yet solve them. The task is to find solutions to known problems.

If problems are assumed to be given, this is in part because they are taken always to have the same form. Problem solving consists in the effort to find means for the achievement of our objectives in the face of the constraints that make such achievement difficult. According to this *instrumentalist* position, there are always objectives, goals, or purposes; these are rooted in human values and are, in a sense, arbitrary, inasmuch as they depend on what we (or others) want to achieve. There are also constraints to the achievement of these objectives, always including the constraint of limited resources. And finally, there are the various available means, the optional courses of action from which we may select the best (or at least an acceptable) path to our objectives. The problem solver, as Simon (1969) has said, is always engaged in searching some problem-space in order to find means well-suited, in the face of constraints, to the achievement of some objective function.

The problem-solving perspective has been very generally adopted by those in our society who, by profession and position, are most powerfully involved in the analysis, design, implementation, and criticism of social policy. Whatever the significant differences may be among economists, administrators, engineers, policy analysts, and planners, in recent years they have all come to regard themselves as problem solvers, in the sense described above. Indeed, the public view of government has come increasingly to include the notion of government as a solver of social problems.[10] In spite of this evolving consensus, however, there are great difficulties with the problem-solving perspective. A sense of its inadequacy has begun to spread among practitioners of social policy and among the public at large. Let me summarize briefly here criticisms which have been made at length elsewhere.

Problems are not given. They are constructed by human beings in their attempts to make sense of complex and troubling situations. Ways of describing problems move into and out of good currency (as the urban problem, for example, tended to be defined in the 1950s as "congestion"; in the 1960s as "poverty"; and in the 1970s as "fiscal insolvency"). New descriptions of problems tend not to spring from the solutions of the problem earlier set, but to evolve independently as new features of situations come into prominence. Indeed, societal problem solving has often created unintended consequences, which come to be perceived as problems in their own right (as public housing, conceived initially as a solution to the problem of housing the temporarily poor, came later to be perceived as a concentration of social pathology). This pattern of solutions creating unanticipated problems casts doubt upon the tenets of instrumentalism. Our efforts to correct errors have not converged upon solutions that are relatively free of error. On the contrary, the iterative cycles of problem setting and problem solving seem to diverge. The social situations confronting us have turned out to be far more complex than we had supposed, and it becomes increasingly doubtful that in the domain of social policy, we can make accurate temporal predictions, design models which converge upon a true description of reality, and carry out experiments which yield unambiguous results. Moreover, the unexpected problems created by our search for acceptable means to the ends we have chosen reveals (as in the cases of health and welfare policies) a stubborn conflict of ends traceable to the problem setting itself. Hence, in the domain of social policy, it has become clear that we ought no longer to avoid the problem of setting the problem.

How, then, are social problems set?

The domain of urban housing is a good one in which to pursue this question. Over the last thirty or forty years, people have told some very different stories about urban housing, and there have been some very dramatic shifts in ideas in good currency about the problem. We shall consider two of these stories, each of which sets out a view of what is wrong and what needs fixing.[11]

Blight and renewal

The first is a story out of the fifties. It is drawn from Justice Douglas's opinion on the constitutionality of the Federal Urban Renewal Program in the District of Columbia.

The experts concluded that if the community were to be healthy, if it were not to revert again to a blighted or slum area, as though possessed of a congenital disease, the area must be planned as a whole. It was not enough, they believed, to remove existing buildings that were unsanitary or unsightly. It was important to redesign the whole area so as to eliminate the conditions that cause slums — the overcrowding of dwellings, the lack of parks, the lack of adequate streets and alleys, the absence of recreational areas, the lack of light and air, the presence of outmoded street patterns. It was believed that the piecemeal approach, the removal of individual structures that were offensive, would be only a palliative. The entire area needed redesigning so that a balanced, integrated plan could be developed for the region including not only new homes, but also schools, churches, parks, streets, and shopping centers. In this way it was hoped that the cycle of decay of the area could be controlled and the birth of future slums prevented. (quoted in Bellush & Haus-knecht, 1967, p. 62)

In this this story, the community itself is one main character, and the planner, or "expert," is another. The community, once healthy, has become blighted and diseased. The planner, beholding it in its decayed condition, conceives the image of the community become healthy once again, with "new homes . . . . schools, churches, parks, streets and shopping centers." But this can be achieved only through redesign of the whole area, under a balanced and integrated plan. Otherwise the area will "revert again to a . . . slum area, as though possessed of a congenital disease."

The slum as natural community

According to the second story, the places called "slums" are not all the same. Some of them are, indeed, decadent and impoverished, the victims of cycles of decay exacerbated by federal policies of "immuring" and of "urban renewal." Others, such as the West End and the North End in Boston, or the East Village in New York City, are true low-income communities which offer to their residents the formal services and informal supports which evoke feelings of comfort and belonging. The task is not to redesign and rebuild these communities, much less to destroy buildings and dislocate residents, but to reinforce and rehabilitate them, drawing on the forces for "unslumming" that are already inherent in them.

This story can be made out in Peggy Gleicher and Mark Fried's summary of their study of West End residents.

In summary, then, we observe that a number of factors contribute to the special importance that the West End seemed to bear for the large majority of its inhabitants:

. . . Residence in the West End was highly stable, with relatively little movement from one dwelling unit to another and with minimal transience into and out of the area. Although residential stability is a fact of importance in itself, it does not wholly account for commitment to the area.

. . . For the great majority of the people, the local area was a focus for strongly positive sentiments and was perceived, probably in its multiple meanings, as home. The critical significance of belonging in or to an area has been one of the most consistent findings in working-class communities both in the U.S. and in England.

. . . patterns of social interaction were of great importance in the West End. Certainly for a great number of people, local space . . . served as a locus for social relationships . . . In this respect, the urban slum community also has much in common with the communities so frequently observed in folk cultures.

. . . These observations lead us to question the extent to which through urban renewal we relieve a situation of stress or create further damage. If the local spatial area and orientation toward localism provide the core of social organization and integration for a large proportion of the working class and if, as current behavioral theories would suggest, social organization and integration are primary factors in providing a base for effective social functioning, what are the consequences of dislocating people from their local areas? Or, assuming that the potentialities of people for adaption to crisis are great, what deeper damage occurs in the process? (Gleicher & Fried, 1967, pp. 126–35)

These are powerful stories, powerful in the sense that they have shaped public consciousness about the issues of housing. Each in its time guided the writing of legislation, the formation of policy, the design of programs, the diligence of planners, the allocation of funds, the conduct of evaluation. Each, moreover, has had its period of dominance. The story of "blight and renewal" shaped public policy in the 1950s when the idea of urban renewal was at its height. In the 1960s, the story of the "natural community and its dislocation" expressed the negative reactions to urban renewal.

Each story conveys a very different view of reality and represents a special way of seeing. From a situation that is vague, ambiguous, and indeterminate (or rich and complex, depending on one's frame of mind), each story selects and names different features and relations which become the "things" of the story – what the story is about: in the first, for example, "community," "blight," "health," "renewal," "cycle of decay," "integrated plan"; in the second, "home," "spatial identity," "patterns of interaction," "informal networks," "dislocation." Each story places the features it has selected within the frame of a particular context – for example, of blight and the removal of blight; of natural communities, their threatened dissolution, and their preservation.

Each story constructs its view of social reality through a complementary process of *naming* and *framing*. Things are selected for attention and named in such a way as to fit the frame constructed for the situation. Together, the two processes construct a problem out of the vague and indeterminate reality which John Dewey (1938) called the "problematic situation." They carry out the essential problem-setting functions. They select for attention a few salient features and relations from what would otherwise be an overwhelmingly complex reality. They give these elements a coherent organization, and they describe what is wrong with the present situation in such a way as to set the direction for its future transformation. Through the processes of naming and framing, the stories make what Rein and Schön (1977) have called the "normative leap from data to recommendations, from fact to values, from 'is' to 'ought'." It is typical of diagnostic/ prescriptive stories such as these that they execute the normative leap in such a way as to make it seem graceful, compelling, even obvious.

How are these functions carried out?

In our two stories, the naming and framing of the urban housing situation proceeds *via* generative metaphor. Just as a paintbrush was seen, in our previous example, as a pump, so here the urban-housing situation is seen first as a disease which must be cured and then as the threatened disruption of a natural community which must be protected or restored. Here, too, the researcher sees *A* and *B*; he takes an existing description of *B* as a putative redescription of *A*. In this case, however, the constellation of ideas associated with *B* is inherently normative. In our ideas about disease and about natural community, there is already an evaluation – a sense of the good which is to be sought and the evil which is to be avoided. When we see *A* as *B*, we carry over to *A* the evaluation implicit in *B*.

Once we are able to see a slum as a blighted area, we know that blight must be removed ("unsanitary and unsightly" buildings must be torn down) and the area must be returned to its former state ("redesigned" and "rebuilt"). The metaphor is one of disease and cure. Moreover, the cure must not be a "mere palliative"; a particular, holistic view of medicine is involved in this metaphor. It would not be enough, the experts said, to remove offensive structures piecemeal.

The entire area needed redesigning so that a balanced, integrated plan could be developed for a region . . . In this way it was hoped that the cycle of decay of the area could be controlled and the birth of future slums prevented.

Effective prophylaxis requires an "integrated and balanced" plan. Just as in medicine one must treat the whole man, so one must "treat" the whole community.

Once we are able to see the slum as a "natural community" (Gleicher and Fried's, 1967, "folk community" or Herbert Gans's, 1962, "urban village"), then it is also clear what is wrong and what needs doing. What is wrong is that the natural community, with its homelike stability and its informal networks of mutual support, is threatened with destruction – indeed, by the very prophylaxis undertaken in the name of "urban renewal." We should think twice about "dislocating people from their local areas"; "natural communities" should be preserved.

Each of these generative metaphors derives its normative force from certain purposes and values, certain normative images, which have long been powerful in our culture. We abhor disease and strive for health. Indeed, popular culture seems often to identify the good life with the healthy life and to make progress synonymous with the eradication of disease (although it may give us pause that "social prophylaxis" has had so strong an appeal for Fascist regimes – such as those of Stalin, Hitler, and the rightist dictatorships of the Third World). We also have a strong affinity for the "natural" and a deep distrust of the "artificial." The idea of Nature, with its Romantic origins in the writings of Rousseau and its deeper sources in pantheism, still works its magical appeal.

A situation may begin by seeming complex, uncertain, and indeterminate. If we can once see it, however, in terms of a normative dualism such as health/disease or nature/artifice, then we shall know in what direction to move. Indeed, the diagnosis and the prescription will seem obvious. This sense of the obviousness of what is wrong and what needs fixing is the hallmark of generative metaphor in the field of social policy.

But that which seems obvious to the unreflecting mind may upon reflection seem utterly mistaken. In so far as generative metaphor leads to a sense of the obvious, its consequences may be negative as well as positive. In the pump-paintbrush example, we emphasized the positive contribution of generative metaphor to the construction of explanations and inventions; but when we see A as B, we do not necessarily understand A any better than before, although we understand it differently than before. How well we understand it has something to do with how well we understand B to begin with, something to do with the ways in which seeing A and B leads us to restructure our perceptions of A, and something to do with the developmental process by which we pass from a pre-analytic detection of similarity between A and B to the construction of a model under which we are able to treat A and B (redescribed) as instances. At any stage of the life cycle of generative metaphor, we may, in seeing A as B, ignore or distort what we would take, upon reflection, to be important features of A. We need, then, to become aware of the generative metaphors which shape our perceptions of phenomena. We need to be able to attend to and describe the dissimilarities as well as the similarities between A and B.

In order to dissolve the obviousness of diagnosis and prescription in the field of social policy, we need to become aware of, and to focus attention upon, the generative metaphors which underlie our problem-setting stories.[12] However, this is not as easy as it sounds, for generative metaphors are ordinarily tacit. Often we are unaware of the metaphors that shape our perception and understanding of social situations.

We may be helped, in attending to underlying generative metaphors, by the presence of several different and conflicting stories about the situation. As in the Japanese film *Rashomon*, one is apt to be puzzled, disturbed, and stimulated to reflection by the telling of several different stories about the same situation, when each story is internally coherent and compelling in its own terms but different from, and perhaps incompatible with, all the others. Such a multiplicity of conflicting stories about the situation makes it dramatically apparent that we are dealing not with "reality" but with various ways of making sense of a reality. Then we may turn our attention to the stories themselves.

In order to bring generative metaphors to reflective and critical awareness, we must construct them, through a kind of policy-analytic literary criticism, from the givens of the problem-setting stories we tell. Indeed, it is through storytelling that we can best discover our frames and the generative metaphors implicit in our frames.

In this process, it is important to distinguish between what one might call "surface" and "deep" metaphors. The language in which the story is told may, as in the two cases we have considered, offer clues to the generative metaphors which set the probem of the story. Justice Douglas, for example, makes explicit reference to health and disease. But the surface language of the story need *not* contain the words "health" and "disease," even though health/disease is the generative metaphor which underlies the story. The deep metaphor, in this sense, is the metaphor which accounts for centrally important features of the story – which makes it understandable that certain elements of the situation are included in the story while others are omitted; that certain assumptions are taken as true although there is evidence that would appear to disconfirm them; and, especially, that the normative conclusions are found to follow so obviously from the facts. Given a problem-setting story, we must construct the deep metaphor which is generative of it. In making such a construction, we interpret the story. We give it a "reading," in a sense very much like the one employed in literary criticism. And our interpretation, is to a very considerable extent, testable against the givens of the story.

Once we have constructed a generative metaphor, once we have concluded that in this story we are seeing A as B, then we can explore and reflect upon similarities and differences between A and B. In doing so, we draw upon a repertoire of additional ways of perceiving and understanding both A and B. Thus, when we are presented with the two housing stories, we may wish to ask the following kinds of questions:

– What does it mean to say that an area is "blighted," when one man's blight may be another man's folk community? What one person sees as "unsanitary and unsightly," another may find comfortable, homelike, or even picturesque. On what criteria of "disease," then, is it appropriate to say that the North End of Boston is diseased?

– What is it that makes communities such as Boston's North and West Ends "natural," whereas the replacement of the old West End is described as "artificial"? Both are man-made and both involve social networks of human interactions. Further, the dislocation of the immigrant from his "natural community" may in some instances (as Gleicher and Fried have suggested) actually contribute to his subsequent achievement of increased autonomy and integration in a different community. Under what conditions, then, is "dislocation" harmful?

Questions such as these call attention to what is metaphorical about generative metaphors. It is precisely because neighborhoods are not literally diseased that one can *see* them *as* diseased. It is because urban communities are not literally natural that one can see them as natural. When in these examples of SEEING-AS we carry over to urban neighborhoods the familiar ideas of disease/health and artifice/nature, we find and construct in the context of these neighborhoods (as they are, as they once were, and as they might be) features and relations organized and evaluated as they are organized and evaluated in the familiar contexts of health and disease, nature and artifice. In this SEEING-AS we construct what is wrong and what needs fixing.

But when we interpret our problem-setting stories so as to bring their generative metaphors to awareness and reflection, then our diagnoses and prescriptions cease to appear obvious and we find ourselves involved, instead, in critical inquiry. We become aware of differences as well as of similarities between the new problematic situation and the familiar situation whose description we have projected upon the new. The glide from facts to recommendations no longer seems graceful or obvious. Attention to generative metaphor then becomes a tool for critical reflection on our construction of the problems of social policy.

Frame awareness, frame conflict, and frame restructuring

From all this, it follows that problem setting matters. The ways in which we set social problems determine both the kinds of purposes and values we seek to realize, and the directions in which we seek solutions. Contrary to the problem-solving perspective, problems are not given, nor are they reducible to arbitrary choices which lie beyond inquiry. We set social problems through the stories we tell – stories whose problem-setting potency derives at least in some cases from their generative metaphors.

It follows, too, that we should become aware of the ways in which we set social problems. We should reflect on the problem-setting processes which are usually kept tacit, so that we may consciously select and criticize the frames which shape our responses.

But what will frame awareness bring? It is likely to bring us into sharper and more explicit confrontation with frame conflict. As we become aware that our social policy debates reflect multiple, conflicting stories about social phenomena – stories which embody different generative metaphors, different frames for making sense of experience, different meanings and values – then we also become aware that frame conflicts are not problems. They do not lend themselves to problem-solving inquiry, in the sense earlier described, because frame conflicts are often unresolvable by appeal to facts. In the case of the two housing stories, for example, the adversaries do not disagree about the facts; they simply turn their attention to *different* facts. Further, when one is committed to a problem frame, it is almost always possible to reject facts, to question data (usually fuzzy, in any case), or to patch up one's story so as to take account of new data without fundamental alteration of the story.

The method of iterative convergent sequences of model building and model testing cannot resolve conflicting frames which are attentive to different features of reality and are able to assimilate new versions of the facts.

I have argued elsewhere (Rein & Schön, 1974, 1977), that, in social policy debates, frame conflicts often take the form of dilemmas – that is, they are situations in which no available choice is a good one, because we are involved in a conflict of *ends* which are incommensurable. Ends are incommensurable because they are embedded in conflicting frames that lead us to construct incompatible meanings for the situation.

What, then, are the possible responses to frame conflicts and to dilemmas? This question is of the utmost importance to us, not only because of the inherent importance of the policy dilemmas themselves, but because these dilemmas often find their social expressions in societal divisions that are sources of anguish in their own right. When frame conflict takes the form of regional, ethnic, and class divisions, it becomes in itself a superordinate policy question.

The question is not, of course, a new one, and various researchers have offered responses to it – responses which take the form of *relativ-*

ism, or of an extended instrumentalism (which would resolve dilemmas by means of technological "fixes" or by the application of tradeoff analysis), or of recourse to types of institutionalized competition (the voting booth, the bargaining table, and the marketplace). Each of these responses seems to me to be radically unsatisfactory. I have argued this case elsewhere, and I do not propose to repeat this argument here. What I do want to emphasize is that each of these responses is presented by its protagonists as an alternative to a certain kind of inquiry. It is because it is thought to be impossible, or unfeasible, to *inquire* into conflicting ends – to subject frame conflict to shared inquiry – that we are thought to have to manage such intractable conflicts by institutionalized competition.

The two-pronged question I should like to ask here is whether frame conflict lends itself to inquiry and, if so, to inquiry of what kind? This is the question which points to the link between the making of generative metaphor and the resolution of conflicting frames.

We do, at least on some occasions, inquire into dilemmas and we do so intuitively in ways that involve cognitive work, occasionally yield insight, and may be judged as more or less well done. Yet, because this sort of inquiry does not fit the dominant model of problem solving, we lack a name for it. We risk denying our intuitive capacity because we cannot describe it.

In this sort of inquiry – which I shall call *frame restructuring* – we respond to frame conflict by constructing a new problem-setting story, one in which we attempt to integrate conflicting frames by including features and relations drawn from earlier stories, yet without sacrificing internal coherence or the degree of simplicity required for action. We do this best, I believe, in the context of particular situations whose information-richness gives us access to many different combinations of features and relations, countering our Procrustean tendency to notice only what fits our ready-made category schemes.

I should like to offer an example of frame restructuring in the domain of housing policy, drawn this time from the experience of developing countries.

Squatter settlements are the shantytowns, the vast spread-out communities in which the poor live in shacks they have built themselves, in the major cities in developing countries throughout the world. In *Housing by People*, Turner (1976) estimates that about one-third of the population of Caracas, one-half the population of Ankara, between one-third and one-half the population of Lusaka, Zambia, and one-third the population of Manila, live in squatter settlements. Such massive phenomena can hardly avoid being seen, but they are seen and interpreted in very different ways.

For the officials of municipal governments and housing agencies, and for many of the well-to-do residents of these cities, the settlements are an eyesore, a mass of debris which has been established by illegal, indeed criminal, action, in violation of property rights, housing codes, and zoning laws. The squatter settlements are, from this perspective, a blight upon the land and a spoiling of the planned city. Public housing projects, on the other hand, are clean, standard, and decent dwellings constructed on land set aside for low-income housing, and built according to regulations for adequate construction. It is true that many low-income persons cannot afford this sort of housing, and that there is too little of it to go around. But there are, in any case, too many poor people in cities who ought to have remained in their villages.

For the partisans of squatter settlements (such as Turner) public housing does not serve those most in need, and produces environments that are often dysfunctional in the extreme.

In the case of the *superbloque* in Caracas . . . built by the Perez Jiminez regime in the 1960's, if it had not been for the very costly programme of community development carried out after the fall of the regime, perhaps all 115 of these monstrous 14-storey buildings would also have had to be pulled down. Before the development of an adequate community infrastructure, they had become scenarios for pitched battles between armed gangs that had taken over the buildings and armoured army units . . . [these cases] highlight the well-known problems of management and maintenance of large schemes, structurally sound but where so many residents become alienated. (Turner, 1976, p. 59)

On the contrary, self-help construction, in the context of squatter settlements, provides an environment of amenity, community, and economic viability.

Thanks to its rent-free accommodation, the family has a small surplus for saving toward its anticipated move, perhaps towards the purchase of a plot of land and construction of its own permanent dwelling. The family pays its share of the utilities . . . the shack is not too great a hardship as long as the roof keeps the rain out – which it does adequately thanks to the use of plastic and other materials culled from the dump. Together with the use of the enclosed and private backyard, the family has plenty of personal space for its domestic life. (Turner & Fichter, 1972, pp. 241–2)

It is true that squatter settlements are sometimes sites for malnutrition, unsanitary conditions, disease. But these are defects in an otherwise natural, user-governed system that meets the actual needs of its inhabitants far better than the public housing created by formal governmental programs.

The two perspectives on squatter settlements are comparable to the perspectives of the partisans and critics of "urban renewal" in the United States, and it is not difficult to detect their resemblance to our familiar housing stories. On the one hand, there is "blight" and the need for its removal through integrated redesign of whole areas. On the other, there are natural communities which provide their members with informal supports, stability, and a sense of home. On the one hand, there is a belief in the efficacy of formal services, professional expertise, governmental programs administered by large bureaucracies. On the other, there is distrust of formal, professional bureaucratized services and a belief in informal practices and informal networks of people who create communities and control environments through their own initiatives.

Considered together, these opposing views evoke a number of policy dilemmas. How is one both to protect property rights, maintain standards of construction and sanitation, and keep total costs within bounds, while at the same time providing housing services to those who need them, allowing people to get shelter at prices they can afford, accommodating the changing needs and capacities of families, and leaving initiative and control in the hands of the users?

Is it possible to integrate these conflicting frames?

Over the last fifteen years or so, a movement has grown up which has tried to do so. The programmatic slogan for this effort is "sites and services." In some cities (Lima, Peru, is an example), some people have considered how squatter settlements might be supported, rather than disrupted, by government action. Confronted with the failures of public-housing programs and with the persistence of squatter invasions, government officials and their advisors have explored what they might design in the way of a mix of formal supports and informal action, of government investment and user initiative.

Turner describes one such venture:

The *barriada* of Huascaran contained an area that was large enough for some twenty single-family dwellings, which the settlement association had acquired and wished to distribute to member families who for lack of their own plots had been living doubled up with relatives or friends in the settlement. When the association approached our agency for funds and technical assistance, Marcial and I suggested to the chief executive . . . that the agency simply lend the plot recipients the cash and let them get on with it under a minimum of supervision . . . The procedure was extremely simple. The local association allocated the plots to bona fide families who had no other urban properties and who contracted to build the minimum units specified within six months of receiving the first of five staged payments. The local recipients also undertook to repay the debt within a fifteen year period on very easy, subsidized interest rate terms. If the property were to be transferred, the debt would also be transferred . . . A new dwelling . . . would . . . be built at far less cost to the public than those built by commercial contractors . . . The total loans were small, just enough for the materials and skilled labor (bricklayer, roofer, electrician, plumber). (Turner & Fichter, 1972, p. 140)

In other, larger projects the government agency provided more than low-interest construction loans:

In one major new settlement, with a site assigned by the central government, well over 100,00 inhabitants were served with graded streets, electric light and power and water mains serving public standpipes in the initial stages of settlement and in consultation with the settlers' association which formed an effective provisional local government. The costs of such simple and basic installations can generally be borne either by the inhabitants or by the government – or by a combination of public subsidies and local contributions. (Turner, 1976, p. 157)

Such a program grows out of a complex coordination of the two perspectives held by municipal officials and by partisans of squatter settlement. The squatters' behavior is seen neither as criminality nor as self-sufficiency, but as initiative that may be both supported and controlled within the constraints of a government program. Individual settlers are seen neither as passive recipients of government services nor as independent violators of governmental regulations, but as responsible participants who can be trusted both to repay loans and avoid being cheated on the purchase of materials. Indeed, Turner reports that

. . . the Huascaran project participants had gotten their bricks with little or no delay. Another participant, a truck driver, took care of deliveries. One of them had a brother in a brick factory who negotiated such a good bargain with his employer that the project participants managed to get themselves a 5 percent better discount than the materials loan program. (Turner & Fichter, 1972, p. 142)

The competitive game formerly played between municipal officials, in which officials seek to control and punish while squatters seek to evade control, gives way here to a collaborative game in which officials and settlers *both* win when houses are built and loans repaid.[13] The choice is no longer conceived of as one between formal governmental interventions, such as public housing, and informal networks of squatters. Rather, a new question is raised as to the ways in which formal government interventions can best complement the informal support system that grows up in squatter settlements. The new question leads to a reframing of the roles of the various parties. Government provides the large-scale infrastructure and the construction loans, while individual squatter families construct their own dwellings, and local associations organize the processes of supply and distribution of resources. As for the role of large industry:

What is being argued is that large organizations should have little or no business building or managing the dwelling environments. Instead, they should be doing a great deal more business installing infrastructure and manufacturing and supplying tools and materials that people and their own small enterprises can use locally. There is plenty of room for debate over the extent to which central administrations are in fact necessary for specific components of infrastructure. (Turner, 1976, p. 129)

Sites-and-services has become an idea in good currency in its own right. The World Bank, for example, has now established loans in many parts of the developing world for sites-and-services programs. The point is not that sites-and-services is a panacea for the problem of housing in the Third World, or even for the problems posed by squatter settlements. Predictably, as the scale of the program has increased, difficulties of organization and management have arisen, which manifested themselves in minor ways, if at all, in the early exploratory programs. Nevertheless, the emergence of this idea, out of the conflicting perspectives associated with municipal housing and with squatter settlements, suggests how social policy dilemmas may yield to frame restructuring.

One may argue, of course, that a dilemma, if it can be resolved, is not a dilemma at all! But what we call a dilemma hinges on the strategies we have for describing the problematic situation and the purposes at stake in it. We can know purposes only as descriptions. If conflicting purposes are redescribed so that they no longer conflict, then we may properly say that the dilemma has been dissolved. By "frame restructuring," however, I do not mean the mere recasting of a problem-setting story so as to escape a dilemma. People do sometimes respond to dilemmas by a kind of surgery, simply leaving out of account values which in an earlier formulation entered into conflict. In such cases the protagonist learns nothing from the dilemma except that it made life difficult. In the sites-and-services example, however, we have what I believe to be an instance of a very different kind of process. Here, two different ways of seeing the housing problem are made to come together to form a new integrating image; it is as though, in the familiar gestalt figure, one managed to find a way to see both vase and profiles at once![14]

It is quite consistent to say both that we are sometimes able to carry out such processes, and that we are usually unable to say how we do it. I believe that the problem-solving perspective blinds us to the few examples in which some of us, at some times, engage intuitively in the restructuring and coordination of conflicting frames. Hence, we lose the few resources available to us for learning how to carry out such processes where we need most desperately to do so. Starting with reflection on these rare intuitive processes, we need to build a full and explicit understanding of them.

It is here that the link between frame restructuring and the making of generative metaphor seems to me to be most critical. Certainly, it would not be surprising, seeing that we often frame social policy problems through generative metaphor, if frame restructuring and coordination strongly resembled the making of generative metaphor. We can explore this possibility by comparing the two examples which have been central to this paper.

In the pump–paintbrush example, we begin with one way of seeing the situation (the brush, the performance gap between the two brushes). Then it is proposed to look at the brush as a pump. The process can be illustrated as in figure 6. In the housing example, we have two ways of seeing squatter settlements (versions of the "disease" and "natural community" frames) which are held by persons who contend with one another over the fate of squatter settlements. Sites-and-services is an integration of these conflicting perspectives, one which reflects a restructuring and coordination of the two frames (see figure 7).

The two cases are quite symmetrical. In both examples, we have the construction of a new description of the phenomenon, one in which the previously conflicting descriptions are restructured and coordinated. In the housing case, however, the two descriptions are initially advanced as conflicting descriptions of the same thing; in the pump–paintbrush example, an existing description of one thing is advanced as a putative description of another.

In both cases, there is a social context in which individuals engage with one another in a kind of reciprocal inquiry through which they reset the problem of their problematic situation. By recapitulating and comparing features of the cognitive work involved in the making of generative metaphor and in the restructuring and coordination of conflicting frames, we can gauge the degree to which these two processes share a family resemblance.

The participants try initially to intermap two different descriptions of a situation, but the descriptions initially resist mapping. The

Figure 6

Figure 7

researchers cannot at first map the elements and relations in "pump" and "paintbrush" onto one another; they cannot see paintbrush as pump. No more can municipal officials in Peru map their descriptions of formal governmental housing programs onto the informal, self-help activities of the squatters; they cannot see the squatter settlement as a housing program. Yet in both cases the two conflicting descriptions are available, and there is energy devoted to considering each in the context of the other. From the moment one of the researchers says, "A paintbrush is a kind of pump!" the others try to discover how this may be so. In the context of squatter settlements, different individuals representing different interests and social groups, contend with one another on the basis of their different descriptions of the situation.

In each case, the cognitive work involves the participants in attending to new features and relations of the phenomena, and in renaming, regrouping, and reordering those features and relations. As the researchers explore the paintbrush in the light of the possibility of its being a kind of pump, they focus on new features of the brush (the spaces between bristles, for example); they regroup and reorder features in relation to one another (perceiving the paint as a liquid that flows through the spaces between bristles); and they rename the new groupings of elements (bristles become the "walls" of "channels"). As the partisans of self-help and the municipal officials contend over the proper response to squatter settlements, some of them begin to regroup housing activities which had been lumped together either as "public housing" or as "squatting." They now decompose "housing development" into the purchasing and distribution of materials, into the construction of individual dwellings, into unskilled and skilled tasks, and into the provision of infrastructure. They now distinguish three kinds of groups as participants in the housing process: individual families, settlers' associations, and municipal agencies. In the new program description, sites-and-services, the newly named components of housing activity are linked with elements in the new grouping of participants: individual families, with construction of dwellings; settlers' associations, with purchasing and distribution of land and materials; municipal agencies, with provision of infrastructure. The participants themselves are also redescribed in ways that capture different features and relations to one another. Settlers are no longer "scavengers" or "passive recipients of service" but become parties to a contract with government, trusted to use cash wisely for the purposes intended. The municipal agency, no longer a policeman or a provider of housing, becomes a lender and builder of roads and sewage lines. The two parties are no longer related as regulator/regulatee but as contractor/contractee. And the housing program becomes a mix of formal and informal services.

In both cases, it is significant that the participants are involved in a particular concrete situation; at the same time that they are reflecting on the problem, they are experiencing the phenomena of the problem. In the pump – paintbrush case, the researchers experimented with what it felt like actually to use the brush. In the housing case, municipal officials were involved with settlers in a particular *barriada*. It is as though the effort to map onto one another descriptions which initially resist mapping causes the participants to immerse themselves, in reality or in imagination, in concrete situations which are information-rich.

The cognitive work of restructuring draws upon the richness of features and relations which are to be found in the concrete situation. There, one can notice the gentle curve of the natural brush and the sharp angle of the synthetic one. One can observe how settlers go about purchasing bricks, how somebody's brother-in-law has a truck that is used to deliver them. These new features can then be incorporated in the new descriptions of the situations. One is not limited to the features captured by the category-schemes with which one began.

The information-richness of particular situations poses a difficulty, however. Although the inquirer has suspended the earlier conflicting descriptions (he is now thinking *about* them rather than seeing the situation in terms of them), he has not yet achieved the restructuring that will enable him to make a new description. In this intermediate state, he needs a way of representing to himself the particularity of the situation in which he is involved – one which is dominated by neither of the descriptions with which he began. At this point, storytelling can play an important part.[15] The inquirer can tell the story of his experience of the situation (can tell it, that is, both to others and to himself) and he can do this before he has constructed a new, coordinated description of the situation. Considered as a strategy for representing the situation, his story captures the juxtaposition of events in time, the "next-next-next" of temporal experience. This strategy of representation permits the inquirer to convey much of the richness of the situation without being constrained by either of the category-schemes with which he begins. The researcher can tell what it feels like to paint with the two brushes. The municipal officials can tell the story of their response to the settlers' association. Subsequently, the inquirers may construct new models of the situation from the stories they have told. Their new, coordinated descriptions may then select out fixed properties which this particular situation shares with others, as in the researchers' model of pumpoids or the planners' model of sites-and-services. But in the midst of the process, when earlier descriptions have been suspended and coordinated descriptions have not yet been developed, the inquirers need strategies of representation which enable them to hang onto and convey the richness of their experience of the events themselves.

From this account, it is reasonable to conclude, I believe, that frame restructuring and the making of generative metaphor are closely related processes. In both kinds of processes, participants bring to a situation different and conflicting ways of seeing – different and conflicting descriptions. There is an impetus to map the descriptions onto one another, but the descriptions resist mapping. In the context of a particular concrete situation, the participants work at the restructuring of their initial descriptions – regrouping, reordering, and renaming elements and relations; selecting new features and relations from their observations of the situation. As this work proceeds, they represent their experience of the situation through strategies which capture the "next-next-next" of temporal experience of events; and from such representations, of which storytelling is a prime example, they draw the restructured groupings and relations of elements which they are able to embed in a new, coordinated description.

It is important also to notice what does *not* happen. The old descriptions are not mapped onto one another by matching corresponding elements in each, for the old descriptions resist such a mapping. Rather, the *restructured* descriptions are coordinated with one another, which is to say that some pairs of restructured elements now match one another, and others are juxtaposed in the new description as components of larger elements. The new description is also not a "compromise," an average or balance of values implicit in the earlier descriptions. One cannot say, for example, that sites-and-services strikes a balance between values attached to "government control" and to "settler initiative"; rather, in the new description, there is a shift in the meanings of these terms, and along with this, a shift in the distribution of the redescribed functions of initiative and control. Finally, we cannot say that the two descriptions are "fused," for the restructuring they undergo is not characterized by the joining of elements and the blurring of boundaries connoted by "fusion."

There is a kind of cognitive work common to the integration of conflicting frames and to the making of generative metaphor, and to this shared process I have given the name "frame restructuring and frame coordination." We find closely related versions of this process in the problem-setting inquiries central to technological invention and to social-policy debate. We are sometimes able to perform such processes intuitively, but our ability to describe and model them is severely limited. I have tried only to describe some of their principal components. Even from these meager beginnings, it is clear that frame restructuring and coordination differs greatly from the processes suggested by such terms as "correspondence mapping," "compromise" and "fusion." The study of frame restructuring and coordination can, and must, be empirically grounded, starting with the careful description and analysis of particular instances of intuitive inquiry.

Two orders of questions seem to me to be critically important for the direction of this research. First, with respect to the workings of the process itself, we need much better descriptions of the component activities which I have called "restructuring" and "coordination." Particular attention ought to be paid to the functions of renaming, regrouping, and reordering, and to the resetting of boundaries, all of which give rise to new perceptions of the elements we call "things" and of the organization of foreground and background. It will be important to characterize the particular kind of *stance* toward the process which enables us to recognize descriptions as descriptions rather than as "reality," and to entertain and juxtapose conflicting descriptions. It will be important to examine the functions of immersion in the concrete experience of the phenomena of the situation, and to explore the strategies of representation which enable us to capture the experienced richness of the situation (its "phenomenology") without forcing it into existing formal categories. And it will be important to inquire into the processes by which we are able to construct new category-schemes, new models, from the information-rich stories we tell.

In all of this, we need to ask what is involved in learning to do this kind of cognitive work? What is its relation, on the one hand, to domain-specific knowledge and, on the other hand, to very general sorts of competence in the use of language? How does the process of frame restructuring and coordination resemble and differ from changes in strategies of representation which occur in the course of cognitive development?

A second group of questions has to do with the conditions favorable to the practice of frame restructuring. In the context of social policy dilemmas, where we most need to learn how to integrate conflicting frames, it is most unlikely that a better understanding of these processes will be sufficient to lead us to undertake them. On the contrary, it is already remarkable how little we draw upon existing cognitive capacity in situations of difficulty and stress. What, then, are the configurations of personal stance toward inquiry, of interpersonal process, and of institutional design, which will be conducive to the use of our understandings of frame restructuring? (For a discussion of some of these conditions, see Schön & Argyris, 1978.)

These two very different lines of inquiry are critical to the improvement of our capacity for engaging social policy dilemmas. If we are to coordinate them, then we must engage in the very process we are studying.

NOTES

1 Ernst Cassirer's work – in particular, his *Language and Myth* (1946) – is central to this tradition.
2 The term was first used in Schön and Bamberger (1976). Schön (1963) was an earlier treatment of this topic.
3 The hermeneutic tradition, developed in late nineteenth-century Germany

by the philosopher Dilthey, has been taken up again in recent years by continental philosophers such as Paul Ricœur (see, e.g., Ricœur, 1970).

4 My interest in problem setting in social policy has been developed through my collaboration with Martin Rein. (See Rein, 1976; and Rein & Schön, 1977.) Others who have written on this topic, with close attention to functions of metaphor, are Nisbet (1969), and R. H. Brown (1976).

5 This example was first described in Schön (1963).

6 There is, of course, the critically important question of the evidence for this assertion. Although I am not primarily concerned here with the problem of interpretation, I have tried to suggest that my construction of the metaphor which informed the work of the researchers may be treated against the date provided by my description of what they actually said and did. My attribution to them of a particular generative metaphor is, I believe, a falsifiable proposition. I shall take up this question again in the discussion of problem setting in social policy.

7 Many authors have noted the economic functions of metaphor conceived both as a kind of utterance and as a way of thinking. See, for example, Cassirer (1946).

8 The notion of SEEING-AS, its relation to "thinking as" and to literal seeing, and its relevance to an understanding of description, have all been set forth by Wittgenstein (1953, especially pp. 193–216).

9 The phrase is Thomas Kuhn's. See Kuhn (1970b).

10 For reference to those who take such a view, and for criticisms of it, see Vickers (1973), Rein (1976), and Schön (1971).

11 For a fuller treatment of this use of "story," see Rein and Schön (1977). Here, I shall simply note that in my usage, "story" does not necessarily connote a narrative of the "Once upon a time . . ." variety. Yet it is a narrative account of some phenomenon, an account in which temporal sequence is central. Explanatory stories are those in which the author, seeking to account for some puzzling phenomenon, narrates a sequence of temporal events wherein, starting from some set of initial conditions, events unfold in such a way as to lead up to and produce the phenomenon in question. A diagnostic/prescriptive story gives an explanatory, narrative account of some phenomenon in such a way as to show what is wrong with it and what needs fixing.

Justice Douglas, in the example that follows, tells a diagnostic/prescriptive story about urban neighborhoods, one framed by the notion of "blight" and "renewal." If Justice Douglas were to *describe* an actual urban neighborhood, I suspect that the things he would say about it — the things he would notice, the features he would select for attention, the ways in which he would group and bound phenomena — would all reflect the fundamental story he had learned to tell about this sort of neighborhood.

12 It is worth pointing out here that although I believe that all problem-setting stories have frames which enable their authors to select out features for attention, it is not necessarily true that all of these frames are metaphorical in nature. The health/disease and nature/artifice frames *are* gen-

erative metaphors for the two stories under consideration here. But many problem-setting stories are framed, for example, by the notion of "mismatch of services to needs" and this is not so obviously an example of generative metaphor.

13 Max Wertheimer (1959) gives a very nice example of the invention of a new game which converts competition to collaboration: He watched two boys playing badminton, one of them very much superior to the other. As the game progressed, each trying to win, the older boy won easily, the younger played worse and worse, until one of the boys then proposed a new game whose objective would be to keep the bird in the air as long as possible. Wertheimer reports that in the course of *this*, while both had to work as hard as they could, the efforts of the older boy were complementary to those of the younger one; both began to feel good about the game, and the younger boy's playing improved.

Not all frame restructuring takes the form of converting games of competition to games of collaboration, however. Wilson (1975) notes the fundamental conflict, in criminal justice policy, between punishment and rehabilitation. But he considers it in the light of the difficulty in drawing conclusions from experimental approaches to the treatment of criminals. After reviewing the evidence, he argues that we know nothing at all about the comparative effectiveness of programs in probation, incarceration, and community care. He finds not only that we do not know but that, in the nature of the case, we cannot know. From this conclusion he moves not to a position of relativism or fatalism but to a reframing of the problem. Emphasis should be placed upon such knowable variables as consistency of sentencing, and the comparative costs of treatment. In short, he argues that because we cannot know what we need to know in order to make the policy choices we have framed, then we must reframe the policy choices so as to make them depend upon what we can know.

14 The gestalt figures are used ordinarily to show how "the same figure" may be seen in very different, incompatible ways. For example, in the well-known figure shown here (figure 8) some people see the two profiles, others the vase. Usually, one can manage (after learning what is there to be seen) to move rapidly from one way of seeing the figure to the other.

Figure 8

It is unusual to find someone who claims to be able to see both at once. Yet this, too, can be managed if one thinks of the figure as two profiles pressing their noses into a vase! It is this integrating image (dreamed up by Seymour Papert) which makes it possible to bring together the two different ways of seeing the figure.

15 Storytelling is employed here as a special case of the use of strategies of representation which Bamberger and I have called "figural." In Schön and Bamberger (1976) we have argued that figural strategies, which group features on the basis of their temporal and/or spatial juxtaposition in a situation, rather than on the basis of fixed properties which they share, play a crucially important role in many kinds of generative processes.

The Conduit Metaphor –
A Case of Frame Conflict in
Our Language about Language

MICHAEL J. REDDY

I should like to respond to Professor Schön's chapter by replaying his theme several octaves lower. In my opinion, he has struck exactly the right set of notes. "Problem setting" should indeed be considered the crucial process, as opposed to "problem solving." And the "stories that people tell about troublesome situations" do set up or "mediate" the problem. And "frame conflict" between various stories should be studied in detail, precisely because it is quite often "immune to resolution by appeal to the facts." It is hard to think of a better overture to genuine advance in the social and behavioral sciences than this. At the same time, it seems to me that Schön has managed to sound these excellent notes only in their overtones, so that the fundamental frequency is barely to be heard – even though, to my ears at least, Schön's kind of thinking is real and long-awaited music.

Quite simply, what I believe is missing is the application of Schön's wisdom – this paradigm-consciousness – to human communication itself. It may seem predictable that I, a linguist, would take such a position. But, if I do, it is hardly disciplinary narrow-mindedness that motivates me. In 1954, Norbert Wiener, one of the originators of information theory, and the "father of cybernetics," stated quite flatly: "Society can only be understood through a study of the messages and communications facilities which belong to it" (Wiener, 1954, p. 16). I have never thought of this statement as referring to things like the size and adequacy of the telephone system. Wiener was talking primarily about the basic processes of human communication – how they work, what sort of wrinkles there are in them, when and why they are likely to succeed or fail. The problems of society, government, and culture depend ultimately on something like the daily box score of such successes or failures to communicate. If there are too many failures, or systematic types of failure, troubles will multiply. A society of near-perfect communicators, though it would no doubt still face conflicts of interest, might well be able to avoid many of the destructive, divisive effects of these inevitable conflicts.

What lies behind Schön's term "frame restructuring," and Kuhn's term "translation" (Kuhn, 1970a) seems to be just this much: better communication. Alleviating social and cultural difficulties requires better communication. And the problem that faces us is, how do we improve our communication? But, if we come around to saying this, then it is high time that we listened to Schön's good advice. It will not do to set out posthaste to "solve the problem" of inadequate communication. The most pressing task is rather to start inquiring immediately about *how that problem presents itself to us*. For problem setting, not problem solving is the crucial process. What kinds of stories do people tell about their acts of communication? When these acts go astray, how do they describe "what is wrong and what needs fixing"?

In this chapter, I am going to present evidence that the stories English speakers tell about communication are largely determined by semantic structures of the language itself. This evidence suggests that English has a preferred framework for conceptualizing communication, and can bias thought process toward this framework, even though nothing more than common sense is necessary to devise a different, more accurate framework. I shall thus be trying to convince you of what may be a disturbing premise: that merely by opening our mouths and speaking English we can be drawn into a very real and serious frame conflict. My own belief is that this frame conflict has considerable impact on our social and cultural problems. If we are largely unable, despite the vast array of communications technologies available to us today, to bring about substantive improvements in human communication, it may well be because this frame conflict has led us to attempt faulty solutions to the problem.

It is, of course, impossible to make such assertions without calling to mind the speculations and arguments of many twentieth-century figures – notably those of Whorf (1956) and of Max Black's (1962d) reluctant but thorough refutation of Whorf. There is an old joke about the Whorf hypothesis to the effect that, if it should be true, then it would be by definition unprovable. For if two human beings not only spoke radically different languages, but also thought and perceived the world differently, well then they would be far too busy throwing rocks and spears at one another to ever sit down and establish this as a fact. The grain of truth in this facetiousness can be found in Schön's dictum that frame conflicts are "immune to resolution by appeal to the facts." As he says, "New facts have a way of being either absorbed or disregarded by those who see problematic situations under conflicting frames." Now, for the past several years, I have been collecting some new facts and talking about them with many different people.

Very slowly, during this period of time, these new facts initiated a frame change in my own thinking about language. I had always been interested in Uriel Weinreich's observation that, "Language is its own metalanguage." But after the frame change, I knew that, as a metalanguage, English, at least, was its own worst enemy. And I knew that there was something more than mysticism to Whorf's ideas. At this point, curiously enough, when everything seemed to fall into place for me, it became much harder to talk to others about the new facts. For now I was speaking across the chasm of frame conflict.

I mention these things because I want to suggest at the outset that the discussion that follows is a marvelous opportunity for one of those failures to communicate which we are concerned to prevent. It is a little bit like the joke about Whorf. If I am right in what I believe about frames, then it may well be difficult to convince you, because the frames I am talking about exist in you and will resist the change. For my part, in writing this, I have made strenuous efforts to remember what it was like before I shifted frames, and how long it took before the "new facts" made sense to me. At the same time, I should like to request that you, on your side, make yourselves receptive to what may be a serious alteration of consciousness. To use Schön's terminology, we are engaged perforce in frame restructuring, and special effort is called for.

The conduit metaphor

What do speakers of English say when communication fails or goes astray? Let us consider (1) through (3), some very typical examples,

    (1) Try to *get* your *thoughts across* better
    (2) None of Mary's *feelings came through to me* with any clarity
    (3) You still haven't *given me* any *idea* of what you mean,

and do as Schön has suggested – take them as problem-setting stories, as decriptions of "what is wrong and what needs fixing." Are there metaphors in the examples? Do these metaphors set the directions for possible problem-solving techniques? Although (1) through (3) contain no fresh metaphors, there is in each case a dead metaphor. After all, we do not literally "get thoughts across" when we talk, do we? This sounds like mental telepathy or clairvoyance, and suggests that communication transfers thought processes somehow bodily. Actually, no one *receives* anyone else's thoughts directly in their minds when they are using language. Mary's feelings, in example (2), can be perceived directly only by Mary; they do not really "come through to us" when she talks. Nor can anyone literally "give you an idea" –

since these are locked within the skull and life process of each of us. Surely, then, none of these three expressions is to be taken completely at face value. Language seems rather to help one person to construct out of his own stock of mental stuff something like a replica, or copy, of someone else's thoughts – a replica which can be more or less accurate, depending on many factors. If we could indeed send thoughts to one another, we would have little need for a communications system.

If there are dead metaphors in (1) through (3), then, they all seem to involve the figurative assertion that language *transfers* human thoughts and feelings. Notice that this assertion, even in its present, very general form, leads already to a distinct viewpoint on communications problems. A person who speaks poorly does not know how to use language to send people his thoughts; and, conversely, a good speaker knows how to transfer his thoughts perfectly via language. If we were to follow this viewpoint, the next question would be: What must the poor speaker do with his thoughts if he is to transfer them more accurately by means of language? The surprising thing is that, whether we like it or not, the English language does follow this veiwpoint. It provides, in the form of a wealth of metaphorical expressions, answers to this and other questions, all of which answers are perfectly coherent with the assumption that human communication achieves the physical transfer of thoughts and feelings. If there were only a few such expressions involved, or if they were random, incoherent figures of speech arising from different paradigms – or if they were abstract, not particularly graphic images – then one might just succeed in dismissing them as harmless analogies. But in fact, none of these mitigating circumstances comes into play.

Typical solutions to the unskilled speaker's communications problems are illustrated by (4) through (8).

(4) Whenever you have a good *idea* practice *capturing it in words*
(5) You have to *put* each *concept into words* very carefully
(6) Try to *pack* more *thoughts into* fewer *words*
(7) Insert those *ideas* elsewhere *in* the *paragraph*
(8) Don't *force* your *meanings into* the wrong *words*.

Naturally, if language transfers thought to others, then the logical container, or conveyer, for this thought is words, or word-groupings like phrases, sentences, paragraphs, and so on. One area of possible difficulty is then the insertion process. The speaker might be generally unpracticed or careless about this, and so be admonished with (4) or (5). As (6) shows, he could fail to put enough meaning in. Or, according to (7), he could put the right meanings in, but put them in the wrong place. Example (8), which stretches common sense most seriously, indicates that he might put meanings into the words which somehow do not fit in them, thus presumably deforming these meanings. It might also be, of course, that the speaker puts too much meaning into words. And there are expressions for this as well.

(9) Never *load* a *sentence with* more *thoughts* than it can hold.

In general, this class of examples implies that, in speaking or writing, humans place their internal thoughts and feelings within the external signals of the language. A more complete listing may be found in the Appendix.

The logic of the framework we are considering – a logic which will henceforth be called the *conduit* metaphor – would now lead us to the bizarre assertion that words have "insides" and "outsides." After all, if thoughts can be "inserted," there must be a space "inside" wherein the meaning can reside. But surely the English language, whatever metaphysical meanderings it may have been guilty of thus far, cannot have involved us in this kind of patent nonsense. Well, a moment's reflection should nudge anyone into remembering that "content" is a term used almost synonymously with "ideas" and "meaning." And that recollection is quite meaning-full (sic) in the present context. Numerous expressions make it clear that English does view words as containing or failing to contain thoughts, depending on the success or failure of the speaker's "insertion" process.

(10) That *thought is in* practically every other *word*
(11) The *sentence was filled with emotion*
(12) The *lines* may rhyme, but *they are empty* of both *meaning* and *feeling*
(13) Your *words are hollow* – you don't mean them.

Or, in general, there is another class of examples that imply that words contain or convey thoughts and feelings when communication is successful. We assert, without batting an eyelash, that "the meaning is right there in the words." Further instances are to be found in the Appendix.

It may be that the fault in a communication failure does not lie with the speaker. Perhaps, somehow, the listener has erred. In the framework of the conduit metaphor, the listener's task must be one of extraction. He must find the meaning "in the words" and take it out of them, so that it gets "into his head." Many expressions show that English does view the matter in this way.

(14) Can you actually *extract* coherent *ideas from* that *prose?*
(15) Let me know if you *find* any good *ideas in* the *essay*
(16) I don't *get* any *feelings* of anger *out of* his *words*.

Curiously, my initial work on these expressions suggests that it is easier, when speaking and thinking in terms of the conduit metaphor, to blame the speaker for failures. After all, receiving and unwrapping a package is so passive and so simple – what can go wrong? A package can be difficult or impossible to open. But, if it is undamaged, and successfully opened, who can fail to find the right things in it? Thus, there are graphic and powerful expressions which blame particularly writers for making the package hard to open, as in (17) through (19).

(17) That *remark is* completely *impenetrable*

(18) Whatever *Emily meant, it's* likely to be *locked up in* that cryptic little *verse* forever

(19) He writes *sentences* in such a way as to *seal up* the *meaning in them.*

But, apart from readers and listeners "not paying attention to what's there in the words," the conduit metaphor offers little explanation for failing to "find" enough thoughts or the right thoughts in "what someone says." Should someone discover too many thoughts, however, we have a wonderfully absurd expression faulting him for this.

(20) You're *reading things into* the poem.

The power of the framework to enforce consistency of rationale even when the results are inane should be apparent here. We must see the reader as having surreptitiously made use of his power to insert thoughts into words when he should have restricted himself purely to extraction. He sneaked those thoughts into the words himself, and then turned around and pretended that he found them there. Perhaps because the problem of too much meaning occurs more often in reading, we have never developed the corresponding expression for speaking – "hearing things into the poem." Instead, we use "reading things into" for both modalities. Once again, further examples appear in the Appendix.

Perhaps we should pause at this point and set up some apparatus for generalizing what we have seen so far. It is not the numbered sentences above that are important, but rather the expressions in italics. These expressions could appear in many different utterances and take many different forms, and we have as yet no way of isolating what is crucial to them. Notice, for instance, that in every example there has been one word, such as "ideas," or "thoughts," or "meanings," or "feeling," which denotes internal conceptual or emotional material. Apart from what seem to be minor stylistic co-occurence restrictions, these and other terms like them can be substituted freely for one another. Thus, it is irrelevant to an example which one of these is present, and it would be helpful to have some abbreviation for the entire group. Let us picture each person as having a "repertoire" of mental and emotional material. This will allow us to say that any term denoting a *repertoire member,* abbreviated "RM," will fit, say, as object in (1) and produce an example utterance. Underlying (1), (2), and (3), then, are what we shall call "core expressions," which can be written as follows.

(21) get RM *across* [underlying (1)]

(22) RM *come through* (to someone) [underlying (2)]

(23) give (someone) RM [underlying (3)].

The parentheses in (22) and (23) indicate optional compliments. Examples (4) through (20), in addition to a term from the RM group, all contain another term, such as "word," "phrase," "sentence," or "poem." These words, in their basic senses at least, designate the external physical patterns of marks or sounds that do pass between speakers. Such energies, unlike the thoughts themselves, are received bodily, and are what information theorists would have called "signals." If we adopt this generic name for the second group, and abbreviate it as "s," then the core expressions for (4) through (6) are,

(24) capture RM *in* s [underlying (4)];

(25) put RM *into* s [underlying (5)];

(26) pack RM *into* s [underlying (6)].

In the Appendix, the core expression is always given first, and then followed by one or two examples. Obviously, each core expression can be responsible for a very large number of different sentences.

The conduit metaphor, and the core expressions which embody it, deserve a great deal more investigation and analysis. My listing of the core expressions is most likely far from complete, and the logical reverberations of this paradigm affect both the syntax and the semantics of many words which are not themselves part of the core expressions. Later on, we shall focus on one such reverberation, which affects the entire s group. Apart from this, however, we shall have to be content to close the present discussion with a brief characterization of some further types of core expression.

Our examples thus far have been drawn from the four categories which constitute the "major framework" of the conduit metaphor. The core expressions in these categories imply, respectively, that: (1) language functions like a conduit, transferring thoughts bodily from one person to another; (2) in writing and speaking, people insert their thoughts or feelings in the words; (3) words accomplish the transfer by containing the thoughts or feelings and conveying them to others; and (4) in listening or reading, people extract the thoughts and feelings once again from the words. Beyond these four classes of expressions, there are a good many examples which have different, though clearly related, implications. The fact that it is quite foreign to common sense to think of words as having "insides" makes it quite easy for us to abstract from the strict, "major" version of the metaphor, in which thoughts and emotions are always contained in something. That is, the major framework sees ideas as existing either within human heads or, at least, within words uttered by humans. The "minor" framework overlooks words as containers and allows ideas and feelings to flow, unfettered and completely disembodied, into a kind of ambient space between human heads. In this case, the conduit of language becomes, not sealed pipelines from person to person, but rather individual pipes which allow mental content to escape into, or enter from, this ambient space. Again, it seems that this extension of the metaphor is aided by the fact that, somewhere, we are peripherally aware that words do not really have insides.

In any case, whatever the cause of the extension, there are three categories of expressions in the minor framework. The categories imply, respectively, that: (1) thoughts and feelings are ejected by speaking or writing into an external "idea space"; (2) thoughts and feelings are reified in this external space, so that they exist independent of any need for living human beings to think or feel them; (3) these reified thoughts and feelings may, or may not, find their way back into the heads of living humans. Some outstanding examples of minor framework expressions are, for the first category,

> *put* RM *down on paper*

(27) Put those thoughts down on paper before you lose them!

> *pour* RM *out*

(28) Mary poured out all of the sorrow she had been holding in for so long.

> *get* RM *out*

(29) You should get those ideas out where they can do some good.

And for the second category,

> RM *float around*

(30) That concept has been floating around for decades.

> RM *find way*

(31) Somehow, these hostile feelings found their way to the ghettos of Rome.

> *find* RM EX LOC

(32) You'll find better ideas than that in the library.

(33) John found those ideas in the jungles of the Amazon, not in some classroom.

> (EX LOC here stands for any locative expression designating a place other than within human beings, that is, an *external locative*.)

And for the third category,

> *absorb* RM

(34) You have to "absorb" Aristotle's ideas a little at a time.
     RM *go over someone's head*
(35) Her delicate emotions went right over his head.
     get RM *into someone's head*
(36) How many different concepts can you get into your head in one evening?

For further examples, see the Appendix.

The toolmakers paradigm

In order to investigate the effect of the conduit metaphor on the thought processes of speakers of English, we need some alternate way of conceiving of human communication. We require another story to tell, another model, so that the deeper implications of the conduit metaphor can be drawn out by means of contrast. Simply speaking, in order to engage in frame restructuring about human communication, we need first an opposing frame.

To begin this other story, I should like to suggest that, in talking to one another, we are like people isolated in slightly different environments. Imagine, if you will, for sake of the story, a huge compound, shaped like a wagon wheel (see figure 9). Each pie-shaped sector of the wheel is an environment, with two spokes and part of the circumference forming the walls. The environments all have much in common with one another – water, trees, small plants, rocks, and the like – yet no two are exactly alike. They contain different kinds of trees, plants, terrain, and so on. Dwelling in each sector is one person who must survive in his own special environment. At the hub of the wheel there is some machinery which can deliver small sheets of paper from one environment to another. Let us suppose that the people in these environments have learned how to use this machinery to exchange crude sets of instructions with one another – instructions for making things helpful in surviving, such as tools, perhaps, or shelters, or foods, and the like. But there is, in this story, absolutely no way for the people to visit each other's environments, or even to exchange samples of the things they construct. This is crucial. The people can only exchange these crude sets of instructions – odd looking blueprints scratched on special sheets of paper that appear from a slot in the hub and can be deposited in another slot – and nothing more. Indeed, since there is no way to shout across the walls of the sectors, the people only know of one another's existence indirectly, by a cumulative series of inferences. This part of the story, the no visiting and no exchange of indigenous materials rule, we shall call the postulate of "radical subjectivity."

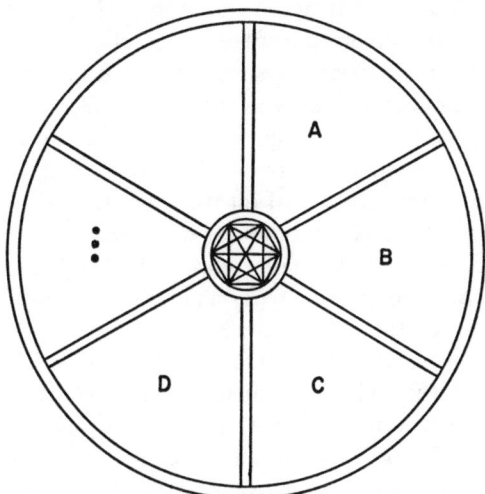

Figure 9. The toolmakers paradigm.

In the analogy, the contents of each environment, the "indigenous materials," represent a person's repertoire. They stand for the internal thoughts, feelings, and perceptions which cannot themselves be sent to anyone by any means that we know of. These are the unique material with which each person must work if he is to survive. The blueprints represent the signals of human communication, the marks and sounds that we can actually send to one another. We shall have to ignore the question of how the system of instructions became established, even though this is an interesting part of the story. We shall simply assume that it has reached some sort of steady state, and shall watch how it functions.

Suppose that person *A* has discovered an implement that is very useful to him. Say he has learned to build a rake and finds he can use it to clear dead leaves and other debris without damaging the living plants. One day person *A* goes to the hub and draws as best he can three identical sets of instructions for fashioning this rake and drops these sets in the slots for persons *B*, *C*, and *D*. As a result, three people struggling along in slightly different environments now receive these curious sheets of paper, and each one goes to work to try to construct what he can from them. Person *A*'s environment has a lot of wood in it, which is probably why he has leaves to rake in the first place. Sector *B*, on the other hand, runs more to rock, and person *B* uses a lot of rock in his constructions. He finds a piece of wood for the handle, but begins to make the head of the rake out of stone. *A*'s original rake head was wood. But since it never occurred to him that anything but wood would be available or appropriate, he did not try to specify wood for the head in his instructions. When *B* is about halfway finished with the stone rake head, he connects it experimentally to the handle and realizes with a jolt that this thing, whatever it is, is certainly going to be heavy and unwieldly. He ponders its possible uses for a time, and then decides that it must be a tool for digging up small rocks when you clear a field for planting. He marvels at how large and strong person *A* must be, and also at what small rocks *A* has to deal with. *B* then decides that two large prongs will make the rake both lighter and better suited to unearthing large rocks.

Quite happy with both his double-bladed rock-pick and his new ideas about what this fellow *A* must be like, person *B* makes three identical sets of instructions himself, for his rock-pick, and inserts them in the slots for *A, C,* and *D.* Person *A,* of course, now assembles a rock-pick following *B*'s instructions, except that he makes it entirely of wood and has to change the design a little if a wooden, two-pronged head is to be strong enough. Still, in his largely rockless environment, he cannot see much use for the thing, and worries that person *B* has misunderstood his rake. So he draws a second set of more detailed instructions for the rake head, and sends them out to everyone. Meanwhile, over in another sector, person *C,* who is particularly interested in clearing out a certain swamp, has created, on the basis of these multiple sets of instructions – the hoe. After all, when you are dealing with swamp grass and muck, you need something that will slice cleanly through the roots. And person *D,* from the same sets of instructions, has come up with a gaff. He has a small lake and fishes quite a bit.

Although it would be interesting to get to know *C* and *D,* the primary heroes of this story are persons *A* and *B.* We return now to them for the climax of the great rake conversation, in which, to everyone's surprise, some real communication takes place. *A* and *B,* who have had profitable interchanges in the past, and thus do not mind working quite hard at their communications, have been caught up in this rake problem for some time now. Their instructions simply will not agree. *B* has even had to abandon his original hypothesis that *A* is a huge man who has only small rocks to deal with. It just does not fit the instructions he is getting. *A,* on his side, is getting so frustrated that he is ready to quit. He sits down near the hub and, in a kind of absent-minded display of anger, grinds two pebbles together. Suddenly he stops. He holds these rocks up in front of his eyes and seems to be thinking furiously. Then he runs to the hub and starts scribbling new instructions as fast as he can, this time using clever iconic symbols for rock and wood, which he hopes *B* will understand. Soon *A* and *B* are both ecstatic. All sorts of previous sets of instructions, not just about rakes, but about other things as well, now make perfect sense. They have raised themselves to a new plateau of inference about each other and each other's environments.

For purposes of comparison, let us now view this same situation once again, as the conduit metaphor would see it. In terms of the radical subjectivist paradigm for human communication, what the conduit metaphor does is permit the exchange of materials from the environments, including the actual constructs themselves. In our story, we would have to imagine a marvelous technological duplicating machine located in the hub. Person *A* puts his rake in a special chamber, pushes a button, and instantly precise replicas of the rake appear in similar chambers for *B*, *C*, and *D* to make use of. *B*, *C*, and *D* do not have to construct anything or guess about anything. Should person *B* want to communicate with *C* and *D* about *A*'s rake, there is no excuse for him sending anything except an exact replica of that rake to these people. There will still be differences in environments, but learning about these is now a trivial matter. Everything *B* has ever sent to *A* has been constructed largely of rock, and *A* is thus perfectly aware of his neighbor's predicament. Even if the marvelous machine should falter now and again, so that artifacts arrive damaged, still, damaged objects look like damaged objects. A damaged rake does not become a hoe. One can simply send the damaged object back, and wait for the other person to send another replica. It should be clear that the overwhelming tendency of the system, as viewed by the conduit metaphor, will always be: success without effort. At the same time, it should be similarly obvious that, in terms of the *toolmakers paradigm*, and the postulate of radical subjectivity, we come to just the opposite conclusion. Human communication will almost always go astray unless real energy is expended.

This comparison, then, brings to light a basic conflict between the conduit metaphor and the toolmakers paradigm. Both models offer an explanation of the phenomenon of communication. But they come to totally different conclusions about what, in that phenomenon, are more natural states of affairs, and what are less natural, or constrained, states. In terms of the conduit metaphor, what requires explanation is failure to communicate. Success appears to be automatic. But if we think in terms of the toolmakers paradigm, our expectation is precisely the opposite. Partial miscommunication, or divergence of readings from a single text, are not aberrations. They are tendencies inherent in the system, which can only be counteracted by continuous effort and by large amounts of verbal interaction. In this view, things will naturally be scattered, unless we expend the energy to gather them. They are not, as the conduit metaphor would have it, naturally gathered, with a frightening population of wrong-headed fools working to scatter them.

As many scholars have pointed out (Kuhn, 1970a; Butterfield, 1965), such shifts in the notion of what a thing does "naturally," that is, if left to its own devices, are the stuff of which scientific revolutions are made. If the earth holds still at some center point, then it is the motions of celestial bodies that must be theorized about and predicted. But if the sun is at that center point, then we must theorize about the motion of the earth. In this regard, the present situation is a little curious. The toolmakers paradigm is very much in accord with the long-postulated connection between information, in the mathematical sense, and the entropy expression of the second law of thermodynamics (Cherry, 1966, pp. 214–17). The second law states that if left to their own devices, all forms of organization always decrease in time. Successful human communication involves an increase in organization, which cannot happen spontaneously or of its own accord. Thus, the shift in viewpoint of the toolmakers paradigm merely seems to bring the model of human communication into line with a previously extant paradigm from the physical sciences. But even though, mathematically, information is expressed as negative entropy, debate and confusion have always surrounded this connection. And it may be that this confusion springs, in part at least, from the dominant position occupied by the conduit metaphor in our language. For the conduit metaphor is definitely in conflict with the second law.

But I do not want to argue too strongly either for or against either of these models in this paper. I do not want to attempt any "appeal to the facts" at this point. For the real question here is to what extent language can influence thought processes. To me, from my vantage point now, it seems that the toolmakers paradigm and radical subjectivism simply form a coherent, common-sense view of what happens when we talk – a common-sense view which finds support in everything from this second law of thermodynamics to recent work in artificial intelligence or cognitive psychology. But if my major claim is true – that the conduit metaphor is a real and powerful semantic structure in English, which can influence our thinking – then it follows that "common sense" about language may be confused. I confess that it took nearly five years for me to come around to radical subjectivism as "common sense." What stood in the way was never a counterargument, but rather the simple inability to think clearly about the matter. My mind would seem to go to sleep at crucial moments, and it was only the mounting weight of more and more evidence that finally forced it to stay awake. Thus, there is the likelihood that arguments about these models either will not be needed, or alternatively, if they are needed, will fall on deaf ears until the biasing effect of the conduit metaphor has been dealt with. Most important, then, is some survey of the evidence that the conduit metaphor can and does influence our thinking.

Semantic pathology

Let us assume now, for the sake of argument, that it is agreed that communication functions as the toolmakers paradigm suggests, and not as the conduit metaphor would have it. And let us assume further that the conflicting implications of the two frames are theoretically interesting or even important. You may well grant me these things and still hold that the conduit metaphor expressions in everyday language do not really influence, or confuse, our thought processes. After all, all of us succeeded in shifting mental gears and thinking about language in terms of the toolmakers paradigm right here in the present discussion. The conduit metaphor did not prevent us from doing this. Where really is the problem? How can anything troublesome arise from a conceptual frame that we were able to discard so easily? This is the question to which we shall address ourselves now. Can the conduit metaphor really bias our thinking? And if so, how?

To begin with, it must be made clear that no speaker of English, not even your author, has discarded the conduit metaphor. Thinking in terms of the toolmakers paradigm briefly may, perhaps, have made us aware of the conduit metaphor. But none of us will discard it until we succeed in bringing about an entire series of linked changes in the English language. The logic of the framework runs like threads in many directions through the syntactic and semantic fabric of our speech habits. Merely becoming cognizant of this in no way alters the situation. Nor does it appear that one can adopt a new framework and develop it while ignoring the cloth of the language. For everywhere one runs into the old threads, and each one pushes conversation and thought back a little way toward the established pattern. No matter how otherworldly this may seem, there is some exceedingly poignant evidence that it has occurred and continues to occur.

The precise claim being made here is important. It has to do, I think, with one of the ways in which people commonly misunderstand the Whorf hypothesis. I do not claim that we cannot think momentarily in terms of another model of the communication process. I argue, rather, that that thinking will remain brief, isolated, and fragmentary in the face of an entrenched system of opposing attitudes and assumptions.

I have not been able to gather hard statistics about the number of core expression arising from the conduit metaphor. Indeed, inasmuch as the concept of a "core expression" is itself somewhat loose, and inasmuch as it is difficult in some cases to decide whether an expression should or should not be listed, I am not sure whether hard statistics can ever be assembled. Nevertheless, the present tally of conduit metaphor expressions is about 140. If one looks about for alternative ways of speaking about communication – ways which are either metaphorically neutral, or metaphorically opposed to the conduit framework – the list of expressions numbers between 30 and 40. A conservative estimate would thus be that, of the entire metalingual apparatus of the English language, at least seventy percent is directly, visibly, and graphically based on the conduit metaphor.

Whatever influence the remaining thirty percent might have appears to be weakened beyond this direct proportionality by several factors. First, these expressions tend to be the multisyllabic, latinate abstractions ("communicate," "disseminate," "notify," "disclose," and so on) which are neither graphic nor metaphorically coherent. Thus, they do not present an alternative model of the communication process, which leaves the notion of "putting ideas into words" as the sole available conception. Second, most of them can be used with the adjunct "in words" ("in s," more generally), thereby losing their neutrality and lending added support to the conduit metaphor. "Communicate your feelings *using* simpler words," for example, succeeds in avoiding the conduit metaphor, whereas, "Communicate your feelings *in* simpler words," does not. And finally, to the extent that etymologies are relevant, many of these expressions have roots which spring directly from the conduit framework ("express," "disclose," etc.). See Part Two of the Appendix for this listing.

The simplest, and perhaps most convincing illustration of our dependence on the conduit metaphor core expressions is a test that can be performed by anyone. Familiarize yourself with the listings in the Appendix. Then begin to become aware of, and try to avoid, conduit metaphors. Every time you find yourself using one, see if you can replace it with a neutral expression, or some circumlocution. My experience in teaching classes which dealt with this subject has been that I am constantly called to account by my students for using the expressions I am lecturing about. If I speak very carefully, with constant attention, I can do fairly well at avoiding them. But the result is hardly idiomatic English. Instead of walking into a classroom and asking, "Did you get anything out of that article?", I have to say, "Were you able to construct anything of interest on the basis of the assigned text?" If one should look, I daresay even the present article is not free from conduit metaphor expressions. I ended the preceding section with a minor framework, category three example, (141) in the Appendix, when I wrote: "The arguments will fall on deaf ears." Practically speaking, if you try to avoid all obvious conduit metaphor expressions in your usage, you are nearly struck dumb when communication becomes the topic. You can say to your wayward student, "Try to communicate more effectively, Reginald," but it will not have nearly the impact of, "Reginald, you've got to learn how to put your thoughts into words."

But even if you could avoid all such obvious conduit "metaphorisms," this would still not free you from the framework. The threads, as I said, are nearly everywhere. To see that they go much deeper than just a list of expressions, I should like to resurrect a concept from pre-transformational semantics. In his *Principles of Semantics*, Stephen Ullmann (1957, p. 122) makes use of the term *semantic pathology*. A semantic pathology arises "whenever two or more incompatible senses capable of figuring meaningfully in the same context develop around the same name." For some time, my favorite English illustration of this was the delicate and difficult problem of distinguishing sympathy from apology. That is, "I'm sorry" can mean either "I empathize with your suffering," or "I admit fault and apologize." Sometimes people expect apologies from us when we only wish to sympathize, in which case saying, "I'm sorry," is either the perfect hedge or the opening line of a fight. Other times, people think we are apologizing when they see no need for us to apologize and respond with, "That's alright, it wasn't your fault."

As I studied the conduit metaphor, however, I came to rely on this example less and less. I kept coming across terms which were ambiguous between what we have here called "repertoire members" and what we have called "signals." I would find a word which, in its basic sense, referred to some grouping of the marks or sounds which we do exchange with one another. But then I would use it in sentences and realize that it could refer just as easily and just as often to segments of human thought or emotions. Consider the word "poem," for example. In (37) through (39),

    (37) The poem was almost illegible
    (38) The poem has five lines and forty words
    (39) The poem is unrhymed,

this word clearly refers to a text, some signals involving either marks

or sounds. For sake of clarity, let us call the *word-sense* operating here
POEM$_1$ (for an operational definition of "word-sense," see Reddy, 1973).
Now notice that, in (40) through (42),

    (40) Donne's poem is very logical

    (41) That poem was so completely depressing

    (42) You know his poem is too obscene for children,

the most probable referent of the word is not a text, but rather the
concepts and emotions assembled in the reading of a text. I say "most
probable" here because it is possible to imagine contexts in which the
referent is actually once again a text. Suppose, for instance, (41) is
uttered by a teacher of penmanship about a child's hasty copy of some
poem. Barring such unusual contexts, however, "poem" in these examples refers to conceptual and emotional material. The word-sense functioning here we shall call POEM$_2$. Example (43) can be read with
either POEM$_1$ or POEM$_2$.

    (43) Martha's poem is so sloppy!

It is easy to see that this ambiguity of the term "poem" is intimately related to the conduit metaphor. If the words in language contain the ideas, then POEM$_1$ contains POEM$_2$, and metonymy, a process of
meaning extension second in importance only to metaphor, takes over.
That is, when two entities are always found together in our experience,
the name of one of them – usually the more concrete – will develop a
new sense which refers to the other. Just as ROSE$_1$ (= the blossom)
developed ROSE$_2$ (= the shade of pinkish red) by metonymy, so
POEM$_1$ gave rise to POEM$_2$. For, in terms of the conduit metaphor, the
two are seen as existing together, the second within the first, and all
the conditions for metonymy are met. As long as we are happy with the
conduit metaphor, then this ambiguity is in no way problematic, and
is certainly not a semantic pathology.

But now consider what happens to the linguistic idealist who wants
to think about communication in terms of the toolmakers paradigm
and radical subjectivism without making any changes in the English
language. In this new model, the words do not contain the ideas, and
so POEM$_1$ does not contain POEM$_2$. Instead, it is of greatest importance
to preserve a principled distinction between POEM$_1$ and POEM$_2$. There
is in most cases only one POEM$_1$, one text, to worry about. But because
of the differences in repertories from one person to the next, and
because of the difficult task of assembling these mental and emotional
materials on the basis of the instructions in the text, it is obvious to
our theorist that there will be as many POEM$_2$'s in existence as there
are readers or listeners. These internal POEM$_2$'s will only come to
resemble one another after the people expend some energy talking

with one another and comparing notes. There is now not the slightest basis for a metonymical extension of POEM$_1$ to POEM$_2$. If we had viewed language in terms of the toolmakers paradigm historically, these two profoundly different concepts would never have been accessed by the same word. Talking about an entire series of slightly, or even terribly, different entities as if there were only one would obviously have led to communicative disaster.

We see, then, that things have taken a troublesome turn for our linguistic idealist. This ambiguity of the word "poem" is for him a real and severe semantic pathology. Other speakers, who accept the conduit metaphor, can be perfectly blasé about it. But he cannot. It befuddles the very distinction he is most concerned to make and bring others to make. More troublesome still is the fact that this pathology is global. It is not an isolated development in the language, involving only the word "poem." I have discussed "poem" here as a paradigm case for the entire class of words in English which denote signals. Analogous examples are available for all of the s words discussed in a previous section – "word," "phrase," "sentence," "essay," "novel," and so on. Even the word "text" has the two senses, as evidenced by (44) and (45).

(44) I am tired of illegible texts

(45) The text is logically incoherent.

In addition, all the proper names of texts, poems, plays, novels, speeches, and the like share this ambiguity. Notice,

(46) The *Old Man and the Sea* is 112 pages long

(47) The *Old Man and the Sea* is deeply symbolic.

As I became aware of this systematic, widespread semantic pathology, I was, of course, far less impressed with the difficulties caused by, "I'm sorry." For here was a case that involved more words than any pathology I had ever heard of. Furthermore, this case showed that semantic structures could be completely normal with respect to one view of reality, and at the same time, pathological with respect to another view. Or in other words, here was some strong evidence that language and views about reality have to develop hand in hand. Finally, I also noticed that this new, potential pathology affected what might be called the "morphosemantics" of the words involved. Suppose, for example, we pluralize the word "poem." As shown in (48),

(48) We have several poems to deal with today,

this produces a form whose most natural referents are a number of POEM$_1$'s, that is, a series of different texts. It would be quite unnatural to utter (48) and mean that there were several internal POEM$_2$'s, Michael's POEM$_2$, Mary's POEM$_2$, Alex's POEM$_2$, and so on, all constructed from the same POEM$_1$, which were to be discussed on a given day. What this means is that, although POEM$_1$, pluralizes with the change in morphology, the other sense, POEM$_2$, is lost in this change. In the case of proper names, pluralization is even more problematic. For most names of texts, there is no morphology defined for the plural. How should our budding radical subjectivist pluralize *The Old Man and the Sea*"? Does he say, "Our internal *The Old Man and the Sea-s*"? Or should it be, "Our internal *Old Men and the Sea*"? And notice that it will not help him very much to use (49), or (50).

(49) Our versions of the poem

(50) Our versions of *The Old Man and the Sea*.

For if, in (49), the word "poem" means POEM$_1$, then this phrase applies to variants of the text – which is not what he wants to say. On the other hand, if "poem" means POEM$_2$, then he is still in trouble. Now it sounds like there is one proper and correct POEM$_2$, available to us all, which we may however, for reasons of taste, alter slightly. The radical subjectivism, the absolute nontransferability of any "correct" POEM$_2$, is muddied completely by (49) and (50). This most important fact, that there is one POEM$_1$ but necessarily many POEM$_2$'s, cannot be expressed easily, consistently, or at all naturally.

This discussion, though it says by no means all that could be said, provides an initial illustration of what would happen to someone who really tried to discard the conduit metaphor and think seriously and coherently in terms of the toolmakers paradigm. He would face serious linguistic difficulties, to say the least, and would quite clearly have to create new language as he restructured his thought. But, of course, he would be likely to do this *only* if he shared our present awareness of the biasing power of the conduit metaphor. So far as I know, none of the thinkers who have tried to present alternate theories of language and the nature of meaning have had this awareness. Thus, the conduit metaphor has undercut them, without any knowledge on their part of what was happening. Of course, the problems caused by this confusion in aesthetics and criticism are legion, and it is easy to document my claims by analysis of works in this area. However, a more convincing documentation – indeed, the most convincing documentation one could wish for is to be found in the historical development of *mathematical information theory*. For here, if ever, with both a concept-free algebra of information, and working machines to use as models, the effect of the conduit metaphor should have been avoided. But, in fact, it was not. And the conceptual basis of the new mathematics, though not the mathematics itself, has been completely obscured by the semantic pathologies of the conduit metaphor.

The framework of mathematical information theory has much in common with our toolmakers paradigm. Information is defined as the ability to make nonrandom selections from some set of alternatives. Communication, which is the transfer of this ability from one place to another, is envisioned as occurring in the following manner. The set of alternatives and a *code* relating these alternatives to physical signals are established, and a copy of each is placed at both the sending and receiving ends of the system. This act creates what is known as an "a priori shared context," a prerequisite for achieving any communication whatsoever. At the transmitting end, a sequence of the alternatives, called the *message*, is chosen for communication to the other end. But this sequence of alternatives is not sent. Rather, the chosen alternatives are related systematically by the code to some form of energy patterns which can travel quickly and retain their shape while they do travel – that is, to the signals.

The whole point of the system is that the alternatives themselves are not mobile, and cannot be sent, whereas the energy patterns, the "signals" are mobile. If all goes well, the signals, when they arrive at the receiving end, are used to duplicate the original selection process and recreate the message. That is, using the relationships of the code and the copy of the original set of alternatives, the receiving end can make the same selections that were made earlier on the transmitting end when the message was generated. Quantification is possible in this framework only because one can set up measures of how much the received signals narrow down the possible choices of preexistent alternatives.

In terms of our toolmakers paradigm, the predefined set of alternatives of information theory corresponds to what we have called the "repertoire." The environments of the persons in the wagon-wheel compound all have much in common – otherwise their system of instructions would not work at all. The "signals" of the mathematical theory are exactly the same as our "signals" – the patterns that can travel, that can be exchanged. In the world of the compound, they are the sheets of paper sent back and forth. Notice now, that, in information theory, as in our paradigm, the alternatives – the "messages" – are not contained in the signals. If the signals were to arrive at the receiving end, and the set of alternatives was damaged or missing, the proper selections could not be made. The signals have no ability to bring the alternatives with them; they carry no little replica of the message. The whole notion of information as "the power to make selections" rules out the idea that signals *contain* the message.

Now, this may be abundantly clear when spelled out in this fashion. And it seems to remain clear as long as information theory is restricted to simple, technical applications. But as most of you know, this theory was hailed as a potential breakthrough for biology and the social sciences. And numerous attempts were made to extend its range of application to include human language and behavior (see Cherry, 1966). Such attempts, of course, were not simple and technical. They required a very clear understanding, not so much of the mathematics of the theory, but rather of the conceptual foundations of the theory. By and large, these attempts were all accounted to be failures. I think that the reason for these failures was the interaction of the conduit metaphor with the conceptual foundations of information theory. As soon as people ventured away from the original, well-defined area of the mathematics, and were forced to rely more on ordinary language, the essential insight of information theory was muddled beyond repair.

The destructive impact of ordinary language on any extensions of information theory begins with the very terms the originators (Shannon and Weaver, 1949) chose to name parts of the paradigm. They called the set of alternatives, which we have referred to here as the "repertoire," the *alphabet*. It is true that in telegraphy the set of alternatives is in fact the alphabet; and telegraphy was their paradigm example. But they made it quite clear that the word "alphabet" was for them a technical coinage which was supposed to refer to *any* set of alternative states, behaviors, or what have you. But this piece of nomenclature is problematic when one turns to human communication. For years I taught information theory in a nonmathematical way to future English teachers, using the term "alphabet." Always this seemed to confuse them, though I never could fathom why, until one year, a student put up her hand and said, "But you can't call the alternatives the *signals*." Now it is strange, on the face of it, that Weaver, particularly, who was very concerned about applying the theory to human communication, would have let this go unnoticed. It confuses the all important distinction between signals and repertoire members. Substituting the present term, "repertoire," for "alphabet" made my teaching much easier.

But another mistake in terminology makes it seem probable that Shannon and Weaver were never quite clear themselves about the importance of this distinction to their own system. Consider the choice of the term "message" to represent the selection of alternatives from the repertoire. "Message," as the following examples show, partakes of the same semantic pathology as "poem."

(51) I got your message (MESSAGE₁), but had no time to read it
(52) Okay, John, I get the message (MESSAGE₂); let's leave him
     alone.

For information theory, this is extremely confusing, because MESSAGE₁ means literally a set of signals, whereas MESSAGE₂, means the repertoire members involved with the communication. For conduit-metaphor thinking, in which we send and receive the MESSAGE₂ within the MESSAGE₁, the ambiguity is trivial. But for a theory based totally on the notion that the "message" (MESSAGE₂) is never *sent* anywhere, this choice of words leads to the collapse of the paradigm. Shannon and Weaver were very careful to point out that the "received signals" were not necessarily the "transmitted signal" because of the possible intervention of distortion and noise. But they blithely wrote the word "message" on the right, or receiving side of their famous paradigm (Shannon & Weaver, 1949, p. 7). At the very least they should have written "reconstructed message" there. In their theory, something is *rebuilt* on that right side which, hopefully, resembles the original message on the left side. The ambiguity of the word "message" should have led them to regard this word as a disaster and never to consider it for use.

If they did not, I believe it is because their thought processes were responding to the biasing effect of the conduit metaphor. Weaver, it seems, could not hold the theory clearly in mind when he spoke of human communication, and used conduit metaphor expressions almost constantly. "How precisely," he asked, "do the transmitted symbols *convey* the desired meaning [italics mine]?" (p. 4) Or he compared two "messages, one of which is *heavily loaded with meaning* and the other of which is pure nonsense." (p. 8) In truth, it seems that he still thought of the MESSAGE₂, the repertoire members, as being sent across the channel, even though this destroys the notion of information as selective power. Weaver hedges significantly when he describes the action of the transmitter. It "changes," he says, "the *message* into the signal [italics Weaver's]." (p. 7) Really, this is a strange description. A code is a relationship between two distinct systems. It does not "change" anything into anything else. It merely preserves in the second system the pattern of organization present in the first system. Marks or sounds are not transmuted into electronic pulses. Nor are thoughts and emotions magically metamorphosed into words. Again, this is conduit-metaphor thinking. There is no justification whatsoever in information theory for talking about communication this way.

It is worth noting that Shannon, who actually originated the mathematics, may have had a more coherent understanding than Weaver. At some points in his own exposition, Shannon used exactly the right ordinary language terms. He wrote, "The *receiver* ordinarily performs the inverse operation of that done by the transmitter, reconstructing the message from the signal" (p. 34). But it still does not seem that he perceived the damage done to the paradigm by his own and Weaver's conduit metaphorisms.

Quite the same thing can be said for other ways of speaking associated with information theory. They do violence to the theory, yet support and uphold the conduit metaphor admirably. Consider "encode" and "decode." These mean to put the repertoire members "into" code, and then take them out of code, respectively. Or think about the term "information content." The theory conceives of information as the power to reproduce an organization by means of nonrandom selections. Signals *do something*. They cannot *contain* anything. If the conduit metaphor is capable of influencing thought processes, then why has an entire generation of information theorists talked in this confusing and detrimental way? One would have to suppose that Weaver and many researchers who have followed him were simply bent on professional destruction. It seems easier to believe that the English language has the power to lead them astray.

A recent anthology collecting psychological and sociological efforts to create a communication theory for human interactions points out in the introduction that "investigators have yet to establish a completely acceptable definition of communication" (Sereno & Mortensen, 1970, p. 2). Then it goes on to say,

Those models based upon a mathematical conception describe communication as analogous to the operations of an information processing machine: an event occurs in which a *source* or *sender transmits a signal* or *message* through a *channel* to some *destination* or *receiver* [italics from anthology]. (p. 71)

Notice the statement, "transmits a signal or message." Here, twenty-one years after Shannon and Weaver, the same confusion persists – can the "message" be sent, or not? And it persists in almost every article of the volume. Consider one more brief example. "The theory [of information] was concerned with the problem of defining the quantity of information contained in a message to be transmitted. . . " (p. 62). Note that here information is *contained* in a transmitted "message." If the author means MESSAGE₁, then he is thinking in terms of the conduit metaphor, and saying that information is contained in the signals. If he means MESSAGE₁, then he is saying that repertoire members, which are transmitted inside of signals, have inside of *them* something called information, which can be measured. Either way, the insight of information theory has been overwhelmed.

Social implications

I should like to conclude with some remarks on the social implications of the situation we have outlined. If the English language has a less than accurate idea of its own workings, and if it has the power to bias thought processes in the direction of this model, what practical impact does this have? We have seen evidence that the conduit metaphor can confuse serious attempts at theory building – but does it matter at all to the man on the street, to mass culture, to federal policymaking?

I must limit myself here to suggesting two ways in which the conduit metaphor does matter to all speakers of English. To discuss the first way, I whould like to return to the "stories" told in an earlier section and add a final sequal.

It came to pass, one year, that an evil magician, who was an expert at hypnosis, flew over the toolmakers' compound. Looking down, he saw that, despite the formidable handicaps, *A*, *B*, *C*, and *D* were doing quite well with their system of instruction sending. They were very aware that communicating was hard work. And their successes were extremely rewarding to them, because they retained a distinct sense of awe and wonder that they could make the system work at all. It was a daily miracle, which had improved their respective standards of living immensely. The evil magician was very upset about this, and decided to do the worst thing he could think of to *A*, *B*, *C*, and *D*. What he did was this. He hypnotized them in a special way, so that, after they received a set of instructions and struggled to build something on the basis of them, they would immediately forget about this. Instead, he planted in them the false memory that the object had been sent to them directly from the other person, via a marvelous mechanism in the hub. Of course, this was not true. They still had to build the objects themselves, out of their own materials – but the magician blinded them to this.

As it turned out, the evil magician's shrewdness was profound. For even though, objectively, the communications system of the compound had not changed one bit, it nevertheless fell very quickly into disuse and decay. And as it crumbled, so did the spirit of harmony and communal progress that had always characterized the relations of *A*, *B*, *C*, and *D*. For now, since they would always forget that they had assembled an object themselves and thus bore a large share of responsibility for its shape, it was easy to ridicule the sender for any defects. They also began to spend less and less time working to assemble things, because, once the mental block descended, there was no feeling of reward for a job well done. As soon as they finished an assembly, the hypnosis would take effect, and suddenly – well, even though they were worn out, still, it was the other fellow who had done all the hard, creative work of putting it together. Any fool could take a finished product out of the chamber in the hub. So they came to resent, and therefore abandon, any assembly jobs that required real work. But this was not the worst effect forseen by the evil magician when he cast his peculiar spell. For, indeed, it was not long before each of the persons came to entertain, privately, the idea that all the others had gone insane. One would send instructions to the others for some device of which he was particularly proud, just as he had always done. Only now of course he believed that he sent, not instructions, but the thing itself. Then, when the others would send him instructions in return, to confirm their receipt of his, he would assemble the object, forget, think that they had returned him the thing itself, and then stare in horror at what he saw. Here he had sent them a wonderful tool, and they returned to him grotesque parodies. Really, what could explain this? All they had to do was to successfully remove his object from the chamber in the hub. How could they change it so shockingly in performing an operation of such moronic simplicity? Were they imbeciles? Or was there perhaps some malice in their behavior? In the end, A, B, C, and D all came privately to the conclusion that the others had either become hostile or else gone berserk. Either way, it did not matter much. None of them took the communications system seriously any more.

Among other things, this sequel attempts to sketch some of the social and psychological effects of believing that communication is a "success without effort" system, when, in fact, it is an "energy must be expended" system. I am sure that no one has failed to realize that, to the extent that the parable applies, the evil magician is the English language, and his hypnotic spell is the bias imparted to our thought processes by the conduit metaphor. This model of communication objectifies meaning in a misleading and dehumanizing fashion. It influences us to talk and think about thoughts as if they had the same kind of external, intersubjective reality as lamps and tables. Then, when this presumption proves dramatically false in operation, there seems to be nothing to blame except our own stupidity or malice. It is as if we owned a very large, very complex computer – but had been given the wrong instruction manual for it. We believe the wrong things about it, and teach our children the wrong things about it, and simply cannot get full or even moderate usage out of the system.

Another point from the story worth emphasizing is that, to the extent that the conduit metaphor does see communication as requiring some slight expenditure of energy, it localizes this expenditure almost totally in the speaker or writer. The function of the reader or listener is trivialized. The radical subjectivist paradigm, on the other hand, makes it clear that readers and listeners face a difficult and highly creative task of reconstruction and hypothesis testing. Doing this work well probably requires considerably more energy than the conduit metaphor would lead us to expect.

But we are still a long way from government policy in these effects. Let us turn, then, to the second example of the impact of the conduit metaphor, which will help to close this gap. The expression employed in (51), number 113 in the Appendix,

(51) You'll *find* better *ideas* than that *in* the *library*,

is derived from the conduit metaphor by a chain of metonymies. That is, we think of the ideas as existing in the words, which are clearly there on the pages. So the ideas are "there on the pages" by metonymy. Now the pages are in the books – and again, by metonymy, so are the ideas. But the books are in the libraries, with the final result that the ideas, too, are "in the libraries." The effect of this, and the many other minor framework core expressions is to suggest that the libraries, with their books, and tapes, and films, and photographs, are the real repositories of our culture. And if this is true, then naturally we of the modern period are preserving our cultural heritage better than any other age, because we have more books, films, tapes, and so on, stored in more and bigger libraries.

Suppose now that we drop the conduit metaphor and think of this same situation in terms of the toolmakers paradigm. From this point of view, there are of course no ideas in the words, and therefore none in any books, nor on any tapes or records. There are no ideas whatsoever in any libraries. All that is stored in any of these places are odd little patterns of marks or bumps or magnetized particles capable of creating odd patterns of noise. Now, if a human being comes along who is capable of using these marks or sounds as instructions, then this human being may assemble within his head some patterns of thought or feeling or perception which resemble those of intelligent humans no longer living. But this is a difficult task, for these ones no longer living saw a different world from ours, and used slightly different language instructions. Thus, if this human who enters the library has not been schooled in the art of language, so that he is deft and precise and thorough in applying instructions, and if he does not have a rather full and flexible repertoire of thoughts and feelings to draw from, then it is not likely that he will reconstruct in his head anything that deserves to be called "his cultural heritage."

Quite obviously, the toolmakers paradigm makes it plain that there is no culture in books or libraries, that, indeed, there is no culture at all unless it is reconstructed carefully and painstakingly in the living brains of each new generation. All that is preserved in libraries is the mere opportunity to perform this reconstruction. But if the language skills and the habit of engaging in reconstruction are not similarly preserved, then there will be no culture, no matter how large and complete the libraries may become. We do not preserve ideas by building libraries and recording voices. The only way to preserve culture is to train people to rebuild it, to "regrow" it, as the word "culture" itself suggests, in the only place it can grow – within themselves.

The difference of viewpoint here between the conduit metaphor and the toolmakers paradigm is serious, if not profound. Humanists appear to be dying these days, and administrators and governments seem to feel few compunctions about letting this occur. We have the greatest, most sophisticated system for mass communication of any society that we know about, yet somehow mass communication becomes more and more synonymous with less communication. Why is this? One reason, at least, may be that we are following our instruction manual for use of the language system quite carefully – and it is the wrong manual. We have the mistaken, conduit-metaphor influenced view that the more signals we can create, and the more signals we can preserve, the more ideas we "transfer" and "store." We neglect the crucial human ability to reconstruct thought patterns on the basis of signals and this ability founders. After all, "extraction" is a trivial process, which does not require teaching past the most rudimentary level. We have therefore, in fact, less culture – or certainly no more culture – than other, less mechanically inclined, ages have had. Humanists, those traditionally charged with reconstructing culture and teaching others to reconstruct it, are not necessary in the scheme of the conduit metaphor. All the ideas are "there in the library," and anyone can go in and "get them." In the toolmakers paradigm, on the other hand, humanists themselves *are* the repositories, and the only real repositories of ideas. In the simplest of terms, the conduit metaphor lets human ideas slip out of human brains, so that, once you have recording technologies, you do not need humans any more.

I am suggesting, then, that, in the same way that "urban renewal" misled the policymakers discussed in Schön's paper, the conduit metaphor is leading us down a technological and social blind alley. That blind alley is mass communications systems coupled with mass neglect of the internal, human systems responsible for nine-tenths of the work in communicating. We think we are "capturing ideas in words," and funneling them out to the greatest public in the history of the world. But if there are no ideas "within" this endless flood of words, then all we are doing is replaying the myth of Babel – centering it, this time, around a broadcasting tower.

APPENDIX

A partial listing of the metalingual resources of English

This appendix is divided into two parts. The first lists expressions arising from the logic of the conduit metaphor; the second lists expressions which are either metaphorically neutral or involve logics alternative to the conduit metaphor. Further search for expressions, along with a more elaborate means of analyzing and classifying, will be required before either collection can be termed complete. In some cases, in Part One, core expressions which I have placed in one category could with justification be placed in a different category as well. These and other niceties must await later exposition. One or two examples follow each expression.

Part One: The conduit metaphor

I. THE MAJOR FRAMEWORK

A. Implying that human language functions like a conduit enabling the transfer of repertoire members from one individual to another.
1. get RM across (to someone)
    "You'll have to try to get your real attitudes across to her better."
    "It's very hard to get that idea across in a hostile atmosphere."
2. put RM across (to someone)
    "If you salesmen can't put this understanding across to the clients more forcefully, our new product will fail."
3. give RM (to someone)
    "You know very well that I gave you that idea."
4. give RM away
    "Jane gives away all her best ideas."
5. get RM from someone
    "Marsha got those concepts from Rudolf."
6. RM get through (to someone)
    "Your real feelings are finally getting through to me."
7. RM come through (to someone)
    "Apparently, your reasons came through to John quite clearly."
    "What comes through most obviously is anger."

8. RM come across (to someone)

"Your concepts come across beautifully."

9. RM make it across (to someone)

"Your thoughts here don't quite make it across."

10. let someone have RM

"Oh come on, let me have some of your great ideas about this."

11. present someone with RM

"Well, you have presented me with some unfamiliar thoughts and I think I should let them settle awhile."

12. send RM (to someone)

"Next time you write, send better ideas."

13. language transfers RM

"Language transfers meaning."

B. Implying that, in speaking or writing, humans place their internal repertoire members within the external signals, or else fail to do so in unsuccessful communication.

14. put RM into s

"It is very difficult to put this concept into words."

15. capture RM in s

"When you have a good idea, try to capture it immediately in words."

16. fill s with RM

"Harry always fills his paragraphs with meaning."

17. pack s with RM

"A good poet packs his lines with beautiful feelings."

18. pack RM into s

"If you can't pack more thought into fewer words, you will never pass the conciseness test."

19. load s with RM

"Never load a sentence with more thought than it can carry."

20. load RM into s

"John loads too much conflicting feeling into what he says."

21. insert RM in s

"Insert that thought elsewhere in the sentence."

22. include RM in s

"I would certainly not include that feeling in your speech."

23. burden s with RM

"You burden your words with rather terribly complex meanings."

24. overload s with RM

"Harry does not exactly overload his paragraphs with thought."

25. stuff RM into s

"You cannot simply stuff ideas into a sentence any old way!"

26. stuff s with RM/full of RM
    "You have only a short time, so try to stuff the essay with all your best ideas."
    "You can stuff the paper full of earthshaking ideas – that man still won't notice."
27. cram RM into s
    "Dickinson crams incredible amounts of meaning into her poems."
28. cram with RM/full of RM
    "He crammed the speech with subversive ideas."
    "Harry crammed the chapter full of spurious arguments."
29. unload RM in s
    "Unload your feelings in words – then your head will be clearer."
30. force RM into s
    "Don't force your meanings into the wrong words."
31. get RM into s
    "I can't seem to get these ideas into words."
32. shove RM into s
    "Trying to shove such complicated meanings into simple sentences is exceedingly difficult."
33. fit RM into s
    "This notion does not seem to fit into any words."

C. Implying that signals convey or contain the repertoire members, or else fail to do this in unsuccessful communication.
    34. s carry RM
        "His words carry little in the way of recognizable meaning."
    35. s convey RM
        "The passage conveys a feeling of excitement."
    36. s transfer RM
        "Your writing must transfer these ideas to those who need them."
    37. s display RM
        "This essay displays thoughts I did not think Marsha capable of."
    38. s bring RM (with it)
        "His letter brought the idea to the French pilots."
    39. s contain RM
        "In terms of the rest of the poem, your couplet contains the wrong kind of thoughts."
    40. s have RM-content/RMa-content
        "The introduction has a great deal of thought-content."
        "The statement appears to have little emotional content."
        "The speech has too much angry content."

("RMa" stands for adjectives appropriate to repertoire members.)

41. RM be in s
   "That thought is in practically every phrase!"

42. s be pregnant with RM
   "His words, pregnant with meaning, fell on receptive ears."

43. s be fraught with RM
   "The poem is fraught with dire thoughts about civilization."

44. s be saturated with RM
   "The last stanza is saturated with despair."

45. s be hollow
   "Your words seem rather hollow."

46. s be full of RM
   "The oracle's words were full of meaning."

47. s be without RM
   "The sentence is without meaning."

48. s have no RM
   "Sam's words have not the slightest feeling of compassion."

49. s be empty (of RM)
   "His lines may rhyme, but they are empty of either meaning or feeling."
   "The sentences are empty; they say nothing to me."
   "What the candidates have said is so much empty sound."

50. s be void of RM
   "The entire chapter is void of all useful ideas."

51. s's RM/RM of s
   "The thought of this clause is somehow disturbing."
   "This paragraph's thought is completely garbled."

52. s be bursting with RM
   "The poem is bursting with ecstasy!"

53. s be overflowing with RM
   "The line is overflowing with pure happiness."

54. RM show up in s
   "This idea shows up in the second paragraph."

55. s hand RM (to someone)
   "But this sentence hands us a completely different idea."

D. Implying that, in listening or reading, humans find repertoire members within the signals and take them into their heads, or else fail to do so in unsuccessful communication.

56. get RM out of s/from s
   "I have to struggle to get any meaning at all out of the sentence."
   "I got the idea of patience from your statement."

57. get the RM in s into one's head

"Everybody must get the concepts in this article into his head by tomorrow or else!"

58. extract RM from s

"Can you really extract coherent thoughts from that incredible prose?"

59. RM arise from s

"The feeling arises from the second paragraph."

60. see RM in s

"We will see this thought several times again in the sonnet."

61. find RM in s

"John says that he cannot find your idea anywhere in the passage."

63. come upon RM in s

"I would be quite surprised if you came upon any interesting concepts in Stephen's essay."

64. uncover RM in s

"John admits that we uncovered those ideas in the ode, but still doesn't believe that Keats put them there."

65. overlook RM in s

"Don't overlook the idea of fulfilled passion later on in the passage."

66. pay attention to RM in s/what's in s

"You rarely pay enough attention to the actual meaning in the words."

"Please pay attention to what's there in the words!"

67. reveal RM in s

"Closer reading reveals altogether uncharacteristic feelings in the story."

68. miss RM in s

"I missed that idea in the sentence completely."

69. s be impenetrable

"The poem is meant to be impenetrable – after all, Blake wrote it."

70. RM be locked up in s

"Whatever she meant, it's likely to be locked up in that cryptic little verse forever."

71. RM be sealed up in s

"It's as if he wrote the sentences in such a way as to seal up the meaning in them."

72. RM be hidden (away) in s

"The attitudes I want to show you are hidden away someplace in the last chapter."

73. RM be/get lost in s

    "Mary has good ideas, but they get lost in her run-on sentences."

74. RM be buried in s

    "Yes, but the man's thought is buried in these terribly dense and difficult paragraphs."

75. RM be sunk in s

    "The thought is there, although I grant that it's sunk pretty deep in paradoxical language."

76. lay bare RM in s

    "John's analysis really lays bare the ideas in the chapter."

77. bare RM in s

    "You have bared the hidden meanings in the sentence."

78. unseal RM in s

    "To unseal the meaning in Wittgenstein's curious phrases is no easy task."

79. expose RM in s

    "You have exposed certain feelings in the essay of which the author would not be proud."

II. THE MINOR FRAMEWORK

E. Implying that, particularly when communications are recorded or delivered in public, speakers and writers eject their repertoire members into an external "space."

80. get RM out

    "I feel some responsibility to get these ideas out where they can do some good."

81. get RM into circulation

    "Try to get your feelings about the merger into circulation among the board members."

82. put RM into circulation

    "We intend to put these new concepts into circulation among actual teachers."

83. put RM forth

    "IBM put forth the idea that they had been mistreated."

84. pour RM out

    "Mary poured out her sorrows."

85. pour RM forth

    "You come over and pour forth your anger and expect me to take it all in!"

86. bring RM out

    "Dr. Williams brings out some unusual thoughts on the matter."

87. s put RM forth

"IBM's legal brief puts forth the idea that they have been mis-
treated."

88. s brings RM out

"The essay brings out unusual thoughts on the matter."

89. bring RM forth

"That child brought forth feelings I couldn't cope with."

90. RM leak out

"Your thoughts will leak out anyway."

91. get RM down on paper

"Get your insights down on paper at once."

92. put RM down on paper

"Perhaps you could put this feeling of sympathy down on
paper and send it to your brother."

93. set RM down on paper

"Can you set the latest idea down on paper and let me take it?"

94. lay RM out on paper

"Lay your thoughts out on paper where you can see them."

95. let RM drop

"Someone let drop the idea of continuing anyway."

96. let RM slip out

"Who let this understanding slip out?"

97. deliver self of RM

"He delivered himself of a great deal of anger."

98. RM pour out

"Interesting ideas just seem to pour out of that man."

99. RM flow out

"Don't let your feelings flow out so freely when he's around."

100. RM gush out/forth

"Let your emotions gush right out – that's what we're here
for."

"All these thoughts can't gush forth at once, you know."

101. RM ooze out

"Her sympathy just oozes out."

102. RM escape someone's lips

"That idea will never escape Mary's lips."

103. throw out RM

"I just want to throw out some new ideas for you folks to
look at."

104. throw RM EX LOC

"You can't just throw ideas onto the page any old way!"

"Mary throws her ideas at the reader too fast."

(EX LOC stands for *external locative*, that is, any expression denoting a place external to the speaker or writer's head.)

105. toss out RM

"I shall begin the class by tossing out some apparently very simple thoughts."

106. blurt out RM

"You always blurt out your feelings before anyone is ready to cope with them."

F. Implying that repertoire members are reified in this external "space," independent of any need for living humans to think or feel them.

107. RM float around

"That concept has been floating around for centuries."

108. RM circulate

"Those precise thoughts began circulating shortly after your birth."

109. RM move

"In America, ideas tend to move from the coasts to the middle of the country."

110. RM make its/their way

"The concept made its way very quickly into the universities."

111. RM find its/their way

"These feelings found their way to the ghettos of Rome."

112. RM arrive

"A fantastic idea arrived in the mail this morning!"

113. RM travel

"The notion traveled from Russia to China that communism would have to be modified."

114. find RM in/at L

"You won't find that idea in any bookstore!"

(L stands for any edifice or room containing reading matter.)

115. RM be in/at L

"I'm sure those thoughts are already in the library."

116. find RM in B

"You can find that idea in several books."

(B stands for those physical objects that normally contain writing – i.e., "magazines," "newspapers," etc., and also expressions like "on microfilm.")

117. RM be in B

"I'm sure those thoughts are in some magazine."

118. RM be on radio/television/tape/records
   "That kind of anger has never been on television."
119. immerse self in RM
   "He immersed himself in the fresher ideas of topology."
120. bury self in RM
   "Don't bury yourself in these concepts in any case."
121. lose self in/among RM
   "She lost herself among her intense feelings."
   "She lost herself in the feeling of grief."
122. wander among RM
   "Harry was now free to wander happily among the ideas of the more learned hedonists."
123. kick RM around
   "We were kicking around some of Dave's ideas."
124. toss RM back and forth
   "They tossed your thoughts back and forth for over an hour, but still could not make sense of them."
125. throw RM around
   "That professor throws around esoteric ideas like it was going out of style."

G. Implying that the reified repertoire members may or may not find their way once again into the heads of living humans.

126. absorb RM
   "You have to absorb Plato's ideas a little at a time."
127. RM sink in
   "Harry just won't let certain kinds of thoughts sink in."
128. take RM in
   "You have to learn to take in your friends' emotions and react sensibly to them."
129. internalize RM
   "Marsha has obviously not internalized these ideas."
130. catch RM
   "It was a notion I didn't catch right away."
131. get RM
   "We didn't get that idea until very late in the semester."
132. RM come to someone
   "Then the thought came to me that you might have already left."
133. RM come to mind
   "Different ideas come to mind in a situation like this."
134. RM come to someone's ears
   "The thought of doing things differently came to my ears in

a very curious fashion."

135. soak up RM

"You should see him soak up ideas!"

136. stuff someone/someone's head with/full of RM

"That have already stuffed his head full of radical ideas."

137. cram (RM)

"I'm cramming history tonight for tomorrow's exam."

"Cramming most of the major ideas of organic in a single night is impossible."

"I'm sorry, but I have to cram this afternoon."

138. shove RM into someone/someone's head

"I've shoved so many ideas into my head today I'm dizzy."

139. RM go over someone's head

"Of course, my ideas went right over his head."

140. RM go right past someone

"It seems like the argument went right past him."

141. RM fall on deaf ears

"Her unhappy feelings fell on deaf ears."

Part Two: Other metalingual resources

Many of the expressions below can be used with common adjuncts to form statements that support the conduit metaphor. Thus, it is only when they are used without these adjuncts that they can be thought of as alternatives. To make this apparent, I shall present starred examples which show how easily the neutrality of these expressions can be lost. There are also expressions which appear to involve the conduit metaphor in one reading, but not in another. These I shall flag with a question mark.

I.   Alternatives to Categories IA, IB, and IE of the Conduit Metaphor: Expressions which do not imply that language functions like a conduit, or that speaking and writing are acts of insertion into the words or ejection into an external space.

1. speak of/about RM (to someone) (NLI s)

"Please speak to me more clearly about your feelings."

(NLI stands for any *non-locative instrumental*, such as "with," "by means of," etc. To be ruled out here are the *locative instrumentals*, "through words," and "in words," which signal the conduit metaphor.)

"Speak to me of your feelings using simpler words."

*"Speak to me of your feelings in simpler words."

2. talk of/about RM (to someone) (NLI s)
   "Mary talked about her new ideas."
   "Harry talked about his ideas using very complex sentences."
   *"Harvey talked about his ideas through very complex sentences."
3. write of/about RM (to someone) (NLI s)
   "John can write of his feelings with real clarity."
   *"Try to write about your feelings in simpler words."
4. state RM (to someone) (NLI s)
   "State your thoughts plainly."
   *"State your thoughts in other words, please."
?5. communicate (of/about) RM (to someone) (NLI s)
   "Is that the feeling you are trying to communicate?"
   *"Why not communicate this thought in the next paragraph?"
6. tell someone of/about RM (NLI s)
   "John told you about those ideas yesterday."
   *"Mary told me about her sorrow in graphic sentences."
7. inform someone of/about RM (NLI s)
   "I informed them of my changing ideas."
   *"Did you inform him of your feelings through words he could understand?"
8. mention RM (to someone) (NLI s)
   "You should never have mentioned the idea to Harry."
   "When I mentioned the thoughts to John, I used the same words I used with you."
   *"When I mentioned the thoughts to John, I did it in the same words I used with you."
9. express RM (to someone) (NLI s)
   "I cannot express these feelings accurately."
   *"Perhaps you should express your concepts through other words."
10. report RM (to someone) (NLI s)
    "You can report your ideas using layman's language."
    *"Report your feelings in different words."
?11. describe RM (to/for someone) (NLI s)
    "Describe those concepts for me again."
    *"Rich described his feelings in beautiful words."
?12. sketch RM (for someone) (NLI s)
    "We only have time to sketch the ideas right now."

*"When you sketch a thought, don't do it in such complicated sentences."

?13. impart RM (to someone) (NLI s)

"It's difficult to impart ideas to a class like this."

*"I'll have to impart the idea in different words."

14. give notice of RM (to someone) (NLI s)

"What she gave notice of was her feeling of isolation."

*"You gave notice of your attitude in words you should not have used."

15. make RM known (to someone) (NLI s)

"When did you make your idea known to her?"

*"You may have tried to make your anger known to them, but you did it in words that were bound to fail."

16. advise someone of/about RM (NLI s)

"Did you advise them about your feelings?"

*"You certainly advised him of your ideas in the right phrases."

17. apprise someone of/about RM (NLI s)

"Mary did not apprise John of her thoughts."

*"John apprised the repairman of his feeling through the simplest of words."

?18. acquaint someone with RM (NLI s)

"I acquainted them with your feelings."

*"You cannot acquaint him with the idea in those words."

19. enlighten someone about RM (NLI s)

"How will you enlighten Mary about your thoughts?"

*"If you enlighten them about the concept in those words, he may never speak to you again."

?20. disclose RM (to someone) (NLI s)

"When you get ready to disclose the ideas, let me know."

*"I would disclose the thoughts first in German, and only later in English."

21. notify someone of/about RM (NLI s)

"Have you notified anyone of these new feelings?"

*"Notify your readers of this idea immediately in the first paragraph."

22. announce RM (to someone) (NLI s)

"You should not announce these attitudes to the group.'

*"You certainly could announce these ideas in different words."

23. bring news of RM (to someone)

"Henry brought news of Jeri's ideas."

24. bring tidings of/about RM (to someone)

"Someone should bring tidings of these thoughts to the world at large."

25. give account of RM (to someone) (NLI s)

"He could not give a clear account of Einstein's ideas."

(Starred examples exist for any core expression with the NLI s adjunct. But since the format of these should be clear by now, I shall cease to provide such examples at this point.)

26. discuss RM (with someone) (NLI s)

"I have never discussed my thoughts with John."

27. converse about RM (with someone) (NLI s)

"You should learn to converse intelligently about your feelings."

28. exchange words about RM (with someone)

"John and I exchanged words about our feelings."

29. have verbal interchange about RM (with someone)

"The class had several verbal interchanges about the new concepts."

?30. publish RM (NLI s)

"When are you going to publish your ideas?"

?31. make RM public (NLI s)

"John does not know how to make his attitudes public."

?32. disseminate RM (NLI s)

"How can we disseminate such ideas?"

II. Alternatives to Categories IC and IF of the Conduit Metaphor: Expressions which do not imply that words contain or convey meanings, or that ideas exist independent of human beings in an abstract "space."

33. s symbolize RM

"Words symbolize meanings."

"Gestures can symbolize various emotions."

34. s correspond to RM

"The sentence corresponds to my thoughts."

35. s stand for RM

"Sentences stand for human thoughts."

?36. s represent RM

"Language represents our thoughts and feelings."

?37. s mean/have meanings (to someone)

"I hope my words mean something to you."

(It appears that we make up for the poverty of this category by reusing many Category I expressions with s words, as opposed to humans, as subjects. Thus, "John's words tell us of his ideas," or "This sentence states your thoughts plainly." Whether this personification of the signals is linked to the conduit metaphor or not, I have not yet determined. The conduit metaphor does view words as containing ideas just as humans do, however, which could provide motivation for the transfer. That is, the signals could be "giving us the ideas they contain," just as, in speaking, humans "give us the ideas they contain." This question will have to await deeper analysis.)

III. Alternatives to Categories ID and IG of the Conduit Metaphor: Expressions which do not imply that reading and listening are acts of extraction, or that reified ideas reenter human heads from an abstract "space."

38. understand s/RM – but not *understand RM in s
"I have some trouble understanding the sentence."
"I can rarely understand his thoughts."
*"I have never understood the meaning in that essay."

39. comprehend s/RM – but not *comprehend RM in s
"Have you comprehended the sentence?"
"She does not comprehend my thoughts."
*"John comprehends few of the thoughts in Mary's paper."

?40. grasp s – but not *grasp RM or *grasp RM in s
"I have not yet grasped the sentence."
*"I have had little time to grasp his thoughts, especially the meaning in the last chapter."

41. construct a reading for s
"It is easy to construct a reading for that sentence."

42. build a reading for s
"How do you build readings for sentences like that?"

?43. get reading for s
"How did you get that reading for that phrase?"

?44. interpret s
"I find it hard to interpret his paragraphs."

45. follow s
"I could follow his sentences easily."

Metaphor, Induction, and Social Policy: The Convergence of Macroscopic and Microscopic Views

ROBERT J. STERNBERG, ROGER TOURANGEAU, AND GEORGIA NIGRO

Metaphor can be studied in many different ways and at many different levels, any one of which may lead to valid insights into the nature of metaphoric generation, comprehension, and appreciation. The insights of any one approach to metaphor are perhaps most convincingly validated when they converge with the insights of a distinctly different approach, leading the student of metaphor to much the same conclusions, without regard to the particular method from which the conclusions derived.

In his lucid and enlightening analysis of generative metaphor, Schön has reached conclusions strikingly similar in many ways to those we have reached in our analyses of metaphor and induction. As anyone might expect, where two independent research programs are involved, there are a number of theoretical issues that are addressed by one of the research programs but not by the other. However, in the central core of overlapping issues, there is clear convergence in the conclusions we have independently drawn. In this chapter we should like to point out and discuss the sources of convergence.

What follows is divided into three sections. In order to relate our work to Schön's, it is necessary in the first section to say something about the motivation, approach, theory, and methods that underlie the work in our laboratory on metaphor and induction. These underpinnings of our research differ in many respects from Schön's. Then, it is possible in the second section to draw parallels between our conclusions and those of Schön regarding metaphor, induction, and social policy. In the third section, we restate five basic questions about metaphor posed by Verbrugge and McCarrell (1977) and by Schön, and discuss how they are answered, or at least addressed, within our view of metaphor.

Metaphor and induction

This section is divided into three parts. In the first two, we describe two different lines of research that address the relationship between metaphor and induction in somewhat different ways. In the third part, we discuss how the theoretical points of view from the two lines of research can be integrated.

Theory of representation

We shall start by discussing a theory of representation in metaphor.[1] The discussion deals with four topics, namely, the motivation, approach, theory, and methods underlying this work.

The basic goals motivating the research are, first, to use a representation for information in semantic memory that is flexible enough to handle metaphors in a variety of domains; second, to propose a small set of rules that account for the differential aesthetic appeal and comprehensibility of metaphors; and third, to relate the representations – and the set of rules operating upon the representations – to their counterparts in a fairly general theory of induction.

Our approach to these problems is in many respects an outgrowth of research on analogical reasoning done by Rumelhart and Abrahamson (1973).[2] These investigators began with the assumption that information can be represented by means of a multidimensional "semantic space" in which each dimension represents some graded characteristic of the set of concepts under consideration. Some limited support for this assumption had been obtained earlier by Henley (1969) in her study of the semantics of animal names. Henley had subjects rate the dissimilarities between all possible pairs of thirty animal names, and then used a multidimensional scaling program to derive a three-dimensional solution that seemed to represent these terms adequately. The three dimensions of the space (in order of appearance and therefore "strength" in the solution) were size, ferocity, and humanness. Animals like *giraffe* and *elephant* were near one extreme on the size dimension, whereas animals like *mouse* and *rabbit* were near the other extreme. The ferocity dimension contrasted animals like *tiger* and *gorilla* with those like *pig* and *cow,* and the humanness dimension contrasted animals like *monkey* and *gorilla* with those like *cow* and *mouse.*

According to Rumelhart and Abrahamson, each term of an analogy problem can be represented by a point in this three-dimensional space. For any analogy problem of the form $A:B::C:?$, there is a concept, I, that is the ideal solution to the analogy in the sense that the vector distance from C to I is the same as that from A to B. The probability of choosing any answer option, X_i, as the best solution to the problem is a monotonic decreasing function of the distance between the locations in the space of I and X_i. Consider, for example, the analogy RAT: PIG::GOAT_____; (A) CHIMPANZEE, (B) COW, (C) RABBIT, (D) SHEEP. There is no animal among these options, or in the semantic space, for that matter, that falls exactly where an ideal solution should. But the animal closest in the space to this hypothetical ideal animal is *cow*, followed by *sheep*, then *rabbit*, and then *chimpanzee*. So if subjects are asked to choose the best solution, the largest proportion of subjects should choose *cow*, then *sheep*, then *rabbit*, and then *chimpanzee*.

The theory of response choice was strengthened by assuming the applicability of Luce's (1959) choice axiom, and by assuming that the probability of choosing an alternative, X_i, as best is an exponentially decreasing function of the distance of that alternative from the ideal point. Thus, a quantitative choice rule is added to supplement the qualitative specification of rank order. With a little bit of mathematics, one can extend the quantitative predictions to all rank orderings, so that if subjects are asked not only to select the best option, but to rank order all the options as well, it is possible to predict the proportion of subjects assigning each rank ordering to each option.

Rumelhart and Abrahamson tested their theory in three ingenious experiments, of which only the first will be briefly summarized here. They asked thirty-five subjects to solve thirty animal-name analogies, rank ordering the options for goodness of fit. The authors then estimated a single parameter for the exponential function, and tested the ability of the mathematical model to account for the response-choice data. In fact, the model provided an excellent fit to the data, suggesting that subjects were indeed following a rank-ordering strategy similar to that proposed by the theory.

We have suspected that a common set of processes and strategies underlie performance on a variety of induction tasks (see, for example, Chapter 13 of Sternberg, 1977b), and so it seemed possible that the same choice rule could be applied to other induction tasks as well. This possibility was investigated experimentally (see Sternberg & Gardner, 1978). Sternberg and Gardner administered thirty animal-name analogies, thirty animal-name series completions, and thirty animal-name classifications to thirty students from the Yale community. The analogies were those from Experiment 1 of Rumelhart and Abrahamson (1973). The series problems took the form exemplified by the problem, RABBIT:DEER:_____; (A) ANTELOPE, (B) BEAVER, (C) TIGER, (D) ZEBRA. Subjects were asked to rank order the options in terms of how well they completed a series from the first term to the second and from the second term to the third. The classification problems took the form exemplified by the problem MOUSE, CHIMPANZEE, CHIPMUNK,_____;

(A) GORILLA, (B) RAT, (C) SQUIRREL, (D) ZEBRA. Subjects were asked to rank order the options in terms of how well they fit in with the three terms preceding the options.

It was hypothesized that in each of the three tasks, subjects would employ a different strategy that was nevertheless aimed at a common goal: the discovery of an ideal point. The strategies can be conceptualized geometrically in terms of the "construction of vectors." In the analogies task, subjects would construct a vector from the first term to the second, and then attempt to construct a vector from the third term to an ideal point such that the new vector was parallel to the first vector and equal to it in length and direction. In the series-completion task, subjects would construct a vector from the first term to the second, and then construct a vector from the second term to an ideal point such that the new vector was collinear with the first vector and equal to it in length and direction. In the classification task, subjects would construct a vector from the first term to the second, another vector from the first term to the third, and then use the centroid of the triangle formed by these vectors as an ideal point. Thus, although the proposed strategies required to arrive at an ideal point differed across the three types of tasks, it was hypothesized that subjects would indeed construct an ideal point in each task, and that the rule by which the subjects rank ordered responses (by relating them to the ideal point) would be the same in each task.

A single exponential parameter was estimated from the response-choice data for each task, and the values from the three estimations were remarkably similar. Moreover, the identical mathematical model provided an excellent fit to the data in each of the three tasks. Apparently, then, Rumelhart and Abrahamson's extension of Luce's choice axiom to the analogies task can itself be extended to other forms of induction tasks as well.

We have viewed metaphoric comprehension and appreciation as inductive in nature, because these global processes seem to involve, at bare minimum, induction of the relationship (s) between the tenor and vehicle of the metaphor. It therefore seems plausible that an approach similar to that employed in the animal-name induction study might be useful in investigating metaphor. Certain problems need to be dealt with, however. First, although the multidimensional scaling paradigm might work well enough in well-delineated semantic fields such as animal names, it seemed less likely to work well, or at least to yield comparable dimensions, across a variety of semantic domains. Second, it seemed necessary to us to generalize the notion of semantic space by introducing a concept of "orders" of spaces in order to accommodate our theory of metaphoric comprehension and appreciation. These orders represent the level of abstraction of the terms in the various spaces. It is to this theory that we now turn.

Imagine an array of "local subspaces" comprising sets of terms, such as U.S. historical figures, modern world leaders, mammals, birds, fish, airplanes, land vehicles, and ships. Each local subspace represents the terms within it as points with coordinates on each of several dimensions. Each of these local subspaces might also be viewed as of roughly the same order (level of abstraction), and as of a lower order than a higher-order hyperspace that contains the lower-order subspaces as points embedded within it. Thus, the points of the higher-order hyperspace map into the lower order subspaces, and can be labeled by the names of these subspaces. This hyperspace can, in turn, be viewed as one of multiple subspaces of some still higher-order hyperspace. However, possible hyperspaces of successively higher orders will not concern us here; we shall need to deal only with local subspaces of a lower order and one hyperspace of a higher order.[3]

We shall also need some rule for restricting the subspaces that map into a single hyperspace, and some way of establishing comparability across subspaces. Both of these goals can be accomplished by requiring all subspaces to have at least one corresponding dimension. [4] Thus, for example, the subspaces of modern world leaders, bird names, and ships must have at least one corresponding dimension if they are to be local subspaces of the same order and of a common hyperspace.

The conventional multidimensional scaling paradigm of requiring, say, dissimilarity ratings between all possible pairs of elements within each of these domains does not seem likely to fill the bill. Viewed in isolation, the domains simply do not seem to bear much resemblance to each other. One possible solution to this problem would be to have subjects rate dissimilarities between all possible pairs of objects both within and between domains, although this procedure quickly becomes impractical with large numbers of objects; moreover, the theoretical status of the cross-domain ratings would have to be thought out. We have followed another alternative, drawing upon the success of Osgood, Suci, and Tannenbaum (1957) and others in achieving uniform dimensions across domains, using the device of the *semantic differential*.

Subjects were asked to rate each of twenty terms within each domain on twenty-one scales, such as *warlike – peaceful, noble – ignoble,* and *strong – weak,* with a different group of sixteen subjects supplying ratings for each of the eight domains. We hoped in this way to obtain a corresponding set of dimensions for the eight domains (U.S. historical figures, modern world leaders, mammals, birds, fish, airplanes, land vehicles, ships). It seemed plausible to us that at least two such corresponding dimensions would obtain: prestige (similar to Osgood et al.'s "evaluative" dimension) and aggression (similar to Osgood et al.'s "potency" or "activity" dimensions). The adjective pairs for each domain were then factor-analyzed.[5]

Visual inspection of the results of the factor analyses supported our hypothesis: Two corresponding dimensions of prestige and aggression appeared for each domain, although the order in which the two dimensions appeared was variable across domains. In order to confirm our visual impression, we computed correlations between the loadings of the adjective pairs on dimensions we believed either to correspond, or not to correspond, across domains. Correlations for corresponding dimensions (prestige in each of two domains or aggression in each of two domains) were very high, and correlations for noncorresponding dimensions (prestige in one domain and aggression in the other) were very low, suggesting that the dimensions did indeed have the statistical properties our visual inspection had suggested they had.

A separate group of thirty subjects rated the eight domain names on each of the twenty-one adjective scales, and these results were also factor analyzed, giving us a three-factor hyperspace with each factor roughly representing a type of content (types of people, types of animals, types of vehicles). The results from this and the preceding factor analyses served as the representational basis for our further theoretical work.

Given our representational framework, what rules might identify metaphors that are either easily comprehensible or aesthetically pleasing? It seems that two basic considerations need to be taken into account in assessing the comprehensibility and aesthetic quality of a metaphor: the superimposed within-subspace distance between the tenor (first term) of the metaphor and the vehicle (second term), and the between-subspace distance.

Consider first the meaning of "superimposed within-subspace distance." Since at least two dimensions are corresponding (or at least, very similar) for each domain, one can imagine superimposing the dimensions of one local subspace onto the corresponding dimensions of another local subspace. Once this superimposition is accomplished, it is also possible to imagine computing the superimposed within-subspace distance between two points that are actually in different subspaces. One simply computes the distance between points as though they were in the same subspace. Thus, if the coordinates of some point in one subspace were (x, y), then the superimposed within-subspace distance to some point in another subspace would be o if that point also happened to occupy location (x, y), and would depart from o as the Euclidean distance of that point from (x, y) increased.

An example may help clarify the concept. The superimposed within-subspace distance from *wildcat* to *hawk* is very small, because the coordinates of *hawk* in the bird subspace are very close to those of *wildcat* in the mammal subspace. The superimposed within-subspace distance from *wildcat* to *robin* is quite large, however, because the coordinates of *wildcat* and *robin* are quite disparate. Similarly, the superimposed within-subspace distance from *wildcat* to *ICBM* is small, whereas the superimposed within-subspace distance from *wildcat* to *blimp* is large.

Consider next the meaning of "between-subspace" distance. In order for the concept to have meaning, it must be possible somehow to compute the distance between a pair of subspaces. This computation is possible, in our representational formulation, because the distance between two subspaces is equal to the distance between the corresponding points within the appropriate hyperspace. Thus, if the coordinates of some local subspace in the hyperspace are (x, y), the distance from that subspace to another subspace increases as the Euclidean distance of that subspace from (x, y) increases.

Let us return to our earlier example to illustrate the concept of between-subspace distance. The between-subspace distance from *wildcat* to *hawk* is the same as that from *wildcat* to *robin*, since both *hawk* and *robin* are in the same local subspace. This distance is small, since mammal and bird names are viewed as relatively close to one another in the hyperspace. The between-subspace distances from *wildcat* to *ICBM* and *blimp* are also the same, since these latter two terms fall within the same local subspace; and this distance is relatively large, since mammal names and names of airplanes are viewed as relatively far from one another in the hyperspace.

Turning now to the theory of metaphor, we propose that *a metaphor is comprehensible to the extent that both the superimposed within-subspace distance and the between-subspace distance between tenor and vehicle are small. A metaphor is aesthetically pleasing to the extent that the superimposed within-subspace distance is small, but the between-subspace distance is large.* Thus, a smaller superimposed within-subspace distance between tenor and vehicle works in favor both of comprehensibility and aesthetic pleasingness, whereas a smaller between-subspace distance works in favor of comprehensibility, but against aesthetic pleasingness.

Consider some example metaphors derived from the terms discussed above:

(1) A wildcat is a hawk among mammals
(2) A wildcat is a robin among mammals
(3) A wildcat is an ICBM among mammals
(4) A wildcat is a blimp among mammals.

What empirical claims does the proposed theory make about each of these metaphors?

A first set of empirical claims addresses the relative comprehensibility of the various metaphors. According to the theory, (1) should be a highly comprehensible metaphor, because both the superimposed within-subspace distance and the between-subspace distance between tenor and vehicle are small. Metaphor (4), on the other hand, should be only poorly comprehensible, because both distances are large. Thus, whereas it is easy to discern relations between a wildcat and a hawk, it is difficult to discern relations between a wildcat and a blimp. Metaphors (2) and (3) should be intermediate in comprehensibility, because in each case, one distance is small but the other is large. *Wildcat* and *robin* occupy locations that are remote with respect to each other in their respective subspaces, but they are located in subspaces that are relatively close to one another (as measured by distance within the hyperspace). Conversely, *wildcat* and *ICBM* occupy locations in their respective subspaces that are quite close to one another, but they are located in subspaces that are relatively remote from one another. The qualitative assumptions of the theory do not distinguish between the comprehensibility of (2) and (3), although the experiments described below will enable us to assign quantitative weights to the use of superimposed within-subspace distance and between-subspace distance in judgments of metaphoric comprehensibility. Our strong expectation is that the former distance will carry a larger weight than the latter one – that larger superimposed within-subspace distance is more destructive to the comprehensibility of a metaphor than is larger between-subspace distance. If this expectation proves to be correct, then (3) will be judged as more comprehensible than (2). To summarize, the metaphors as ordered from most comprehensible to least comprehensible are (1), (3), (2), (4).

A second set of empirical claims address the relative aesthetic pleasingness (or quality) of the various metaphors. According to the theory,

(3) should be the metaphor of highest quality, since although *wildcat* and *ICBM* are quite close to one another in terms of superimposed within-subspace distance, they are from distant local subspaces. Metaphor (2) should be lowest in quality, because the tenor and vehicle occupy discrepant positions in their respective subspaces, and are from proximal subspaces. Metaphors (1) and (4) should be intermediate in quality. Again, we expect superimposed within-subspace distance to carry more weight than between-subspace distance. Hence, we expect metaphor (1) to be perceived as higher in aesthetic quality than metaphor (4), since the greater superimposed within-subspace distance should be more destructive to the quality of the metaphor than the lesser between-subspace distance. To summarize, the metaphors as ordered from most to least aesthetically pleasing are (3), (1), (4), (2).

Although the theory that we are advancing may well not apply to all metaphors of all kinds, we do believe that it is fairly general and applicable to metaphors whose tenors and vehicles may not be from obvious semantic subspaces (like those for mammals or modern world leaders). Donne's famous metaphor (or conceit) linking lovers to stiff twin compasses, for example, is not readily comprehensible, according to our theory, because although the superimposed within-subspace distance between lovers and stiff twin compasses is small (at least within the context of "A Valediction: Forbidding Mourning"), the between-subspace distance is large. But it is precisely this pair of properties that renders the metaphor so aesthetically pleasing and, ultimately, so memorable. "The moon is a ghostly galleon" has also survived (perhaps too long!) because although one does not usually link heavenly bodies to ships at sea (large between-subspace distance), one can easily visualize an eerie orb sailing through the sky, impervious to the demands made upon ordinary sailing vessels.

At the opposite end of the spectrum, the theory can also explain why some statements are utter failures as metaphors. A literal statement or definition such as, "An ICBM is an intercontinental ballistic missile," fails as a metaphor because although *ICBM* and *intercontinental ballistic missile* occupy identical locations within their respective local subspaces (and hence the superimposed within-subspace distance is 0), the subspaces are identical (and hence the between-subspace distance is also 0), so that whereas satisfaction of one criterion for a good metaphor is maximized, satisfaction of the other criterion is minimized. An anomalous statement equating two seemingly unrelated concepts, such as, "An ICBM is a haystack," fails as a metaphor because although

ICBM and *haystack* come from subspaces that presumably are quite distant from one another, their locations in these subspaces are quite discrepant.

Our theory may require supplementation in order fully to account for either the comprehensibility or aesthetic quality of certain metaphors. For example, we are attracted to Ortony's notion (see Ortony, 1979, and this volume) that good metaphors tend to be those in which salient properties of the vehicle are linked to nonsalient properties of the tenor. In our representational framework, the relative salience of a property is a function of the relative order in which that property emerges as a dimension. In a standard principal component or factor solution, factors are ordered in terms of their relative strength in accounting for variation in the data. Stronger (more salient) dimensions appear earlier.

It would be possible to supplement our proposed theory (although we have not yet done so) with weights that take into account the possible interaction between the order in which a dimension appears and its role in the metaphor. Dimensions establishing the principal correspondence between tenor and vehicle (that is, the earliest corresponding dimensions) would be weighted as contributing to the goodness of the metaphor if they were both early dimensions of the vehicle and later dimensions of the tenor; dimensions would be weighted as contributing to the badness of the metaphor if they were both early dimensions of the tenor and later dimensions of the vehicle. An aesthetically pleasing metaphor, then, would be one in which the principal correspondence is between an earlier dimension of the vehicle and a later dimension of the tenor.

It should be pointed out that our theory is only one of a class of theories that may be derived from the general representational framework that we have proposed. One could imagine alternative theories in which either superimposed within-subspace distance or between-subspace distance are weighted zero, or in which predictions about which way these distances should go are either opposite or orthogonal to our own predictions. An appealing alternative to our hypothesis regarding the relation between between-subspace distance and aesthetic quality of a metaphor has been suggested by Michael Gardner. His suggestion is that the function is curvilinear rather than linear: The best metaphors are ones in which the between-subspace distance is moderate. If the distance is too small, the connection appears to be trivial, but if the distance is too large, the connection appears to be remote; or possibly, after a certain point, the dimensions cease to match up at all. One might imagine a rubber band stretched further and further, until it snaps: Beyond a certain distance, the metaphor simply cannot withstand the strain. To summarize, the representational framework is flexible enough to accommodate a variety of rules for operating upon that framework, but is not so flexible as to be vacuous: It does make empirical claims as to what kinds of distances should affect the comprehensibility and quality of a metaphor.

We are conducting two experiments designed to test some of the empirical claims and implications of the theory we have described (Tourangeau and Sternberg, 1978). Each of the experiments looks at the theory in a slightly different way.

In the first experiment, subjects are presented with sixty-four metaphors, such as, "A wildcat is a hawk among mammals," and are asked to rate, among other things, the aesthetic quality or comprehensibility of each metaphor. The basic independent variables for predicting these two dependent variables (via multiple regression) are superimposed within-subspace distance and between-subspace distance. Other variables, such as the dimensional salience variable mentioned earlier, may also be considered if the initial two appear to need supplementation. Each subject also received two ability tests, one measuring skill in verbal analogical reasoning (e.g., PATIENT:CLIENT::_____; (A) SURGEON:ACTOR, (B) HOSPITAL:PENITENTIARY, (C) DOCTOR:LAWYER, (D) TUBERCULOSIS:FELONY) and the other measuring skill in judging the quality of poetry (Rigg, 1937). Subjects are presented with two passages of poetry, one by a famous poet, the other (doggerel) by the author of the test, and are asked to select the better verse. We plan to use the tests to determine whether individual differences in measured verbal abilities are predictive of differences in parameters of the model (i.e., differential weights assigned by individual subjects to the superimposed within-subspace distance and the between-subspace distance).

In the second experiment, subjects are divided into two groups, each of which receives one of two types of items. In both groups, subjects receive a metaphor in which a tenor is supplied, but the vehicle is missing. Subjects in one group are offered four alternative vehicle completions, all from the same local subspace. The subjects' task is to rank order these completions in terms of their aesthetic quality. Subjects in the other group are also offered four alternative vehicle completions; the completions are each from a different local subspace, but they are approximately matched in terms of their locations within their local subspaces. Thus, the alternatives in the items presented to the first group are at an approximately constant between-subspace distance from the tenor, but at a variable superimposed within-subspace distance; the alternatives in the items presented to the second group are at an approximately constant superimposed within-subspace distance from the tenor, but at a variable between-subspace distance. The theory makes clear qualitative predictions regarding the rank orders subjects should give for each type of item: Lower ranks (signifying better metaphors) should be assigned to completions that minimize superimposed within-subspace distance and maximize between-subspace distance. In these studies, it is possible to supplement the qualitative predictions with quantitative predictions as well. By extending the Rumelhart-Abrahamson adaptation of Luce's choice axiom to the present situation, we hope to predict the proportion of subjects who should assign each ranking to each option. If this application of the choice axiom is successful, then it will appear that the same decision rule that is used in a variety of induction tasks (analogies, series completions, and classifications) is used in the metaphor task as well. Indeed, metaphoric comprehension and evaluation might then be viewed as inductive processes in much the same way that analogical, serial, and classificational reasoning are. The induction can proceed either from tenor to vehicle or from vehicle to tenor. Thus, the second experiment might equally have been conducted (and further research will be conducted) in such a way that the tenor rather than the vehicle is missing. Such a study, in addition to testing the generalizability of the theory from both ends of the metaphor, would enable one to investigate Ortony's (1979) hypotheses regarding asymmetry in metaphor.

Theory of information processing

The theory of representation that we have described addresses itself to the form in which information is represented, and to rules that act upon that form of representation. It does not, however, specify an information-processing model for metaphoric comprehension and appreciation. In this part of the paper,[6] we discuss a theory of information processing in metaphor. This discussion, like the preceding one, deals with four topics; namely, the motivation, approach, theory, and methods underlying our work.

The basic goals motivating our research parallel those in the research on representation. These goals are, first, to construct a theory of information processing that is flexible enough to handle metaphors in a variety of domains; second, to propose a small set of processes that account for time to comprehend and evaluate metaphors, in conjunction with rules that explain why some metaphors are more easily comprehended, or more highly regarded, than others; and, third, to relate the information processes to their counterparts in a fairly general theory of induction.

Our approach to the problems listed above is in many respects an outgrowth of earlier research on analogical reasoning (Sternberg, 1977a, 1977b). Thus, the approach to information processing, like the one to representation, began with a theory of analogical reasoning, although the two theories of analogical reasoning (Rumelhart and Abrahamson's, and Sternberg's) deal with virtually nonoverlapping theoretical issues.

According to the "componential" theory of analogical reasoning, solution of analogies of the form $A:B::C:D_1 \ldots D_k$ is accomplished through the execution of up to six component processes. Consider, as an example, the analogy,

WASHINGTON : ONE : : LINCOLN : _____; (A) TEN, (B) FIVE.

An individual solving this analogy must *encode* the terms of the problem, identifying the terms and retrieving from long-term memory the attributes and values that may be relevant for analogy solution. The individual must also *infer* the relation between the first two analogy terms, ascertaining what it is that *"Washington"* and *"one"* have in common (e.g., that Washington was the first president, or that Washington's is the portrait on a one-dollar bill). Next, the individual must *map* the relation from the first term to the third, recognizing what it is that links the *domain* (or first half) of the analogy, which is about Washington, and the *range* (or second half) of the analogy, which is about Lincoln. Then the individual must *apply* the inferred relation as mapped to the range of the analogy from the third analogy term to each answer option, determining which option bears the same relation to *Lincoln* that *one* does to *Washington*. Optionally, the individual may need to *justify* one of the options as preferred, but nonideal. The individual may find, for example, that neither option meets his or her criterion for an acceptable response, and therefore may need to check previous operations to determine whether there were any errors of omission or commission. An example of an error of omission would be one in which the individual inferred the ordinal position of Washington's presidency, but failed to infer that Washington's is the portrait on a one-dollar bill. An example of an error of commission would be one in which the individual believed that Lincoln's is the portrait on a two- rather than a five-dollar bill, and thus failed in application. Finally, the subject must *respond*, communicating his or her answer choice.

This theory was tested in a series of three experiments, using schematic-picture, verbal, and geometric analogies (see Sternberg, 1977b). Subjects were asked to solve analogies of varying difficulty and content under various experimental conditions that permitted isolation of the hypothesized component processes. The results of the experiments lent strong support to the theory, suggesting that response times to analogies of various types can be viewed as the sum of the times spent on each of the component processes specified by the componential theory of analogical reasoning.

It seemed plausible that this information-processing theory of analogical reasoning, like the Rumelhart-Abrahamson theory of representation and response choice, could be extended to other induction tasks as well. So in a series of nine experiments, the generalizability of the theory has been tested on analogies, series completions, and classifications with schematic-picture, verbal, and geometric content (Sternberg, 1978). A typical classification problem took the form:

(A) N.J., N.Y.   (B) N.C., S.C.
PA.

The subject's task was to determine whether the target item, here, *Pa.*, belonged more appropriately in category A or in category B. According to the componential theory of induction, the individual must encode the terms of the problem, infer the relation between *N.J.*, and *N.Y.*, infer the relation between *N.C.* and *S.C.*, map the differences that distinguish between the two categories, apply this relation to *Pa.* to determine in which category *Pa.* belongs, optionally, justify one of the categories as preferred, and then respond. A typical series completion problem took the form:

LOUIS XIII: LOUIS XIV: LOUIS XV

TRUMAN: (A) EISENHOWER, (B) ROBESPIERRE.

The subject's task was to determine which of the answer options should follow the last term, here, *Truman*, in the series. Subjects must recognize the relation of succession for the French kings, and then use this relation of succession for American presidents. According to the theory, the individual must encode the terms of the problem, infer the relation between *Louis XIII* and *Louis XIV*, infer the relation between *Louis XIV* and *Louis XV* (using only those attributes that are still deemed revelant after the first inference between *Louis XIII* and *Louis XIV*), map the relation from *Louis XV* to *Truman*, apply the inferred relation as mapped to the range of the problem from *Truman* to each answer option, optionally, justify one of the answer options as preferred, and finally, respond. To summarize, the same component process seem to be involved in the solution of each of the three kinds of induction problems. Are these same processes involved in metaphoric understanding and appreciation? The information-processing theory about to be described suggests that they are.

We propose that the componential theory of induction can be extended to the comprehension and evaluation of metaphors (Sternberg and Nigro, 1978). What are the processes involved in comprehending and evaluating metaphors? Consider the metaphor, "Bees in a hive are a Roman mob (a) in the streets, (b) in the coliseum." The individual faced with a choice between the two completions must encode the terms of the metaphor, infer the relation between *bees* and *hive*, map the relation between *bees* and *a Roman mob*, and apply the inferred relation from *a Roman mob* to *in the streets* and *in the coliseum*.[7] Presumably, the individual will choose the latter as the preferred completion because a coliseum encloses a multitude in a way somewhat analogous to the way a hive encloses a multitude. Neither completion seems ideal, however, so that the individual may spend some time justifying *in the coliseum* as preferred but nonideal. Finally, the individual responds. Thus, the metaphor considered here is analogical in nature, and seems to require the same processes to comprehend it as does an analogy.

Not all metaphors are stated in analogical form. For example, the metaphor "My head is an apple without a core" is missing a term. The individual attempting to comprehend the metaphor must infer the relation between *apple* and *core*, map from *apple* to *head*, and then apply the previously inferred relation to *head*, completing the metaphor with the missing *brains* (or some such). In this metaphor, comprehension requires insertion rather than selection of a missing term. Consider four variants of the "bees and Romans" metaphor:

(5) Bees in a hive are a Roman mob in the coliseum
(6) Bees in a hive are a Roman mob
(7) Bees are a Roman mob in the coliseum
(8) Bees are a Roman mob.

In the first metaphor, all terms are supplied. In the second and third metaphors, one term is missing, and in the fourth metaphor, two terms are missing. What effects do the missing terms have upon the comprehensibility and aesthetic quality of the metaphor? We believe, with Miller (this volume), that when terms are deleted, the individual must insert the missing terms, attempting to place constraints upon the metaphor that render it interpretable. Deleting terms decreases the ease with which the metaphor is comprehended, because of the extra cognitive processing involved in the generation of missing terms. If the subject is unable to insert missing terms, or inserts inappropriate missing terms, comprehension may be thwarted altogether.

Deleting terms, however, is proposed to increase the aesthetic quality of the metaphor. Part of what makes a metaphor pleasing, we believe, is the insertion of the missing terms or constraints. Part of the beauty of Donne's metaphor linking lovers to stiff twin compasses, for example, seems to derive from the cognitive work required to insert the links between lovers and stiff twin compasses. In the language of the theory of representation stated earlier, this work is expended toward bridging the between-subspace distance.

Appreciation of a metaphor requires a certain amount of active participation on the part of the comprehender, which is reduced in the interpretation of literal statements (where the between-subspace distance is zero or close to it), and this active participation, we believe, cannot be separated from any beauty that may be "inherent" in the metaphor. As mentioned earlier, the perceived beauty of the metaphor may only increase with between-subspace distance up to a certain point, beyond which the metaphor may become utterly opaque. This point seems likely to differ for different individuals. The preferred distance between tenor and vehicle may be greater for highly verbal or trained individuals than for modestly verbal or trained individuals. Active participation contributes to the beauty of a metaphor only if the participation is in the bridging of between-subspace distance. Greater superimposed within-subspace distance can only destroy the beauty of a metaphor.

To summarize, the information-processing theory proposed here, like the representational theory proposed earlier, derives from a theory of analogical reasoning that was first extended to series completion and classification tasks, and then to metaphor. The proposed theory is flexible enough to accommodate a variety of types of metaphor, but not so flexible as to fail to make well-specified empirical claims. This theory, like the representational theory, is only in the earliest stage of testing, and is thus readily subject to change if the data demand it. It is to a description of two initial experimental tests of the theory that we now turn.

In a first experiment, designed to isolate the components of information processing (Sternberg and Nigro, 1978), subjects are presented with metaphors such as "Bees in a hive are a Roman mob _____ (a) in the streets, (b) in the coliseum." Subjects are asked to select the preferred completion as quickly as they can while still making a carefully reasoned choice. The metaphors are always presented in trials consisting of two parts. The second part always consists of the full metaphor. The content presented in the first part differs as a function of the experimental condition.

Each subject receives half the metaphors in each of two conditions. In the first condition, the first part of the trial consists merely of presentation of a blank field. Subjects press a button when they are ready to see the full metaphor. After they press the button, the full metaphor appears immediately, and the subjects solve it as quickly as they can.

In the second condition, the first part of the trial consists of presentation of the first half of the metaphor, for example, "bees in a hive." Again, subjects press a button when the are ready to see the full metaphor, and the metaphor appears immediately after the button is pressed. The purpose of having the two conditions is to enable us to separate component processes that otherwise would be confounded. (See Sternberg, 1977b, for the rationale of componential task decomposition.) Subjects also receive tests of verbal reasoning, including a standard analogies test, which are used to assess the extent to which individual differences in component information processing in the metaphorical reasoning task are related to individual differences in verbal – and particularly verbal analogical – reasoning ability.

In a second experiment, designed to investigate the determinants of metaphoric comprehensibility and pleasingness, subjects are presented with metaphors taking the four forms described earlier for the "bees and Romans" metaphor. Although each metaphor is presented in each of the four forms, a given subject sees a particular metaphor in only one of the four forms. Each subject receives equal numbers of metaphors in each of the four forms. The subject's task is to rate either the aesthetic quality, or the comprehensibility, of each metaphor presented. A given subject supplies only one kind of rating. Unbeknownst to the subjects, they are being timed while making their ratings. Our expectations are that (a) aesthetic quality will decrease with increasing numbers of explicitly presented terms, (b) comprehensibility will increase with increasing numbers of explicitly presented terms, and (c) time to respond will decrease with increasing numbers of explicitly presented terms, despite the slightly increased reading load, because of the reduced amount of cognitive work required, i.e., there is less need to insert missing terms.

Integration of theories of representation and information processing

The theories of representation and information processing that we have presented look at metaphoric comprehension and appreciation from distinct but complementary points of view. These points of view can be integrated. In *encoding*, the individual locates the tenor and vehicle of the metaphor in their respective local subspaces. In *inference*, the subject constrains those dimensions of the tenor that are likely to be relevant. *Mapping* is the heart of metaphoric comprehension and appreciation: The subject "computes" the superimposed within-subspace distance and the between-subspace distance between tenor and vehicle. In *application*, the subject constructs or selects a completion to the vehicle that satisfies the same constraints as those inferred for the tenor. If the subject is unable to find such a completion, then *justification* is used to construct or select the best possible, nonoptimal completion. Finally, the subject offers whatever kind of *response* is required.

The comprehensibility and quality of a metaphor can be influenced in all but the last (response) stage of metaphoric reasoning. If a term is particularly difficult to encode, then the comprehensibility and aesthetic quality of a metaphor may be reduced. Terms in remote local subspaces (i.e., in remote regions of the hyperspace), terms whose coordinates are unknown, or terms that are particularly ambiguous and thus may not have a unique set of coordinates, are all likely to be difficult to encode. Requiring insertion of a missing term during inference will generally decrease the comprehensibility of a metaphor while increasing its quality. If, however, explicit constraints are presented that are highly unusual or conceptually opaque, then comprehensibility may actually be reduced by supplying the subject with the difficult-to-process constraints. Mapping is without question the major source of variance in metaphoric comprehensibility and quality: A metaphor is highly comprehensible if both superimposed within-subspace distance and between-subspace distance are small, and highly pleasing if superimposed within-subspace distance is small but between-subspace distance is large. Requiring insertion of a missing term during application will generally reduce the comprehensibility of a metaphor while increasing its quality. Requiring selection of one of several metaphoric completions, none of which is very satisfactory, will increase the amount of justification required, and reduce the comprehensibility and quality of the metaphor. To summarize, we speculate that although comprehensibility and aesthetic quality are determined primarily by the outcome of the mapping process, each is complexly determined, as our analysis has shown.

Metaphor, induction, and social policy

In his analysis of generative metaphor, Schön attacks the problem of metaphor at a global level. Nevertheless, he points out that "with respect to the workings of the process itself, we need much better descriptions of the component activities [of] 'restructuring' and 'coordination.' " The analysis presented in the preceding section was an attempt to provide such description – an attempt to analyze at a *microscopic level* the elements of metaphor that Schön has analyzed at a *macroscopic level*. There is no one correct level of analysis: Each level of analysis is capable of providing its own unique form of enlightenment. The present section is divided into five parts in each of which we take one of Schön's macroscopic constructs and explicate it in terms of the more microscopic constructs proposed in the present theories.

Generative metaphor

Schön conceives of the central construct in his theory, generative metaphor, as the " 'carrying over' of frames or perspectives from one domain of experience to another." Not all metaphors are generative: Some merely capitalize upon already existing ways of seeing things. A generative metaphor, however, actually generates "new perceptions, explanations and inventions." The perception of the relation between tenor and vehicle creates in the perceiver a fresh way of viewing the nature of the tenor of the metaphor.

In our information-processing account of metaphor, the process most directly giving rise to what Schön calls "generative metaphor" is mapping, a term Schön himself uses. In structural terms, the perceiver sees a correspondence between a term located at a particular point in one local subspace and some other term located at the corresponding point in another local subspace. The metaphor is generative by virtue of the correspondence never having been perceived before: thus it results in a new perspective on the tenor of the metaphor.

Consider a few examples. A metaphor presented earlier, "A wildcat is an ICBM among mammals," might result in a new perception of a wildcat, one of a deadly hurling projectile whizzing in a long arc through the air, about to strike and destroy an unsuspecting victim. Schön cites another example of interest, "Man is a wolf." This metaphor may result in a new or enhanced perception of man as a fierce, untamed, destructive animal, ready to pounce in an instant upon his unsuspecting victims. The example is also of interest for the structural theory proposed earlier, because it calls attention to a new situation, one in which the tenor and vehicle of the metaphor seem, at least on the surface, to be at different levels of abstraction. In our implementation of the structural theory, *man* was at a higher level of abstraction, and thus in a higher-order space, than *wolf*. *Wolf* was an element in the local subspace of mammals, whereas *man* might have been considered as a higher-order space containing *modern world leaders* and *U.S. historical figures* as local subspaces. How does the structural theory handle metaphors constructed from terms of seemingly different levels of abstraction?

We believe that in comprehending this metaphor, the individual does not assign to every man (or woman) he or she has known the properties of a wolf. *Man* is not defined in terms of its full exten-

sional meaning, any more than "wolf" is. Rather, the individual constructs two prototypes, one for "man" and one for "wolf," that represent composites of the attributes associated with each term. Most of us
today do not have highly differentiated notions about, or diverse
acquaintances with, wolves, so that the prototype for "wolf" may be
nothing more than an already assigned point for *wolf* in a single local
subspace. (Among hunters, wolves might comprise a whole subspace of
their own.) "Man," on the other hand, is likely to be a highly differentiated concept, and the prototype may be viewed as the centroid of
the points corresponding to the salient men we know or know of. The
centroid need not be, and probably is not, an unweighted average of
coordinates. We suspect it is a weighted average, with the weights
influenced by context. In this case, "wolf" sets up a minimal context.
Thus, the dimension of aggression noted earlier may well receive a
higher weight than that of prestige. These prototypes are used as the
basis for mapping. Note that the formation of the prototype is by what
was earlier called the encoding process – that process by which the
location of a point in space (in this case, the centroid corresponding to
the prototype) is identified.

Problem setting versus problem solving

Schön believes that the major difficulties in social policy are in problem setting rather than in problem solving. The greater challenge is to
frame the purposes to be achieved rather than to select optimal means
of achieving them. He cites case-study examples in which the way the
problem was framed was largely responsible for the way in which the
problem was solved. Schön's examples reminded us of Graham Allison's
(1969) classic paper, in which Allison compared different frames in
which the Cuban missile crisis might have been viewed, each of which
suggested a different conception of the enemy (primarily the Soviet
Union) and of how to deal with it.

We think Schön is almost certainly correct in this regard. In his
words, "Problems are not given. They are constructed by human
beings in their attempts to make sense of complex and troubling situations." In terms of our proposed structural and process theories, problem-setting style can be determined by any of a number of predilec-
tions. Consider the forms individual differences in each of the component processes of metaphorical reasoning might take.

The policymaker has a number of options in encoding the available
information. First, he or she may view certain dimensions as more sali-

ent than others. For example, some individuals seem to view the aggression dimension as particularly salient, adopting a "cold war" mentality wherever possible. Second, individuals may differ in their placements of points within a particular local subspace. For example, *Brezhnev* was scaled as the most aggressive of the modern world leaders included in our sample of leaders. However, *Brezhnev*'s location in the subspace was computed as an average for the individuals supplying ratings. Some individuals might see him as less aggressive, resulting in a very different perception of him as the tenor of an implicit metaphor.

Policymakers may also differ in their inferences about the topics of their metaphors. For example, a pacifist might be viewed either as a lion or a mouse, depending upon whether the individual constructing the metaphor inserts as implicit terms "among senators" or "in the Senate" on the one hand, or "among soldiers" or "on the battlefield" on the other. Either metaphor might be acceptable, depending upon the constraining context the individual chose to insert.

Mapping can also influence the way in which problems are set. Presumably, everyone tries to match terms as closely as possible in their respective local subspaces; but there may be substantial individual differences in preferred distances between subspaces. As was noted earlier, it seems plausible that highly verbal or literate individuals might prefer larger between-subspace distances than do less verbal or literate individuals. Similarly, some individuals may have greater vision in reaching beyond the mundane metaphors that can be formed from very close local subspaces.

Policymakers may also differ in the constraints they apply to the vehicle of the metaphor. To continue with an earlier example, viewing a pacifist as a lion might mean very different things, depending upon whether the lion is viewed as being in its native jungle habitat or in the captivity of a cage at the zoo. A politician compared to a Spartan might be viewed either as a jingoist in the legislature, or as an austere individual in his personal life, depending upon whether the Spartan is viewed in the context of the battlefield or the home.

Finally, like everyone else, policymakers may differ in their tolerance of imperfection in metaphor, where imperfection is viewed in terms of the superimposed within-subspace distance between two points. Stated otherwise, policymakers may differ in their willingness to justify as valid, metaphors of varying degrees of imperfection. Gerald Ford, for example, often compared himself to Harry Truman, a comparison that seems shaky at best. It would seem that an intermediate degree of willingness to justify metaphors as acceptable would be best. Very high willingness to justify metaphors might result in outright distortion of the facts, whereas very low willingness to justify metaphors might result in tunnel vision.

Frame awareness, frame conflict, and frame restructuring

Schön argues that there are "certain pervasive, tacit generative metaphors" that govern thinking about social policy problems, and that "we ought to become critically aware of these generative metaphors, to increase the rigor and precision of our analysis of social policy problems by examining the analogies and 'disanalogies' between the familiar descriptions . . . and the actual problematic situations that confront us." Once again, we are in agreement with Schön's position. We cannot evaluate the quality of our solutions to problems without knowing what the problem is that we have set out to solve. And this problem is one of our own construction. We have structured external events, although we may not know how. In terms of the structural and process theories described above, we are only dimly aware (if that) of the structure and content of our various orders of subspaces, and of the operations we perform on them. Surely, the research of Nisbett and Wilson (1977) on our awareness of internal processes suggests minimal access to these processes. We should like to believe that although the internal representations and processes are not accessible to conscious introspection, they are accessible to the kinds of experimental analyses that we have described.

Frame conflict, according to Schön, arises when "several different stories about the same situation" are constructed; "each story is internally coherent and compelling in its own terms but different from and perhaps incompatible with all the others." Schön provides an example of frame conflict, showing how an urban slum can be viewed either as blighted and decayed or as healthy and natural. In terms of our own theories, frame conflict can arise because of different encodings of terms, different inferred constraints, different between-subspace mappings, different applied constraints, or different tolerances in justification of nonzero superimposed within-subspace distances.

Now, according to Schön, frame conflict is resolved by frame restructuring, in which "we respond to frame conflict by constructing a new problem-setting story, one in which we attempt to integrate conflicting frames by including features and relations drawn from earlier stories, yet without sacrificing internal coherence or the degree of simplicity required for action." In terms of the theories proposed earlier, there seem to be two major ways of resolving frame conflict. The first is to seek new encodings, inferences, mappings, applications, and justifications that resolve conflict by selective inattention to conflicting details. A "frame story" is created that integrates only those features of two previous stories that are consistent with each other. The second is to create new aspects of the stories that resolve inconsistencies. For example, a sly general initially compared to a fox turns out to be ruthless on the battlefield. He is then compared to a rabid fox. An insertion further describing the vehicle restructures the metaphor to render it minimally acceptable.

A domestic example of the development of a generative metaphor may help show the course of frame awareness, frame conflict, and frame restructuring. The example is one of policymaking "in the small." One of us (Sternberg) recently had to decide whether to buy a house. The major problem with the house seemed to be that its price was at the very limit of affordability; the house might therefore be difficult to maintain. This particular house happened to be located on a cul-de-sac named Wolf Tree Drive. The owners mentioned one day that a wolf tree is a tulip tree. That same day, Sternberg looked up "tulip tree" in a dictionary and found it to be a tree with pretty flowers resembling tulips. This definition resulted in the generation of a metaphor comparing the house to a tulip tree, a metaphor that was very pleasing. Sternberg then looked up "wolf tree," and found it to be "a forest tree whose size and position cause it to prevent the growth of many small and potentially more valuable trees around it by usurping their space, light, and nourishment." This definition also led to generation of a metaphor, and an unpleasant one at that: By buying the house, Sternberg and his wife were investing in a wolf tree that would restrict their ability to do a number of things in life that were important to them. Travel and family plans, for example, might have to be postponed because of the cost of the house. They became aware not only of the two frames, but of the obvious conflict between them. They resolved the conflict, eventually, with the discovery that the flowers of the tulip tree appear only very high on the tree and when the tree is fully mature. They thus concluded that after a few years had passed and their financial position had become more secure, their investment would flower! They had resolved the conflict by means of the first way of resolving frame conflict. They had ignored those aspects of the wolf tree that were inconsistent with the tulip tree. How else could they justify their decision to buy the house?

Life cycle of a generative metaphor

Schön proposes that a generative metaphor has a life cycle all its own. In the earlier stages of the life cycle, one notices or feels that A and B are similar, without being able to say similar with respect to what. Later on, one may come to be able to describe relations of elements present in a restructured perception of both *A* and *B* which account for the pre-analytic detection of similarity between *A* and *B*, that is, one can formulate an *analogy* between *A* and *B*. Later still, one may construct a general model for which a redescribed *A* and a redescribed *B* can be identified as instances.

Note that Schön, too, sees the construction of a metaphor as tantamount to the formulation of an analogy. His account of the life cycle of a metaphor is consistent in several respects with our laboratory findings regarding the "life cycle," or information-processing model of analogy solution.

First, analytic solution of analogies via attribute-by-attribute comparison does appear to be accompanied by what has been variously called holistic processing or a preliminary scan (Sternberg, 1977a, 1977b). This processing is pre-analytic in the sense that the comparison does not rely on serial, "reasoned" attribute comparisons. Thus, dual processing of both a pre-analytic and an analytic nature appears to be common to the processing of both standard analogies and generative metaphors.

Second, it has been found that in analogy solution, subjects are not only unaware of what they have mapped from the domain (first half) to the range (second half) of the analogy, but are unaware of having mapped at all! In contrast, subjects are at least marginally aware of having encoded, inferred, applied, or justified, although they are often unaware of the particular attributes they have processed. The *A* to *C* mapping in analogy solution corresponds to the *A* to *B* similarity recognition in metaphor generation referred to by Schön. In analogy solution, as in metaphor generation, one can later state the similarity relations that may have been used. Consider, for example, the analogy WASHINGTON:ONE::LINCOLN:FIVE. Subjects will have no difficulty recognizing that Washington and Lincoln are similar in a number of ways. But they will not be aware of having generated these similarities during the course of analogy solution.

Third, a subject, after reflection, may well be able to describe the two terms as special cases, in the example analogy, of presidents whose faces appear on currency. In terms of the proposed structural theory of metaphor, the subject recognizes the dimensions of similarity that overlap between local subspaces and that form the basis for mapping. The individual may even recognize the hyperspace in which the local subspaces reside. But these recognitions follow rather than precede the detection of relations that makes possible understanding of an analogy or generation of a metaphor.

Surface metaphors versus deep metaphors

Schön distinguishes between surface and deep metaphors. The surface metaphor is that contained in the explicit language of a story about some object or phenomenon. But this language may not disclose what lies beneath the story.

The deep metaphor, in this sense, is the metaphor which accounts for centrally important features of the story – which makes it understandable that certain elements of the situation are included in the story while others are omitted, that certain assumptions are taken as true although there is evidence that would appear to disconfirm them; and, especially, that the normative conclusions are found to follow so obviously from the facts. Given a problem-setting story, we must construct the deep metaphor which is generative of it.

How do people ascertain the deep metaphor that underlies one or more surface metaphors? We suspect people do so by filling in terms of an implicit analogy.

Consider, as a first example, John Dean's description of the Nixon presidency and Dean's relation to it as told in Dean's congressional testimony. Dean conveys to President Nixon his fear of a cancer on the presidency. This surface metaphor, and the story surrounding it, seem intended to suggest a deep metaphor of John Dean as cancer surgeon. Dean's first function, in many ways the most difficult of all, is the recognition that a cancer exists. His second function is to excise the cancer, operating in a way that will remove the cancer while at the same time doing minimal damage to the patient's healthy organs. His final function is to restore the patient to an appearance of good health, stitching up any incisions that may have been made and making the patient presentable to the outside world. In this account, the blemishes signifying a cancerous state reappear because the root causes of the cancer – the internal dispositions of Nixon and the (other) men who surrounded him – were beyond the cancer surgeon's control. But an alternative reading is also possible, one of John Dean as cosmetic surgeon. As cosmetic surgeon, Dean first recognizes the appearance of external blemishes, and shows no concern for the internal malignant state that may have been responsible for these blemishes. Next, Dean performs cosmetic surgery, attempting to remove the blemishes while remaining oblivious to the internal states that may have generated them. Finally, Dean restores the patient to his preblemished appearance, substituting healthy-looking skin for the now-removed blemished skin. In this account, the blemishes quickly reappear because nothing was done to correct the internal state that generated them.

Consider as a second example the case of the White House "plumbers" operating during the Nixon administration. Again, there are two alternative readings of the actions of the so-called plumbers. In the White House – sponsored reading, the plumbers were plugging leaks in the flow of information along the pipeline that conveys state secrets from one security agency (for example, the FBI) to another (for example, the CIA). Leaks in the pipeline could be disastrous to national security, and thus needed to be corrected immediately and often without much regard as to the means used to correct them. In the alternative reading, the pipeline being treated was not one between security agencies, but between informants and the press. The information traveling along this pipeline was not state secrets, but secrets damaging to Nixon's prestige and possibly his longevity as president as well. Most importantly, the proper deep metaphor was not one of plumbers plugging leaks in pipelines, but one of demolition experts blowing up the pipelines that provide information to the press and thus protect our rights under the First Amendment.

In deciding between the appropriateness of two or more alternative deep metaphors, one has to decide between the appropriateness of two or more implicit analogies. Consider the case of John Dean. The two implicit analogies are:

(1) External actions of Dean:Internal state of Dean::External actions of cancer surgeon:Internal state of cancer surgeon;

(2) External actions of Dean:Internal state of Dean::External actions of cosmetic surgeon:Internal state of cosmetic surgeon.

The two analogies are identical in their A and B terms (domains). They differ only in their C and D terms (ranges). Thus, the major difficulty in choosing between analogies is in deciding upon the preferred mapping from domain to range of the analogy. There are other difficulties, however. First, the A term of the analogy may be incompletely or incorrectly given: Dean's account of his actions may be wholly inadequate, and must be checked against other sources of information. Second, the content of the B term is not a given, but must be inferred from the content of the A term. But it is difficult to infer internal states from external actions. Any of a number of inferences is usually possible, and the choice of inferences may well determine the mapping that is made. Third, neither analogy can be expected to be perfect, and so the individual will have to decide which is better, and whether the better analogy is close enough to a perfect analogy to justify it as being valid. To summarize, the construction of a deep metaphor is fraught with difficulties – difficulties that can be characterized in terms of the components of the information-processing theory of analogical reasoning described earlier.

We have attempted to take the major concepts in Schön's broadly based and conceptually rich theory of metaphor, and to show how they relate to concepts in both the theories of metaphor and of analogy (and induction) presented in the preceding section of this paper. We believe that the major difference between Schön's research and ours is one of approach rather than substance. His approach might be characterized as macroscopic, ours as microscopic. But the commensurability of the conclusions reached by the two different approaches is a powerful argument in favor of their validity. Converging operations have led to converging conclusions, suggesting that there is a common core of knowledge that transcends specific methodologies. With time, we can hope to see the substance of this core extended.

Conclusion

We shall conclude our discussion of metaphor, induction, and social policy by re-posing five major issues in the theory of metaphor posed by Verbrugge and McCarrell (1977) and by Schön, and by showing how the theories of representation and processing described in this paper deal with these issues.

One issue posed by Verbrugge and McCarrell is that of how semantic information is represented. We have proposed a spatial representation in which local subspaces can be mapped into points of higher-order hyperspaces, and vice versa. This representation is more flexible than conventional spatial representations because of its ability to characterize terms of different levels of abstraction. We have proposed that a common set of dimensions underlies many (although almost certainly not all) of the local subspaces, and our factor-analytic data were consistent with this notion.

A second issue posed by Verbrugge and McCarrell is that of what makes some metaphors more successful than others. We have proposed two rules that we believe govern successful, i.e., aesthetically pleasing, metaphors. The first is that the superimposed within-subspace distance between tenor and vehicle be minimized; the second is that the between-subspace distance be maximized (at least within that range of distances for which the dimensions of the local subspaces remain correspondent). Comprehensibility, unlike aesthetic quality, is maximized by minimization of both superimposed within-subspace distance and between-subspace distance.

A third issue posed by these authors is that of how the tenor and vehicle of a metaphor interact. There seem to be three sources of interaction in the proposed theory. The first is an interaction between superimposed within-subspace distance and between-subspace distance: Aesthetically pleasing metaphors minimize the first while maximizing the second. The second source is in the constraints placed by the inference and application processes. It has been proposed that the explicit or implicit constraints set by the context of the metaphorical sentence result in tenor and vehicle being perceived in restricted ways that delimit their possible relations to each other. The third source of interaction was not discussed in this paper for lack of space, although it is discussed elsewhere in the context of research on reasoning by analogy (Sternberg, 1977a, 1977b; Sternberg & Rifkin, in press). There exist alternative process models by which individuals can encode, infer, map, and apply attributes. At one extreme is a completely noninteractive model, in which the outcome of each operation is independent of the outcome of every other operation. At the other extreme is a completely interactive model, in which the outcome of each operation can influence the outcome of every other operation. It seems likely that metaphors are comprehended in a highly interactive way, with the results of operations directly affecting each other.

A fourth issue, this one posed by Schön, is that of how we decide whether people are using generative metaphors, and if they are, what these generative metaphors are. In two of the experiments we have described, subjects were asked to choose among alternative completions for metaphors. Preferences could thereby be discerned. But in both of these experiments, subjects were given at least part of the metaphor as stimulus material. We have not yet attempted to infer subjects' implicit metaphors when the subjects are given no experimentally controlled stimulus material at all.

A fifth issue, also posed by Schön, is that of discovering how people generate metaphors. The theories proposed here only begin to answer this fundamental question. We have proposed a structure and rules for operating upon this structure. In the mapping process, individuals will generate metaphors that minimize superimposed within-subspace distance and meet their preference for between-subspace distance. We have suggested that individuals may differ in this latter preference. Individuals may also differ in the ways in which they encode, infer, and apply attributes. Different encodings of an urban slum, to take Schön's example, result in very different generative metaphors. But we are certainly a long way from a full description of what leads people to generate certain metaphors, and in particular, those metaphors rather than others.

We have attempted to demonstrate in this paper a convergence between macroscopic and microscopic views of metaphor, induction, and social policy. The demonstration began with a description of the microscopic views we have adopted, continued with an integration of these views with the macroscopic views of Schön, and ended with a discussion of how the microscopic view deals with some fairly macroscopic questions about metaphoric generation, comprehension, and appreciation. The convergence of Schön's views with our own strengthens our conviction that an understanding of metaphor can be attained that is independent of the means used to attain that understanding.

NOTES

Some of the ideas we present evolved out of conversations of the first author with Amos Tversky who has investigated similar hypotheses regarding semantic domains and their relations to metaphorical goodness. We acknowledge his contribution with gratitude. We are also grateful to Andrew Ortony, to Sandra Scarr, and to the members of Robert Sternberg's research seminar at Yale for comments on an earlier draft of this chapter. Preparation of this chapter was supported by a contract from the Office of Naval Research to Robert Sternberg.

1 The research described in this section has been done as a collaboration between Roger Tourangeau and Robert Sternberg (see Tourangeau & Sternberg, 1978).

2 Our thinking about and approach to metaphor has been influenced by the notions of others as well, including those of interaction between tenor and vehicle (Black, 1962b) and of basic natural categories (Rosch, 1975b; Rosch, Mervis, Gray, Johnson & Boyes-Braem, 1976).

3 Although the spatial representation described here has provided a useful theoretical basis and heuristic for our thinking about metaphor, we believe it likely that the theory could be mapped into other forms of representation as well, such as a feature representation (Tversky, 1977) or an attribute-value representation (Sternberg, 1977a, 1977b).

4 Dimensions may correspond in the sense that a common label applies to them. The dimensions are not viewed as equivalent, however: "Prestige" in the domain of modern world leaders may not mean the *same* thing as "prestige" in the domain of mammal names.

5 Factor analyses were performed via principal-factor solutions rotated to the varimax criterion.

6 The research described in this section has been done as a collaboration between Robert Sternberg and Georgia Nigro (see Sternberg & Nigro, 1978).

7 The metaphor may also be set up so that inference occurs in the vehicle and application in the tenor. The nature of the task determines the order of processing.

METAPHOR
AND
SCIENCE

Metaphor and Theory Change:
What is "Metaphor" a Metaphor for?

Introduction

In the now classic paper "Metaphor" (Black, 1962b), Max Black considers and rejects various formulations of the "substitution view" of metaphor, according to which every metaphorical statement is equivalent to a (perhaps more awkward, or less decorative) literal statement. Black devotes most of his critical attention to a special case of the substitution view, the "comparison view," according to which a metaphor consists in the presentation of an underlying analogy or similarity. It is clear from Black's discussion that he understands the comparison view as entailing that every metaphorical statement is equivalent to one in which some quite definite respect of similarity or analogy is presented, and that successful communication *via* metaphor involves the hearer understanding the same respect(s) of similarity or analogy as the speaker.

Black argues that, except perhaps in cases of *catachresis* – the use of metaphor to remedy gaps in vocabulary – the comparison view is inadequate. As an alternative, Black proposed the adoption of an "interaction view" of metaphor. According to this view, metaphors work by applying to the principal (literal) subject of the metaphor a system of "associated implications" characteristic of the metaphorical secondary subject. These implications are typically provided by the received "commonplaces" about the secondary subject. Although Black's position has many facets, it is clear that, at a minimum, it differs from the comparison view in denying that the success of a metaphor rests on its success in conveying to the listener or reader some quite definite respects of similarity or analogy between the principal and secondary subjects: metaphors are, on Black's view, more openended (this is not his terminology) than the comparison view would suggest.

In certain passages, Black appears to suggest even stronger points of divergence between his view and the comparison account. In addition to denying that successful metaphors must convey to the reader or hearer some quite definite respect of similarity or analogy, he also denies that any analysis of an interaction metaphor in terms of explicit analogies or similarites, however elaborate, can capture the cognitive content which it is capable of conveying (Black, 1962b, p. 46). He even suggests (p. 37) that in some cases it is revealing to understand metaphors as *creating* the similarities (or, presumably, analogies) upon which they depend. In any event, Black sees these features of metaphor as indicative of an important difference between metaphorical uses of language and those uses which have the features of explicitness characteristic of scientific usage.

We need the metaphors in just those cases where there can be no question as yet of the precision of scientific statements. Metaphorical statement is not a substitute for formal comparison or any other kind of literal statement but has its own distinctive capacities and achievements. (p. 37)

In particular, in this view, one should expect that when metaphorical language is employed in a scientific context, its function should either lie in the pretheoretical (prescientific?) stages of the development of a discipline, or in the case of more mature sciences, it should lie in the realm of heuristics, pedagogy, or informal exegesis, rather than in the realm of the actual articulation or development of theories.

In formulating my own views about the role of metaphor in theory change, I have found it valuable to compare and contrast my understanding of scientific metaphors with Black's account of metaphors in general. Roughly speaking, what I should like to argue here is this: There exists an important class of metaphors which play a role in the development and articulation of theories in relatively mature sciences. Their function is a sort of catachresis – that is, they are used to introduce theoretical terminology where none previously existed. Nevertheless, they possess several (though not all) of the characteristics which Black attributes to interaction metaphors; in particular, their success does not depend on their conveying quite specific respects of similarity or analogy. Indeed, their users are typically unable to precisely specify the relevant respects of similarity or analogy, and the utility of these metaphors in theory change crucially depends upon this open-endedness.

On the other hand, I shall argue, this particular sort of open-endedness or inexplicitness does not distinguish these metaphors from more typical cases of scientific terminology, nor is it the case that these metaphors forever resist complete explication of the relevant respects of similarity and analogy; such explication is typically an eventual consequence of successful scientific research. The impression that metaphors must lack the precision characteristic of scientific statements reflects, I shall argue, an extremely plausible but mistaken understanding of precision in science.

More precisely, what I shall argue is that the use of metaphor is one of many devices available to the scientific community to accomplish the task of *accommodation of language to the causal structure of the world*. By this I mean the task of introducing terminology, and modifying usage of existing terminology, so that linguistic categories are available which describe the causally and explanatorily significant features of the world. Roughly speaking, this is the task of arranging our language so that our linguistic categories "cut the world at its joints"; the "joint" metaphor is misleading only in that it obscures the fact that the relevant notion of "joint" may be context, or discipline, relative. An important special case of this task of accommodation (not under that description) has recently been investigated in some detail by Kripke (1972) and Putnam (1975a, 1975b), who have emphasized the ostensive character of some of the mechanisms by which the reference of certain natural-kind terms is fixed. Although their accounts of the "causal theory of reference" differ in important details, each of them emphasizes that it is by virtue of the ostensive character of these reference-fixing mechanisms that it is possible for natural-kind terms to refer to kinds which are determined by explanatory or "real" essences, rather than by definitional or "nominal" essences: that is, their account explains how it is possible for natural-kind terms to play a role in what I am calling *accommodation*. The accounts which Putnam and Kripke offer are particularly well suited to cases in which the reference of a term is specified by display of one or more examples of a substance whose real essence is its internal constitution. What I shall argue here is that the employment of metaphor serves as a nondefinitional mode of reference fixing which is especially well suited to the introduction of terms referring to kinds whose real essences consist of complex relational properties, rather than features of internal constitution.

If I am right, this conclusion does more than shed light on the role of metaphor in science and provide an additional example of nondefinitional reference fixing. It also provides the basis for a clearer understanding of the (itself metaphorical) notion that reference fixing in the case of theoretical terms in science involves *ostension*. I shall suggest that the notion of ostension, and indeed the notion of reference itself, are fundamentally epistemological notions, and that the issue of reference for a general term is the issue of its role in making possible socially coordinated *epistemic access* to a particular sort of thing or natural phenomenon. In terms of the notion of epistemic access, I believe, one can formulate an account of linguistic precision in science which allows an adequate treatment of ostensively defined terms in general and metaphor in particular. I also hope to indicate ways in which the role of metaphor in science illustrates the objective, public, and programmatic character of much of the tacit, or inexplicit, basis of scientific work.

Examples of metaphor in science

There is, no doubt, a considerable variety of sorts of metaphor which play a role in science, and in theory change. Certain metaphors, which might be plausibly termed exegetical or pedagogical metaphors, play a role in the teaching or explication of theories which already admit of entirely adequate nonmetaphorical (or, at any rate, less metaphorical) formulations. I have in mind, for example, talk about "worm-holes" in general relativity, the description of the spatial localization of bound electrons in terms of an "electron cloud," or the description of atoms as "miniature solar systems."

The first two of these metaphors are insufficiently suggestive or insightful theoretically to serve more than the function of pedagogical exegesis or instruction for visualization; simultaneous interactive reflection on annelid worms and space-time structures does not produce fundamental insights in physics, nor is an analogy to meteorology especially useful in the development of quantum mechanics.

In the case of the third metaphor, theoretical insight is not lacking (the metaphor summarizes Bohr's fundamental theoretical conception), but the insight does not arise from the aptness of the metaphor, nor from its open-endedness: one can say *exactly* in what respects Bohr thought atoms were like solar systems without employing any metaphorical devices, and this was true when Bohr's theory was proposed.

The fact that these metaphors, and others like them, do not convey theoretical insights not otherwise expressible does not indicate that they play no important role in theory change. Kuhn's work has made it clear that – at least insofar as the actual social practices of scientists are concerned – the establishment of a fundamentally new theoretical perspective is a matter of persuasion, recruitment, and indoctrination. It cannot be irrelevant to those enterprises that there is a body of exegetically, or pedagogically, effective metaphors. It is also perhaps true that, in the case of metaphors like the atom-as-solar-system example, the quite specific analogy between the cognitive content of a proposed theory and one already accepted may provide some evidential support for the new theory.

Nevertheless, it seems to me that the cases of scientific metaphor which are most interesting from the point of view of the philosophy of science (and the philosophy of language generally) are those in which metaphorical expressions constitute, at least for a time, an irreplaceable part of the linguistic machinery of a scientific theory: cases in which there are metaphors which scientists use in expressing theoretical claims for which no adequate literal paraphrase is known. Such metaphors are *constitutive* of the theories they express, rather than merely exegetical. It might seem doubtful that such theory-constitutive metaphors exist; after all, it is at least plausible that metaphorical language is fundamentally pretheoretical, and lacks the explicitness and precision characteristic of scientific theories. Still, if one looks at theory construction in the relatively young sciences like cognitive psychology, one finds theory-constitutive metaphors in abundance. The examples that I know best are metaphors in cognitive psychology that are drawn from the terminology of computer science, information theory, and related disciplines. The following examples are but a small subset of the actual cases:

1. the claim that thought is a kind of "information processing," and that the brain is a sort of "computer";
2. the suggestion that certain motoric or cognitive processes are "preprogrammed";
3. disputes over the issue of the existence of an internal "brain-language" in which "computations" are carried out;
4. the suggestion that certain information is "encoded" or "indexed" in "memory store" by "labeling," whereas other information is "stored" in "images";
5. disputes about the extent to which developmental "stages" are produced by the maturation of new "preprogrammed" "subroutines," as opposed to the acquisition of learned "heuristic routines," or the development of greater "memory storage capacities" or better "information retrieval procedures";
6. the view that learning is an adaptive response of a "self-organizing machine";
7. the view that consciousness is a "feedback" phenomenon.

I do not want to maintain that *all* of these examples are of fundamental importance to theoretical psychology. Nevertheless, the prevalence of computer metaphors shows an important feature of contemporary theoretical psychology: a concern with exploring analogies, or similarities, between men and computational devices has been the most important single factor influencing postbehaviorist cognitive psychology. Even among cognitive psychologists who despair of actual machine simulation of human cognition, computer metaphors have an indispensable role in the formulation and articulation of theoretical positions. These metaphors have provided much of the basic theoretical vocabulary of contemporary psychology (Neisser, 1966; G. A. Miller, 1974).

Moreover, it is clear that these computer metaphors are theory-constitutive: psychologists do not, generally speaking, now know how to offer literal paraphrases which express the same theoretical claims. This absence of available literal paraphrases is made clearly evident by the current discussion among psychologists and philosophers about the doctrine called "functionalism" (Block & Fodor, 1972; Block 1977; Boyd, 1978; Fodor, 1965, 1968; Lewis, 1971; Putnam, 1967, 1975b, 1975f; Shoemaker, 1975b). It is widely agreed that some version or other of the doctrine that mental and psychological states are functional states of organisms represents the cognitive content of the metaphorical statement that the brain is a sort of computer. But even among psychologists and philosophers who are convinced that functionalism is true, there is profound disagreement about important issues regarding its interpretation. Thus, this metaphor, and other computer metaphors employed in psychological theorizing, share with more typical interaction metaphors, at least for a time, the property that their cognitive content cannot be made explicit.

In important respects, however, these theory-constitutive metaphors are highly atypical. In the first place, they undergo a sort of public articulation and development that is uncharacteristic of literary metaphors. Typically, a literary metaphor has its "home," so to speak, in a specific work of a specfic author; when the same metaphor is employed by other authors, a reference to the original employment is often implicit. When the same metaphor is employed often, by a variety of authors, and in a variety of minor variations, it becomes either trite or hackneyed, or it becomes "frozen" into a figure of speech or a new literal expression (see Black on "orange"). Literary interaction metaphors seem to lose their insightfulness through overuse: the invitation to explore the various analogies and similarities between the primary literal subject and the metaphorical secondary subject becomes pointless or trite if repeated too often. Theory-constitutive scientific metaphors, on the other hand, become, when they are successful, the property of the entire scientific community, and variations on them are explored by hundreds of scientific authors without their interactive quality being lost. They are really conceits rather than metaphors – and conceits which extend not through one literary work, but through the work of a generation or more of scientists.

There is another closely related respect in which theory-constitutive metaphors are atypical. As Black points out, the task of offering explicit and literal paraphrases of literary metaphor is the appropriate task of literary critics and other commentators, but represents an enterprise relatively distinct from the production of the literary works in which the metaphors occur: The task of explication of metaphor is typically separate from the task of production and is often pursued by a quite different group of practitioners. In the case of scientific metaphors, on the other hand, especially in the case of theory-constitutive metaphors, this division of tasks and division of labor does not obtain. It is part of the task of scientific theory construction involving metaphors (or any other sort of theoretical terminology) to offer the best possible explication of the terminology employed. Although this task is sometimes also the preoccupation of professional philosophers (as in the case of functionalism), it is certainly the routine responsibility of working scientists. Indeed, as recent work in philosophy of psychology has shown, it is not, in general, possible to draw a methodologically significant line between philosophical investigation of the concepts of scientific psychology, and the articulation of psychological theory, nor to draw a nonarbitrary line between psychologists and philosophers of psychology. The sciences in general, and psychology in particular, are self-reflective disciplines, and the explication of theoretical concepts – metaphorical or not – is an essential part of the task of scientific inquiry.

Finally, whatever the merits of the claim that the cognitive content of literary metaphors can never be captured by literal paraphrase, there seems to be no reason to doubt that such explication is possible in the case of theory-constitutive metaphors, nor is there any reason to doubt that complete explications are often the eventual result of the attempts at explication which are central to scientific inquiry. Thus, for example, although a priori optimism about future research is no doubt unwarranted, there is no a priori reason to doubt that our understanding both of human physiology and psychology and of self-organizing and problem-solving programs will progress to the point where we will be in a position to say in exactly what respects human beings are like computers.

These systematic differences between theory-constitutive metaphors and literary interaction metaphors are, I believe, all reflections of an important difference in the ways in which metaphors of the two different sorts are open-ended. Literary interaction metaphors display what might be termed *conceptual open-endedness*: They work by inviting the reader (or hearer) to consider the principal subject of the metaphor in the light of associated implications characteristic – typically – of the commonplace conception of the secondary subject. Even in those cases in which the metaphor depends upon esoteric information about the secondary subject, the information is of the sort the sufficiently sophisticated reader might be expected to possess (sophisticated commonplaces, so to speak); indeed, the whole point of most literary metaphors would be lost if this sort of knowledge on the part of readers could not be presupposed. The function of literary metaphor is not typically to send the informed reader out on a research project.

Exactly the opposite is the case with theory-constitutive metaphors. They display what might be called *inductive open-endedness.* Although the intelligibility of theory-constitutive metaphors rests on the reader's being able to apply to his current understanding of the primary subject some of the associated implications appropriate to his current conception of the secondary subject, the function of the metaphor is much broader. The reader is invited to explore the similarities and analogies between features of the primary and secondary subjects, including features not yet discovered, or not yet fully understood. Thus, for example, the metaphorical claims that men are computers, and that thought is information processing, are initially intelligible because the reader knows enough about men and computers to have some idea what similarity or analogy might be suggested, but part of the function of this metaphor as a theoretical statement is to suggest strategies for future research by asserting that, as investigations of men and machines progress, additional, or, perhaps, entirely different, important respects of similarity and analogy will be discovered. This programmatic research-orienting feature of theory-constitutive metaphors explains, I believe, the ways in which such metaphors both resemble and differ from ordinary interaction metaphors. Theory-constitutive metaphors are introduced when there is (or seems to be) good reason to believe that there are theoretically important respects of similarity or analogy between the literal subjects of the metaphors and their secondary subjects. The function of such metaphors is to put us on the track of these respects of similarity or analogy; indeed, the metaphorical terms in such metaphors may best be understood as referring to features of the world delineated in terms of those – perhaps as yet undiscovered – similarities and analogies. Thus, it is hardly surprising that, at least for a time, it is not known exactly what the relevant respects of similarity or analogy are; many have yet to be discovered or understood. Similarly, it is unsurprising that theory-constitutive metaphors can retain their interactive quality even though they are employed, in a number of variations, by a number of authors, and over a long time. Repeated employment of such metaphors does not consist (as it would in the case of more typical interaction metaphors) of merely repetitive and trite invitations to once again explore the same understanding of the principal subject in the light of the same body of associated implications about the secondary subject. Instead, the use of theory-constitutive metaphors encourages the discovery of new features of the primary and secondary subjects, and new understanding of theoretically relevant respects of similarity, or analogy, between them.

Precisely because theory-constitutive metaphors are invitations to future research, and because that research is aimed at uncovering the theoretically important similarities between the primary and secondary subjects of the metaphors, the explication of these similarities and analogies is the routine business of scientific researchers, rather than of some specialized body of commentators. Indeed, the explication of such metaphors is essentially an automatic consequence of success in the research programs that they invite. For this reason, and because we cannot know a priori that such investigations will not ultimately be completely successful with respect to the issues raised by any particular metaphor, we have no reason to deny that complete explication of theory-constitutive metaphors is possible. They do, however, share with literary metaphors the important property that their utility does not depend on the (even tacit) availability of such an explication. Indeed, the utility of theory-constitutive metaphors seems to lie largely in the fact that they provide a way to introduce terminology for features of the world whose existence seems probable, but many of whose fundamental properties have yet to be discovered. Theory-constitutive metaphors, in other words, represent one strategy for the accommodation of language to as yet undiscovered causal features of the world.

Accommodation and reference fixing

The possibility that linguistic usage in science might be accommodated to as yet unknown "joints" in the causal structure of the world is at least as old as the seventeenth century. In Book III (and, to a lesser extent in Books II and IV) of the *Essay Concerning Human Understanding* (Locke 1690/1959), Locke explores the consequences of the proposal that substance terms should be taken to refer to the "real essences" of substances in the sense suggested by Boyle's corpuscular theory of matter: that is, that terms like "gold" or "water" should be understood to refer to specific kinds of corpuscular structure. Locke's rejection of this proposal in favor of the view that general terms must refer to kinds specified by "nominal essences," that is, by criteria of membership fixed by definitional convention, has formed the basis for all subsequent empiricist discussions of meaning and reference.

It is important to remember that empiricist accounts of meaning and reference, from Locke to the present, have rested on what are essentially "verificationist" principles. It is insisted that the kinds referred to by general terms must be delineated by "nominal essences" precisely because attempts to delineate kinds by "real essences" or "secret powers" (Hume's phrase) would make knowledgeable use of language impossible. Thus, for example, Locke rejects the possibility of classifying substances on the basis of their atomic structure on the grounds that the limitations of the senses precludes our ever discovering atomic structures. He also concludes that, in general, our inability to discern the hidden inner constitution of things makes knowledge of general laws impossible (although, like all empiricists, he restrains such skepticism where it suits his own philosophical purposes).

More recent empiricists have departed from both Hume and Locke in holding that verificationism *is* compatible with the view that knowledge of general laws is possible. Nevertheless, contemporary versions of Locke's account of general terms – doctrines to the effect that the reference or cognitive content of general terms must be fixed by "operational definitions," "criterial attributes," "law-clusters," "reduction sentences," and the like – still have a verificationist foundation. We are to understand the kinds referred to by general terms to be specified by definitional conventions because – so the argument goes – knowledge of unobservable underlying "powers" or "inner constitutions" is impossible.

In recent years there has been a movement in the philosophy of science away from the instrumentalism implicit in this sort of position and toward the "scientific realist" position that knowledge of "unobservables" and of causal powers is indeed possible (Boyd, 1973, and forthcoming; Putnam, 1973, 1975f, Smart, 1963). To a large extent, this realist tendency has resulted from analyses of the actual findings and methods of the empirical sciences. More recently, it has also been associated with the development of distinctly non-Humean positions in epistemology: causal theories of perception, causal theories of knowledge generally, the increased realization that Locke and Hume were correct in insisting that inductive generalization is unfounded unless our categories correspond to causal powers or natural necessity, and the recognition that knowledge of general laws in science is – typically, at least – impossible without some knowledge of unobservable entities or powers (Boyd, 1973, and forthcoming; Goldman, 1967, 1976; Harre & Madden, 1975; Shoemaker, 1975a).

One of the most interesting aspects of this realist tendency has been the recently renewed interest in alternatives to the standard empiricist accounts of language. It has long been recognized that considerations of circularity preclude *all* general terms possessing reference-fixing descriptive definitions. Logical positivists, for example, typically assumed that general terms for qualities of sense-data (e.g., "orange" as a description of the qualitative character of sensation) and their reference (or extension) are fixed ostensively, that is, by association with examples of the relevant sensory qualities, rather than by verbal definition. A number of philosophers, most notably Kripke and Putnam, have recently defended and developed the view – which has occasionally tempted certain of the more realist logical empiricists like Feigl – that the reference of natural-kind terms (like "water" and "gold"), and of theoretical terms in science, might be fixed "causally" or ostensively rather than by definitional convention. Such a view accords with the realistic position that knowledge of "unobservable" causal powers and constituents of matter is possible, and with Quinean dicta to the effect that there are no analytic definitions, no truths by convention. These dicta, in turn, have been confirmed by the experience of philosophers of science, who have found it extraordinarily difficult to find rationally defensible grounds for deciding which measurement procedures are operational definitions or which laws are in law-clusters or which statements are reduction sentences: that is, by the experience of philosophers who have found it impossible in practice to distinguish scientific truths-by-convention from high level empirical truths.

Putnam's account of ostensive reference for theoretical terms (Putnam, 1975a, 1975b) is the most highly developed to date (although, as he points out, it represents a preliminary discussion). The examples of ostensive reference fixing on which he concentrates are those in which terms are introduced that refer to substances like water, or to fundamental physical magnitudes like electrical charge. In these cases, on his view, we may think of the reference of terms like "water" or "electrical charge" as being fixed by "dubbing" or naming ceremonies (the latter terminology is Putnam's, the former, Kripke's) involving the association of the term in question with a sample or exemplary causal effect of its referent, or with a description of stereotypical samples or causal effects. One might, for example imagine a ceremony in which someone says "Let's call 'water' whatever substance is present in this bucket over here" or "Let's call 'electrical charge' whatever fundamental physical magnitude is responsible for the deflection of the needles on meters of this sort." Of course, no general terms are actually introduced precisely by such ceremonies, but as an idealization such an account does indicate how unambiguous (or nearly unambiguous) reference could be achieved without explicit definition in terms of necessary-and-sufficient conditions, criterial attributes, or operational procedures. If the stuff in the bucket is nearly pure water, then we may take the dubbing to have fixed the reference of "water" as the chemical substance water, even though no one at the time of the dubbing may know what property is really essential to water (i.e., no one might know that water is H_2O and that ice and steam are, therefore, species of water). Similarly, if electrical charge is the only one fundamental magnitude which is the principal determinant of the position of needles in the meters in question, then we might think of the reference of "electrical charge" as having been fixed as electrical charge – even if no one knew how to detect electrical charge generally, nor what its most fundamental properties are, nor how, in other circumstances, to distinguish the effects of charge from the effects of other fundamental magnitudes. This sort of ostensive reference fixing, then, can be understood as a procedure aimed at accommodation of linguistic usage to as yet undiscovered causal structures: We introduce terminology for substances and fundamental magnitudes by appealing to situations in which we believe they are exemplified, prior to our discovery of their fundamental or essential features (that is, prior to the discovery of those properties which would have to be mentioned in an extensionally correct explicit definition).

The success of the particular style of ostensive reference fixing by citation of samples or exemplary effects also depends on the particular sorts of kinds at which the ostension "aims." It is possible to employ samples in fixing the reference of substance terms precisely because relatively pure samples of substances are possible – because it is possible to have situations in which only one kind of the sort in question is significantly present. However, in cases where terms are to be introduced ostensively to refer to kinds whose essential properties include causal relations to, and co-occurrence with, other kinds of the same sort, one must typically think of their reference as being fixed by dubbings with a more complicated structure than the dubbings considered by Putnam. The avoidance of quite fundamental ambiguity requires that one think of the idealized dubbing ceremonies as involving features which serve to disambiguate the references of each introduced term between two or more kinds of the same sort, all of which are manifested in the exemplary samples, or situations. There must, therefore, be differences between the introducing ceremonies corresponding to the differences in essential properties between the kinds referred to.

The rationale for ostensive introduction of general terms is to permit reference to kinds whose essential properties may not yet by known – and thus to accommodate linguistic categories to as yet only partially understood causal features of the world. It is thus typically impossible that the differences between the essential properties of such co-occurring kinds should be marked, either in actual reference fixing or in idealized models of dubbing, by entirely accurate and complete descriptions of their respective essential properties.

If I am right, one of the important roles of theory-constitutive metaphors is to accomplish nondefinitional reference fixing of this sort. If the fundamental properties of the metaphorical secondary subjects of a body of related metaphors are sufficiently well understood, then these metaphors can be employed – together perhaps with exemplary circumstances of application – to fix nonliteral referents for the metaphorical expressions they contain. If the differences in essential properties of the secondary subjects are sufficiently great, analogy or similarity with them may suffice to disambiguate the (new) reference of the terms thus introduced. Subsequent metaphors which develop the same metaphorical theme may be used to report discoveries or theoretical speculations regarding the kinds to which the new reference of the metaphorical terms so introduced has been fixed. In such cases, as in the case of ostensive introduction of terms for substances, linguistic terminology is accommodated to the structure of natural phenomena whose fundamental features are not yet fully understood.

The case of computer metaphors in cognitive psychology, I believe, illustrates this sort of ostensive introduction of theoretical terminology. Mental and psychological states and processes are, almost certainly, among the sorts of kinds whose essential properties are relational – they are functional states or processes. Furthermore, it seems reasonable to hold about many psychological states and processes that their causal relations to *other psychological states and processes* are among their essential properties. (These claims make up what is least controversial about the doctrine called "functionalism.") Theoretical terms in psychology, then, are among those for which reference fixing must typically involve disambiguation between several quite different but co-occurring kinds of the same sort. Computational states and processes of the sort which are the secondary metaphorical subjects of computer-metaphors in psychology are also functional states and processes: Typically their essential properties are their causal relations to other computational states or processes or to the inputs and outputs of the machines which realize or manifest them. What I am suggesting is that – when computer metaphors in cognitive psychology are successful – the metaphorically employed computer terms come to have new referents in the context of psychological theory-construction. They refer to functionally defined psychological states or processes which bear to each other functional relations analogous to those which the literal referents of these terms bear to one another. If the metaphors are apt, and if they are drawn in sufficient detail, the differences in functional (relational) properties of the literal referents of the computer terms will serve – by analogy – to disambiguate the referents of these terms in their theory-constitutive metaphorical applications.

Consider, for example, the metaphorical claims that thought is information processing, that consciousness is a matter of feedback, and that memory involves addressing of information and its later retrieval by a search of semantically relevant addresses. Suppose, for the sake of argument, that these metaphorical claims reflect real insight into human cognition. There will be features of human cognitive activity analogous in important respects to information processing, feedback, semantically addressed memory storage, and semantic heuristics in information retrieval, as these processes or states are realized in computing machines. These cognitive states or processes will bear to each other, and to other psychological states and processes, distinguishing functional relations, closely analogous to the functional relations that distinguish the computational states and processes to which they correspond. According to the view I am advancing, we should understand these theory-constitutive metaphorical expressions – when they are used in psychological theory – as referring to the functional features of human cognition which correspond to their literal referents. Here the importance of metaphor in reference fixing is especially clear. If the metaphors in question are descriptive of fundamental features of human cognition it will almost never happen that any of these fundamental cognitive processes occur in isolation from others, nor will it often happen that a particular effect will be caused by only one of these processes. Thus the ostensive introduction of terms referring to these kinds of fundamental processes must involve devices for disambiguation of reference between the several psychological states and processes that are simultaneously present in any exemplary situation. The metaphorical employment of computer terminology allows for this disambiguation – relying on analogies to the distinguishing features of various kinds of computational states and processes – even though a definitive theory of the distinguishing characteristics of cognitive states and processes is not yet available.

The example of computer metaphors has several features that illustrate the programmatic character of theory-constitutive metaphors and,

indeed, of nondefinitionally introduced theoretical terminology generally. In the first place, when we inquire about the referents of theory
constitutive metaphorical expressions, it is necessary to inquire about
the aptness or insightfulness of the metaphors in which they are
employed. The introduction of theory-constitutive metaphors, like the
introduction of any theoretical terminology, represents an estimate
that natural phenomena of the right sorts exist (see Putnam, 1975a, p.
224–5). Computer metaphors are introduced into psychological theory
on the basis of an informed "guess" that there are important similarities or analogies between their primary and secondary subjects. The
aim of the introduction of such terminology is to *initiate investigation*
of the primary subjects in the light of an informed estimate of their
properties. In cases where a theoretical metaphor proves not to represent a real insight, we need no more inquire about the new referents of
its metaphorical terms than we do with respect to the referent of the
term "vital force": in such cases the "guess" does not work out, and
the relevant terms do not refer at all. If there are no features of human
cognition closely analogous to the fundamental features of machine
computation, then, for example, there is nothing which is the referent
of "information processing" in its use as a term of psychological theory.

It is also possible to see an important relation between the programmatic inductive open-endedness of theory-constitutive metaphors and
their role as reference-fixing devices. Computer metaphors are introduced in order to make possible investigation of the similarities and
analogies between human cognition and machine computation. These
metaphors are (at least for a while) open-ended precisely because the
research program they help to initiate is incomplete: We still do not
know in exactly what respects human cognition resembles machine
computation. What metaphorical uses of computer terminology permits is that we introduce at a relatively early stage theoretical terms to
refer to various plausibly postulated computerlike aspects of human
cognition, which then become the objects of further investigation. Two
features of this sort of use of metaphors are worth remarking on here.
First, it is by no means necessary – in order that fundamental ambiguities among the new referents of the metaphorical terms by avoided –
that the fundamental or essential properties of their literal (nonmetaphorical) referents be fully understood. The relation between "indexing" of memory items and subsequent "information retrieval" is not
fully understood by computer specialists, for example, but this does
not prevent the notions of "indexing" and "retrieval" from playing a
role in successful psychological metaphor. Indeed, this sort of case illustrates the important point that successful theory-constitutive meta-

phors can have programmatic importance for the development of research about their metaphorical secondary subjects, as well as for research about their primary subjects and the new referents of their metaphorical terms. There is no doubt that analogies between human cognition and computer functioning have provided useful heuristics for programmers as well as for psychologists.

The second point worth noting is that subsequent developments in the research program initiated by the employment of theory-constitutive metaphors may well lead to further articulation of the metaphor in question, to the introduction of new theoretical terminology (metaphorical or not) and to a consequent refinement of usage and further reduction in ambiguity of such terminology. Thus, for example, the notion of "feedback," in its information-processing and computer usage, seems to cover a variety of sorts of phenomena, ranging from simple feedback circuits in analogue devices to "system monitoring" functions in complex computational devices (indeed, the former represents the most standard usage, even though something like the latter is suggested by the proposition that consciousness is a feedback phenomenon). If there is some insight in the claim that consciousness is a sort of feedback, then one might expect that, as both applied computation theory and psychology progress, new terminology will be introduced (perhaps, but not necessarily, by employment of further computer metaphors), which will permit the drawing of finer distinctions among those cognitive processes that are analogous to the machine processes now grouped under the term "feedback."

These programmatic features of theory-constitutive metaphors – the fact that they introduce the terminology for future theory construction, refer to as yet only partially understood natural phenomena, and are capable of further refinement and disambiguation as a consequence of new discoveries – explain the fact that repeated employment and articulation of these metaphors may result in an increase in their cognitive utility rather than in a decline to the level of cliché.

What is significant is that these programmatic features of theory-constitutive metaphorical expressions are, in fact, typical of theoretical terms in science (in fact, they are true of general terms, generally). Normally, we introduce terminology to refer to presumed kinds of natural phenomena long before our study of them has progressed to the point where we can specify for them the sort of defining conditions that the positivist's account of language would require. The introduction of theoretical terms does require, however, some tentative or preliminary indication of the properties of the presumed kinds in question. Any such terminology must possess a sort of programmatic open-endedness, inasmuch as its introduction fixes a presumed topic for future research. Thus the introduction of theoretical terminology generally requires just the features that theory-constitutive metaphors provide. One way of providing a tentative and preliminary account of the properties of presumed kinds – and of disambiguating terms referring to presumed kinds of the same general sort – is by open-ended analogy to kinds whose properties are in some respects better understood. One way of expressing such analogies is by metaphorical use of terms referring to those better understood kinds. Theory-constitutive metaphors, then, simply represent one strategy among many for the preliminary stages of theory construction.

Given the initial plausibility of the view that metaphorical uses of language are insufficiently precise to be scientific, it is surprising that the use of metaphors in science is so unsurprising. The fact of their utility in science is philosophically important, not because they represent an especially unusual phenomenon, but, instead, because they provide an especially apt illustration of ubiquitous but important features of scientific language generally.

Metaphor and linguistic precision: challenges for a theory of reference

Black argues, and common sense concurs, that metaphorical language lacks the precision of scientific language. Metaphors must play only an ancillary role – a merely heuristic or pedagogical role – in scientific theory-construction. Against this eminently plausible position, I have proposed that there exist theory-constitutive metaphors in abundance, and that a nondefinitional "causal" or "ostensive" account of reference of the sort advanced by Kripke and Putnam can be employed to defend the view that the metaphorical terms occurring in theory-constitutive metaphors actually refer to natural kinds, properties. magnitudes, and so on – hereafter referred to simply as "kinds" – which constitute the nonliteral scientific subject matter of such metaphors. I suggested that, in fact, the use of theory-constitutive metaphors represents a nondefinitional reference-fixing strategy especially apt for avoiding certain sorts of ambiguity.

Is this the whole story? Is the intriguing issue of metaphor and theory construction, in reality, reducible to a footnote to an already extant theory of scientific language? Is it a mistake to believe that important theoretical questions are raised by the issue of metaphor in scientific theory-construction?

That the answer to these questions is no is suggested not only by common sense, but also by the following consideration: nothing in the application of the causal theory of reference to theory-constitutive metaphors directly addresses Black's claim that metaphorical language lacks scientific precision. Supposing it to be established that there are theory-constitutive metaphors, and that their metaphorical terms are to be understood referentially, the question still remains why their apparent imprecision does not render them unsuitable for scientific theory construction. No alternative to the common-sense understanding of linguistic imprecision has been offered. Furthermore, this deficiency – which the issue of theory-constitutive metaphors forces us to examine – reflects, not a defect in my presentation, but rather a serious limitation in the existing accounts of the casual theory of reference.

There are, broadly speaking, two rival accounts of the ways in which reference is fixed for natural-kind terms and the other sorts of general terms that occur in scientific and everyday discourse. According to the empiricist account, for all but a special class of primitive terms, all general terms are to be understood as governed by stipulatory definitional conventions. Certain sentences (operational definitions, law-clusters, meaning conventions) involving such terms are true by stipulation, are known a priori, and fix the meaning (and the extension or reference) of the terms they define. According to the rival causal or ostensive accounts, for many general terms, reference is fixed by an appropriate sort of causal interaction between users of the term and instances of the kind to which it refers.

The empiricist account readily supplies criteria of linguistic precision. Two uses of the same term (or of two lexicographically different terms for that matter) are coreferential or co-extensive only when they are governed by the same definitional conventions. Vagueness arises from inexplicitness or intersubjective variation in definitional conventions, and ambiguity from the association of a single term with two or more nonequivalent definitional conventions. Both sources of linguistic imprecision have the same remedy: each general term should be associated with a single, quite explicit, and definite conventional definition which is accepted by the relevant linguistic community *prior to* the employment of the term in question. Linguistic precision can be identified with the existence of explicit, detailed, and intersubjectively accepted conventional definitions.

The empiricist account of general terms has other important consequences as well. It entails that there are certain (definitional) statements which are immune from revision or refutation by experimental evidence. It entails that these definitional truths can be established by convention prior to the conduct of experimental investigations. Furthermore, it entails that necessary truths are almost always a priori definitional truths, and (as Kuhn, 1970a, brilliantly observed, especially pages 101–2) it entails that major changes in scientific theories are almost always to be diagnosed as changes in subject matter or conceptual framework, rather than as new discoveries. Finally, although the empiricist account of general terms may be construed as a theory of *reference,* in important respects it represents a nonrealist, nonreferential account of general terms. The extensions of the "natural" kinds, or values of the magnitudes which are the referents of general terms are – according to the empiricist conception – largely fixed by arbitrary and empirically unrevisable definitional conventions. General terms are not understood as referring to independently existing kinds or magnitudes. Indeed, an antirealist and verificationist perspective has provided the defense of the empiricist account of language since its proposal by Locke (see, Locke, 1690/1959, especially, Book III). Characteristically, the empiricist account of language treats even precisely defined nonobservational ("theoretical") general terms as playing a merely heuristic, or conceptual (but nonreferential), role in scientific theory-construction.

With the decline of logical empiricism, especially within the philosophy of science, each of these consequences of the empiricist account of language has come to seem unacceptable to a number of philosophers. It is the unacceptability of these consequences that has led philosophers like Kripke and Putnam (and, much earlier, Feigl – see Feigl, 1956) to advance causal or ostensive theories of reference. The reasoning goes something like this: The empiricist account of language has unacceptable philosophical consequences; on the other hand, if the reference of some general terms is fixed nondefinitionally, in a way somewhat analogous to ostension, baptism, or the employment of stereotypical "definitions," then one can accommodate the variety of anti-empiricist findings of recent philosophy of science and philosophy of language. Thus, a nondefinitional account of reference fixing is probably correct for a wide variety of general terms.

There is nothing wrong with this sort of reasoning. Indeed, the proposal that reference-fixing mechanisms are typically nondefinitional promises to be one of the most important achievements of recent analytical philosophy. What has not happened, however, is the articulation of a genuine causal *theory* of reference as an alternative to the received empiricist theory. It is proposed that reference is somehow a nondefinitional causal relation, but no general theory of nondefinitional reference in the literature integrates all of the proposed nondefinitional reference-fixing strategies into a single unifying theory of reference. In particular, existing proposals lack an adequate account of ambiguity and coreferentiality, and, thus provide no account either of the nature of linguistic precision, or of the methodological or linguistic practices which are apt for achieving it. The causal account of reference arises from an attempt to defend the position that general terms (especially "theoretical" terms in scientific theories) should typically be understood referentially, that general terms can refer even though they do not possess unrevisable conventional definitions, and (importantly) that tokens of a term employed in different contexts, as different historical times, within different paradigms, or in different "possible worlds" may be coreferential, even though they are not associated with equivalent conventional definitions. The independent philosophical justification for these doctrines warrants the acceptance of a causal account of reference, but it remains true that no available account offers a satisfactory treatment of the crucial issues of coreferentiality, ambiguity, and linguistic precision. In particular, one must reject the "obvious" criterion for coreferentiality of ostensively introduced terms: that two tokens of a term are coreferential only when they are each connected (by a historical causal chain of speakers' intentions to corefer) to the same dubbing or introducing ceremony. There are almost never actual events which can be identified with idealized introducing ceremonies, and, furthermore, painful human linguistic experience makes it abundantly clear that good intentions are not sufficient to avoid unintended ambiguity or shifts in reference.

Arguably, the absence of an adequate account of coreferentiality does not seriously undermine the cogency of the considerations which favor a causal account of reference. The causal account does avoid unacceptable consequences of the empiricist theory of language, and the judgments about reference and about coreferentiality which the causal account protects – even if they are not assimilated into a general theory of reference – are quite well justified by independent philosophical, linguistic, and historical considerations. On the other hand, if we are concerned about the role of theory-constitutive metaphors in science, the situation is reversed. Both common sense and the best available treatments of metaphor suggest that metaphorical language must be imprecise. nonreferential, and essentially heuristic, just as the empiricist theory of language would suggest. In the previous section, I showed that it is *possible* to maintain that the metaphorical terms in theory-constitutive metaphors refer, even though they lack explicit definitions, by adopting a nondefinitional account of the way in which they refer. I have not, however, shown that such metaphorical terms *must* be understood referentially and, in particular, I have not replied to the plausible rebuttal that – precisely because their imprecision precludes their sustaining a definite reference over time, and from one occasion of use to another – metaphorical terms in science should be understood *nonreferentially*, and scientific metaphors should be seen as playing a largely heuristic role in theory construction. Existing causal theories of reference do not provide the machinery for a reply to this challenge.

In an important respect this challenge to a referential and nonheuristic treatment of theory-constitutive metaphors represents a challenge to a whole realist and anti-empiricist project in the philosophy of science. The considerations that have persuaded many recent philosophers of science to abandon the empiricist (and especially the verificationist) position that theoretical terms play a heuristic or conceptual but nonreferential role in scientific theories are quite general and, if sound, should apply to almost all cases of theoretical language in successful scientific theory construction (see, for example, Boyd, 1973, and forthcoming; Byerly & Lazara, 1973; Feigl, 1956; Fodor, 1968; MacCorquodale & Meehl, 1948; Putnam, 1975a, 1975b; Smart, 1963). If considerations of linguistic precision should dictate a nonreferential and heuristic treatment of theory-constitutive metaphors, serious questions would be raised at least about the generality of the currently accepted anti-empiricist account of scientific theory-construction. If the considerations that support a referential treatment of theoretical terms, and that support the rejection of Kuhn's paradigm relativism regarding the meaning and reference of such terms, are sound then they should be applicable as well to metaphorical terms in science, and it should be possible to extend them to a general theory of reference which adequately treats the issue of coreferentiality and precision. I shall address the following questions which reflect the challenge we have just examined:

1. Given that it is *possible* to employ a nondefinitional account of reference fixing as an alternative to both the verificationist accounts of empiricists, and the related relativist accounts of Kuhn (1970a) and Hanson (1958), why is such a position preferable to a nonreferential treatment according to which the role of theoretical terms is purely heuristic or conceptual?

2. How do the considerations that constitute the answer to 1 apply to the especially difficult case in which the theoretical terms in question are metaphorical terms occurring in theory-constitutive metaphors?

3. Given that ambiguity and linguistic imprecision are real possibilities in the use of scientific language, what account of ambiguity, coreferentiality, and linguistic precision can the defenders of nondefinitional

reference fixing offer as an alternative to the received empiricist account?

4. How does this alternative account treat the especially difficult issue of imprecision in theory-constitutive metaphors?

In order to answer these questions, it will be necessary to develop, at least in outline, a general theory of nondefinitional reference and a nondefinitional alternative to the received empiricist accounts of co-referentiality, ambiguity, and linguistic precision. The development of this general theory will require a substantial digression from the specific topic of metaphor to more fundamental topics in the philosophy of language. This digression will, I believe, prove fruitful. Scientific metaphors raise truly fundamental issues about language and linguistic competence, and the theory of reference required to understand them has several quite startling consequences, which are important both to an understanding of metaphorical language, and to an understanding of language in general. We shall discover, for example, that there is, in an important sense, no such thing as *linguistic* precision; there are rational strategies for avoiding referential ambiguity, but they are not a reflection of rules of linguistic usage (as the empiricist theory suggests). Rather, they reflect essentially nonlinguistic principles of rational inquiry. We shall also discover that a nonreferential but heuristic treatment of metaphorical language in science is ruled out (as are similar paradigm-relativistic treatments of theoretical terminology of the sort advocated by Kuhn) by quite general epistemological considerations. Finally, we shall see that the alternative nonempiricist account of reference leads to strikingly novel suggestions about the nature of linguistic competence, which may be especially relevant to our understanding of how "theoretical" or metaphorical language works.

Epistemic access: the basis of a theory of reference

Let us then begin our digression into the philosophy of language by addressing the general question: What is reference? What relation between the use of terminology and features of the world is at issue when the question of reference is raised? What sorts of phenomena is a theory of reference supposed to explain? One way to approach the issue of the nature of reference is to examine some of the doctrines about reference which have produced so much recent excitement in philosophy. It is clear that we sometimes refer by pointing, or by employing definite descriptions. If what Putnam and Kripke say is basically correct, then we can also refer to things by employing terminology which bears the right sort of historical relation to antecedent introduction ceremonies, or by employing stereotypical descriptions which look very much like definite descriptions, but are not. In his provocative papers, Field (1973, 1974) suggests that there is a relation of *partial denotation* between certain words and features of the world which is importantly like reference. Putnam (1975e) argues that a *principle of benefit of doubt* is appropriate when assessing the reference of terms in the work of previous scientists, and that a *division of linguistic labor* involving deference to scientists and other experts is essential to reference (Putnam, 1975a).

If these doctrines are even approximately correct (and I believe that they are) then the phenomenon of reference has some quite striking properties: It can be manifested by pointing, by explicitly defining, by dubbing, or by stereotyping; it is essentially connected to the knowledge-gathering efforts of experts and specialists; and it admits of partial manifestation. It is reasonable to ask what sort of relation between language use and the world it is, that has such varied manifestations. Indeed, it is reasonable to ask what the justification is for the presumption that there is a *single* phenonemon of reference with all these different manifestations.

So far as I have been able to ascertain, this question has almost never been explicitly addressed in the literature on reference. The one place in which I have found it treated is Putnam (1975a), where it is suggested that reference and truth should be "so construed that, at least in the 'paradigm case', at least for important classes of sentences, at least if things go as they should, sentences will tend to be accepted in the long run if and only if they are true." This standard for theories of reference and truth is seen as consonant with the "scientific realism" in epistemology defended in Boyd (1973). This principle is, as Putnam remarks, especially suited to explaining the principle of benefit of the doubt and other doctrines which link the notion of reference to issues regarding the opinions and investigations of experts.

The account of reference offered here (which was developed independently of the position of Putnam, 1975a) has Putnam's position as a special case, and may be viewed both as an explanation and a justification for Putnam's position, and as an extension of it which can provide a theoretical basis for a wider variety of recent discoveries about reference. I shall not attempt here to provide an analytic definition of reference, nor to establish necessary and sufficient conditions for a word's referring to a particular thing or kind. On Quinean grounds, I doubt that such analytic definitions or specifications of necessary and sufficient conditions are ever to be found in the case of philosophically important concepts. Furthermore (following Field), I believe that it is a misleading idealization to portray the referential relation between language and the world as being constituted by relations of determinate reference between words and their unique referents. What I shall do is to try to describe the essential features of reference in such a way as to illuminate as much as possible the issues raised by discussions of reference in the recent philosophical literature.

A general account of reference should, it seems to me, account for the plausibility of a number of doctrines in the philosophy of language (and related areas of epistemology) which may not themselves be mutually consistent. I shall be especially concerned to learn from, and to explicate, the grain of truth in each of the following doctrines:

1. Operationalism;

2. The law-cluster account of "meaning" and reference for theoretical terms;

3. Putnam's (1975a) claim that there is a "division of linguistic labor" involved in reference fixing;

4. The suggestion of Quine and Ullian (1970) that language "extends the senses";

5. Gibson's (1966) claim that perception is detection of "ambient information";

6. Putnam's principle of benefit of the doubt;

7. Putnam's suggestion that those who introduced general terms like "water" intended to name an explanatory real essence if there was one;

8. Field's claim that there is a relation of "partial denotation" which may obtain between a general term and more than one kind of natural phenomenon at a time when the distinction between those kinds has not yet been drawn;

9. Causal theories of knowledge and perception (Goldman, 1967, 1976) and the suggestion that they are closely related to causal theories of reference (especially the view that the general reliability of belief-producing mechanisms or methods is a crucial feature of knowledge);

10. The suggestion (Feigl, 1956; Byerly & Lazara, 1973) of a causal theory of detection and measurement for physical magnitudes analogous to causal theories of perception;

11. The view that a realist account of scientific theories (i.e., one which treats theoretical terms as referring to real kinds) is essential to a satisfactory account of the epistemology and method of science. Here we are especially concerned with the view that "theoretical" considerations are essential to the reliable assessment of evidence in science, that the reliability of such theoretical considerations rests on the approximate truth of the body of "collateral theories" upon which they

depend, and that rational scientific practice, when successful, eventuates in the adoption of successively more accurate approximations to the truth. (For a defense of this realist and cumulative account of method with respect to issues of measurement, see Cronbach & Meehl, 1956; for a similar treatment of ontological issues in science, see MacCorquodale & Meehl, 1948; for a realist treatment of principles of experimental design and assessment of experimental evidence, see Boyd, 1973, and forthcoming).

12. The suggestion of Goldstein (1978) that the metaphor of "ostension" in nondefinitional accounts of reference fixing for theoretical terms is to be understood in terms of the role of those terms in "pointing out" or indicating directions for future research programs.

It seems to me that the grains of truth in these doctrines can best be explained by an account of the essence of reference which generalizes the doctrine of Quine and Ullian that language extends the senses, the doctrine of Gibson that the senses are detectors of ambient information, and the doctrine of Feigl that "verifying evidence is to be viewed as causally related to the evidence's 'theoretical' entities" (Feigl, 1956, p. 17). In the light of these considerations, I propose to defend the following:

1. The notion of reference is fundamentally an epistemological notion. *Semantic Theory – insofar as it is a branch of Philosophy – is a branch of epistemology.*

2. The central task of a theory of reference is to explain the role of language in the acquisition, assessment, improvement, and communication of knowledge, especially the role of language in making possible social cooperation and rational deliberation within these activities. *What is to be explained is our (collective) capacity to successfully detect and discover facts about the world.*

3. The causal theory of reference is true not, primarily, because reference involves causal connections to dubbing or introducing ceremonies, but rather because the referential connection between a term and its referent is typically sustained by a variety of epistemically relevant causal connections both between users of the term and examples of its referent (measurement, perception, detection, experimental manipulation, etc.) and between different users (reporting, deliberating, justifying, disputing, etc.). *A causal theory of reference is true precisely because reference is an epistemological notion and causal theory of knowledge is true.*

4. In deciding issues in the theory of reference it is, therefore, appropriate to make use of the best available epistemological theories. *The true theory of reference will be a special case of the true theory of*

knowledge: The true theory of reference for theoretical terms in science will be a special case of the true theory of the epistemology of science.

It also seems to me essential that one adopt a *dynamic* and *dialectical* conception of reference, in contrast to conceptions of reference which present a *synchronic, piecemeal,* and *nondialectical* idealization of the relation between individual words and features of the world. I intend to criticize conceptions of reference according to which the referential relation between a natural language and the world is entirely constituted by those relations of reference which obtain between particular words, and quite definite kinds.

One consequence of such accounts is to treat as nonreferential those connections between words and features of the world which (like Field's partial denotation) do not link words to unique referents. Equally important is the consequence that diachronic changes in linguistic usage, which alter relations of definite reference, are not themselves constitutive of the phenomenon of reference; they must be diagnosed as "changes of reference" in a sense which necessarily contrasts with "report of new discovery." One of the consequences of this sort of picture of reference is the plausibility of the empiricist doctrine that the definiteness and constancy of reference must be guaranteed by explicit and purely conventional definitions for all nonprimitive general terms. The remaining three claims are in opposition to this static conception of reference.

5. The accommodation of our language and conceptual categories to the causal structure of the world ("cutting the world at its joints") is essential in order that knowledge be possible. Since – in the absence of perfect causal knowledge – such accommodation cannot be accomplished by explicit and conventional definitions, nondefinitional procedures for accommodating language to the world are essential to knowledge. Since knowledge gathering is the essential core of reference: *The processes of linguistic accommodation are essential components of reference.*

6. Ostensive reference fixing, and other nondefinitional reference-fixing mechanisms – in the absence of perfect knowledge – will often establish referential connections between a word and more than one thing or kind. Routinely, terms with this sort of "imprecision" play a vital role in the socially coordinated discovery and communication of knowledge; indeed, the employment of terms of this sort appears to be essential to scientific inquiry (and rational inquiry generally). Thus, if reference is the relation between language and the world which ex-explains the role of language in the acquisition and communication of

knowledge: *Nondeterminate referential connections between words and features of the world are essential components of reference.*

7. It is also routine that the acquisition of new knowledge, and the exploration of new areas of inquiry, require that linguistic usage be modified so as to mark newly discovered causal features of the world. This sort of dialectical modification of language use (which has what Field, 1973, calls "denotational refinement" as a special case) is essential to the process of accommodation of language to (newly discovered features of) the causal structure of the world, and is thus an essential component of reference. *Reference has an essential dynamic and dialectical aspect. Changes in language use – when they reflect the dialectics of accommodation – do not represent changes of reference in any philosophically puzzling sense of that term. Instead, such dialectical changes of reference are characteristic of referential continuity and represent perfectly ordinary vehicles for the reporting of new discoveries.*

In order to defend this epistemological account of reference, I propose to analyze the notion of reference in terms of the notion of *epistemic access*. I hold that, for any particular general term, the question of reference is to be understood as the question: To which kind (or kinds), or property (or properties) or magnitude (or magnitudes), . . . and so on, does our use of this term afford us epistemic access? When we conduct rational inquiry intended to discover facts about the referent of this term, about what kind(s) do we in fact gather information? A better picture of the relevant notion of epistemic access or information gathering can be obtained by first considering very simple cases of language use which illustrate Quine and Ullian's claim that language extends the senses. Consider, for example, the case of cries issued by sparrows to warn others of approaching predators. Such crying "extends the senses" in a perfectly straightforward sense. Sparrows, hearing such cries, are able to detect indirectly the presence of predators outside their line of sight through the efforts of others. The detection of predators takes on a social character: sparrows have, in such cases, socially coordinated epistemic access to certain kinds of predators. Even though it may be inappropriate to talk of "reference" in such cases, a "warning cry" is a warning cry rather than a mating call precisely because sparrows (a) can detect predators by sight with fair reliability, (b) typically issue warning cries only when they do so, and (c) typically respond to hearing warning cries in much the same way that they respond to seeing a predator.

The sort of epistemic access afforded by certain words in human languages (like "red" or "cold," for example) is quite analogous. Central to our employment of the term "red" are the facts that most speakers of English can detect the presence or absence of the color red, use the term "red" to report the presence of that color, and (under normal circumstances) take others' reports of "red" as indicative of the presence of the color red.

To these simple cases of language extending the senses, we may add cases in which the relevant "detection" skills are cognitive rather than merely perceptual (consider the case of the general term "refrigerator"), and where "discovery" rather than "detection" may be the more appropriate term (but not, I insist, "construction"). More relevant to the issue of reference for theoretical terms in science are cases in which epistemic access, the discovery of facts about the referents of terms, requires scientific investigation and serious theory construction. In such cases, the role of general terms in the social coordination of knowledge acquisition is substantially more complex. It remains true in these cases that one may be afforded a passive extension, if not of one's senses, then of one's research. I am, for example, able to know that DNA carries the genetic code in mammals, by relying on the testimony of experts whose research demonstrated this fact about the referent of "DNA." Inasmuch as this is the only way I can obtain such information about the substance which is the referent of "DNA," however, the sort of epistemic access which I have to its referent is not central to determining the reference of "DNA."

What is important is the epistemic access which the term "DNA" affords to DNA in virtue of the role that term plays in the organization of research. Here there are at least three distinguishable ways in which use of the term "DNA" makes it possible for the relevant scientific community to make of itself an instrument for the detection (or discovery, if you prefer) of information about DNA:

1. Its use permits scientists to report to each other the results of studies of DNA.

2. Its use permits the public articulation, justification, criticism, debate, and refinement (in the light of justification, criticism, debate *and* experimentation) of theories concerning DNA, thus making the interpretation of data and the evaluation of proposed theories – as well as the reporting of results – into a social enterprise.

3. Finally, the use of the term "DNA" makes possible verbal reasoning concerning DNA with respect to questions of data interpretation, theory evaluation, experimental design, and so forth. That is, the use of language makes possible not merely the formulation of theories and publicity and cooperation in their assessment; it makes it possible for reason-

ing (whether individual or public) to be *verbal* reasoning: to take place in words.

In discussing simpler cases of epistemic access, it was necessary to appeal to the general and typical reliability of the human senses, or the commonplace cognitive ability to, for example, recognize refrigerators. In the context of theoretical terminology, the analogous factors are somewhat more complex. In the first place, of course, the epistemic reliability which is involved is (typically) that of the community of scientific experts, rather than that of particular individuals, especially laymen. Furthermore, the scope of the relevant notion of epistemic reliability must be formulated with some circumspection. Scientific terms must be understood as providing the sort of epistemic access appropriate to the level of epistemic success typical of scientific discoveries. Historical evidence suggests that the theories which are accepted by the scientific community are rarely entirely correct in every respect, even when they reflect the discovery of fundamentally important truths. What is typical of successful scientific investigations is successive improvements in partial but significant knowledge: scientific progress typically arises from the replacement of revealing (though only approximately accurate) theories with more revealing (and more nearly accurate) theories. Similarly, it is true that the history of science reveals a number of plausible but fundamentally mistaken "false starts" which are only corrected over time, (for example, Darwin's belief in inheritance of acquired characteristics, or the theory of vital forces). Thus the sort of success which is characteristic of epistemic access in the case of a theoretical term in science involves the capacity of the scientific community, typically and over time, to acquire increasingly accurate knowledge about the referent of that term.

The mark of reference, then, is epistemic access, and the mark of epistemic access is the relevant sort of socially coordinated epistemic success. Roughly, a general term, T, affords epistemic access to a kind (species, magnitude, and so on) k to the extent that the sorts of considerations which are (in the relevant historical context) rationally taken as evidence for statements involving T are, typically, indicative in an appropriate way of features of k. The following mutually supporting epistemic relations between a term T and a kind, k, are characteristic (but by no means definitive) of the sorts of relations which constitute epistemic access:

1. Certain of the circumstances or procedures which are understood to be apt for the perception, detection, or measurement of T are, in fact, typically apt for the perception, detection, or measurement of k.[1]

2. Some of the circumstances which are taken to be indicative of cer-

tain features or properties of manifestations of T are, in fact, typically indicative of those features or properties of manifestations of k.

3. Certain significant effects attributed to the referent of T by experts (or generally, in the case of nontheoretical terms) are in fact typically produced by k.

4. Some of the most central laws involving the term T are approximately true if they are understood to be about k.

5. There is some generally accepted, putative, definite description of the referent of T which is in fact true of k and of no other kind.

6. The sorts of considerations which rationally lead to modifications of, or additions to, existing theories involving the term T are, typically and over time, indicative of respects in which those theories can be modified so as to provide more nearly accurate descriptions, when the term T is understood as referring to k, so that the tendency over time is for rationally conducted inquiry to result in theories involving T which are increasingly accurate when understood to be about k.

It is, of course, possible for a term T to afford epistemic access to several quite different kinds. The term "demon" probably afforded epistemic access to a great variety of kinds of natural phenomena for centuries. What I am suggesting is that it is correct to talk of the referent of a general term precisely in those cases in which the term affords substantial epistemic access to a single kind or, at any rate, to a family of closely related ones. The mark of reference is continued epistemic success with respect to information gathering about a particular kind. In the case of general terms employed in the theoretical sciences, such continued success is typically reflected in theoretical advances and in new discoveries, but it is important to realize that the same phenomenon of continued epistemic success is reflected in a more mundane fashion in the case of everyday general terms. Even in the absence of profound discoveries or theoretical advances regarding refrigerators, the color blue, or candlesticks, it remains true that we daily succeed in conveying to each other new and reliable information regarding refrigerators, blue things, and candlesticks, by employing the terms "refrigerator," "blue," and "candlestick."

I want to defend the view that reference is constituted by just this sort of epistemic access, in part, by showing how such a view can make sense of our seemingly incompatible philosophical intuitions regarding reference. But it should be said at the outset that the analysis of reference in terms of epistemic access has considerable independent plausibility. It is hard to see how language could serve the vital social functions it does if epistemic access were not a central feature of its use, and – given the limits of human knowledge – it is hard to see how the relevant sort of epistemic access could be other than that which involves gradual improvement of knowledge. Furthermore, a referential treatment of theoretical terms – and a treatment which explains how reference is possible prior to definitive knowledge – is apparently essential to any adequate treatment of the role of theoretical considerations in the assessment of scientific evidence (Boyd, 1973). Thus, considerations of both everyday and scientific epistemology favor an account of reference in terms of epistemic access. It remains to show that such an account also makes sense of the received body of philosophical truisms about reference.

In the first place, an account of reference in terms of epistemic access avoids the necessity for idealized reference to dubbing ceremonies. The kind to which a general term refers is determined by the role that term plays in socially coordinated inquiry, rather than by any particular features of an introducing ceremony, or the intentions of the speakers who first introduced it. It is true, of course, that the history of a term's use, and the intentions of those who use it, will play a role in determining the kind(s) to which it affords epistemic access, but we are able to offer an account of reference which does not make introducing ceremonies or speakers' intentions definitive in this regard.

Similarly, we can see how an epistemic-access account of reference accommodates the insights of the two most important logical empiricist accounts of the meaning of theoretical terms: operationalism and the "law-cluster" account. Operationalism insists that the reference (or the cognitive content – many early defenders of operationalism rejected a referential treatment of theoretical terms) is determined by conventionally fixed procedures of detection or measurement. It is mistaken in holding that detection and measurement procedures are definitive in reference fixing, and even more mistaken in holding that the reliability of measurement or detection procedures is a matter of linguistic convention. Nevertheless, if an epistemic-access account of reference is correct, there is an important grain of truth in operationalism. In typical cases, substantial epistemic access to a natural kind or physical magnitude rests on the possession of relatively reliable detection or measurement procedures. Furthermore, the sort of continued theoretical understanding characteristic of reference for theoretical terms will typically result in the acquistion of even more sophisticated and accurate techniques of detection or measurement. This sort of centrality of detection or measurement to referential epistemic access represents the important grain of truth in operationalism.

In the case of the law-cluster account, there are several grains of truth which can be accommodated to the epistemic-access account. In the first place, of course, if continued epistemic success is characteristic of reference, then the intuition is vindicated that there is something absurd in the suggestion that all of our most fundamental beliefs about a "theoretical entity" might be fundamentally mistaken. Substantial and sustained epistemic access guarantees that we cannot be entirely mistaken all the time. Furthermore, in as much as scientific investigations tend to be influenced by those theoretical beliefs that the scientific community considers most fundamental, continued epistemic success provides strong indication that those beliefs are, in some respects at any rate, correct. None of these considerations, of course, support the view that fundamental laws are true by linguistic convention, or that it is always true when reference occurs that most of them are even approximately correct.

The central importance of law-clusters in reference is also explained by a central feature of scientific methodology. Scientific methodology is heavily theory-determined: for example, one tests a proposed theory by trying to identify those alternative theories which are – in the light of the best available theoretical knowledge – most likely to be true, and by designing experiments or observational studies with the aim of choosing between a proposed theory and its *plausible* rivals (this is a point which Putnam has often emphasized). There is every reason to believe that this procedure for theory assessment is crucial to the success of scientific practice (Boyd, 1973). Because the plausibility judgments involved in the practice of this methodological principle depend on applications of the best available theories, the most fundamental laws which the scientific community accepts about a given kind will play a methodologically crucial role in the discovery of new knowledge. Indeed, the approximate truth of such collateral theoretical beliefs is part of the explanation for future epistemic success. We have thus identified another important grain of truth in the law-cluster view: The approximate truth of many of the most important laws in a given subject area is not only a probable consequence of the sustained epistemic-access characteristic of reference, in many cases, it provides the explanation for the success of scientific method in producing the epistemic successes which constitute that epistemic access. Here again, of course, the doctrine that law-clusters are true by stipulation need not be invoked; indeed, that doctrine is contrary to the methodological picture of sustained experimental *and* theoretical criticism and subsequent modification of existing theories.

There are still more grains of truth in the law-cluster view; I shall mention two quite briefly. First, in the case of theoretical terms, epistemic access is typically achieved through the efforts of trained experts.

For precisely the methodological reasons just mentioned, the training of those experts necessarily involves, as a critical component, the learning of the most fundamental laws currently accepted by the scientific community. Secondly, it is often fruitful to distinguish between those nonexperts who have had the benefit of passive epistemic access to some relatively esoteric natural phenomenon and those who have not. Both the man who has read about black holes in *Scientific American*, and the man who says, "My neighbor studies black holes, whatever they are," can refer to black holes by using the term "black holes," but only the former understands anything about them. We sometimes say that nonexperts in the former category "understand the meaning" of the term "black hole" whereas members of the latter category do not. No doubt this use of the term "meaning" to distinguish informed from uniformed laymen represents one of the many nondeviant uses of the term "meaning." In any event, understanding the "meaning" of a term in that sense will typically involve knowing the law-clusters associated with the general terms in the relevant field, because those fundamental discoveries are the results of scientific investigations that are most likely to be made available to the educated layman.

It is also apparent that the epistemic-access account of reference offers an explanation for many of the less empiricistic doctrines regarding reference and knowledge, which appear on the list with which I began this section. Indeed, the epistemic-access account straightforwardly incorporates causal theories of perception, detection, and knowledge; Quine and Ullian's doctrine that language extends the senses; realist accounts of scientific methodology; and Goldstein's suggestion that ostension involves indication of research directions.

The epistemic-access account also provides an important elaboration of Putnam's talk of a division of linguistic labor. Experts play a crucial role in reference for theoretical terms (and relatively esoteric terms generally) precisely because it is they who provide nonpassive epistemic access to the referents of those terms. In this regard, it is worth remarking that what occurs is not really a division of *linguistic* labor at all. Instead, what is involved is the social division of mental (or, better yet, cognitive) labor: some of us are auto mechanics and know what "accelerator pump" means, others of us are nurserymen and know what "beech" means, whereas still others are physicists who know what "black hole" means. This division of labor is not primarily a linguistic phenomenon, nor is it primarily an epistemological phenomenon: Instead, as Putnam insists, it represents facts about social organization of labor at a certain stage of historical development. The division of cognitive labor is related to the issue of reference only because it is reflected in the ways people have of gathering information about features of the world, and because the notion of reference is essentially an epistemic notion.

To insist that the division of labor is not really linguistic is not merely to quibble over words; rather, it is essential to an understanding of the full implications of Putnam's account of reference.

In the first place, recognizing that there is a social division of cognitive labor – that different members of society afford to society as a whole, epistemic access to different sorts of phenomena – and recognizing that this division of labor is essential for reference to esoteric kinds, allows Putnam's observations about division of linguistic labor to be assimilated to a broader epistemic account of reference generally. Recognizing that the divided labor is cognitive labor allows us to see more clearly the fundamental issue of the relation between philosophy of language and theory of knowledge, which has always been one of Putnam's primary concerns.

Secondly, such an understanding of the fundamental role in reference of deference to experts has significant implications for issues of language and concept acquisition and for our understanding of the notion of "linguistic competence." According to classical empiricist views of language and concepts, linguistic competence with respect to a given general term is achieved by learning to associate with it the corresponding concept; concepts, in turn, are thought of as sets of defining attributes, law-clusters, and the like. A postempiricist account of language which denies the existence of definite criterial attributes, et cetera, must eventually provide an alternative account of the acquisition of linguistic competence. The epistemic-access account of what Putnam calls the "division of linguistic labor" allows us to see an important – and even a surprising – feature of that alternative account. Part of one's linguistic competence with respect to an esoteric general term outside one's own field is manifested in one's ability to achieve passive epistemic access to the referent of that term by deferring to the relevant experts. Part of my linguistic competence with respect to the term "black hole" lies in my capacity to use that term to find out more about black holes. At least, this is so if by linguistic competence with respect to a general term, one intends the ability to use the term in such a way that its use accomplishes the most important social function of language use (viz., epistemic access). Part of my linguistic competence with respect to the term "black hole," then, lies in my having the ability to rely on the finding of experts (in this case, astrophysicists) who know about black holes, whenever I want information about them.

What is significant is how this particular important aspect of my linguistic competence with respect to the term "black hole" contrasts with the picture of linguistic competence arising from the empiricist tradition. According to the empiricist views, if I am competent with respect to the term "black hole," I achieved that competence by coming to have a quite special competence with respect to that particular term itself (that is by acquiring the particular concept of a black hole and associating it with the term "black hole"). In the contrasting epistemic access account of competence there is no special competence with respect to the term "black hole" *itself* which accounts for my linguistic competence with respect to it.

I am able to achieve epistemic access to black holes *via* the term "black hole" (and thus to participate in the most important features of reference with respect to that term), because I have learned to defer to experts in such matters. But I never did learn to defer to experts with respect to the term "black hole," nor did I learn to defer to experts with respect to "beech tree" or "accelerator pump." I did not acquire many thousand different skills and inclinations of deference – one for each esoteric general term outside my field which I can use. Instead, I acquired a much smaller number of intellectual and social skills which are not particular to any special term, or even to any particular vocabulary or branch of inquiry: I learned a fundamental principle of rational inquiry – that one should ask people who are likely to be knowledgeable in areas outside one's competence.

I learned lots of facts about the social division of intellectual labor in my own society, which make it relatively easy for me to find expertise when I want it. I learned something about how to proceed when there is controversy about expertise. I learned certain social and technical skills necessary to employ the strategy of deferring to experts (ranging from conversational skills to skill in the use of card catalogues). Finally, I, like everyone else, learned a lot of background information of the sort necessary to make sense of lots of things I read and hear. None of these skills or inclinations is specific to any particular word, or even to the vocabulary of any special branch of human inquiry.

Nevertheless, the most crucial component of my linguistic competence with respect to the term "black hole" arises precisely from my acquisition of those nonspecific skills and inclinations. There simply is nothing I did which was *acquiring* linguistic competence (or, at any rate, referential competence) with respect to the term "black hole" except learn that the expression was in my language. (Consider: Tonight I read the headline "Ultra-dwarf Mezars Discovered," then I am already linguistically competent with respect to the term "ultra-dwarf mezar" *automatically*, in virtue of the social and intellectual skills that I already have.)

Here then is the first major surprise that follows from an epistemic-access interpretation of the division of linguistic labor: Empiricist accounts of linguistic competence are more profoundly wrong about general terms than we might at first have thought. Linguistic competence with respect to a given general term is not acquired by learning to associate that term with a criterial definition – that is hardly surprising. But, in fact, linguistic competence with respect to a particular general term is not *acquired* at all! Aside from recognizing its grammatical category, what is essential to linguistic competence with respect to a particular general term amounts to the possession of a variety of quite general social and intellectual skills which are in no way specific to the term itself. Herein lies the second surprise: Much of linguistic competence is not distinctly linguistic. Beyond a knowledge of grammar and of the general semantic rules of one's language (already a lot, of course), most of the competence necessary to make one a successful language user may consist of general social and intellectual skills, which have application outside the realm of language use, and which are in no obvious sense *linguistic* skills at all. Deference to knowledgeable experts is, for example, a general principle of rationality. Indeed, the principle of deference to experts has quite clear application to cases in which language need not be employed at all: learning a skill by watching someone else perform it, or, even, learning about the behavior of a species of fish by watching carefully the behavior of an animal who is adept at capturing fish of that sort.

I should like to turn now to the three remaining intuitions about reference on the list with which I began this section: Putnam's plea for "benefit of the doubt" in assessing reference, his claim that the earliest users of general terms like "water" intended to refer to the secret inner constitution of the substance in question, and Field's defense of a notion of partial denotation. If I am right, all three represent commentaries on the dialectical aspects of reference: the accommodation of language to the causal structure of the world.

What I am calling "accommodation" is a response to an epistemological problem, whose discovery represents the principle epistemological achievement of early empiricism: inductive generalization is reliable (or, at any rate, is nonaccidentally reliable) only if the categories in terms of which generalizations are formulated correspond in the right way to the causal powers of things in the material world (Locke, 1690/1959, Book IV, Chap. iii, Sections 14, 25, 29; Hume, 1739/1973, pp. 90–1). If all A's I have so far examined have produced the effect

B under circumstances *C*, and I conclude on that basis that *A*'s always produce effect *B* under circumstances *C*, I am going to be right (barring pure luck) only if the categories *A*, *B*, and *C* correspond in the right way to the kinds of causal powers that operated to produce the effects, that I observed in the sampled cases. I can go wrong, for example, if all the observed *A*'s actually belong to a smaller kind *D*, and in fact, only *D*'s have the causal power to produce *B* under circumstances *C;* I can go wrong if the category *C* is too broad to capture the causal contribution which the observed instances of *C* made to the observed effect, or if the category *B* is so narrow that it excludes some of the very effects which are sometimes produced by the very mechanisms which were involved in the sample situations. As Locke and Hume (somewhat inconsistently) recognized, it follows that knowledge of general laws is impossible unless we are able to succeed at the "metaphysical" task of "cutting nature at its joints."

It was the fond hope of twentieth-century logical empiricists that a non-"metaphysical" nonrealist account of the meaning of scientific theories would prove to be compatible with an acceptable account of the possibility of their rational confirmation by experiment and observation. The failure of positivist philosophy of science indicates that this was a vain (if well motivated) hope. The emergence of realist conceptions of scientific epistemology reflect the recognition that Hume was right after all: It is impossible to understand scientists as being in the business of achieving nonaccidental success at inductive generalization without understanding them to be in the business of learning about (typically "unobservable") causal powers and underlying mechanisms of structures (Boyd, 1973, and forthcoming).

It follows, then, that the business of inductive generalization must be the business of "cutting the world at its joints" – the business of describing and classifying natural pheonomena in ways which in fact correspond to underlying causal powers or mechanisms. In other words, the accommodation of language to the world is essential for linguistically mediated epistemic access. It is for this reason that I insist that the dialectical process of accommodation – the introduction of linguistic terminology, or the modification of current usage so that general terms come to afford epistemic access to causally important features of the world – is an essential component of reference. The sorts of epistemic success that are characteristic of reference are only possible in cases where general terms afford epistemic access to kinds which are "natural" in the sense of corresponding to important causal features of the world.

We are, thus, in a preliminary way, able to offer an explication of

Putnam's doctrine that the earliest users of terms like "water" intended to name the underlying real essence, if any, which explained the observable properties of their samples of water. Taken literally, this claim is patently false. What is true, however, is that the earliest users of "water" were embarked on an enterprise – the socially coordinated and linguistically mediated discovery and transmission of information about natural substances – whose rational conduct eventually required the deployment of a general expression which holds of just the inner constitution of the substance which predominated in the samples they called "water." Although they were not in a position to intend, to know, or even to imagine it, the rational conduct of the enterprise upon which they were embarked was to require the employment of terminology coextensive with our term "H_2O."

In a somewhat similar way, we can explicate Putnam's principle of the benefit of the doubt. Suppose that earlier practitioners of some science have achieved a certain measure of success: Suppose, for example, that they have come to be able to make relatively accurate predictions about a significant range of observable phenomena. In the light of the best available accounts of scientific epistemology, we may say that it is overwhelmingly likely (as a partial explanation for their success) that the linguistic terminology of their field afforded them epistemic access to (at least many of) those kinds of natural phenomena that are crucial in the causal determination of the phenomena that they have been able to predict successfully.

Their terminology must have, with some success, "cut the world at its joints." Suppose that we are now in possession of an even more sophisticated theory of the same subject area – an even more sophisticated account of those "joints." If we now ask the question: "To which natural kinds did the terminology of those earlier scientists afford them epistemic access?" we shall (quite properly) answer the question in the light of the best available current theory about what natural kinds causally determine the phenomena at issue. In many typical cases, the most plausible answer will be that their terms were – in all or most cases – coreferential with the same terms as we currently use them. Such an answer – when it is justified – will constitute part of a causal explanation of the epistemic success of earlier researchers – an explanation informed both by historical data and by the best available account of the structure of the world they were studying. Such an account of Putnam's dictum accords perfectly with the claim that what a theory of reference should explain is the role of language in the acquisition, improvement, and communication of knowledge.

We are now in a position to see the wisdom of Field's talk about partial denotation. Consider how accommodation of linguistic usage to the causal structure of the world works in cases where existing practice reflects real errors in classification of natural phenomena. There seem to be two relatively distinct types of error-correcting procedures, which correspond to two different sorts of error.

In type one cases, we have classified together (say, as A's) certain things which have no important similarity, or we have failed to classify together things which are, in fact, fundamentally similar. In cases of this sort, we typically revise our classifications and say that the things in the first instance really weren't A's after all, and that the things in the second instance really were A's after all.

In type two cases, the situation is more complicated. We have classified things as A's and have met with success in certain sorts of causal generalization or theory construction. We later discover that for certain other theoretical or practical purposes, the things we have classified as A's do not form so natural a kind. Instead, we are led to employ a classification which partly overlaps those cases which we have earlier classified as A's. It may later turn out that one or the other of these two classifications seems the more fundamental, in the sense that it plays a role in the more significant general laws, but it remains true that each of the categories is appropriate for the formulation of interesting generalizations or laws. (I have formulated the description of these two types of error as though the terms in question referred to natural kinds of things. Obviously, similar cases obtain for properties, kinds of properties, magnitudes, and so on.)

If all cases of classificatory error were of the first type, then the two proposals of Putnam which we have been discussing would be entirely plausible. In such cases, it is plausible to say that we are correct in saying that the erroneous misclassifications represented saying of a non-A that it is A and saying of an A that it is not an A. Precisely because there is no other natural kind close to A which includes the deviant cases, it is plausible to say that the referent of A has remained the same, and that we simply learned more about it. There would be only one kind which might plausibly be thought of as the referent of "A," even before the anomalies were discovered, and it would be reasonable both to claim (in the metaphorical sense) that it had been the "intended" referent all along, and therefore to apply the principle of benefit of the doubt and to say that earlier speakers' use of "A" had been coreferential with our more sophisticated use. Cases of type one are cases in which no new kind has been discovered; rather they are cases in which the boundary of a previously known kind are fixed with greater accuracy.

Unfortunately, cases of type two are not so clear-cut. Consider the term "fish." At one time, whales and porpoises were classified under the term "fish." Later it was discovered that whales and porpoises are mammals and are quite distinctly unlike other marine vertebrates in many important respects. We now say that whales and porpoises are "not fish" or that they are "not true fish." It remains true, however, that porpoises and bonefish do have many interesting nonphylogenetic features in common. For purposes of many sorts of investigations (of fishing industries, or animal locomotion, for example) it may be perfectly rational to classify whales and porpoises together with the bone and cartilaginous fish.

Suppose that the response to the anatomical, behavioral, physiological, and evolutionary findings that make it rational to distinguish fish from marine mammals had instead been that people had begun to say that there were two importantly different sorts of fish: furry fish and scaled fish (with subsequent modifications of terminology to distinguish "true scaled fish" from, for example, sharks and rays), and that the general term "fish" had continued to be universally applied to bone fish, sharks, rays, porpoises, and whales alike. Suppose, that is, that the important biological discoveries about aquatic animals that we have discussed had not resulted in a change in the animals which people termed "fish," and that the term "fish" had retained its prescientific usage, rather than being employed as a relatively technical term approximately coextensive with "osteichthyes." Under the circumstances we are imagining people would not have said, for example, "Whales really aren't fish after all," but they would have marked, with different terminology, the same distinctions between kinds of aquatic animals which we now make. Provided that our imaginary linguistic community gets its biological theories right in other respects, it is unreasonable to say that they are mistaken in saying, "Whales are fish." If it is also unreasonable to say that we are wrong in saying, "Whales are not fish," then we have constructed a situation in which Putnam's principle of benefit of the doubt is inapplicable, even though the linguistic communities in question have made no scientific errors. After all, the two communities have the same linguistic history prior to the relevant biological discoveries, and each could – with equal justification – apply the principle of benefit of the doubt to enshrine its own *current* usage as exemplary of the earlier reference of the term "fish."

Two facts are made obvious by examples of this sort. In the first place, the schemes of classification, or modes of measurement, that are inductively appropriate for the acquisition of general knowledge in one field of inquiry may be quite different from those that are appropriate to another. We can and must "cut nature at its joints," but the boundaries between joints are themselves context-specific. Ways of classifying animals which are appropriate for evolutionary biology may be inappropriate for commerce, or for ethological studies. To use Goodman's terminology, "projectability" is a context-of-inquiry relative property of predicates.

Secondly, when it first becomes evident that it is necessary to draw a distinction between kinds where none has been drawn before, it is often the case that nothing in previous linguistic usage or intellectual practice dictates which of the newly marked kinds, if any, should be referred to by whatever the relevant previously used general term is, and which should be referred to by newly introduced terminology. It is, for example, undetermined whether the old terminology should be co-opted for the more technical, or the less technical, of the subsequent distinctions. In the case of "fish" the term has come to be used in a relatively technical way, whereas in the case of the term "jade," the term has retained its old commercial usage, and new technical terms ("jadite" and "nephrite") were introduced to mark the relevant technical distinction. (This example is from Putnam, 1975a.) As we have seen, neither of these choices were dictated by constraints of rational usage: All that rationality required was that the relevant distinction be marked in the language.

This phenomenon illustrates, I believe, what Field calls partial denotation. It often happens that a term affords epistemic access to two (or more) relatively similar — but clearly distinguishable — kinds during the period before the relevant distinctions have been drawn. Prior to the discoveries that give rise to the drawing of those distinctions, substantial information is gathered about the kinds in question — and formulated with the aid of the general term in question — so that the epistemic access afforded by that term is often crucial to the discoveries in question. After the relevant discoveries have been made, relevant changes in linguistic usage are made, but linguistic and scientific rationality do not dictate a unique new referent for the term in question. These refinements of usage represent the paradigm case of the accommodation of language to the causal structure of the world.

It is clear that the epistemic-access account of reference fully explicates Field's notion of partial denotation. Field is right to think of partial denotation as very closely related to typical cases of reference, because partial denotation involves not only epistemic access but also – in the sort of cases we are discussing – the sort of epistemic successes characteristic of reference. Indeed, the eventual resolution of partial denotation in favor of ordinary reference is typically achieved in the light of those successes. It is precisely this sort of "denotational refinement" (Field's term) that one would expect to be commonplace when theory-constitutive metaphorical terms are introduced at early stages of theory construction. As I suggested earlier, the term "feedback" in psychology is a likely candidate.

Field is right in another way. If we think of reference as being the relation between expressions of language and features of the world by virtue of which communication and linguistically mediated discovery are possible, then partial denotation – and indeed epistemic access in general – must be counted as part of that relation between language and the world, and so must the process of linguistic accommodation. There are two reasons why these dialectical elements must be understood as part of the phenomenon of reference itself. First, what is central in reference is epistemic access and epistemic success, and both of these can be achieved to a considerable extent in cases of partial denotation. Second, the accommodation of linguistic categories to the causal structure of the world is essential to the very possibility of the epistemic success characteristic of reference. To think of the phenomenon of reference as excluding these dialectical elements, and as somehow consisting solely of cases in which a term affords epistemic access to only one kind, would be a denial of the basically epistemic character of reference, and might, as well, lead to the absurd conclusion that in early prescientific communities many extremely useful terms have no referential interpretation at all.

There is an even more important consequence of understanding the accommodation of language to the world to be a routine feature of the process of reference, and a routine response to the acquisition of new knowledge. According to the empiricist conception of general terms, there are two quite distinct sorts of changes in the ways we use language. On the one hand, we may use general terms in a way which preserves their current referents, in order to revise, modify, amend, or contradict things we have previously said. On the other hand, we may change our usage in such a way that one or more general terms change their referents (that is, we can "adopt" new criterial attributes, law-clusters, operational definitions, or reduction sentences for such terms). Only the former sort of change, according to an empiricist understanding of reference, represents an appropriate vehicle for the assertion of new discoveries or the refutation of former beliefs. Changes in linguistic practice of the second sort – which involve changes in the referents of the relevant terms – amount, on the empiricist view, to a decision to speak a language which is, with respect to the terms in question, a new language altogether. According to such a view, sentences containing those terms which are uttered before the change in reference are in no straightforward way comparable with sentences containing the same terminology after the linguistic shift: They have a quite different subject matter and their acceptance represents simply the adoption of a new linguistic convention (this is the essence of Kuhn's treatment of the term "mass" during the change from Newtonian mechanics to special relativity; Kuhn 1970a, pp. 101-2).

Against this empiricist relativism, it is possible to insist, as an epistemic-access account of reference does, that law-clusters, operational definitions, and reduction sentences are not definitive of the referent of a general term, are not established by defining conventions, and can be modified or disconfirmed without changing the entity to which a term affords epistemic access (and, thus, without changing its referent if it refers). Nevertheless, cases like those which provide counterexamples to Putnam's principle of benefit of the doubt *are* cases in which it seems impossible to maintain that the relevant term referred to just the same kind before and after the important change in language use.

What are we to say about these cases? Are they cases in which what has occurred is a change in linguistic convention (or "world view," or "conceptual scheme") *and not a discovery*? Or, alternatively, are we – having recognized that Putnam's principle of benefit of the doubt fails in these cases – forced to treat pre-Linnaean uses of "fish" and pre-Einsteinian uses of "mass" nonreferentially on the grounds that there is no unique kind or magnitude (respectively) to which such earlier uses afforded epistemic access? Are we to say that "fish" and "mass" did not refer at all? Or, similarly, are we to say that psychologists' uses of the term "feedback" do not refer because there may be several feedback-like psychological processes?

According to the view that I am defending here (whether one chooses to say that these terms partially denoted in their earlier usage, or, alternatively, that they referred, but lacked unique referents), the important fact is that they provided substantial and sustained epistemic access to a sufficiently small number of kinds that their use resulted in sustained increases in knowledge (and eventually in the discovery that crucial distinctions had to be drawn between those kinds to which they did afford epistemic access). This sort of linguistically mediated epistemic success – *which necessarily includes modification of linguistic usage to accommodate language to newly discovered causal features of the world* – is the very core of reference. It is just a fact that circumstances arise relatively frequently in which a term affords epistemic access to two or more natural phenomena which are importantly different but which are similar enough in certain respects. Consquently, a considerable amount of theoretically and practically useful knowledge about them can be gathered before the relevant distinctions come to light. The epistemic access provided by such terms plays a crucial role in the acquisition of this information, and in the discovery of the relevant differences; furthermore, such sustained epistemic access is characteristic of reference. Thus, both the relation which such terms bear to the world originally, *and* the modification of usage which accommodates the relevant parts of language more precisely to the causal structure of the world in the light of subsequent discoveries, are central features of the phenomenon of reference.

Two conclusions now follow: In the first place, if we are interested in the "microstructure" of reference – the relations between individual words and the world which go together to constitute the referential relation between language as a whole and the world – then the notions of epistemic access and accommodation are more important than the notion of an individual word's possessing a distinct referent. The situation in which a term affords substantial epistemic access to more than one partial denotation, until more precise accommodation is achieved in the light of later discoveries, is so commonplace that we may think of it as one of the typical ways in which language is connected to the world.

In the second place, we can now see how to answer questions about the distinction between discovery, on the one hand, and the adoption of new linguistic conventions on the other, in cases of accommodation involving partially denoting terms. Contrary to the empiricist account, alterations in the reference (or the partial denotation) of general terms is a perfectly ordinary way of expressing the discovery of new natural kinds. Situations like that of "fish," "jade," and "mass," in which a partially denoting term comes to have a more definite referent as language is accommodated to newly discovered features of the world, are absolutely commonplace. Far from representing the adoption of a new and incomparable language with respect to the terms in question, such developments are marks of referential *success*: these partially denoting terms have facilitated the discovery of new and relevant features of the world.

Having developed an epistemic-access theory of reference, we are now in a position to address the questions regarding coreferentiality, ambi-

guity, and linguistic precision, which were posed at the beginning of
this section and to return to the issue of theory-constitutive metaphors.

Consider first the question of why one should prefer to understand
the reference of theoretical terms as continuous during scientific revolutions rather than as changing in ways which make comparison
between successive theories impossible. This amounts to the question
of why one should apply Putnam's principle of benefit of the doubt.
We have just seen in some detail how Putnam's principle, amended in
the light of Field's notion of partial denotation, is a consequence of an
epistemic-access account of reference. Two points in favor of the continuity account are especially relevant because of their relation to the
corresponding question about metaphors. First, according to the epistemic-access account, there are no particular features of the use of a
theoretical term (like, for example, a law-cluster, or a particular set of
measurement procedures, or a set of reduction sentences) which are
conventionally definitive of its referent. Thus, we are not obliged to
conclude that the referent of a theoretical term has changed whenever
there has been a radical change in the relevant theory, provided that
there is some reason to treat the change in theory as a response to additional evidence.

Secondly, in cases of scientific revolutions, the fact that the subsequent theory resembles the previous one in some important respects
provides part of the evidence in support of the latter theory, and this
evidential consideration makes sense only on the view that what is
involved is the replacement of one approximately accurate and well-
confirmed theory by another even better theory *with basically the same
subject matter.*

This last point can be put in another way: Certainly, in the case of
the development of the theory of relativity, the earlier Newtonian
theory served a valuable heuristic role in the development of the later
theory. Newtonian mechanics provided a valuable guide to the construction of a new theory to account for new and surprising data.
What the present account of scientific epistemology dictates is the conclusion that the overwhelmingly likely explanation of the heuristic
value of a theory in such a situation is that its terms refer (or partially
denote); that it is in important respects true; and that for that reason
it can serve as a guide to the formulation of an even more nearly true
theory *with relevantly the same subject matter,* that is, one in which
most terms preserve their earlier referents (Boyd 1973, and forthcoming). The typically positivist move of distinguishing between a theory's
being approximately true, and its merely providing a heuristically valuable way of looking at data, fails: In all but contrived and scientifically

atypical situations, the only plausible explanation for a theory's heuristic value is that its terms refer, and that it is in some important respects approximately true.

Conclusion

We can now ask the corresponding question about theory-constitutive metaphors: Given that it is possible to employ a nondefinitional account of reference to defend the view that theory-constitutive metaphorical expressions should be understood as referring, why is this view preferable to the view that theory-constitutive metaphorical expressions are nonreferential and are merely heuristically useful?

First, the fact that we are typically unable to provide an explication of theory-constitutive metaphors – that we are typically unable to *define* the relevant respects of similarity or analogy between the primary and secondary subjects of these metaphors – does not, in the light of an epistemic-access account of reference, provide any reason to doubt that the relevant metaphorical expressions refer. The existence of explicit definitions is not characteristic of referring expressions, and is not even a typical accompaniment to sustained epistemic access.

Secondly, the option of treating theory-constitutive metaphorical expressions as serving a merely heuristic role, rather than treating them referentially, is ruled out by general epistemological considerations from the philosophy of science. If the articulation and refinement of a body of metaphors all involving the same metaphorical theme proves to be genuinely fruitful in scientific theory-construction, then the only epistemologically plausible explanation is that most of the relevant metaphorical expressions refer, and that the metaphorical statements in question – when interpreted in the light of the nonstandard referents of their metaphorical terms – express important truths.

Finally, Field's notion of partial denotation, which the epistemic-access account explains, makes it possible to treat metaphorical expressions referentially without ignoring the strong intuition that it is unlikely that such expressions always refer to a single definite kind. The view that the metaphorical terms in successful theory-constitutive metaphors should be understood referentially, but perhaps as affording epistemic access to more than one kind, amounts to an understanding that the epistemic-access account of reference dictates for theoretical terms generally.

At the beginning of the last section, I raised the question of what the standard of continuity of reference was if the empiricist standard of preservation of law-cluster, operational definition, or reduction sentences is not correct. The epistemic-access account provides an answer: Reference is continuous if the term in question continues to provide epistemic access to the same kind. Similarly, several roughly simultaneous uses of the same term are coreferential if they are embodied in patterns of usage which afford epistemic access to the same kind(s).

It must be understood that the issue of epistemic access (and thus of reference) for a particular term is a perfectly ordinary scientific question. One is inquiring about the complex causal relationships between features of the world and the practices of the relevant linguistic community; whether, how, and/or to what extent they, in turn, give rise to the relevant sort of epistemic relations between the term in question and one or more kinds.

In typical cases, one might expect the outcome of such an inquiry to be an independent specification of the kinds to which the term in question affords epistemic access. In the case of theory-constitutive metaphorical expressions, this outcome is precluded (at least until later research makes the explication of the metaphor possible) inasmuch as an independent specification of the relevant kinds would amount to the sort of analysis or explication of which theory-constitutive metaphors typically do not admit. Nevertheless, when we inquire whether a single metaphorical expression occurring in a variety of different theory-constitutive metaphors which develop the same theme, has the same referent (or the same partial denotata) in each of those metaphors, we can have evidence for a positive answer, even though an independent specification of its referent may be impossible. For precisely the epistemological reasons which justify a realist conception of scientific theories, we know that the only plausible explanation for genuinely substantial heuristic value in such an extended series of metaphors is that there is a relatively small number of kinds to which their constituent terms afford epistemic access. Thus, whenever an extended series of related scientific metaphors has genuine scientific value, the overwhelmingly plausible explanation lies in the assumption that each of their constituent metaphorical expressions affords epistemic access to at most a small number of kinds – that is, that reference is constant from one employment of such a metaphorical expression to the other.

Thus, if an epistemic-access account of reference is sound, we have every good reason to hold, in the case of genuinely fruitful theory-constitutive metaphors, that all or most of their constituent metaphorical terms refer and that each of them has the same referent (or approximately the same set of partial denota) in each of its applications within the relevant theoretical context.

Let us turn now to the question of exactness, or linguistic precision, as it arises in the case of theory-constitutive metaphors. Black holds that metaphors lack the "precision of scientific statements," and that they must therefore play a role in language different from the role played by the theoretical statements of science. It is evident that it is the open-endedness and inexplicability of interaction metaphors which leads Black to this conclusion. If, as I have argued here, such open-endedness and inexplicitness is typical of theoretical statements and of theoretical terms whose reference is not definitionally fixed, the question arises: What is the right account of linguistic precision in science?

According to the empiricist understanding of scientific terms and scientific method, there are two quite distinct kinds of precision in scientific practice. On the one hand, there is precision in the use of scientific language. Since Locke, the empiricist view has been that this sort of precision is achieved to the extent to which general terms are associated with fixed, conventional, and explicit definitions of their extensions or referents. On the other hand, there is what might be called methodological precision: precision in reasoning, careful experimental design, diligent reporting of data, proper control of experimental variables, precision in measurement, and so forth. The first sort of precision is wholly a matter of the proper following of linguistic rules, whereas the second is a matter of care in treating epistemological issues. Black's insistence that metaphors lack scientific precision must, I believe, stem from a recognition that the use of metaphorical terminology fails to meet the first of these empiricist tests of precision.

Against this view of precision in science, I want to maintain that there is only one sort of scientific precision – methodological, or epistemological precision – and that precision in the use of scientific language is merely one feature, and one consequence, of this methodological precision. There is no purely *linguistic* precision, no mere following of *linguistic* rules, which account for precision in the use of theoretical terms.

We may, at the outset, see why the empiricist account of linguistic precision is fundamentally mistaken. The aim of this account is to set standards of linguistic precision which guarantee that each general term will refer to exactly one quite definite kind. The referent (or the extension) of a general term is supposed to be precisely fixed once and for all by conventionally adopted defining criteria. Given human ignorance, it would inevitably be the case (as Locke and Hume recognized) that almost none of the terms introduced according to such pure conventions would correspond to "natural kinds," almost none would "cut nature at its joints." As both Locke and Hume recognized, such terms would in fact prove to be almost useless for the acquisition of any general knowledge whatsoever, and would thus be scientifically useless; indeed, it is hard to see what viable social arrangements could sustain the practice of abiding by such self-defeating conventions.

If the empiricist criterion of precision is a failure, we may still ask what sorts of linguistic difficulties it was designed to avoid. It seems that there are two sorts of linguistic imprecision against which empiricist standards of linguistic precision were directed, although the distinction between them does not seem to have been carefully drawn, even by Locke who may well be the most careful of the empiricists in discussing misuses of language.

On the one hand, there is the difficulty which would arise from idiosyncratic uses of a general term – from circumstances in which someone uses a general term with a different referent or extension from the referent or extension which it has in the idiolects of the typical speakers of his language, or from circumstances in which there was a corresponding sort of mismatch between the uses of a term in two communities which share the same language. On the other hand, there is the sort of difficulty which would arise if the linguistic community as a whole used a general term in an ambiguous or vague way – in a way which left it without any definite referent or extension. Empiricism proposes the same solution – definitional linguistic conventions – to both of these problems.

From the point of view defended here, the first of these problems takes on a somewhat different cast. Because, on the epistemic-access view, reference is a social rather than a private phenomenon, fewer circumstances fit the first of these cases than Locke, say, might have thought. For example, many cases in which an individual has atypical evidential standards for the application of a general term, but in which he also relies on indirect evidence provided by the testimony of others, would be diagnosed as cases in which his use of the term afforded him epistemic access primarily to the same kind to which others referred, but in which his own beliefs about the kind in question were seriously mistaken.

Similarly (and even more obviously), cases in which two communities employed different evidential standards in applications of the same term – standards which were in fact apt for the detection of two different kinds, but in which this fact went unnoticed, so that members of each community relied on reports from members of the other – would often be diagnosed as cases of partial denotation, rather than cases in which definite but different referents could be assigned to the term in the voluntary of each community. Nevertheless, difficulties of the first sort no doubt do occur, and it is reasonable to inquire what remedy exists for them if an epistemic-access account of reference is correct. Here, interestingly, the remedy involves principles of rational inquiry, which are not distinctly linguistic principles: Assess evidence in the light of the best available *generally* accepted theory unless compelling evidence dictates its rejection. Rely on the advice of recognized experts. When your standards of evidence contrast sharply with those of others, seek to identify the source of the conflict, and so on. These are independently justifiable methodological principles, but the consistent application of principles of this sort provides the only rational procedure for uncovering or preventing the difficulties we have been discussing.

The second sort of difficulty arises when the use of a general term affords epistemic access to two or more quite distinct kinds, or (worse yet) to no particular kinds at all. What is to be avoided, then, are situations in which a general term partially denotes rather than refers, or situations in which it affords such diffuse epistemic access that even partial denotation is not achieved. The empiricist solution to this problem is to erect contrived categories as the referents of general terms at the cost of abandoning the project of "cutting nature at its joints." The alternative solution is provided by the ongoing project of continuous accommodation of language to the world in the light of new discoveries about causal powers. Here, the examples of the terms "demon," "fish," "jade," and "mass" are revealing. In each of these instances, a case of quasi-reference or worse was resolved by either a subsequent refinement of usage, or by the abandonment of a term altogether. In each case, the improvement in linguistic usage resulted from new discoveries about the world, rather than from attention to linguistic rules or conventions. In general, this sort of accommodation is achieved by careful and critical research about the structure of causal relations, and in particular by the pursuit of questions like: How reliable are the detection and measurement procedures which we now use? When we take several different procedures to be reliable tests for the same kind, or reliable measures for the same magnitude, are we right in believing that they are all indicative of the same kind or magnitude? How similar are the things we now classify together, and in what respects? How different? What new and undiscovered natural kinds, magnitudes, ond so on, must be postulated to account for new data? It is in the *methodologically* precise and diligent pursuit of these scientific questions – rather than in any distinctly *linguistic* practices – that the solution to the problem of diffuse epistemic access lies.

Indeed, all of these questions, as well as the remedies for idiosyncratic usage, are a reflection of a single methodological principle: Always inquire, in the light of the best available knowledge, in what ways your current beliefs about the world might plausibly be incomplete, inadequate, or false, and design observations or experiments with the aim of detecting and remedying such possible defects. All of the principles which serve to prevent diffuse epistemic access are special cases of this principle, and there is no application of it which is irrelevant to the dialectical task of accommodation. I conclude, therefore, that there are no distinct principles of *linguistic* precision in science, but rather that linguistic precision is one of the consequences of methodological precision of a quite general sort.

Turning now to the issue of metaphor in science, we can see what realist standards of precision should govern their use. One should employ a metaphor in science only when there is good evidence that an important similarity or analogy exists between its primary and secondary subjects. One should seek to discover more about the relevant similarities or analogies, always considering the possibility that there are no important similarities or analogies, or alternatively, that there are quite distinct similarities for which distinct terminology should be introduced. One should try to discover what the "essential" features of the similarities or analogies are, and one should try to assimilate one's account of them to other theoretical work in the same subject area (that is, one should *attempt* to explicate the metaphor). Such principles of methodological precision are, of course, not importantly different from those that properly govern the use of any sort of theoretical terminology in science, and it is for that reason that we may conclude that the "imprecision" of metaphors does not preclude their employment as constituents of scientific theories.

A final remark about the inexplicitness of theory-constitutive metaphors: Theory-constitutive metaphorical terms – when they refer – refer implicitly, in the sense that they do not correspond to explicit definitions of their referents, but instead indicate a research direction toward them. The same thing is apparently true of theoretical terms in science generally.

Now, Polanyi and others have popularized an *idealist* conception of scientific understanding, which treats implicit features of scientific knowledge as tacit, personal, and constructive, rather than as objective and intersubjective. It is beyond the scope of this essay to explore Polanyi's views in any detail. But it is interesting to reflect that the implicit character of scientific metaphors does not demand any such idealist interpretation. They refer by virtue of *social* and intersubjective (as opposed to personal) mechanisms, which connect scientific research with independently existing ("objective") features of the world.[2] Furthermore, when we understand a theory-constitutive metaphor, there is no reason to believe that we somehow *tacitly* understand the similarities and analogies to which its constituent terms afford epistemic access, just as there is no reason to believe that Newton tacitly understood the Einsteinian account of the referents of his theoretical terminology. These considerations are, of course, not conclusive with respect to an idealist and subjective conception of science; but, taken together with the independent evidence for a realist conception of scientific theories, the fact that an idealist explanation is not required in so obvious an area as that of metaphor in science should give a thoughtful idealist pause.

NOTES

The present chapter is for Herbert Feigl and James J. Gibson. In it I have focused on the question: How can we explain the role of metaphor in the articulation of new scientific theories? I have not addressed the question: What role does metaphorical thinking play in theory invention? I find the second question no less important, but I do not have anything interesting to say about it.

Especially in developing my views on epistemic-access and reference I have benefited from advice and criticism from a number of colleagues. I want especially to thank William Alston, Alex Goldstein, Hilary Kornblith, Barbara Koslowski, Richard Miller, Sydney Shoemaker, Robert Stalnaker, and Nicholas Sturgeon.

1 Here, and in other entries on this list, I have abused the use – mention distinction. The reader will have no difficulty in providing (somewhat tedious) but correct reformulations of these points.

2 It is important to understand in just what respect natural kinds are "objective" or "independently existing." According to the account offered here, natural kinds are discipline-or-interest relative. That is, the "naturalness" of a natural kind consists in the fact that its members have relevantly similar causal powers (or causal histories, etc.). Relevance of similarity is assessed with respect to the sort of everyday reports, inductive generalizations, or theory constructions that are required for the particular practical or theoretical projects that the relevant linguistic community undertakes. Thus "jade" denotes a commercial and "gemological" natural kind, even though for purposes of geology, jadite and nephrite are quite distinct kinds. Indeed, the notion of a natural kind can be fully explicated in terms of the notion of linguistic accommodation in the setting of particular practical or theoretical projects.

This project-relativity of natural kinds represents the *only* grain of truth

in Locke's claim that, while nature makes things similar, men rank them
into kinds (Locke, Book III, Chap. iv, Sections 35–8). In no other respect
are kinds un-"objective." The causal structures to which our language is
accommodated exist quite independently of our conceptual schemes or
theory construction. We do not decide by convention where the boundaries
of natural kinds lie. Neither do we, in any important sense, "construct" the
world when we adopt linguistic or theoretical frameworks. Instead *we*
accommodate *our* language to the structure of a theory-independent world
(contrast Kuhn, 1970; Putnam, 1977).

Metaphor in Science

THOMAS S. KUHN

If I had been preparing the main paper on the role of metaphor in science, my point of departure would have been precisely the works chosen by Boyd: Max Black's well-known paper on metaphor (Black, 1962b), together with recent essays by Kripke and Putnam on the causal theory of reference (Kripke, 1972; Putnam, 1975a, 1975b). My reasons for those choices would, furthermore, have been very nearly the same as his, for we share numerous concerns and convictions. But, as I moved away from the starting point that body of literature provides, I would quite early have turned in a direction different from Boyd's, following a path that would have brought me quickly to a central metaphor-like process in science, one which he passes by. That path I shall have to sketch if sense is to be made of my reactions to Boyd's proposals, and my remarks will therefore take the form of an excessively condensed epitome of parts of a position of my own, comments on Boyd's paper emerging along the way. That format seems all the more essential inasmuch as detailed analysis of individual points presented by Boyd is not likely to make sense to an audience largely ignorant of the causal theory of reference.

Boyd begins by accepting Black's "interaction" view of metaphor. However metaphor functions, it neither presupposes nor supplies a list of the respects in which the subjects juxtaposed by metaphor are similar. On the contrary, as both Black and Boyd suggest, it is sometimes (perhaps always) revealing to view metaphor as creating or calling forth the similarities upon which its function depends. With that position I very much agree and, lacking time, I shall supply no arguments for it. In addition, and presently more significant, I agree entirely with Boyd's assertion that the open-endedness or inexplicitness of metaphor has an important (and I think precise) parallel in the process by which scientific terms are introduced and thereafter deployed. However scientists apply terms like "mass," "electricity," "heat," "mixture," or "compound" to nature, it is not ordinarily by acquiring a list of criteria necessary and sufficient to determine the referents of the corresponding terms.

With respect to reference, however, I would go one step further than Boyd. In his chapter, the claims for a parallel to metaphor are usually restricted to the theoretical terms of science. I suppose that they often hold equally for what used to be called observation terms, for example "distance," "time," "sulphur," "bird," or "fish." The fact that the last of these terms figures large in Boyd's examples suggests that he is unlikely to disagree. He knows as well as I that recent developments in philosophy of science have deprived the theoretical/observational distinction of anything resembling its traditional cash value. Perhaps it can be preserved as a distinction between antecedently available terms and new ones introduced at particular times in response to new scientific discoveries or inventions. But, if so, the parallel to metaphor will hold for both. Boyd makes less than he might of the ambiguity of the word "introduced." Something with the properties of metaphor is often called upon when a new term is *introduced into* the vocabulary of science. But it is also called upon when such terms – by now established in the common parlance of the profession – are *introduced to* a new scientific generation by a generation that has already learned their use. Just as reference must be established for each new element in the vocabulary of science, so accepted patterns of reference must be reestablished for each new cohort of recruits to the sciences. The techniques involved in both modes of introduction are much the same, and they therefore apply on both sides of the divide between what used to be called "observational" and "theoretical" terms.

To establish and explore the parallels between metaphor and reference fixing, Boyd resorts both to the Wittgensteinian notion of natural families or kinds and to the causal theory of reference. I would do the same, but in a significantly different way. It is at this point that our paths begin to diverge. To see how they do so, look first at the causal theory of reference itself. As Boyd notes, that theory originated and still functions bests in application to proper names like "Sir Walter Scott." Traditional empiricism suggested that proper names refer by virtue of an associated definite description chosen to provide a sort of definition of the name: for example "Scott is the author of *Waverley*." Difficulties immediately arose, because the choice of the defining description seemed arbitrary. Why should being the author of the novel *Waverley* be a criterion governing the applicability of the name "Walter Scott" rather than a historical fact about the individual to whom the name, by whatever techniques, does refer? Why should having written *Waverley* be a necessary characteristic of Sir Walter Scott but having written *Ivanhoe* a contingent one? Attempts to remove these difficulties by using more elaborate definite descriptions, or by restricting the characteristics on which definite descriptions may call, have uniformly failed. The causal theory of reference cuts the Gordian knot by denying that proper names have definitions or are associated with definite descriptions at all.

Instead, a name like "Walter Scott" is a tag or label. That it attaches to one individual rather than to another or to no one at all is a product of history. At some particular point in time a particular infant was baptized or dubbed with the name "Walter Scott," which he bore thereafter through whatever events he happened to experience or bring about (for example, writing *Waverley*). To find the referent of a name like "Sir Walter Scott" or "Professor Max Black," we ask someone who knows the individual about whom we inquire to point him out to us. Or else we use some contingent fact about him, like his authorship of *Waverley* or of the paper on metaphor, to locate the career line of the individual who happened to write that work. If, for some reason, we doubt that we have correctly identified the person to whom the name applies, we simply trace his life history or lifeline backward in time to see whether it includes the appropriate act of baptism or dubbing.

Like Boyd, I take this analysis of reference to be a great advance, and I also share the intuition of its authors that a similar analysis should apply to the naming of natural kinds: Wittgenstein's games, birds (or sparrows), metals (or copper), heat, and electricity. There is something right about Putnam's claim that the referent of "electric charge" is fixed by pointing to the needle of a galvanometer and saying that "electric charge" is the name of the physical magnitude responsible for its deflection. But, despite the amount that Putnam and Kripke have written on the subject, it is by no means clear just what is right about their intuition. My pointing to an individual, Sir Walter Scott, can tell you how to use the corresponding name correctly. But pointing to a galvanometer needle while supplying the name of the cause of its deflection attaches the name only to the cause of that particular deflection (or perhaps to an unspecified subset of galvanometer deflections). It supplies no information at all about the many other sorts of events to which the name "electric charge" also unambiguously refers. When one makes the transition from proper names to the names of natural kinds, one loses access to the career line or lifeline which, in the case of proper names, enables one to check the correctness of different applications of the same term. The individuals which constitute natural families do have lifelines, but the natural family itself does not.

It is in dealing with difficulties like this one that Boyd makes what I take to be an unfortunate move. To get around them he introduces the notion of "epistemic access," explicitly abandoning in the process all use of "dubbing" or "baptism" and implicitly, so far as I can see, giving up recourse to ostension as well. Using the concept of epistemic access, Boyd has a number of cogent things to say both about what justifies the use of a particular scientific language and about the relation of a later scientific language to the earlier one from which it has evolved. To some of his points in this area I shall be returning. But despite these virtues, something essential is lost, I think, in the transition from "dubbing" to "epistemic access." However imperfectly developed, "dubbing" was introduced in an attempt to understand how, in the absence of definitions, the referents of individual terms could be established at all. When dubbing is abandoned or shoved aside, the link it provided between language and the world disappears as well. If I understand Boyd's chapter correctly – something I do not take for granted – the problems to which it is directed change abruptly when the notion of epistemic access is introduced. Thereafter, Boyd seems simply to assume that the adherents of a given theory somehow or other know to what their terms refer. How they can do so ceases to concern him. Rather than extending the causal theory of reference, he seems to have given it up.

Let me therefore attempt a different approach. Though ostension is basic in establishing referents both for proper names and for natural kind terms, the two differ not only in complexity but also in nature. In the case of proper names, a single act of ostension suffices to fix reference. Those of you who have seen Richard Boyd once will, if your memories are good, be able to recognize him for some years. But, if I were to exhibit to you the deflected needle of a galvanometer, telling you that the cause of the deflection was called "electric charge," you would need more than good memory to apply the term correctly in a thunderstorm or to the cause of the heating of your electric blanket. Where natural-kind terms are at issue, a number of acts of ostension are required.

For terms like "electric charge," the role of multiple ostensions is difficult to make out, for laws and theories also enter into the establishment of reference. But my point does emerge clearly in the case of terms that are ordinarily applied by direct inspection. Wittgenstein's example, games, will do as well as another. A person who has watched chess, bridge, darts, tennis, and football, and who has also been told that each of them is a game, will have no trouble in recognizing that both backgammon and soccer are games as well. To establish reference in more puzzling cases – prize fights or fencing matches, for example – exposure is required also to members of neighboring families. Wars and gang rumbles, for example, share prominent characteristics with many games (in particular, they have sides and, potentially, a winner), but the term "game" does not apply to them. Elsewhere I have suggested that exposure to swans and geese plays an essential role in learning to recognize ducks (Kuhn, 1974). Galvanometer needles may be deflected by gravity or a bar magnet as well as by electric charge. In all these areas, establishing the referent of a natural-kind term requires exposure not only to varied members of that kind but also to members of others – to individuals, that is, to which the term might otherwise have been mistakenly applied. Only through a multiplicity of such exposures can the student acquire what other authors in this book (for example, Cohen and Ortony) refer to as the *feature space* and the knowledge of *salience* required to link language to the world.

If that much seems plausible (I cannot, in a presentation so brief, hope to make it more), then the parallel to metaphor at which I have been aiming may be apparent as well. Exposed to tennis and football as paradigms for the term "game," the language learner is invited to examine the two (and soon, others as well) in an effort to discover the characteristics with respect to which they are alike, the features that render them similar, and which are therefore relevant to the determination of reference. As in the case of Black's interactive metaphors, the juxtaposition of examples calls forth the similarities upon which the function of metaphor or the determination of reference depend. As with metaphor, also, the end product of the interaction between examples is nothing like a definition, a list of characteristics shared by games and only games, or of the features common to both men and wolves and to them alone. No lists of that sort exists (not all games have either sides or a winner), but no loss of functional precision results. Both natural-kind terms and metaphors do just what they should without satisfying the criteria that a traditional empiricist would have required to declare them meaningful.

My talk of natural-kind terms has not yet, of course, quite brought me to metaphor. Juxtaposing a tennis match with a chess game, may be part of what is required to establish the referents of "game," but the two are not, in any usual sense, metaphorically related. More to the point, until the referents of "game" and of other terms which might be juxtaposed with it in metaphor have been established, metaphor itself cannot begin. The person who has not yet learned to apply the terms "game" and "war" correctly can only be misled by the metaphor, "War is a game," or "Professional football is war." Nevertheless, I take metaphor to be essentially a higher-level version of the process by which ostension enters into the establishment of reference for natural-kind terms. The actual juxtaposition of a series of exemplary games high-lights features which permit the term "game" to be .applied to nature. The metaphorical juxtaposition of the terms "game" and "war" high-lights other features, ones whose salience had to be reached in order that actual games and wars could constitute separate natural families. If Boyd is right that nature has "joints" which natural-kind terms aim to locate, then metaphor reminds us that another language might have located different joints, cut up the world in another way.

Those last two sentences raise problems about the very notion of joints in nature, and I shall return to them briefly in my concluding remarks about Boyd's view of theory change. But one last point needs first to be made about metaphor in science. Because I take it to be both less obvious and more fundamental than metaphor, I have so far emphasized the metaphor-like process which plays an important role in fixing the referents of scientific terms. But, as Boyd quite rightly in-sists, genuine metaphors (or, more properly analogies) are also funda-mental to science, providing on occasions "an irreplacable part of the linguistic machinery of a scientific theory," playing a role that is "*con-stitutive* of the theories they express, rather than merely exegetical." Those words are Boyd's, and the examples which accompany them are good ones. I particularly admire his discussion of the role of the meta-phors which relate cognitive psychology to computer science, informa-tion theory, and related disciplines. In this area, I can add nothing useful to what he has said.

Before changing the subject, however, I would suggest that what Boyd does say about these "constitutive" metaphors may well have a bearing wider than he sees. He discusses not only "constitutive" but also what he calls "exegetical or pedagogical" metaphors, for example those which describe atoms as "miniature solar systems." These, he sug-gests, are useful in teaching or explaining theories, but their use is only heuristic, for they can be replaced by nonmetaphorical techniques. "One can say," he points out, "*exactly* in what respects Bohr thought atoms were like solar systems without employing any metaphorical devices, and this was true when Bohr's theory was proposed."

Once again, I agree with Boyd but would nevertheless draw atten-tion to the way in which metaphors like that relating atoms and solar systems are replaced. Bohr and his contemporaries supplied a model in which electrons and nucleus were represented by tiny bits of charged matter interacting under the laws of mechanics and electromagnetic theory. That model replaced the solar system metaphor but not, by doing so, a metaphor-like process. Bohr's atom model was intended to be taken only more-or-less literally; electrons and nuclei were not thought to be exactly like small billiard or Ping-Pong balls; only some of the laws of mechanics and electromagnetic theory were thought to apply to them; finding out which ones did apply and where the similarities to billiard balls lay was a central task in the development of the quantum theory. Furthermore, even when that process of exploring potential similarities had gone as far as it could (it has never been completed), the model remained essential to the theory. Without its aid, one cannot even today write down the Schrödinger equation for a complex atom or molecule, for it is to the model, not directly to nature, that the various terms in that equation refer. Though not prepared here and now to argue the point, I would hazard the guess that the same interactive, similarity-creating process which Black has isolated in the functioning of metaphor is vital also to the function of models in science. Models are not, however, merely pedagogic or heuristic. They have been too much neglected in recent philosophy of science.

I come now to the large part of Boyd's chapter that deals with theory choice, and I shall have to devote disproportionately little time to my discussion of it. That may, however, be less of a drawback than it seems, for attention to theory choice will add nothing to our central topic, metaphor. In any case, with respect to the problem of theory change, there is a great deal about which Boyd and I agree. And in the remaining area, where we clearly differ, I have great difficulty articulating just what we disagree about. Both of us are unregenerate realists. Our differences have to do with the commitments that adherence to a realist's position implies. But neither of us has yet developed an account of those commitments. Boyd's are embodied in metaphors which seem to me misleading. When it comes to replacing them, however, I simply waffle. Under these circumstances, I shall attempt only a rough sketch of the areas in which our views coincide and in which they appear to diverge. For the sake of brevity in that attempt, furthermore, I shall henceforth drop the distinction on which I have previously insisted between metaphor itself and metaphor-like processes. In these concluding remarks, "metaphor" refers to all those processes in which the juxtaposition either of terms or of concrete examples calls forth a network of similarities which help to determine the way in which language attaches to the world.

Presupposing what has already been said, let me summarize those portions of my own position with which I believe Boyd largely agrees. Metaphor plays an essential role in establishing links between scientific language and the world. Those links are not, however, given once and for all. Theory change, in particular, is accompanied by a change in some of the relevant metaphors and in the corresponding parts of the network of similarities through which terms attach to nature. The earth was like Mars (and was thus a planet) after Copernicus, but the two were in different natural families before. Salt-in-water belonged to the family of chemical compounds before Dalton, to that of physical mixtures afterwards. And so on. I believe, too, though Boyd may not, that changes like these in the similarity network sometimes occur also in response to new discoveries, without any change in what would ordinarily be referred to as a scientific theory. Finally, these alterations in the way scientific terms attach to nature are not – logical empiricism to the contrary – purely formal or purely linguistic. On the contrary, they come about in response to pressures generated by observation or experiment, and they result in more effective ways of dealing with some aspects of some natural phenomena. They are thus substantive or cognitive.

These aspects of Boyd's and my agreement should occasion no surprise. Another one may, though it ought not. Boyd repeatedly emphasizes that the causal theory of reference or the concept of epistemic access makes it possible to compare successive scientific theories with each other. The opposing view, that scientific theories are incomparable, has repeatedly been attributed to me, and Boyd himself may believe I hold it. But the book on which this interpretation is imposed includes many explicit examples of comparisons between successive theories. I have never doubted either that they were possible or that they were essential at times of theory choice. Instead, I have tried to make two rather different points. First, comparisons of successive theories with each other and with the world are never sufficient to dictate theory choice. During the period when actual choices are made, two people fully committed to the values and methods of science, and sharing also what both concede to be data, may nevertheless legitimately differ in their choice of theory. Second, successive theories are incommensurable (which is not the same as incomparable) in the sense that the referents of some of the terms which occur in both are a function of the theory within which those terms appear. There is no neutral language into which both of the theories as well as the relevant data may be translated for purposes of comparison.

With all of this I believe, perhaps mistakenly, that Boyd agrees. If so, then our agreement extends one step further still. Both of us see in the causal theory of reference a significant technique for tracing the

continuities between successive theories and, simultaneously, for revealing the nature of the differences between them. Let me provide an
excessively cryptic and simplistic example of what I, at least, have in
mind. The techniques of *dubbing* and of *tracing lifelines* permit astro-
nomical individuals – say, the earth and moon, Mars and Venus – to
be traced through episodes of theory change, in this case the one due to
Copernicus. The lifelines of these four individuals were continuous
during the passage from heliocentric to geocentric theory, but the four
were differently distributed among natural families as a result of that
change. The moon belonged to the family of planets before Copernicus, not afterwards; the earth to the family of planets afterwards, but
not before. Eliminating the moon and adding the earth to the list of
individuals that could be juxtaposed as paradigms for the term
"planet" changed the list of features salient to determining the referents of that term. Removing the moon to a contrasting family
increased the effect. That sort of redistribution of individuals among
natural families or kinds, with its consequent alteration of the features
salient to reference, is, I now feel, a central (perhaps the central) feature of the episodes I have previously labeled scientific revolutions.

Finally, I shall turn very briefly to the area in which Boyd's metaphors suggest that our paths diverge. One of those metaphors, reiter-
ated throughout his chapter, is that scientific terms "cut [or can cut]
nature at its joints." That metaphor and Field's notion of quasi-reference figure large in Boyd's discussion of the development of scientific
terminology over time. Older languages succeeded, he believes, in cutting the world at, or close to, some of its joints. But they also often
committed what he calls "real errors in classification of natural phenomena," many of which have since been corrected by "more sophisticated accounts of those joints." The older language may, for example,
"have classified together certain things which have no important similarity, or [may] have failed to classify together, things which are, in
fact, *fundamentally* similar," (italics added). This way of talking is,
however, only a rephrased version of the classical empiricists' position
that successive scientific theories provide successively closer approximations to nature. Boyd's whole chapter presupposes that nature has one
and only one set of joints to which the evolving terminology of science
comes closer and closer with time. At least, I can see no other way to
make sense of what he says in the absence of some theory-independent
way of distinguishing *fundamental* or *important* similarities from those
that are *superficial* or *unimportant*.[1]

To describe the successive-approximation view of theory change as a presupposition does not, of course, make it wrong, but it does point to the need for arguments missing from Boyd's paper. One form such arguments might take is the empirical examination of a succession of scientific theories. No pair of theories will do, for the more recent could, by definition, be declared the better approximation. But, given a succession of three or more theories directed to more-or-less the same aspects of nature, it should be possible, if Boyd is right, to display some process of bracketing and zeroing in on nature's real joints. The arguments which would be required are both complex and subtle. I am content to leave open the question to which they are directed. But my strong impression is that they will not succeed. Conceived as a set of instruments for solving technical puzzles in selected areas, science clearly gains in precision and scope with the passage of time. As an instrument, science undoubtedly does progress. But Boyd's claims are not about the instrumental effectiveness of science but rather about its ontology, about what really exists in nature, about the world's real joints. And in this area I see no historical evidence for a process of zeroing in. As I have suggested elsewhere, the ontology of relativistic physics is, in significant respects, more like that of Aristotelian than that of Newtonian physics. That example must here stand for many.

Boyd's metaphor of nature's joints relates closely to another, the last I shall attempt to discuss. Again and again, he speaks of the process of theory change as one which involves "the accommodation of language to the world." As before, the thrust of his metaphor is ontological; the world to which Boyd refers is the one real world, still unknown but toward which science proceeds by successive approximation. Reasons for being uneasy with that point of view have already been described, but this way of expressing the viewpoint enables me to phrase my reservations in a different way. What is the world, I ask, if it does not include most of the sorts of things to which the *actual* language spoken at a given time refers? Was the earth really a planet in the world of pre-Copernican astronomers who spoke a language in which the features salient to the referent of the term "planet" excluded its attachment to the earth? Does it obviously make better sense to speak of accommodating language to the world than of accommodating the world to language? Or is the way of talking which creates that distinction itself illusory? Is what we refer to as "the world" perhaps a product of a mutual accommodation between experience and language?

I shall close with a metaphor of my own. Boyd's world with its joints seems to me, like Kant's "things in themselves," in principle unknowable. The view toward which I grope would also be Kantian but without "things in themselves" and with categories of the mind which could change with time as the accommodation of language and experience proceeded. A view of that sort need not, I think, make the world less real.

NOTES

1 In revising the manuscript to which this paragraph and those following are addressed, Boyd has pointed out that both natural kinds and nature's joints may be context- or discipline- or interest-relative. But, as note 2 to his paper will indicate, that concession does not presently bring our positions closer together. It may do so in the future, however, for the same footnote undermines the position it defends. Boyd concedes (mistakenly, I think) that a kind is "un-'objective'" to the extent that it is context- or discipline-dependent. But that construal of "objective" requires that context-independent bounds be specified for context-dependence. If any two objects could, in principle, be rendered similar by choice of an appropriate context, then objectivity, in Boyd's sense, would not exist. The problem is the same as the one suggested by the sentence to which this footnote is attached.

Metaphorical Imprecision and the "Top-Down" Research Strategy

ZENON W. PYLYSHYN

In discussing Boyd's interesting and provocative thesis concerning the role of metaphor in the development of scientific understanding, I shall focus on several issues which strike me as particularly relevant to the new discipline of cognitive science (which takes a computational approach to the study of cognition). In doing so, I shall occasionally adopt a translation of some of his terminology into terminology more familiar to me, thus perhaps exhibiting some metaphorical usage of my own.

The four main points that I shall address are the following. First, I suggest that important as it is, the accommodation of linguistic usage is only one part of the sort of accommodation of conceptual schemata that occurs in ontogenetic development, and which in my opinion, remains as deep a mystery as it was in Socrates' time. Second, as I wonder why I find some of Boyd's own metaphors enlightening without at the same time compelling me to accept some of his conclusions, I suggest that in cases where views differ, "aiming at" will not substitute for detailed argument. Third, since I find Boyd's discussion of imprecision to be particularly interesting, I try to relate this notion to my own bias concerning the utility of certain kinds of imprecision (referential, not logical) in the development of cognitive theory. And finally, recognizing that Boyd and I do not share the same view concerning particular examples of metaphors in cognitive psychology, I speculate on what gives some scientific descriptions the right to bear the ascription "literal" – and suggest that computation is a literal rather than metaphorical view of cognition.

Conceptual accommodation and linguistic usage

Boyd's presentation can be viewed as related to a question of long standing in psychology as well as in the philosophy of science. It is that adaptive equilibrium between two essential but antagonistic processes by which our mental world comes to terms with our experiences. Piaget calls these processes "assimilation" and "accommodation." "Assimilation" refers to the process by which the environment is made cognitively accessible by incorporating some of its effects into relatively stable intellectual systems called "schemata." Accommodation, on the other hand, refers to the slower but no less systematic and presistent manner in which the schemata themselves change in response to the demands of the environment.

One way of presenting the difficult and far-reaching problem posed by this opposition – which some might even call the basic paradox of adaptation and learning – is in terms of the question: How is it possible to acquire new knowledge? If one's intellectual apparatus consists of a set of concepts or conceptual schemata which are the medium of thought, then one can only learn (or apprehend) what can be expressed in terms of these concepts. On the other hand, if it were possible to observe and to acquire new "knowledge" without benefit of these concepts, then such "knowledge" would not itself be conceptual or be expressed in the medium of thought, and therefore it would not be cognitively structured, integrated with other knowledge, or even comprehended. Hence, it would be intellectually inaccessible.

This paradox, in one form or another, has been with us at least since the time Socrates offered his "learning as recollecting" solution in the Meno. Almost every major cognitive theoretician – from Hume to Newell and Simon (1976) – has had a crack at it. Recently Fodor (1975) has made a strong case against the whole class of empiricist accounts of concept acquisition, thus giving the Socratic position new life.

The paradox arises because we need terms or categories or concepts in order to structure our experience and to serve as a vehicle for tokens of thought. But then we immediately run into the problem of explaining how it is possible to think about new things, and especially how new ways of carving up our experiences are possible. The universal solution in contemporary experimental psychology (as well as much of artificial intelligence) has been to consider new concepts as being characterized in terms of old ones (plus logical connectives) – i.e., a definitional view of concept acquisition. But this view, as many have argued (e.g., Fodor, 1975; Fodor, Fodor & Garrett, 1975; Kintsch, 1974), and as Boyd concurs, is fundamentally incapable of dealing with the problem. For one thing, since definitions are logically eliminable, this approach does not actually add new concepts but merely alters the accessibility to combinations of already available ones. For another, it simply appears to be an inconvenient fact of life that, with very few exceptions, there are no criterial definitions available for natural concepts.

In some psychological circles a recent response to this difficulty (and other closely related ones) has been to abandon, or at least to augment, conceptual schemata by introducing a number of *metaphorical* devices – such as internal analogues, images, prototypes, and the like. Now, one might wonder why I have been referring to concepts as literal things and then in the last sentence why I have switched to talking about analogues and images as metaphorical. At this point, I simply wish to present an example of an evaluative use of the term "metaphor" from my point of view (a sort of ostensive reference to metaphor) so that I can pick up this theme again later. For the present, I shall simply offer the claim that none of these expedients addresses the assimilation – accommodation paradox but merely postpones it in one way or another.

Before turning to Boyd's proposal, I should point out that in my view, Boyd only addresses a part of the problem – and not even what I take to be the most crucial part – because he confines himself almost exclusively to discussing the use of linguistic terms (verbal labels) rather than to the general case of the acquisition of internal concepts. This may partly reflect his concern in this essay with linguistic issues (metaphor in particular). But it may also be that he accepts the philosophical position to which many of the people Boyd cites subscribe – which denies the existence of such abstract private terms.

For these people, thoughts are thought in English or some other natural language, not in a language-free "mentalese" – though many of these people reluctantly and uneasily leave open the possibility that images or some other sorts of entities may also play an as yet undetermined role (e.g., both Boyd and Fodor imply this possibility). I shall not take time to argue for the plausibility (or, indeed, the necessity) of such an abstract private conceptual system (but see Pylyshyn, 1978a; and Fodor, 1975). I do want to briefly suggest, however, that although some of Boyd's discussion may be relevant to concepts as well as to linguistic terms, much of it is not, so that the assimilation – accommodation problem is not resolved. The only aspect of this problem that is directly addressed is that of linguistic accommodation – and, more specifically, that of accommodating linguistic usage.

In comparing the problem of linguistic usage with that of conceptual assimilation and accommodation, one might note several striking differences. Consider, for example, the process whereby the use of terms in the public natural language accommodates to various constraints. According to the view advocated by Boyd (which, as I understand it, is essentially that of Putnam, 1975a), we begin by applying a term to paradigm situations where we believe its referent is exemplified, and continue to refine and adjust the scope of the term as we discover new essential features of situations in which it seems appropriate to use that term.

Thus, when we use the term "water" to refer to the stuff in the bucket we are really "aiming at" a deeper essence (which we cannot yet define) and so are prepared to accommodate our use of the term when we discover that ice and steam contain the same essential substance (at least from certain perspectives relevant, say, to scientific theories and perhaps also to other contexts as well). In other words, a prerequisite for such accommodation is that our use of the term is not fixed by stable perceptual or biological conditions but depends on various kinds of common-sense considerations (such as who is likely to know best, where one can find out the relevant facts, how similar this is to other situations, what a plausible guess might be, and so on). Any change in usage therefore, involves understanding, plausible reasoning, and decision.

Such, however, is not the case for terms in the private language – for concepts – especially those for which there are no corresponding lexical items in the public vocabulary. Let us accept for the moment the need for a distinct internal vocabulary of symbols, which are amodal and refer to such things as equivalence classes of perceptual patterns and also serve as objects of such things as beliefs, desires, and fears. Whatever such terms are, it would seem that unlike public linguistic terms, there is no room here for reasoning about them and choosing the scope of their referents. While I may decide to call both *this* and *that* by the same name (for example, water and ice) I cannot in the same sense *decide* on the basis of evidence that *this* and *that* are really cognitively equivalent (that is indiscernible) and therefore fall under the same concept.

The reason for this difference between concepts and words is that the former are by hypothesis the elements over which our perception, comprehension, memories, beliefs, and reasoning take place. They are the *atomic* symbols which distinguish the content of our mental representation. Although we do have representations of words as lexical items, as phonetic shapes, as graphical shapes, and so forth, as well as independent representations of what words refer to (the latter being a prerequisite to learning the association of words with things, as well as prerequisite for some sense of reasoning in nonverbal organisms), we do not have such dual representations of concepts – at pain of infinite regress. To use a computer metaphor, concepts are terms of the wired-in machine language. That is why concepts, unlike words, cannot have the kind of ambiguity associated with homonyms or homographs.

Yet this dual representation or meta-access to concepts is what we would need in order to rationally alter the referents of concepts in response to changing beliefs. In other words, this suggests that we do not reason, or have beliefs about, *concepts* but only about what they refer to. A fortiori, we cannot change what the referents of concepts are in the same manner as we can change the way we publicly express such beliefs or the way we *use* linguistic terms. The difference is that in the case of *words* there is a component of reason and choice which mediates between cognitive content and outward expression. I can choose what words I use, whereas I cannot in the same sense choose the concepts in terms of which I represent the world.

All this, of course, is not to suggest that the concepts in terms of which our knowledge is structured are fixed, or that they cannot change in response to new knowledge. Indeed, it is the fact that they do change which raises the assimilation – accommodation problem in the first place. However, it suggests that the mechanisms by which concepts change their referents (or by which percepts and thoughts change their content) may not be the same as those by which the use of linguistic terms changes. Thus Boyd's paper is a contribution to understanding how *language usage* accommodates: The assimilation–accommodation puzzle of greatest concern to cognitive psychologists remains.

Reference and the metaphor of epistemic access

According to Boyd, reference fixing is a process of linguistic accommodation, whose goal is to provide continuing *epistemic access* to an intended essential aspect of some situation. Because language "extends the senses" by giving us indirect knowledge (such as shared social knowledge and reports of findings), by focusing our joint efforts (say to investigate certain phenomena) and enabling us to discuss referents of terms, Boyd takes this sort of reaching out for knowledge – or epistemic access – to be "the mark of reference." Though one might quarrel with the exclusive attention given to the communative use of language, there is no doubt that providing access to knowledge is one of the fundamental values of language. By focusing on this aspect of language, Boyd does weave an interesting account of how language use evolves adaptively under certain pressures.

For example, the establishment of a reference for general terms (i.e., terms other than proper names) begins with an ostensive example or "dubbing" and the use of the term then gradually evolves under subtle pressure from its use by others (particularly experts) and by the demands of nature. Consequently (at least in science), the term eventually accommodates to the "causal structure of the world." Thus, general terms can truly be said to *refer*, even though what they refer to cannot be explicitly defined, because it is something like the functional essence of the exemplar – i.e., it is that aspect which enters into causal relations, which has yet to be explicated in any detail, and to which linguistic usage will eventually accommodate.

This is an interesting and, in many ways, illuminating account of linguistic usage and its relation to the reasoned search for knowledge. It has a number of useful consequences quite apart from sharpening some technical issues in the philosophy of language. One is that the disturbingly variable and uncertain relation that (superficially) appears to exist between terms and what we think of as their referents is given an account in terms of a real underlying, currently "inarticulable," referent, together with pragmatic, social, and common sense reasoning principles, which tend to produce a convergence of usage onto these real underlying referents. This realist position has natural implications for viewing theory change in science (to which I shall return later).

Another consequence is that by denying a number of prevalent distinctions – such as that between modification of linguistic usage and genuine empirical discoveries, or that between linguistic and methodological precision – Boyd is able to illuminate an underlying unity among a variety of phenomena by relating them to the dialectical process of acquisition of knowledge or epistemic access. And finally, this view of the relationship between terms and their referents leads Boyd to locate a natural place for metaphor in science. Metaphor is seen as simply providing an alternative to ostension for initiating the reference fixing process by which linguistic usage eventually accommodates to the "causal structure of the world." By this account, metaphors are not qualitatively different from other general terms in science. They are all seen as having real underlying referents and serving as stages in the ongoing process of providing epistemic access.

Though this is an elegant story, there are nonetheless a number of things about it which are, at least, discomforting. For instance, I am somewhat uneasy about the recursive flavor of the discussion of metaphor, wherein the account itself is distinctly metaphorical. If I were to accept Boyd's conclusion, I would naturally appreciate the essential contribution which his theory of constitutive metaphors makes to his presentation. On the other hand, if I should find the metaphors (say, the metaphor of "aiming at") to be unilluminating, then I suppose I should not accept the claims about the value of metaphor in such arguments. This gives me a certain dizzy feeling, because I do find Boyd's metaphors illuminating, and yet at the same time, I feel that his long paper has been somewhat like the proverbial Chinese feast and that in a short time I shall be hungry again.

My problem is that while I enjoyed the insights and agree with much of what Boyd has to say, I do not see how this type of argument, which appeals to notions as seemingly diffuse as that of epistemic access, can be made to carry much explanatory weight. One must distinguish between the general programmatic enterprise of trying to illuminate a new phenomenon and the much more demanding goal of establishing the validity of an explanatory theoretical principle. For example, some quite specific strong claims that Boyd makes demand much more than the sort of "aiming at" treatment afforded by metaphorical discussion (however appealing that might be): They demand an argument.

Consider, for example, the claim that there is continuity of reference during scientific revolutions, rather than a change of reference, as many people have claimed (for example, that classical terms like "mass," "length," "time," and so on continued to have the same referents with the advent of special relativity or quantum mechanics). Now there is surely a sense in which the acquisition of knowledge about *something* continues undisturbed through revolutionary theory change. Furthermore, this something is doubtlessly somehow epistemically related to the use of the crucial terms. Thus, if reference is to be identified with epistemic access, I suppose one would be entitled to say that reference is maintained. But that seems like a distinctly unenlightening conclusion, inasmuch as it is more a stipulation of linguistic policy (i.e., on how to use the word "reference") than a fact about theory change. Of course, if we knew what it was that the terms were intended to designate, then we could say whether the referents had changed, but in the epistemic-access view this is not possible.

I do not see how the epistemic access story allows one to draw the continuity conclusion. We can either attend to the common features of terms before and after the theory change, and conclude that they had always referred to the same essence, or else we can attend to their differences and conclude that the use of the same name was incidental. For example, the continued use of the same terms could be viewed as a consequence of trying to make the new referent intelligible in terms of old concepts, or it may be a retrospective rationalization of the earlier enterprise. At least, such alternatives are not a priori implausible – especially since the exegesis of earlier scientific and technical work is notorious in its tendency to rewrite history so as to give the appearance of unrelenting progress (cf. Smith, 1970).

According to such an alternative approach, metaphor might even be invoked to help build a bridge between two world views – not, as Boyd says, to introduce terminology for putative new features of the world, but to help make the two views mutually intelligible by emphasizing, or even inducing, a similarity between them. I am not seriously proposing this as a view of theory change but merely pointing out that so long as we confine our discussion of these issues to such general metaphorical levels as are involved when we invoke epistemic access, the arguments have little force over other plausible ways of talking.

What all this suggests to me is that while metaphors may be interesting and insightful in certain contexts and relative to certain goals, there are other contexts in which they are quite powerless to settle an issue. I think this is related to the notion of imprecision in science and to the way it can be exploited for progress. Because Boyd and I are in agreement that this is an important notion, I propose to devote the next section to it.

Precision and the "top-down" strategy

In arguing for the importance of the computational approach to cognitive psychology recently (Pylyshyn, 1978a), one of my points was related to the precision issue. Because I want to refer to this point later in the discussion, I shall begin by quoting what I wrote then.

... just as there are two sources of understanding – the empirical and the rational – so there are two corresponding loci of rigor. One can be rigorous by operationally defining one's constructs and sticking close to the experimental data. One can also be rigorous by ensuring that one's theoretical ideas are complete, consistent, and logically sound. One can then try to capture one's intuitions and bring everyday knowledge to bear on the development of theoretical ideas with some confidence that they are neither incoherent nor contradictory, and furthermore with some way of exploring what they entail. The point is that there are better and worse places for introducing rigor into an evolving discipline.

What I was arguing for was the benefit, at certain stages in development of the theory, of what is sometimes referred to as a "top-down strategy." There are various ways of understanding and pursuing a top-down research strategy. Functional analysis as typically practiced is one sort of top-down approach. It attempts to account for the behavior of a system as a "black box," in terms of the interaction of smaller black boxes, which carry out subfunctions, and each of which is also explained in a similar way. Typically the regress ends when the function carried out by a black box is sufficiently simple, and its function can be subsumed under physical principles (for example, they are instantiated in a machine). This strategy is not only typical of functional analysis, but it is also fundamental to synthesis or design of systems. In computer science it is called "structured programming" and is the standard method of designing computer programs. Furthermore, some version of this sort of top-down approach is ubiquitous in scientific progress.

As Simon (1969) remarks,

We knew a great deal about the gross physical and chemical behavior of matter before we had a knowledge of molecules, a great deal about molecular chemistry before we had an atomic theory, and a great deal about atoms before we had any theory of elementary particles . . . This skyhook-skyscraper construction of science from the roof down to the yet unconstructed foundations was possible because the behavior of the system at each level depended on only a very approximate, simplified, abstracted characterization of the system beneath. This is lucky, else the safety of bridges and airplanes might depend on the correctness of the "Eightfold Way" of looking at elementary particles. (p. 17)

It is useful to recognize several different dimensions which correspond to the top-down "direction." The functional analysis case and the examples cited by Simon emphasize the *systematic reduction* aspect. It is not that one gains precision in descending the explanatory reduction hierarchy. What one gains is a deeper, more general, and therefore a more *complete*, explanation. In artificial intelligence (a discipline generally viewed as committed to a top-down analysis of intelligent action), the primary goal is to discover methods which are sufficient for some particular problem domain, and to postpone concern over a number of other important questions, such as its detailed similarity to human mechanisms. As a methodology for theory construction in cognitive psychology, it contrasts with the more traditional bottom-up approach, which has typically been to infer isolated mechanisms to account for experimental results, while postponing the question of how these mechanisms might be employed, or how they might arise as part of a more general method.

Another traditional approach has been to operationally define properties or parameters that can be used to predict experimental results, while postponing the explanation of how these properties come about, or what more general role they might have in cognition. The difference between top-down and bottom-up approaches in this case is again not a question of precision so much as a question of the priority of various criteria and of what sort of incompleteness is considered most tolerable. The top-down approach of cognitive science and artificial intelligence tolerates incompleteness in specifiability of detailed correspondence with experiments in favor of accounting for the possibility of certain performance skills.

The latter way of putting it shows the top-down dimension to be rather closely related to the strategy, which Boyd discusses, involving the use of metaphor, and which he contrasts with the empiricist position. Use of metaphor is intended to "provide a way to introduce terminology for features of the world whose existence seems probable, but many of whose fundamental properties have yet to be discovered." This initiates a direction of research beginning with diffuse epistemic access and hopefully converging onto important causal entities. This convergent focusing strategy is a top-down approach, which like the other examples cited above, postpones certain crucial commitments (such as entailed by operational definitions) with the intention of avoiding the most costly potential dead ends.

There is a general principle behind this strategy which is recognized in artificial intelligence and variously referred to as the "principle of least commitment" or the "principle of procrastination" or the "wait and see strategy" (see, for example, Marr, 1976). This is a computational strategy applied to methods of visual processing, problem solving, and language analysis, which says, roughly, that one should proceed in such a way as to avoid, whenever possible, doing something (e.g., making an inductive guess) which subsequent discoveries may force one to undo. This, it seems to me, is the heart of most of the top-down strategies and contrasts with the empiricist method which, in Boyd's words, "erects contrived categories as the referents of general terms at the cost of abandoning the project of 'cutting nature at its joints'." Inasmuch as cutting nature at its joints is, however, a prerequisite to formulating general causal laws, the "contrived categories" frequently have to be changed, or else very complex systems have to be erected ad hoc as discoveries are made.

Despite the general top-down theme that is shared by the various examples cited above, there are significant differences among them. These differences, I believe, account for why I personally find some particular cases of top-down strategies to be more fruitful than others, and why I find certain types of imprecision to be more promising steps towards scientific progress than others. What I am trying to propose here is some way to distinguish between metaphors that I find revealing and those that I find stultifying.

Earlier, I referred to concepts and schemata as literal entities, whereas internal analogues, images, and the like, I took to be metaphors. Because I suspect that some people may feel that the converse is the case, it may be worthwhile to see whether there is anything systematic underlying such intuitions. I believe that there is more to this difference than mere idiosyncratic intuition or a commitment to a different theoretical system. I think what is at stake is a qualitative difference in the *type* of imprecision these terms entail – and here I believe that part of Boyd's discussion provides a useful basis for the comparison.

In addition to the obvious differences among various undefined terms and metaphors – for example, that some capture deeper underlying causal structures – is a difference in (1) the degree and the manner in which their referents are constrained, and (2) the extent to which they invite certain kinds of further explication. I shall try to elaborate briefly on these two aspects, which I believe differentiate different types of theoretical imprecision.

1. Systematic constraints

Many terms which appear in cognitive science – such as "schemata," "proposition," "representation," "control structure," "goal," and the like – are usually not given an explicit definition, and certainly not an operational definition in the empiricist sense. They are typically introduced by ostension in a context in which their essential properties are usually pretty clear to those familiar with the field. They are, in addition, usually rather tightly constrained in their possible referents by virtue of the fact that they must partake in an elaborate system. (This is related to the point I was driving at in my passage quoted above).

For example, suppose I have a theory of perception that claims that a certain class of scene is perceived in terms of entities which I shall call "visemes," of which there are eleven distinct types. Furthermore, the physical structure of objects is such that only certain specified arrangements of these visemes can occur in an image. Even if I am unable to give an operational definition of a viseme, or of its different types, the system as a whole is rather severely constrained, for it must be able to account for the appropriate set of equivalence classes of percepts. For example, these elements together with the system of rules or procedures must be capable of producing the correct perceptual distinctions and the correct discription of the scene. Furthermore, they must form a *coherent system*, which remains fixed as the perceptual cases it is asked to deal with are changed. Such a set of units is not arbitrary – in fact, the demands are so severe that working examples such as this one are very rare.[1] A similar (though not so dramatic) story can be told about schemata, concepts, propositions, and so on, as these are used in cognitive science. Because their exemplars typically occur in large theoretical systems, the requirement that the system be coherent imposes tight constraints on their potential properties.

Such is generally not the case with other types of general terms (e.g., "analogue," "image," "prototype," and so forth). Though these are no less precise, their exemplars do not (at least not yet) play a part in large, intricate systems, whose coherence provides strong intrinsic constraints on their properties.

2. Openness to explication

The difference among metaphors or general terms with respect to the kinds of further explication they invite seems to me to be an even more important differentiating property. If one believes, as I do, that the appropriate kind of explanation of cognitive phenomena is one which proceeds along the functional-analysis and systematic-reduction lines sketched earlier, then any practice which tends to discourage this process would be viewed as counterproductive. For instance, any metaphor which leaves one feeling that a phenomenon has been "explained," even though only a superficial level of functional reduction or process explanation has been offered, is, to my mind (and presumably also by Boyd's criteria), unproductive. This would, for instance, be the case with certain of Boyd's examples, such as "demon," or with the Freudian metaphors of energy and flow.

Closer to home, I believe that it is also the case with a large number of metaphors in cognitive psychology. It is, in my view, particularly serious in those cases where the metaphor makes prediction possible without affording explanation. For example, there is a view that mental comparison (of, say, sizes or colors) is performed by an "internal psychophysics," wherein images of the objects in question are compared in the "mind's eye." Because empirical generalizations concerning psychophysical comparison of external stimuli are available (for example, the time it takes to make a comparison is linearly related to the similarity of the objects compared), these can then be used to make predictions and are therefore taken as accounts of the mental-comparison cases. Although the detailed explanations of this and other cases involving mental comparisons and mental manipulation are considerably more complex than this illustration, they nevertheless invariably come to rest on the same set of metaphors involving the "mind's eye," or the metaphor of "mental access" as a species of internalized perception.

Despite the fact that every time I raise this point I am accused of attacking a straw man, and although the latest appeals to imagery as an explanatory notion have been more carefully hedged, I have seen no reason to revise the view I held in 1973 (Pylyshyn, 1973) that the apparent cognitive satisfaction of these accounts rests on a comfortable metaphor. That the accounts involve metaphor is, as Boyd has emphasized in his chapter, not a sign of ultimate deficiency. But that the accounts come to *rest* on it because of its subjective comfort *is* to my mind a more serious problem.

I might add that the metaphor here is not unproductive of research – any more than the Freudian, or for that matter, the demonic, ones (taking a liberal view of "research"). On the contrary, the very intuitiveness of the metaphor inspires a bumper crop of experimental research. What it does tend to inhibit, however, is the process of functional reduction. Consider the following example, which has occupied me personally for several years (see, e.g., Pylyshyn, 1978b). The story goes that in order to judge whether two differently oriented figures are identical in shape one "mentally rotates" a mental image of one of them until it is in the same orientation as the other and then tests them for congruence – presumably by superimposition or template matching. This account nicely "explains" why the comparison time is a linear function of the relative orientation of the two figures (it takes more time to rotate through a larger angle) and a lot of other experimental findings as well. Now, the term "rotate" is clearly a metaphor here since there is no spatially extended rigid object to rotate. However, there is little pressure to explicate the metaphor by further functional reduction. There seems to be no need to explain *how* rotation occurs as a cognitive process, because it is obvious how rotation occurs in the subsidiary subject of the metaphor (that is, in the case of real rotation of physical objects).

Elsewhere (Pylyshyn, 1978c) I argue that this is not a matter of methodological sloppiness or mere heuristics. The difference between those who accept the sort of cognitive metaphors illustrated above and those who, like myself, do not, lies deeper – in differing views concerning what, in principle, would constitute an ideal complete explanation. It may be that no theory-building enterprise can, or should, avoid metaphors any more than it should avoid general terms with which – as Boyd has argued – they share a great deal in common. But some resting places are more sound than others, and I believe that there are principled reasons for preferring some types of imprecision to others (in particular, for preferring imprecision that occurs in a framework that clearly marks it as an explanatory I.O.U.). But a detailed argument for that claim is a topic for another occasion.

Literal descriptions as world views

The last point I shall take up was prompted by the fact that it appears that Boyd and I have differing views concerning what constitute instances of the use of metaphor in science. I want to challenge the examples Boyd has chosen to illustrate the use of metaphor in cognitive psychology – since many of these examples do not seem to me to be metaphors at all. But to do this, we need to have some idea of what it would mean for a theoretical system to be a *literal* account. And this, in view of the very generality of the process of reference fixing which Boyd introduces, seems to be an even more difficult notion to explicate than is metaphor. Metaphor, as a type of reference-fixing process affording epistemic access to relational complexes, is apparently to be found whenever general relational notions are introduced (even possibly when relational terms are introduced by ostension, inasmuch as that can be viewed as an instance of the metaphor implied in the comparison statement "X shall refer to all things that are essentially like *this*"). But where are the *literal* uses of general terms in science?

Clearly, there are uses of language – other than simple statements using proper names and definite descriptions – that deserve to be called "literal." Indeed one of the defining characteristics of Boyd's theory-constitutive metaphors is that they "express theoretical claims for which no literal paraphrase is known." Later Boyd adds that "complete explications are often the eventual result of the attempts at explication that are central to scientific inquiry."

But one may well ask what distinguishes a metaphor from its complete explication – or, for that matter, from any literal description. Surely not the syntax of the description – for instance, the presence of comparative construction or the violation of selectional restrictions. Neither is the difference likely to rest on implied imprecise comparisons or on the vagueness of descriptions, since surely we can be literal in our intention though vague in the way we formulate our description. Are explicit criteria for distinguishing literal from metaphoric description possible, or must *that* distinction itself be (as Boyd's title implies) metaphorical?

As an illustration of how this distinction might be problematic, consider the following example of Boyd's of a metaphor which is not theory constitutive (but merely exegetic) because a literal paraphrase *is* available. According to Boyd the metaphor that atoms are "miniature solar systems" is theoretically eliminable, because "one can say *exactly* in what respects Bohr thought atoms were like solar systems without employing any metaphorical devices." Though I agree with this conclusion it seems to me that we need some way to justify this claim. One could surely argue that any of the ways of explicating the solar-system metaphor itself involves other, perhaps more familiar, metaphors. For instance, it is not clear that reference to electrons as *objects* travelling in elliptical *orbits* in a three dimensional *space* does not itself involve a metaphorical extension of our notions of object, orbit, and space to include subatomic domains, which are prima facie very different from the objects, orbits, and space with which we are familiar in macrophysics. Indeed, even the leap from the mechanics of middle-sized objects to astronomy was vigorously resisted in Galileo's time, for there is a sense in which a metaphor-like extension of reference was called for.

If this is the case, then there does remain a problem of distinguishing literal from nonliteral descriptions. Without some clearer explication of the metaphor of "metaphor" we are not in a good position to discuss, say, why certain approaches of cognitive science appear metaphorical to Boyd whereas I see them as literal.

My own tentative feeling is that the difference between literal and metaphorical description lies primarily in such pragmatic considerations as (a) the stability, referential specificity, and general acceptance of terms; and (b) the perception, shared by those who use the terms, that the resulting description characterizes the world *as it really is*, rather than being a convenient way of talking about it, or a way of capturing superficial resemblances. The first of these is in line with Boyd's notion of epistemic access becoming less diffuse and more focused on true causal entities as the scientific enterprise progresses. The second consideration — the perception-as-reality of the description — is, however, no less important. It represents what might be thought of as a perceptual phenomenon rather than a research strategy, and reflects the tacit acceptance of a certain view regarding what an ultimate explanation of certain puzzles will have to be like.

The case of space, to which I have already alluded, provides a revealing example of the latter pheonomenon. Our current scientific conception of space is a projection of geometry onto the observations of mechanics. But plane geometry was well known and widely used by the ancient Egyptians in surveying and building. Later it was developed into an exquisite formal system by the Greeks. Yet, for the Egyptians, it was a way of calculating, like a system of ciphers, whereas, for the Greeks, it was a demonstration of the perfect Platonic order. It was not until two millennia later that Galileo began the transformation which eventually resulted in the view that is so commonplace and mundane today that virtually no vestige remains of the Aristotelian ideas of natural motions and natural places. Everyone imagines space as that perfectly empty infinite isotropic three-dimensional receptacle, quite independent of the earth or any object, and capable of locating such mathematical entities as points and infinite straight lines. Such a strange idea was literally unthinkable before the seventeenth century. In fact not even Galileo totally accepted it. For him a straight line was still bound to the earth's surface. It was not until Newton that the task of "geometrization of the world" (to use Butterfield's, 1965, phrase) was completed.

The transformation that led to the reification of geometry – to accepting the axioms of Euclid as a literal description of physical space – profoundly affected the course of science. Both Hanson (1958) and Polanyi (1966) have argued that the importance of accepting a system as a literal account of reality is that it enables scientists to see that certain further observations are possible and others are not. It goes beyond merely asserting that certain things happen in certain ways and becomes a way of seeing. It is thus quite distinct from metaphor, which by contrast remains a rather self-conscious imposition of an unrelated extrinsic system believed to reflect important aspects of similarity to the primary phenomena. Whereas metaphor *induces* a (partial) equivalence between two known phenomena, a literal account describes the phenomenon in the authentic terms in which it is "seen."

The reason I have gone into this digression concerning the reification of geometry is that for me the notion of computation stands in the same relation to cognition as geometry does to mechanics: It is not a metaphor but part of a literal description of cognitive activity. This is not to say that there are not also metaphorical uses of computer concepts. Indeed most contemporary writing about cognition (especially by philosophers!) does make extensive use of the computer as a metaphor for the brain, and of software as a metaphor for mind.

But is seems to me that *computation*, and all that it entails regarding rule-governed transformations on intentionally interpreted symbolic expressions, applies just as literally to mental activity as it does to the activity of digital computers. Such a term is in no sense a literal description of the operation of electronic computers that has been metaphorically transported to the primary subject of mind. The relation between computation and artifacts is just as abstract as the relation between computation and mental activity (the same can be said of the term "information"). Both require that we give terms an interpretation in these domains, precisely the way Euclidian axioms are given a realistic interpretation in classical space, and the axioms of non-Euclidean geometry are given a realistic interpretation in the space of special relativity. I see no significant differences here which would lead me to characterize computation, but not geometry, as metaphor.

Of course, accepting computations as a literal account imposes a special burden on those who take that road (and currently they are not all that numerous). We can no longer get away with certain kinds of permanent imprecision. Being committed to the view that we are literally describing mental activity we take on the responsiblity of giving an explanation by functional reduction – an explanation which does not itself terminate with an appeal to metaphor, empirical generalizations, stipulated properties of different media, (e.g., analogue media), similarity spaces, and the like, *except* as these are clearly marked to be explanatory debts to be repaid at a later time and in a particular manner (that is, as further explicated computations). Thus, imprecision is permitted – as it must be if science is to develop – but within a clearly circumscribed top-down research strategy, and with the character of the ultimate explanatory terms specified by the particular realist view of the enterprise.

Naturally a great deal more needs to be said concerning this position – and I have already said some of it elsewhere (Pylyshyn, 1978c). For the present purposes, my point is that although Boyd's account of the utility of metaphor in science is insightful, it might be of additional value to distinguish among various kinds of imprecision associated with metaphor, and to try to characterize what constitutes literal usage along the lines I have sketched – especially for those cases which are not in the empiricist mold of linguistic rigor and consequently might appear to the outsider to be cases of theory-constitutive metaphor.

NOTE

1 This example is a slightly disguised reference to the work of Waltz (1975) who designed an elegant system for perceiving scenes consisting of polyhedral objects and shadows. The "visemes" in this case were edges which were classified into eleven labeled categories. Grammarlike constraints on co-occurrence of different label combinations at various types of vertices, further constrained when two vertices share a common edge, made "parsing" the image straightforward.

METAPHOR
AND
EDUCATION

Metaphor and Learning

HUGH G. PETRIE

Metaphor in education

There seem to be two main views of the role of metaphor in education. On the one hand, there is the idea that metaphors are primarily of aesthetic value, with perhaps some secondary utility as heuristic aids. This view concentrates on metaphors along with other linguistic forms, such as analogies, similes, and synecdoche, as figures of speech in literature, especially poetry. The poet's insight is often expressed through metaphor. Occasionally, proponents of the aesthetic value of metaphor also admit that it has some heuristic value in educational contexts outside of literature. For example, some of metaphor's relatives, like analogies and models are often used as teaching aids. The solar-system model of the atom is familiar to high-school physics students. But even in such a positive view of the pedagogical value of metaphors, it is usually claimed that although possibly useful and often ornamental, the metaphors and models are not essential to a cognitive understanding of what is being taught and learned. This is at least part of the position held by those whom Black calls in this volume, the appreciators of metaphor.

On the other hand, metaphors occasionally receive bad press in education. Metaphors are used when one is too lazy to do the hard, analytic work of determining precisely what one wants to say. Consequently, metaphors encourage sloppy thought. In addition, metaphors can be tremendously misleading. There are a number of different ways in which metaphors can be taken and so the possibility of mistake abounds. If metaphors are eliminated, there will be fewer mistakes. Finally, metaphors and their close cousins, slogans, are often used to cloud educational issues and reduce complex matters to simple-minded banalities. In short, as has been noted in other connections, metaphors have all the advantage over explicit language as does theft over honest toil (for example, R. M. Miller, 1976). Such views are often held by those whom Black has called the depreciators of metaphor.

Notice that both appreciators and depreciators of metaphors in education tend to agree that the *cognitive* significance of metaphor is severely limited. The main home of metaphor is in poetic insight and any more general cognitive function is ideally better served by explicit analytic language. At best, metaphors may be nice, but they are scarcely necessary for comprehension, communication, or coming to know (but, cf. Ortony, 1975). Yet it is precisely this view that I wish to challenge.

There are two different sources from which the challenge can be issued. On the one hand, it can be argued that metaphor enables one to transfer learning and understanding from what is well-known to what is less well-known in a vivid and memorable way, thus enhancing learning. This claim is essentially a psychological one, asserting a connection between vividness, or more precisely, imageability, and learning (Paivio, 1971). It is an important point if explicit analytic modes of presentation lead to less memorable learning than vivid metaphorical teaching strategies. For even if we grant the possible misuse and misleadingness of metaphor and assume the goal of making what is learned explicit, it follows that we ought to teach metaphorically for increased memorability, guard against misleading interpretations, and only later make things explicit. Thus even though metaphors may turn out to be dispensable to a logical characterization of the subject being taught and learned, they may be indispensable to the pedagogical process of acquiring that subject.

The view that metaphors may be nice, but are not necessary, can also be challenged from a different quarter. It can be claimed that the very possibility of learning something radically new can only be understood by presupposing the operation of something very much like metaphor. This is not just the heuristic claim that metaphors are often useful in learning, but the epistemic claim that metaphor, or something like it, renders intelligible the aquisition of new knowledge.

Plato first posed the problem in his famous paradox of the *Meno*:

> You argue that a man cannot enquire either about that which he knows or about that which he does not know; for if he knows, he has no need to enquire; and if not, he cannot; for he does not know the very subject about which he is to enquire. (Plato, *Meno* 80E; Jowett translation)

How *is* it possible to learn something radically new? — a question also raised by Pylyshyn (this volume).

There is an educational formulation of the issue raised in the *Meno* paradox. If we assume, as was done in the nineteenth century, that we can simply pour knowledge into the heads of students, then we are faced with the problem of how those students can ever recognize what they receive as knowledge, rather than as something to be rote-memorized. If, however, we insist, as current conventional wisdom would have it, that learning must always start with what the student presently knows, then we are faced with the problem of how the student can come to know anything radically new. It is my thesis that metaphor is one of the central ways of leaping the epistemological chasm between old knowledge and radically new knowledge (see also Petrie, 1976).

The belief that there is such an epistemological chasm depends upon certain presuppositions for which I shall not here argue. Although controversial, three of these presuppositions are widely accepted. First, experience is never directly of the world as it is, but is always in part constituted by our modes of representation and understanding. For example, we experience the chairs upon which we sit as dense and impenetrable, although they are, physicists tell us, composed of clouds of very tiny particles. Second, most learning consists of processing that which impinges on us in terms of a context of rules or schemata. These contexts of rules form our modes of understanding. Much learning is thus being able to experience in terms of contexts. We learn about the Civil War by seeing it is a war within a nation. Third, on some occasions we learn by actually changing the contexts of understanding. The result of changed structures of understanding is what I call radically new knowledge. This latter phenomenon is graphically illustrated by the so-called ambigious figures. Figure 10 can be seen as either a duck or as a rabbit. Piaget notes the distinction between these two kinds of learning by distinguishing between assimilation and accommodation. During assimilation, we learn by changing experience to fit our concepts and modes of understanding. During accommodation, we learn by changing our concepts and modes of understanding to fit our experience.

The problem posed by the *Meno* paradox occurs with accommodation. If understanding and learning involve being able to put that which is learned in a context, then how can we ever rationally come to *change* our contexts of understanding? It seems we would either have to presuppose that we already possess, at least implicitly, the context which renders intelligible the radically new thing we are attempting to learn, or else we would have to admit that the learning of something radically new is arbitrary and subjective. Both alternatives, unfortunately, have considerable precedent in education. What I shall suggest here is a third alternative – that metaphor can provide a

Figure 10

rational bridge from the known to the radically unknown, from a given context of understanding to a changed context of understanding.

There are probably devices other than metaphor that serve a bridge from the known to the unknown, such as analogies, models, and theories. There are, no doubt, important differences between metaphors and such other devices, which a full treatment would have to explore. Conversely, there are many features of metaphor itself with which I shall not be directly concerned. The central question for me is, "How is radically new knowledge possible?" With the presuppositions noted above that question becomes, "How is rational change of contexts of understanding possible?" Finally, these "How?" questions are to be taken in the epistemic and not the psychological sense. In other words, the question is, "How is one to make intelligible the acquisition of new knowledge?" not, "What are the processes involved?"

My concern with metaphor is derivative from this central educational concern. I believe an examination of metaphor will show that it does, on occasion, play this crucial epistemic role of rendering the acquisition of radically new knowledge intelligible. Analogies, models, and exemplary problem solutions also sometimes perform this function and, I think, in very similar ways to metaphor. The feature that all of these have in common is that they invite the use of a familiar rule-governed device for dealing with the material to be learned in ways which require the bending or even breaking of the familiar rules. Metaphor is one crucial way this happens; analogies, models, and exemplars are others. Whether one wishes to elevate this central epistemic role of rendering intelligible changes in cognitive structure into a new principle of grouping these disparate devices as all being a form of metaphor is

not my concern. My purpose is rather to argue that metaphor as traditionally understood often plays a central role in the acquisition of radically new knowledge.

Metaphor

There are two issues in the voluminous literature on metaphor which
are of particular interest for my purposes. The first is the distinction
between comparative and interactive metaphors. On the comparative
view of metaphor, what a metaphor does is to say implicitly that two
apparently dissimilar things have a similarity in common after all.
Thus, in speaking of the "flow" of electricity, despite the obvious dissimilarities between electricity and liquids, it is held that there is a
fundamental similarity – they both move in a fluid kind of way. On
this view, a metaphor is an implicit comparison, whereas a simile or an
anology is an explicit comparison (Green, 1971). Metaphors transfer
meaning and understanding by comparison. It should be noted that
comparative metaphors would not serve to make intelligible the
acquisition of radically new knowledge. For, by hypothesis, radically
new knowledge is that knowledge which results from a change in cognitive structures, whereas comparisons must occur within a given cognitive structure which renders the comparison sensible. The comparative
level of metaphor might allow for extensions of already existing knowledge, but it would not provide a new form of understanding.

There are, however, problems with attempting to construe all metaphors as implicit comparisons. Consider the example (Haynes, 1975),
"Virginity is the enamel of the soul." Is the implicit comparison to be
between the positive features of clarity, strength, and protectiveness, or
the negative features of rigidity, brittleness, and enclosure? Nothing in
the metaphor tells us and only nonlinguistic contextual knowledge of
speaker or hearer seems useful. For reasons such as this, many writers
have claimed that there is also an interactive level of metaphor. Black
says,"It would be more illuminating in some of these cases to say that
the metaphor creates the similarity then to say that it formulates some
similarity antecedently existing" (Black, 1962b, p. 37). The interactive
level of metaphor is peculiarly appropriate for my purposes, because if
it *creates* similarities, then it could provide the bridge between a student's earlier conceptual and representational schemes and the later
scheme of the totally unfamiliar subject to be learned by the student.
Interactive metaphor would allow truly new forms of knowledge and
understanding to be acquired by the student without presupposing the
student already knows, in some sense, that which is being learned.

The discussion so far points to the fact that a metaphor, comparative or interactive, depends on the cognitive scheme presupposed for understanding the metaphor. One and the same metaphor can be comparative *and* interactive, depending on the point of view taken. An educational metaphor like, "The atom is a miniature solar system," is probably a comparative metaphor from the point of view of the teacher. The teacher already knows both about the solar system and about atoms and is relying upon the similarity between them which already exists in our collective understanding. But from the point of view of the student just beginning atomic physics, the metaphor, assuming it is successful, will be interactive. It will (help) create the similarity *for the student*. And remember I have rejected the view that such similarities are simply given to common human experience, independently of how different people represent their experience. Thus, the fact that the metaphor can be interactive for the student is crucial. For it may provide a way of understanding how the student's modes of representation and understanding can be changed, although granting that experience is dependent on a particular mode or scheme of understanding.

The second general issue concerning the nature of metaphor that I wish to discuss is whether a metaphor can be identified by some set of linguistic features independent of its use on particular occasions. The appropriate category for metaphor, at least for educational purposes, seems to be not that of formal linguistic sentence meanings, but rather utterance meanings or speech acts (Searle, 1969, p. 16). Such a categorization is suggested by the necessity of taking account of the context of understanding in deciphering a metaphor. Given the current typology of speech acts, there is not one which corresponds to speaking metaphorically. One could probably add such a category and give conditions for its employment (Loewenberg, 1975a); however, I am more concerned at present with looking at the connection of uttering a metaphor with making an assertion.

Assertions are speech acts that are properly assessed in the true–false domain. Considered as a potential assertion, the utterance of a metaphor will always turn out to be false, because the world just is not the way it is represented as being by the words in the utterance if those words are given their literal interpretation. A basic convention of language is that people intend to utter meaningful, useful, and in the case of assertions, true, statements. When a teacher utters a metaphorical statement in a typical educational context, the student's first thought tends to be that the teacher is asserting something. That is, the student tries to assimilate the utterance to literal schemata, rules, and conventions. But in attempting such an assimilation, the statement turns out to be fairly obviously false. Is the teacher just confused or mistaken? That is certainly one way students sometimes cope with the recognition that the teacher has produced a false utterance. As educators, we hope, however, that the student will try to make sense of the utterance in a different way, making use of clues that the teacher is serious and attempting to say something important and useful. Such clues are standard in the educational context.

If the student already possesses a cognitive structure sufficient to render intelligible the implicit comparison contained in a comparative metaphor, then the disturbance caused by the recognition that the statement is false is easily removed. The student transfers those literal features of the metaphor being singled out for comparison to the new subject matter. Thus the literal orbits of the solar system are transferred to the electron orbits of the atom. This is a case of extending one's existing cognitive schemes to cover new cases. There is no radically new knowledge, for the cognitive structures remain the same; only their field of application has changed.

Sometimes, however, the student does not possess the cognitive structure that would enable him or her to interpret the metaphor in a comparative way. In these cases, the disturbance created by the recognition that the metaphorical statement is literally false becomes an anomaly, in that it cannot be assimilated to the student's existing cognitive structure. The student will have to accommodate his or her cognitive structure to account for the anomaly. If the student is somehow "in the presence" of the new material to be learned, then the student can try to deal with the material as if the metaphor were literally true. In the case of the flow of electricity, for example, this would involve looking at rates of flow, ways flow can be dammed up, perhaps stored, and so on. As the student attempts such a literal focusing on the material, the teacher and the material itself can provide corrections to the knowledge that does not transfer directly. I shall have more to say about how the student utilizes the metaphor to change his or her cognitive structure, but for now I simply want to emphasize that it is the *anomalous* character of an interactive metaphor, anomalous in terms of the student's *current* set of rules for understanding, which distinguishes the way metaphor transfers chunks of experience from the way in which literal language or comparative metaphor transfers chunks of experience. Literal language requires only assimilation to existing frameworks of understanding. Comparative metaphor requires simple extensions of the framework in the light of a more comprehensive framework. Accommodation of anomaly requires changes in the framework of understanding. It is this general requirement of a change in cognitive framework that provides the distinction between the ways interactive metaphor and literal language are to be understood and secures the importance of metaphor in considering how radically new knowledge is acquired.

Metaphor and the growth of science

This brief description of how an interactive metaphor creates an anomaly for a student and leads the student toward changes in cognitive structure bears a striking analogy to Kuhn's description of the workings of science during scientific revolutions (Kuhn, 1970a). During the periods of normal science, puzzles and problems are solved by the use of the accepted paradigm of the moment. Occasionally, such problems or disturbances resist current paradigm efforts to solve them, and they become anomalies. The scientist then searches for a new metaphor or model which can remove the anomaly. The main difference between the scientist on the frontiers of knowledge and the student is that in the student's case the metaphor provided by the teacher, if it is a good one, is likely to be more immediately helpful than are the variants tried out by the scientist. But except for a kind of trust in the teacher, the student does not really know any more about where he or she will end up than does the scientist. This seems to me to go directly against the educational dogma that one should always lay out in advance for the student exactly what the goals of the learning experience are taken to be. For in cases where the goals are to change significantly the student's current cognitive structure, it will not be possible to lay out in advance learning outcomes the student can initially understand. Only metaphorically and ex post facto can the student be brought to understand the goals expressed in the terms and categories of the to-be-learned subject matter.

One of the crucial senses of "paradigm" for Kuhn is what he calls an exemplar. What is an exemplar? It is a concrete problem with its solution, which together constitute one of the scientific community's standard examples. Acquiring these exemplars is a critical part of the scientist's training, and they serve the absolutely central function of allowing the student to "apply theory to practice," although, as I shall show, this is a misleading way of making the point. The exemplar is what enables the student to deploy the symbolic generalizations of the theory being learned in particular problem situations. This role is extremely important, because on Kuhn's view, we do not always link up theory and observation statements by means of correspondence rules, nor is there any direct access to the world independent of our theoretical language. In short, having denied a direct perceptual link to the world "as it is," and having accepted the fact that observation is theory-laden, another account of the link between our beliefs and nature must be provided. Kuhn's suggestion is that, in an important sense, exemplars serve this function.

How do exemplars work? Kuhn has given an extended example of a young boy learning to recognize ducks, swans, and geese by repeated ostensive definition and correction of mistakes (Kuhn, 1974). His account goes no further than the simple observation that this is indeed how such learning often happens. Kuhn claims that what the boy has done is not learn "rules" of application, but rather the boy has learned a primitive perception of similarity and difference. This perception precedes any linguistic formulation of the similarity relations. Can these nonlinguistic similarity relations be spelled out in more detail? If so, perhaps a third alternative, besides direct access and correspondence rules between theory and observation, can be given some plausibility as a way of accounting for the link between observation and nature or between theoretical language and observational language about nature.

What I wish to suggest is that understanding an interactive metaphor includes, as an essential part, activities similar to those involved in acquiring an exemplar. For when a metaphor has effected a change of cognitive structure (where the "rules" of the cognitive structure need not be explicitly formulated or formulatable), the student has a new way of dealing with, describing, and thinking about nature, just as the science student in acquiring an exemplar has a new way of deploying symbolic generalizations in nature.

The key to both processes is that they are bound up with *activities* on the part of the student. It is not simply a case of hearing words, understanding them literally, and applying them directly. It is a case of *acting* in the ecology. For the science student, this is brought out by Kuhn's insistence that in acquiring exemplars the student requires diagrams, demonstrations, and laboratory exercises and experiments. Even the young boy learning about ducks, swans, and geese is doing something. He is classifying and being corrected. Of course, language is involved, not as a kind of labeling, but as a prod to *activities* of sorting, classifying, and perceiving similarities and differences. I believe my subsequent discussion of interactive metaphor in a pedagogical situation, especially as viewed from the student's perspective, will be directly relevant to Kuhn's claims that exemplars provide the way of understanding how language relates to the world.

Thus the educational functions I am proposing for metaphor are that it does, indeed, make learning more memorable, and that it does, indeed, help move one from the more familiar to the less familiar. But I am also claiming that metaphor is what enables one to pass from the more familiar to the unfamiliar in the sense that it provides one mechanism for changing our modes of representing the world in thought and language. It provides this mechanism not through a direct labeling, nor through explicit rules of application, but rather because in order to understand an interactive metaphor, one must focus one's *activities* on nodes of relative stability in the world. Language bumps into the world at those places where our activity runs up against similar boundaries in diverse situations.

How do educational metaphors work?

Let me begin this section by quoting a fairly lengthy parable from Donald Campbell (1963).

Let us pose to a hypothetical animal psychologist the problem of diagnosing the habits of an aged and experienced rat shipped to him from another laboratory. What would happen? The process would be a hit-or-miss, random, trial-and-error procedure. The foreign rat under varying degrees of deprivation would be placed in all the likely pieces of apparatus available in the diagnostic laboratory. Knowledge that the rat shared some common culture, i.e., that it was a university-psychology rat, would make the selections of apparatus somewhat less random. The rat would be tried in a lever-pressing Skinner box, while buzzers buzzed and lights flashed, and any combinations that resulted in increased lever pressing would be taken as symptoms of some habit. The rat might be placed on a Lashley jumping stand while various colors and designs were placed in the card slots; and if jumping occurred, an effort would be made to find to which cue cards the jumping was most consistent. Multiple T and Y maze segments would be tried. The process would be one of random search, and the presence of a common culture merely serves to limit the range of things tried or to make certain guesses more probable. And no matter how clever the research, there would still be the possibility that important and highly routinized habits of the rat went unnoticed by the diagnostician.

The diagnostician makes the initial definition of stimuli and the initial classification of response. They represent classes of objects and behaviors which the experimenter can consistently discriminate, and which he guesses the animal might also. Once he finds some evidence of the stimulus-response consistency on the part of the rat, the experimenter would typically start varying stimuli and varying his classification of muscle movements in order to approximate more closely the appropriate *genus proximum* for the habit; that is, he would try and find out whether certain subtleties discriminable by him were also discriminable and being discriminated by the rat. Thus, if he found that the rat jumped to a yellow circle, he would start varying the shape and the color of the stimulus card to find which degree of yellow, if any, maximized the response, which shape maximized it, or whether shape made any difference. At the same time, he would strive to learn the appropriate classification of the consistency of response. Was it a consistency of muscle contraction, or a consistency of locomotor achievement, an object consistency, etc.? Gradually, by trial and error, the diagnostician would obtain a more specific and appropriately labeled stimulus-response correlation. The final classification, however, would still be in the scientist's terms, and would be limited to discriminations that the scientist could make. (pp. 101–2)

This parable could be used as an analogy to illustrate the problems of the teacher in diagnosing the student's conceptual scheme, so that lessons and learning experiences can be designed accordingly. However, I want to suggest that it is even more fruitful to look at the parable as an analogy to the *student's* position in being faced with a teacher attempting to pass on a part of our collective understanding, which requires not merely an elaboration of the student's existing conceptual scheme, but rather a fundamental change in that conceptual scheme. And remember, I am accepting the theory-ladenness of observation and, hence, forswearing any attempt to teach the student by means of assembling "building blocks" of basic perception. The building blocks themselves will have to be constructed or modified in the course of the learning experience. On this view, the student is analogous to the experimenter and the teacher to the university rat whose habits the experimenter is trying to establish. Such a switch in the more usual way of looking at teacher and student may be salutary in itself. With this in mind, how might Campbell's parable read?

Let us pose to a hypothetical student the problem of diagnosing the habits of an aged and experienced professor teaching a new course for the student, where the student has no information about prior environments and reinforcements of the professor. The process would be a hit-and-miss, trial-and-error process. Knowledge that the professor shared some common culture, i.e., that it was a university psychology professor, would make the selections of apparatus somewhat less random. The professor would be placed in a classroom while questions would be asked about different aspects of the course, and any combination of types of questions which produced increased enthusiasm and nods of the head by the professor would be taken as symptoms of some habit. The professor might be placed at a desk while various student papers were used as discrimination cards and if any markings of "A" occurred, an effort would be made to find which papers were most frequently marked in that way. In similar fashion, office visits, and examination answers would be explored by the student. The presence of the university culture would serve simply to limit the range of things tried by the student, or to make certain guesses more probable. But no matter how clever the research by the student, there would still be the possibility that important, highly specific, and stable habits of the professor would go unnoticed by the student.

The initial definition of stimulus and classification of response are the student's. They represent classes of objects and classes of behaviors which the student can consistently discriminate, and which he guesses the professor can also. Once he finds some evidence of stimulus-response consistency on the part of the professor, he would typically start varying stimuli and varying his classification of movements in order to approximate more closely the optimal description of the habit. Thus, if he found that the professor marked "good" at a place in a paper which questioned suppositions, he would start varying suppositions questioned and the depth of the questioning to find what maximized the contingency. Likewise, he would try to discern the appropriate classification of response. Does the professor want clarity of originality, or what? Gradually, by trial and error, the student would obtain a more specific and appropriately labeled conceptual map of the subject being taught. The final classifications would still be in the student's terms and would be limited to classifications which the student could make.

What I believe this parable illustrates is the kind of triangulating of thought and activity which can lead through a succession of iterations from a given way of conceiving a situation to a radically different way of conceiving the situation. And all the while, the modes of representation are the scientist's or student's. There is no direct contact with the world "as it is." There is only conjecture and correction in a process that ultimately focuses, not necessarily on "the truth," but on a representational structure that is adequate for the scientist or student in dealing with the world. It is, I believe, in this way that one learns something radically new.

In almost all cases, bringing to bear thought and action in their ordinary literal guises is all that is necessary to resolve the problematic situation. The kind of learning that goes on in such cases is what I have called ordinary learning. It is primarily the utilization of existing cognitive structures to deal with our experience.

In cases involving the use of a metaphor that is comparative from the point of view of the student, the process is only slightly more complicated. Since the metaphor is literally false, the recognition of that falsehood will constitute part of the problematic situation for the student. Since I am assuming, however, that the metaphor is comparative for the student, the construal of it is relatively straightforward. The larger cognitive structure in terms of which the implicit comparison makes sense is brought to bear and the similarities noted. One may have extended one's cognitive structure, but that is about the only change that has occurred.

In a few cases, however, neither ordinary learning nor a simple extension of cognitive frameworks allows the student to deal with the problematic situation. In such cases, a change of cognitive structure, or as I have called it, the acquisition of radically new knowledge, is necessary. The problematic situation is in this case more properly described as an anomaly by analogy with Kuhn's discussion of paradigm shifts in science. Because I am discussing the construal of interactive metaphors which do lead to a change of cognitive structures, I shall call the problematic situation, an anomaly, even though in the vast majority of cases the problems can be, and are, resolved far short of a change in cognitive structure.

Nevertheless, the continuum briefly sketched above, from ordinary learning to construing comparative metaphors to the structural changes consequent on construing an interactive metaphor (probably with a lot of other steps between), is very important. For it shows that one need not be consciously aware of metaphors or the need for radical change in one's cognitive structure nor anything else so esoteric. In this sense, the process of construing a metaphor is, as Searle says in this book, a natural extension of ordinary thought and activity. Educationally, we can start with what we know, and by an iteration of triangulations of thought and activity on our experience, end up with radically new knowledge.

Now, this process of triangulation to achieve a more adequate fit between thought and action can surely proceed without the use of metaphors, narrowly conceived. Scientists occasionally change their cognitive structures in response to problems posed by their investigations. Surely no one has provided them with a metaphor to guide these changes. Of course, they often have guiding models or analogies or theories which may serve the same role as metaphors, but that is not here at issue. The important thing is that metaphor is one way of performing this function of guiding cognitive changes, and, furthermore, it is a way which can be intentionally used by a teacher in bringing about structural changes in the cognitive apparatus of students. So, in what follows, I shall be speaking of this process of altering cognitive schemes using the language of construing a metaphor. This is, I think, what happens in many cases of direct tuition and these are the ones of most immediate concern to educators.

Let me now try to break this process of acquiring radically new knowledge by means of triangulation on the world into its major components. Consider again the student diagnosing the psychology professor's habits. The first component I shall call the "anomaly step." This consists subjectively of the student's perception of the situation as problematic enough to require a minimal amount of cognitive activity.

Objectively, the activity will need to be of a sufficient magnitude to require a change in cognitive structure, although as I have mentioned, the student need not be aware of this. The student in taking the new course may be wholly unaware that the end product will be a partial restructuring of his or her cognitive schemes.

Assuming, then, that attempts at assimilating the problematic situation to ordinary cognitive structures have failed, and there really is an anomaly, in the technical sense of a problem requiring a change of cognitive structure, the second step, which I shall call "providing a metaphor" begins.

Acting as an experimenter, the student tries out various alternative classifications of the professor's behavior. These alternatives are focused to some extent by general background knowledge and the fact that the anomaly is occurring at a certain place in the student's conceptual scheme. Of course, the most important source of an alternative classification for the student is the metaphor provided by the teacher. Yet in the sense that the variant cognitive structure, at the time of the variation, need not contain the final solution or diagnosis, the learning process will necessarily be interactive for the student. Although the metaphor being used by the teacher may be comparative from the teacher's point of view, it is an interactive metaphor from the student's point of view. The student may trust that the teacher is trying to provide a guide, but that merely helps remove the possibility that the clearly false assertion is to be assimilated to, for example, teacher confusion. But the metaphor is a guide in that it essentially says, "Look at and deal with this new situation as if it were like one you already know about." Thus, the second step in the process of understanding a metaphor is conceiving of possible variant classifications as if they were like what is already known. This is what occurs as the student begins conceiving of the course in terms already familiar to the student, or in terms appropriate if the metaphor were literally true.

The third step in the process is actually acting in the world and observing the results. An interactive metaphor is not going to succeed unless activity takes place. The activity is guided by the metaphor. On the first trial, one can conceive of the activity taking place as if the metaphor were literally true. One behaves in the new area as one would have behaved in the area in which the metaphor is literally true. The point of the metaphorically suggested activity is to see if *it* will remove the anomaly. Does the teacher respond positively to the student's papers, questions, and examination answers? If not, does the response indicate that the activity was close?

Notice that each of the steps thus far mentioned, recognizing an anomaly, conceiving the problematic situation as if the metaphor were literally true of it, and acting on the situation in those terms, provides a triangulation on the problematic situation. The anomaly step focuses on the situation in terms of the existing framework and characterizes the situation in existing-framework terms. The metaphor suggests a new characterization of the situation, and activity on the situation provides a third triangulation. Of course, some of the steps may be combined, as when a good metaphor creates the anomaly because it is literally false and simultaneously creates a new characterization that can guide subsequent activity.

The fourth step in construing an educational metaphor is the correction of the activity. Typically, the first activity carried out in terms of the metaphor's suggested conceptualization will not be quite right; yet, from the point of view of the anomaly, it will show promise. The teacher, typically, will provide such a correction, and a new activity – close to, but slightly different from, the original – will be attempted. For example, the professor's encouragement of arguing for presuppositions, instead of merely expressing them, will be discovered. The corrected activity provides another triangulation of the problematic situation and reflects back on the metaphorical conception, beginning to show in what sense the ultimately correct conceptualization will differ from the initial metaphorically suggested conceptualization. Likewise, the corrected activity reflects back on the original conception of the situation as anomalous, showing the extent to which the anomaly is being removed by the corrected activity and its evolving conceptualization. And then the process starts all over again. To what extent is there still an anomaly? The anomaly is now defined by the extent to which the metaphorical conceptualization is still inadequate; this points to a modification of conceptualization, which in turn brings about slightly modified activity, with a new balance of triangulation on the problematic situation. To the extent that corrections are still needed, the process may be repeated several times. Figures 11 through 14 illustrate the process. It is essentially the iterated process of triangulation of conceptualization, and activity powered by the perception of remaining anomaly, that enable the student gradually to change conceptual schemes to accommodate totally new experiences. And it is the reaching of a final equilibrium of conceptualization and activity that is the test of the success of the metaphor, not whether we can explain the meaning of the metaphor (R. M. Miller, 1976). For whether or not we can explain the meaning of the metaphor tells us nothing about whether the student has grasped that meaning.

The same steps are present when one considers metaphor from the external point of view of the teacher, but the steps look somewhat dif-

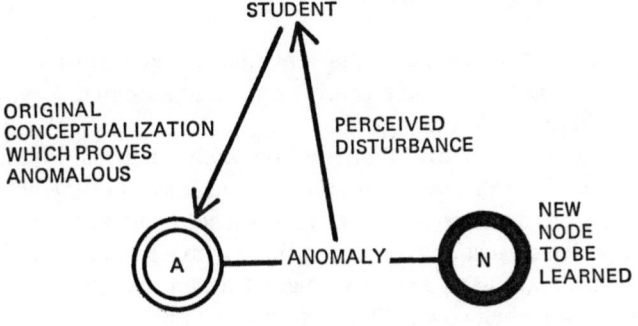

STUDENT

ORIGINAL
CONCEPTUALIZATION
WHICH PROVES
ANOMALOUS

PERCEIVED
DISTURBANCE

A — ANOMALY — N

NEW
NODE
TO BE
LEARNED

Figure 11

STUDENT

METAPHORICAL
CONCEPTION
IF TAKEN LITERALLY

ORDINARY
REFERENT
OF METAPHOR

A

M_1

N

Figure 12

STUDENT

FIRST ACTIVITY
A_1

A

M_1 A_1

N

Figure 13

STUDENT

M_2 A_2

A

M_1 A_1

N

Figure 14

ferent. In the first place, since the metaphor is comparative from the teacher's standpoint, the whole process can be represented most perspicuously in a single figure (see figure 15).

The teacher must pay special attention to both the initial intelligibility to the student of the metaphor and the appropriateness of the activity for triangulation on the new material. The teacher must also consider the ecology in which corrections leading ultimately to a reflective equilibrium in the student take place. For in triangulating on the new material, the student will stop when conception and activity have combined to remove the anomaly. There are equilibria which do not match the collective understanding the teacher is trying to impart, and these are the ones that must be avoided. Probably the best way, in general, to avoid such a possibility is to provide an ecology rich in opportunities to apply the student's newly established equilibrium of conceptualization and activity. For if the student's triangulation is just a bit off, then in dealing with a variety of cases, such errors are more likely to become apparent to the teacher.

The power of metaphor as one of the ways of intentionally bringing about conceptual change should now be apparent. The teacher presumably has a grasp both of the student's current ways of structuring his or her experience, and of the conceptual structure as it is found in the material to be taught to the student. The teacher can, therefore, choose instructional metaphors that will serve to create an anomaly for the student, as well as suggest initial conceptual guides to removing the anomaly. Furthermore, activities for the student can be chosen with a

Figure 15

view to guiding the successive triangulations of thought and action toward the material to be learned. Students can learn something radically new without metaphors, but only if their variant conceptualizations serve the same function as metaphors – providing new ways of looking at old material.

The conceptual power of the notion of successive triangulation as the way in which pedagogical metaphors work can be brought out in the following way. Recall that I have rejected the view that one attaches language to the world through some kind of direct perceptual access, which in turn, provides the foundation for observation terms. On the contrary, observation is itself a mode of representing reality, and it depends on the concepts we use. Observational categories can and do change over time. If this is so, then both observational and theoretical representational systems will be intimately bound up with our conceptual frameworks. I believe a kind of equilibrium among these systems is the best we can hope for under these conditions. However, a great number of people believe such a perspective seriously threatens the objectivity of science and knowledge (e.g., Scheffler, 1967). For, how can one change one's equilibria in response to the way the world is if observation is theory-dependent? The answer suggested here is that one triangulates on reality with one's representational schemes, and some of these representational schemes, require activity in the world which may well be frustrated if the observational representation is inadequate. If all we had to do was think about the world, then indeed, one might fear for objectivity, but since we must *act* in the world and coordinate our activity with our thought so that activity and thought triangulate on nodes of stability in the world, objectivity and conceptual change are possible at the same time.

Returning for a moment to Kuhn, the importance of his exemplars or concrete problem solution is now apparent. For these are the *activities* that provide one of the crucial legs in the triangulation of conceptualization and activity on the subject area. Such problem solutions are indeed how the science student learns to deploy the disciplinary matrix in dealing with the world. And the four-step process I have outlined of anomaly, metaphor, activity, and correction can be seen as construing Kuhn's ostensive definition as an activity in which the student must *construct* the experience the definition is to apply to. At the same time, if the process of learning a new paradigm is at all like what I have described as the process of a student coming to change conceptual frameworks through the operation of interactive metaphor, then the process of paradigm shift is both intelligible and intelligent. It is intelligible as an iteration of triangulations of thought and action on the world. It is intelligent in that it proceeds *from* the rules of reasonableness currently held by the scientist/student at any point in the historical process. Thus the charges of radical subjectivism leveled against at least my emendations of Kuhn do not stand.

Frames of reference: an example

One of the interesting features that seems to characterize most people's unreflective concept of motion is that there is no difficulty in deciding whether something is in motion or not. One simply looks and sees. Yet, an essential feature of motion is that it is properly describable only relative to a coordinate system. Where the observer happens to be located when trying to decide whether something is in motion is essential to understanding motion. It at least seems plausible that to acquire the concept of motion relative to a coordinate system would require a change of conceptual structure on the part of most high-school students and not merely an assimilation of experience to existing structure. It is clear to science teachers that the idea of judging motion relative to a coordinate system will require, for many students, a quite new way of processing experience.

How do secondary-school science texts approach this problem? Let me illustrate in some detail how one randomly chosen text treats relative motion (Fisk & Blecha, 1966, pp. 217–18). After having noted several examples of motion, the text suggests that one look at a nearby object, for example, a chair, and decide whether or not it is moving. The authors assume the answer will be no, and then they point out that the chair is on the earth's surface, and the earth is moving, so is not the chair moving after all? This step fairly clearly fits the idea of introducing an anomaly into the student's conceptual scheme. They ask if the chair is moving, assume the student will judge that it is not, but then point out to the student the chair is on the earth and the earth moves. Does the chair move or does it not?

The authors have to assume two things about the student here; first, that the standard unreflective judgment of the student will be that the chair is not moving, and second, that the student knows the earth moves. Without those two assumptions, the attempt to introduce an anomaly into the student's view of the world will fail, for the student will simply reject one of the things he or she is being invited to consider, probably the claim that the earth moves. What this illustrates is that an anomaly will *be* an anomaly only from the standpoint of a conceptual scheme. If the student does not know about the earth's movement, no anomaly will occur.

The authors of the text seem implicitly to recognize this problem, for their next paragraph straightforwardly reminds the student about the earth's movement, both rotational and orbital. They are not sure how many of their students will have the appropriate knowledge to recognize the thought experiment as creating an anomaly. The authors are also still a bit worried about the student's really understanding that the chair moves in virtue of its being on the earth. So the next paragraph is concerned with making the same point in terms of a book on the seat of a moving car. Does the book move or not? From the point of view of the car, no; from the point of view outside the car, yes. Surely, most modern students will have had experience with cars, both inside of them and outside of them.

Next, the authors try to make the anomaly explicit by suggesting it may seem strange to say the book is both moving and not moving. Here they are relying on the idea that everyone probably finds contradictions anomalous. The metaphor to be used to solve the anomaly is then introduced. The book's moving and not moving seems strange only because the book is being observed from two different *frames of reference*. I take it that the metaphorical term here is "frame of reference." This is the step I have called providing the metaphor.

The authors next define "frame of reference" as "a place or position from which an object's motion may be observed and described" (Fisk & Blecha, 1966, p. 218). It might be objected that since "frame of reference" is being explicitly defined, it is not a metaphor at all. I grant that "frame of reference" probably *is* a technical literal term for people *who already know how to use it*. For the student, however, it may have no literal referent at all. Does it mean that the student is to put up a picture frame and block out part of his or her experience? That would be one "literal" meaning. The point is crucial for pedagogy. A technical term may have a literal meaning for those who understand the subject but be completely metaphorical for the student just learning the subject.

But it will be objected that the term was *given* a literal definition and so still fails to be metaphorical. The plausibility of this objection rests on the presupposition that the students, possibly through the first couple of thought experiments with earth and car movement, have already grasped the notion of *different points of view* – which is, after all, the core of the frame of reference idea. If they have, then "a place or position from which an object's motion may be observed and described" makes sense as referring to different places at the same time with putative observers at those places at the same time. But if the student has not yet grasped the notion of different points of view, then "a place or position from which an object's motion may be observed" may literally mean to the student, the student's *own* place or position. Thus, unless one presupposes that most of the work of grasping the metaphor has already occurred, the "literal" definition may not do the trick at all.

This point can be brought out another way. I have suggested that activity guided by the metaphor is what comes next, at least in terms of the logic of understanding the operation of the metaphor. In the current case, that activity is largely confined to thought experiments (as it necessarily must be in most written materials). The student is asked to imagine the chair on the earth's surface and the book on the car's seat as both moving. The former experiment is *only* capable of being performed as a thought experiment, given current technology, whereas the latter – the book on the car seat – is something that virtually all students will have experienced. In this way, the thought experiments take on the logical role of the activity that helps one to triangulate on motion. The metaphor "frame of reference," however that is initially understood by the student, provides the other leg of the triangulation. If the thought experiments do not provide sufficient activity for the student to get a triangulation on the idea of relative motion, they could be supplemented by actual activities of the same type.

The fourth requirement is correction. The first attempts at triangulation may result in fairly gross approximations, and corrections may be needed. The authors in this text refer back to the chair example and now, using frame of reference language, explicitly suggest that one look at the chair from a position in space near the moon, and as they put it, somewhat hopefully, "You would probably say that the chair is moving because the earth is moving" (p. 218). They are implicitly correcting a possible mistake with the chair–earth example, which they anticipate some students may have initially made.

In addition to the metaphor of frames of reference, the text uses this interesting diagram (figure 16) to supplement in a perceptual way the new conceptualization suggested by the metaphor. Through the sequence of pictures, the authors try to show how important "point of view" is. They take it for granted the student would, if in the spaceship, say the book fell to the floor. By presenting a schematic series of pictures of the spaceship ascending, an anomaly is created, for the floor is also rising, But the pictures also illustrate the alternative conceptualization which can solve the problem. The pictures quite plainly *demand* that one take up a point of view outside the spaceship, and it is that "other point of view" that is the point of the lesson. Again the activity is left to thought experiments. However, the caption of the

Figure 16

illustration provides an opportunity for correcting potential student mistakes. *Both* "book falling" and "floor rising" seem appropriate from the point of view from which the pictures are seen. For the students to check out their ideas on such a fairly subtle point provides opportunity for correction and successive triangulations.

The overall point of this example is that, if successful, the student's conceptual framework has been changed in a fairly fundamental way through the use of the metaphor of a "frame of reference." The notion was given a literal definition in terms of place of observation, but the appropriateness of that definition depended upon the *nonlinguistic* ability to take up alternative points of view (another metaphor?), so that place of observation did not simply mean to the student "where *I* happen to be at the time." In learning to take up alternative points of view, the students acquire the ability to see the similarities involved in viewing the chair as motionless and as in movement, the book in the car as motionless and as in movement, and so on. Indeed the students *may* say something like, "Ah, it depends on how you look at it," but the verbal formula is unlikely to be *what* it is they have learned in learning to take up alternative points of view. Indeed, the verbal formula at best refers to what they have learned.

It would, furthermore, be a mistake to suppose that I have merely redescribed common sense. On the one hand, of course, any new theory or idea must accord, at least in large measure, with common sense, even the common sense of textbook writing. For after all, common sense is not likely to be completely wrong. What a new theory, or a new way of looking at common sense, does is to provide a possibly different way of going on in *new* cases. And I think my view of metaphor as a key pedagogical tool does do that. For it suggests that in some cases, those in which the desired learning is of a relatively new and different cognitive structure, explicit definition, for example, will be appropriate only *after* the basic idea is grasped, probably initially in a nonlinguistic way. Metaphor, activity, and correction are the appropriate tools and using them in new cases does not seem to me to constitute current educational common sense. According to the view presented here, it will not always be possible to lay out educational goals for a student in terms that the student can initially understand. The understanding will only come with the new cognitive structures which are to be learned. So the theory of metaphor as a pedagogical tool does have an empirical "bite."

Conclusion

I have tried to sketch the educational centrality of metaphor for bridging the gap between old and new knowledge. Educational metaphors need to be viewed from two perspectives – that of the student, and that of the teacher. From the latter standpoint, the metaphor may look like a concealed analogy, but what the teacher must never forget is that from the student's point of view, in those cases in which the metaphor really is to effect a cognitive change, it will *not* be merely an analogy.

Metaphors in education have traditionally been viewed as occasionally heuristically useful but essentially ornamental, and sometimes as downright pernicious. I have argued that metaphors are essential for learning in a number of ways. They may provide the most memorable ways of learning and thus be our most efficient and effective tools. But further, they are epistemologically necessary in that they seem to provide a basic way of passing from the well-known to the unknown. However, such a formulation is somewhat misleading. For the crucial use of metaphor is in moving from one conceptual scheme with its associated way of knowing to another conceptual scheme with *its* associated way of knowing. Finally, and of suggestive importance for current philosophy of science, it seems that the activity phase of understanding metaphors has much in common with exemplars – concrete problem solutions – in providing an alternative to immediate observation as one of the crucial legs for triangulating our theories and observations on the world.

Two features in current views of the nature of metaphor are of particular interest to a discussion of their educational implications. First, one and the same metaphor can be comparative from the point of view of the teacher and interactive from the point of view of the student. This possibility provides an understanding of how students' conceptual schemes can rationally be changed. Second, metaphors seem *not* to be formal linguistic entities, but rather belong to the category of speech acts. This feature shows how metaphors can be used to create an anomaly for the student, how they can provide a new view of the situation, and how they can be judged better or worse without having to speak of "metaphorical truth"; rather, one judges them as successful or unsuccessful actions.

My positive account of how educational metaphors work contains four steps. First, an anomaly is created for the student, often through the fact that the metaphor treated as a straightforward assertion would have to be false and teachers at least try not to utter falsehoods. The metaphor provides one leg of a triangulation by suggesting a way of looking at new, unknown material as if it were old, known material. In addition to the new view, opportunity to be active with the new material is critical. Often this activity may be in the form of thought experiments only, but the activity, the acquisition of nonlinguistic similarity relationships, is essential in providing the other leg for triangulating on the material to be learned. Corrections of initial triangulations and iterations of the whole process provide a mechanism whereby eventually the student's cognitive understanding of the material to be learned and his or her manner of acting on the material provide a triangulation that is significantly different from where the student began, and significantly like the triangulation enshrined in the disciplinary, collective understanding of the material, to justify our claim that the student has learned something radically new. The metaphor has been successful, not when we can say what it means, but when the triangulation allows the student to make judgments similar to those of experts in similar specific cases. Thus understanding the process involved in construing metaphor is what makes intelligible the ability to learn something new while admitting we must always start with what and how we already know.

Learning without Metaphor

THOMAS F. GREEN

Professor Petrie wishes to establish the claim that metaphor is "epistemologically necessary" for "learning something that is radically new." I believe that his attempt is unsuccessful. Seeing *that* it fails, however, is neither as difficult nor as interesting as seeing *why*. To discover the sources of his failure, we may begin with the following, rather complex, conditional. If one holds to a very narrow and limited conception of the reach of reason and inference in ordinary life; and if one is captured by the paradox of the *Meno* into believing that there is a particular mystery in understanding how anyone can learn something radically new; and if, finally, one discovers that metaphor is often pedagogically helpful in leading a student to bridge the gap between the known and the unknown, then one is likely to conclude that metaphor is "epistemologically necessary" to learning something radically new.

It seems to me that this sequence of thinking sets forth pretty well the path that Petrie follows. I wish to propose a counterpath, one that might reveal the reasons why Petrie believes that metaphor is epistemologically necessary and why we may believe that it is not. That path begins with a reconsideration of how large and inclusive is the role of reason in ordinary life. But more of that in a moment. We must first consider what it is that Petrie means by "learning something radically new."

Petrie, I understand, is referring to learning that has two important features. First, it is learning something that is not strictly implied by anything that we already know; and secondly, it is learning something that has the result of reorganizing what we do already know. So this is not any mere accretion of information that he has in mind. It is not, for example, like arriving at the doctor's office and learning that he is out. There may be mystery in that kind of learning; but if there is, it is not the mystery that he has in mind. Neither does he have in mind the sort of surprise that comes upon us from time to time when we discover a theorem in logic that, despite its everlasting presence, was once concealed to our consciousness and is now revealed. That is still a learning of something that is implied by what we know already. Nor, I believe, does Petrie have in mind that rare case of somebody learning something that is not entailed by *anything* that *anybody* knows. These are cases that might better be described as "discovery," "invention" "creation," or even "inspiration," but surely not as "learning." We would not say that Newton "learned" Newtonian mechanics in the same sense that students learn it now.

Petrie has in mind the experience of students who need to learn something that is not implied by anything that *they* may know, even though it is, no doubt, well understood by their teachers. Such learning is surely the most important kind that we try to bring about by teaching. If we cannot make that kind of learning understandable, then surely we cannot make the most lofty aims of pedagogy intelligible.

Petrie suggests that this kind of learning is quite common. I suspect that it is not. Consider carefully what it would mean to learn something that is not entailed by *anything* that one already knows. That, it seems to me, is a fairly rare occurrence in teaching, although when it does occur, it is terribly important. But add to that the second condition, namely, that learning something radically new is that kind of learning that has the consequence of reorganizing what we already know. This too, is an experience that we all can recognize. But, in my own memory at least, the most drastically reorganizing ideas or concepts have been those that are derivable from what I had known already. Indeed, that is where part of the power of such learning enters. It turns out, as students sometimes say, that "I knew it all along." When we put together these *two* features of learning something radically new – logical independence and the capacity to reorganize what is already known – then we have, it seems to me, an experience that is quite extraordinary. It rarely happens in the day-to-day affairs of teaching. But it is immensely important when it does occur. It seems to me that the paradigm case of learning something radically new in Petrie's sense would occur in the case of religious teaching. I do not see how one can come to possess religious knowledge as more than an agreeable possibility except through the use of metaphor. Yet this quite unusual occurrence is clearly not what Petrie has in mind, even though it could quite clearly be described as "learning something radically new."

But let us begin to construct the counterpath. My point is not that metaphor is never useful in leading a student to learn something radically new. My point is rather that all we need to understand how such learning occurs in the normal course of teaching, *and perhaps even to bring it about,* is contained in the standard logical categories of truth, argument, and inference. Reason has a much larger role in ordinary life and in everyday teaching than Petrie is willing to acknowledge. Consider the simple observation that even jokes, for the most part, are arguments. The very possibility of their existence rests upon the human capacity to reason. Comedians even use the language of arguments in discussing the comedic art. First, they say, you must establish the premise. Sometimes, having established the premise, and having waited for the hearer to draw *his* conclusion, the joke is then produced by introducing an entirely different conclusion, a conclusion no less valid, but for all that, unexpected. A man goes to the doctor and says, "Doctor, I am dead." The remark immediately suggests both diagnosis and treatment. The doctor replies, "You will agree, won't you, that dead men do not bleed?" "Of course." The doctor then pierces the patient's finger and draws blood. Whereupon the patient says, "I was wrong, doctor, dead men do bleed." The argument of the joke is so explicit that it can be formalized with ease. Its presence needs no comment.

But jokes do not always depend upon this possibility of drawing multiple inferences from a set of established premises. Sometimes the turn comes from the sudden exposure of a missing or ambiguous premise. A man enters a country inn to take a room for the night. He registers at the desk and turns to go upstairs, but the way is blocked by a pipsqueak of a dog barking furiously. The visitor turns to the innkeeper. "Does your dog bite?" "Certainly not!" And so the visitor turns to ascend the stairs and is promptly bitten. (Notice the anomaly. The dog bites; the dog does not bite.) "You told me your dog doesn't bite!" "Ah, yes! But that's not my dog." (Note the disappearance of the anomaly.) Here the joke has the structure of an enthymeme. The joke is delivered by revealing the missing premise.

I suppose that there are exceptions to this general rule that jokes are always arguments. But I would venture to guess that the exceptions are fewer than we might think. Even sight gags contain a kind of argument. There is a difference between seeing a person of slovenly demeanor and mean disposition slip on a banana peel and seeing a person dressed as a banker do the same. Different premises are established by dress and manner and thus different inferences are drawn by the person watching. Can anyone honestly suppose that Laurel and Hardy, those masters of the sight gag, paid no attention to their dress and to the character presented by their actions? I doubt it. Serious attention to such matters is essential in establishing the premises of the sight gag. Even one-liners have their argument. When a sociologist kisses his beloved does he multiply her face into a crowd? When philosophers make love do they advance a proposition? The inferences are multiple, and yet they are clearly present. The success of the joke depends upon which inferences are drawn from an established set of premises. I repeat: A joke is an argument.

What happens if the inferences of the joke are not negotiated? We have a perfectly familiar way of describing the result. We say, "I don't get it!" Recall, if you can, the sense of dismay and helplessness that we all experience on hearing that announcement. It is a kind of signal to make the argument of the joke explicit, yet we know, even before starting, that making it explicit is precisely what is sufficient to destroy the joke. If you don't "get it," then you cannot make the argument of the joke explicit. If you do "get it," then the argument of the joke does not need to be made explicit. And finally, if you do make the argument explicit, then there is no longer any joke "to get."

These observations about the arguments of jokes parallel almost exactly Petrie's remarks when he presents his strongest claims for the epistemological necessity of metaphor in learning something radically new. In his carefully developed example of how students might learn the concept of relative motion, he says, "Unless one presupposes that most of the work of grasping the metaphor has already occurred, the 'literal' definition may not do the trick at all." Unless the student has, in large measure, already "got it," the verbal definition will not help. And in another place, when discussing what is involved in learning to take up alternative points of view, he writes, "Indeed the students *may* say something like, 'Ah, it depends on how you look at it,' but the verbal formula is unlikely to be *what* it is that they have learned in learning to take up alternative points of view."

Notice the close parallel of these remarks of Petrie's to my own observations about the claim that a joke is an argument. My claim, recall, is that what Petrie says about the role of metaphor in learning something radically new can be said quite satisfactorily with sole reference to the categories of argument and inference. Part of the reason that the presence of arguments in jokes so often escapes our attention is that we all clearly recognize that *telling* a joke is by no means the same as *giving* an argument. *Telling* a joke is something like a speech act. Giving the argument of the joke is not. Giving the argument of the joke is so distant a thing from *telling* the joke that, in fact, we all recognize it is the quickest way to destroy the joke. Nonetheless, if we wish to *remember* a joke that we have heard and have "got," then the best way to do it is to remember the argument of the joke, that is, the premises and the conclusion. Likewise, when we learn what it means to think of relative motion, then *what* we have learned is not any verbal formula or definition. The definition is merely the summary of what we have already learned, but now put in a form that is orderly and systematic so that we can remember, and better use, what we have learned.

Now, there is something about this last point that seems to me correct, profound, and surprising. Petrie, early in his paper, reminds us of a view that we are all familiar with. It is the view that the function of metaphor in education is to make memorable, in a compact expression, what we have learned through literal, but more extended, language. This is the view that metaphor is a mnemonic or heuristic device. And surely, that is sometimes true. But now comes Petrie. And, if I understand him correctly, he says precisely the opposite. It is through the metaphor that we learn — in several stages — and the literal rendering of what we have learned, rather than metaphor, is the mnemonic device, the summary.

If I have represented him faithfully, then I believe that this insight of Petrie's is true and profoundly important for pedagogy. If I have not represented him faithfully, then I apologize, but still declare that he has taught something radically new *to me* about the practice of teaching. What I have learned, I may now express. What, as a teacher, I have often thought was to be learned by the students, I now see was only the mnemonic device; and what I thought sometimes was merely a mnemonic device, I now see was what really advanced learning. That confusion is like supposing that in telling the *argument* of a joke, I was telling the *joke*.

Yet, there is something about my comments on the argument of a joke that does not quite fit with Petrie's topic. What is that lack of fit? Petrie finds it necessary to use a rather extended and enlarged sense of the term "metaphor." He says that his meaning will include such things as models, similes, physical objects of certain sorts, and even theories. I mean to make no such enlargement of the concepts of arguments and inference. Jokes are arguments in a quite literal and standard sense of "arguments." If my meaning seems to involve an extended meaning of "argument" that is simply due to the profound difference between telling the joke and telling the argument of the joke. These indeed, are not the same. But there is this further peculiarity about jokes. In telling them, we rely heavily upon our capacity to establish the premises. That is possible only within a context of discourse in which references and allusions have a high probability of eliciting the same inferences in the minds of many hearers. Thus, the telling of jokes depends upon a shared experience and a generally predictable pattern of reasoning about the shared experience. There must, in short, be nothing conceptually new in the argument of a joke. Thus, it may seem, these observations about the arguments of jokes do not shed light on what it means to learn something radically new. Jokes do not take us beyond what we already know and what we are already disposed to conclude from what we know. They must rely heavily upon our shared common experience, and they go only most cautiously beyond those limits. Thus, to continue exploring my counterthesis, we need a fresh start from a different direction.

Let us consider the steps that Petrie actually describes. He says there are four. Metaphor figures in all four, but is predominant in only one. The four steps are: *anomaly, metaphor, action,* and *correction.* Let us begin with Petrie's account of this first step and see where the argument will lead. In only one place, as far as I can see, does he give us an example of what he means by an anomaly. And in that case – the example from the physics text – he is quite clear that the anomaly appears, *for the student* not because the student's conception of the world is anomalous, but precisely because it is not. Because we can rely upon the student's conception of the world to produce a rather standard set of inferences, and to include a rather standard and widely accepted set of premises, therefore, it is possible for us to introduce a contradiction in the mind of the student. *And this contradiction* is, according to Petrie, what constitutes the anomaly. It is clearly not the metaphor that creates the anomaly. Nor is the anomaly created by the fact that the student's conceptualization of the world is anomalous. On the contrary, the introduction of the anomaly is accomplished by constructing an argument that rests upon a set of inferences that we believe students, in general, will make. It rests, therefore, upon our conviction that the students' conceptualizations of the world are not anomalous.

The point is that Petrie's account of anomalies is confusing. I am trying to take the step of action and correction by seeing what sorts of inferences we are, and are not, permitted to make on the basis of what he says. Let us see, then, what he actually describes as a case of learning something radically new. The curious fact is that his own illustration fits the counterthesis that I have been exploring more precisely than it fits his own.

Petrie describes the introduction of an anomaly. But what he describes, in fact, is a process by which we introduce an argument – or a pair of arguments – whose conclusion Petrie describes as a contradiction. In doing this, the teacher – the textbook writer – like the teller of jokes, takes care to see that the premises of the argument are premises established in the minds of the students. This is a chair, and it is at rest. This is a chair; it is on the surface of the earth; the earth is moving; therefore, the chair is moving. *Conclusion*: The chair is moving and the chair is at rest. Petrie says of this step that it "fairly clearly fits the idea of introducing an anomaly into the student's conceptual scheme."

On this point, I think that Petrie makes a mistake. We have not *introduced* an anomaly at all. Assuming that the students' beliefs are quite usual, and not anomalous in *that* sense, we seek to expose those premises that they are already disposed to accept and to draw those inferences that they are already disposed to make. Petrie describes the result as the introduction of a contradiction, saying, "Everyone probably finds a contradiction anomalous." I suggest that it is a pedagogical mistake to speak thus of *introducing* the contradiction. Rather we uncover it, we elicit it, and in speaking thus, we are already taking the view of the student. And that is what Petrie wants us to do. Only later, by his view, do we introduce something into the mind of the student.

But it is a mistake of another sort to suggest that in this step we elicit a contradiction. What is produced, in this case, is not a contradiction but a paradox. The difference may seem small, but it is enormously important, especially for our understanding of pedagogy. A contradiction is usually understood as a pair of propositions which, *as a minimum*, cannot both be true. The pedogogical purpose of exposing a contradiction might then be to lead the student to reject one or the other side of the contradiction. There is a place for such a thing in teaching. But that is not the purpose here at all.

A paradox, in contrast to a contradiction, is produced by the juxtaposition of a pair of propositions that *appear* to be contradictory, but which are, in fact, both true. Clearly, what is wanted in Petrie's example is not the dsecription of the anomaly as a contradiction, but its description as a paradox. What we want is to lead the student to see a way of holding to the truth of *both* propositions about the chair — that it is in motion, and that it is at rest — without thinking they are in opposition. The teacher who follows Petrie's account on this point, will make a substantial mistake in pedagogy.

The tension that the student experiences, and that Petrie speaks of, is not then created by a metaphor. Rather it is created by an argument, or series of arguments, that establish a paradox in the mind of the student on the basis of premises that he already accepts. What is needed to remove that tension is the introduction of some premise that will permit the student to hold on to both sides of the paradox as true. Introducing that premise is what Petrie describes as "solving the anomaly." If we want students to learn something radically new, then what we must do, according to Petrie's illustration, is to cast about for the paradox from which the new concept, formulated as a premise, will provide an escape. First, we expose to the student a paradox implicit in what he already believes Then we show the student how to escape from it by introducing a fresh premise into the argument in the mind of the student. This last step may require metaphor as a kind of practical necessity or it may not. But it will certainly require something like Petrie's steps of test and correction. *What* the student must test are the inferences permitted by the escape from the paradox. *What* he must correct are mistaken inferences. Being able to make the correct inferences permitted by the escape from the paradox is precisely what we mean by having learned something radically new. When that happens, the student has learned, as Petrie puts it, "to make the same moves as the professor."

Introducing the premise needed to escape the paradox is the step that, I believe, Petrie wants to say *requires* metaphor. I can certainly understand and appreciate his inclination to that view. No doubt, such a step does require imagination on the part of the student. We may even say that it requires invention or discovery. Here we are with another person, "caught" as it were, in a paradox quite of his own making. Now we are asking him to find a way out, and unless there is something for us to do, we are quite helpless in offering any assistance. The problem is not that the task is ill-defined. On the contrary, it is quite well-defined by the paradox itself. One wants to find some way of maintaining both that the chair is in motion and that it is at rest, without these claims being in apparent contradiction. How are we to help anyone who is faced with such a difficult task to find the right way? How are we to help anyone to "get it"? About the best that we can do is to present a symbol, a model, a verbal formula of some kind, which the "drowning victim" can grab ahold of and with which he can begin to reason – throw out a suggestion that he can grab to start the steps of testing and correction. Indeed, it seems that what is needed is an interactive metaphor, one that *creates* likenesses, comparisons, and aids in creating the inferences that are to be tested in the search for rescue.

But how can Petrie settle on the metaphor as the *necessary* step? I think it goes something like this. One of the conditions of the problem that Petrie sets is that the premise needed to escape the paradox must be something new. If it is not, then we do not have a case of learning something radically new. It follows that *whatever* we do to bring about the rescue must be something so new *to the student,* so much a fresh addition to his understanding of the world, that it will have some of the features of a metaphor. Even though the idea of relative motion is old hat to us, it is not to the student who is captured by the paradox.

It turns out then that *anything* that works will have some of the features of metaphor, whether it is a symbol, or a statement, or a physical model, or whatever. If it works, then it must be new to the student, not derivable from what the student knows already, and it must create the needed similarities to permit the reasoning to begin that constitutes the steps of testing and correction.

It turns out then that the *necessity* of metaphor flows from the terms of the problem that Petrie sets. It is simply analytic that *anything* that works *must* have the properties of an interactive metaphor, because the properties of interactive metaphor are simply defined as those that work in the effort to effect rescue from the paradox. Now Petrie knows very well that there are, in fact, many things other than metaphors, in the normal sense of "metaphor," that will work, and so he finds it necessary to his view that the concept of "metaphor" be extended to include them. I suspect that *whatever* device of rescue we may find successful, Petrie will expand his list to include metaphor. It turns out that anything that works to effect rescue from the paradox will be included as metaphor. This, I believe, is how he develops the view that metaphor is epistemologically necessary for learning something radically new.

But of course, there are other ways of introducing to the student the premise needed to escape the paradox. We can, for example, cast about for *other* experiences on which to base *other* premises in the mind of the student, from which the testing and correction of inferences can begin. *And this is precisely what the textbook writers in Petrie's example do.* They ask the students, "Have you ever been in a car, a bus, or a train and felt that the vehicle was moving when it was not moving? If so, what happened to cause the feeling of movement?" This is a move that is precisely of the same order as the moves made in the lesson to establish the premises of the arguments producing the paradox. Petrie describes this step in the text as a "fairly difficult extension of the concept." But that is his account. My own is that this step is an effort to find the premise already established in the mind of the student, from which reasoning may begin to test a possible escape from the paradox. It still requires imagination on the part of the student, and perhaps even a kind of invention. But I see no reason to say that there is here any metaphor involved.

Petrie's presentation is full of excellent advice to anyone who will take his teaching seriously. It is full of good advice to writers and students also. Indeed, on the conduct of teaching, Petrie's presentation contains more wisdom than I have seen in any similar work for many years. I believe, however, that we may accept that advice, and even cherish it, without accepting any of the account of metaphor in learning that goes with it.

For example Petrie says that he has *shown* that "an anomaly will *be* an anomaly only from the standpoint of a conceptual scheme." Now, I think that what he says here is true in a quite limited sense, but that he has not *shown* it to be true in any sense. The claim that the chair is in motion and that it is at rest is a paradox in *any* conceptual scheme, though it is true that it is not *paradoxical* except to some people. What Petrie wants us to grasp is that we who are teachers know the way out, and that what we must do to be effective teachers is to make sure that we present the paradox, or develop it in teaching, so that it will indeed have the force of paradox to the students, and even so that once again it may strike *us* as paradoxical. That requires that we forget, for the moment, that we as teachers know the way out. But this need, though extremely important to point out, is also quite understandable from the perspective of the conventional categories of argument and inference. It is also understandable from the requirements of telling jokes. The premises must be established in the minds of the hearers. We cannot expect "in jokes" to be successful when told to an "out group." But that is only because the premises of the argument of the joke cannot be established in such a group. It is good advice to both humorists and teachers to keep that fact in mind.

There is, of course, in both teaching and learning, such a thing as the exercise of imagination. I have already suggested that in introducing to the student the premise that he needs to escape the paradox, something even like discovery and invention is called for. This element is an essential requirement that must be acknowledged in any theory of pedagogy.

I have students, for example, who are so "literal-minded" and "empirically biased" by their studies that they seem unable to entertain imaginary circumstances that would reveal important truths to them, because they see such imaginary circumstances only as patently contrary to well-known fact. Sometimes, I find that metaphor, even the effort to revive dead metaphors, is helpful in overcoming this difficulty. Whenever I encounter it, it always strikes me as something particularly odd. It seems a strange kind of incapacity to entertain counterfactual conditionals. Suppose we lived in a world where there was no work at all. What would it be like? How would we, as humans, be different creatures if there were no death and no birth in the world? What would be missing from the world if we were missing the capacity for memory? Yet, it usually happens that students who have difficulty entertaining such questions read science fiction and have no similar problem in grasping what their friends may mean when they say, "If today were Saturday, I would be swimming."

The "thought experiment" that Petrie describes is a similar exercise. "How would the chair appear, if I were on the moon?" He points out that the thought experiment, that is, the capacity to entertain a counterfactual conditional, may not work. I agree. If it does not work, then one must find another way to establish the premise needed to generate the paradox. But what really is the difference between, "If I were on the moon, then . . . " and "If today were Saturday, then . . . "? Why is the imagination free always to consider the one, but not the other?

I suspect that it is due to something peculiar in the classroom setting, something there that tends to inhibit the "epistemic conditions" of learning something radically new. After all, the role of the teacher is a peculiarly authoritative one. Both student and teacher share the belief that the teacher knows the way out of the paradox, even though the students do not. And furthermore, what is wanted is to "get" the way out. So the tendency of the teacher is to forget the necessity of exploiting the premises needed and already implicitly present in the mind of the student. And the student is likely to be impatient, knowing that after all, it is not the premises that are important. It is "the way out" that counts.

Perhaps in this way of viewing the matter, we have a description of what often happens with both bad students and bad teachers. They omit the step that requires the exercise of imagination and forge on to what is to be understood literally as true. What both leave out of the process is thinking. Truth passes from the professor's notes to the student's notes without going through the head of either. Perhaps that is why, as we all know, students from time to time are able to identify the teacher that they admire and why they are so often just those teachers who, as the students say, "make them think."

Petrie has described what is needed to "make them think." I accept his advice. What he has not described is any epistemological necessity for metaphor. Rather he has been able to help us see how metaphor might be useful sometimes in that essential step of learning that I have described as "exercising imagination," or entertaining the counterfactual conditional, or "getting" the premise needed to escape the paradox.

In short, I believe that what Petrie has taught us about learning something radically new is quite understandable through traditional concepts of argument and inference. Learning something radically new is quite understandable – as understandable as it can be – without the introduction of metaphor at all. Metaphors are nice; sometimes they are needed; oftentimes they are useful; but epistemologically necessary they are not. If there is any setting in which metaphors come closest to being absolutely indispensable, it would be, I believe, in those settings where they are used by religious teachers. But that is another topic entirely.

Still, there may be something missing in this quite traditional and conventional account that I have given. I still do not know how they "get it." But here Petrie and I are on equal ground. If either of us needs an account of "getting it," then both of us do. He does not explain how anyone "gets the metaphor." But neither can I explain how anyone "gets the joke," or "gets the parable," or "gets" the premise needed to escape the clutches of paradox. Perhaps, after all, it turns out on this point that the best we can do is to say there are those who have eyes to see and ears to hear, who are gifted, inspired, talented, or inventive. And, of course, all this is true. There are such people. Petrie is one of them. But the fact that we may have to rest at this point, and the fact that some do not "get it" is no excuse for sloppy, slovenly, or unskillful teaching, anymore than it is an excuse for telling jokes badly. Petrie has described such skillful teaching, even though, it seems to me, he has not described the role of metaphor in learning something radically new. Perhaps, on the other hand, my conclusion should be more modest. It does not seem to me, that Petrie, by his metaphors, has described the role of metaphor in learning any better than I have without them.

Educational Uses of Metaphor

THOMAS G. STICHT

As educators, the goal of our inquiries into the nature of cognitive processes is to achieve an understanding of these processes that can be put to use in improving students' learning through improved educational practice. In Petrie's presentation the inquiry focuses on the improvement of educational practice by the more effective use of metaphor. Petrie discusses three topics: (1) the nature of metaphor (as "speech act" rather than "linguistic entity"); (2) the manner in which metaphor "works" (by creating a cognitive anomaly in the listener); and (3) a prescription for the teacher's use of metaphor (first create an anomaly; next offer opportunity for the student to actively discuss or otherwise become active with the new ideas addressed by the metaphor; and then provide corrective feedback, with several iterations if necessary, to get the student to understand the relationships between the knowledge domains addressed in the metaphor).

In this chapter. I shall follow Petrie's lead and comment on the nature and mechanism of action of metaphorical speech acts. I will make my comments within the context of a discussion of metaphor as a tool for communication and thought. Evidence will be presented to suggest that children and marginally literate adults who lack skills in analytical thinking can be taught aspects of these skills in relatively brief training periods, and that such training can improve their ability to produce and comprehend metaphors. This discussion extends Petrie's consideration of the educational use of metaphor to include the development of students' abilities to produce and comprehend metaphors as tools of communication and thought.

Metaphors as tools for communication

To understand the nature of metaphor as a speech act, we need to understand how metaphors serve as linguistic tools for overcoming certain cognitive limitations – limitations that we all have by virtue of the way we are built. As with other tools, metaphors provide a way of extending our capacities, in this case, for communication. Just as the tool function of the hammer is to extend the strength of the arm and the hardness of the fist, and just as the tool function of the telescope is to extend the range of the eye, so the tool function of the metaphor is to extend the capacity of active memory *using the medium of speech.*

The fact that speech is a fleeting, temporally linear means of communicating, coupled with the fact that, as human beings, we are limited in how much information we can maintain and process at any one time in active memory, means that as speakers we can always benefit from tools for efficiently bringing information into active memory, encoding it for communication, and recoding it, as listeners, in some memorable fashion. Metaphors appear to serve as one of a variety of special linguistic devices facilitating these activities. Other such devices for overcoming the ephemeral nature of speech include rhyme and rhythm, both of which apparently aid in the learning of speech, as in the memorizing of poetry.

Ortony's (1975) discussion of metaphor elaborates on the role of metaphor as a tool for overcoming active memory limitations in the use of spoken language. Ortony discusses three different theses to explain how metaphor may facilitate learning: the *compactness thesis,* in which it is asserted that metaphors work by transferring chunks of experience from well-known to less-well-known contexts; the *vividness thesis,* which maintains that metaphors permit and impress a more memorable learning due to the greater imagery or concreteness or vividness of the "full-blooded experience" conjured up by the metaphorical vehicle; and the *inexpressibility thesis,* in which it is noted that certain aspects of natural experience are never encoded in language and that metaphors carry with them the extra meanings never encoded in language.

Both the compactness and inexpressibility theses are compatible with the view that metaphor has its origins in the oral language and that it serves as a tool for cognitive economy by helping to transfer information in large chunks. Furthermore, the mnemonic function of metaphor as expressed in Ortony's vividness thesis also points to the value of metaphor as a tool for producing durable learning from unenduring speech.

The importance of metaphor as a tool for active memory may be demonstrated by the use of a key metaphor for bringing coherence to discourse. Here is an example from *Moby Dick* (cited by Upton, 1973):

Queequeg and I were mildly employed weaving what is called a sword-mat, for an additional lashing to our boat. . . . As I kept passing and repassing the filling or woof of marline between the long yarns of the warp, using my own hand for the shuttle, and as Queequeg, standing sideways, ever and anon slid his heavy oaken sword between the threads, and idly looking off upon the water, carelessly and unthinkingly drove home every yarn: I say so strange a dreaminess did there then reign all over the ship and all over the sea, only broken by the intermitting dull sound of the sword, that it seemed as if this were the Loom of Time, and I myself were a shuttle mechanically weaving and weaving away at the Fates. There lay the fixed threads of the warp subject to but one single, ever returning, unchanging vibration, and that vibration merely enough to admit of the crosswise interblending of other threads with its own. This warp seemed necessity; and there, thought I, with my own hand I ply my own shuttle and weave my own destiny into these unalterable threads. Meantime, Queequeg's impulsive, indifferent sword sometimes hitting the woof slantingly, or crookedly, or strongly, or weakly, as the case might be; and by this difference in the concluding blow producing a corresponding contrast in the final aspect of the completed fabric; this savage's sword, thought I, which thus finally shapes and fashions both warp and woof; this easy, indifferent sword must be chance – aye, chance, free will, and necessity – no wise incompatible – all interweavingly working together. The straight warp of necessity, not to be swerved from its ultimate course – its every alternating vibration, indeed, only tending to that: free will still free to play her shuttle between given threads; and chance, though restrained in its play within the right lines of necessity, and sideways in its motions directed by free will, though thus prescribed to by both, chance by turns rules either, and has the last featuring blow at events.

In this example, two vivid chunks, or domains of knowledge, one dealing with weaving, the other with human destiny, are brought into juxtaposition in active memory and are discussed in an extended manner. In this case, the metaphor initiates an interactive mode of thought between the two domains that is distinctly different from the linear processing that precedes and follows the metaphor. This has the effect of producing a certain saliency in the discourse which makes it "stick together" or cohere. In this regard, the metaphor serves a similar function to various discourse structures which are currently being shown to affect comprehension and learning (for instance, Frederiksen, 1977).

The educational implications of metaphor as a tool for efficient communication are mentioned, in passing, by Petrie, but he does not elaborate upon them. Instead, he focuses on the use of metaphor as a tool of thought for creating new knowledge, and he concentrates on the teacher's use of metaphor, which induces considerable cognitive anomaly or puzzlement on the part of students.

However, when teachers use metaphors as efficient tools of communication it is *not desirable* to produce excessive puzzlement in students. Rather, the effective use of metaphor for efficient communication requires the teachers to know that students possess the knowledge addressed in the metaphor. It also requires the teacher to have a technique for determining that this knowledge is recalled and structured according to the metaphor. Indeed, determining that students understand what is being said is a crucial problem in all teaching. But it is a particularly important consideration for metaphor, because the metaphor is itself frequently used as a way of trying to explain something else. This problem is compounded in schools with students from widely varying cultural backgrounds. It also takes on different dimensions with students of different ages. Young children are not as well-equipped to comprehend the wide variety of metaphors that depend upon the extra meaning addressed in Ortony's inexpressibility thesis (Winner, Rosenstiel & Gardner, 1976).

Perhaps an example from a classic metaphor will help convey the importance of the teacher's understanding of students' knowledge for choosing metaphors that are efficient communication tools. Consider the well-known example: "The Lord is my shepherd. . . " In this case, we can imagine that the psalmist who is trying to convey his feelings about the Lord faces crowds who are familiar with the ways of shepherds. They know that shepherds take care of sheep, they protect them, take them to good pastures, and so forth. The psalmist wonders how he can convey something about the Lord to his audience. So he thinks, "Well, the Lord takes care of me like a shepherd takes care of sheep." Without hesitation then, the psalmist tell the audience: "The Lord is *my* shepherd . . ." and so on. In this case, he intends the audience to recognize that the Lord is someone who will take care of them, protect them, love them, and so forth. It is generally assumed that the context of the statement and the situation will guide the audience to the intended interpretation of the statement in an efficient manner. Additionally, it may be at least tacitly understood by the psalmist that the use of metaphor is likely to cause the audience to make inferences beyond those statements that can be literally expressed, as in Ortony's inexpressibility thesis, and hence a degree of affect may accompany the interpretation which would be lost if the psalmist simply listed the important features of the Lord.

The use of metaphor in written text is a particularly hazardous venture for both the teacher and the reader. Typically, the teacher as writer has only the most global notions of who the potential readers might be. Thus, when transferred to the written language, particularly in the mass production of textbooks, metaphors, like other more-or-less "context-bound" figures of speech, run the risk of leading to misunder-standing, because a large number of readers may not share the required experiences for receiving the large chunks of information to be transferred by the metaphor. Typically, the author is not available, and so readers cannot resolve ambiguities through question-and-answer techniques. This may well lead to many activities to reduce the feeling of anomaly, as Petrie suggests, but these activities reflect a lack of understanding, which might not occur if a metaphor which fitted the reader's experiences were used. To the extent that the writer can better understand who the reader is, and what experiences the reader has had that are relevant to the material to be presented, the more skillfully the writer should be able to use metaphor to facilitate learning.

From the point of view of the student, the metaphor is something to be comprehended. To comprehend the metaphor, the student must first infer that the teacher means the student to shift from a mode of cognition in which ideas are being fitted to an existing knowledge structure, to a metaphorical mode in which the construction of a third knowledge structure consisting of the relations educed between the two domains referenced by the metaphor is accomplished.

Petrie identifies, correctly I believe, one of the cues for inferring the need for metaphorical thinking: a cognitive anomaly created by a state-ment that does not fit well into the knowledge structure being devel-oped in response to the language preceding the metaphor. The infer-ence that metaphorical thinking is called for by the cognitive anomaly requires that the student rely on his or her understanding of the con-ventions of language use, which as Petrie also notes, includes the notion that people try to make sensible utterances. If the student has no reason to think that the teacher is mistaken or confused, then the inference that sense should be made of what was said by applying met-aphorical thinking may be appropriate.

In metaphorical thinking, the student must strive to find some basis for similarity between the two domains in the metaphor, the juxtaposi-tion of which created the cognitive anomaly. Analysis of a traditional Aristotelian "proportional" metaphor (Upton, 1973, p. 76), in which two seemingly disparate domains are shown to be related to one another by virtue of some similarities in structure, function, or some derived relation, illustrates this type of thinking.

In this example, imagine an educator who states that "the teacher is the fertilizer of budding minds."[1] To comprehend the metaphor, it is necessary for the student to understand something about teachers, where they work, with whom, what they do; and it is necessary to understand something about fertilizers, where they work, with what,

what they do. The domain of knowledge about teachers (Knowledge Domain I) and the domain of knowledge about fertilizers (Knowledge Domain II) must be searched to discover some basis for establishing a relation, or set of relations, between teachers and fertilizers, as required in the metaphor. This search leads to the discovery of the analogical relationship that the teacher is to children's minds ($A:B$) what fertilizer is to plants ($C:D$); that is, a stimulant to growth.

What the student now constructs in his or her mind is a knowledge structure that is not signaled at all in the language of the speaker, that is, "A teacher stimulates the growth of children's minds." This structure is a third structure consisting of relationship(s) understood to hold between the two given domains. Whether it is the precise knowledge structure the teacher had in mind cannot be certain to the student without additional information. However, if the teacher has carefully considered what it is the student is to learn about a topic, in this case teaching, and what domains of knowledge the student possesses that can be used to reason analogically, then communication should be fairly efficient, and the student's learning should be facilitated both through the mnemonic powers of metaphor and through engagement in the analytical thought processes involved in metaphorical thinking.

Metaphors as tools for thought

In the preceding section, metaphor was discussed as a tool for communication. It was noted that the metaphor is a linguistic device particularly well suited to overcoming problems involved in using an ephemeral medium like speech. Ortony's (1975) compactness thesis deals with metaphor as a means of efficiently transmitting large chunks of information, so that active memory processing is made more efficient, while his vividness thesis points to the role of metaphor as tool for making information more memorable through the mnemonic powers of vivid images. Both the chunking and the mnemonic functions are illustrated by the passage of *Moby Dick* which "coheres" a segment of prose into a vivid, recallable chunk.

When metaphor is considered as a tool for communication, attention is focused on its use for the exchange of information among speakers and listeners. The consideration of metaphor as a tool for thought, on the other hand, is concerned with the discovery of relationships between seemingly disparate domains and an exploration of the extent to which they can be related. For instance, the metaphor "the brain is a computer," discussed by both Boyd and Miller in this volume, is based upon some similarities in structure and function that are easily identified between the domains of knowledge about brains and computers. However, the attempt to exhaustively enumerate the similarities and differences between these domains may lead to the discovery of relationships or differences not thought of at the time the metaphor was formed. Here, Ortony's (1975) inexpressibility thesis seems relevant, because the continued consideration of a metaphor may lead to the recognition and explicit formulation of similarities and differences latent in a metaphor.

To understand the function of metaphor as a tool for thought, we have to distinguish between the tool functions of metaphors when they are used in an intuitive manner, and those tool functions involved in the use of metaphor as a "metacognitive" tool for creative problem solving (as discussed by Schön in this volume), for rhetorical purposes, for literary effect, or for the types of educational purposes with which Petrie is concerned.

It seems to me that the function of metaphor as a tool for thought, when used intuitively, is to extend our capacities for perceiving relationships in the perceptual domain to the conceiving of relationships in the conceptual domain. Let me explain this notion a bit.

In the domain of visual perception, the fact that we perceive both the onset and the offset of a light suggests that we react to stimulus change, i.e., relative stimulus values, rather than to the stimulus energy per se. Similar examples hold in other sensory modalities. Perceptually, then, we are built to perceive relationally.

At the level of conception, examples such as metaphor, simile, analogy, suggest that we are likely to be able to conceive only on a relative basis. That is, we can only know something in relation to our knowledge of something else. Metaphor, as condensed simile, permits us to think about one thing or event being like (and in that regard related to) something else. From the speaker's point of view, the metaphor permits the use of language to express conceived relations in a less than exhaustively analyzed fashion, as Ortony's inexpressibility thesis suggests. In the act of placing conceptions into language, there is a clarification and stabilization of similarities which may have earlier been only vague conceptions. In the same way as a stereoscope brings a third dimension to what would otherwise have been a flat picture, the juxtaposition of two seemingly disparate domains of knowledge may produce a stable third domain made up of conceptual relationships between the first two. In both cases, the whole is greater than the sum of its parts – the parts are essentially incomplete descriptions.

From the listener's point of view, a metaphor provides both a cue to what kind of thinking should be done (a search for similarities of some sort), and two domains of knowledge, or relative conceptual positions, from which to conduct the mental search.

While metaphors contain the ingredients for producing new knowledge domains from old ones, as Petrie indicates, there is no guarantee that students will be able to perform this task without considerable interaction with the teacher. Indeed, there is evidence that many adults may lack skill in forming categories into which objects or events may be sorted on the basis of some similarity. For instance, figure 17 presents a task, having commonalities with metaphor production and comprehension, on which adults having low literacy skills perform poorly. In this task, the person studies Parts *A* and *B* to understand that the matrix of Part *B* is constructed from information in Part *A*. The person's task is then to study Part *C* and construct a matrix as Part *D*. Notice that this task, like the proportional metaphor discussed above, is an analogy problem of the sort *A:B::C:D*. The student's task is to discover by studying the *A:B* terms that the column headings of Part *B* are superordinate category names for the elements contained in the column. In solving the *C:D* problem, the person must study *C*, tentatively identifying features of the things being referred to in the paragraph. The person must develop a hypothesis about a superordinate category label, check some more of the elements, confirm the hypothesized category label or generate a new one; and then, given appropriate category labels, elements in the paragraph must be sorted into the appropriate columns of the matrix.

That this is a difficult task, highly related to literacy level, is indicated by data for adult men in a remedial literacy program who attempted the task. Men reading at the fourth grade level, or below, got less than twenty percent correct, those reading at the sixth grade level got nearly fifty percent correct, whereas men reading at the tenth grade level or higher got nearly one hundred percent correct.

Table 2 presents an analysis of the types of errors made by men at these three different reading ability levels on the matrix task. Clearly, the problem of developing appropriate headings for matrix columns is highly related to the making of errors in sorting elements into cells, as evidenced by the data for men reading below the fifth grade level. However, the data for the better readers, those scoring at the ninth grade or higher, clearly indicate that even though proper column headings may be inferred from study of the passage, this does not necessarily guarantee that elements will be identified and sorted into cells correctly.

The results of six weeks of literacy training, in which students reading below the fifth grade level practiced producing classification matrices based on reading text passages, and then inferring superordinate

A

Types of Bars

Crowbars are used for moving timbers and rocks. They are available in 4 and 5 foot lengths with a diameter of 1 or 1-1/4 inches. Pinch bars are from 12 to 36 inches long and are used for prying out spikes and nails. Pinch bar diameters range from 1/2 to 1 inch depending on their length. Wrecking bars have diameters of 1/2 to 1-1/8 inches and are available in lengths from 12 to 60 inches. They are used for the same things as crowbars. Pry bars are used for prying out gears and bushings. They are 16 inches long and have a diameter of 1-1/16 inches.

B

Type	Use	Length	Diameter
Crowbar	Moving timbers and rocks	4-5 feet	1 or 1-1/4 inches
Pinch bar	Prying out spikes and nails	12-36 inches	1/2 to 1 inch
Wrecking bar	Moving timbers and rocks	12-60 inches	1/2 to 1-1/8 inch
Pry bar	Prying out gears and bushings	16 inches	1-1/16 inches

C

When You Are Lost - EAT PLANTS

If you are lost and out of food there are many types of plants that you can eat. Marsh marigolds are best during early spring. They are found in swamps and in streams. The leaves and stems are the only parts that you should eat. The leaves, stems, and flowers of the rock rose are all good to eat. You can find them along streams and lakes in early spring. Fireweed is also good to eat. It is usually found in burned-over areas during spring and summer. You can eat the leaves and flowers of the fireweed but not the stem. The roots of the mountain willow are also good to eat. Mountain willow is found in high mountains in early summer.

D

Figure 17. Analogical reasoning task similar to that involved in metaphorical thinking.

Table 2. *Types of errors made by literacy students from three levels of reading skill on the analogies task*

Errors	Reading levels		
	Less than 5 ($n = 10$)	5–8 ($n = 10$)	9 and greater ($n = 10$)
Format			
Did not use matrix	2	0	0
Column headings copied from sample	5	0	0
Missing headings	1	1	0
No headings	2	3	1
Table cells			
Copied sample cell information	5	0	0
Cell information missing:			
Types of plants	9	2	2
Locations of plants	8	3	3
Edible parts	9	4	2
Time of year	9	4	3
Information combined in cells	5	2	2

categories, resulted in a forty percent increase in the number of people getting ninety percent correct or better on the task of Figure 17. This training was very similar to that used by Silverman, Winner, and Gardner (1976) to teach sensitivity to style in art, and comprehension and production of metaphoric language, to pre-adolescents. It consisted essentially of group discussion in which students and teachers talked about picking out things in a text that in some respects are similar. Thus, discussions of various attributes that things can differ on, or resemble each other on, were discussed, and the need to develop semantic category labels was stressed.

The method of Silverman, Winner, and Gardner for teaching children to produce metaphors and the method for teaching literacy students to represent information in matrices, incorporated most of Petrie's prescription of the teacher's use of metaphor. In each case, a "cognitive anomaly" is established by posing a challenging task requiring problem solving. Opportunity is given for the students to become active with the problem, to try solutions, to learn about related matters, such as categorization skills and semantic categories, and to receive corrective feedback from the teacher or peers. Thus, Petrie's method for improving the educational utility of metaphor is not uniquely reserved for the use of metaphor. Though this weakens its value as a specific instructional methodology, it is of value to recognize that this generally used instructional method, which is a basic form of inquiry, may be fruitfully applied using metaphor. Empirical evidence regarding the value of this type of application is yet to be adduced.

The fact that pre-adolescents and marginally literate adults can so readily be taught certain of the analytic skills used in producing representation formats such as matrices and metaphors, suggests that what is being learned is not some fundamentally new, difficult mode of thinking. Rather, it appears that what is happening is that students are learning metacognitive skills of categorization applied to situations where the propensity for such activities is low. Cole and Scribner (1974) point out that apparently one function of schooling is to increase the range of situations in which people use the fundamental cognitive processes involved in classification; schooled persons seek relationships in a greater variety of situations by appealing to a broader range of ways in which things, events, and processes could be related.

As an intuitive tool for thought, metaphor embodies the principles of semantic growth identified by Slobin (1971): "New forms first express old functions, and new functions are first expressed by old forms" (p. 317). These principles appear to fit neatly into Piaget's processes of assimilation and accommodation, identified by Petrie as mechanisms underlying the function of metaphor in producing new knowledge from old. By Slobin's principles, children first acquire a conceptualization that they intend to express. Then they acquire the linguistic means of expressing it, the form. Soon they acquire a new function or conceptualization. Not yet having the form necessary to express this new function, children may use a simile or metaphor, as an old form of expression. The use of such figures of speech is reinforced because of their effectiveness in overcoming active-memory limitations.

When the use of metaphor is made explicit as a metacognitive tool for thought, then it is more likely to serve the process of accommodation when it is used intuitively to assimilate new functions by use of old forms. The training of analysis skills underlying the specifications of relations between semantic categories, as in the literacy and metaphor-training programs discussed, may facilitate the development of metacognitive skill in the use of metaphor to stimulate knowledge *invention* not simply knowledge *retention*, which is a major function for metaphor when communicating in the ephemeral medium of speech.

Metaphor as a tool for knowledge invention seems to underlie Black's concept of the "interactive" metaphor, as discussed by Petrie. It also seems to be the aim of Petrie's prescription for the teacher's use of metaphor. This assumes the analytical skills that I have discussed.

In Petrie's scheme, metaphor is used as a metacognitive tool by the teacher to produce a cognitive anomaly and to provide the potential for resolving the anomaly by use of the domains expressed in the metaphor. For the student, Petrie's paradigm calls for going beyond some superficial similarities between the domains to an extended consideration of the full ramifications of the metaphor. Often, considerable surprise may be experienced as the implications of a metaphor are understood, and an "accommodation" of thought may occur. However, such surprise is not a unique feature of metaphor; it also occurs in the most "literal" languages, mathematics and formal logic, when a long argument reveals a surprising, through perfectly predictable, conclusion.

The metacognitive knowledge of how to manipulate ideas explicitly in metaphor so as to transform either one's own or another's knowledge into new knowledge makes metaphor a major tool for extending our capacities for analytical thought, while at the same time changing us as tool users. Though the types of changes produced by the use of metaphor as a tool for thought may not yet be fully understood, it can be argued by analogy that just as the repeated use of a hammer may strengthen the arm, the repeated use of metaphors may strengthen the powers of analysis and synthesis. Also, much as the telescope may produce knowledge that changes our basic assumptions about ourselves and the nature of our universe, the use of metaphors may, as Petrie has argued, bring about basic changes in how we understand ourselves and the world around us.

NOTES

The ideas and opinions expressed herein are those of the author and do not represent the opinions and/or policies of the National Institute of Education or the Department of Health, Education, and Welfare. Helpful comments on an earlier version of this presentation were received from NIE colleagues Carl Frederiksen, Marcia Whiteman, and Joe Dominic.

1 I am indebted to Virginia Koehler, Chief of the Teaching Division, NIE, for this insightful metaphor. It is recognized that the analysis of the metaphor given in the text is oversimplified and incomplete, e.g., the use of terms such as "budding mind" and "growth of children's minds" are themselves metaphorical. While the appearance of metaphors within metaphors complicates metaphorical thinking, no new processes of thought seem to be implicated.

BIBLIOGRAPHY

Abraham, W. 1975. *A linguistic approach to metaphor*. Lisse, The Netherlands: Peter de Ridder Press.

Allison, G. T. 1969. Conceptual models and the Cuban missile crisis. *American Political Science Review, 63*, 689–717.

Anderson, C. C. 1964. The psychology of the metaphor. *Journal of Genetic Psychology, 105*, 53–73.

Anderson, J. R., and Bower, G. H. 1973. *Human associative memory*. Washington, D.C.: Winston and Sons.

Anderson, R. C., and Ortony, A. 1975. On putting apples into bottles: A problem of polysemy. *Cognitive Psychology, 7*, 167–80.

Aristotle. 1952a. [*Rhetoric*]. Translated by W. R. Roberts. In W. D. Ross (ed.), *The works of Aristotle* (vol. 11): *Rhetorica, De rhetorica ad Alexandrum, Poetica*. Oxford: Clarendon Press.

   1952b. [*Poetics*]. Translated by I. Bywater. In W. D. Ross (ed.), *The works of Aristotle* (vol. 11): *Rhetorica, De rhetorica ad Alexandrum, Poetica*. Oxford: Clarendon Press.

Arnheim, R. 1969. *Visual thinking*. Berkeley: University of California Press.

Asch, S. E. 1958. The metaphor: A psychological inquiry. In R. Tagiuri and L. Petrullo (eds.), *Person perception and interpersonal behavior*. Stanford, Calif.: Stanford University Press.

Austin, J. L. 1961. Truth. In J. L. Austin, *Philosophical Papers*. Oxford: Clarendon Press.

Bach, K., and Harnish, R. *A theory of speech acts*. New York: Crowell, forthcoming.

Bain, A. 1888. *English composition and rhetoric*. New York: D. Appleton and Co.

Bartlett, F. C. 1932. *Remembering*. Cambridge: Cambridge University Press.

Beardsley, M. C. 1958. *Aesthetics: Problems in the philosophy of criticism*. New York: Harcourt Brace and Co.

   1962. The metaphorical twist. *Philosophy and Phenomenological Research, 22*, 293–307.

   1967. Metaphor. In P. Edwards (ed.), *Encyclopedia of philosophy* (vol. 5). New York: Macmillan.

Begg, I. 1972. Recall of meaningful phrases. *Journal of Verbal Learning and Verbal Behavior, 11*, 431–9.

Bellush, J., and Hausknecht, M. (eds.). 1967. *Urban renewal: People, politics and planning*. Garden City, N.Y.: Doubleday Anchor.

Berger, P. L., and Luckmann, T. 1966. *Social construction of reality: A treatise in the sociology of knowledge*. Garden City, N.Y.: Doubleday.

Berlyne, D. E. 1960. *Conflict, arousal and curiosity*. New York: McGraw-Hill.

Billow, R. M. 1975. A cognitive developmental study of metaphor comprehension. *Developmental Psychology, 11*, 415–23.

    1977. Metaphor. A review of the psychological literature. *Psychological Bulletin, 84*, 81–92.

Binkley, T. 1974. On the truth and probity of metaphor. *Journal of Aesthetics and Art Criticism, 33*, 171–80.

Black, M. 1962a. *Models and metaphors*. Ithaca, N.Y.: Cornell University Press.

    1962b. Metaphor. In M. Black, *Models and metaphors*. Ithaca, N.Y.: Cornell University Press.

    1962c. Models and archetypes. In M. Black, *Models and metaphors*. Ithaca, N.Y.: Cornell University Press.

    1962d. Linguistic relativity: The views of Benjamin Lee Whorf. In M. Black, *Models and metaphors*. Ithaca, N.Y.: Cornell University Press.

Block, N. 1977. Troubles with functionalism. In C. W. Savage (ed.), *Minnesota studies in the philosophy of science* (vol. 9). Minneapolis: University of Minnesota Press.

Block, N., and Fodor, J. A. 1972. What psychological states are not. *Philosophical Review, 81*, 159–81.

Blumer, H. 1969. *Symbolic interactionism; perspective and method*. Englewood Cliffs, N.J.: Prentice-Hall.

Boyd, R. 1973. Realism, underdetermination and a causal theory of evidence. *Nous, 7*, 1–12.

    1978. Materialism within reductionism. In N. Block (ed.), *Readings in philosophy of psychology*. New York: Harper & Row.

Boyd, R. *Realism and scientific epistemology*. Cambridge: Cambridge University Press, forthcoming.

Boyle, R. R. 1954. The nature of metaphor. *Modern Schoolman, 31*, 257–80.

Bransford, J. D., and McCarrell, N. S. 1975. A sketch of a cognitive approach to comprehension. In W. B. Weimer and D. S. Palermo (eds.), *Cognition and the symbolic processes*. Hillsdale, N.J.: Erlbaum.

Bréal, M. 1899. *Essai de semantique*. Paris: Hachette.

Bresnan, J. 1978. A realistic theory of transformation grammar. In M. Halle, J. Bresnan, and G. A. Miller (eds.), *Linguistic theory and psychological reality*. Cambridge, Mass.: M.I.T. Press.

Brewer, W. F. 1975. Memory for ideas: Synonym substitution. *Memory and Cognition, 3*, 458–64.

Brooks, C., and Warren, R. P. 1938. *Understanding poetry*. New York: Holt, Rinehart and Winston.

Brown, R. H. 1976. Social theory as metaphor. *Theory and Society, 3*, 169–98.

Brown, R. W. 1958. *Words and things.* Glencoe, Ill.: Free Press.

Brown, S. J. 1927. *The world of imagery.* London: Kegan Paul, Trench, Trubner.

Butterfield, H. 1965. *The origins of modern science* (rev. ed.). New York: Free Press.

Byerly, H. C., and Lazara, V. A. 1973. Realist foundations of measurement. *Philosophy of Science, 40,* 1–27.

Campbell, D. T. 1963. Social attitudes and other acquired behavioral dispositions. In S. Koch (ed.), *Psychology: A study of a science* (vol. 6). New York: McGraw-Hill.

Carroll, J. D., and Wish, M. 1974. Multidimensional perceptual models and measurement methods. In E. C. Carterette and M. P. Friedman (eds.), *Handbook of perception.* New York: Academic Press.

Cassirer, E. 1946. *Language and myth.* New York: Dover.

Cavell, S. 1976. *Must we mean what we say?* Cambridge: Cambridge University Press.

Cherry, C. 1966. *On human communication* (2nd ed.). Cambridge, Mass.: M.I.T. Press.

Chomsky, N. 1964. The logical basis of linguistic theory. In H. G. Lunt (ed.), *Proceedings of the Ninth International Congress of Linguistics.* The Hague: Mouton.

1965. *Aspects of the theory of syntax.* Cambridge, Mass.: M.I.T. Press.

1971. Deep structure, surface structure, and semantic interpretation. In D. D. Steinberg and L. A. Jakobovits (eds.), *Semantics: An interdisciplinary reader in philosophy, linguistics, and psychology.* Cambridge: Cambridge University Press.

Chomsky, N., and Halle, M. 1968. *The sound pattern of English.* New York: Harper & Row.

Clark, H. H. and Lucy, P. 1975. Understanding what is meant from what is said: A study in conversationally conveyed requests. *Journal of Verbal Learning and Verbal Behavior, 14,* 56–72.

Cohen, L. J. 1970. *The implications of induction.* London: Methuen.

1971. Some remarks on Grice's views about the logical particles of natural language. In Y. Bar-Hillel (ed.), *Pragmatics of natural languages.* New York: Humanities Press.

1977a. Can the conversationalist hypothesis be defended? *Philosophical Studies, 31,* 81–90.

1977b. *The probable and the provable.* Oxford: Clarendon Press.

Cohen, L. J., and Margalit, A. 1972. The role of inductive reasoning in the interpretation of metaphor. In D. Davidson and G. Harman (eds.), *Semantics of natural language.* Dordrecht, The Netherlands: D. Reidel.

Cohen, T. 1976. Notes on metaphor. *Journal of Aesthetics and Art Criticism, 34,* 249–59.

Cole, M., and Scribner, S. 1974. *Culture and thought.* New York: Wiley.

Cronbach, L. J., and Meehl, P. E. 1956. Construct validity in psychological tests. In H. Feigl and M. Scriven (eds.), *Minnesota studies in the philosophy of science* (vol. 1). Minneapolis: University of Minnesota Press.

Cushing, S. 1977. *Discourse, logical form, and contextual model selection: The unity of semantics and pragmatics in presupposition and anaphora.* Discussion paper. Higher Order Software, Cambridge, Mass.

Dewey, J. 1938. *Logic: The theory of inquiry.* New York: H. Holt and Company.

Dubois, J.; Edeline, F.; Klinkenberg, J. M.; Minguet, P.; Pire, F.; and Trinon, H. 1970. *Rhétorique générale.* Paris: Larousse.

Eberle, R. 1970. Models, metaphors and formal interpretations. In C. M. Turbayne (ed.), *The myth of metaphor* (rev. ed.). Columbia: University of South Carolina Press.

Empson, W. 1951. *The structure of complex words.* New York: New Directions. (Reprinted by the University of Michigan Press, 1967.)

Feigl, H. 1956. Some major issues and developments in the philosophy of science of logical empiricism. In H. Feigl and M. Scriven (eds.), *Minnesota studies in the philosophy of science* (vol. 1). Minneapolis: University of Minnesota Press.

Field, H. 1973. Theory change and the indeterminacy of reference. *Journal of Philosophy, 70,* 462–81.

1974. Quine and the correspondence theory. *Philosophical Review, 83,* 200–28.

Fisk, F. G., and Blecha, M. K. 1966. *The physical sciences.* River Forest, Ill.: Doubleday.

Fodor, J. A. 1965. Explanations in psychology. In M. Black (ed.), *Philosophy in America.* Ithaca, N.Y.: Cornell University Press.

1968. *Psychological explanation.* New York: Random House.

1975. *The language of thought.* New York: Crowell.

Fodor, J. A., Fodor, J. D., and Garrett, M. F. 1975. The psychological unreality of semantic representations. *Linguistic Inquiry, 6,* 515–31.

Fraser, B. 1977. *An account of metaphor.* Unpublished manuscript, Boston University.

Fraser, B. *On requesting: An essay on pragmatics,* forthcoming.

Frederiksen, C. 1977. Structure and process in discourse production and comprehension. In M. Just and P. Carpenter (eds.), *Cognitive processes in comprehension.* Hillsdale, N.J.: Erlbaum.

Gans, H. 1962. *The urban villagers.* New York: Free Press.

Gazdar, G. 1976. *Formal pragmatics for natural language implicature, presupposition and logical form.* Doctoral dissertation, University of Reading, Reading, England.

Geertz, C. (ed.). 1974. *Myth, symbol and culture.* New York: Norton.

Gibson, J. J. 1966. *The senses considered as perceptual systems.* Boston: Houghton Mifflin.

Gleicher, P., and Fried, M. 1967. Some sources of residential satisfaction in an urban slum. In J. Bellush and M. Hausknecht (eds.), *Urban renewal:*

People, politics and planning. Garden City, N.Y.: Doubleday Anchor.

Goldman, A. 1967. A causal theory of knowing. *Journal of Philosophy, 64,* 357–72.

    1976. Discrimination and perceptual knowledge. *Journal of Philosophy, 73,* 771–91.

Goldstein, A. 1978. *Meaning reference and theory change.* Doctoral dissertation, University of Michigan.

Goodman, N. 1968. *Languages of art.* Indianapolis: Bobbs-Merrill.

Green, T. 1971. *The activities of teaching.* New York: McGraw-Hill.

Greimas, A. J. 1970. *Du sens. Essais sémiotiques.* Paris: Editions du Seuil.

Grice, H. P. 1975. Logic and conversation. In P. Cole and J. L. Morgan (eds.), *Syntax and semantics* (vol. 3): *Speech acts.* New York: Academic Press.

Hanson, N. R. 1958. *Patterns of discovery.* Cambridge: Cambridge University Press.

Harre, R., and Madden, E. 1975. *Causal powers.* Totowa, N.J.: Rowman and Littlefield.

Harwood, D. L., and Verbrugge, R. R. 1977. *Metaphor and the asymmetry of similarity.* Paper presented at the Annual Meeting of the American Psychological Association, San Francisco.

Haviland, S. E., and Clark, H. H. 1974. What's new? Acquiring new information as a process in comprehension. *Journal of Verbal Learning and Verbal Behavior, 13,* 512–21.

Haynes, F. 1975. Metaphor as interactive. *Educational Theory, 25,* 272–7.

Hebb, D. O. 1949. *The organization of behavior.* New York: Wiley.

Hempel, C. G. 1965. *Aspects of scientific explanation and other essays in the philosophy of science.* New York: Free Press.

Henle, P. (ed.). 1965. *Language, thought, and culture.* Ann Arbor: University of Michigan Press.

Henley, N. M. 1969. A psychological study of the semantics of animal terms. *Journal of Verbal Learning and Verbal Behavior, 8,* 176–84.

Herbart, J. H. 1898. *[Letters and lectures on education].* Translated by H. M. Felkin and E. Felkin. London: Sonneschein.

Honeck, R. P.; Riechmann, P.; and Hoffman, R. R. 1975. Semantic memory for metaphor: The conceptual base hypothesis. *Memory and Cognition, 3,* 409–15.

Horn, L. R. 1976. *On the semantic properties of logical operators in English.* Bloomington: Indiana University Linguistics Club.

Hume, D. 1973. *A treatise of human nature.* Edited by L. Selby-Bigge. London: Oxford University Press. (Originally published 1739.)

Hymes, D. 1973. *Towards linguistic competence.* Working paper in sociolinguistics, 16. Austin: University of Texas, Department of Anthropology.

Jakobson, R., and Halle, M. 1956. *Fundamentals of Language.* The Hague: Mouton.

Johnson, M. G. 1970. A cognitive-feature model of compound free associations. *Psychological Review, 77,* 282–93

1977. *The abstraction of meaning from complex pictures.* Paper presented at the Annual Meeting of the Psychonomic Society, Washington, D.C.

Kant, E. 1963. *[Critique of pure reason].* Translated by N. K. Smith. London: Macmillan. (Originally published 1787.)

Karttunen, L., and Peters, S. 1975. Conventional implicature in Montague Grammar. In *Proceedings of the First Annual Meeting of the Berkeley Linguistics Society.* Berkeley: University of California.

Katz, A. N. 1976. *Verbal concept identification: Disentangling the dominance effect.* Doctoral dissertation, University of Western Ontario.

Katz, A. N., and Paivio, A. 1975. Imagery variables in concept identification. *Journal of Verbal Learning and Verbal Behavior, 14,* 284–93.

Katz, J. J. 1966. *The philosophy of language.* New York: Harper & Row.

1977. *Propositional structure: A study of the contribution of semantic meaning to speech acts.* New York: Crowell.

Katz, J. J., and Fodor, J. A. 1963. The structure of a semantic theory. *Language, 39,* 170–210.

Kennedy, J. M. 1976. *Pictorial metaphor: A theory of movement indicators in static pictures.* Paper presented at the Information through Pictures Symposium, Swarthmore College, Swarthmore, Pa.

Khatchadourian, H. 1968. Metaphor. *British Journal of Aesthetics, 8,* 227–43.

Kintsch, W. 1972. Notes on the structure of semantic memory. In E. Tulving and W. Donaldson (eds.), *Organization of memory.* New York: Academic Press.

1974. *The representation of meaning in memory.* Hillsdale, N.J.: Erlbaum.

Klee, H., and Eysenck, M. W. 1973. Comprehension of abstract and concrete sentences. *Journal of Verbal Learning and Verbal Behavior, 12,* 522–9.

Koen, F. 1965. An intra-verbal explication of the nature of metaphor. *Journal of Verbal Learning and Verbal Behavior, 4,* 129–33.

Koestler, A. 1964. *The act of creation.* New York: Macmillan.

Kripke, S. A. 1972. Naming and necessity. In D. Davidson and G. Harman (eds.), *The semantics of natural language.* Dordrecht, The Netherlands: D. Reidel.

Krumhansl, C. L. 1978. Concerning the applicability of geometric models to similarity data: The interrelationship between similarity and spatial density. *Psychological Review, 85,* 445–63.

Kuhn, T. S. 1970a. *The structure of scientific revolutions* (2nd ed.). Chicago: University of Chicago Press.

1970b. Reflections on my critics. In I. Lakatos and A. Musgrave (eds.). *Criticism and the growth of knowledge.* Cambridge: Cambridge University Press.

1974. Second thoughts on paradigms. In F. Suppe (ed.), *The structure of scientific theories.* Urbana: University of Illinois Press.

Lakoff, G. 1971. On generative semantics. In D. D. Steinberg and L. A. Jakobovits (eds.), *Semantics: An interdisciplinary reader in philosophy, linguistics and psychology.* Cambridge: Cambridge University Press.

Langer, S. K. 1942. *Philosophy in a new key.* Cambridge, Mass.: Harvard University Press. (Reprinted by Mentor Books, New York, 1948.)

Levi, J. N. 1974. On the alleged idiosyncracy of nonpredicate NP's. In *Papers from the Tenth Regional Meeting, Chicago Linguistic Society*. Chicago: University of Chicago.

Lévi-Strauss, C. 1963. [*Structural anthropology*]. Translated by C. Jacobson and B. G. Schoepf. New York: Basic Books.

Levin, S. R. 1977. *The semantics of metaphor*. Baltimore, Md.: Johns Hopkins University Press.

Lewis, D. 1971. An argument for the identity theory. In D. M. Rosenthal (ed.), *Materialism and the mind-body problem*. Englewood Cliffs, N.J.: Prentice-Hall.

Locke, J. 1959. *An essay concerning human understanding*. Edited by A. C. Fraser. London: Dover. (Originally published 1690.)

Loewenberg, I. 1973. Truth and consequences of metaphors. *Philosophy and Rhetoric, 6*, 30–46.

    1975a. Denying the undeniable: Metaphors are *not* comparisons. *Mid American Linguistics Conference Papers*. Pp. 305–16.

    1975b. Identifying metaphors. *Foundations of Language, 12*, 315–38.

Luce, R. D. 1959. *Individual choice behavior*. New York: Wiley.

MacCorquodale, K., and Meehl, P. E. 1948. On a distinction between hypothetical constructs and intervening variables. *Psychological Review, 55*, 95–107.

Malgady, R. G., and Johnson, M. G. 1976. Modifiers in metaphors: Effects of constituent phrase similarity on the interpretation of figurative sentences. *Journal of Psycholinguistic Research, 5*, 43–52.

Marr, D. 1976. Early processing of visual information. *Philosophical Transactions of the Royal Society of London, 275*.

Marschark, M., and Paivio, A. 1977. Integrative processing of concrete and abstract sentences. *Journal of Verbal Learing and Verbal Behavior, 16*, 217–32.

Matthews, R. J. 1971. Concerning a "linguistic theory" of metaphor. *Foundations of Language, 7*, 413–25.

Miller, G. A. 1974. Towards a third metaphor for psycholinguistics. In W. B. Weimer and D. S. Palermo (eds.), *Cognition and the symbolic processes*. Hillsdale, N.J.: Erlbaum.

    1978. Semantic relations among words. In M. Halle, J. Bresnan, and G. A. Miller (eds.), *Linguistic theory and psychological reality*. Cambridge, Mass.: M.I.T. Press.

Miller, G. A., and Johnson-Laird, P. N. 1976. *Language and perception*. Cambridge, Mass.: Harvard University Press.

Miller, R. M. 1976. The dubious case for metaphors in educational writing. *Educational Theory, 26*, 174–81.

Mooij, J. J. A. 1976. *A study of metaphor*. Amsterdam: North-Holland.

Morgan, J. L. 1978. Two types of convention in indirect speech acts. In P. Cole (ed.), *Syntax and semantics* (vol. 9): *Pragmatics*. New York: Academic Press.

Murry, J. M. 1931 Metaphor. In J. M. Murry, *Countries of the mind*. London: Oxford University Press.

Neisser, U. 1966. Computers as tools and as metaphors. In C. R. Dechert (ed.), *The social impact of cybernetics*. Notre Dame, Ind.: University of Notre Dame Press.

1967. *Cognitive Psychology*. New York: Appleton-Century-Crofts.

Newell, A., and Simon, H. A. 1976. Computer science as empirical inquiry: Symbols and search. *Communications of the Association for Computing Machinery, 19*, 113–26.

Nicolson, N., and Trautmann, J. (eds.). 1976. *The letters of Virginia Woolf* (vol. 2): *1912–1922*. New York: Harcourt Brace Jovanovich.

Nisbet, R. A. 1969. *Social change and history*. New York: Oxford University Press.

Nisbett, R. E., and Wilson, T. D. 1977. Telling more than we can know: Verbal reports on mental processes. *Psychological Review, 84*, 231–59.

Norman, D. A.; Rumelhart, D. E.; and the LNR Research Group. 1975. *Explorations in cognition*. San Francisco: W. H. Freeman.

Nowottny, W. 1962. *The language poets use*. London: Athlone Press.

Oakeshott, M. 1959. *The voice of poetry in the conversation of mankind*. London: Bowes and Bowes.

Olson, D. R. 1970. Language and thought: Aspects of a cognitive theory of semantics. *Psychological Review, 77*, 257–73.

O'Neill, B. J., and Paivio, A. 1978. Semantic constraints in encoding judgments and free recall of concrete and abstract sentences. *Canadian Journal of Psychology, 32*, 3–18.

Ortony, A. 1975. Why metaphors are necessary and not just nice. *Educational Theory, 25*, 45–53.

1976. On the nature and value of metaphor: A reply to my critics. *Educational Theory, 26*, 395–8.

1979. Beyond literal similarity. *Psychological Review, 86*, 161–80.

Ortony, A.; Reynolds, R. E.; and Arter, J. A. 1978. Metaphor: Theoretical and empirical research. *Psychological Bulletin, 85*, 919–43.

Ortony, A.; Schallert, D. L.; Reynolds, R. E.; and Antos, S. J. 1978. Interpreting metaphors and idioms: Some effects of context on comprehension. *Journal of Verbal Learning and Verbal Behavior, 17*, 465–77.

Osgood, C. E. 1953. *Method and theory in experimental psychology*. New York: Oxford University Press.

1963. Language universals and psycholinguistics. In J. Greenberg (ed.), *Universals of language* (2nd ed.). Cambridge, Mass.: M.I.T. Press.

Osgood, C. E.; Suci, G. J.; and Tannenbaum, P. H. 1957. *The measurement of meaning*. Urbana: University of Illinois Press.

Paivio, A. 1963. Learning of adjective-noun paired associates as a function of adjective-noun word order and noun abstractness. *Canadian Journal of Psychology, 17*, 370–9.

1971. *Imagery and verbal processes*. New York: Holt, Rinehart, and Winston.

1975a. Coding distinctions and repetition effects in memory. In G. H. Bower (ed.), *The psychology of learning and motivation*, (vol. 9). New York: Academic Press.

1975b. Imagery and synchronic thinking. *Canadian Psychological Review, 16*, 147–63.

Paivio, A., and Begg, I. 1971. Imagery and comprehension latencies as a function of sentence concreteness and structure. *Perception and Psychophysics, 10*, 408–12.

Paivio, A., and Yarmey, A. D. 1966. Pictures versus words as stimuli and responses in paired-associate learning. *Psychonomic Science, 5*, 235–6.

Petrie, H. G. 1976. Metaphorical models of mastery: Or how to learn to do the problems at the end of the chapter in the physics textbook. In R. S. Cohen, C. A. Hooker, A. C. Michalos, and J. W. vanEvra (eds.), *Proceedings of the Philosophy of Science Association, 1974*. Dordrecht, The Netherlands: D. Reidel.

Plato. 1937. *Meno*. In B. Jowett (ed. and trans.), *The dialogues of Plato*. New York: Random House.

Polanyi, M. 1966. *The tacit dimension*. Garden City, N..Y: Doubleday.

Pollio, H. R., and Burns, B. C. 1977. The anomaly of anomaly. *Journal of Psycholinguistics Research, 6*, 247–60.

Preminger, A. 1974. *The Princeton encyclopedia of poetry and poetics*. Princeton, N.J.: Princeton University Press.

Price, H. H. 1950. *Perception*. London: Methuen.

Putnam, H. 1967. Psychological predicates. In W. H. Capitan and D. D. Merrill (eds.), *Art, mind and religion*. Pittsburgh, Pa.: University of Pittsburgh Press.

1975a. The meaning of meaning. In H. Putnam, *Mind, language and reality*. Cambridge: Cambridge University Press.

1975b. Explanation and reference. In H. Putnam, *Mind, language and reality*. Cambridge: Cambridge University Press.

1975c. The nature of mental states. In H. Putnam, *Mind, language and reality*. Cambridge: Cambridge University Press.

1975d. Philosophy and our mental life. In H. Putnam, *Mind, language and reality*. Cambridge: Cambridge University Press.

1975e. Language and reality. In H. Putnam, *Mind, language and reality*. Cambridge: Cambridge University Press.

1975f. The mental life of some machines. In H. Putnam, *Mind, language and reality*. Cambridge: Cambridge University Press.

1977. Realism and reason. *Proceedings and Addresses of the American Philosophical Association, 50*, 483–98.

Pylyshyn, Z. W. 1973. What the mind's eye tells the mind's brain: A critique of mental imagery. *Psychological Bulletin, 80*, 1–24.

1978a. Complexity and the study of human and machine intelligence. In M. Ringle (ed.), *Philosophical perspectives in artificial intelligence*. New York: Humanities Press.

1978b. Imagery and artificial intelligence. In C. W. Savage (ed.), *Minnesota studies in the philosophy of science* (vol. 9): *Perception and cognition: Issues in the foundations of psychology*. Minneapolis: University of Minnesota Press.

1978c. *On the explanatory adequacy of cognitive process models* (Mimeo). Paper presented at the M.I.T. Workshop on Representation, Massachusetts Institute of Technology, January 1978.

Quine, W. V., and Ullian, J. S. 1970. *The web of belief*. New York: Random House.

Reddy, M. J. 1969. A semantic approach to metaphor. In *Papers from the Fifth Regional Meeting, Chicago Linguistic Society*. Chicago: University of Chicago, Department of Linguistics.

1973. Formal referential models of poetic structure. in *Papers from the Ninth Regional Meeting, Chicago Linguistic Society*. Chicago: University of Chicago, Department of Linguistics.

Reese, H. W. 1968. *The perception of stimulus relations: Discrimination learning and transposition*. New York: Academic Press.

Rein, M. 1976. *Social science and public policy*. New York: Penguin.

Rein, M., and Schön, D. 1974. *The design process*. (Mimeo.) Massachusetts Institute of Technology.

1977. Problem-setting in policy research. In C. H. Weiss (ed.), *Using social research in public policy making*. Lexington, Mass.: D. C. Heath.

Reinhart, T. 1976. On understanding poetic metaphor. *Poetics, 5,* 383–402.

Richards, I. A. 1936a. *The philosophy of rhetoric*. London: Oxford University Press.

1936b. Metaphor. In I. A. Richards, *The philosophy of rhetoric*. London: Oxford University Press.

Ricœur, P. 1970. *Freud and philosophy: An essay in interpretation*. New Haven, Conn.: Yale University Press.

Rigg, M. 1937. The relationship between discrimination in music and discrimination in poetry. *Journal of Educational Psychology, 28,* 149–52.

Rosch, E. 1975a. Cognitive reference points. *Cognitive Psychology, 7,* 532–47.

1975b. Cognitive representations in semantic categories. *Journal of Experimental Psychology: General, 104,* 192–233.

Rosch, E.; Mervis, C. B.; Gray, W. D.; Johnson, D. M.; and Boyes-Braem, P. 1976. Basic objects in natural categories. *Cognitive Psychology, 8,* 382–439.

Rumelhart, D. E., and Abrahamson, A. A. 1973. A model for analogical reasoning. *Cognitive Psychology, 5,* 1–28.

Rumelhart, D. E., and Ortony, A. 1977. The representation of knowledge in memory. In R. C. Anderson, R. J. Spiro, and W. E. Montague (eds.), *Schooling and the acquisition of knowledge*. Hillsdale, N.J.: Erlbaum.

Russell, B. 1956. *Logic and knowledge*. Edited by R. C. Marsh. London: Allen & Unwin.

Sadock, J. M. 1976. Methodological problems of linguistic pragmatics. In *Problems in linguistic metatheory*. East Lansing: Michigan State University, Department of Linguistics.

1978. On testing for conversational implicature. In P. Cole (ed.), *Syntax and semantics* (vol. 9): *Pragmatics*. New York: Academic Press.

Sapir, E. 1921. *Language: An introduction to the study of speech*. New York: Harcourt, Brace and World.

Sapir, J. D. 1977. The anatomy of metaphor. In J. D. Sapir and J. C. Crocker (eds.), *The social use of metaphor: Essays on the anthropology of rhetoric*. Philadelphia: University of Pennsylvania Press.

Scheffler, I. 1967. *Science and subjectivity*. New York: Bobbs-Merrill.

Schön, D. 1963. *Displacement of concepts*. New York: Humanities Press.

1971. *Beyond the stable state*. New York: Random House.

Schön, D., and Argyris, C. 1978. *Organizational learning: A theory of action perspective*. Reading, Mass.: Addison-Wesley.

Schön, D., and Bamberger, J. 1976. *The figural/formal transaction: A parable of generative metaphor*. (Mimeo.) Cambridge, Mass.: M.I.T., Division for Study and Research in Education.

Searle, J. R. 1969. *Speech Acts*. Cambridge: Cambridge University Press.

1975. Indirect speech acts. In P. Cole and J. L. Morgan (eds.), *Syntax and semantics* (vol. 3): *Speech acts*. New York: Academic Press.

1978. Literal meaning. *Erkenntnis, 13*, 207–24.

Segal, A. U. 1976. *Verbal and nonverbal encoding and retrieval differences*. Doctoral dissertation, University of Western Ontario.

Sereno, K., and Mortensen, C. (eds.). 1970. *Foundations of communication theory*. New York: Harper & Row.

Shannon, C. E., and Weaver, W. 1949. *The mathematical theory of information*. Urbana: University of Illinois Press.

Shepard, R. N. 1974. Representation of structure in similarity data: Problems and prospects. *Psychometrika, 39*, 373–421.

Shibles, W. A. 1971. *Metaphor: An annotated bibliography and history*. Whitewater, Wis.: Language Press.

Shoemaker, S. 1975a. *Causality and properties*. Unpublished manuscript, Sage School of Philosophy, Cornell University.

1975b. Functionalism and qualia. *Philosophical Studies, 27*, 291–315.

Silverman, J.; Winner, E.; and Gardner, H. 1976. On going beyond the literal: The development of sensitivity to artistic symbols. *Semiotica, 18*, 291–312.

Simon, H. A. 1969. *The sciences of the artificial*. Cambridge, Mass.: M.I.T. Press.

Skinner, B. F. 1957. *Verbal behavior*. New York: Appleton-Century-Crofts.

Slobin, D. 1971. Developmental psycholinguistics. In W. O. Dingwall (ed.), *Survey of linguistic science*. Stamford, Conn.: Greylock Publications.

Smart, J. J. C. 1963. *Philosophy and scientific realism*. London: Routledge & Kegan Paul.

Smith, T. M. 1970. Some perspectives on the early history of computers. In Z. W. Pylyshyn (ed.), *Perspectives on the computer revolution*. Englewood Cliffs, N.J.: Prentice Hall.

Sperber, D. 1975. [*Rethinking symbolism*]. Translated by A. L. Morton. Cambridge: Cambridge University Press.

Stalnaker, R. C. 1972. Pragmatics. In D. Davidson and G. Harman (eds.), *Semantics of natural language*. Dordrecht, The Netherlands: D. Reidel.

Stern, G. 1965. *Meaning and change of meaning*. Bloomington: Indiana University Press. (Originally published in Sweden 1932.)

Sternberg, R. J. 1977a. Component processes in analogical reasoning. *Psychological Review, 84*, 353–78.

1977b. *Intelligence, information processing, and analogical reasoning: The componential analysis of human abilities*. Hillsdale, N.J.: Erlbaum.

1978. *Components of inductive reasoning*. Unpublished manuscript, Yale University.

Sternberg, R. J., and Gardner, M. K. 1978. *A unified theory of inductive reasoning in semantic space*. Unpublished manuscript, Yale University.

Sternberg, R. J., and Nigro, G. 1978. *Component processes in metaphoric comprehension and appreciation*. Unpublished manuscript, Yale University.

Sternberg, R. J., and Rifkin, B. 1979. The development of analogical reasoning processes. *Journal of Experimental Child Psychology*, in press.

Stevens, W. 1957. *Opus posthumous*. New York: Knopf.

Thoreau, H. D. 1937. Walden. In H. S. Canby (ed.), *The works of Thoreau*. Boston: Houghton Mifflin.

Thorndike, E. L. 1924. Reading as reasoning: A study of mistakes in paragraph reading. *Journal of Educational Psychology, 15*, 323–32.

Tourangeau, R., and Sternberg, R. J. 1978. *What makes a good metaphor?* Unpublished manuscript, Yale University.

Tulving, E. 1972. Episodic and semantic memory. In E. Tulving and W. Donaldson (eds.), *Organization of memory*. New York: Academic Press.

Turner, J. F. C. 1976. *Housing by people*. New York: Pantheon Books.

Turner, J. F. C., and Fichter, R. (eds.). 1972. *Freedom to build*. New York: Macmillan.

Turner, V. W. 1974. *Dramas, fields and metaphors: Symbolic action in human society*. Ithaca, N.Y.: Cornell University Press.

Tversky, A. 1977. Features of similarity. *Psychological Review, 84*, 327–52.

Ullmann, S. 1957. *The principles of semantics* (2nd ed.). London: Basil Blackwell.

Underwood, B. J., and Richardson, J. 1956. Some verbal materials for the study of concept formation. *Psychological Bulletin, 53*, 84–95.

Upton, A. 1973. *Design for thinking*. Palo Alto, Calif.: Pacific Books.

Verbrugge, R. R., and McCarrell, N. S. 1977. Metaphoric comprehension: Studies in reminding and resembling. *Cognitive Psychology, 9*, 494–533.

Vickers, G. 1973. *Making institutions work*. New York: Wiley.

Waltz, D. 1975. Understanding line drawings of scenes with shadows. In P. H. Winston (ed.), *The psychology of computer vision*. New York: McGraw-Hill.

Werner, H., and Kaplan, B. 1963. *Symbol formation: An organismic developmental approach to the psychology of language and the expression of thought.* New York: Wiley.

Wertheimer, M. 1959. *On productive thinking.* New York: Harper and Row.

Whatley, J. 1961–2. 'Like.' *Proceedings of the Aristotelian Society, 62,* 99–116.

Whorf, B. L. 1956. *Language, thought, and reality.* Edited by J. B. Carroll. Cambridge, Mass.: M.I.T. Press.

Wiener, N. 1954. *The human use of human beings: Cybernetics and society* (2nd ed.). Garden City, N.Y.: Doubleday Anchor.

Wilson, J. Q. 1975. *In thinking about crime.* New York: Basic Books.

Winner, E.; Rosenstiel, A.; and Gardner, H. 1976. The development of metaphoric understanding. *Developmental Psychology, 12,* 289–97.

Winokur, S. 1976. *A primer of verbal behavior: An operant view.* Englewood Cliffs, N.J.: Prentice-Hall.

Wittgenstein, L. 1953. *Philosophical investigations.* New York: Macmillan.

1961. [*Tractatus logico-philosophicus*]. Translated by D. F. Pears and B. F. McGuiness. London: Kegan Paul & Routledge. (Originally published 1921.)

NAME INDEX

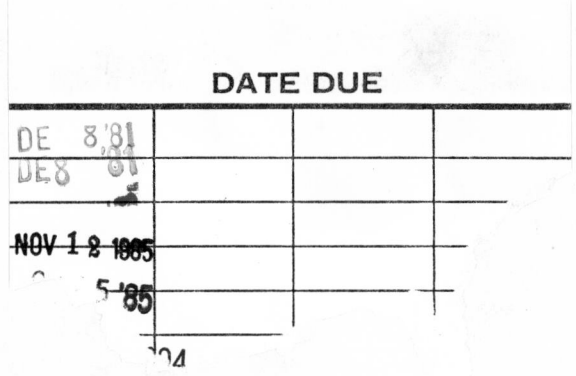